The SAGE Encyclopedia of

EDUCATIONAL RESEARCH, MEASUREMENT, AND EVALUATION

Editorial Board

The SAGE Encyclopedia of

EDUCATIONAL RESEARCH, MEASUREMENT, AND EVALUATION

1

Editor

Bruce B. Frey
University of Kansas

⑤SAGE reference

Los Angeles | London | New Delhi | Singapore | Washington DC | Melbourne

FOR INFORMATION:

SAGE Publications, Inc.
2455 Teller Road
Thousand Oaks, California 91320
E-mail: order@sagepub.com

SAGE Publications Ltd.
1 Oliver's Yard
55 City Road
London, EC1Y 1SP
United Kingdom

SAGE Publications India Pvt. Ltd.
B 1/I 1 Mohan Cooperative Industrial Area
Mathura Road, New Delhi 110 044
India

SAGE Publications Asia-Pacific Pte. Ltd.
3 Church Street
#10-04 Samsung Hub
Singapore 049483

Printed in the United States of America.

Library of Congress Cataloging-in-Publication Data

Names: Frey, Bruce B., editor.

Title: The Sage encyclopedia of educational research, measurement, and evaluation/editor, Bruce B. Frey, University of Kansas.

Description: Thousand Oaks, California : SAGE Publications, Inc., [2018] | Includes bibliographical references and index.

Identifiers: LCCN 2017042016 | ISBN 978-1-5063-2615-3 (hardcover : alk. paper)

Subjects: LCSH: Education—Research—Methodology.

Classification: LCC LB1028 .S139 2018 | DDC 370.72—dc23 LC record available at https://lccn.loc.gov/2017042016

Acquisitions Editor: Andrew Boney
Developmental Editor: Shirin Parsavand
Assistant Editor: Jordan Enobakhare
Reference Systems Manager: Leticia Gutierrez
Production Editor: David C. Felts
Copy Editor: Hurix Digital
Typesetter: Hurix Digital
Proofreaders: Lawrence W. Baker, Barbara Coster, Eleni Georgiou, Sally Jaskold
Indexer: Joan Shapiro
Cover Designer: Anupama Krishnan
Marketing Manager: Jennifer Bourque

18 19 20 21 22 10 9 8 7 6 5 4 3 2 1

Contents

Volume 4

List of Entries

Reader's Guide

Assessment

Assessment Issues

Accessibility of Assessment
Accommodations
African Americans and Testing
Asian Americans and Testing
Cheating
Ethical Issues in Testing
Gender and Testing
High-Stakes Tests
Latinos and Testing
Minority Issues in Testing
Second Language Learners, Assessment of
Standards for Educational and Psychological Testing
Test Security
Testwiseness

Assessment Methods

Ability Tests
Achievement Tests
Adaptive Behavior Assessments
Admissions Tests
Alternate Assessments
Aptitude Tests
Attenuation, Correction for
Attitude Scaling
Basal Level and Ceiling Level
Benchmark
Buros *Mental Measurements Yearbook*
Classification
Cognitive Diagnosis
Computer-Based Testing
Computerized Adaptive Testing
Confidence Interval
Curriculum-Based Assessment
Diagnostic Tests
Difficulty Index
Discrimination Index

English Language Proficiency Assessment
Formative Assessment
Intelligence Tests
Interquartile Range
Minimum Competency Testing
Mood Board
Personality Assessment
Power Tests
Progress Monitoring
Projective Tests
Psychometrics
Reading Comprehension Assessments
Screening Tests
Self-Report Inventories
Sociometric Assessment
Speeded Tests
Standards-Based Assessment
Summative Assessment
Technology-Enhanced Items
Test Battery
Testing, History of
Tests
Value-Added Models
Written Language Assessment

Classroom Assessment

Authentic Assessment
Backward Design
Bloom's Taxonomy
Classroom Assessment
Constructed-Response Items
Curriculum-Based Measurement
Essay Items
Fill-in-the-Blank Items
Formative Assessment
Game-Based Assessment
Grading
Matching Items
Multiple-Choice Items

Score Linking
Standard Setting
Table of Specifications
Vertical Scaling

Organizations and Government Agencies

American Educational Research Association
American Evaluation Association
American Psychological Association
Educational Testing Service
Institute of Education Sciences
Interstate School Leaders Licensure
    Consortium Standards
Joint Committee on Standards for Educational
    Evaluation
National Council on Measurement in Education
National Science Foundation
Office of Elementary and Secondary Education
Organisation for Economic Co-operation
    and Development
Partnership for Assessment of Readiness for
    College and Careers
Smarter Balanced Assessment Consortium
Teachers' Associations
U.S. Department of Education
World Education Research Association

Professional Issues

Accountability
Certification
Classroom Observations
Compliance
Confidentiality
Conflict of Interest
Data-Driven Decision Making
*Diagnostic and Statistical Manual of Mental
    Disorders*
Educational Researchers, Training of
Ethical Issues in Educational Research
Ethical Issues in Evaluation
Ethical Issues in Testing
Evaluation Consultants
Federally Sponsored Research and Programs
Framework for Teaching
Guiding Principles for Evaluators
Licensure
Professional Development of Teachers
Professional Learning Communities

School Psychology
*Standards for Educational and Psychological
    Testing*
Teacher Evaluation
Teachers' Associations

Publishing

Abstracts
APA Format
Authorship
Demographics
Dissertations
Journal Articles
Literature Review
Methods Section
Research Proposals
Results Section

Qualitative Research

Auditing
Delphi Technique
Discourse Analysis
Document Analysis
Ethnography
Field Notes
Focus Groups
Grounded Theory
Historical Research
Interviewer Bias
Interviews
Market Research
Member Check
Narrative Research
Naturalistic Inquiry
Participant Observation
Qualitative Data Analysis
Qualitative Research Methods
Transcription
Trustworthiness

Research Concepts

Applied Research
Aptitude-Treatment Interaction
Causal Inference
Data
Ecological Validity
External Validity
File Drawer Problem

Fraudulent and Misleading Data
Generalizability
Hypothesis Testing
Impartiality
Interaction
Internal Validity
Objectivity
Order Effects
Representativeness
Response Rate
Scientific Method
Type III Error

Research Designs

ABA Designs
Action Research
Case Study Method
Causal-Comparative Research
Cross-Cultural Research
Crossover Design
Design-Based Research
Double-Blind Design
Experimental Designs
Gain Scores, Analysis of
Latin Square Design
Meta-Analysis
Mixed Methods Research
Monte Carlo Simulation Studies
Nonexperimental Designs
Pilot Studies
Posttest-Only Control Group Design
Pre-experimental Designs
Pretest–Posttest Designs
Quasi-Experimental Designs
Regression Discontinuity Analysis
Repeated Measures Designs
Single-Case Research
Solomon Four-Group Design
Split-Plot Design
Static Group Design
Time Series Analysis
Triple-Blind Studies
Twin Studies
Zelen's Randomized Consent Design

Research Methods

Classroom Observations
Cluster Sampling

Control Variables
Convenience Sampling
Debriefing
Deception
Expert Sampling
Judgment Sampling
Markov Chain Monte Carlo Methods
Quantitative Research Methods
Quota Sampling
Random Assignment
Random Selection
Replication
Simple Random Sampling
Snowball Sampling
Stratified Random Sampling
Survey Methods
Systematic Sampling
Weighting

Research Tools

Amos
ATLAS.ti
BILOG-MG
Bubble Drawing
C Programming Languages
Collage Technique
Computer Programming in Quantitative Analysis
Concept Mapping
EQS
Excel
FlexMIRT
HLM
HyperResearch
IRTPRO
Johari Window
Kelly Grid
LISREL
Mplus
National Assessment of Educational Progress
NVivo
PARSCALE
Programme for International Student Assessment
Progress in International Reading Literacy Study
R
SAS
SPSS
Stata

Quantitative Literacy
Reading Comprehension
Scaffolding
School Leadership
Self-Directed Learning
Service-Learning
Social Learning
Socio-Emotional Learning
STEM Education
Waldorf Schools

Theories and Conceptual Frameworks

Ability–Achievement Discrepancy
Andragogy
Applied Behavior Analysis
Attribution Theory
Behaviorism
Cattell–Horn–Carroll Theory of Intelligence
Classical Conditioning
Classical Test Theory
Cognitive Neuroscience
Constructivist Approach
Data-Driven Decision Making
Debriefing
Educational Psychology
Educational Research, History of
Emotional Intelligence
Epistemologies, Teacher and Student
Experimental Phonetics
Feedback Intervention Theory
Framework for Teaching
g Theory of Intelligence
Generalizability Theory
Grounded Theory
Improvement Science Research
Information Processing Theory
Instructional Theory
Item Response Theory
Learning Progressions
Learning Styles
Learning Theories
Mastery Learning
Multiple Intelligences, Theory of

Naturalistic Inquiry
Operant Conditioning
Paradigm Shift
Phenomenology
Positivism
Postpositivism
Pragmatic Paradigm
Premack Principle
Punishment
Reinforcement
Response to Intervention
School-Wide Positive Behavior Support
Scientific Method
Self-Directed Learning
Social Cognitive Theory
Social Learning
Socio-Emotional Learning
Speech-Language Pathology
Terman Study of the Gifted
Transformative Paradigm
Triarchic Theory of Intelligence
True Score
Unitary View of Validity
Universal Design in Education
Wicked Problems
Zone of Proximal Development

Threats to Research Validity

Falsified Data in Large-Scale Surveys
Hawthorne Effect
Instrumentation
Interviewer Bias
John Henry Effect
Maturation
Mortality
Nonresponse Bias
Observer Effect
Placebo Effect
Reactive Arrangements
Regression Toward the Mean
Restriction of Range
Selection Bias
Threats to Research Validity
Treatment Integrity

Sara Miller McCune founded SAGE Publishing in 1965 to support the dissemination of usable knowledge and educate a global community. SAGE publishes more than 1000 journals and over 800 new books each year, spanning a wide range of subject areas. Our growing selection of library products includes archives, data, case studies and video. SAGE remains majority owned by our founder and after her lifetime will become owned by a charitable trust that secures the company's continued independence.

Los Angeles | London | New Delhi | Singapore | Washington DC | Melbourne

About the Editor

Bruce B. Frey, Ph.D., is an award-winning researcher, teacher, and professor of educational psychology at the University of Kansas. He is the author of *There's a Stat for That!, Modern Classroom Assessment,* and *100 Questions (and Answers) about Tests and Measurement* for SAGE and associate editor of SAGE's *Encyclopedia of Research Design.* He also wrote *Statistics Hacks* for O'Reilly Media. His primary research interests include classroom assessment, instrument development, and program evaluation. In his spare time, Bruce leads a secret life as Professor Bubblegum, host of *Echo Valley,* a podcast that celebrates bubblegum pop music of the late 1960s. The show is wildly popular with the young people.

Contributors

Tineke A. Abma
VU University Medical Center

Samuel E. Abrams
National Center for the Study of Privatization in Education

Phillip L. Ackerman
Georgia Institute of Technology

Robert A. Ackerman
University of Texas at Dallas

Christopher M. Adams
Fitchburg State University

Allison Jennifer Ames
James Madison University

Ji An
University of Maryland, College Park

Samantha F. Anderson
University of Notre Dame

Heidi Arnouts
University of Antwerp

Raman Arora
Johns Hopkins University

Diana J. Arya
University of California, Santa Barbara

Patricia Teague Ashton
University of Florida

Tony Attwood
The Minds and Hearts Clinic

Marilyn M. Ault
University of Kansas

Karen Badger
University of Kentucky

Alison L. Bailey
University of California, Los Angeles

Ella G. Banda
University of Massachusetts Amherst

Brian R. Barber
Kent State University

Nicole Barnes
Montclair State University

Gail Vallance Barrington
Barrington Research Group, Inc.

Jordan R. Bass
University of Kansas

A. Alexander Beaujean
Baylor University

Danielle M. Becker
University of Minnesota

Thomas J. Beckman
Mayo Clinic

Eric T. Beeson
Northwestern University

Linda S. Behar-Horenstein
University of Florida

John Bell
Michigan State University

Aarti Bellara
University of Connecticut

Nicholas F. Benson
Baylor University

Peter M. Bentler
University of California, Los Angeles

Dale E. Berger
Claremont Graduate University

Jacquelyn A. Bialo
Georgia State University

Magdalena Bielenia-Grajewska
University of Gdansk

Scott Bishop
Questar Assessment Inc.

Bruce E. Blaine
St. John Fisher College

Shane D. Blair
University of Kansas

Lorraine Blatt
Johns Hopkins University

Joseph K. Blitzstein

Linda Dale Bloomberg
Teachers College, Columbia University

David Bloome
The Ohio State University

Clive R. Boddy
Middlesex University

Christian Bokhove
University of Southampton

Stella Bollmann
Ludwig Maximilians University

Edward L. Boone
Virginia Commonwealth University

Marc H. Bornstein
National Institute of Child Health and Human Development

Robert Boruch
University of Pennsylvania

Frank A. Bosco Jr.
Virginia Commonwealth University

Alex J. Bowers
Teachers College, Columbia University

Richard E. Boyatzis
Case Western Reserve University

Michelle L. Boyer
University of Massachusetts Amherst

Nancy N. Boyles
Southern Connecticut State University

Laine Bradshaw
University of Georgia

Alisa Palmer Branham
University of Kansas

Mason Lee Branham
University of South Carolina

Michael T. Brannick
University of South Florida

Markus Brauer
University of Wisconsin-Madison

Robert L. Brennan
University of Iowa

Tonya Breymier
Indiana University East

Ali S. Brian
University of South Carolina

Sharon Brisolara
Shasta College

Angela Broaddus
Benedictine College

Alex Brodersen
University of Notre Dame

Jeanne Brooks-Gunn
Teachers College, Columbia University

James Dean Brown
University of Hawaii at Manoa

Julie C. Brown
University of Minnesota, Twin Cities

Mary T. Brownell
University of Florida

Alan W. Brue
Capella University

Jennifer A. Brussow
University of Kansas

Kelley Buchheister
University of Nebraska–Lincoln

Frederick Burrack
Kansas State University

Gervase R. Bushe
Simon Fraser University

Andrew C. Butler
University of Texas at Austin

Yuko Goto Butler
University of Pennsylvania

Li Cai
University of California, Los Angeles

Meghan K. Cain
University of Notre Dame

Gregory L. Callan
Ball State University

Mitchell Campbell
University of Wisconsin-Madison

Emily Cantwell
University of Kansas

Kimberly Capp
Nova Southeastern University

Nicole Mittenfelner Carl
University of Pennsylvania

Thomas R. Carretta
Air Force Research Laboratory

Arthur Charpentier
Université du Québec à Montréal

Walter Chason
University of South Florida

Helen L. Chen
Stanford University

Jie Chen
University of Kansas

Yi-Hsin Chen
University of South Florida

Ying Cheng
University of Notre Dame

Yuk Fai Cheong
Emory University

Monaliza M. Chian
University of California, Santa Barbara

Shriniwas Chinta
South West Sydney Area Health Service

Mary M. Chittooran
Saint Louis University

Theodore J. Christ
University of Minnesota

Christine Ann Christle
University of South Carolina

Amy Clark
University of Kansas

Nathan H. Clemens
University of Texas at Austin

Hamish Coates
University of Melbourne

Jill S. M. Coleman
Ball State University

Zachary K. Collier
University of Florida

Eric Alan Common
University of Kansas

Zachary Conrad
Kansas Multi-Tier System of Supports

Bryan G. Cook
University of Hawaii at Manoa

Kyrsten M. Costlow
National Institute of Child Health and Human Development

Matthew Gordon Ray Courtney
Melbourne Graduate School of Education

Nelson Cowan
University of Missouri

Jana Craig-Hare
University of Kansas

Bonnie Cramond
University of Georgia

Kent J. Crippen
University of Florida

Kevin Crouse
Rutgers Graduate School of Education

Toni Crouse
University of Kansas

Zhongmin Cui
ACT, Inc.

Steven Andrew Culpepper

Arthur J. Cunningham
St. Olaf College

Nicholas A. Curtis
James Madison University

Joshua A. Danish
Indiana University Bloomington

Cynthia S. Darling-Fisher
University of Michigan

Judith Davidson
University of Massachusetts Lowell

Jennifer Davidtz
Nova Southeastern University

Larry Davis
Educational Testing Service

Michael E. Dawson
University of Southern California

Anita B. Delahay
Carnegie Mellon University

Christine E. DeMars
James Madison University

Leah Dembitzer
Rutgers, The State University of New Jersey

Angelo S. DeNisi
Tulane University

Justin A. DeSimone
University of Cincinnati

Maria DeYoreo
Duke University

Ronli Diakow
New York City Department of Education

Kathryn Doherty Kurtz
University of Massachusetts Boston

Thurston A. Domina
University of North Carolina at Chapel Hill

Ashley Donohue
Baylor University

Neil J. Dorans
Educational Testing Service

John F. Dovidio
Yale University

Lyman L. Dukes III
University of South Florida St. Petersburg

Danielle N. Dupuis
University of Minnesota

Stephanie Dyson Elms
University of Kansas

John Joseph Dziak
Pennsylvania State University

Meghan Ecker-Lyster
University of Kansas

Julianne Michelle Edwards
Azusa Pacific University

Anna J. Egalite
North Carolina State University

Thorlene Egerton
The University of Melbourne

Valeisha M. Ellis
Spelman College

Susan E. Embretson
Georgia Institute of Technology

Amy S. Gaumer Erickson
University of Kansas

Eduardo Estrada
Camilo José Cela University

Kimberly Ethridge
Nova Southeastern University

Howard T. Everson
SRI International

Leandre R. Fabrigar
Queen's University

Carl Francis Falk
Michigan State University

Fen Fan
University of Massachusetts Amherst

Anna C. Faul
University of Louisville

John M. Ferron
University of South Florida

David Fetterman
Fetterman & Associates

W. Holmes Finch
Ball State University

Roger Fischer
Montana State University

Helenrose Fives
Montclair State University

Sara A. Florence
Nova Southeastern University

Timothy Franz
St. John Fisher College

Bruce B. Frey
University of Kansas

Alon Friedman
University of South Florida

Catherine O. Fritz
University of Northampton

Kyra N. Fritz
University of Louisville

John Mark Froiland
Pearson

Danling Fu
University of Florida

Matthew B. Fuller
Sam Houston State University

Gavin W. Fulmer
University of Iowa

Joseph Calvin Gagnon
University of Florida

April Galyardt
University of Georgia

Copelan Gammon
National Institutes of Health

Alejandra Garcia
University of Massachusetts Amherst

Andrea M. Garcia
University of Kansas

Rachel Darley Gary
University of Massachusetts Amherst

Pat J. Gehrke
University of South Carolina

Nicholas W. Gelbar
University of Connecticut

Claudia A. Gentile
NORC at the University of Chicago

Elizabeth T. Gershoff
University of Texas at Austin

Dean R. Gerstein
Independent Scholar

Iman Ghaderi
University of Arizona

Graham R. Gibbs
University of Huddersfield

Drew Gitomer
Rutgers Graduate School of Education

Lina Goldenberg
University of Kansas

Samantha B. Goldstein
National Institute of Child Health and Human Development

Juana Gómez-Benito
University of Barcelona

Roland H. Good
Dynamic Measurement Group

Jacqueline D. Goodway
The Ohio State University

Brian S. Gordon
University of Kansas

Chad M. Gotch
Washington State University

Bruce Granshaw
Victoria Universtiy

Judith L. Green
University of California, Santa Barbara

Jennifer C. Greene
University of Illinois at Urbana-Champaign

Judith M. S. Gross
University of Kansas

Fei Gu
McGill University

Cassandra Guarino
University of California, Riverside

Daniel B. Hajovsky
University of South Dakota

Kevin A. Hallgren
University of Washington

Marc Hallin
Université libre de Bruxelles

Lawrence C. Hamilton
University of New Hampshire

K. Chris Han
Graduate Management Admission Council

Carl B. Hancock
The University of Alabama

Gregory R. Hancock
University of Maryland, College Park

Maggie Quinn Hannan
University of Pittsburgh

Brenda Hannon
Texas A&M University-Kingsville

David M. Hansen
University of Kansas

Shlomo Hareli
University of Haifa

Lisa L. Harlow
University of Rhode Island

Jeffrey R. Harring
University of Maryland, College Park

Heather D. Harris
James Madison University

Judith R. Harrison
Rutgers, The State University of New Jersey

Jessica P. Harvey
Southern Illinois University Edwardsville

Richard D. Harvey
Saint Louis University

John D. Hathcoat
James Madison University

Clifford E. Hauenstein
Georgia Institute of Technology

Ellen Hazelkorn
Dublin Institute of Technology

Dan He
University of Kansas

Lauren M. Henry
National Institute of Child Health and Human Development

Socorro Herrera
Kansas State University

Michael Herriges
University of Minnesota

Salome Heyward
Salome Heyward and Associates

Tyler Hicks
University of Kansas

M. Dolores Hidalgo
University of Murcia

Rana S. Hinman
University of Melbourne

John M. Hintze
University of Massachusetts Amherst

Tyrell Hirchert
University of Northern Colorado

David C. Hoaglin
University of Massachusetts Medical School

Michael F. Hock
University of Kansas

Janice A. Hogle
University of Wisconsin-Madison

Søren Holm
University of Manchester

S. Jeanne Horst
James Madison University

Jessica Hoth
Universität Vechta

Carrie R. Houts
Vector Psychometric Group, LLC

Kenneth R. Howe
University of Colorado Boulder

Lindsay Till Hoyt
Fordham University

Mei Hoyt
University of North Texas

Hsiu-Fang Hsieh
Fooyin University

Bo Hu
University of Kansas

Anne Corinne Huggins-Manley
University of Florida

Ben P. Hunter
University of Kansas School of Medicine-Wichita

R. Shane Hutton
Vanderbilt University

Dragos Iliescu
University of Bucharest

Paul B. Ingram
Texas Tech University

Dianne Nutwell Irving
Georgetown University

S. Earl Irving
Kia Eke Panuku, The University of Auckland

Dan Ispas
Illinois State University

Jessica N. Jacovidis
James Madison University

Justin Jager
Arizona State University

Lilli Japec
Statistics Sweden

Gerard Michael Jellig
University of Pennsylvania

Patricia A. Jenkins
Albany State University

Rebecca Jesson
University of Auckland

Jennifer L. Jewiss
University of Vermont

Hong Jiao
University of Maryland, College Park

Daniela Jiménez
Pontificia Universidad Católica de Chile

Maria Jimenez-Buedo
Universidad Nacional de Educación a Distancia

Adam Michael Johansen
University of Warwick

Jeffrey P. Johnson
Educational Testing Service

Matthew S. Johnson
Teachers College, Columbia University

Paul E. Johnson
University of Kansas

Robert L. Johnson
University of South Carolina

Tessa Johnson
University of Maryland, College Park

Natalie D. Jones
Claremont Graduate University

Nathan D. Jones
Boston University

Seang-Hwane Joo
University of South Florida

Jeanette Joyce
Rutgers, The State University of New Jersey

Diana Joyce-Beaulieu
University of Florida

George Julnes
University of Baltimore

Hyun Joo Jung
University of Massachusetts Amherst

Uta Jüttner
Hochschule Luzern

David Kahle
Baylor University

Irene Kaimi
Plymouth University

Matthew P. H. Kan
Queen's University

Jeffrey D. Karpicke
Purdue University

Arunprakash T. Karunanithi
University of Colorado Denver

Meagan Karvonen
University of Kansas

Kentaro Kato
Benesse Educational Research and Development

Daniel Katz
University of California, Santa Barbara

Ian Katz
Saint Louis University

Irvin R. Katz
Educational Testing Service

Mira B. Kaufman
National Institute of Child Health and Human Development

Walter Keenan
University of Connecticut

Harrison J. Kell
Educational Testing Service

Jessie Kember
University of Minnesota

Ana H. Kent
Saint Louis University

Ryan J. Kettler
Rutgers, The State University of New Jersey

Haeyoung Kim
Korea University

Hyung Jin Kim
University of Iowa

Hyung Won Kim
University of Texas Rio Grande Valley

Minkyoung Kim
Indiana University Bloomington

Yoon Jeon Kim
Massachusetts Institute of Technology

Neal Kingston
University of Kansas

Allyson J. Kiss
University of Minnesota

Karla Kmetz-Morris
University of South Florida St. Petersburg

Olga Korosteleva
California State University, Long Beach

Rachel Elizabeth Kostura Polk
University of Kansas

Laura M. B. Kramer
University of Kansas

Parvati Krishnamurty
NORC at the University of Chicago

Jeffrey D. Kromrey
University of South Florida

Ivar Krumpal
University of Leipzig

B. Venkatesh Kumar
Tata Institute of Social Sciences

Swapna Kumar
University of Florida

Michael Kung
University of Florida

Lori Kupczynski
Texas A&M University-Kingsville

Carrie La Voy
University of Kansas

Chi Yan Lam
Queen's University

Kathleen Lynne Lane
University of Kansas

Hongling Lao
University of Kansas

Lotta C. Larson
Kansas State University

Norman J. Lass
West Virginia University

Brandon LeBeau
University of Iowa

James M. LeBreton
Pennsylvania State University

Thomas Ledermann
Utah State University

Kerry Lee
University of Auckland

Lina Lee
University of New Hampshire

Lisa Lee
NORC at the University of Chicago

Won-Chan Lee
University of Iowa

Walter L. Leite
University of Florida

Hildie Leung
The Hong Kong Polytechnic University

Janet Tsin-yee Leung
The Hong Kong Polytechnic University

Daniel Lewis
Pacific Metrics Corporation

Chen Li
University of Maryland, College Park

Isaac Y. Li
University of South Florida

Jianqiang Liang
The Hong Kong Polytechnic University

Rosemary Luyin Liang
The Hong Kong Polytechnic University

Dandan Liao
University of Maryland, College Park

Gregory Arief D. Liem
National Institute of Education, Nanyang Technological University

Nicholas K. Lim
Spalding University

TickMeng Lim
Open University Malaysia

Li Lin
The Hong Kong Polytechnic University

Sheila K. List
Virginia Commonwealth University

Haiyan Liu
University of Notre Dame

Jingchen Liu
Columbia University

Shengtao Liu
Hunan University

Xiaofeng Steven Liu
University of South Carolina

Yang Liu
University of California, Merced

Sarah Lockenvitz
Missouri State University

Jill Hendrickson Lohmeier
University of Massachusetts Lowell

Stephen W. Loke
University of Kansas Medical Center

Patricia D. López
San José State University

Sue Lottridge
Pacific Metrics Corporation

Patricia A. Lowe
University of Kansas

Richard M. Luecht
University of North Carolina at Greensboro

Lars Lyberg
Lyberg Survey Quality Management Inc.

Cecilia Ma
The Hong Kong Polytechnic University

David P. MacKinnon
Arizona State University

Joseph Madaus
University of Connecticut

Patrick Mair
Harvard University

Matthew C. Makel
Duke University

Christoforos Mamas
University of California, San Diego

Gregory J. Marchant
Ball State University

Michael O. Martin
Boston College

Phillip K. Martin
University of Kansas School of Medicine–Wichita

Julie Masterson
Missouri State University

Andrew Maul
University of California, Santa Barbara

Brendan Maxcy
Indiana University–Purdue University Indianapolis

Joseph A. Maxwell
George Mason University

Scott E. Maxwell
University of Notre Dame

Rebecca Mazur
University of Massachusetts Amherst

Dominica McBride
Become

Michael A. McDaniel
Virginia Commonwealth University

Andrew McEachin
RAND Corporation

Elizabeth H. McEneaney
University of Massachusetts Amherst

Ryan J. McGill
College of William and Mary

Jamie C. McGovern
University of Kansas Medical Center

Mary L. McHugh
Angeles College

Alex McInturff
University of California, Berkeley

James McLeskey
University of Florida

Miles Allen McNall
Michigan State University

David E. Meens
University of Colorado Boulder

Valerie Meier
University of California, Santa Barbara

Daryl F. Mellard
University of Kansas

Krystal Mendez
University of Kansas

Sylvia L. Mendez
University of Colorado Colorado Springs

Natalja Menold
GESIS–Leibniz Institute for the Social Sciences

Margaret Kristin Merga
Murdoch University

Gabriel J. Merrin
University of Illinois at Urbana-Champaign

Craig A. Mertler
Arizona State University

Audrey Michal
Northwestern University

Milica Miočević
Arizona State University

Gregory Mitchell
University of Virginia

Monica Morell
University of Maryland, College Park

David Morgan
Spalding University

Demetri L. Morgan
Loyola University Chicago

Grant B. Morgan
Baylor University

Carl N. Morris
Harvard University

Peter E. Morris
Lancaster University and University of Northampton

Kristin M. Morrison
Georgia Institute of Technology

Wilfridah Mucherah
Ball State University

Jamie R. Mulkey
Caveon, LLC

Ina V. S. Mullis
Boston College

Karen D. Multon
University of Kansas

Sohad Murrar
University of Wisconsin-Madison

Angela K. Murray
University of Kansas

Brittany Murray
University of North Carolina at Chapel Hill

Dorothy J. Musselwhite
University of Georgia

Jessica Namkung
University of Nebraska–Lincoln

Oksana Naumenko
University of North Carolina at Greensboro

Mario A. Navarro
Claremont Graduate University

Kelli L. Netson
University of Kansas School of Medicine–Wichita

Kirsten Newell
University of Minnesota

Joan Newman
University at Albany

Anh Andrew Nguyen
Queen's University

Thu Suong Nguyen
Indiana University–Purdue University Indianapolis

Joseph R. Nichols
Saint Louis University

Nicole M. Nickens
University of Central Missouri

Kyle Nickodem
University of Minnesota

Kathleen H. Nielsen
University of Washington

Christopher R. Niileksela
University of Kansas

Kim Nimon
University of Texas at Tyler

Patricia M. Noonan
University of Kansas

Anthony Odland
Sanford Health

Laura O'Dwyer
Boston College

Insu Paek
Florida State University

Qianqian Pan
University of Kansas

Ming Fai Pang
The University of Hong Kong

Eugene T. Parker
University of Kansas

Sarah Parsons
University of Southampton

Tracy Paskiewicz
University of Massachusetts Boston

Meagan M. Patterson
University of Kansas

Michael Quinn Patton
Utilization-Focused Evaluation

Trena M. Paulus
University of Georgia

Phillip D. Payne
Kansas State University

Melissa Pearrow
University of Massachusetts Boston

Mark Pedretti
Claremont Graduate University

Beverly Pell
University of Kansas

Peng Peng
University of Nebraska–Lincoln

Marianne Perie
University of Kansas

Laura Pevytoe
National Institutes of Health

Lia Plakans
University of Iowa

Anthony Jason Plotner
University of South Carolina

Jonathan A. Plucker
Johns Hopkins University

Kelvin Terrell Pompey
University of South Carolina

Michael I. Posner
University of Oregon

Dmitriy Poznyak
Mathematica Policy Research

Ludmila N. Praslova
Vanguard University of Southern California

Christopher Prickett
Texas A&M University, College Station

Susan Prion
University of San Francisco

Joshua N. Pritikin
Virginia Commonwealth University

Ana Puig
University of Florida

Elisabeth M. Pyburn
James Madison University

Patrick Radigan
University of Colorado Colorado Springs

Kelsey Ragan
Texas A&M University

Sharon F. Rallis
University of Massachusetts Amherst

Jennifer Randall
University of Massachusetts Amherst

David L. Raunig
ICON Clinical Research

Sharon M. Ravitch
University of Pennsylvania

Jason Ravitz
Google Inc

Randall Reback
Barnard College

Lynne M. Reder
Carnegie Mellon University

Malcolm James Ree
*Our Lady of the Lake
University*

Charles M. Reigeluth
Indiana University Bloomington

Sally M. Reis
University of Connecticut

Rachel L. Renbarger
Baylor University

Matthew R. Reynolds
University of Kansas

Melissa N. Richards
*National Institute of Child
Health and Human
Development*

John T. E. Richardson
The Open University, UK

Robert D. Ridge
Brigham Young University

Rigoberto Rincones-Gómez
*University of North Carolina
Wilmington*

Joseph A. Rios
Educational Testing Service

Francisco L. Rivera-Batiz
Columbia University

Andrew T. Roach
Georgia State University

L. Danielle Roberts-Dahm
*University of South Florida
St. Petersburg*

Michael C. Rodriguez
University of Minnesota

Liliana Rodríguez-Campos
University of South Florida

Mary Roduta Roberts
University of Alberta

Bradley D. Rogers
University of South Carolina

Jonathan D. Rollins
*University of North Carolina at
Greensboro*

Jeanine Romano
*American Board
of Pathology*

Benjamin D. Rosenberg
Chapman University

Jeffrey N. Rouder
University of Missouri

Amber Rowland
University of Kansas

David J. Royer
University of Kansas

Donald B. Rubin
Harvard University

Cort W. Rudolph
Saint Louis University

Jennifer Lin Russell
University of Pittsburgh

Tonya Rutherford-
Hemming
*University of North Carolina at
Greensboro*

Thomas G. Ryan
Nipissing University

Falak Saffaf
Saint Louis University

Stephen Keith Sagarin
Berkshire Waldorf School

Johnny Saldaña
Arizona State University

Asmalina Saleh
*Indiana University
Bloomington*

Courtney B. Sanders
James Madison University

Massimiliano Sassoli de Bianchi
*Laboratorio di Autoricerca di
Base*

Dorothea Schaffner
*University of Applied Science
Lucerne*

Anne M. Schell
Occidental College

Heather Schmitt
Michigan State University

Stephanie Schmitz
University of Northern Iowa

Rachel Watkins Schoenig
Cornerstone Strategies, LLC

Ryan W. Schroeder
*University of Kansas School
of Medicine–Wichita*

Michael A. Seaman
University of South Carolina

Kathleen Sexton-Radek
Elmhurst College

Nichola Shackleton
University of Auckland

Priti Shah
University of Michigan

Sarah Shannon
University of Washington

Can Shao
University of Notre Dame

Daniel Tan-lei Shek
*The Hong Kong Polytechnic
University*

Mark D. Shermis
*University of Houston–Clear
Lake*

Galit Shmueli
*National Tsing Hua
University*

Nicholas J. Shudak
University of South Dakota

Boaz Shulruf
*University of New South
Wales*

Vivian Shyu
University of Colorado Denver

Jason T. Siegel
Claremont Graduate University

Satoko Siegel
Western University of Health Sciences

Timothy C. Silva
Claremont Graduate University

Julius Sim
Keele University

Lucinda Simmons
Elmhurst College

Stephen G. Sireci
University of Massachusetts Amherst

Julie Slayton
University of Southern California

Stephanie Snidarich
University of Minnesota

Brian Song
California State University, Long Beach

Nancy Butler Songer
Drexel University

J. E. R. Staddon
Duke University and the University of York

Laura M. Stapleton
University of Maryland, College Park

Rachel M. Stein
University of California, Santa Barbara

Douglas Steinley
University of Missouri

Robert J. Sternberg
Cornell University

David W. Stewart
Loyola Marymount University

David W. Stockburger
Missouri State University

Vera Lynne Stroup-Rentier
Kansas State Department of Education

Richard R. Sudweeks
Brigham Young University

Cindy Suurd Ralph
Queen's University

Sruthi Swami
University of California, Santa Barbara

Cara N. Tan
Claremont Graduate University

Ser Hong Tan
National Institute of Education

Michael Tang
University of Colorado Denver

Maciej Taraday
Jagiellonian University

Charlotte Tate
San Francisco State University

Mohsen Tavakol
The University of Nottingham, School of Medicine

Mark S. Teachout
University of the Incarnate Word

David Teira
Universidad Nacional de Educación a Distancia

Lee Teitel
Harvard University

Alexandru C. Telea
University of Groningen

Michael S. Ternes
University of Kansas

Jordan Thayer
University of Minnesota

Lori A. Thombs
University of Missouri

W. Jake Thompson
University of Kansas

Martha L. Thurlow
University of Minnesota

Gail Tiemann
University of Kansas

Rebecca Tipton
Baylor University

Sara Tomek
The University of Alabama

David Torres Irribarra
Pontificia Universidad Católica de Chile

Meng-Jung Tsai
National Taiwan University of Science & Technology

Kayla Tureson
Sanford Health

Yvonne H. M. van den Berg
Behavioural Science Institute, Radboud University

Thomas I. Vaughan-Johnston
Queen's University

Frank R. Vellutino
University at Albany

Aldert Vrij
University of Portsmouth

Jonathan Wai
Duke University Talent Identification Program

Breanna A. Wakar
Mathematica Policy Research

Zachary Walker
National Institute of Education

Jacqueline Remondet Wall
American Psychological Association

Ryan W. Walters
Creighton University

Lisi Wang
University of Texas at Austin

Xi Wang
University of Massachusetts Amherst

Yan Wang
University of South Florida

Emily Ward
Baylor University

Jackie Waterfield
Keele University

Kathryn Weaver
University of New Brunswick

David J. Weiss
University of Minnesota

Craig Stephen Wells
University of Massachusetts Amherst

Jenny C. Wells
University of Hawaii at Manoa

Megan E. Welsh
University of California, Davis

Brian C. Wesolowski
University of Georgia

Colin P. West
Mayo Clinic

David Westfall
Emporia State University

Anna Wieczorek-Taraday
Nencki Institute of Experimental Biology

Christina Wikström
Umeå university

Magnus Wikström
Umeå university

Immanuel Williams
Rutgers, The State University of New Jersey

Pamela Williamson
University of North Carolina at Greensboro

Linda Wilmshurst
The Center for Psychology

Stefanie A. Wind
The University of Alabama

Steven L. Wise
Northwest Evaluation Association

Sara E. Witmer
Michigan State University

James Wollack
University of Wisconsin-Madison

Kenneth K. Wong
Brown University

Rebecca H. Woodland
University of Massachusetts Amherst

Heather H. Woodley
New York University

Annette Woods
Queensland University of Technology

Florence Wu
The Hong Kong Polytechnic University

Jing Wu
The Hong Kong Polytechnic University

Yi-Fang Wu
ACT, Inc.

Gongjun Xu
University of Minnesota

Inbal Yahav
Bar Ilan University

Ji Seung Yang
University of Maryland, College Park

Yang Lydia Yang
Kansas State University

Yanyun Yang
Florida State University

Brandon W. Youker
Grand Valley State University

Jing Yu
University of California, Santa Barbara

Elizabeth R. Zell
Stat-Epi Associates, Inc.

April L. Zenisky
University of Massachusetts Amherst

Hao Helen Zhang
University of Arizona

Kun Zhang
Carnegie Mellon University

Zhiyong Zhang
University of Notre Dame

Fei Zhao
The Citadel

Chunmei Zheng
Pearson

Xiaodi Zhou
University of Georgia

Qingqing Zhu
University of Kansas

Xiaoqin Zhu
The Hong Kong Polytechnic University

Michele F. Zimowski
NORC at the University of Chicago

Bruno D. Zumbo
University of British Columbia

Introduction

Educational Research, Measurement, and Evaluation

The title of this encyclopedia seems to cover at least three distinct fields, each of which could easily fill several volumes of its own. Indeed, there are several fine reference works that cover social science research methods, statistics, assessment and measurement, and program evaluation. Some of the nicer examples are already published by SAGE, in fact. Several encyclopedias cover the field of education in general, with a moderate amount of methodological entries, as well. However, these areas, in terms of their methods, activities, and typical variables of interest, are strongly entwined. Program evaluators use methods developed by educational researchers and develop instruments following measurement best practice. Many, maybe most, of the basic measurement statistics and foundational measurement principles were first conceived and developed by educational researchers. Program evaluators tend to be educational researchers, as well, and, of course, use the tools of social science research to reach their conclusions.

The strongest evidence, perhaps, of the symbiotic relationship among educational research, measurement, and program evaluation can be found in the faculty and courses at research universities. It is often the same professors who teach the research courses, the assessment courses, and the evaluation courses. The same is true of the scholarly journals in educational research, measurement, and evaluation. These journals routinely publish studies across all three areas.

Producing a single encyclopedia that covers the wide range of topics across these connected areas allows for a unique contextual dimension that promotes deeper understanding and allows for more effective learning. In addition to reference works, there are textbooks, handbooks, monographs, and other publications focused on various aspects of educational research, measurement, and evaluation, but to date, there exists no major reference guide for students, researchers, and grant writers new to the field or a particular methodology. The encyclopedia fills that gap. This is the first comprehensive A-to-Z reference work that fully explores methods specific to educational research, assessment, measurement, and evaluation. *The SAGE Encyclopedia of Educational Research, Measurement, and Evaluation* is comprehensive and integrates the three methodological areas of scholarship in the science of education. In an era of constant changes in state and federally driven curricular standards and high-stakes testing, a growing need for innovative instructional methods, increased reliance on data-driven decision-making and calls for accountability in research, a shared understanding of the methods of educational research, measurement, and evaluation is more important than ever.

Making an Encyclopedia

A project of this size takes many people and a long time. Once a publisher, like SAGE, realizes there is a need for a multi-volume reference work like this, they choose an editor, like me. I was likely chosen because I've taught and published across these areas of educational research, measurement, and evaluation.

My first step was to recruit a world-class group of expert advisors, leaders in their field who teach and publish in educational research, measurement and evaluation. I was fortunate to form an Advisory Board of these five nice and wise folks:

- Dr. Rebecca Woodland, University of Massachusetts Amherst
- Dr. Neal Kingston, University of Kansas

- Dr. Jill Lohmeier, University of Massachusetts Lowell
- Dr. William Skorupski, University of Kansas
- Dr. Jonathan Templin, University of Kansas

Together, we began to shape the encyclopedia. What topics or broad categories should be covered? We wanted the emphasis to be on methodology in educational research, measurement, and evaluation, but we also wanted the encyclopedia to cover important theories and common research variables. What entries should be included? Encyclopedia publishers call entry titles "headwords," and choosing these headwords was critical. In a four-volume encyclopedia there is only room for so many headwords (about 700), each headword can only be a certain number of words (about 500 to 3,000), and the right length of each headword varies depending on the importance of the entry. At the end of this process, we identified these broad topics as a framework for what belongs in the encyclopedia:

Assessment

Cognitive and Affective Variables

Data Visualization Methods

Disabilities and Disorders

Distributions

Educational Policies

Evaluation Concepts

Evaluation Designs

Human Development

Instrument Development

Organizations and Government Agencies

Professional Issues

Publishing

Qualitative Research

Research Concepts

Research Designs

Research Methods

Research Tools

Social and Ethical Issues

Social Network Analysis

Statistics

Teaching and Learning

Theories and Conceptual Frameworks

Threats to Research Validity

The reader's guide, near this introduction, lists all the entries, grouped by these categories, so you can find what you want quickly. Based on these topics, we began identifying entries that an encyclopedia of educational research, measurement, and evaluation should include. We then needed to find hundreds of experts to write the 691 entries in this work. The advisory board suggested names and reserved some entries for themselves, I took a few for myself and began identifying potential authors, and, in what turned out to be a smart move, I hired a bright doctoral student, Alan Nong, to help with the search process. For some entries, there were clear leaders in the field, or authors of key studies to recruit. For other general entries, we searched education, educational psychology, curriculum, and statistics departments at universities throughout the globe. We have some of the top scholars in their field among the authors of these entries.

Acknowledgments

Among the experts who authored entries for the encyclopedia are Robert Brennan writing about testing, Craig Mertler writing about standardized scores, Bruno Zumbo writing about psychometrics, Joseph Maxwell writing about mixed methods research and qualitative data analysis, Laura O'Dwyer and Donald Rubin writing about experimental design, Peter Bentler writing about structural equation modeling, and David Fetterman and Michael Quinn Patton writing about evaluation. And literally hundreds of others were willing to contribute, for which I am grateful. You can see a list of all contributors at the front of this encyclopedia. About two years was spent in the recruitment and writing process and the initial stages of review and editing before the encyclopedia was copyedited. I am so impressed with the quality and value of the work done by our authors. Thanks, sincerely, to all of them.

I am most grateful for the fine work and guidance of the friendly people at SAGE. It was Jim

Brace-Thompson who, as acquisition editor, promoted the idea to SAGE and first got me involved, and Andrew Boney who took the project on, worked with layout and design, and kept things running smoothly. Jordan Enobakhare helped get things going. Anna Villaseñor taught me how to use the remarkable software system that lets people make encyclopedias. Most of the heavy lifting during the first year or two of this process was done by Susan Moskowitz, who somehow handled the recruitment and enlistment of hundreds of scholars, shepherded their submissions, and worked with their schedules. Shirin Parsavand agreed to be the developmental editor and, though I don't think we've ever met (or been at the same conference at the same time), it seems like we shared an office and this has truly been a team effort with her. As we neared the finish line, David Felts, the production editor for the encyclopedia, took the reins to move us through the final gates. Thank you, SAGE editors and staff, as you all are really first rate and so good at what you do. Finally, I am so thankful for the material and moral support of my wife, Bonnie Johnson. She is a finer scholar than I.

Bruce B. Frey

a PARAMETER

The *a* parameter, or the discrimination parameter, is one of the key item parameters in many item response theory (IRT) models. This entry discusses how the *a* parameter is defined and interpreted. For this discussion, properties of the *a* parameter are introduced in the unidimensional IRT framework in which items in a test measure one and only one construct, with a focus on dichotomous item responses. Realistically, items in a test are considered to be unidimensional as long as a single construct accounts for a substantial portion of the total score variance.

Unidimensional IRT framework is the focus of this entry because it is the foundation of its multidimensional counterpart, and basic principles in unidimensional IRT framework can be straightforwardly interpreted in the multidimensional context. In addition, this discussion concentrates on dichotomous item response models because they can be considered as the special cases of polytomous models, and when item responses become binary, polytomous models reduce to dichotomous models.

Defining the *a* Parameter

Using a mathematical formula, the IRT theory defines the probability of an examinee's correct response to an item as a function of the latent ability of the examinee and that item's properties. This function, the item characteristic curve (ICC), is also referred to as the item response function. An ICC defines a smooth nonlinear relationship between latent trait constructs (θ) and probability of a correct response. If assumptions are met, the ICCs can be stable over groups of examinees, and the θ scale also can be stable even when the test includes different items. A graphical representation of an ICC is given in Figure 1.

The generic mathematics function for Figure 1 is shown in Equation 1.

$$P(x_i = 1 \mid \theta) = c_i + (1 - c_i) \frac{\exp(a_i(\theta - b_i))}{1 + \exp(a_i(\theta - b_i))}, \quad (1)$$

where θ is the examinee ability parameter, c_i is often referred to as the pseudo-guessing or lower asymptote parameter with a value typically between 0 and 0.25, b_i is the location or difficulty

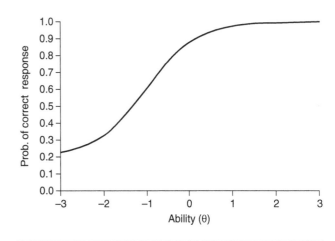

Figure 1   Example of an ICC

1

parameter, and a_i is the discrimination or slope parameter. The parameter a_i indicates the steepness of ICC at $\theta = b$, where probability of correctly answering an item changes most rapidly. The logistic function presented in Equation 1 is called the three-parameter logistic (3PL) model, which was presented by Allan Birnbaum in a pioneering work by Frederic Lord and Melvin Novick in 1968. The two-parameter logistic (2PL; Equation 2) and one-parameter logistic (1PL) model (Equation 3) can be considered as special cases of the 3PL IRT model. As indicated in the corresponding formula, the 2PL model only has the *a* and the *b* parameter, whereas the 1PL model only has the *b* parameter and the *a* parameter is fixed.

$$P(x_i = 1 \mid \theta) = \frac{\exp(a_i(\theta - b_i))}{1 + \exp(a_i(\theta - b_i))}, \qquad (2)$$

$$P(x_i = 1 \mid \theta) = \frac{\exp(\theta - b_i)}{1 + \exp(\theta - b_i)}. \qquad (3)$$

Interpreting the *a* Parameter

Figure 2 represents ICCs for three dichotomous items under the unidimensional 3PL IRT model. Among these 3 items, all *b*'s = 0 and all *c*'s = 0.2, but *a* values differ: $a_1 = 0.5$, $a_2 = 1$, and $a_3 = 1.5$.

As shown in Figure 2, the slope of Item 1, at the location where examinees' abilities are about the same as the item's difficulty ($\theta = b = 0$), is the flattest among the three items, whereas the slope of Item 3 at the same location is the steepest. Therefore, Item 1 has the lowest discrimination value among the three and Item 3 has the highest. If identifying two examinees of whom one has an ability larger than zero and one smaller than zero on the ability axis, the difference between the probabilities of the two students answering Item 3 correctly will be greater than Item 1 or 2. It is therefore easier to discriminate between the two examinees using Item 3, compared to Item 1 or 2. With all else equal, Item 3 can be concluded as more desirable because it can effectively distinguish among examinees differing in ability.

Using the item information function, similar information can be verified via a different angle. Generally speaking, information stands for precision. If the amount of information is large at a given ability level, an examinee whose true ability at that level can be estimated with the greatest precision. Figure 3 shows the item information functions for the 3 items previously shown in Figure 2. As shown in Figure 3, when the *b* parameter and the *c* parameter are the same across items as in the example, Item 3 has the largest item information because the *a* parameter associated with Item 3 has the largest value among the 3 items.

The *a* parameter interpretation in the 2PL model is very similar to its interpretation in the 3PL model. However, because the location parameter

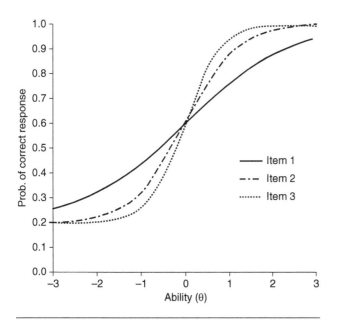

Figure 2 ICCs for three example items

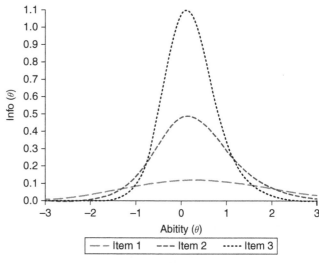

Figure 3 IIFs for the same three example items

for the 2PL model indicates the ability level at which examinees have a 50% chance of answering an item correctly, the *a* parameter indicates the item discrimination information specifically at this ability level. The item discriminations are considered equal across items in the 1PL model because all *a* parameters are fixed. Therefore, if a group of items' ICCs are presented together under the 1PL model, the curves will not cross each other. Overall, items can be maximally informative at any part of the ability (θ) continuum, but interpretation of the *a* parameter will be most meaningful when interpreted in conjunction with the *b* and/or *c* parameter for the same item.

The item responses are said to be polytomous when more than two categories exist. Representative models in this group include graded response model, generalized partial credit model, and nominal response model. For polytomous item responses, the probability of an examinee reaching a score category can be described by one of these polytomous IRT models. Interpretation of the discrimination parameter in polytomous response models is very similar to its counterparts in the binary response models arena because polytomous item response models are developed by extending the general underlying IRT premise to items scored in two or more categories.

Fei Zhao

See also *b* Parameter; *c* Parameter; Item Response Theory

Further Readings

Baker, F. B., & Kim, S. H. (2004). *Item response theory: Parameter estimation techniques.* New York, NY: Marcel Dekker.

Birnbaum, A. (1968). Some latent trait models and their use in inferring an examinee's ability. In F. M. Lord & M. R. Novick (Eds.), *Statistical theories of mental test scores* (pp. 397–479). Reading, MA: MIT Press.

Bock, R. D. (1972). Estimating item parameters and latent ability when responses are scored in two or more nominal categories. *Psychometrika, 37*(1), 29–51.

Muraki, E. (1992). A generalized partial credit model: Application of an EM algorithm. *Applied Psychological Measurement, 16,* 159–176.

Samejima, F. (1969). Estimation of ability using a response pattern of graded scores. *Psychometrika Monograph Supplement, 34*(4 part 2), 100.

ABA Designs

ABA designs, also known as *reversal designs*, are among a family of single-case experimental designs most often used by behavioral scientists and educators to evaluate the effectiveness of clinical or educational interventions. This entry first describes ABA designs and provides an example, then discusses phase changes in ABA designs, how ABA designs are used to identify treatment effects, and the limitations of ABA designs.

In a typical ABA design, a relevant dependent variable, such as frequency of tantrums, self-injurious behaviors, or correct academic responses, is measured continuously over some period of time for a single participant. Observation and measurement of this behavior initially occurs under a *baseline* condition (A in the ABA sequence), in which no independent variable, or treatment, is presented. During this baseline condition, the behavior of interest is assumed to be occurring at its natural level, prior to introduction of the independent variable. After this behavior has demonstrated stability, showing no discernible upward or downward trend during baseline, the treatment or intervention phase (B) is introduced, and measurement of the dependent variable continues. Finally, a return to baseline (A) is programmed, allowing for assessment of the dependent variable once again in the absence of treatment.

The ABA design can be seen as a formalization of the common "before and after" observations that many of us make of ourselves in response to changes in diet, exercise routines, and other efforts at self-improvement. Such designs are common experimental methods in the natural sciences and were advocated by Claude Bernard, the father of experimental medicine. The general logic of single case experimentation was adopted by psychologist B. F. Skinner as a powerful method for the continuous analysis of learning processes in real time. Beginning in the late 1930s, Skinner pioneered a branch of natural science he called the experimental analysis of behavior, whose products include the contemporary profession of applied behavior analysis.

Applied behavior analysts have been longtime proponents and practitioners of ABA designs, as their work involves the application of basic learning principles to socially significant behavior across many domains, including schools, workplaces, and the home. Behavior analysts utilize single-case ABA designs in order to evaluate the effectiveness of treatments, especially in the area of autism and developmental disabilities. ABA designs are experimental designs that support causal inferences, and the data produced by such designs contribute to our knowledge of evidence-based interventions in the behavioral sciences.

A hallmark of the ABA design is its focus on the behavior of the individual. Behavior analysts consider single-case designs and continuous measurement superior to large-scale group designs in resolving the nuances of moment-to-moment behavior–environment interactions that are often the target of such interventions. Behavior often responds both quickly and dramatically to changes in environmental variables, and the ABA design is a powerful method for assessing these changes. In fact, use of ABA designs can often identify environmental events that correspond to changes in behavior with as much regularity as the lights turn off and on in a room with each flip of a light switch. Each change in condition, from baseline to treatment, or from treatment to baseline, becomes an opportunity to observe a functional relationship between the treatment and the behavioral variable. In addition, further phase changes can be programmed to replicate this functional relationship; thus, ABA designs have intraparticipant replication built into them, and this is an extremely important criterion for developing evidence-based practices.

Example of ABA Design

The essential logic of the ABA designs is fairly intuitive and can be depicted in a hypothetical example. Maria, a successful CEO of a marketing firm, having learned that she is at risk for developing heart disease due to family history, has decided to initiate a regular exercise regimen. She joins a local gym and, being an observant and detail-oriented person, keeps track of her total time spent exercising for 2 weeks. Maria's interest is in increasing her overall duration of cardiovascular exercise, not any specific kind of workout, so she varies her exercise routines (e.g., swimming, riding a stationary bike, walking on a treadmill) and times of her workouts, adding up the total time for each week.

At the end of a 2-week period, Maria sees that her exercise duration varies from day to day, but it doesn't seem impressive to her, and she would like to set her goals much higher. Like most of us, Maria lives a very busy life, raising two children and putting in the long hours of an executive officer, and realizes that increasing her exercise amount is going to be a challenge. In order to provide additional motivation, Maria recruits the help of a close friend. She writes her friend a check for a very large amount, more than she would feel comfortable losing, and tells her friend that if she (Maria) doesn't increase her total exercise duration by at least 20% by the end of the next week, her friend is to give the money to an organization for which Maria has nothing but contempt. In essence, Maria is using a potentially aversive consequence, losing a sizable amount of money, in order to motivate her to increase her exercise. Although self-imposed, she is manipulating an independent variable (threat of lost money) in order to alter measurable aspects of a dependent variable, in this case her total amount of weekly exercise.

Figure 1 is a time-series graph, often used by behavioral scientists to depict behavior change in response to programmed treatments or interventions. The graph is called a time-series graph because time, in this case represented in successive days, is represented on the x-axis. The primary dependent variable, total duration of exercise per week, is plotted on the y-axis. The vertical lines drawn through the data paths represent changes in conditions, the first line depicting initial implementation of the monetary contingency (potential loss of money) and the second line depicting removal of this monetary contingency or return to baseline.

The first week's data represent Maria's baseline level of exercise. Although Maria's exercise duration shows some degree of variability from day to day (a near guarantee for almost any behavior), there are no obvious trends upward or downward during this first week. Maria's disappointment in her exercise amount prompts her to enlist her friend and a simple behavioral contingency in an effort to enhance her exercise. The first vertical line, then, separates the first two weeks, or baseline period, from the initial treatment week, in which the potential monetary loss is in effect. Finally, after the intervention week, Maria decides

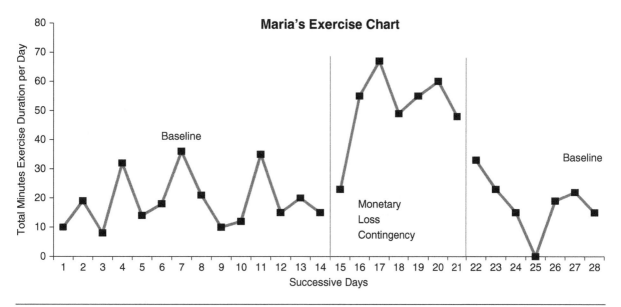

Figure I Maria's exercise chart

to revert to the baseline condition, in which the potential monetary loss contingency is no longer in effect. This return to baseline is conceptualized as a replication of this nontreatment condition, and it serves as a comparison for the previous treatment condition.

Phase Changes

In single-case experimental designs, individual participants serve as their own controls, meaning their behavior is evaluated under both treatment and nontreatment conditions. This comparison is logically similar to comparing control and experimental groups in a more conventional large group experimental design. In the ABA design, visible change in the data path following a phase change (baseline to treatment or treatment to baseline) is suggestive of an effect of independent variable presentation (treatment) or removal (return to baseline).

The logic of the design actually allows for multiple alternations between baseline and treatment, so that although the design is called ABA, there are no formal limits on how many phase changes can be produced. Two presentations and subsequent removals of treatment, for example, would result in an ABABA design. Although this many phase changes may not be common, multiple phase changes are advantageous because each phase change represents a replication of an earlier condition change. Single-case experimental designs

derive their inferential power from such replications, not through null hypothesis testing and statistical inference.

Identifying Treatment Effects

The hypothetical real-time data provided by Maria in Figure 1 would be subjected to visual analysis and possibly quantitative effect size measures in order to identify treatment effects. When analyzing such time-series data, researchers consider a number of characteristics of the data path. One possible comparison is to draw a horizontal line through the mean of a baseline phase and an adjacent treatment phase. The difference between these lines is interpreted as a change in level. In addition, a data path can be evaluated for trend, which is visible as clear movement up or down in the data path.

As stated earlier, it is important to ensure that no obvious trend is present in baseline data, as this would render any comparison of these data with initial treatment data problematic. For instance, if Maria's exercise duration demonstrated a clear increase near the end of the first phase (A) in Figure 1, additional increases during the first intervention (B) could not be easily interpreted as a treatment effect. However, if baseline data remain stable and increase only in treatment phases, a stronger argument can be made for a treatment effect. In addition to visual inspection of data paths, a number of quantitative analyses have been developed for evaluating effect sizes in single-case experimental designs.

In the example presented earlier, Maria transitioned from a baseline condition to a treatment condition and finished with a return to baseline. The basic logic of the ABA design, however, allows for changing this sequence if necessary. In many instances, the behavior being targeted may be especially aversive, even dangerous, for the client or others in the client's environment. When this is the case, and a substantial baseline period of observation is considered unethical (recall that baseline means that there is no treatment being delivered), a treatment condition can actually be instituted first, followed by a brief baseline period and a final treatment period. This effectively produces a BAB design rather than an ABA design.

Limitations of ABA Designs

ABA or reversal designs are powerful and flexible for identifying treatment effects in education and behavior analysis, but they are not without limitations. Many behaviors, especially those acquired in academic settings, are not easily reversed when interventions are removed. Imagine, for example, delivering a new reading readiness program to preschoolers. One would not expect the skills acquired during this program to disappear during a subsequent return to baseline. And, as mentioned previously, when the behavior of interest is potentially dangerous, it would be unethical to withdraw what appeared to be an effective treatment. For this reason, frequent reversals to baseline are not always feasible in applied settings. When this is the case, ABA designs are not advisable. Other single-case experimental designs, however, such as multiple-baseline designs, changing criterion designs, and alternating treatment designs, can be relied on to assess treatment effectiveness. These designs also utilize the principal tactic of replication to demonstrate treatment effects but do so in procedurally different ways and both within and across individual participants.

David Morgan

See also Applied Behavior Analysis; Behaviorism; Replication; Single-Case Research

Further Readings

Bailey, J. S., & Burch, M. R. (2002). *Research methods in applied behavior analysis.* Thousand Oaks, CA: Sage.

Blampied, N. M. (2012). Single-case research designs and the scientist-practitioner ideal in applied psychology. In G. Madden (Ed.), *APA handbook of behavior analysis.* Washington, DC: American Psychological Association.

Cooper, J. O., Heron, T. E., & Heward, W. L. (2007). *Applied behavior analysis* (2nd ed.). Upper Saddle River, NJ: Pearson.

Morgan, D. L., & Morgan, R. K. (2009). *Single-case research methods for the behavioral and health sciences.* Thousand Oaks, CA: Sage.

Richards, S. B., Taylor, R. L., & Ramasamy, R. (2014). *Single subject research: Applications in educational and clinical settings.* Belmont, CA: Wadsworth.

Smith, J. D. (2012). Single-case experimental designs: A systematic review of published research and current standards. *Psychological Methods, 17*(4), 510–550.

ABILITY TESTS

An ability test is an objective and standardized measure of a sample of behaviors at a specific point in time. Broadly defined, ability tests assess the innate and acquired capacity to perform mental or motor functions. This entry discusses the history of ability tests, their classification and standardization, the criteria for evaluating ability tests, and controversies over their use.

The modern scientific study of human cognitive abilities is often attributed to French psychologist Alfred Binet, who developed the Binet-Simon intelligence test, and to the World War I Army Alpha and Beta tests in the United States. The Army Alpha and Beta tests were used to assess cognitive ability for U.S. military recruits during World War I. The Army Beta test is noteworthy in that it was used to evaluate recruits who were illiterate, unschooled, or non-English speaking. This is considered an early example of cognitive tests that do not rely on verbal skills or learned content. An important consequence of the Army Alpha and Beta tests was the popularization of group-administered aptitude tests.

Debate on the structure of abilities began in the early 1900s and continues to the present. An important milestone in this debate was the development and application of factor analysis to determine the extent to which aptitudes were distinct from one another. Applying factor analyses, Louis Leon Thurstone proposed seven primary mental abilities. Others later reanalyzed Thurstone's data and demonstrated a single, general ability factor that influenced the seven primary abilities. Despite this finding, the development of multiple aptitude tests thrived. Examples of these tests are the Differential Aptitude Tests, Multiple Aptitude Tests, and Comprehensive Ability Battery.

In the last part of the 20th century, the advent of fast and inexpensive computers played a major role in both test construction and test administration. Previously, test statistics were computationally burdensome, prone to errors, and time-consuming. Computers enabled test construction to be done more quickly with fewer errors while also making results available much sooner. It also has allowed for computer adaptive testing. In computer adaptive testing, a question is asked, the response is scored immediately, and the next item is selected to best suit the ability level of the examinee. This continues until an accurate measure of ability is obtained.

Computer adaptive testing has been implemented by governments and commercial endeavors. Three examples are the National Council Licensure Examination of the National Council of State Boards of Nursing, the Armed Services Vocational Aptitude Battery, and the GRE General Test. In 2011, the GRE General Test became adaptive only for groups of questions.

Classification of Ability Tests

A general distinction is often made between ability tests, sometimes referred to as intelligence or aptitude tests, and achievement tests. Although ability, intelligence, and aptitude are sometimes used synonymously, there are subtle distinctions. Ability and intelligence tests are usually considered as tapping more into fundamental abilities, while aptitude tests may include more of an accumulation of cognitive and motor abilities. In addition, intelligence tests are often defined in broad categories such as verbal and quantitative abilities, whereas aptitude tests are usually defined in more specific ways combining ability and accumulated knowledge (e.g., mechanical, musical, and spatial).

The following are two important factors that differentiate aptitude from achievement tests: (1) the prior experience of the examinee that is considered by the test developer and (2) the purpose for which the test scores are used. Early conceptions of these tests reflected a simplistic distinction based on heredity versus the environment. Aptitude tests were based on innate capacity or traits, independent of learning, while achievement tests were based on more specific learning.

Rather than considering ability and achievement as independent concepts, a useful approach is to consider ability tests on a continuum. All are developed abilities, differentiated by the type of prior experience that is considered in constructing the test items. At one end of the continuum, aptitude is acquired over years of education, experience, and life activities. Therefore, prior experience of the examinee is defined quite broadly and over a longer term. Some consider aptitude tests long-term achievement tests. At the other end of the continuum, achievement tests measure specialized knowledge or skills acquired through formal or informal education or training. Hence, prior experience is typically considered narrower and shorter term.

The second distinction is the purpose for which the test scores are used. While both are a snapshot of an attribute at a specific time, aptitude tests are designed for predictive purposes while achievement tests are designed for descriptive purposes. A typical aptitude or intelligence test is designed to assess the capacity of the examinee to learn both cognitive and motor skills in order to predict the potential to learn and use those skills in future situations, such as an educational, training, or work setting. An achievement test may examine mastery of knowledge or a motor skill to determine the level of competency of the examinee. For example, knowledge of regulations and driving ability are tested to obtain a driver's license, a language test is administered to select an interpreter, and state licensing exams are used for many professions such as the medical and legal professions.

Both aptitude and achievement are developed abilities. Aptitude tests describe knowledge and skills and measure attributes intended to predict future learning. Achievement tests measure the mastery of more specific subject matter. In practice, there may be confusion when there is overlap between the content and purpose of a test. That is, some tests may contain elements of both aptitude and achievement. When learned contents are used in aptitude tests, the blend becomes evident. Achievement tests are sometimes misused for predictive purposes.

Aptitude Tests

Some aptitude tests purport to measure a single aptitude, while others purport to measure multiple aptitudes. Typically, most aptitude tests measure a relatively standard set of constructs reflecting cognitive and motor skills. Cognitive skills are unobservable and represent different capacities for mental activity, information processing, understanding, and problem solving. Content may include verbal, numerical, spatial, abstract reasoning, and comprehension. Motor skills are observable and represent the ability to perform physical tasks that do not require a cognitive skill to understand. These are motor coordination, finger dexterity, and manual dexterity.

Some motor skill tests require the use of cognitive skills to make a physical response. For example, a block design test requires the examinee to view a picture of how blocks should look when assembled and then to assemble them as quickly as possible replicating the design in the picture. Some aptitude tests use composite scores obtained by combining two or more subtests. Scores can be interpreted as a unique test score and as part of a composite. For example, intelligence test scores are verbal intelligence (using verbal, numerical, and spatial aptitude) and performance intelligence (using abstract reasoning and object manipulation tasks). Other aptitude composites are verbal comprehension, perceptual organization, processing speed, and working memory.

Examples of aptitude tests are the Stanford–Binet Intelligence Scales, Wechsler Adult Intelligence Scale, Wechsler Intelligence Scale for Children, Wechsler Preschool and Primary Scale of Intelligence, Otis-Lennon School Ability Test, Differential Ability Scales, and the Woodcock-Johnson Tests of Cognitive Abilities.

There are ways of measuring aptitude without learned content such as the Raven's Progressive Matrices and a procedure measuring the speed of neural processing. Raven's Progressive Matrices is a test of abstract reasoning based on a series of geometric figures and is frequently regarded as "culture free." An individual's speed of neural processing can be assessed by having the individual look at a computer screen while a light is flashed and the speed with which a single nerve conducts the impulse is measured.

Admissions tests are used in the application process at private elementary and secondary schools, as well as at most colleges and universities. These are used to predict the probability of student success in these academic settings. Examples for secondary school include the High School Placement Test. Tests for undergraduate admission are the SAT and ACT. In addition, there are numerous admission exams for graduate and professional school, including the Graduate Management Admission Test (GMAT) used by business schools, GRE General Test, Law School Admission Test, and Pharmacy College Admission Test.

Achievement Tests

Tests of specific knowledge, professional certification, and licensing are not aptitude tests but rather achievement tests. Achievement tests measure specialized knowledge or skills acquired through formal or informal education or training. Thousands of achievement tests are developed and used nationally by states and local entities. Examples are the Wechsler Individual Achievement Test, Kaufman Test of Educational Achievement, Woodcock-Johnson Tests of Achievement, and Peabody Individual Achievement Test. Many states use specifically designed achievement tests for certification of teachers and principals as well as for medical and legal professions.

For public schools, the National Assessment of Educational Progress is used, whereas state achievement tests may be required for schools that receive federal funding. There also may be tests required for high school graduation such as the

New York State Regents Examination. Other achievement tests include the GED test, which is taken to certify academic skills in lieu of a high school diploma. Tests created by private institutions are often used to monitor progress in K–12 classrooms.

Praxis certification exams for teacher certification measure academic skills in reading, writing, and mathematics. The Praxis Subject Assessments measure subject-specific content knowledge and the Praxis Content Knowledge for Teaching Assessments assess specialized content knowledge for K–12 teaching.

Finally, language proficiency exams such as the Test of English as a Foreign Language (TOEFL) are used to assess international students for admission to colleges and universities where English is used as the primary language.

Standardization of Ability Tests

Most ability tests are standardized and designed to provide an objective assessment of an individual's abilities relative to data collected on a relevant reference group (i.e., normative group). This is known as a norm-referenced test. Comparing the examinee's score to that of the normative group permits the interpretation of the score relative to the normed population, whether a raw score, standard score, or percentile. The normed group must be meaningful as a basis for comparison. For example, it would be misleading to compare high school student test scores to scores from a normative group of elementary school students because the high school student results would appear to be much higher than if compared to a more relevant norm group of their own age.

Tests often have more than one normative group. For example, a test designed for elementary school children may have a normative group of students for each grade. Subsequent examinee scores can then be compared to see whether they've scored at, above, or below their grade level. Norms are also often developed for gender and ethnicity.

Developing normative information is time-consuming and costly. Often an appropriate normative group is not available for comparison, so users must choose the most relevant norm group available. Another issue is that normative

information may be out-of-date. The accuracy and usefulness of normative interpretations may decline as the age of the normative data increases.

Achievement tests may also be standardized, but unlike ability tests where test scores are compared to a normative population (e.g., high school graduates), achievement test scores are usually compared to a minimum acceptable score. Tests that are interpreted by comparing the examinee's score to a predetermined standard or cutoff score are called criterion-referenced tests. For example, to obtain a driver's license in most states, one must receive a minimum score on a test of traffic and safety rules.

Criteria for Evaluating Ability Tests

Three points of evaluation of ability tests are reliability, validity, and applicability for the examinees. Reliability creates consistency of measurement. Although there are several methods for determining reliability, the most obvious is test–retest, repeating the same test on two occasions with the same people and calculating the correlation between the scores.

The validity of a test is concerned with what the test measures and how well it measures it. There are several aspects of validity that are particularly relevant to ability tests, including predictive validity, content-based validity, and construct-based validity. Predictive validity determines whether the test predicts some important outcome such as success in a school course. Content-based validity arguments focus on the items or tasks that make up the test itself and the degree to which they appropriately sample from the universe of all possible items. Construct-based validity argues that the test scores represent the construct of interest within a theoretical framework.

Evaluation of reliability and validity depends on the use of the test scores. Rough rules of thumb for reliability are based on coefficient α, a common index of internal consistency: .5 is acceptable for research, .7 for group decisions, and .8 for decisions about individuals. Validity can be evaluated in several ways, but often the strongest evidence comes from correlations with other measures. Does the ability test show a statistically significant correlation with an external criterion test? Evaluation of reliability and validity is complex, however, and is not driven by one or two criteria.

Controversies in Ability Testing

Controversies in ability testing have a long history. Among the longest controversies is whether ability is unitary or made up of many separate parts (multiple abilities), and the way theories organize these parts. The controversy is sometimes cast in the model of general ability (g) versus specific abilities (s). This has implications for construction and use of ability measures. Early 20th century models of ability emphasized g but did not exclude the concept of s. Mid-century models focused on s which is reflected in the development of multiple abilities theories. This lead to the development of multiple ability test batteries that found their way into public schools as early as1935. The existence of a general ability factor is widely accepted, but the utility of g versus s is still debated.

Other controversies include the differences in mean test scores among groups and the impact of race, ethnicity, gender, and culture on ability test scores. These controversies have been widely studied and discussed in the professional literature. While group mean differences exist, there is no evidence that the predictive power of tests differs among and between groups. Additionally, there is empirical evidence that ability and achievement tests measure the same constructs for the various identifiable groups in the population.

More recently, the use of so-called high-stakes testing has become controversial, especially with the nationwide implementation of the No Child Left Behind Act of 2001, which was replaced in 2015 by the Every Student Succeeds Act. It is of note that New York state instituted high-stakes testing in secondary school with the Regents Examinations in the 19th century and that even before the No Child Left Behind Act of 2001 some states had school accountability systems that included public reporting of standardized test scores and sanctions for low performance.

Ability test misuse is frequently related to four deficiencies. The first is poor training and practice by the examiner. Some examiners will have been trained in past decades by experts whose training was completed decades before that. Therefore, they will not be knowledgeable about changes in scores and their meanings. Second, proper interpretation of scores depends on the knowledge of the situation in which the constructs measured will be relevant. Third is failure to evaluate the construct validity of the test. The claim of the test developer is not a sufficient substitute for examining the articles and reports that support the claims that an ability test actually measures the targeted ability. Finally, continuing education on changes in statistical methods in testing needs to take place.

*Mark S. Teachout, Malcolm James Ree,
and Thomas R. Carretta*

See also Achievement Tests; Aptitude Tests; Computerized Adaptive Testing; Intelligence Tests; Reliability; Stanford–Binet Intelligence Scales; Validity

Further Readings

Anastasi, A., & Urbina, S. (1997). *Essentials of psychological testing* (7th ed.). Upper Saddle River, NJ: Prentice Hall.

Dubois, P. (1970). *A history of psychological testing.* Boston, MA: Allyn and Bacon.

Fleishman, E. A., & Quaintance, M. K. (1984). *Taxonomies of human performance: The description of human tasks.* Orlando, FL: Academic Press.

Jensen, A. R. (1980). *Bias in mental testing.* New York, NY: The Free Press.

Jensen, A. R. (1998). *The g factor: The science of mental ability.* Westport, CN: Praeger.

Zhang, H. (1988). Psychological measurement in China. *International Journal of Psychology, 23,* 101–117.

ABILITY–ACHIEVEMENT DISCREPANCY

The ability–achievement discrepancy is defined as a statistically significant difference between a child's score on a measure of achievement in one or another academic domain such as reading or math and the child's score on a measure of intellectual ability, typically in the form of IQ. For a considerable period of time, the IQ-achievement discrepancy was the central criterion used by educators, school psychologists, and educational researchers to define specific learning disabilities in otherwise normal children. This entry discusses the history of the ability–achievement discrepancy, the origin of its use, and problems with its use to identify individuals with specific reading disability.

The use of the ability–achievement discrepancy criterion has a long history that dates back to Samuel Kirk and Barbara Bateman's suggestion that learning disabilities can be defined as a collection of developmental disorders of neurological origin that affect various types of school-based learning in children who are not mentally challenged or impaired by extraneous impediments to learning such as sensory deficits, emotional disorders, or socioeconomic disadvantage. The Education for All Handicapped Children Act (U.S. Public Law 94–142, later renamed the Individuals with Disabilities Education Act), adopted in 1975, mandated that learning disabilities be defined as the occurrence of achievement deficits in otherwise normal children who have at least average intelligence.

The Education for All Handicapped Children Act had significant impact because it led to the use of intelligence as a defining criterion in most state definitions of learning disability, typically in the form of an IQ-achievement discrepancy in one or another academic domain. The IQ-achievement discrepancy eventually became widely adopted as a basic prerequisite for diagnosing learning disabilities in schools and other institutions and for defining learning disabilities in empirical research studying the etiology and nature of hypothesized impediments to success in school learning.

Origin of the IQ-Achievement Discrepancy Definition of Learning Disability

The definition of learning disability specified in U.S. Public Law 94–142 and the widespread use of the IQ-achievement discrepancy as the central criterion for diagnosing learning disabilities were in large measure influenced by the work of Michael Rutter, William Yule, and their associates. These investigators conducted a large-scale epidemiological study evaluating the etiology of reading disability—the most common form of learning disability—and found that the percentage of children whose scores on measures of reading ability were two standard errors or more below the scores that were predicted by their ages and IQs was significantly higher than the percentage of children who were expected to fall in this range on

the assumption of normality (i.e., 2.3%), thereby creating a "hump" in the tail end of the distribution of residual scores.

Rutter and Yule hypothesized that there were two types of impaired readers: one said to be afflicted by "specific reading retardation," as defined by a significant discrepancy between observed reading achievement and expected or IQ-based reading achievement, along with the absence of general learning difficulties, and a second said to be afflicted by "general reading backwardness," as defined by general learning difficulties along with the absence of any significant discrepancy between observed and expected reading achievement. Rutter and Yule's distinction between specific reading retardation and general reading backwardness was in keeping with Kirk and Bateman's seminal definition of learning disability, and it subsequently became the basis for what can be called "exclusionary definitions" of reading and other learning disabilities having the IQ-achievement discrepancy as their central defining criterion.

Problems With Discrepancy Definitions of Reading Disability

The use of the IQ-achievement discrepancy as the basis for defining specific reading disability, also referred to as dyslexia, has qualified empirical justification at best. For example, Eve Malmquist reviewed results from a large number of studies that evaluated the relationship between intelligence and reading achievement and found that correlations between these two variables were modest, ranging only from .40 to .60. Malmquist obtained correlations of comparable magnitudes in a large multivariate study of first-grade, poor, and normal readers. Guy Bond and Robert Dykstra obtained similar results with a randomly selected sample of first graders.

Although several studies have obtained higher correlations between intelligence and reading achievement with older participants, the intelligence tests used in these studies consisted of items with high verbal content and/or depended on skill in reading. Thus, observed correlations between the measures of intelligence and the measures of reading achievement used in these studies, in many cases, may have been an artifact of shared variance contributed by language-based abilities underlying performance on both sets of measures. Additional support for this possibility is provided by a study conducted by Frank Vellutino and his associates with elementary and middle school-age children in which it was found that correlations between measures of reading subskills and a commonly used test of intelligence were significantly higher when the intelligence test evaluated verbal abilities than when it evaluated nonverbal abilities. Thus, discrepancy definitions of the types motivated by Rutter and Yule's work may have been based on inaccurate conceptualization of the relationship between intelligence and reading achievement resulting from faulty analysis of the cognitive abilities underlying performance on both intelligence tests and reading tests.

Even more compelling evidence against using the IQ-achievement discrepancy to define reading and other learning disabilities is provided by results from several other studies that have addressed the question. First, a study conducted by Rodgers failed to replicate the type of bimodal distributions obtained by Rutter and Yule. This finding was replicated by David Share and his associates, and it was suggested that Rutter and Yule's findings may have been an artifact of floor and ceiling effects on the reading measures used in their studies. This possibility was later given some credibility in independent studies conducted by A. van der Wissel and F. E. Zegers and by Share and his associates, in which it was found that bimodality in each of several distributions of IQ-reading residual scores could be artificially induced by creating false ceilings on the reading scores. These findings question the reliability of the results obtained by Rutter and Yule and, thereby, question the validity of using both IQ scores to estimate expected reading achievement and the validity of using an IQ-achievement discrepancy to define reading and other learning disabilities. More definitive evidence against these practices comes from several other studies that have appeared in the literature.

For example, in a study conducted by Jack Fletcher and his associates, it was found that impaired readers who had no significant IQ-achievement discrepancies performed no differently than impaired readers who did have significant IQ-achievement discrepancies, either on measures of reading achievement or on measures of cognitive abilities believed to underlie

reading achievement (e.g., phonological awareness, verbal memory, word retrieval, and visual analysis). Not surprisingly, each of these groups performed significantly below a group of nondiscrepant typically developing readers on both sets of measures. However, of special interest is Fletcher and colleagues' finding that a group of children who would have been classified as "disabled readers" by virtue of significant IQ-achievement discrepancies (i.e., above average IQs coupled with at least average reading achievement) performed as well as nondiscrepant typical readers not only on tests of reading achievement but also on tests of reading-related cognitive abilities. Fletcher and colleagues were doubtful that the children in the former group had a reading disability and suggested that the IQ-achievement discrepancy risks either overidentifying or underidentifying children as disabled.

Results discussed thus far quite naturally raise two important questions: (1) To what degree can an individual's IQ set upper limits on or predict the individual's ability to learn to read? (2) To what degree can an individual's IQ predict response to remedial intervention? The first of these questions was addressed in independent studies conducted by Linda Siegel and by Share and his associates. In the study conducted by Siegel, children with and without reading disability across a broad age range (7–16 years) were administered a large battery of tests evaluating reading achievement and reading-related language and language-based skills, in addition to measures of verbal and nonverbal intelligence. The children in both groups were then stratified in one of four IQ subgroups (IQ < 80, IQ = 80–90, IQ = 91–109, and IQ > 110) and thereafter compared on the reading and cognitive measures.

Siegel found that within each IQ stratification the children with reading disability performed significantly below the children without reading disability on all cognitive measures. This finding is important because it indicates that readers with and without reading disability can be found within different IQ ranges, including those falling below the average range. This is contrary to the view that intelligence is highly correlated with reading ability and therefore sets upper limits on reading achievement.

Share and his associates later conducted a longitudinal study that replicated Siegel's findings and also addressed the question of whether IQ can predict rate of growth in reading. The investigators tracked an unselected group of aged children from 3–13 years and periodically evaluated their reading achievement at ages 7, 9, 11, and 13. Intelligence in these children was assessed at ages 3 and 5. A composite measure based on these estimates was used to group the children into six IQ ranges and the children in each range were assessed at age 13 years on a measure of word recognition. In accord with results obtained by Siegel, Share found that IQ and reading ability were not highly correlated insofar as the full range of reading ability was represented within each IQ range. In addition, no strong or consistent differences were found among the different groups in rate of growth in reading.

The question of whether intelligence test scores can predict response to remedial intervention was initially addressed in a large-scale intervention study conducted by Vellutino and his associates that was published in 1996. In this study, reading growth in children identified as struggling readers in mid-first grade was tracked from the beginning of kindergarten until the end of fourth grade—that is, before and after they were identified as struggling readers. A randomly selected group of these children were provided with daily individual tutoring and the rest were provided with whatever remedial services were available at their home schools. Intervention was initiated in mid-first grade and was terminated at the end of first grade for children who were found to be readily remediated and in mid-second grade for children who were found to be more difficult to remediate. After one semester of project-based intervention, children who received this intervention were rank ordered on the basis of measures of growth in reading during that semester and thereafter separated into four groups designated as follows: "very good growth," "good growth," "limited growth," and "very limited growth."

For purposes of comparison, two groups of typically developing readers were also identified in mid-first grade: one group consisting of children with average intelligence and a second group consisting of children with above average intelligence. Reading growth in these children was also tracked from the beginning of kindergarten through the end of fourth grade. In addition, all groups were compared on measures of intelligence and reading related cognitive abilities in kindergarten, first, and third grade. Vellutino and colleagues found that the children in the four tutored groups did not differ on the measures of intelligence, especially those evaluating nonverbal intelligence, nor did they differ from the typical readers with average intelligence on these measures. In contrast, the children who were found to be difficult to remediate differed significantly from the children who were found to be readily remediated on measures of language-based skills, especially phonological skills that are important for learning to read (e.g., knowledge of letter names and sounds, phoneme awareness, letter–sound decoding, verbal memory, and name retrieval). In addition, the typical readers with average and above average intelligence did not differ on measures of basic word-level skills (i.e., word identification and word attack).

These findings were essentially replicated in a second major intervention study conducted by Vellutino and his associates, and the combined results from these two studies provide strong and compelling evidence that responsiveness to intervention may be a more valid means of identifying specific learning disability as compared with the IQ-achievement discrepancy. Research conducted more recently provides considerable support for this suggestion.

Frank R. Vellutino

See also Ability Tests; Achievement Tests; Aptitude Tests; Evidence-Based Interventions; Flynn Effect; Intelligence Quotient; Intelligence Tests; Learning Disabilities; Stanford–Binet Intelligence Scales; Wechsler Intelligence Scales; Woodcock-Johnson Tests of Achievement

Further Readings

Bond, G. L., & Dykstra, R. (1967). The co-operative research program in first grade reading instruction. *Reading Research Quarterly, 2,* 5–142.

Fletcher, J. M., Shaywitz, S. E., Shankweiler, D. P., Katz, L., Liberman, I. Y., Steubing, K. K., . . . Shaywitz, B. A. (1994). Cognitive profiles of reading disability: Comparisons of discrepancy and low achievement definitions. *Journal of Educational Psychology, 86*(1), 6–23.

Kirk, S. A., & Bateman, B. (1962–1963). Diagnosis and remediation of learning disabilities. *Exceptional Children, 29,* 73–78.

Malmquist, E. (1960). *Factors related to reading disabilities in the first grade of the elementary school.* Stockholm, Sweden: Almqvist Wiksell.

Rodgers, B. (1983). The identification and prevalence of specific reading retardation. *British Journal of Educational Psychology, 53,* 369–373.

Rutter, M., & Yule, W. (1975). The concept of specific reading retardation. *Journal of Child Psychology and Psychiatry, 16,* 181–197.

Share, D. L., McGee, R., McKenzie, D., Williams, S., & Silva, P. A. (1987). Further evidence relating to the distinction between specific reading retardation and general reading backwardness. *British Journal of Developmental Psychology, 5,* 35–44.

Siegel, L. S. (1988). Evidence that IQ scores are irrelevant to the definition and analysis of reading disability. *Canadian Journal of Psychology, 42,* 201–215.

U. S. Office of Education. (1977). Assistance for states for education for handicapped children: Procedures for evaluating specific learning disabilities. *Federal Register, 42,* G1082–G1085.

van der Wissel, A., & Zegers, F. E. (1985). Reading retardation revisited. *British Journal of Developmental Psychology, 3,* 3–9.

Vellutino, F., Scanlon, D., & Lyon, G. R. (2000). Differentiating between difficult-to-remediate and readily remediated poor readers: More evidence against the IQ-achievement discrepancy definition of reading disability. *Journal of Learning Disabilities, 33,* 223–238.

Vellutino, F. R., Scanlon, D. M., Sipay, E. R., Small, S. G., Pratt, A., Chen, R., & Denckla, M. B. (1996). Cognitive profiles of difficult to remediate and readily remediated poor readers: Toward distinguishing between constitutionally and experientially based causes of reading disability. *Journal of Educational Psychology, 88*(4), 601–638.

Vellutino, F. R, Scanlon, D. M., Zhang, H., & Schatschneider, C. (2008). Using response to kindergarten and first grade intervention to identify child at risk for long-term reading difficulties. *Reading and Writing: An Interdisciplinary Journal, 21,* 437–480.

ABSTRACTS

An abstract is a brief summary of a text—a journal article, conference paper, or dissertation—that highlights its most important claims and findings. Since first appearing in medical journals in the 1960s, they have become common in every field of study except the humanities, where they are nonetheless not altogether absent.

Function

Abstracts serve different functions for different readerships:

> For ordinary readers, they summarize the text, allowing readers to decide whether to read the entire piece and organizing their comprehension by providing a "road map."

> For journal editors and reviewers, they offer a ready-to-hand reference for evaluating a text for publication.

> For indexers, professional abstract writers, and information management professionals, they offer guidance for classifying and sorting a text.

> For conference organizers, editorial boards, and funding agencies, they "advertise" and "sell" a research project or paper.

Most abstracts can be described as *informative, indicative,* or *critical.* An informative abstract presents research findings directly; an indicative abstract describes the text's discussion of a topic. Whereas an informative abstract might say, "we conclude that peer support networks can improve teachers' motivation," and an indicative abstract would simply say, "implications for teachers are discussed." Critical abstracts function like executive summaries, addressing strengths, and weaknesses of a text.

Length

The form of an abstract varies from field to field and even from journal to journal (guidelines are often included in a journal's instructions to authors). At variance is often the length: While traditional abstracts are typically about 150 words long, structured abstracts can be anywhere from 250 to 400 words, and abstracts for short communications, such as conference proceedings or technical notes, can be as short as 50 words.

Abstracts are typically written retrospectively, toward the end of the composing process, to represent completed work. But abstracts can also be prospective; when scholars apply for conference presentations or grant funding, they often submit abstracts for work yet to be done. In these cases, the abstract functions as a proposal or research trajectory. Such prospective abstracts can be 500 words or longer, depending upon guidelines provided.

Structure

Despite their different lengths, most abstracts attempt to make five rhetorical "moves":

1. introduce the topic, its context, and its importance;

2. present the research question or purpose;

3. describe methods and materials used;

4. present key results and findings; and

5. discuss the significance of the findings for relevant audiences.

Abstracts for short communications will emphasize moves 3 through 5. A structured abstract, by contrast, will separate each move into its own paragraph with a subheading. Because structured abstracts tend to be longer, they provide more information to readers and are considered to be more useful. Structured abstracts have only been in use since the 1980s but are becoming increasingly common.

Mark Pedretti

See also Dissertations; Journal Articles; Literature Review; Methods Section; Results Section; Significance

Further Readings

Cremmins, E. T. (1996). *The art of abstracting* (2nd ed.). Arlington, TX: Information Resources Press.

Hofmann, A. H. (2013). *Scientific writing and communication: Papers, proposals, and presentations* (2nd ed., Chap. 14). Oxford, UK: Oxford University Press.

Huckin, T. (2001). Abstracting from abstracts. In M. Hewings (Ed.), *Academic writing in context: Implications and applications* (pp. 93–103). Birmingham, UK: University of Birmingham Press.

Swales, J. M., & Feak, C. B. (2009). *Abstracts and the writing of abstracts.* Ann Arbor: University of Michigan Press.

Accessibility of Assessment

Accessibility originates from the field of architecture that aims to make buildings and the physical environment accessible to the whole population, including people with and without physical disabilities. For example, curb cuts help people in wheelchairs cross a street, but the same curb cuts also benefit people who are not in wheelchairs. Similarly, educational assessments that are accessible provide students with the opportunity to demonstrate their knowledge and skills on the construct being assessed, regardless of personal characteristics unrelating to what is being assessed. In contrast, an assessment with poor accessibility introduces barriers based on personal characteristics. There can be negative consequences when assessment results reflect those personal characteristics and not just the construct being assessed. This entry further defines *accessibility* as the term is used in assessment and discusses the related concepts of accommodation and universal design for assessment (UDA). It then discusses the accessibility of computer-based assessments, the relationship of accessibility to validity, and ways to maximize the accessibility of assessment.

Accessibility is a characteristic of the assessment, but it requires consideration of the test taker's interaction with items or tasks. Each test taker might experience individual barriers during the assessment process. For example, a student with low vision may have difficulty reading items printed in a standard font size on a paper and pencil test, while a student with very little computer experience might have difficulty navigating and choosing answers in a computer-based test. Accessibility is also a consideration in other types of assessments, not just tests. For example, consider a performance assessment that consists of giving an oral presentation, where grading criteria include speed and fluency of oral communication. This assessment could introduce barriers to students with speech disorders and nonnative language speakers who are still working toward language proficiency.

When individual characteristics present barriers during the assessment, these characteristics limit the test taker's ability to demonstrate what they know. As a result, examinees' true knowledge and skills tend to be underestimated. This in turn limits the validity of inferences that can be made based on the scores. Therefore, it is important to ensure the assessment is as accessible as possible to everyone regardless of language proficiency, disability status, or other unique characteristics that might detract from the assessment. Steps can be taken to promote accessibility at the assessment design, administration, and scoring and reporting phases.

Related Concepts

Accessibility is related to concepts such as accommodation and UDA, but it is still a distinct concept. All three of these concepts have the same objective, which is to maximize test takers' opportunities to demonstrate their knowledge or skills of the construct being tested—removing the influence of knowledge or characteristics unrelated to the construct while also not changing the construct being assessed. However, test accommodations and UDA are different from accessibility of assessment in some respects.

Accommodation refers to a change in the assessment administration methods or environment for test takers with disabilities or limited language proficiency. There are a variety of test accommodations that change the student's experience with the assessment. Accommodations may be made in timing and scheduling, setting, presentation, and/or response. However, accommodations are designed to alter the student's experience after the assessment is designed and are only granted by exception. Test accommodations are only applied to examinees who are eligible under relevant laws (e.g., in the United States, the Individuals with Disabilities Education Act, and Section 504 of the Rehabilitation Act cover accommodations for individuals with disabilities). Decisions about which accommodations should be provided are made on a case-by-case basis.

UDA is a framework for promoting accessibility through all stages of assessment design and delivery. UDA often starts by considering inclusiveness of the population that is intended to be eligible for the assessment. The ultimate goal of UDA is to enhance the accessibility of the test, thereby improving the fairness of the assessment for all students and the validity of inferences made from test scores for all test takers. Both UDA and accessibility of assessment apply to the whole population, including people with and without disabilities or limited language proficiency. Accessibility of assessment can be regarded as one facet of UDA, focusing on the interaction of the test taker and the assessment content. Features of the items themselves and supports made available to test takers both facilitate accessibility.

Accessibility of Computer-Based Assessments

Computer-based assessments are becoming more prevalent in large-scale assessment programs and in classrooms. In addition to benefits such as cost and time savings, computer-based assessments also provide new opportunities to support accessibility. For example, it is much easier to customize item delivery methods and response formats via computer-based assessment than paper and pencil assessment. Additionally, computers increase the availability and flexibility of the use of accessibility supports. Some computer-based assessments treat accessibility features as tools that test takers may enable or disable on demand. For example, a student may turn on a magnification tool when viewing a diagram and turn it back off when reading a paragraph. Other common tools include on-screen highlighters, text-to-speech functions that read text aloud, changes to color configurations, and overlays that mask parts of the information on screen. Some systems are also compatible with assistive technology devices that allow individuals with disabilities to interact independently with the computer even without a standard keyboard and mouse.

While computer-based assessments can improve accessibility, there is also a risk of measuring knowledge and skills that are unrelated to the assessment. Test takers must be familiar with the testing platform and with the accessibility supports that are used. A test taker who lacks basic computer skills or access to computers in daily life may not be able to use an online system without some practice or coaching in advance. And when it comes to accessibility tools, more is not necessarily better. The test taker should be familiar with the tool, and the tool should not introduce distraction or confusion. Test developers can provide guidance to test administrators and test takers on the accessibility tools in order to promote good decisions about the use of tools to minimize barriers. Organizations such as the iMS Global

Learning Consortium promote the use of common standards for accessibility across technology platforms in various sectors including education.

Relationship of Assessment Accessibility to Validity

Evidence of an assessment's accessibility influences the validity of inferences that may be made about its results. An accessible assessment measures the intended construct and avoids measuring unrelated characteristics. Sources of construct-irrelevant variance that occur in assessments with poor accessibility include item bias, unclear presentation of information in instructions, and lack of or inappropriate use of supports.

It is important to avoid construct-irrelevant variance because poor estimation of a student's true knowledge and skills can lead to negative consequences. For example, if results of a high school mathematics exam are used to determine whether a student has met graduation requirements and the items contain complex vocabulary unrelated to mathematics, a student with limited language proficiency may fail to pass the exam and meet the graduation requirements even while possessing the relevant mathematics knowledge and skills. An assessment is biased when it presents barriers to a subgroup of students and their results are negatively impacted despite their having the same construct-relevant knowledge and skills as other test takers.

Maximizing the Accessibility of Assessment

The accessibility of an assessment is maximized when the issue is considered at all phases of the assessment's life span: during assessment design and development, during administration, and after results are available. Accessibility may be planned or evaluated at each of these steps.

During the Assessment Design and Development Phase

During the test development stage, developers can promote accessibility using an evidence-centered design framework. Using evidence-centered design, test developers carefully describe the construct being assessed and detail the behaviors that

are required to demonstrate understanding of the construct. These descriptions can be reviewed before they are used to guide item writing in order to ensure there are no unintended barriers to demonstrating knowledge of the content for subgroups of individuals. Once items are developed, they can also be reviewed for evidence of barriers related to construct-irrelevant factors (e.g., unique cultural knowledge that would be required to answer the question, use of complex vocabulary unrelated to the measured content).

In addition to considering accessibility during item development, the test as a whole may be designed to minimize barriers. For example, test developers should make sure directions are clear and that the items are displayed in ways that minimize confusion. Assessment developers also define the supports that may be made available to increase accessibility without advantaging any subgroups. Items should not be easier or harder for examinees who choose to use extra supports.

In the prototype or early test design phrases, cognitive labs are a common method to evaluate whether items or tasks elicit the intended cognitive process. In a cognitive lab, test takers report their thoughts (i.e., think aloud) when they are reading, interpreting, and responding to an item. This method helps test developers evaluate whether item features are performing as intended and check for problems with clarity of the item content. Cognitive labs and observation methods can also be used to evaluate whether accessibility supports have the intended effect.

During the Assessment Administration Phase

During the assessment administration phase, educators and students play roles in ensuring accessibility is maximized. Educators must understand the supports that could be provided to each student. When they also choose supports for individual students, their choices should match the students' current needs and preferences. Supports selected to meet a student's need should not introduce unintended barriers. For example, enlarged font may be helpful for test takers with low vision; however, if the item cannot be shown in one page, the need for scrolling or reading an item across pages may introduce unintended barriers. When test takers themselves have the opportunity to choose the supports they use, they need enough information about the support to make informed decisions. Selected supports should be familiar to the student, either through use during instruction or through opportunities to practice similar activities prior to testing. Finally, educators may be responsible for providing some supports directly during an assessment. For example, an educator may read items aloud or help a student enter answers for a computer-based test. In these cases, educators need to administer the supports with fidelity and follow instructions for standardized administration.

During the test administration phase, teacher surveys, teacher interviews, and observations may be used to evaluate accessibility. Observations can determine whether an educator can implement accessibility supports with fidelity and whether the student was able to use the supports as intended. Through interviewing or surveys, teachers can provide their suggestions on usability, effectiveness, and suggestions for supports that tend to improve the accessibility of assessment.

After Administration

Once an assessment is administered to enough students, it is possible to evaluate accessibility even further. For example, there are statistical techniques that can be applied to determine whether items may be biased for subgroups of students. Differential item functioning analysis is commonly used to detect whether different groups of test takers with the same true ability have performed differently on items. Differential item functioning analysis can be used to check for potential item bias—for example, for groups of students with limited language proficiency, lower socioeconomic status, or disability. There are different statistical procedures to detect differential item functioning items, such as logistic regression and Mantel–Haenszel statistics. Items that are found to function differently for different subgroups of students should be investigated further. For example, a panel of educators could convene to review items and identify features that may be disadvantaging students. These techniques require data based on large samples, so they are most appropriate for large-scale assessments.

Although assessment developers may have accessibility as a goal during the design phase, planning for accessibility does not guarantee that the goal was met. Collecting evidence related to item and test features, and student experiences with accessibility supports, allows for ongoing evaluation and improvement of assessments for all students.

Qianqian Pan and Meagan Karvonen

See also Accommodations; Differential Item Functioning; English Language Proficiency Assessment; Intellectual Disability and Postsecondary Education; Second Language Learners, Assessment of; Test Bias; Universal Design in Education

Further Readings

Beddow, P. A., Kurz, A., & Frey, J. R. (2011). Accessibility theory: Guiding the science and practice of test item design with the test-taker in mind. In S. N. Elliott (Ed.), *Handbook of accessible achievement tests for all students: Bridging the gaps between research, practice, and policy* (pp. 163–182). London, UK: Springer Science & Business Media.

Iwarsson, S., & Ståhl, A. (2003). Accessibility, usability and universal design: Positioning and definition of concepts describing person-environment relationships. *Disability and Rehabilitation, 25*(2), 57–66.

Ketterlin-Geller, L. R. (2005). Knowing what all students know: Procedures for developing universal design for assessment. *The Journal of Technology, Learning and Assessment, 4*(2). Retrieved from http://www.jtla.org

Ketterlin-Geller, L. R. (2008). Testing students with special needs: A model for understanding the interaction between assessment and student characteristics in a universally designed environment. *Educational Measurement: Issues and Practice, 27*(3), 3–16.

Russell, M. (2011). Accessible test design. In M. K. Russell (Ed.), *Assessing students in the margin: Challenges, strategies, and techniques* (pp. 407–424). Charlotte, NC: Information Age Publishing.

Thompson, S. J., Johnstone, C. J., & Thurlow, M. L. (2002). *Universal design applied to large scale assessments* (Synthesis Report 44). Minneapolis: University of Minnesota, National Center on Educational Outcomes. Retrieved from http://www.cehd.umn.edu/nceo/onlinepubs/Synthesis44.html

Thurlow, M. L., & Kopriva, R. J. (2015). Advancing accessibility and accommodations in content assessments for students with disabilities and English learners. *Review of Research in Education, 39*, 331–369.

Websites

iMS Global Learning Consortium https://www.imsglobal.org/

ACCOMMODATIONS

Accommodations are defined as adjustments for variances. As such, educational accommodations, the topic of this entry, are strategies utilized to remove content irrelevant variance from an assignment or test, allowing students to demonstrate what they have learned in relation to the specific academic content standard being targeted, without noise associated with any impairment related to a disability. For example, students with delayed processing may be given extended time on a standardized assessment in order to more accurately assess what they have learned rather than how rapidly the student can process the questions and retrieve the answers.

This entry further defines educational accommodations and looks at some of the issues surrounding the selection and use of accommodations. It then discusses the use of accommodations in classrooms and in testing, strategies for selecting accommodations, and selection of alternative interventions to teach students skills needed to address impairment for which accommodations are typically provided.

Accommodations are often confused with modifications given to students with disabilities. Although these terms are sometimes used interchangeably, they are not the same. Modifications represent a difference in what the student is expected to learn, as in having a student learn multiplication facts up to 5× while the class learns multiplication facts up to 10×. Conversely, the use of accommodations does not lower standards or change expectations. The use of accommodations provides a differential boost between those with and without disabilities. Thus, when students with and without disabilities utilize an accommodation, a greater increase in performance should be evident for students with the disability than for students without the disability. For example, if a student is deaf and communicates with American Sign Language, it is highly probable that the student's performance will increase with an American Sign Language interpreter interpreting instruction and interactions in the classroom, but it is not likely that the performance of students in the classroom who are not deaf will be affected.

Accommodations typically are changes in how the task or test is presented (e.g., questions read aloud), how the student is expected to respond (e.g., dictating answers), and the time allowed for the task (e.g., time and a half). For testing situations, an accommodation may be granted for students to take the test in a smaller group setting or in a distraction-free room. They may also be situation-specific. That is, the student may be provided extra time on writing tasks but not for math problem sheets.

An increased focus on accountability and use of high-stakes testing in schools, along with greater inclusion of students with disabilities in general education settings and the need to assure equal access to the general education curriculum and grade-level content standards, all heighten the need to understand the process of accommodating for impairment associated with disabilities. Teachers are expected to teach the same content to all students, those with and without disabilities, and students are expected to demonstrate proficiency on all standards. At the same time, assessment scores must represent what students have learned specific to the content being evaluated and not be affected by extraneous variance associated with a disability, such as the effects of a reading disability when interpreting a math word problem assessment. Thus, for students with disabilities served by special education, individualized education program (IEP) teams are charged with selecting appropriate accommodations.

However, issues exist with the selection and use of accommodations. Although federal law mandates the use of accommodations, research is far behind and provides minimal support to educators for the selection of specific accommodations for specific areas of impairment. In addition, an overreliance on accommodations exists and IEPs lack interventions specifically to teach strategic skills needed to decrease the negative effects of the disability on academic performance. A third concern about accommodations is a philosophical one. Changing or individualizing an assessment for some students conflicts with the goals of universal design that prefers a single assessment that is "accessible" to all students. Accommodations and universal design share an underlying principle, however, which is that the scores from assessments should be equally valid for all.

History of Accommodations

The history of educational accommodations is intertwined with the history of the inclusive education movement in the United States. Until the first federal special education law was adopted in 1975, schools in the United States first denied students with disabilities an education and then marginalized them to institutional or classroom "holding pens." The federal Education for All Handicapped Children Act referred to the "least restrictive environment," which indicated that students should be educated, whenever educational benefit could be achieved, in general education classrooms with their age-equivalent peers.

This language was further strengthened in the reauthorizations of the act in 1990 (the Individuals with Disabilities Education Act) and in 2004 (the Individuals with Disabilities Education Improvement Act). With this encouragement to educate students with disabilities in general education classrooms with support, the need to reduce the cognitive load of tasks and assessments to the most salient elements led to further development of accommodations. These accommodations are student-specific and are codified in an IEP or Section 504 plan.

Over the years, courts have established that school staff members are responsible for implementing the accommodations described in the IEP. The teacher responsible for teaching the child-specific content for which accommodations are specified on the IEP is legally bound to provide the accommodation. If an IEP team selects an accommodation and includes it in the student's IEP and the accommodation is not implemented, then the child did not receive a free appropriate public education. If school districts do not inform teachers of the student's IEP, then the district may be liable; and if the teacher elects not to implement the accommodations, then the teacher may be liable. If a teacher believes that an accommodation on an IEP is not in the best interest of a student, then the teacher should request an IEP meeting to discuss the accommodation rather than changing or disregarding the accommodations as

written. Two methods of selecting accommodations are discussed in the next section.

Selecting Accommodations

Following best practice procedures, accommodations are selected based on the strengths and needs of the child identified on the child's IEP under the category of Present Levels of Academic and Functional Performance, the grade-level standards, and the instructional tasks being used to assess proficiency on the standards. The Present Levels of Academic and Functional Performance is a section in the IEP that identifies "how the child's disability affects the child's involvement and progress in the general education curriculum" [IDEA Sec. 614 (d) (1) (A) (i) (I)].

However, reviews of IEPs published by Craig Spiel and colleagues (2014) and Connie Schnoes and colleagues (2006) suggest little rhyme or reason to the accommodations included on most IEPs. It appears, from these studies and anecdotal evidence, that educators select many accommodations from a laundry list without considering the impairment that is interfering with academic progress or the feasibility of all of the accommodations being implemented by teachers in classrooms. In fact, as of 2016, there are IEP writing software packages that include pull-down menus, allowing practitioners to "shop" for accommodations. Although these are editable, many practitioners report defaulting to the options provided in the software.

One of the accommodations most frequently listed in IEPs is the provision of extra time. Many students, regardless of their strengths and weaknesses, receive extra time on assignments and assessments, although empirical evidence is lacking as to whether this accommodation improves performance across the spectrum of disabilities.

One means of addressing this issue is for educators to follow procedures outlined in the accommodations manual published by the Council of Chief State School Officers to select, administer, and evaluate the outcomes associated with accommodations. The accommodation manual was written to provide guidelines to states for the selection and administration of accommodations and is written in such a way that state-level rules can be added as needed.

The accommodation guide provides four steps for selecting and implementing accommodations supplemented by 11 tools. The steps are to (a) expect students with disabilities to achieve grade-level academic content standards, (b) learn about accommodations for instruction and assessment, (c) select accommodations for instruction and assessment for individual students, and (d) administer accommodations during instruction and assessment. Potentially, there is room for a fifth step in which the benefits of the administered accommodations are considered and the selection revised as indicated.

The third step, select accommodations, is the focus of this section and suggests that IEP teams should consider seven factors when selecting accommodations: (1) student characteristics identified in the Present Levels of Academic and Functional Performances, (2) inclusion characteristics that need accommodation, (3) strategies to include the student in the process, (4) effectiveness of prior accommodations, (5) accommodations for instruction and assessment, (6) individual test characteristics, and (7) state accommodation policies. Specifically, IEP teams first consider student strengths and weaknesses and then the impact of the impairment associated with the disability on the student's learning. Additionally, the team must determine the type of specialized instruction needed to master the grade-level content standards, drawing from the results of prior tasks when the specific accommodation was used.

Potential problems with the accommodations, and the perceptions of teachers and the student regarding the need and effectiveness of the accommodation, help to determine whether the accommodation should be included in the IEP. Finally, teams should consider the willingness of the student to utilize the accommodation, the need for the accommodation across educational settings, and the acceptability of the accommodation on high-stakes assessment. Accommodations used on high-stakes testing should be the same as those used in the classroom. Introducing students and teachers to a new accommodation on a high-stakes test is not effective.

Along the same lines, another model for selecting strategies for inclusion in IEPs, including accommodations, was developed by Judith Harrison and her colleagues. This model targets the use of accommodations that are being provided to students with the potential to learn the missing skill for which accommodations are being provided. One example would be teaching a student to take notes, as opposed to accommodating inattention to class discussion by providing a student with a copy of teacher notes, eliminating the need to take notes or as a supplement to notes taken by the student. It is assumed that these students can, in fact, improve their note-taking skills with scaffolding. Alternatively, this approach is not appropriate when accommodations are needed for a skill that cannot be taught, such as when a student is deaf and needs a sign language interpreter.

The model developed by Harrison and colleagues is founded on the life-course model for mental health treatment selection developed by Steven Evans and colleagues. The premise behind the LCM is that services are provided to increase the acquisition of skills needed across the life span, focusing on both short- and long-term concerns. Similarly, Harrison and colleagues' model for IEP strategy selection is designed to assist IEP teams in selecting strategies designed to teach skills and provide accommodations only when the student does not have the capacity to learn the skills, or expectations need to be adjusted at the start of an intervention and faded with mastery of the skill.

An example of the use of Harrison and colleagues' model would be if a student is in an inclusive history class and does not attend and take notes effectively, the teacher could teach the student to self-monitor attention to task and note-taking skills. However, while she is teaching note-taking skills, she continues to teach content associated with grade-level content standards. In order for the student to keep up with the instruction while he is learning note-taking strategies, the teacher could give him a copy of her notes (an accommodation).

In this model, students are provided the accommodation until they have mastered the skill needed, after such time the accommodation is no longer needed. The length of this time period is dependent on the individual student. Accommodations are selected that directly address targeted areas of impairment and progress is monitored and accommodations changed if sufficient progress is not documented. For example, students with attention-deficit/hyperactivity disorder frequently struggle with completing and submitting homework due to organizational skill deficits. To address this issue, the child might meet with a counselor each morning before school, who would help her organize her binder. The counselor would continue to help the child with organization using a structured checklist to guide the process. However, the counselor would scaffold assistance, withdrawing support as the student learns to organize the binder without assistance.

Potential Accommodations

As previously mentioned, multiple accommodations are often recommended without any empirical evidence to support their effectiveness or usefulness in accommodating for impairment. In the following section, examples of potential accommodations (potential, as research is needed to determine whether the strategies truly provide a differential boost) are described for the four areas of accommodations: presentation, response, timing/scheduling, and setting. However, accommodations must be selected based on the criteria described earlier, with a strong focus on student need. In addition, emphasis is placed on progress monitoring to determine that the student is benefiting from the use of the accommodation and that the accommodation does not cause harm, such as a reduction in effort or motivation.

Presentation accommodations are changes in the manner in which instruction, assignments, and/or assessments are presented to the student. For example, test or assignment questions might be read to a student, removing the need for the student to read the question by him- or herself. It is a frequent accommodation for students with reading disabilities to have math word problems read to them. In addition, recent evidence suggests that reading tests aloud to students with attention-deficit/hyperactivity disorder helps the student maintain attention to task even when the student does not have a reading disability. Students who have visual or hearing impairments frequently receive presentation accommodations, such as enlarged or magnified content or audio amplification, in order to access the information being taught.

Response accommodations are changes in the manner in which students respond to instruction via assignments, assessments, or organizational devices used by the student to determine and write a response. For example, a student who struggles with formulating written responses might be allowed to answer questions verbally instead of writing them on a test. This form of response might or might not include a scribe who writes the answers for the student or voice to text software to formulate a response to a question or to write a paper. Several potential response accommodations are considered methods of increasing active engagement for an entire class of students, such as choral response using whiteboards to respond to teacher questions or clickers to be used with an interactive whiteboard. Additionally, there are many technology-based strategies that can be used as response accommodations or as simply good teaching strategies to increase engagement classwide.

Timing and scheduling accommodations, those that change the amount or organization of time for an assignment or a test, are the most frequent accommodations. In fact, the one most frequently found accommodation on IEPs, extended time, falls within this category. Extended time is the provision of extra time for a task. For example, students who process information or read more slowly than others might be given 90 minutes instead of 60 minutes to complete a timed assessment. Recent research suggests that extended time is not an effective accommodation for students with behavioral disorders such as attention-deficit/hyperactivity disorder. Other timing accommodations include frequent breaks and giving tests at specific times of the day, such as in the morning.

Setting accommodations are those that change the location in which the assignment or test is completed. For example, students who are easily distracted frequently have accommodations of testing in small groups or in a distraction-free environment.

Alternative Interventions

Following the model of strategy selection for IEPs developed by Harrison and colleagues, interventions to teach skills are included prior to or in conjunction with accommodations. For example, students who struggle with initiating and maintaining attention to task are frequently given extra time to complete tasks with the rationale that more time is needed to compensate for the time spent off task. However, this does not teach the student the skill of attending; it merely reduces the expectation to complete tasks in the same amount of time as typically developing peers. Self-management is an intervention that can be tailored to teach students to attend to task. Specifically, students can be taught to self-monitor and document whether they were paying attention at a given interval over a set number of intervals. Students are taught not only to self-monitor but to set a goal for the number of intervals in which they will attend and then reward themselves when they meet their goal.

Accommodations are intended to facilitate demonstration of academic mastery by a student with disabilities, minimizing the impact of the specific disability on the student's performance. These accommodations relate to how the task is presented to the student as well as how the students make their response and differ from modifications that change what is asked of the student. When paired with strategic interventions such as described earlier, accommodations have the potential to be beneficial to teachers and learners. However, there is some indication that this is not always being carried out as intended and much more research and diligence in practice is needed.

Judith R. Harrison and Jeanette Joyce

See also Attention-Deficit/Hyperactivity Disorder; Individualized Education Program; Individuals with Disabilities Education Act; Least Restrictive Environment; Progress Monitoring; Universal Design in Education; Universal Design of Assessment

Further Readings

Christensen, L., Carver, W., VanDeZande, J., & Lazarus, S. (2011). Accommodations manual: How to select, administer, and evaluate use of accommodations for instruction and assessment of students with disabilities (3rd ed.). Washington, DC: Assessing Special Education Students State Collaborative on Assessment and Student Standards, Council of Chief State School Officers.

Evans, S. W., Owens, J. S., Mautone, J. A., DuPaul, G. J., & Power, T. J. (2014). Toward a comprehensive life-course model of care for youth with attention-deficit/hyperactivity disorder. In *Handbook of School Mental Health* (pp. 413–426). Springer.

Harrison, J. R., Bunford, N., Evans, S. W., & Owens, J. (2013). Educational accommodations for students with behavioral challenges: A systematic review of the literature. *Review of Educational Research, 83*(4), 551–597. doi:10.3102/0034654313497517

Schnoes, C., Reid, R., Wagner, M., & Marder, C. (2006). ADHD among students receiving special education services: A national survey. *Exceptional Children, 72*, 483–496. doi:10.1177/001440290607200406

Spiel, C. F., Evans, S. W., & Langberg, J. M. (2014). Evaluating the content of individualized education program and 504 Plans of young adolescents with attention deficit/hyperactivity disorder. *School Psychology Quarterly, 29*, 452–468. doi:10.1037/spq0000101

Spiel, C. F., Mixon, C. S., Holdaway, A. S., Evans, S. W., Harrison, J. R., Zoromski, A. K., & Sadler, J. M. (2016). The effect of reading tests aloud on the performance of youth with and without ADHD. *Remedial and Special Education, 37*(2), 101–112. doi:10.1177/0741932515619929

ACCOUNTABILITY

Accountability is a theory of action on raising student performance by applying pressure on, and providing support for, schools and districts that do not meet academic standards. Annual or periodic reporting on school performance forms the basis of actions to address academic needs. Simply put, what gets measured and reported receives attention from stakeholders in the public arena. This entry further defines accountability in the context of public education before describing the federal role in school accountability in the United States and how it has changed since the mid-20th century.

In the United States, accountability is defined in the context of a decentralized public education system. With a federal system of governance, states assume a leading role in primary and secondary education. The constitution in each of the 50 states affirms state responsibility in this policy domain. States and their localities continued to provide about 90% of the funding in public education. States exercise control over their academic content standards, educator preparation and recruitment, and the scope of intervention in low academic performance.

State dominance notwithstanding, accountability in public education has become a shared state–federal function. The 1960s marked the beginning of an active federal role to address educational inequity and the achievement gap between students from low- and high-income families. The U.S. Congress has established a grants-in-aid system to target federal support for students with particular needs, such as low-income students, English-language learners, Native Americans, and students with learning disabilities.

Grants from the federal government account for about 10% of total public school spending. In return for federal dollars, states and school districts are required to comply with federal standards on assessing students. Federal involvement in accountability intensified in 2001 when Congress passed the No Child Left Behind Act (NCLB). With the 2015 passage of the Every Student Succeeds Act (ESSA), states have regained some control over accountability policy.

NCLB expanded the federal role in educational accountability. The federal law required annual testing of students at the elementary grades in core subject areas, mandated the hiring of "highly qualified teachers" in classrooms, and granted states and districts substantial authority in taking "corrective actions" to turn around low-performing schools. Further, the law provided school choice to parents to take their children out of failing schools. Equally significant was NCLB's intent to close achievement gaps among racial and ethnic subgroups as well as subgroups based on income, limited English proficiency, and special education.

Under NCLB, to determine whether a school met adequate yearly progress (AYP), student achievement for each school was aggregated by grade and subject area. All students in Grades 3–8 and one additional grade in high school were tested annually in mathematics and in reading/English-language arts. In addition, students in select grades were tested in science. The school-level report included the percentage of students proficient in each of the core-content areas, student participation in standardized testing, attendance rates, and graduation rates.

Equally prominent is the equity focus on NCLB. Depending on their socioeconomic characteristics, schools were required to report the academic proficiency of students of the following subgroups: economically disadvantaged students, students from major racial and ethnic groups, students with disabilities, and limited English proficiency students. In this regard, for accountability purposes, the NCLB promoted transparency on student progress. Schools that persistently failed to meet AYP were subject to a gradation of intervention, including school closure or conversion to a charter school.

The federal accountability agenda, as articulated in NCLB, encountered implementation problems. Tension occurred between the theory of accountability based on the federal intent and the practice of accountability at the state and local level. More specifically, the decentralized education system allows for varying degrees of policy specification and academic rigor across states. Within each state, the decision-making process allowed for multiple stakeholders to weigh in on the rigor, scope, timing, and cost of student academic assessment. Consequently, state assessments vary widely in terms of the level of rigor, as indicated by the substantial gap in many states between student proficiency on state tests and their performance on the National Assessment of Educational Progress, a set of standardized tests used throughout the United States.

Further, the NCLB accountability agenda encountered social constraints. The extent to which a district or a school met AYP was affected by the presence of student subgroups, including low-income students, English-language learners, students with disabilities, and racial and ethnic minorities. One study of AYP data in California and Virginia found that schools with more student subgroups experienced more difficulty in meeting AYP.

Recognizing the implementation problems with NCLB, in 2011, the Obama administration began granting waivers to states that exempted them from some provisions of the law, including meeting the target that 100% of students demonstrate proficiency on state tests by the end of the 2013–2014 school year. Over 40 states received the waivers.

States that received waivers still had to test students in certain core subjects annually, especially in Grades 3–8 and in one high school grade, and hold schools accountable for performance standards. In addition, states had to adopt reading/language arts and mathematics standards that were common to a number of states or had to show that their standards were certified by a state network of higher education institutions.

The simplest way to meet the waiver requirement on academic standards was to adopt the Common Core State Standards, which had already been adopted by many states. States were also encouraged to adopt the Common Core in exchange for federal funding as part the Race to the Top grant competition begun in 2009. With the Common Core, states can compare their academic progress to that in other states, improve economies of scale in terms of technical assistance, and streamline teacher recruitment and support. At the same time, there have been problems with the implementation of Common Core, including concerns that teachers were not adequately trained in the standards and the assessments aligned to them. In addition, many have criticized the use of financial and deregulatory incentives to encourage adoption of the Common Core as federal intrusion in state and local academic affairs.

In late 2015, the U.S. Congress replaced NCLB with the ESSA. To be sure, ESSA continues to build on the NCLB accountability policy. In particular, states will continue to conduct annual testing of core subjects in students of Grades 3–8 as well as in one grade in high school. States are required to issue annual report cards that show the performance of students from various subgroups, including students from low-income families, English-language learners, children with learning disabilities, and various minority groups.

Departing from NCLB, ESSA signals the return of some state control over accountability. ESSA places limits on federal prescriptions on intervening in low-performing schools. Under the law, states are required to adopt "challenging" standards, but the U.S. education secretary cannot use incentives encouraging states to adopt a particular set of standards. In addition, the law does not require states to set up teacher-evaluation systems that incorporate students' test scores, as they were required to do to receive waivers from NCLB. ESSA also allows states to use multiple measures to assess student performance.

Under ESSA, states have gained control over several important aspects of education accountability.

States can decide on academic standards, including developing their own standards and multiple measures of academic assessment. States can also establish criteria in identifying low-performing schools for direct intervention, although ESSA expects that states will focus on the bottom 5%. Evaluation of teachers will be determined by states, which do not have to use student test results as the basis for the evaluation.

Kenneth K. Wong

See also Accreditation; Achievement Tests; *Brown v. Board of Education*; Common Core State Standards; Every Student Succeeds Act; Great Society Programs; High-Stakes Tests; National Assessment of Educational Progress; No Child Left Behind Act; Partnership for Assessment of Readiness for College and Careers; Race to the Top; Smarter Balanced Assessment Consortium; Standards-Based Assessment

Further Readings

Cohen, D., & Moffitt, S. (2009). *The ordeal of equality.* Cambridge, MA: Harvard University Press.

Hess, F., & Petrilli, M. (2006). *No child left behind primer.* New York, NY: Peter Lang Publishing.

Kim, J., & Sunderman, G. (2005). Measuring academic proficiency under the No Child Left Behind Act: Implications for educational equity. *Educational Researcher, 34* (8), 3–13.

Manna, P. (2010). *Collision course.* Washington DC: Congressional Quarterly Press.

Wong, K. K., & Nicotera, A. (2007). *Successful schools and educational accountability.* Boston, MA: Pearson Education.

ACCREDITATION

Designed to protect public health, safety, and interest, accreditation provides a system of quality assessment and improvement. In the United States, educational, human services, and health-care programs and institutions undergo accreditation review. Although each of these three sectors has unique accreditation processes, accreditation generally consists of a process of voluntary, external review that occurs and results in a decision based upon the institution's consistency with accepted standards. This entry discusses the history of accreditation in the United States, the process of accrediting U.S. higher education institutions, criticisms of the accreditation system in higher education, and supporters' responses to these criticisms.

Many accrediting practices provide recommendations to increase compliance and, therefore, offer opportunities for program improvement to those undergoing review. The accreditation process has evolved over the years in the United States and offers advantages and disadvantages for higher education and other professional entities. Accreditation started in higher education in the late 19th century as a way to verify student qualifications for entry into colleges and universities. This led to the formation of regional groups of higher education administrators to evaluate secondary education practices.

The federal government entered accreditation with the Servicemen's Readjustment Act, commonly known as the GI Bill, in 1944 by providing educational funding for World War II servicemen. In 1952, this legislation was reauthorized and included a process of peer review to establish the legitimacy for institutions offering educational services. Since then, the role of the federal government has continued through legislation enacted, establishing the U.S. Department of Health, Education, and Welfare in 1953. In 1979, when the U.S. Department of Education (ED) was created, the US Department of Health, Education, and Welfare was separated. The ED is designated to establish educational policy, to coordinate federal assistance to the educational enterprise, to enforce civil rights legislation in education, and to collect information on schools within the United States.

The emphasis placed on actions by the ED is to promote achievement of students and make schools accountable. The ED does not establish academic institutions or programs, nor does it perform accreditation. However, the Higher Education Act (1965) and subsequent amendments to the Higher Education Opportunity Act (2008) authorize the U.S. secretary of education to publish lists of recognized accrediting agencies. These recognized accrediting bodies not only provide ratings of educational quality, but many also allow students to access federal funding established by Title IV in the Higher Education Act. Specifically, Title IV authorizes programs to accept government monies to allow access to higher education; this funding requires state licensure of the institution and accreditation by an ED-recognized accreditor.

In addition to the ED, the Council for Higher Education Accreditation provides recognition of accrediting agencies. Council for Higher Education Accreditation, a voluntary membership organization with more than 3,000 institutions represented, establishes the quality of agencies that accredit programs and institutions that are regional, faith-based, career-focused, and specialty/programmatic in nature.

Accreditation in Higher Education

In the United States, higher education accreditation incorporates three separate pathways, termed *the triad*: the federal government, state governments, and accrediting organizations. Established to provide public protection through combined regulation processes set by governments and the development of peer-evaluation systems, these processes may be focused on the institution or on individual programs of study. States provide authorization and regulate educational institutions that operate within state boundaries. Accreditors evaluate educational system inputs as well as the effectiveness of education through examining student achievement and outcomes of the process. Accrediting bodies may be regional associations that review entire institutions; national associations that primarily evaluate career, vocational, and trade schools; or specialty and programmatic accreditors that examine individual programs of study (e.g., medicine, dentistry, and teaching). Accreditation by some national and specialty accreditors and all regional accreditors provides access to Title IV funding.

The review processes typically begin with the institution or program being accredited, creating a self-evaluation. These self-evaluations are reports demonstrating compliance with standards or guidelines developed by the accrediting body. Next, it is common to have the self-evaluation reviewed and a visit to the site following this review. Volunteer peers not affiliated with the program or institution undergoing evaluation conduct these visits, reports from which are sent to the accrediting organization for review. The accrediting body then examines all information provided to measure compliance with a set of accreditation standards. Those programs and institutions meeting the standards are granted a limited time period of accreditation before they are reviewed. Most require information reported during this time and operate under a set of complex guidelines in the accreditation process.

In some countries, accreditation is a mandated government process, while in the United States, accreditation is founded on voluntary participation. Therefore, for the publics served by accredited programs and institutions, accreditation serves to indicate that the standards of quality are being met and the program or institution operates in accord with the agreed upon policies, procedures, and practices of the accrediting body. Irrespective of the authority and type of accreditation, the process represents a formal evaluation of an organization, a program, or a service against the best practice standards.

Accreditation standards are exemplars of quality standards that are developed by those within the area being assessed or subject matter experts. Subject matter experts develop these standards through an iterative process, reflecting that which is being evaluated in a manner that is acceptable to the broader group establishing and supporting the method of evaluation.

Although the system of accreditation provides a basis for ensuring that graduates of programs have the knowledge, skills, and abilities warranted for the type of education, the process is not without its critics. Some allege that the accreditation system is not understandable to the public; others complain that it remains difficult to compare institutions and that the process is not well received by many who are subject to it. Some institutions see it as a burdensome and costly process, without substantive benefit. One challenge in evaluating educational quality is that student behavior, for example, motivation, in combination with inherent traits, ultimately influences learning and, therefore, achievement and outcomes. Even with such challenges, though, the present system maintains that it establishes an acceptable level of quality and accountability. Supporters state that for more than a century, the peer-review process effectively and collegially provided an approach to evaluate educational programs and institutions.

Jacqueline Remondet Wall

See also Certification; Program Evaluation

Further Readings

Association of Specialty and Programmatic Accreditors. (n.d.). *About accreditation: Resources, documents and definitions.* Retrieved from http://www.aspa-usa.org/about-accreditation/

U.S. Department of Education. (n.d.). *Accreditation in the United States.* Retrieved from http://www2.ed.gov/admins/finaid/accred/index.html?exp=2

U.S. Department of Education. (n.d.). *The database of accredited postsecondary institutions and programs.* Retrieved from http://ope.ed.gov/accreditation/Agencies.aspx

Websites

Council for Higher Education Accreditation http://www.chea.org

Achievement Tests

The term *achievement tests* refers to tests designed to measure the knowledge, skills, and abilities attained by a test taker in a field, in a subject area, or in a content domain in which the test taker has received training or instruction. This entry first clarifies the difference between achievement tests and aptitude tests and introduces a brief history of achievement tests in the United States. It then describes the purposes of achievement tests, types of tests, and major steps in developing and administering achievement tests. The entry concludes with an overview of the benefits and limitations of achievement tests.

Achievement Tests Versus Aptitude Tests

Before the 21st century, achievement tests were not always distinguished from aptitude tests. William H. Angoff asserted that in educational assessments, there is neither a very clear distinction between achievement and aptitude nor a sharp difference between measures of achievement and measures of aptitude. The aim of aptitude tests is to indicate a test taker's readiness to learn or to develop proficiency in some particular area if instruction or training is provided; achievement tests can serve the same purpose.

The main difference between the two constructs is that the achievement test is confined to a single subject area more completely than is the aptitude test. That is, while items and tasks on the achievement tests are based on specific content standards or are dependent on the materials in the curriculum that examinees are expected to learn in a subject area, those on aptitude tests may be based on skills not explicitly taught in school. Depending on the intended purposes for which the test was developed, the results from an achievement test can be used, for example, for assessing proficiency levels, diagnosing strengths and weaknesses, assigning grades, certification, licensure, course placement, college admission, curriculum evaluation, and school accountability.

Brief History of Achievement Tests in the United States

In 1845, the Boston School Committee led by Samuel G. Howe initiated a large-scale, group-administered written examination to facilitate comparisons across classrooms and to monitor schools' effectiveness. This test is probably the prototype of contemporary achievement tests in the United States, although the term *achievement tests* was not prevalent at the time. This test, which was intended to efficiently measure the knowledge and skills of a great number of students, carried many of the features relevant to the large-scale state and district tests in the late 20th and early 21st centuries. In addition to monitoring the effectiveness of schools, achievement tests of the mid-19th century were designed for selection purposes.

The publication of arithmetic and handwriting tests by Edward L. Thorndike and his students in 1908 symbolized the inception of the unceasing achievement testing movement. At the beginning of the 20th century, there had been some hundreds of achievement tests available for use in elementary and secondary schools; nearly 100 of them were standardized and a variety of content areas were measured: arithmetic, English, geography, handwriting, history, Latin, mathematics, modern languages such as French and Spanish, reading, science, and spelling. The development of achievement test batteries that were designed to inform the public about student learning and school effectiveness across multiple grade levels arose around that time.

The Stanford Achievement Tests developed by Truman L. Kelley, Giles M. Ruch, and Lewis M. Terman in 1923 was one of the first achievement test batteries for multiple grades. Another early test battery was the Iowa Every Pupil Examination for elementary and middle school students, which was developed in 1929 by Everett F. Lindquist and later became the Iowa Tests of Basic Skills. In 1945, Lindquist developed the Iowa Tests of Educational Development for high school learners. These tests were intended to assess students' achievement and to help teachers improve their quality of teaching.

The development of the National Assessment of Educational Progress, first launched in the early 1960s, was a landmark in the history of achievement tests. It is the largest nationally representative assessment designed to assess and monitor what American students know and can do in core subjects. The Elementary and Secondary Education Act of 1965 (ESEA) was enacted to offer equitable educational opportunities to disadvantaged students in the United States. Title I of the law, which provides assistance to school districts for the education of low-income students, has evolved over time and influenced education reforms and testing throughout K–12 education.

In the 1960s and 1970s, the use of standardized achievement tests to meet the ESEA assessment requirements developed incrementally. Standardized tests are administered under conditions that are consistent for all test takers and test scores are norm-referenced, reporting student performance in relation to others from the same population.

The desire to ensure that individual students reached an acceptable minimal level of proficiency resulted in the growth of state-mandated, minimum-competency testing programs throughout the 1970s and has continued to contribute to the spread of standardized achievement tests since then. State-mandated tests are tests and other assessments that the law requires to be administered to all students at designated grade level(s). This wave further triggered the use of criterion-referenced score interpretation for achievement tests.

Beginning in the 1980s, the education reform movement shifted the focus from minimum competency to the expectation of high levels of performance from all students. For achievement tests, this change resulted in a shift from an emphasis on knowledge of basic facts to a focus on more sophisticated reasoning and higher order thinking skills. It also led to changes in item format so that there was some movement away from a reliance on multiple-choice items toward increased use of performance assessments.

The reauthorization and renaming of the ESEA with the passage of the No Child Left Behind Act of 2001 forced state and local educational agencies to be accountable for student achievement and progress. The No Child Left Behind Act, like the original ESEA, aimed to improve the educational experience of disadvantaged populations, and it dramatically expanded the role of state-mandated, standardized achievement tests. Efforts to develop rigorous standards and assessments aligned to them were not new, but the movement toward standards-based testing accelerated after the passage of the No Child Left Behind Act; high levels of student achievement and academic institution accountability were both expected.

Scores on achievement tests can be interpreted using norms, criteria, and/or standards. Standards-based testing has dominated state-level testing since the early 21st century and will likely continue its popularity and influence under new education reforms.

Essentials of Achievement Tests

Summative and Formative Purposes

Achievement tests may be incorporated into the learning process and instructional materials at different times. For summative purposes, testing is done at the end of the instructional process. The test results are viewed as the summation of all knowledge or skills acquired by test takers during a particular subject unit. Judgments about the quality or worth of test takers' achievement are made after the instructional process is completed.

For formative purposes, testing occurs constantly during the learning process so that teachers can evaluate the effectiveness of teaching methods and assess students' performance at the same time. The test results are used to improve teachers' teaching and to help guide students' next learning steps. Judgments about the quality of students' achievement are obtained while the students are still in the process of learning.

Types of Tests

Achievement tests can take either the form of a single subject assessment that focuses on achievement in a single area or the form of a survey battery that typically consists of a group of subject area tests designed for particular grade levels. In a classroom setting, teachers can use tests associated with textbooks as part of their formative and summative assessments to diagnose students' problems and to measure students' mastery. For admission purposes, achievement tests can offer a uniform measure of college readiness such that colleges can identify promising students who are deserving of admission. Furthermore, they provide admissions officers a means to distinguish between well- and poorly prepared applicants.

Survey or Test Battery

Achievement tests are not necessarily standardized tests. In the United States, however, achievement tests produced by test publishers in the form of a survey or a test battery, or the state-mandated tests that not only measure student achievement in K–12 for making instructional decisions but are also known to report public accountability, usually have a high degree of standardization.

Single-level standardized tests for one course or subject, sometimes called surveys, are developed for assessing achievement at only one education level or for one course (e.g., geometry). Usually they are stand-alone tests and are not associated with tests for other courses. For example, the California Standards Tests for Science, available for Grades 5, 8, and 10, are used to assess students' achievement against California's academic content standards in science.

Test batteries or survey batteries contain different tests that assess several curricular areas. There are often multiple levels, indicating that the test content spans several grade levels. For example, the Iowa Assessments are designed for students in kindergarten through the 12th grade. The tests are written for multiple grade levels, with each test level consisting of a series of content areas designed to measure specific skills. The TerraNova by CTB/McGraw-Hill and Data Recognition Corporation is a series of standardized achievement tests designed to assess K–12 student achievement in reading, language arts, mathematics, science, social studies, vocabulary, spelling, and other areas. The ACT Aspire, another example, can be modular or a battery, which provides a means to measure students' learning outcomes in English, mathematics, reading, science, and writing from Grade 3 through early high school.

Often, school districts use a standardized achievement battery to acquire supplementary information useful in curriculum and lesson planning. Achievement tests can serve diagnostic purposes—teachers may use the results of a single test or test battery to suggest areas for individual student development.

Classroom Use

Teacher-made tests and textbook or curricular accompaniments are also achievement tests. Teachers can craft tests to measure the specific learning goals the curriculum framework emphasizes, and the test content can be derived from the course syllabus, the class objectives, or textbook. Also, in teacher's editions, there are usually tests at the end of textbook chapters, at the back of the book, built into instructional materials, or supplied separately with textbook series. These non-standardized tests are designed to measure students' mastery of a specific learning domain such that teachers can learn information about the skills of individual students that are most and least developed, followed by decision-making on the competency, placement, and/or advancement of the students; diagnostic purposes of achievement tests are fulfilled in this way.

Classroom achievement tests are often considered to be criterion-referenced since a student's scores are compared against some standard, such as the learning objectives for a book chapter, rather than compared with the score of other students in the class. These tests are helpful for teachers to make timely instructional decisions because the turnaround time is controlled by the teacher.

Higher Education Admission

In addition to serving diagnostic purposes, achievement tests can also be prognostic tests used to predict achievement or future performance in a particular area or at a specific time. For example, the ACT and SAT are globally recognized college admission tests. The ACT consists of subject area tests designed to measure academic achievement in English, mathematics, reading, science, and writing. The SAT also tests students' knowledge and skills learned in school, including reading, writing, and mathematics. For admissions officers, these two college admissions tests provide a predictive tool to distinguish between applicants who are likely to perform well or poorly in college.

College admissions tests are prevalent all over the world. Certainly, the college admissions tests from various countries differ in many ways and they evolve over time, but one constant characteristic of these tests remains: They are high stakes, competitive, and stressful.

Development and Administration

The use of achievement tests involves several major steps, including item development and test assembly, administration, scoring and score interpretation, and reporting. The methods used to design achievement tests must address constructs to be measured in terms of knowledge, skills, and cognitive processes. Item writers are content experts who usually begin with a list of content standards that specify what students are expected to know and learn in a given grade level. The number and type of test items can be determined by the grade-level content standards.

Item Types

Typically on a paper-and-pencil test, the item types used on achievement tests include multiple-choice items, true-false questions, short-answer open-ended items, and essay questions. Due to advancements in technology, test delivery can be done not only by paper but via computer and other electronic devices. For example, technology-enhanced items are computer-delivered items to which test takers respond based on interactions such as dragging and dropping, editing, highlighting, ordering, and sorting.

The choice among various item types is typically made on the assumption that some particular knowledge, skill, ability, or mental process can be measured by each of these item types. Whatever educational achievement that can be measured well by one type of test item can probably also be measured quite well by some other types. In practice, choosing among item types often takes into account development costs as well as testing and scoring time, which often works in favor of objective test items (e.g., multiple-choice items).

Administration

Most achievement tests, especially in education, are administered in group settings. For high-stakes or mandatory achievement tests, standardization is required such that the testing conditions are the same for all test takers; it is also common to establish norm-based score scales for interpreting test performance against a representative sample of individuals from the population with which the test is intended to be used. Individuals approved for test accommodations may be provided with a specialized version of a test, such as large type print, braille, audio, or Spanish language, or given an extended time to take a test.

Ideally, test takers should understand what the test requires them to do, attain an environment in which they can motivate themselves to do as well as they can, and have an equal opportunity to demonstrate their best efforts to achieve good performance. It is also important that achievement tests avoid being unduly speeded. Most test takers should have enough time to complete the test, which often enables the best performance on the tests and the most accurate predictions of subsequent achievement.

Scoring

In terms of scoring, each item type presents unique methods and problems for scoring. For teacher-crafted tests, answers to multiple-choice and true-false questions as well as other objective-item types can be marked directly on the test copy and later be scored by hand. For state-level or large-scale tests, scoring can be facilitated if the answers are provided by marking on a separate answer sheet such that they can be scored more quickly and accurately by electrical scoring machines. For open-ended items (e.g., short-answer questions) and essay questions, scoring rubrics are developed for the questions and used to train human raters or to program computer scoring algorithms. For short-answer questions, a scoring key that shows the kinds of answers eligible for full credit or partial credit is often recommended.

Essay scoring rubrics can be analytic or holistic. Irrelevant factors, such as the quality of handwriting, verbal fluency, and rater interests or biases should be avoided in the scoring process. In general, essay scoring takes considerably more time and is much more costly than the scoring of objective items.

Score Interpretation and Reporting

The meaning and interpretation of achievement test scores can be relative, absolute, or both. A norm-reference framework, which interprets test scores in a relative sense, indicates how the achievement of a particular student compares with the achievement of a well-defined group of other test takers (i.e., the norm group) who have taken the same test. Derived scores commonly used for the norm-referenced tests include percentile ranks; linear, normalized, or developmental standard scores; and grade equivalents.

A criterion-reference framework offers an absolute score interpretation by inferring the kinds of performance a student can do in a domain. The results of criterion-referenced testing can be presented by, for instance, the percentage of correct responses, the percentage of objectives mastered, the predefined quality level of student achievement (e.g., "excellent," "mastery," rating of "A" or "5"), or the precision of performance. For standards-based referenced scores and interpretation, performance-level descriptions are unique to the achievement test for which they define levels of performance such as "basic," "proficient," and "advanced." A certain range of test scores is carefully associated with each of the achievement levels in a subject; the percentage of test takers at each level of proficiency is of the most interest.

Finally, score reporting typically contains at least three elements: types of scores provided on score reports, other information provided on or with the score reports (e.g., interpretive guides for students, parents, teachers, or principals), and other supporting information that may be available (e.g., technical reports). Accurate, efficient scoring and reporting makes the test score interpretation clearly communicated and strongly supportable and provides more directly useful information to guide instructional decisions and promote learning.

Benefits and Limitations

Achievement tests are standardized or nonstandardized tests used to measure acquired learning. A well-constructed test yields valid and reliable results, providing test takers with an opportunity to demonstrate what they have learned in school and to show to themselves and others the knowledge and skills that they have accumulated. The development of test specifications needs to be aligned with curriculum or professional content standards in a clear and coherent way. Following the specifications, items, questions, or tasks on the tests can then present the targeted procedural knowledge and cognitive processes.

Rigorous test administration helps with the interpretation of scores. The results of achievement tests serve as indicators of examinee progress. Score results can help examinees confirm their strengths and weaknesses. Also, a well-written, valid test equipped with efficient scoring and reporting will give teachers valuable information regarding students' needs and abilities, offer teachers a useful measure of how well the students have achieved the course objectives, and assist teachers in evaluating teaching effectiveness. As outlined, achievement tests are also one of the many useful tools to predict college performance.

Concern has arisen over the increased use of standardized tests in schools, with some arguing that test takers may become anxious and frustrated from taking and preparing for the tests, which may subsequently lower their motivation to learn. Whether the content coverage and relevance as well as the construct representativeness of the tests are solid and sound is sometime a concern to the public. In addition, if items do not present a challenge to the test takers, the test may become meaningless since test users might question whether the test items adequately represent the content domain and the quality of performance such that we can assure successful performers on the tests actually meet the content standards.

However, even if the test is well written and content valid, the degree to which the achievement measure is authentic is sometimes doubted. Authenticity is limited due to the cost of test construction and the acceptable administration time. Items on achievement tests are often expressed in verbal or symbolic terms. Meanwhile, the knowledge obtained by direct perceptions of objects, events, feelings, or relationships, as well as mental and behavioral skills, such as leadership and friendship, are not assessed by most achievement tests.

Also, achievement tests may be able to measure what a person knows but not necessarily how effectively he or she uses that knowledge in practice. In addition, items do not necessarily reflect the actual, full picture of the learning outcomes from a classroom setting. It is not possible for an achievement measure to cover all knowledge and skills or to represent the whole of human achievement. A student with higher achievement scores is more likely to succeed than another student with low achievement scores, but high scores cannot guarantee future success.

Finally, one of the intended purposes for using K–12 standardized achievement tests is to provide information for public accountability. In some schools, test results are also used to evaluate teachers, although there is ongoing debate about the legitimacy of using standardized tests for this purpose. In any case, it is clear that standardized achievement test results should not become the single most important indicator of school performance or teacher evaluation. An overemphasis on test scores can result in pressure that can potentially lead to cheating by administers and teachers, which invalidates the whole idea of achievement testing.

Yi-Fang Wu

See also Ability Tests; ACT; Criterion-Referenced Interpretation; Formative Assessment; Norm-Referenced Interpretation; SAT; Standardized Tests; Standards-Based Assessment; Summative Assessment

Further Readings

AERA, APA, & NCME. (2014). *Standards for educational and psychological testing*. Washington, DC: AERA.

Angoff, W. H. (1971). Scales, norms, and equivalent scores. In R. L. Thorndike (Ed.), *Educational measurement* (2nd ed., pp. 508–600). Washington, DC: American Council on Education.

Brookhart, S. M., & Nitko, A. J. (2014). *Educational assessment of students* (7th ed.). Upper Saddle River, NJ: Pearson.

Ebel, R. L., & Frisbie, D. A. (1991). *Essentials of educational measurement* (5th ed.). Englewood Cliffs, NJ: Prentice Hall.

Ferrara, S., & DeMauro, G. E. (2006). Standardized assessment of individual achievement in K–12. In R. L. Brennan (Ed.), *Educational measurement* (4th ed., pp. 579–621). Westport, CT: American Council on Education/Praeger.

Haladyna, T. M., & Downing, S. M. (Eds.). (2006). *Handbook of test development.* Mahwah, NJ: Erlbaum.

Koretz, D., & Hamilton, L. S. (2006). Testing for accountability in K–12. In R. L. Brennan (Ed.), *Educational measurement* (4th ed., pp. 531–578). Westport, CT: American Council on Education/Praeger.

Monroe, W. S., DeVoss, J. C., & Kelly, F. J. (1917). *Educational tests and measurements.* New York, NY: Houghton Mifflin.

Nitko, A. J. (1983). *Educational tests and measurement: An introduction.* New York, NY: Harcourt Brace Jovanovich.

Resnick, D. P. (1982). History of educational testing. In A. K. Wigdor & W. R. Garner (Eds.), *Ability testing: Uses, consequences, and controversies, Part II* (pp. 173–194). Washington, DC: National Academy Press.

The College Board. (2016). The SAT®. Retrieved from https://sat.collegeboard.org/home

Thomas, J. Y., & Brady, K. P. (2005). Chapter 3: The Elementary and Secondary Education Act at 40: Equity, accountability, and the evolving federal role in public education. *Review of Research in Education, 29,* 51–67. doi:10.3102/0091732X029001051

Whipple, G. M. (Ed.). (1918). *The seventeenth yearbook of the National Society for the Study of Education, Part II: The measurement of educational products.* Bloomington, IL: Public School Publishing Company.

ACT

The American College Testing Program (ACT) is a curriculum- and standards-based educational and career planning tool assessing students' academic readiness for college. The ACT comprises five tests, including four subject tests (English, mathematics, reading, and science) and an optional writing test. Depending on whether the optional writing test is taken, the total testing time is either 2 hours and 55 minutes or 3 hours and 35 minutes. Each of the five tests is scored on a scale from 1 to 36. A composite score of the four nonwriting subjects is also based on a scale from 1 to 36.

The ACT is created and administered by a nonprofit company, ACT, Inc. (formerly known as American College Testing). ACT scores are accepted by all 4-year colleges and universities in the United States. Students can also take the ACT overseas, and it is administered multiple times each year, both inside and outside of the United States. This entry discusses the history of the test, its components, methods of preparing for the test, and how the test is used.

History

On November 7, 1959, the first-ever ACT was taken by 75,460 high school students looking forward to joining college. Although another college admissions test (the SAT, then known as the Scholastic Aptitude Test) did exist at that time, the ACT was different because it was a test of achievement and did not purport to measure innate intelligence or intelligence quotient. Being unsatisfied with the existing system of admissions testing, E. F. Lindquist and Ted McCarrel cofounded the ACT (now ACT, Inc.) and created the first college admission test based on information taught in schools.

Since its inception, the ACT has grown rapidly. Since 1960, ACT has been taken in all 50 states. In 2012, for the first time, the number of students taking the ACT surpassed the number of students taking the SAT. In 2012, over half of the country's high school graduates took the ACT. Part of the growth can be attributed to statewide administrations of the ACT. In 2001, Colorado and Illinois became the first states to adopt the ACT as part of their statewide assessment programs to measure students' progress toward meeting state learning standards. Other states soon followed. For the 2014–2015 school year, the ACT was administered as part of a state assessment to students in 21 U.S. states.

In spring 2013, ACT announced enhancements to the ACT based on evidence from the ACT National Curriculum Survey and to reflect changes in the education market. These enhancements are as follows: (a) the online administration of the ACT, (b) the addition of questions on the reading test, addressing whether students can integrate knowledge and ideas across multiple texts, (c) the inclusion of additional statistics and probability items in the mathematics test for reporting of student achievement in this area, and (d) additional scores and indicators (STEM score, progress toward career readiness indicator, English language arts score, and understanding complex texts indicator). However, the 1–36 score scale remains. In fall 2015, enhancements were made to the design of the writing test and new writing scores were introduced. The score scale has been changed from 2–12 to 1–36. Instead of one holistic score, students receive four analytic scores (also known as domain scores) which are used to compute the writing score on the 1–36 scale.

Test Description

The ACT consists of four multiple-choice tests: English, mathematics, reading, and science. The ACT with writing includes the four multiple-choice tests and a writing test. All multiple-choice items have four choices except for those on the mathematics test which have five choices. Each item will have only one best answer (i.e., the correct answer). Students score one point by choosing the correct answer, with no penalty for incorrect answers.

The English test measures standard written English and rhetorical skills. The test consists of five essays or passages, each of which is accompanied by a sequence of multiple-choice test questions. It comprises 75 questions, and examinees have 45 minutes to finish them. Students' performances on the English test are reported on a scale from 1 to 36. In addition to the total test score, two subscores (usage/mechanics and rhetorical skills) are provided.

The mathematics test measures mathematical skills students have typically acquired in courses taken up to the beginning of Grade 12. It consists of 60 questions and examinees have 60 minutes to finish them. Students' performances on the mathematics test are reported on a scale from 1 to 36. In addition to the total test score, three subscores (pre-algebra/elementary algebra, intermediate algebra/coordinate geometry, and plane geometry/trigonometry) are provided.

The reading test measures reading comprehension. It consists of 40 questions, and examinees have 35 minutes to finish them. Students' performances on the reading test are reported on a scale from 1 to 36. In addition to the total test score,

two subscores (social studies/natural sciences and arts/literature) are provided.

The science test measures the interpretation, analysis, evaluation, reasoning, and problem-solving skills required in the natural sciences. It consists of 40 questions, and examinees have 35 minutes to finish them. Students' performances on the science test are reported on a scale from 1–36. There are no subscores for the science test.

Starting from fall 2016, reporting category scores are also provided to students. The reporting categories for the English test include production of writing, knowledge of language, and conventions of standard English. The reporting categories for the mathematics test include preparing for higher math, number and quantity, algebra, functions, geometry, statistics and probability, integrating essential skills, and modeling. The reporting categories for the reading test include key ideas and details, craft and structure, and integration of knowledge and ideas. For the science test, the reporting categories include interpretation of data, scientific investigation, evaluation of models, and inferences and experimental results.

The optional writing test measures writing skills emphasized in high school English classes and entry-level college composition courses. It consists of one prompt that typically presents conversations around contemporary issues and offers three diverse perspectives that encourage critical engagement with the issue. Students have 40 minutes to develop and compose an argument that puts their perspective in dialogue with others. Student writing is evaluated in four domains: ideas and analysis, development and support, organization, and language use. The four domain scores are used to compute the subject-level writing score that, like other subject scores, is on a scale from 1 to 36.

Preparing for the ACT

To help students prepare for the ACT, ACT, Inc. publishes an official prep book, *The Real ACT Prep Guide*. In addition to information on how to register and prepare for the test day, this book includes five practice tests, each with an optional writing test, which were used in previous actual test administrations. For all multiple-choice items, this book explains why an answer choice is right or wrong. For the writing prompt, the book explains how it is scored. A review of important topics in English, mathematics, science, and writing is also included.

ACT, Inc. also publishes an electronic tool to help students prepare for the ACT, ACT Online Prep, available on both desktop computers and tablet computers. It is not an electronic copy of the official prep book, but an interactive tool to help students become familiar with the ACT, to know their strengths and weaknesses, and to improve. Using ACT Online Prep, students can take a short-form ACT to get a predicted score range. Based on students' performance on the short-form ACT and their unique needs (e.g., the available preparation time before the test), the system can create a personalized learning path to guide the students through a library of learning content in the most efficient way possible. Students have different ways to learn, including flash cards, lessons, and practice questions. A dashboard is available for students to keep track of their progress and to get feedback on their strengths and weakness and how to improve. This tool also includes a full-length ACT, which was used in previous actual test administrations, to help students get familiar with the test and predict their performance.

Both *The Real ACT Prep Guide* and ACT Online Prep are available for purchase, though ACT provides low-income students with free access to its ACT Online Prep program. A free copy of *Preparing for the ACT* is available for download at the ACT website. This document includes test information, a complete practice test, and a sample writing prompt. It allows students to become familiar with the test before turning to the two more extensive test preparation tools.

There are many other test preparation companies that sell test preparation materials and offer preparation courses or training opportunities for students to prepare for the ACT (e.g., Kaplan, Inc.; Princeton Review). In addition to the ACT, these companies typically offer preparation services for various other tests. Although they typically claim coaching courses help increase their scores, there is no solid support for such claims from research.

ACT conducted several studies between the early 1990s and 2003 to examine ACT score increases attributable solely to short-term test preparation activities (e.g., commercial test preparation courses, commercial workbooks, test preparation computer software, test preparation workshops offered by local schools) using repeat test takers and cross-sectional samples of students who took the test at given time points. The results from these studies show that short-term test preparation activities have a relatively small positive impact on the ACT composite score when compared to long-term activities. The best preparation for the ACT is to take a rigorous core curriculum in high school.

Using the ACT

The ACT is designed to give students an indication of how likely they are to be ready for college-level work. ACT suggests that these scores or higher scores indicate readiness for college: English, 18; math, 22; reading, 21; and science, 24. Mean scores on the ACTs are about 20, with standard deviations of about 4½. Research has shown that students with higher ACT scores tend to be better prepared for college-level work as shown by higher first-year GPAs in college.

Like any other achievement test, the ACT neither measures everything students have learned in high school nor measures everything necessary for students to know to be successful in their next level learning. Such a test simply does not exist, so admissions decisions should not be made solely based on a single test. The reported scale score for an examinee is only an estimate of that examinee's true score because of some measurement error. The ACT demonstrate very high reliability, however, and observed scores are considered very close to students' "true" scores.

The ACT can be used for numerous and diverse purposes. Distinct validity evidence, however, is needed for each intended use, according to the *Standards for Educational and Psychological Testing* of the American Educational Research Association, American Psychological Association, and National Council on Measurement in Education. The most common uses, according to the *Technical Manual* published by ACT, are to measure educational achievement in particular subjects, make college admission and college course placement decisions, evaluate the effectiveness of high schools in preparing students for college, and evaluate students' likelihood of success in the first year of college and beyond. For usage not covered by ACT's *Technical Manual*, it is advised that users support their usage by validity arguments.

Zhongmin Cui

See also Achievement Tests; College Success; SAT; *Standards for Educational and Psychological Testing*

Further Readings

ACT, Inc. (n.d.). News and FAQs. Retrieved from http://www.act.org/actnext/

ACT, Inc. (n.d.). Our products. Retrieved from http://www.act.org/content/act/en/products-and-services.html

ACT, Inc. (2016). Preparing for the ACT test. Retrieved from https://www.act.org/aap/pdf/Preparing-for-the-ACT.pdf

ACT, Inc. (n.d.). The Act Test for students. Retrieved from http://www.actstudent.org/

ACT, Inc. (2012). What kind of test preparation is best? Retrieved from https://www.act.org/research/policymakers/pdf/best_testprep.pdf

ACT, Inc. (2014). Technical manual. Retrieved from https://www.act.org/research/policymakers/pdf/best_testprep.pdf

ACT, Inc. (2015). Using your ACT results. Retrieved from http://www.act.org/aap/pdf/Using-Your-ACT-Results.pdf

American Educational Research Association, American Psychological Association, & National Council on Measurement in Education. (2014). *Standards for educational and psychological testing*. Washington, DC.

Strauss, V. (2012). Why ACT overtook SAT as top college entrance exam. Retrieved from https://www.washingtonpost.com/blogs/answer-sheet/post/how-act-overtook-sat-as-the-top-college-entrance-exam/2012/09/24/d56df11c-0674-11e2-afff-d6c7f20a83bf_blog.html

ACTION RESEARCH

Action research is a form of reflective inquiry with intended use and users; practitioners in their own educational settings conduct it in order to improve their own professional practice and outcomes for students. Through action research, educators identify pressing problems of professional practice and engage in data collection, analysis, and interpretation, with the intention of understanding gaps between desired and actual results and achieving genuine improvements in the quality of their instruction and student learning. The action research process and resultant findings can equip practitioners with the knowledge they need to make real-time, evidence-based decisions about schooling, teaching, and learning. This entry discusses the development of action research as a method of inquiry, how and why action research is used in PreK–16 schools and barriers to the action research use in these schools.

Educators engage in action research in order to continuously test their working theories as to what works and what doesn't in schools and classrooms. It is the individuals' immediate use of data to inform and/or improve their practice that most distinguishes "action" research from more traditional academic research where educators may have little input into study design, data collection, or interpretation. This method of inquiry is most common among professionals in PreK–16 educational settings, including regular and special education teachers, school principals, district superintendents, instructional coaches, school counselors, and school psychologists.

Action research is arguably the most valid, powerful, and important tool that professionals in PreK–16 settings have at their disposal to make meaningful, ongoing, and sustained positive changes to their practice intended to bring about essential outcomes. Action researchers can acquire greater congruity between the values they espouse and the values they enact in practice in classrooms and across systems. Action research is ideal for those who hold participatory, democratic, and improvement-oriented worldviews concerned with the development of rich, valid, contextually useful information for the improvement of teaching, learning, and schooling.

Background

The term *action research* was first used in the early 20th century to characterize group research activities that resulted in changed community practices. A theoretical framework for action research emerged from Kurt Lewin and his studies of the workplace in the 1930s. He conceived of action research as an ongoing process of thinking and doing by organizational stakeholders, bringing about increases in employee morale and their work ownership. In time, the principles of action research began to be integrated into the examination of pedagogical and educational reform activities. Today, action research stands in marked contrast to traditional educational research (or "pure" research), in which an outside investigator examines an issue, disseminates findings (perhaps through publication in peer-reviewed journals), and then leaves it up to practitioners to locate, access, interpret, and implement the results.

Action research is increasingly recognized as a legitimate form of social science research. One such measure of legitimacy are peer-reviewed venues for publication on the topic. *Action Research*, an international, interdisciplinary, peer-reviewed journal that publishes articles on the theory and practice of action research, was launched in 2003. The journal publishes accounts of action research projects and articles that explore the philosophical underpinnings and methodology of action research. Action research, as a job-embedded process, stimulates the ingenuity of educators and cultivates their ability to creatively and collaboratively address immediate problems of practice. Educators who conduct action research experience intellectual and professional growth, develop more positive attitudes toward their colleagues, and improve their pedagogical skills.

Action Research for Informed Decision Making

Educators make hundreds of complex decisions every day, the most important of which are made in a quick and intuitive fashion during the act of instruction. Given the high-stakes and multifaceted nature of learning environments, whose outcomes have immediate and long-standing ethical implications for individuals and society, educators cannot afford to practice their craft in an unexamined fashion. Decisions about what to teach and how to go about the business of teaching and learning are too often based on recollections of events, anecdotal information, ideas found through happenstance, and casual observations.

Through action research, school-based professionals can examine and interpret the learning environment in order to make informed decisions about curriculum, instruction, and assessment. It is the systematic collection and analysis of a variety of contextualized classroom- and school-based data, including observations, student artifacts, interviews, journal entries, formative assessment results, and video of teaching, considered in light of established theory that helps to transform typical and less rigorous forms of reflective practice into action research.

Cycle of Action Research

In a cycle of action research, an educator or team of educators will (a) identify a theory or argument about what is important and makes a difference in student learning; (b) formulate specific questions about teaching and learning related to their theory or argument; (c) identify and define the variables, terms, and concepts at the heart of their questions; (d) understand the already available key literature or studies that shed light on the questions of interest; (e) develop a hypothesis or supposition about what their studies' findings might reveal; (f) collect and analyze data about the variables, terms, and concepts in their research questions; (g) interpret the results and make decisions about what or how to change or improve practice; (h) revisit, revise, and refine their original theory or argument; and (i) repeat a–h as an ongoing part of their regular professional work.

Action Research as Professional Development

Action researchers are working professionals who use applied social science data collection and analysis methods to explore and test new ideas, methods, and materials and assess the effectiveness of curricular approaches. Action research is most effective when it is conceived of as a regular and routine part of their professional practice, that is, when educators initiate and facilitate systematic inquiry as part of their teaching and administrative responsibilities. When educators undertake their own places of work, action research can become an exceptional vehicle for job-embedded professional development. School leaders can support action research activities by reserving space and time to enable educators to jointly carry out the cycle of action research. In addition, school leaders can incorporate the process and results of teacher action research into the more formal systems of supervision and evaluation. Teachers can use documentation of their individual or team-level cycle of action research as the mechanism for setting, monitoring, and reporting their instructional practice and student learning goals required by state and local educator evaluation systems.

Barriers to Action Research

If action research is one of the most effective means through which teachers and administrators can improve their practice, student achievement, and schooling, why is engagement in action research infrequent in schools? Although action research is an effective strategy for a continuous organizational and pedagogical improvement, there are few powerful federal or state-level policy proponents or legislative mandates that support it. As a result, educators do not typically have the resources or the impetus they need to carry out action research studies.

A significant resource in short supply is time. A significant amount of time is needed in order for educators to use action research to improve instruction and enhance student learning. Although there is no rule for how much time is needed for action research to be productive, studies suggest that any professional development endeavor in which teachers are engaged for less than an average of 8 hours *per month* will likely have little or no impact on instructional practice and student learning. In addition to a lack of resources such as time, educators may also lack the skills necessary for conducting high-quality, quantitative and qualitative data collection and analysis at the core of all social science research methods.

Rebecca H. Woodland

See also Applied Research; Conceptual Framework; Mixed Methods Research; Professional Development of Teachers; Qualitative Research Methods; Quantitative Research Methods

Further Readings

Mills, G. (2014). *Action research: A guide for the teacher researcher* (4th ed.). Pearson.

Parson, R., & Brown, K. (2002). *Teacher as reflective practitioner and action researcher*. Belmont, CA: Wadsworth.

Sagor, R. (2000). *Guiding school improvement with action research*. Alexandria, VA: ASCD.

Wei, R. C., Darling-Hammond, L., & Adamson, F. (2010). *Professional development in the United States: Trends and challenges*. Dallas, TX: National Staff Development Council.

Yoon, K. S., Duncan, T., Lee, S. W. Y., Scarloss, B., & Shapley, K. (2007). Reviewing the evidence on how teacher professional development affects student achievement (Issues & Answers Report, REL 2007–No. 033). Washington, DC: U.S. Department of Education, Institute of Education Sciences, National Center for Education Evaluation and Regional Assistance, Regional Educational Laboratory Southwest. Retrieved from http://ies.ed.gov/ncee/edlabs

Active Learning

This entry describes active learning, addresses its benefits and challenges, and offers strategies for implementing active learning in classroom settings. Active learning shifts the focus of learning from passively receiving content information to diligently participating in learning activities. Student engagement in learning increases retention and understanding of course content and enhances the quality of learning outcomes. In active learning, with the guidance and assistance of the teacher, students learn and practice new concepts and use them meaningfully.

Although there are many definitions of active learning, it can be described as a student-centered approach to instruction. According to Charles Bonwell and James Eison, active learning is "anything that involves students in doing things and thinking about the things they are doing" (p. 2). The key elements of active learning are student involvement in the learning process and critical reflection on course material. Unlike the teacher-centered approach where students simply listen to lectures and take notes, in active learning, students engage with the course material, participate in the class, and collaborate with others. The process affords students the opportunity to explore and develop new concepts through meaningful discussions and problem-solving situations.

In active learning, teachers must shift their roles from "sage on the stage" to "guide on the side." They are no longer information providers; rather, they are facilitators helping students understand a concept, demonstrate it, and apply it in the real-world situations. In active learning, students become autonomous and self-directed learners taking charge of their own learning by taking initiative, monitoring progress, and evaluating learning outcomes. Consequently, students not only develop knowledge and skills, they also show high motivation and good attitudes toward learning.

In today's classrooms, there is increasing emphasis on equipping students with 21st-century skills, including critical thinking, creativity, communication, and collaboration. Critical thinking is often promoted through higher order thinking that requires students to use cognitive skills to understand, synthesize, evaluate, and make use of information to create content. Critical thinking helps students gain control of their own learning and make better informed decisions as to what, when, and how to learn. Furthermore, active learning promotes social interactions, allowing students to work collaboratively with their peers and teachers. Increased peer-to-peer and student-to-teacher interaction helps to build a learning community through which students develop, share, and exchange perspectives.

Challenges of Using Active Learning

Although active engagement empowers students to create their own learning experiences and is believed to enhance the quality of learning, both students and teachers perceive challenges. Some students may not be willing to abandon their passive roles of listening to lectures. Students may not have skills required, such as learning strategies and critical thinking, to participate in active learning. Class of large sizes can prevent teachers from implementing active learning due to limited class time. Teachers are preoccupied by not being able to cover the amount of course material or feeling a loss of control. They also fear that students may resist active learning. Other barriers include a lack of needed materials, equipment, or resources. The challenges of using active learning can be overcome by offering teachers effective strategies and techniques.

Strategies for Implementing Active Learning in Teaching

To effectively use active learning, teachers first need to openly communicate with students about their instructional goals and strategies. A common instructional strategy for active learning is to integrate student-centered activities into the traditional lecture. To maintain student attention span during the lecture, a combination of instructional techniques can be used, such as open-ended questions, small group discussions, and reflective responses. At the end of the lecture, students are asked to answer teacher-made questions called "minute paper," allowing them to reflect on that day's course material.

Several techniques are considered effective for active learning, including collaborative learning, problem-based learning, project-based learning, and technology-based learning. Collaborative learning activities allow students to work together with others to achieve a common goal, whereas problem-based learning, a student-centered approach, enables students to gain knowledge and skills through the experience of solving difficult and complex problems. Problem-based learning requires critical thinking, self-regulation, and self-motivation on the part of students.

Another way to embrace active learning is by using flipped learning. Due to the increasing availability of digital technology, teachers can easily prepare short video lectures for students to view and learn course material, at home before the class session. Flipped learning emphasizes students' learning responsibility. It allows teachers to free up class time to explore the challenging aspects of course content and engage students with the content, using various types of active learning activities such as open-ended discussions in pairs or small groups. In the flipped classroom, teachers provide personalized learning and meet individual student needs. Through active engagement with anytime and anywhere access to video lectures, students learn at their own pace to master the concept.

Lina Lee

See also Constructivist Approach; Instructional Theory; Mastery Learning; Social Learning

Further Readings

Barkley, E. (2010). *Student engagement techniques*. San Francisco, CA: Jossey-Bass.

Bonwell, C. C., & Eison, J. A. (1991). Active learning: Creating excitement in the classroom (ASHE-ERIC Higher Education Report No. 1). Washington, DC: The George Washington University, School of Education and Human Development.

Carr, R., Palmer, S., & Hagel, P. (2015). Active learning: The importance of developing a comprehensive measure. *Active Learning in Higher Education, 16*(3), 173–186.

Mayer, R. E. (2008). *Learning and instruction* (2nd ed.). Upper Saddle River, NJ: Pearson Merrill Prentice Hall.

Wenger, E. (1998). *Communities of practice: Learning, meaning and identity*. New York, NY: Cambridge University Press.

ADA

See Americans with Disabilities Act

ADAPTIVE BEHAVIOR ASSESSMENTS

Adaptive behavior refers to a group of basic skills that people must master in order to function and survive. These skills are conceptual, social, and practical skills used in daily life. Assessment of adaptive behavior skills is necessary as a component of the diagnosis or classification for having an intellectual disability.

People with an intellectual disability typically have significant deficits in their conceptual, social, and/or practical skills. These deficits can prevent them from being fully independent. Adaptive behavior measures can be used to help determine the level of impairment. This entry first looks at how the criteria for diagnosing intellectual disabilities have changed and now include deficits in adaptive functioning. It then describes the two main rating scales used to assess adaptive behavior skills, the Adaptive Behavior Assessment System (ABAS) and the Vineland Adaptive Behavior Scales.

Intellectual Disabilities and Adaptive Behavior Skills

A deficit in adaptive behavior skills has not always been a part of assessment for intellectual disabilities. When the American Psychiatric Association first published the *Diagnostic and Statistical Manual of Mental Disorders* (*DSM*) in 1952, the classification category of *mental deficiency* was introduced to account for cases that were primarily a defect of intelligence present at birth with no known organic brain disease or known prenatal cause for the deficits. Cases were to include only individuals with familial or idiopathic (unknown origin) mental deficiencies, and severity was to be determined by IQ scores in the following three ranges: *mild* (an IQ of approximately 70–85), *moderate* (IQ 50–70), and *severe* (IQs below 50). Although IQ scores were necessary to determine the range and expectations, the *DSM* noted the importance of considering other factors.

When the second edition of *DSM* (*DSM-II*) was first published in 1968, the term *mental retardation* (MR) replaced *mentally deficient*. The *DSM-II* better aligned with what was then called the American Association on Mental Retardation (now the American Association on Intellectual and Developmental Disabilities) and supported five ranges of severity (borderline, mild, moderate, severe, and profound), with the borderline range for IQ scores in the 68–85 range. It listed clinical codes for 9 subcategories for the disorder, based on the circumstances of origin (e.g., following infection and intoxication; following trauma or physical agent).

In 1980, the *DSM-III* placed MR in a new section titled "Disorders Usually First Evident in Infancy, Childhood or Adolescence." The three main criteria for a diagnosis of MR remained consistent with the previous version (i.e., impaired IQ, impaired adaptive behaviors, and onset during the developmental period); however, these criteria were further refined at this time. Subnormal intelligence was now set two standard deviations below the mean (IQ of 70), instead of one standard deviation (IQ of 85) with the addition of a five-point interval to be considered (IQ 65–75) to account for the standard error of measure. Onset during the developmental period was defined as occurring below 18 years of age. Impairments in adaptive functioning were required; however, the *DSM* noted that the then-current measures were not considered valid to be used in isolation to make this decision and recommended that clinical judgment should evaluate adaptive functioning in individuals relative to similar aged peers.

In the *DSM-IV*, first published in 1994, the three criteria for diagnosing MR were retained from the previous version. The criterion of adaptive functioning was further defined as requiring deficits in two of 10 possible areas: (1) functional academic skills, (2) social/interpersonal skills, (3) communication skills, (4) self-care, (5) home living, (6) use of community resources, (7) self-direction, (8) work, (9) leisure, and (10) health/safety. These deficits were determined by an individual's score on an adaptive measure that was 2 standard deviations (*SD*s) below the norm. These criteria remained consistent in the subsequent text revision of the *DSM-IV-TR* in 2000.

In 2002, the American Association on Mental Retardation made the landmark decision to change the way it defined the severity of MR, moving away from classifying levels based on intellectual functioning to levels of supports needed (*intermittent, limited, extensive,* or *pervasive*) to close the gap between problems in adaptive functioning and enhancing an individual's capabilities. The Supports Intensity Scale was developed to measure the need for supports and includes 49 life activities grouped into six subscales: Home Living, Community Living, Lifelong Learning, Employment, Health and Safety, and Social Activities. In 2008, the American Association on Mental Retardation reported that SIS has a .87 inter-rater reliability coefficient, which the organization said put the scale in an "excellent range" of reliability in assessment instruments. Recent research suggests that proper training in the administration of the SIS increases the reliability of the instrument.

There were many changes in the way that disorders are conceptualized with the publication of the *DSM-5* in 2013. In an attempt to move away from a purely categorical classification system and to incorporate more of a dimensional approach to regarding disorders along a continuum, the *DSM-5* is organized using a developmental framework. The section labeled "Disorders Usually First Diagnosed in Infancy, Childhood, or Adolescence," in the *DSM-IV* was removed and in its place a new section called "Neurodevelopmental Disorders" was added. The term *MR* was replaced by *intellectual disabilities*, also known as *intellectual developmental disorders*, which include categories for global developmental delay (for children under 5 years who demonstrate delays and have not yet been assessed) and unspecified intellectual disability (for cases over 5 years of age where assessment cannot be conducted due to other factors such as severe behavior problems or sensory/motor impairments). The *DSM-5* continues to use specifiers (mild, moderate, severe, and profound) to identify the severity of the disorder; however, unlike previous versions of the *DSM*, the severity no longer is based on IQ scores but now refers to levels of adaptive functioning in the conceptual, social, and pragmatic domains.

Rating Scales

Adaptive behavior rating scales are used to obtain feedback from parents, caretakers, teachers, and employers. It is important to obtain feedback from multiple sources. If a child has two parents, it is customary to ask each parent to complete a rating scale. Professionals have found that parents can differ in their viewpoint of a child's abilities. Parents also sometimes yield scores higher than those from other sources because parents may overestimate their child's ability or may not be able to compare their child to a child without adaptive behavior deficits as easily as a teacher can because teachers also spend time with students who do not have delays.

If adaptive scores from parents are inconsistent with a teacher scale and other information gathered, it is often wise to consider following up with an interview. Another parent adaptive rating scale may be used and administered in an interview format. By questioning a parent and providing examples of what the item is asking, feedback may be provided that more readily matches a child's deficits.

There are two major rating scales used to assess adaptive behavior in children, adolescents, and adults: Adaptive Behavior Assessment System, Third Edition (ABAS-3) and Vineland Adaptive Behavior Scales, Third Edition (Vineland-3).

ABAS

The ABAS-3, published by WPS, is one of the leading adaptive behavior measures. The measure, authored by Patti Harrison and Thomas Oakland, was updated in 2015. The ABAS-3 includes five rating forms: Parent/Primary Caregiver Form (for ages 0–5 years), Teacher/Daycare Provider Form (for ages 2–5 years), Parent Form (for ages 5–21 years), Teacher Form (for ages 5–21 years), and an Adult Form (for ages 16–89 years).

Parents, close family members, teachers, day care staff, supervisors, or others who are familiar with the daily activities of the person being evaluated can complete any of these forms. Eleven adaptive skill areas are assessed by the ABAS-3; either nine or 10 skill areas are included on each form, depending on the age of the person being rated. The three adaptive domains that are addressed are conceptual, social, and practical. In addition, the test provides an overall General Adaptive Composite. All scores are categorized descriptively as extremely low, low, below average, average, above average, or high.

The conceptual composite consists of the following skill areas: communication, functional academics, and self-direction. The communication skill area assesses how well one speaks using appropriate grammar. It also looks at the ability one has in stating information about oneself and how well one converses with others. Functional academics assesses how well one performs the basics in academics in order to function daily at school, home, and the community. Self-direction assesses how well one acts responsibly. For example, this can include completing schoolwork and chores, controlling anger and frustrations appropriately, and making responsible choices in spending money.

The Social Composite Scale consists of information regarding the following skill areas: leisure and social. Leisure includes things one does when not in school or doing chores at home. Examples could include the following: reading a book or putting together a puzzle, playing games with friends, joining in sports activities, and/or joining some type of club. Social involves the ability to make friends and maintain friendships. It also assesses how well one is aware of other people's feelings and appropriate actions taken in certain situations.

The Practical Composite Scale measures the following skill areas: community use, home living, health and safety, and self-care. Community use assesses how well one functions in the community. For example, this can include using the library and mailing letters at the post office. Home living evaluates how well one is able to do things at home for oneself. Making the bed, preparing food for oneself, and washing one's dishes are all examples of this skill area. Health and safety is an important skill in that it looks at one's ability to be healthy and safe in everyday situations. This may include following rules: using caution around a hot stove and seeking help when someone is hurt. Self-care assesses how well one functions independently in taking care of self. One must be able to do everyday things on one's own, such as dressing oneself, bathing, and using the bathroom.

The ABAS-3 standardization was completed using 7,737 research forms completed by the respondents who rated the adaptive behavior of 4,500 individuals. Sample sizes were 1,420 for the Infant and Preschool Forms, 1,896 for the Parent and Teacher Forms, and 1,184 for the Adult Forms. The sample represented the 2012 United States population in terms of ethnicity, gender, and household education level, and all geographic regions were represented. Compared to the U.S. Census, there was an overrepresentation of White individuals and those with a higher level of education.

Internal consistency, which indicates the degree to which test items correlate with each other and is often treated as an estimate of reliability, is excellent. The α reliability coefficients range for the broad adaptive domains was 0.90–0.98 on the Teacher/Daycare Provider Form, 0.93–0.99 on the Teacher Form, 0.85–0.98 on the Parent/Primary Caregiver Form, 0.94–0.99 on the Parent Form, 0.94–0.99 on the Adult self-report form, and 0.96–0.99 on the Adult rated by others form. For the adaptive skill areas, the reliability coefficient range was 0.72–0.97 on the Teacher/Daycare Provider Form, 0.82–0.99 on the Teacher Form, 0.76–0.97 on the Parent/Primary Caregiver Form, 0.81–0.99 on the Parent Form, 0.80–0.99 on the Adult self-report form, and 0.82–0.99 on the Adult rated by others form.

Test–retest reliability refers to the stability of test scores over a time period. The correlations on this measure are very good. The average corrected test–retest correlations on the Parent/Primary Caregiver Form are .70 for the adaptive skill area scaled scores, .76 for the adaptive domain standard scores, and .82 for the General Adaptive Composite. The average corrected test–retest correlations on the Parent Form are .77 for the adaptive skill area scaled scores, .80 for the adaptive domain standard scores, and .86 for the General Adaptive Composite. The average corrected test–retest correlations on the Teacher/Daycare Provider Form are .80 for the adaptive skill area scaled scores, .80 for the adaptive domain standard scores, and .86 for the General Adaptive Composite. The average corrected test–retest correlations on the Teacher Form are .80 for the adaptive skill area scaled scores, .81 for the adaptive domain standard scores, and .84 for the General Adaptive Composite. The average corrected test–retest correlations on the Adult Form (self-report) are .76 for the adaptive skill area scaled scores, .85 for the adaptive domain standard scores, and .87 for the General Adaptive Composite. The average corrected test–retest correlations on the Adult Form (rated by others) are: .75 for the adaptive skill area scaled scores, .85 for the adaptive domain standard scores, and .89 for the General Adaptive Composite.

Vineland Adaptive Behavior Scales

The Vineland-3, published by Pearson, is another leading adaptive behavior measure. The measure, authored by Sara Sparrow, Domenic Cicchetti, and Celine Saulnier, was updated in 2016. The Vineland-3 includes three rating forms: interview form (for ages 3 to adult), parent/caregiver form (for ages 3 to adult), and a teacher form (for ages 3–21). Parents, close family members, teachers, day care staff, supervisors, or others who are familiar with the daily activities of the person being evaluated can complete any of these forms. Test items may be read aloud to those with poor vision or poor reading skills. The Vineland-3 offers online and paper administration options for all forms and computerized or hand scoring for all forms. Administration time is approximately 20 minutes for the Interview Form and 10 minutes for the Teacher Form.

The remainder of this section provides information on the Vineland-2 because the Vineland-3 was not published at the time this entry was written. Nine adaptive skill areas are assessed by the Vineland-2. The three adaptive domains that are addressed include communication, daily living skills, and socialization; there are optional motor skills and maladaptive behavior domains. In addition to domain scores, the test provides an overall adaptive behavior composite. All scores are categorized descriptively as low, moderately low, adequate, moderately high, or high.

The communication domain score consists of the following subdomains: receptive, expressive, and written. The receptive subdomain assesses how an individual listens and pays attention and what the individual understands. The expressive subdomain assesses what an individual says and how the individual uses words and sentences to gather and provide information. The written subdomain assesses what an individual understands about how letters make words and what the individual reads and writes.

The daily living skills domain score consists of the following subdomains: personal, domestic, and community. The personal subdomain assesses how an individual eats, dresses, and practices personal hygiene. The domestic subdomain assesses what household tasks an individual performs. The community subdomain assesses how an individual uses time, money, the telephone, the computer, and job skills.

The socialization domain score consists of the following subdomains: interpersonal relationships, play and leisure time, and coping skills. The interpersonal relationships subdomain assesses how an individual interacts with others. The play and leisure time subdomain assesses how an individual plays and uses leisure time. The coping skills subdomain assesses how an individual demonstrates responsibility and sensitivity to others.

The Vineland-2 standardization was completed using 3,695 individual cases. The norm sample was stratified based on demographic variables such as sex, race/ethnicity, socioeconomic status, and geographic region. Recruitment was based on the 2001 U.S. population demographic data. All regions of the United States were represented. Sample sizes were 1,085 for ages 0:0–4:11; 2,290 for ages 5:0–21:11; and 320 for ages 22:0–90.

Internal consistency is good. The reliability coefficient range for the communication domain is .84 to .93; in the subdomains, it was .59 to .80 for receptive, .76 to .93 for expressive, and .73 to .85 for written. The reliability coefficient range for the daily living skills domain is .86 to .91; in the subdomains, it was .66 to .83 for personal, .72 to .85 for domestic, and .77 to .83 for community. The reliability coefficient range for the socialization domain is .84 to .93; in the subdomains, it is .76 to .87 for interpersonal relationships, .58 to .83 for play and leisure time, and .78 to .88 for coping skills.

Test–retest reliability correlations are very good. The average adjusted test–retest correlation across all forms is .88 for domains; it is .88 for the communication domain, .89 for the daily living skills domain, and .85 for the socialization domain. The average adjusted test–retest correlation across all forms is .85 for subdomains. Within the communication domain, it is .89 for receptive, .84 for receptive, and .87 for written. Within the daily living skills domain, it is .85 for personal, .89 for domestic, and .87 for community. Within the socialization domain, it is .82 for interpersonal relationships, .79 for play and leisure time, and .80 for coping skills.

Inter-interviewer reliability is good for the Survey Interview Form. The average correlation between interviewers is .73 for domains; it is .68 for the communication domain, .80 for the daily living skills domain, and .72 for the socialization domain. Across all forms, the mean correlation is .70 for subdomains. Within the communication domain, it is .69 for receptive, .77 for receptive, and .74 for written. Within the daily living skills domain, it is .77 for personal, .75 for domestic, and .67 for community. Within the socialization domain, it is .71 for interpersonal relationships, .53 for play and leisure time, and .63 for coping skills.

Inter-rater reliability (Parent/Caregiver Rating Form) is good for the Survey Interview Form. The average correlation between raters is .77 across domains, .77 for the communication domain, .71 for the daily living skills domain, and .78 for the socialization domain. Reliability across all forms is .77 for subdomains. Within the communication domain, it is .82 for receptive, .72 for receptive, and .81 for written. Within the daily living skills domain, it is .63 for personal, .78 for domestic, and .85 for community. Within the socialization

domain, it is .73 for interpersonal relationships, .74 for play and leisure time, and .73 for coping skills.

Alan W. Brue and Linda Wilmshurst

See also *Diagnostic and Statistical Manual of Mental Disorders*; Diagnostic Tests; Rating Scales

Further Readings

American Association on Intellectual and Developmental Disabilities. (2008). Supports Intensity Scale™ Information. Retrieved from https://aaidd.org/docs/default-source/sis-docs/latestsispresentation.pdf?sfvrsn=2

Brue, A. W., & Wilmshurst, L. (2016). *Essentials of intellectual disability assessment and identification.* Hoboken, NJ: Wiley.

Wilmshurst, L., & Brue, A. W. (2010). *The complete guide to special education: Expert advice on evaluations, IEPs, and helping kids succeed* (2nd ed.). San Francisco, CA: Jossey-Bass.

ADEQUATE YEARLY PROGRESS

Adequate yearly progress (AYP) is a federal accountability measure established under the No Child Left Behind Act of 2001 (NCLB). Under the AYP system, states established timelines for improving the academic achievement level of over 12 years, at the end of which 100% of students in all subgroups should perform at the proficient level or better. This entry first discusses the regulations establishing the AYP measure and the reception of the AYP process by administrators, parents, and educators. It then looks at the impact of AYP on student achievement, how the percentage of schools failing to make AYP increased over the years, and the waiver system introduced in 2011.

Regulations

Each state's department of education sets the AYP targets for each state's public schools. Private schools were not required to participate in the AYP system. NCLB requires each state's targets to follow a timeline ensuring that by the end of the

2013–2014 school year, 100% of students, including 100% of students in identified subgroups, were meeting or exceeding the state-defined level of proficiency on academic achievement assessments. With the December 2015 authorization of the Every Student Succeeds Act, the AYP system was replaced by state-determined long-term goals.

According to the federally mandated schedule, states were required to align their tests with their chosen state academic standards and begin testing students. Students in Grades 3–8 were tested annually in reading and math, and those in Grades 10–12 were tested at least. Additionally, a sample of fourth and eighth graders in each state are expected to take the National Assessment of Educational Progress reading and mathematics tests every other year. The National Assessment of Educational Progress data were used to make cross-state comparisons and compile a national report card showing aggregate levels of student proficiency.

Annual AYP targets were set separately for reading and for math achievement. Overall state targets were set for the total population of students, and separate targets were set for the subgroups of economically disadvantaged students, students of identified major racial and ethnic groups, students with disabilities, and students with limited English proficiency. The process of improving student subgroups' attainment of academic proficiency at a rate faster than the overall improvement rate is sometimes referred to as "closing the gap."

In order for a school to be considered to be making AYP, three conditions had to be met. First, at least 95% of overall students as well as 95% of the students in each subgroup with 45 or more students must have been tested. Additionally, the overall population of students as well as each subgroup of students was required to meet or exceed the state-determined objectives or increase the percentage of students meeting or exceeding the target by at least 10%. Federal guidance indicated that students can be counted more than once when determining proficiency rates. Finally, the school also had to meet the minimum annual state target for attendance rate for elementary and middle schools and graduation rate for high schools.

Using these targets, state departments of education were responsible for determining the schools and districts considered to be making AYP. When schools failed to make AYP for multiple years in a row, they were subject to the following system of penalties outlined in NCLB. Title I schools that failed to make AYP for 2 consecutive years were enrolled for the program improvement process and were designated as schools in need of improvement. Parents of children in those schools were given the choice to transfer their children to other schools that were not identified for improvement and not identified as persistently dangerous. Priority in school choice was mandated to be given to low-achieving children from low-income families. If all schools in a district were classified as in need of improvement, districts were encouraged to cooperate with neighboring districts in order to provide school choice.

After 3 years of failing to make AYP, the school was required to provide tutoring and other supplemental services for low-income students in addition to providing parents with the option of school choice. After 4 years of failing to make AYP, schools were subject to additional corrective actions. These actions included replacement of specific school staff relevant to the failure, institution of a new curriculum, the appointment of outside experts to advise the school, extension of the school year and/or school day, and internal restructuring.

Failure to make AYP in the 5th year led to development of a plan to reopen the school as a charter school, replace most or all school staff, turn over school operations to the state or to a private company, or enact some other major restructuring. After 6 years of failing to make AYP, the school is expected to implement the plan designed in the previous year. In practice, most schools opted for the "other major restructuring" option rather than completely replacing the staff or surrendering operations to an external entity. A school was eligible to exit the program improvement process when it had met AYP for 2 out of the past 3 years.

Reception

The accountability measures under NCLB and the AYP system met with resistance from many school administrators, educators, and parents. Although many lauded the legislation's goal of having 100%

of students in all demographic subgroups score proficient or better by the end of 2014, this goal was quickly criticized as impossible to attain, especially for subpopulations such as students with disabilities and students with limited English proficiency.

Some evidence suggested that the AYP system was causing beneficial increases in schools' attention to the alignment between curriculum and instruction. However, there was also concern that apart from imposing penalties, the schools failing to make AYP were systematically stripped of needed resources instead of providing them with assistance, thus setting up a cycle of failure. Additionally, some school buildings that had performed well on other measures of success struggled to meet the proficiency benchmarks required for AYP, which caused confusion surrounding the assessment practices driving the accountability process.

As increasing numbers of buildings failed to make AYP, some observers became convinced that the AYP system overidentified schools as being in need of improvement. Additionally, several reports indicated that states were employing a variety of strategies to slow or reverse the trend of increasing numbers of schools failing to make AYP, which included changing state testing policies by lowering cut scores, adopting new tests, and revising test administration policies. By implementing these strategies, some states managed to successfully reduce their number of buildings failing to make AYP. However, such changes to the testing process subverted the intention of the accountability system to accurately measure and improve student achievement consistently through time.

The increased testing schedule mandated in NCLB was another cause for concern. Although only 19 states had annual reading and mathematics tests in place in 2002, all states had adopted this testing schedule by 2006. This increase in time spent on testing drew concern from some parents and educators. Moreover, many parents and educators felt that the need to meet the consistently rising achievement goals set through the AYP process pressured classroom instructors to narrow their curriculum in order to address test content, thus decreasing the attention paid to subjects other than reading and math and to content that did not appear on the test, thereby depriving children of a balanced education. Finally, many states reported that they lacked sufficient funds or staff needed to implement the requirements of the AYP system, especially the corrective actions mandated for schools in the program improvement process. As a result of these concerns, several articles and reports called for the abolishment of the accountability system and the AYP measure.

Impact

The percentage of students nationwide performing at or above the proficient level on state tests increased for many subgroups of students under NCLB. In addition, scores on the National Assessment of Educational Progress generally improved since the adoption of NCLB, although critics of the law argue that the trend of performance improvement had already been established before the NCLB took effect.

Despite state-level gains in the percentage of students performing at or above the proficient level, an increasing percentage of schools failed to make AYP as time went on and the proficiency targets grew closer to 100%. From 2010 to 2011, the percentage of U.S. public schools failing to make AYP increased from 39% to 48%, which was the highest percentage since NCLB took effect in 2002, and it represented an increase of 19 percentage points over the 2006 rate of 29% of schools failing to make AYP. In 2011, at the state level, 21 states and the District of Columbia had more than half of their schools failing to make AYP. In 2011, the percentage of schools failing to make AYP varied widely by state, from 7% in Wyoming to 91% in Florida.

Waivers

As a result of the increasing percentage of schools failing to make AYP, the U.S. Department of Education introduced a formal process for waiving accountability requirements in 2011. The waiver process allowed states flexibility in setting new annual measurable objectives to use in determining AYP and waived the penalties for schools failing to make AYP. Waivers initially granted states flexibility in meeting the provisions of NCLB through the end of the 2013–2014 school year, though states could apply for an extension through the 2014–2015 school year. At the end of the 2014–2015 school year, states had the option to request a 3-year renewal of flexibility. By 2014, a total of 43 states, the District of Columbia, Puerto Rico, and a group of California school districts received approval for the waivers.

Jennifer A. Brussow

See also Accountability; High-Stakes Tests; National Assessment of Educational Progress; No Child Left Behind Act; Standardized Tests; U.S. Department of Education

Further Readings

No Child Left Behind Act of 2001: Part A—Improving Basic Programs Operated by Local Educational Agencies, Pub. L. No. 107-110, 20 U.S.C. § 1111 (2005). Retrieved from http://www2.ed.gov/policy/elsec/leg/esea02/pg2.html#sec1111

Riddle, R., & Kober, N. (2011). *State policy differences greatly impact AYP numbers.* Washington, DC: Center on Education Policy. Retrieved from http://www.cep-dc.org/displayDocument.cfm?DocumentID=414

U.S. Department of Education. (2015). *ESEA flexibility.* Retrieved from http://www2.ed.gov/policy/elsec/guid/esea-flexibility/index.html

Usher, A. (2012). *AYP results for 2010–11—November 2012 update.* Washington, DC: Center on Education Policy. Retrieved from http://www.cep-dc.org/displayDocument.cfm?DocumentID=414

Websites

The Nation's Report Card: https://www.nationsreportcard.gov/

ADHD

See Attention-Deficit/Hyperactivity Disorder

ADMISSIONS TESTS

Admissions tests usually refer to tests designed to find candidates suitable for higher education. Such tests and other forms of entrance examinations can be made mandatory for applicants in a country or region to take or they may be specific to a university or a university program. This entry first discusses the roles and importance of admissions tests, the principles on which they are based, and their history. It then looks at how admissions tests can be characterized and issues in admissions testing.

In an admission decision, there are two fundamental roles that a test can fulfill: to identify candidates who have sufficient knowledge to be able to complete an education (eligibility) and to rank the candidates and to make a selection in cases where there are more eligible candidates than there are available slots (selection). A test can be designed to meet either of these two roles, although most admissions tests are used only for selection purposes. Admissions tests can be further categorized with respect to the construct or constructs they are assumed to measure. Standardized aptitude tests measure aptitude in general cognitive skills and are designed to determine a person's ability to learn. Entrance examinations are generally achievement oriented and focus on what a candidate has learned.

Having a fair selection model is of greatest importance in a democratic society. Although modern higher education often can be regarded as education for large parts of the population, universities are still institutions educating those who will hold important positions and influence society. An important question is how the number of slots at these universities should be distributed and what constitutes a fair admissions system, as this is not an easy or uncontroversial question to answer.

Fairness and Meritocracy

Fairness is closely connected to distributive justice, which concerns a socially just allocation of goods. There are several types of distributive norms describing how goods can be allocated such as equity, equality, power, need, and responsibility. In selection to higher education, there are different views on what can be considered a fair system.

Although not uncontroversial, it is common to base admissions systems on the idea of meritocracy. Applicants are ranked by their merits, usually measured by test scores or previous grades. But there may also be influences from a utilitarian approach, where equality, need, and responsibility also become important. Universities may aim for a selection that makes the student body more representative of society as a whole or in some other way more balanced.

There may be practical and ethical problems with following principles other than the meritocratic because it may be regarded as unfair to give certain groups advantages even if they are underrepresented in higher education. Often, it is prohibited to set quotas for certain groups in selection situations, irrespective of whether the group in question is underrepresented. An exception can be when the selection is made between two individuals with equal merits. In order for the meritocratic principle to be maintained, the challenge is therefore to find or develop instruments for eligibility and selection that measure the relevant construct or constructs without any bias related to student background. This has proven to be very difficult, as all measurement instruments, including grades and tests, are known to have error and often work differently for different groups of individuals.

History of Admissions Tests

Just how long higher education entrance examinations have existed is a source of debate. It has been claimed that such tests were first introduced in France in the 18th century. This fits well with the historical situation at the time when principles of equality were stressed in connection to the French Enlightenment. *Meritocracy* became a leading word. It would no longer be burden and privilege that decided who was to enter higher education. Rather, it was the best performance in terms of preparation or preknowledge that would determine selection.

Other sources indicate, however, that entrance examinations to higher education were introduced much earlier, for example, in Spain in the late 1500s. In England and Germany, admissions testing was introduced in the mid-19th century. But despite the early introduction of testing, the emergence of admissions tests was still modest at this time. Although there were meritocratic ambitions in training and selection, money and privilege were still the best entry tickets to higher education well into the 1900s, especially into the more prestigious schools.

Emergence of Standardized Testing in Admissions

Even if tests have existed for a long time and in many countries, the United States should be considered the country where admissions tests were first developed on a larger scale. There, admissions tests have been in use for a long time, with the Scholastic Aptitude Test (SAT) as the first and most important of a number of different tests.

The SAT was developed by the College Board in the United States during the 1920s in order to standardize the selection process for higher education. It was originally based on the Army Alpha test, which was used in the recruitment of soldiers during World War I. The Army tests were descendants of IQ tests. For that reason, the early versions of the SAT were quite similar to IQ tests.

World War II increased the need for testing for military purposes. The demand for skilled labor increased and a large number of war veterans aimed for higher education, which boosted the industry of testing for educational purposes. Up to that point, scoring was performed manually, but by 1939, scoring became automated, which simplified the procedures surrounding the SAT.

By 1941, the SAT was psychometrically advanced, with normed and standardized scores in order to enable comparisons over time, which should be considered unique for the time period. In 1947, the Educational Testing Service was established, and since then, it has been responsible for the development and administration of the SAT. As a consequence of increased demand for higher education, the educational sector in the United States expanded significantly. This had the consequence that the market for eligibility and selection tests flourished, and during this period, the organization the American College Testing Program was formed. The company, now ACT, Inc., developed ACT as a competitor to the SAT. Both of these tests have since received great recognition and been of great importance to education in the United States, when it comes to both higher education and various preparatory courses.

Use of Admissions Tests Today

The United States is not the only country that has developed entrance examinations to higher education. But no other country has done it in the same scientific, large-scale, and standardized way. Admission tests are available in many countries, but it is then common for universities to use smaller scale tests targeted to specific training. However, there are some entrance examinations similar to the American selection tests in design and purpose, including tests used in Sweden, Israel, and Georgia.

Admission tests are usually used in conjunction with other selection instruments, and there are a large number of different models applied throughout the world. As mentioned, in the United States, the SAT and ACT are common tests to take if one wants to enter university education. Schools use tests in combination with other materials, such as secondary school performance and recommendation letters. A few other countries use aptitude-like tests such as Sweden (SweSAT) and Israel (PET). These countries also rely on other material in the selection process. In Sweden, one third of the students are admitted by the SweSAT and the remaining students are admitted by upper secondary school grades. In Israel, the PET is combined with national secondary leaving exams.

A common model used in many countries is to require students to take entrance examinations. National exams are used in countries such as China and Georgia. Turkey and Spain use national exams in combination with high school performance, while Japan and Russia use multiple examinations where one part constitutes a national exam and other parts institutionally conducted examinations.

Finally, some countries do not rely on entrance examinations at all. In those instances, high school performance is the most important selection instrument. One example where there are no tests involved is Norway. In the case of entrance examinations, the contents vary by country and institution. In some institutions, the entrance examination covers a wide field of knowledge, whereas in other countries and institutions, the exams cover more specific areas connected to the university program that is being applied for.

Characterization of Admissions Tests

The distinctions between different types of tests have to do with what one wants to measure and how one wants to use the results. A test can be classified in several ways. Tests used in the admission context are what are called indirect measurements.

This means that the test asks questions about knowledge or skills, which in turn are indicators of some kind of superior knowledge, skill, or ability.

A second distinction concerns test type. Admission tests are usually norm referenced. This means that the result of the test is interpreted purely in comparison to the results of other test takers. The score on a norm-referenced test does not tell whether an individual qualifies in terms of knowledge. It merely indicates whether the individual scored higher or lower than the individual's peers. This is natural because the purpose of admission tests is usually to rank individuals or at least to separate them. The opposite of norm-referenced tests is called criterion-referenced tests. In this case, the purpose is to measure knowledge in relation to a predetermined criterion. Such tests give information about what a person can or cannot do. The latter types of tests are sometimes used in admissions, to establish whether a candidate meets eligibility conditions.

A third characterization of tests concerns what type of question is posed, referred to as item type. Most commonly, admission tests contain closed format items such as multiple-choice items, where a respondent answers the questions by selecting one out of several prespecified alternatives. However, there are several different item formats used, and often a multiple-choice test cannot provide information that is relevant for the selection at hand. One example of this is if a selection to an artistic school is being made. In this case, it is very difficult to use a multiple-choice test because such a test will not be able to test the skills required, for example, how well a person plays the violin. In such cases, standardized multiple-choice tests may still be used but only in conjunction with other measurement of skills such as an audition.

Multiple-choice tests may also give limited information in other respects. An alternative to prespecified answer alternatives is to use an open question format, where the test taker writes an answer. This is used in some of the major admission tests such as the SAT where a writing assignment is included in the test. From a general point of view, the choice of item formats can be seen as a trade-off, where multiple-choice items have the advantage of being simple to score and considered objective in the sense that there is no human involvement in scoring, whereas open questions may have greater realism at the expense of being subjective and harder to score.

A fourth characterization concerns the format of the test. When tests use a paper-and-pencil format, the respondent takes the test in a school or test center and a proctor collects the answer sheets at the end of the test. Computerized tests have some advantages over paper-and pencil tests: A test can be scored immediately after the testing session, it is easier to vary the order of which items are presented among test takers to prevent cheating, and adaptive testing can be implemented to shorten the number of items necessary to establish a final score. One major drawback with computerized tests is that they are considered expensive and difficult to implement on a large scale.

Issues in Admissions Testing

Despite the long use of admission tests in higher education selection, there is an ongoing debate about the usefulness and the drawbacks of tests compared to other ways of ranking students. Below, two areas where the debate is continuing are discussed.

Test Validity

The meritocratic principle means that individuals who have the best chances of completing a university education should be those who are admitted. The instruments used in the selection of candidates should therefore be capable of predicting what candidates will be successful in higher education. Predictive validity is used in psychometrics as a concept to reflect the extent to which a test score predicts an outcome, in this case, how successful students will be at their academic studies.

To operationalize predictive validity, researchers and other investigators measure whether the score on the instrument correlates with academic achievement. There are numerous correlation studies made with regards to admission tests. In the American context, studies are usually performed by correlating the score on the SAT (or ACT) with achievement in higher education, usually measured as the grade point average after Year 1 in university. Most studies find that admission tests, to some extent, can predict academic achievement. However, there is no consensus of exactly how well admission tests serve in this respect.

Admission test scores can also be compared to other admission instruments, such as high school grades. Comparisons of grades and test scores in their ability to predict future performance usually show that grades predict academic achievement better than test scores, but both instruments have been shown to have predictive power, indicating that using both instruments to predict academic achievement is better than just using one of the instruments.

Coaching and Cheating

In comparison with previous academic performance, one potential drawback with using tests is that the examiner cannot observe the candidate for a longer time period and is therefore less certain that the candidate has the required skills. Although the modern tests are designed so as to limit coincidence or luck, it is nevertheless problematic that candidates vary with respect to things such as test anxiety. Some individuals do not perform well when they are exposed to high-stakes tests. To limit anxiety, a candidate may benefit from learning about the test format and content.

Receiving professional coaching on the contents of a test has become increasingly popular. Although it is beneficial for the candidate in the short run, it may be detrimental for learning as well as time-consuming. In those instances where admission tests are used as the only selection instrument, learning in high school may well be hampered by the focus on a single exam. To what extent coaching is harmful for learning has yet to be determined.

A general problem with tests is cheating, such as by obtaining test questions beforehand. New technology makes cheating easier. There are examples of spy-like technology having been used to obtain the test items during a session, which then are delivered to other test takers using earpieces. Preventing and detecting cheating is very important because the aim of a test is to rank individuals to find the most suitable candidates.

Magnus Wikström and Christina Wikström

See also Achievement Tests; ACT; Aptitude Tests; Predictive Validity; SAT; Standardized Tests

Further Readings

Code of Fair Testing Practices in Education. (2004). Washington, DC: Joint Committee on Testing Practices.

Helms, R. M. (2009). University admissions: Practices and procedures worldwide. International Higher Education, 54, 5–7.

Lemann, N. (1999). *The big test: The secret history of the American meritocracy*. New York, NY: Farrar, Straus and Giroux.

Linn, R. (2001). A century of standardized testing: Controversies and pendulum swings. *Educational Assessment, 7*, 29–38.

Zwick, R. (2002). *Fair game? The use of standardized admissions tests in higher education*. New York, NY: RoutledgeFalmer.

ADOLESCENCE

Adolescence is a transition period from childhood to adulthood, typically spanning approximately from 12 to 18 years of age. Development during adolescence involves attaining physical and sexual maturity, along with increased complexity of thought and social behavior. Understanding adolescent development is critical for the development of policy and practice related to secondary education. This entry discusses the history of the construct of adolescence, developmental contexts and tasks of adolescence, the stages of adolescence, and major domains of adolescent development.

History

The notion of a distinct developmental stage between childhood and adulthood is a relatively new concept. In the late 19th century, theorists such as G. Stanley Hall began promoting the idea of adolescence as a distinct life stage. Prior to this time, there was a sense of youth (roughly the period from one's midteens through early 20s) as an important and impressionable period of development, but not the modern sense of adolescence as a time of identity exploration and relative lack of adult responsibilities. The increasing availability of public education and decline in child labor contributed to the view that a period of transition from childhood to the assumption of adult roles was necessary.

Throughout much of the 20th century, adolescence was viewed as a period of "storm and stress," in which adolescents struggled to manage their emotions, had frequent conflicts with parents and other authority figures, and engaged in high-risk behaviors. Despite this popular view, researchers have argued that the notion of adolescence as a time of high drama is largely exaggerated. Although adolescents do report more negative moods and more frequent mood swings than either adults or younger children, the majority of adolescents report feeling happy and confident most of the time.

Researchers operating from the perspective of positive youth development argue that the traditional view of adolescence has been overly negative and focused on deficits (e.g., mental illness, alcohol and drug use). Positive youth development theorists argue that researchers and practitioners should instead focus on adolescents' strengths and structure environments such that these strengths are tapped and promoted.

Developmental Tasks and Contextual Demands

Developmental tasks are fundamental abilities and achievements that must be acquired for optimal development at a given life stage and appropriate progress toward the next phase of life. Key developmental tasks of adolescence include development of realistic self-perceptions (awareness of one's strengths and weaknesses in various domains), identity development (including development of a vocational identity in preparation for a career), establishing autonomy from parents, engaging in appropriate peer relationships (belonging to a peer group, forming and maintaining friendships), navigating sexuality and romantic relationships, and development of coping skills (such as conflict resolution and decision making).

As in other life stages, one key determinant of individual outcomes is the goodness of fit between the individual's needs and capabilities and what is required of the individual by the environment. Due to their developmental needs, adolescents often desire greater autonomy and flexibility from their environments than children do. Parents and teachers can promote optimal development for adolescents by allowing autonomy and choice while still acting as a source of emotional support and monitoring adolescents' behavior and emotional states.

Stages

Researchers typically divide adolescence into three stages: early, middle, and late adolescence. Early adolescence typically begins around 11–12 years of age and continues through approximately age 14. Early adolescence is a time of rapid physical changes associated with puberty. Along with these physical changes, there are important social changes, most often including greater emotional independence from parents and increasing reliance on friends as sources of social and emotional support. During middle adolescence (approximately ages 14–16), pubertal changes near completion. Consistent with their greater physical maturity, middle adolescents often show increasing interest in romantic and sexual relationships. By late adolescence (approximately ages 16–18), pubertal changes are complete and adult appearance is in place. Late adolescents have a firmer sense of identity than younger adolescents and are clearly moving toward assumption of adult roles and responsibilities.

The onset of puberty is a key marker of the transition from childhood to adolescence. Multiple factors, including heredity, nutrition, and overall physical health, influence when an individual goes through puberty. Pubertal changes include overall body growth (in both height and weight), the onset of menstruation for girls, and the development of secondary sexual characteristics (including development of body hair, facial hair growth for boys, and breast development for girls). Typical pubertal development takes approximately 4 years.

Girls tend to begin and complete puberty earlier than boys; thus, it is not unusual for girls to be taller, heavier, and more mature in appearance than boys of the same age during early adolescence. These biological changes, combined with media images emphasizing beauty and thinness as key determinants of women's worth, may contribute to negative body image and decreased self-esteem among adolescent girls.

Puberty may impact other aspects of development, such as self-concept and peer relationships. The timing of puberty seems to be particularly important, with early puberty relative to peers having a negative impact for girls but a more positive impact for boys.

Brain Development

Shortly before the onset of puberty, the brain experiences a growth spurt of sorts, with rapid growth of synapses (the connections between neurons that allow for the transmission of signals across the brain). During adolescence, those synapses that are not used are pruned and disappear. Throughout adolescence, the amount of myelin (a fatty sheath that increases the speed of communication between neurons) in the brain also increases.

These processes of synapse generation, synaptic pruning, and myelination occur throughout the brain during adolescence but particularly in the frontal cortex. The maturation of the frontal cortex contributes to increased executive function capabilities (including control of attention, inhibition of impulses, and improved decision making) over the course of adolescence. The frontal lobe of the brain is one of the last areas of the brain to mature fully, and the relative immaturity of this structure may contribute to risk taking among adolescents.

Neural connections between various brain regions increase in strength during adolescence. These strengthened connections contribute to the cognitive advances seen in adolescence, including improvements in attention, planning, problem-solving, and self-regulation.

The brain's sensitivity to certain neurotransmitters also shifts during adolescence. These changes mean that adolescents respond to both stressful and pleasurable events more strongly than do younger children or adults. Increased sensitivity to neurotransmitters may contribute to certain risk-taking behaviors (such as drug use) and to psychological disorders such as depression.

Cognitive, Social, and Identity Development

Cognitive Development

Cognition in the adolescent stage shows many advances over childhood cognition. These include increases in abstract thinking, scientific reasoning, planning, hypothetical reasoning (including thinking about the future), perspective taking, and metacognitive skills. Executive function skills, including selective attention, inhibition, and cognitive self-regulation, also improve. Thus, thinking in adolescence is more abstract, logical, flexible, and well-organized than children's thinking. The increasing ability to consider hypothetical outcomes may lead adolescents to be especially idealistic in their thinking, particularly regarding abstract concepts such as justice or discrimination.

Social Cognition

The social, environmental, and biological changes that occur in adolescence lead to a greater variety of relationships and social encounters. Along with these changes come greater awareness of and interest in other people. In some cases, this awareness may lead adolescents to become self-conscious and preoccupied with how others view their appearance and behavior. This increasing self-awareness, combined with the view that one is unique and particularly worthy of others' attention, comprises the phenomenon of adolescent egocentrism.

Identity Development

As individuals move through adolescence, their self-concepts become more accurate, detailed, and nuanced. Compared to children, adolescents have a better sense of their individual strengths, weaknesses, and capabilities across a variety of domains. Across the course of adolescence, individuals become increasingly aware of and are able to consider ways in which they may have a different self in different contexts (e.g., being outspoken with friends but reserved with family members). Adolescents who have warm, supportive relationships with their parents tend to have more positive views of themselves than do adolescents whose parents are harsh, critical, or uninvolved. Similarly, encouragement from teachers, coaches, or nonparental relatives can help to promote positive self-views for adolescents.

Identity development is one of the most widely studied aspects of development in the adolescent stage. In his theory of psychosocial development, Erik Erikson describes the central psychological conflict of adolescence as identity versus identity confusion. The major developmental task of this stage is for adolescents to explore various aspects of identity (such as vocational aspirations, political beliefs, and cultural or ethnic identity) and to ultimately commit to a personal identity that is coherent and well integrated. This process often involves questioning one's own previously held beliefs or the beliefs of family and community members. A well-established identity, in Erikson's view, provides a sense of who one is and where one is going in life. Adolescents whose families provide support while encouraging exploration and self-expression tend to have a positive sense of identity. Close, supportive relationships with friends can also facilitate the identity development process.

Sexuality

Negotiating sexual identity and sexual behavior is another key developmental task of adolescence.

Adolescents often spend a great deal of time and energy thinking about romantic and sexual relationships. By age 18, approximately two thirds of adolescents report having had at least one sexual partner. Adolescents who are involved in serious or exclusive dating relationships tend to initiate sexual activity earlier than those who are not involved in such relationships.

For adolescents who identify as gay or lesbian, the average age of "coming out" (disclosing one's sexual orientation to others) is 16–17 years. Most youth come out to friends before disclosing to parents or other relatives. Coming out now typically occurs several years earlier than in previous decades, largely due to greater visibility and acceptance of gay and lesbian individuals.

Family Relationships

Although adolescents generally rely less on parents for social and emotional support than younger children, parents are still an important source of support and guidance through the adolescent years. Adolescents who have warm, supportive relationships with their parents tend to have positive outcomes in the areas of peer relationships, identity development, and academic achievement.

Responding to the adolescent's increasing desire for autonomy is often a challenge for parents. A cooperative parent–child relationship, open communication, and continued parental monitoring of adolescents' behavior (e.g., knowing where the child is after school, enforcing curfews) are associated with positive outcomes for adolescents.

Peer Relationships

Peers become an increasingly important source of social and emotional support during adolescence. Over the course of adolescence, friendships become more focused on intimacy (such as being able to disclose thoughts and feelings) and loyalty. This emphasis on emotional closeness in friendships is especially strong for girls. Close, supportive relationships with friends can promote positive identity development and engagement with school. Friendships tend to be closer and more intimate than romantic relationships, particularly for early and middle adolescents.

Parents and teachers are often concerned about peer pressure among adolescents. Although adolescents (particularly early adolescents) are somewhat more likely to conform to peers than younger children or adults, this is not always detrimental. For example, adolescents tend to conform to their peers in domains such as academic engagement and participation in extracurricular activities. Adolescents whose parents use an authoritative parenting style (including a balance of warmth and appropriate limits on behavior) tend to be more resistant to antisocial peer influence.

Mental Health

Many mental illnesses, such as depression, schizophrenia, and eating disorders, tend to emerge for the first time during adolescence. Depression is the most common psychological problem seen among adolescents. Both physical and environmental factors can contribute to the development and emergence of mental illness; risk factors include a family history of the disorder, high levels of family conflict, harsh or uninvolved parenting, experiences with trauma (such as abuse, sexual assault, or death of a loved one), and peer rejection. Adolescents who are gay or lesbian may be at greater risk of psychological problems such as depression or substance abuse, particularly if their family or other environments are unsupportive.

Meagan M. Patterson

See also Adultism; Childhood; Erikson's Stages of Psychosocial Development; Puberty

Further Readings

Casey, B. J., Jones, R. M., & Hare, T. A. (2008). The adolescent brain. *Annals of the New York Academy of Sciences, 1124*, 111–126.

Dubas, J. S., Miller, K., & Petersen, A. C. (2003). The study of adolescence during the 20th century. *History of the Family, 8*, 375–397.

Eccles, J. S., Midgley, C., Wigfield, A., Buchanan, C. M., Reuman, D., Flanagan, C., & Mac Iver, D. (1993). Development during adolescence: The impact of stage-environment fit on young adolescents' experiences in schools and in families. *American Psychologist, 48*, 90–101.

Larson, R. W. (2000). Toward a psychology of positive youth development. *American Psychologist, 55*, 170–183.

Steinberg, L. (2001). We know some things: Parent–adolescent relationships in retrospect and prospect. *Journal of Research on Adolescence, 11*, 1–19.

Steinberg, L. (2005). Cognitive and affective development in adolescence. *Trends in Cognitive Sciences, 9*, 69–74.

Tomasik, M. J., & Silbereisen, R. K. (2012). Social change and adolescent developmental tasks: The case of postcommunist Europe. *Child Development Perspectives, 6*, 326–334.

Zimmerman, M. A., Stoddard, S. A., Eisman, A. B., Caldwell, C. H., Aiyer, S. M., & Miller, A. (2013). Adolescent resilience: Promotive factors that inform prevention. *Child Development Perspectives, 7*, 215–220.

ADULTISM

Adultism refers to all attitudes and actions that flow from the idea that adults are superior to young people and have the right to control and punish them at will. These attitudes are embedded in institutions, customs, child rearing practices, and relationships between young people and adults. Psychologist Jack Flasher is generally credited with first using the term in this sense in a 1978 journal article. Although not widely accepted, the concept of adultism has received attention in the children's rights movement and within critical psychology.

Adultism is pervasive, often unconscious, and deeply influences relationships between youth and adults. It is difficult to identify, challenge, and eliminate precisely because everyone has experienced it to some degree and because much adultist behavior is considered natural and normal by most people. This entry describes examples of adultism in society; its effects, including its emotional legacy and links to other forms of societal mistreatment; and how individuals and organizations, including schools, can assess their level of adultism and find ways to avoid it.

Understanding Adultism

Children are for the most part highly controlled by adults, who tell them what to eat, what to wear, when they can talk, that they will go to school, and which friends are OK. Even as they grow older, young people are punished freely by adults, their opinions are not valued, and their emotions are often considered immature. Adults reserve the right to threaten young people, take away their "privileges," and ostracize young people as part of disciplining them; in some cultures, even beating children is considered acceptable as part of discipline.

The fact that adults genuinely have enormous importance in and responsibility for the lives of young people may make it difficult to understand adultism. Not everything adults do in relation to young people is adultist. Young people need love, guidance, rules, expectations, teaching, role modeling, nurturance, and protection. The attitude that defines adultist behavior is disrespect for the young person's intelligence or autonomy; this attitude allows adults to treat young people in a way that they would never treat another adult.

Adults' approaches to young people are based partly on culture, ethnicity, gender, class, and religion, complicating the identification of adultism. Different cultures accept or reject different behaviors from children and youth; different cultures accept different degrees of harshness by adults in the punishment of unacceptable childhood behavior. Virtually no culture has identified and accepted the concept of adultism as an oppressive set of attitudes and behaviors to be understood and rejected. Something can be considered adultist if it involves a consistent pattern of disrespect and mistreatment.

Examples of Adultism

In the extensive research literature on children and youth, there is very little stating that young people are an oppressed group, with parallels to other oppressed groups. Those who do see prevalent attitudes toward young people as comparable to racism and sexism point to common statements and occurrences as examples of adultism. Common statements that show disrespect are the following: "You're so smart for 15!" "When are you going to grow up?" and "What do you know? You haven't experienced anything!"

Physical and sexual abuse of children is all too common. Physical punishments such as hitting, beating, and constraining children for bad behavior are widely accepted, even when illegal. Nonphysical punishments that show disrespect include

routinely criticizing or yelling at young people and arbitrarily grounding them or denying them privileges. Punishment often becomes more severe if young people protest against the mistreatment.

On the other end of the spectrum, far from punishment but disrespectful nonetheless, adults often pick up little children and kiss or tickle them without asking them or allowing for the treatment to be mutual. Adults often grab things out of children's hands without asking. These actions are not ill intended but rather conditioned by the wider culture.

Adults often talk down to children, talk about them in their presence as though they were not there, and give young people orders or lay down rules with no explanation. Although adults expect young people to listen to them, they generally do not take young people's concerns as seriously as those of adults. Adults typically do not respect the way young people think in the way they respect adult thinking.

Adultism in Schools

Schools use hall passes, detention, suspension, expulsion, and other penalties to control students. All communities need rules to live by, but the rules in most school communities are imposed on young people and enforced by adult staff, with no input from the children or youth. Teachers sometimes yell at students and are not disciplined, but students who yell at teachers generally are disciplined. In cases of a teacher's word against a student's, in many schools, the teacher's version typically prevails. Students are graded and those grades can, over time, cause them to internalize a lifelong view of themselves as "smart" or "average" or "dumb"—with a profound impact on their lives. Students, however, do not assign grades to their teachers, and when a student gets a poor grade, it is typically assumed that the student and not the teacher is to blame.

Regardless of whether school is an effective learning environment for a particular young person, an American student must attend school until at least age 16 years (and in many states until 18 years), unless parents exercise the demanding option of homeschooling. Most elementary and secondary schools give students little to no voice, power, or decision-making avenues to make significant changes.

Youth Roles and the Youth Market

Throughout U.S. society, young people find few decision-making roles and no real opportunities for developing policy or holding political power. At the same time, however, the youth market is exploited for profit as the manufacturing and entertainment industries manipulate styles, fads, and other aspects of mass culture to appeal to young people.

Effects of Adultism

The main negative messages young people receive from the treatment described earlier are that they are not as important as adults, are not taken seriously, and have little or no power. The emotional legacy of this kind of treatment, depending on its intensity, may leave scarring including anger, feelings of powerlessness, insecurity, inferiority, depression, lack of self-confidence and self-respect, and hopelessness. These emotional states can lead to unhealthy behavior. Some young people respond to these feelings by bullying, being prone to violence, or rebelling against the norm. Some become self-destructive and commit suicide, abuse alcohol or drugs, become depressed, or engage in behaviors such as cutting. Some isolate themselves, feel lonely, don't ask for help, don't trust, and have few close relationships. Other factors, such as poverty, trauma, serious physical or mental abuse, disability, or poor health, may also produce these results. But systematic disrespect and mistreatment over years simply because of being young contributes to feelings of powerlessness and low self-esteem.

Adultism has links to other forms of prejudice, including that mistreatment can condition people to act out against others who are less powerful. In this way, adultism conditions young people to play their respective roles in the other structures of oppression, such as sexism and racism. All of these structures of oppression reinforce each other, and how young people are treated or mistreated is closely tied to their class, gender, and ethnicity. Yet the phenomenon of being disrespected simply because of being young holds true across diverse backgrounds and environments.

Assessing Adultism

It is useful to examine youth–adult interactions, program practices, policies, and power relationships through the lens of adultism. One might ask questions such as "Would I treat an adult this way?" "Would I use the same tone of voice?" "Would I grab this out of an adult's hand?" "Would I listen to an adult friend's problem in this same way?" The opposite of adultist behavior includes listening attentively to young people; asking them questions about what they think and implementing some of their ideas; curbing the inclination to take over; giving them freedom to make mistakes, within safety limits; and supporting their initiative. Parents and teachers can reexamine their approach to discipline to discern possible adultism.

On an organizational basis (e.g., school, classroom, and youth program), the following questions can help assess the level of adultism: How are young people involved in decision making? What is the evidence that young people's capabilities and intelligence are being respected? How balanced are the power relationships between adults and young people? Have the discipline policies and practices been reexamined for adultism? Do young people have an appropriate engagement in policies? For example, in schools, are elementary students' assessments of their teachers systematically gathered or are high school students involved in staff hiring, curriculum assessment, or teacher evaluation? Are the opinions and ideas of young people valued in obvious ways?

John Bell

See also Corporal Punishment; Educational Psychology; Emotional Intelligence; Erikson's Stages of Psychosocial Development; Kohlberg's Stages of Moral Development

Further Readings

Bell, J. (1995). *Understanding adultism: A key to developing positive adult-youth. relationships.* Somerville, MA: YouthBuild.

Burman, E. (2008) *Deconstructing developmental psychology* (2nd ed.). London, England: Brunner-Routledge.

Flasher, J. (1978). Adultism. *Adolescence, 13*(51), 517–523.

Krey, K. (2015). Adults just don't understand: Checking out our everyday adultism. Retrieved from http://everydayfeminism.com/2015/02/everyday-adultism/

Sazama, J. (2004). *Get the word out!* Somerville, MA: Youth on Board. Retrieved from https://youthonboard.org/publications

Sazama, J., & Young, K. (2006). 15 points to successfully involving youth in decision-making. Somerville, MA: Youth On Board. Retrieved from https://youthonboard.org/publications

Wright, J. (2001). Treating children as equals. New Renaissance Magazine. Retrieved from http://www.ru.org/index.php/education/371-treating-children-as-equals

ADVOCACY IN EVALUATION

Advocacy in evaluation involves a set of inherent tensions in the commissioning and practice of policy and program evaluation. The two primary tensions are (1) advocacy for particular social goods, or what are the most legitimate *values* that can be advanced in evaluation studies and (2) advocacy for particular constituencies, or who comprises the most important *audiences* for evaluation studies. These tensions arise because evaluation is both a technical and a social practice that typically takes place in politicized contexts and because evaluations of programs, especially public programs, have multiple legitimate interested audiences. This entry concentrates on evaluations of public programs and policies wherein the issues of advocacy are most salient and consequential.

Evaluation as the Social Practice of Valuing

Evaluation is a technical activity that relies on various methodologies and tools of social science. Evaluators conduct experiments, surveys, and case studies, and they use assessments, questionnaires, interviews, and observations as primary data collection techniques. Yet, as distinct from most social science research, evaluation is *also* a social practice of valuing, as it explicitly involves making *judgments of quality* regarding the program being evaluated.

The core logic of evaluation, as articulated by evaluation expert Michael Scriven, involves the comparison of data gathered to established criteria or standards of goodness. These criteria define, for that evaluation study, a good or effective program. For example, criteria for judging the quality of a new high school biology curriculum could include strong student average test performance, favorable teacher ratings of the substantive and pedagogical attributes of the curriculum, or the documented success of the new curriculum in attracting students from groups traditionally underrepresented in the sciences to biology as a field of study and possible career.

Further, various criteria convey different values regarding a good or effective program. In an evaluation of an educational program, a criterion that specifies acceptable student performance, *on average*, advances the values of egalitarianism. A criterion that addresses the *reach of this program to all students* advances values of social equity. And so the selection of criteria for judging program quality inevitably involves the advancement, or the advocacy, of some values and not others.

Recognized Audiences and Purposes for Evaluation

Audiences for evaluation are also known as evaluation stakeholders, or individuals and groups who have a legitimate stake or vested interest in the program being evaluated. There are three recognized groups of legitimate evaluation stakeholders: (1) those responsible for authorizing and funding the program—policy and other decision makers; (2) those responsible for implementing the program—administrators, staff, and volunteers; and (3) the intended beneficiaries of the program, their families, and communities as well as the broader public.

Stakeholders characteristically have different interests in and thus different evaluative questions about the program. Different evaluation questions are further linked to different evaluation purposes. Decision makers usually want to know if the program "worked," that is, achieved its intended programmatic and policy *outcomes*. Program implementers typically want to know how they could *improve* the design and implementation of the program, for example, to reach more people or to adapt program materials for newly arrived immigrant families. And program participants are usually interested in how well the program's *promised benefits match their own particular needs*.

Evaluation audiences and purposes are linked, in part, to the developmental stage of an educational program. A new computer technology program that provides a laptop computer and related instruction for every child in Grades 3–5 in a particular urban school district would be evaluated for the purposes of program improvement and thus for audiences of program developers, administrators, and staff. An established technology-oriented after-school program that has been through several cycles of implementation and improvement would be most appropriately evaluated to assess its outcomes, both intended and unintended, for broad audiences of educational policy makers and community families alike.

The selection of audiences for an evaluation study is further contingent on additional contextual factors that include policy priorities, funding, and sociocultural factors. Even so, the evaluator has both the authority and the responsibility to contribute to the identification of key evaluation audiences and purposes. And so, beyond programmatic and contextual contingencies, the selection of audiences for an evaluation study involves the privileging, or advocacy, of some stakeholder priorities over others.

Evaluators' Responsibilities for Advocacy

Social policy and program evaluations are nearly always initiated by those responsible for funding, implementing, or critically reviewing a given social, educational, or health program. Evaluators are then called in to conduct an evaluation that is already substantially framed and bounded by extant priorities and expectations. This framing usually includes expectations of the criteria to be used to make judgments of quality, the primary purposes and audiences for the evaluation, and the key questions to be addressed.

Often, all of the factors that frame an evaluation are not explicitly stated. Even so, it is the evaluator's responsibility to ensure that the advocacy in that evaluation—which values are advanced and whose interests are addressed—is defensible, fair, and serves the broader public good.

Jennifer C. Greene

See also Democratic Evaluation; Ethical Issues in Evaluation; Evaluation Versus Research; Values

Further Readings

Cronbach, L. J., Ambron, S. R., Dornbusch, S. M., Hess, R. D., Hornik, R. C., Phillips, D. C., . . . Weiner, S. S. (1980). *Toward reform of program evaluation.* San Francisco, CA: Jossey-Bass.

Greene, J. C. (1997). Evaluation as advocacy. *Evaluation Practice, 18,* 25–35.

House, E., & Howe, K. (1999). *Values in evaluation and social research.* Thousand Oaks, CA: Sage.

Scriven, M. (1981). *The logic of evaluation.* EdgePress.

AEA

See American Evaluation Association

AERA

See American Educational Research Association

AFRICAN AMERICANS AND TESTING

This entry describes issues related to African Americans and testing and discusses possible reasons for the relatively low average performance of African Americans on standardized tests. The difference in test performance, or *achievement gap*, between African American students and European American students has been the subject of much research. Many factors may contribute to the achievement gap, including socioeconomic differences, the home environment, parent educational level, and teacher perceptions of students' academic abilities. Understanding and addressing the reasons for lower test performance among African Americans is important because of the use of test results in diagnosing learning problems, determining a student's academic level, and making other significant decisions about schools and students.

Importance of Testing

Various kinds of decision making are involved in teaching. It is necessary for teachers to know their students' performance in the classroom. Testing is one way of doing this. Testing allows a teacher to compare one student's performance on a particular task with a set standard or the performance of other students by gathering information about student learning. Many people can design a test, including a classroom teacher; local, state, or federal government agencies such as school districts; or commercial test development firms. When done properly, testing can provide unbiased data for decision making, giving it a large role in many classroom decisions.

Testing became more common in K–12 classrooms, with the No Child Left Behind Act of 2001, which used the results of standardized tests to measure school performance. Test results are also used to make many decisions about individual students. Achievement tests are common measures given to students and are meant to measure a student's level of learning in specific content areas such as reading comprehension, language usage, computation, science, social studies, mathematics, and logical reasoning.

Admission to kindergarten; promotion from one grade to the next; high school honors, Advanced Placement classes and graduation; access to special programs; placement in special education classes; teacher licensure and tenure; and school funding may all be affected by test results. In making these decisions, it is of great importance to consider the quality of the test itself and the way the test is used. For example, many African Americans are inappropriately identified as needing remedial instruction, and a majority are placed in special education classes.

It is important to know the consequences of choosing one test over another for a particular purpose with a given group. Of equal significance is understanding how the test scores of minority-group students will be interpreted and the effect of testing on each of the students. In addition, we need to be cognizant of what we mean by intelligence, competence, and scholastic aptitude and what implications come with each of these. Do our views agree with those implied by the tests we use to measure these constructs? How will other information about the individual be integrated with test results to make major decisions or judgments? Responding to these questions requires choices based on values as well as accurate information about what tests can and cannot tell us.

African American Students and Test Performance

Research evidence shows African American students underperform on academic tests due to a variety of reasons including socioeconomic differences, the home environment, parent education, teaching practices, teacher perceptions, and anxiety. The increase in child poverty and a greater emphasis on low-level skills in high-poverty schools may be worsening this gap.

When compared to students from low-socioeconomic families, students from higher socioeconomic families are rated as having higher academic ability. African American students tend to be over-represented in the lower socioeconomic status. One possible explanation as to why there is a significant difference by socioeconomic status in teacher perceptions of students' academic ability is the mismatch between what the test measures and what the teacher is evaluating. For instance, research shows African American students and students from low-socioeconomic families possess a smaller vocabulary than European American students and students from middle-/high-socioeconomic families. Socioeconomic status may be a proxy for vocabulary differences that teachers may be incorporating into their perceptions of students' academic ability, which are not captured by the tests and teacher perceptions.

Depending on the teacher–student interaction, the skills and habits that a student demonstrates may be rewarded differently. Parents and students with higher socioeconomic status tend to possess higher levels of cultural capital that is valued in the school and testing settings. The cultural capital that a teacher may reward in the classroom includes social and behavioral skills.

Some researchers point to institutional-based racism toward African American students in educational testing as another reason for the achievement gap, with some of these researchers using the mathematics teaching in schools as an example. They argue that approaches to mathematics are mainly driven by what works for European American students, and the poor achievement test scores in predominantly African American schools are a reflection of this institutional racism. One way to address this problem is to intentionally include components of the cultural history of African Americans that could be applied to mathematics.

Research examining various factors that contribute to the achievement gap between African

American and European American students has shown that teachers' perceptions of students' academic ability is a significant factor in the observed gap. Research evidence reveals that in addition to academic skills, teachers' valuations of students include their work habits, motivation, effort, and behavior, commonly referred to as social and behavioral skills.

African American students tend to receive lower ratings on measures of social and behavioral skills than European American students even when controlling for other characteristics such as students' socioeconomic status, gender, age, family structure, test scores, and prior social and behavioral skills. Teacher reports of social and behavioral skills are seemingly more important for teacher perceptions of student academic ability for African American students than for European American students. In other words, classroom behavior has a larger influence on how teachers perceive the academic ability of African American students than it does for European American students. According to research in this area, teacher perceptions of students' academic ability are sustained over time.

Anxiety appears to play a significant role in the achievement gap between African American and European American students. A study examining the achievement gap between minority and majority racial groups in schools sought to measure academic test results and anxiety related to those tests among diverse high school students. The study results showed that European American students performed better on the tests, and race accounted for 9–23% of the variance, even after controlling for educational opportunities and socioeconomic status.

African American students are often anxious about negative consequences of failing, such as not receiving a regular diploma and having restricted access to college or trade school. Another aspect of anxiety that may be experienced by African American students during testing is stereotype threat, which refers to the risk of confirming a negative stereotype of one's group. A seminal 1995 study by Claude Steele and Joshua Aronson found that African American students did better on a test composed of difficult verbal questions from the GRE General Test when they were told it was for research on psychological factors in problem-solving than when they were told it measured their verbal abilities. Numerous studies have since been published on stereotype threat among a range of groups.

High-Stakes Testing and African American Students

High-stakes testing may have further widened the gap between the scores of African American and European American students. Decisions affected by test scores are so critical that many educators call this process high-stakes testing. High-stakes testing refers to standardized tests whose results have powerful influences when used by school administrators, other officials, or employers to make decisions. For example, high-stakes test results can be used to hold teachers, schools, and administrators accountable for student performance.

It is reasonable to expect that a test measures what has been taught due to the weight of what rides on test results. However, research shows that fewer than 10% of the items in students' curricula overlapped with both the textbooks and the standardized tests students were given. In response to this mismatch, some teachers have resorted to "teaching to the test."

Because of the average difference between the test scores of African American and European American students, teachers of predominantly African American students are most likely to teach to the test in an effort to narrow the achievement gap. This emphasis on test performance may, however, lead to increased dropout rates among African American students if they feel they are going to fail the exam that many states require for high school graduation. Without the expectation of graduating, they see no point in continuing to attend school.

Finally, African American students may underperform on achievement tests because teaching strategies and academic content often do not align with their lived experiences. African American students may perform better on tests if teaching strategies align closely with the specific types of problems that the students will encounter on the test and are embedded in a culturally responsive pedagogy.

Wilfridah Mucherah

See also Achievement Tests; Alignment; Anxiety; Asian Americans and Testing; Cultural Competence; Culturally Responsive Evaluation; Gender and Testing; High-Stakes Tests

Further Readings

Chavous, T. M., Bernat, H., Schmeelk-Cone, K., Caldwell C. H., Kohn-Wood, L., & Zimmerman, M. A. (2003). Racial identity and academic attainment among African American adolescents. *Child Development, 74*(4), 1076–1090.

Davis, J., & Martin, D. B. (2008). Racism, assessment, and instructional practices: Implications for mathematics teachers of African American students. *Journal of Urban Mathematics Education, 1*(1), 10–34.

Herman, M. R. (2009). The black-white-other achievement gap: Testing theories of academic performance among multiracial and mono-racial adolescents. *Sociology of Education, 82*(1), 20–46.

Minor, E. C. (2014). Racial differences in teacher perception of student ability. *Teachers College Record, 116*(10), 1–22.

Osborne, J. W. (2001). Testing stereotype threat: Does anxiety explain race and sex differences in achievement? *Contemporary Educational Psychology, 26*(3), 291–310.

AGE EQUIVALENT SCORES

An age equivalent (AE) score is a type of norming that provides an estimate of the chronological age (CA) at which a typically developing child demonstrates the skills displayed by the child being assessed. Scores are intended to convey the meaning of test performance in terms of what is typical of a child at a given age based on the mean raw score on a test obtained by the group of children in the normative sample at a specific age. This entry describes how AE scores are calculated and discusses their limitations.

AE scores are often expressed in years and months (e.g., 5;0 for 5 years, 0 months). In simple terms, if on average children at 36 months of age obtain a score of 10 correct responses on a particular test, then any child obtaining a score of 10 correct will receive an AE of 36 months.

Limitations

Despite the wide use of AE scores, there are several well-documented limitations associated with these scores. First, in contrast to standard scores and percentile ranks, AE scores do not take into consideration the range of normal performance for individuals whose scores fall within the average range. Rather, these scores represent the age at which a given raw score is average. It would be expected that half of the examinees on a test will achieve a higher AE score than their corresponding CA. Similarly, half of the examinees should receive a lower than average AE score.

The lack of consideration for a range of normal performance results in AE scores implying a false standard of performance. For example, one might expect a 4-year-old child to earn an AE score of 4;0. However, due to the nature of AE scores, half of the 4-year-old examinees will earn an AE score that is below their CA. A child who receives a standard score or percentile rank that is below the mean for a given age-group may be performing well within the range of normal or within 1 standard deviation away from the mean. This same examinee might earn an AE score that is significantly below the examinee's CA. Therefore, AE scores make no attempt to describe a normal range of performance, therefore these types of scores are ineffective in case management decisions.

A second reported limitation of AE scores is that these scores promote typological thinking. AE scores compare children to the "average *x*-year-old." However, the average *x*-year-old does not exist. Rather, the term *average* represents a range of performance for a particular age-group.

A third serious limitation of AE scores is the lack of information about a test taker's performance on a given test. When two children earn the same AE score, the examiner cannot assume that the children responded the same way to the stimulus items on the test. Earning the same AE score simply means that these two children answered correctly the same number of questions. Although a 5-year-old and a 10-year-old may earn the same AE score, these two children may have approached the stimulus items differently. That is, they may have demonstrated varying performance patterns. It is likely that the younger child performed lower level work with greater consistency, reaching a ceiling early on. The older child likely attempted more problems but performed at a lower accuracy level. Consequently, AE scores would be ineffective in making inferences about what can be expected from these children regarding their language abilities. AE scores may also be ineffective in assessing children with severe developmental delays or mental retardation. AE scores are not valid when evaluating children with Down syndrome because these children may use different underlying processes when approaching stimulus items. If the development of these two groups of children is not comparable, AE scores are no longer valid for children with Down syndrome. In other words, the fact that a child with Down syndrome has an AE score that is similar to that of a much younger typically developing child does not mean that the child with Down syndrome is using the same underlying processes as the younger child.

A fourth commonly reported limitation of AE scores is the derivation method of these scores. AE scores are derived through interpolation and extrapolation. For example, when deriving AE scores for a test, the test developers may examine a group of children in the normative sample whose CAs fall between 5;0 and 5;5. These children's scores are plotted and smoothed into a graph. Using this graph, the AE scores for children at each month interval are estimated or extrapolated. The AE score for each age represents the average raw score for that age-group of children. Thus, when AE scores are calculated, they represent a mean score of a group of children who were not actually tested.

A fifth problem with AE scores is that these scores falsely imply that abilities increase at a constant rate from year to year. Unlike standard scores, which follow an equal-interval scale, AE scales are ordinal, with a flattening of the curve as the age increases. That is, as age increases, similar differences in AE scores are due to the smaller and smaller differences in raw scores. For example, a difference in AE scores of 3 months for a 4-year-old is more significant than a difference of 3 months for a 14-year-old. Therefore, AE scores cannot be used to demonstrate change in a child's skills over time.

Zachary Conrad

See also Grade Equivalent Scores; Norming; Scales

Further Readings

Elliott, C. D., Smith, P., & McCulloch, K. (1996). *British Ability Scales Second Edition (BAS II).*

Administration and scoring manual. London, UK: Nelson.

Maloney, E., & Larrivee, L. (2007). Limitations of age-equivalent scores in reporting the results of norm-referenced tests. *Contemporary Issues in Communication Science and Disorders, 34,* 86–93.

McCauley, R. J., & Swisher, L. (1996). Use and misuse of norm-referenced tests in clinical assessment: A hypothetical case. *Journal of Speech and Hearing Disorders, 49,* 338–348.

Salvia, J., Ysseldyke, J., & Bolt, S. (2006). *Assessment: In special and inclusive education.* Boston, MA: Houghton Mifflin.

ALIGNMENT

In educational assessment, alignment refers to how well assessments measure what is taught or intended to be taught. In 2002, Norman Webb described alignment as the "extent to which expectations and assessments are in agreement and serve in conjunction with one another to guide the system toward students learning what they are expected to know and do" (p. 1). This entry discusses the models used to measure and understand alignment and the reasons why alignment is important.

Most alignment models consider the match or overlap between curriculum (in the form of content standards or curriculum guides), tests or other assessment tools, and classroom instruction. Because of this, measures of alignment are best thought of as a form of content-related evidence of validity. According to Stephen Haynes, David Richard, and Edward Kubany, content-related validity is understood to be how well an assessment instrument reflects the particular construct that is being measured by the instrument. Although the concept of alignment can be applied in a variety of contexts (e.g. credentialing, employment tests), its most frequent application has been in the realm of K–12 standards-based accountability.

Among the many provisions in the No Child Left Behind Act of 2001, perhaps none received as much attention as the requirement that states develop and administer annual statewide standardized tests in Grades 3–8 and at least once in high school. These tests were intended to measure both students' knowledge and their progress toward meeting state-defined performance standards. The idea behind the testing requirement was that combining student achievement data with strong accountability consequences for schools, districts, and state education agencies would result in improved academic outcomes. To achieve this objective, educational systems needed to ensure (and were federally mandated to demonstrate) the alignment between their content standards and standardized assessments.

The Council of Chief State School Officers issued a monograph that reviewed the three frameworks most commonly used by states and test developers for evaluating alignment: (1) the Webb model, (2) the surveys of enacted curriculum model, and (3) the Achieve model. Each of these frameworks involves expert review of standards and assessments that results in a series of indices characterizing the extent of match or overlap in state standards, assessments, and (in the case of the surveys of enacted curriculum) classroom instruction.

It is important to note that alignment is not a dichotomous variable (i.e., aligned *vs.* not aligned). Rather, the information produced by alignment studies can be used by policy makers, test developers, and educators to make adjustments to test content or instructional practices to improve the extent of alignment with the curricular expectations outlined in content standards.

Clearly, an insufficient degree of alignment (i.e., a significant mismatch between content standards and test content) can result in fragmentation and confusion for educators and students. For example, in the absence of alignment, how are educators to determine the skills and knowledge most important to teach? Moreover, if test content does not match what was taught to students in class, they may experience frustration and failure on required assessments. A lack of alignment between these elements also calls into question any inferences drawn from assessments. Without demonstrating adequate alignment between tests and content standards, it is impossible to determine whether a school's success or failure in demonstrating adequate yearly progress can be attributed (at least in part) to the quality and content of classroom instruction.

Although other models have been proposed for understanding alignment, the intended curriculum model developed by Alexander Kurz and Stephen Elliott is the most recent and comprehensive one. The model demonstrates curricular expectations expressed at different levels in the educational system: system-wide, classroom, and individual student.

According to the intended curriculum model, two types of curriculum exist at the system level: the *intended curriculum* and the *assessed curriculum*. Intended curriculum refers to subject- and grade-specific content and skills that are outlined in content standards, teacher's manuals, or curriculum guides. The second system-wide curriculum is the assessed curriculum, representing the content actually measured during testing. Both of these system-level curricula could be viewed as policy tools sending messages to educators and students about the skills and concepts that are valued and important. For example, teachers may make decisions about the topics to be emphasized based on what they know or believe will be on the subsequent high-stakes test.

Moving from the system level, Kurz and Elliott define a series of curricula at the teacher and student level. The *planned curriculum* represents the teacher's actually teaching plans based on the content outlined in the standards, whereas the *enacted curriculum* represents the content the teacher subsequently delivers during instruction.

The planned and enacted curricula can introduce substantial variation in alignment across the system. For example, a number of factors (e.g., teacher expertise, student skill level) may result in an individual teacher's decision to emphasize some aspects of the intended curriculum while simultaneously de-emphasizing or skipping others. The most widely used alignment evaluation frameworks (the Webb model, the surveys of enacted curriculum model, and the Achieve model) focus on alignment at the intended curriculum model's system level and (sometimes) the teacher level.

Kurz, however, indicates that variation at the individual student level may influence alignment as well. The *engaged curriculum* consists of instructional content on which a student is productively engaged. Student engagement might be influenced by a variety of factors including difficulty level of the task, classroom behavior, or the quality of teachers' classroom management. Only instruction that is provided in a manner and context that facilitates productive engagement is likely to become part of students' *learned curriculum* and subsequently part of their *demonstrated curriculum*.

The demonstrated curriculum represents the skills and understanding students are able to produce as part of the standardized test or other assessment strategies. Factors beyond quality of instruction and student engagement also influence students' ability to demonstrate their learning. If assessment items are poorly designed or the needed testing accommodations are not made available, students may be unable to produce responses that represent the true scope of their learning.

Andrew T. Roach and Jacquelyn A. Bialo

See also Adequate Yearly Progress; Content-Related Validity Evidence; No Child Left Behind Act

Further Readings

Haynes, S. N., Richard, D. C. S., & Kubany, E. S. (1995). Content validity in psychological assessment: A functional approach to concepts and methods. *Psychological Assessment, 7*, 238–247.

Kurz, A. (2011). Access to what should be taught and will be tested: Students' opportunity to learn the intended curriculum. In S. N. Elliott, R. J. Kettler, P. A. Beddow, & A. Kurz (Eds.), *Handbook of accessible achievement tests for all students* (pp. 99–129). New York, NY: Springer.

Kurz, A., Elliott, S. N., Wehby, J. H., & Smithson, J. L. (2009). Alignment of the intended, planned, and enacted curriculum in general and special education and its relation to student achievement. *The Journal of Special Education, 44*, 131–145.

Kurz, A., Talapatra, D., & Roach, A. T. (2012). Meeting the curricular challenges of inclusive assessment: The role of alignment, opportunity to learn, and student engagement. *International Journal of Disability: Development and Education, 59*, 37–52.

Martone, A., & Sireci, S. G. (2009). Evaluating alignment between curriculum, assessment, and instruction. *Review of Educational Research, 79*, 1332–1361.

Roach, A. T., Niebling, B. C., & Kurz, A. (2008). Evaluating the alignment among curriculum, instruction, and assessments: Implications and applications for research and practice. *Psychology in the Schools, 45*, 158–176.

U.S. Department of Education. (2004). *NCLB: Title I—Improving the academic achievement of the disadvantaged.* Retrieved from http://www2.ed.gov/policy/elsec/leg/esea02/pg1.html#sec1001

Vockley, M. (2009). *Alignment and the states: Three approaches to aligning the national assessment of educational progress with state assessments, other assessments, and standards.* Washington, DC: Council of Chief State School Officers.

Webb, N. L. (2002). *Alignment study in language arts, mathematics, science, and social studies of state standards and assessments for four states.* Washington, DC: Council of Chief State School Officers.

Alpha Level

In statistical hypothesis testing (or *tests of significance*), one assumes that the null hypothesis is true about a reference population and attempts to reject it by seeking evidence for the alternative hypothesis. This is done by taking a sample and evaluating whether the sample provides evidence to support the alternative hypothesis. To do so, it is customary to compute the p value. The rejection of the null hypothesis depends on the comparison of the p value with a threshold probability value (chosen by the experimenter), which is referred to as the α *level* (or *level of significance*) of the test and is symbolized as the Greek letter α. This entry discusses the calculation and interpretation of the α level, the history of its use in statistics, statistical hypothesis testing using the rejection region, and misconceptions surrounding the α level.

Comparing a p value with a chosen α level allows one to make a conclusion about the statistical significance of results. Suppose that the p value associated with a sample is very small. This means that the sample outcome (a statistic of the sample) is very unlikely under the assumption that the parameter is the value stated in the null hypothesis, and it serves as evidence favorable to the alternative hypothesis. Suppose contrarily that the p value associated with a sample is not small. This means that the sample outcome is not unlikely under the same assumption and that the data fail to serve as evidence for the alternative hypothesis.

To determine how small a p value has to be to reject the null hypothesis, one needs a threshold value: α. That is, if the p value is less than the α, one is able to reject the null hypothesis; but if the

p value is greater than the α, one cannot reject the null hypothesis. While customary α levels are .001, .01, .05, or .1, in most applications .05 or .01 is specified. If, for example, $\alpha = .05$, then the confidence level that the test would lead one to the correct conclusion that the null hypothesis is true when it is in fact true is $.95$ ($=1 - \alpha$). It is important that a researcher specify the α level prior to setting up the statistical test. This is because it is ethically problematic to choose an α level after identifying the p value, which would allow a researcher to manipulate the conclusion.

Underlying Meaning and Interpretation of α Level

An α level of .05 means that we allow a 5% risk of rejecting the null hypothesis even if it is true, and the difference between the obtained outcome statistic and the parameter specified in the null hypothesis is due to sampling error. The α level of .05 defines what results are improbable enough to allow an experimenter to take the risk of rejecting the null hypothesis when it is true. That is, if the p value is less than .05, one would conclude that the observed effect actually reflects the characteristics of the reference population rather than just sampling error. Contrarily, if the p value is greater than .05, one would fail to make this conclusion. Other α levels, such as .1 or .01, may be adopted, depending on the field, the nature, and the circumstances of the study. Compared to the α level of .05, the α value of .01 is more cautious, while the α value of .1 is less cautious.

The process of making conclusions entails the possibility of two types of errors: (1) concluding that the observed effect of a statistical outcome (an observed value) occurred due to actual changes in the reference population when the effect is actually due to sampling error alone and (2) concluding that the observed effect of a statistical outcome occurred due to sampling error alone when the effect is actually due to a change in the parameter. These are referred to as Type I and Type II errors, respectively.

Charles Henry Brase and Corrinne Pellillo Brase have stated that the α level of a test (the probability of rejecting the null hypothesis given that it is actually true) may be defined, in terms of *risk* and *error*, as the probability at which one is willing to risk a Type I error. While a Type I error depends solely on the choice of α level, a Type II error depends on a Type I error (the α level selected before the test), the initial estimation of changes in the parameter, and the sample size. The probability of committing a Type II error is denoted by the Greek letter β.

Hypothesis testing methods require controlling α and β values to keep them as small as possible. Depending on the nature and context of the test, controlling one type of error may be more important and viable than controlling the other type. Setting the α level at .05 means setting the probability of making a Type I error (or the conditional probability of rejecting the null hypothesis given that the null hypothesis is true) at 5%. Represented graphically in terms of area, an α level of .05 means that the area in which the evidence leads to a rejection if the sample statistic falls into it is 5% of the total area of the sampling distribution.

History

The idea of significance testing in statistics was initiated and outlined by a British statistician, Ronald Fisher, in the early 20th century. In 1925, Fisher published *Statistical Methods for Research Workers*, where he suggested the probability of .05 (1-in-20 chance) as a cutoff level to reject the null hypothesis. Later, Fisher changed this recommendation, suggesting that the cutoff level should be chosen by the experimenter depending on the specific circumstances of the experiment and the field. Two other early to mid-20th-century statisticians, Jerzy Neyman and Egon Pearson, collaboratively contributed to the development of hypothesis testing theory and laid the foundation of modern statistical hypothesis testing. In particular, they noted the importance of setting the α level prior to any data collection.

Statistical Hypothesis Testing Using Rejection Region

A null hypothesis can be considered as the default statement that indicates no change in the parameter of interest. As shown earlier, one way to determine whether a null hypothesis should be rejected (or retained) is to compare a p value with an α level. Another way involves considering the *rejection region*.

The graphical representation of the α level is as part of the total area under the probability curve of the test distribution; the part corresponding to the α level is the rejection region. A *critical value* is the point where the rejection region is cut off from the nonrejection region. In order to decide whether a null hypothesis should be rejected, one can compare the test statistic (calculated from the statistic of the sample) with the critical value. If the test statistic falls in the rejection region, it leads to the conclusion that the null hypothesis should be rejected. In a one-tailed test, the rejection region for an α level of .05 would be allocated to one side (or one tail) of the test distribution and take up 5% of the area under the density curve. In a two-tailed test, the rejection region for an α level of .05 still takes up 5% of the area under the density curve but is divided between the two ends (the tails) of the test distribution, each with 2.5% of the area.

Misconceptions

The α level of a hypothesis test should be interpreted as the probability of rejecting the null hypothesis when the null hypothesis is true. Common misinterpretations of the α level include that it instead indicates the level at which the null hypothesis is proven improbable or false, or, conversely, true; the level of the probability of accepting the null hypothesis when it is true; or the level of confidence in the probability of the null hypothesis being false.

Hyung Won Kim

See also Hypothesis Testing; Inferential Statistics; *p* Value; Significance; Type I Error

Further Readings

Brase, C. H., & Brase, C. P. (2003). *Understandable statistics: Concepts and methods* (7th ed.). Boston, MA: Houghton Mifflin.

Castro Sotos, A. E., Vanhoof, S., Van den Noortgate, W., & Onghena, P. (2009). How confident are students in their misconceptions about hypothesis tests? *Journal of Statistics Education, 17*(2). Retrieved from www.amstat.org/publications/jse/v17n2/castrosotos.html

Everitt, B. S. (2006). *The Cambridge dictionary of statistics.* New York, NY: Cambridge University Press.

Fisher, R. A. (1925). *Statistical methods for research workers.* Edinburgh, Scotland: Oliver and Boyd.

Johnson, B., & Christensen, L. (2008). *Educational research: Quantitative, qualitative, and mixed approaches.* Thousand Oaks, CA: Sage.

Leon-Guerrero, A., & Frankfort-Nachmias, C. (2014). *Essentials of social statistics for a diverse society.* Los Angeles, CA: Sage.

Moore D. S. (2003). *The basic practice of statistics* (Vol. 3). New York, NY: W. H. Freeman.

ALTERNATE ASSESSMENTS

Alternate assessments are measures of academic content or English proficiency intended for students with disabilities. Alternate assessments are different in one or more ways from general assessments intended for the majority of students in schools, including students with disabilities. This entry describes the three types of alternate assessments for students with disabilities that have been identified in federal laws or regulations. It examines each type in terms of the students for whom it was intended, its use in states, and the technical qualities it was expected to meet. The entry concludes with evidence of the consequences that have been attributed to one of the types of alternate assessments, the alternate assessment based on alternate achievement standards, which by 2015 was the only alternate assessment recognized in federal law.

In the early 1990s, alternate assessments were initially used by some states as a way to include all students with disabilities in large-scale assessments designed to measure the academic achievement of students on state-defined content standards. Students with disabilities are a diverse group of students, with varying disability characteristics. Among the most prevalent of the disabilities that qualify students for special education under federal law are specific learning disabilities, speech and language impairments, autism, emotional disabilities, other health impairments, and intellectual disabilities. Among the least prevalent of these disabilities are visual impairments, hearing impairments, and orthopedic impairments.

Depending on the disability a student has, the student may need to be assessed with accessibility supports or accommodations that may be different from those needed by another student with a disability. Small numbers of students with disabilities may need to be assessed with an assessment that is different in some way from the general assessment that most students with disabilities take either with or without accessibility supports and accommodations. These other assessments may be in a different format or require the student to meet different expectations from the general assessment.

In the 1997 reauthorization of the Individuals with Disabilities Education Act, alternate assessments were first introduced in federal law. The requirements for alternate assessments have been defined and refined because they were first introduced as assessments for those students with disabilities unable to participate in general assessments even with accommodations. Accommodations are changes in testing materials or procedures that provide access to the assessment without changing what the test is intended to measure.

Because the Individuals with Disabilities Education Act required the development of state alternate assessments for students with disabilities, three types of alternate assessments have been identified in federal regulations for the Elementary and Secondary Education Act (ESEA), which was reauthorized in 2002 as the No Child Left Behind Act and in 2015 as the Every Student Succeeds Act (ESSA). These are alternate assessments based on alternate achievement standards (AA-AAS, also referred to as alternate assessments based on alternate academic achievement standards), alternate assessments based on grade-level achievement standards (AA-GLAS, also referred to as alternate assessments based on grade-level academic achievement standards), and alternate assessments based on modified achievement standards (AA-MAS, also referred to as alternate assessments based on modified academic achievement standards). These alternate assessments varied in terms of the performance standards (called achievement standards) on which they were to be based for judging student performance. All of the alternate assessments have been required to be based on the same grade-level content that is assessed by general assessments. The requirements for the achievement standards were defined through regulations tied to the ESEA.

AA-AAS

Alternate achievement standards are standards for performance that are different in complexity from the GLAS held for students taking general assessments. For example, when a student in the general assessment is asked to provide an extended written response to a prompt, the student participating in the AA-AAS might be asked to enter picture cards into a graphic organizer to convey a response.

Students Intended to Take the AA-AAS

The AA-AAS is intended for a small group of students who have significant cognitive disabilities. This group of students does not comprise a disability category but is generally recognized to include primarily students with intellectual disabilities, autism, and multiple disabilities but not all students in those categories. Students with significant cognitive disabilities have disabilities that affect their intellectual functioning and adaptive behavior. Adaptive behavior refers to the knowledge and skills needed for living independently and functioning safely in daily life.

Under No Child Left Behind Act accountability rules setting targets for the percentage of students testing proficient in English and math, no more than 1% of tested students could be considered proficient based on their performance on an AA-AAS. Because of this, it was sometimes referred to as the 1% assessment. In 2015, when Congress replaced the No Child Left Behind Act with ESSA, the AA-AAS was incorporated as an expected part of assessments used for school accountability. Participation in the AA-AAS was limited to 1% of the total student population at each grade to ensure that only students with the most significant cognitive disabilities were included in the assessment. In addition, the AA-AAS was the only alternate assessment recognized by ESSA for inclusion in school accountability systems. Neither the AA-GLAS nor the AA-MAS could be used for school accountability purposes under the requirements of ESSA.

Use of AA-AAS in States

All U.S. states, along with the District of Columbia, Puerto Rico, Virgin Islands, Guam, and other jurisdictions that receive federal special education funding, have developed AA-AAS for their students with significant cognitive disabilities. These assessments are primarily item-based assessments, similar to states' general assessments, although some are body-of-evidence portfolios and some are rating scales. All states have AA-AAS for English language arts, mathematics, and science, as required by federal law. Some states also have AA-AAS for other content areas, such as social studies.

Clarification of the Qualities of AA-AAS

AA-AAS are to meet the same technical quality requirements as other assessments in which students with disabilities participate. These technical quality requirements include validity, reliability, fairness, and accessibility, and others that address alignment to content standards, test design and item development, scoring, and test security. Addressing these technical quality requirements evolved over time as the understanding of students with significant cognitive disabilities improved and expectations for their performance increased.

Alternate Assessments Based on Grade-Level Achievement Standards (AA-GLAS)

GLAS are standards for performance that are the same as the GLAS held for students taking general assessments. This type of assessment addressed the need for different procedures for demonstrating grade-level performance, such as completing a portfolio or participating in a performance assessment to demonstrate the same level of proficiency as could be demonstrated on traditional general assessments that included multiple-choice and extended response items.

Few states ever developed an AA-GLAS. Instead, they relied on accommodations to ensure that assessments were appropriate for their students with disabilities working on GLAS. In 2015, ESSA eliminated this alternate assessment as an optional assessment for English language arts, mathematics, and science.

Although AA-GLAS were eliminated for content area assessments, federal guidance released in 2014 confirmed that states needed to have alternate assessments for some English learners with disabilities taking the state English language proficiency assessment. The guidance required that these alternate assessments be based on the same criteria for proficient performance as English

language proficiency assessments for English learners without disabilities.

Students Intended to Take the AA-GLAS

The AA-GLAS was intended for students with disabilities who needed a different way to demonstrate their grade-level performance. Among the students identified as needing a different way to demonstrate the same level of performance as demonstrated by other students were students with significant motor disabilities, disabilities that hypothetically would prevent them from responding to a paper and pencil or computer-based test.

Use of AA-GLAS in States

Only one state developed and implemented an AA-GLAS that was considered by the U.S. Department of Education to meet the requirements for a technically adequate assessment of GLAS. That state used a portfolio approach to hold students to the same achievement standards as students taking the general assessment.

Clarification of the Qualities of AA-GLAS

Defining the qualities necessary for an AA-GLAS is more difficult than defining the technical qualities of a more traditional assessment. Further, with the push in ESSA to include in the general assessment items that are delivered in the form of projects, portfolios, and extended performance tasks, the distinction of an AA-GLAS disappeared because all students were considered to have access to these different procedures for assessing students' knowledge and skills.

AA-MAS

In 2007, modified achievement standards were introduced through federal regulation. They were defined as reduced, less difficult expectations for students with disabilities on challenging assessments aligned to grade-level content. AA-MAS were presented as an optional assessment that states could elect to develop for a small group of students with disabilities. With this option, states could count up to 2% of all students as proficient who met the AA-MAS proficiency standards. Because of this, it was sometimes called the 2% assessment. The allowance for the AA-MAS was rescinded through federal regulation in August 2015, just months before the reauthorization of ESEA eliminated it as an optional assessment for states to develop for students with disabilities.

Students Intended to Take the AA-MAS

Defining the students for whom an AA-MAS was appropriate was challenging for states. The AA-MAS regulation indicated that students with disabilities who participate in an AA-MAS could be from any disability category. Further, the students were described as ones who had access to quality grade-level instruction but who were unlikely to achieve grade-level proficiency within the time period covered by their IEPs.

Use of AA-MAS in States

The number of states that developed and implemented AA-MAS varied over the years when it was allowed for ESEA accountability. In 2012, 5 years after states were first allowed to develop this optional assessment, there were 12 states using it for some of their students with disabilities. The participation policies in these states differed, but most of them included previous poor performance on state assessments, or on state assessments and other measures, for defining which students should participate in the AA-MAS.

Clarification of the Qualities of AA-MAS

AA-MAS were to meet the same quality requirements as other assessments in which students with disabilities participate. These requirements were difficult for states to meet because of the difficulty identifying less difficult but challenging performance for students with disabilities. Research confirmed this difficulty. Considerable evidence was accumulated that indicated the lowest performing students with disabilities often were assigned to the AA-MAS in 1 year, then to the AA-AAS in another year, and sometimes to the general assessment in another year.

Evidence of the Consequences of AA-AAS for Students With Significant Cognitive Disabilities

The AA-AAS, which as of 2015 was the only alternate assessment to continue to be allowed for purposes of federal ESEA accountability, has resulted in significant changes in understanding the characteristics of students with significant cognitive disabilities and in providing grade-appropriate academic instruction to these students. These changes, in turn, have affected understanding of how to best assess grade-level academic content for these students.

With the development of new, more rigorous AA-AAS and the collection of data on the students participating in the assessment, the characteristics of students with significant cognitive disabilities were examined. These examinations revealed that most students with significant cognitive disabilities communicate with symbolic-level skills, both receptively and expressively, and also responded to social interactions. Most students with significant cognitive disabilities also were able to read text with basic understanding and compute numbers, either with or without a calculator. Further, most had normal vision, hearing, and motor function, with or without correction. Fewer than 10% of the students who participated in the AA-AAS were viewed as communicating primarily through cries, facial expressions, or changes in muscle tone or as having no social interactions with others or even not being aware of them.

Unlike assessments developed in the late 1990s that focused primarily on functional skills, by 2015 states' AA-AAS focused on grade-level English language arts, mathematics, and science content, with standards set to reflect alternate achievement of the content. Students with significant cognitive disabilities were being held to much more rigorous expectations and in general tended to be on the path to meeting those expectations.

Martha L. Thurlow

See also Accommodations; Every Student Succeeds Act; Individuals with Disabilities Education Act; No Child Left Behind Act

Further Readings

Kleinert, H., & Kearns, J. *Alternate assessment for students with significant cognitive disabilities: An educator's guide.* Baltimore, MD: Paul H. Brookes.

Lazarus, S. S., Thurlow, M. L., Ysseldyke, J. E., & Edwards, L. M. (2015). An analysis of the rise and fall of the AA-MAS policy. *Journal of Special Education, 48*(4), 231–242.

Perie, M. (Ed.). (2010). *Alternate assessments based on modified achievement standards (AA-MAS): Research, best practices and recommendations for their design and development.* Baltimore, MD: Paul H. Brookes.

Thurlow, M. L., Lazarus, S. S., & Bechard, S. (Eds.). (2013). *Lessons learned in federally funded projects that can improve the instruction and assessment of low performing students with disabilities.* Minneapolis: University of Minnesota, National Center on Educational Outcomes.

Thurlow, M. L., & Quenemoen, R. F. (2016). Alternate assessments for students with disabilities: Lessons learned from the National Center and State Collaborative. In C. Wells & M. Faulkner-Bond (Eds.), *Educational measurement: From foundations to future.* New York, NY: Guilford.

Wiener, D. (2006). *Alternate assessments measured against grade-level achievement standards: The Massachusetts "competency portfolio"* (Synthesis Report 59). Minneapolis: University of Minnesota, National Center on Educational Outcomes.

AMERICAN EDUCATIONAL RESEARCH ASSOCIATION

The American Educational Research Association (AERA) is the nation's largest professional organization dedicated to education research. Founded in 1916, the primary focus of AERA is to facilitate the creation of rigorous education research for the improvement of educational practices, experiences, and outcomes. Education research is examining the process of education and learning throughout the life span while considering individual and contextual differences. This entry further describes AERA, including its structure and function, and then discusses its Graduate Student Council (GSC) and annual meeting.

AERA has a total membership of approximately 25,000, including researchers, students, and practitioners from around the world. Although the majority of the association is made up of education researchers (approximately 74%), some members conduct research in other disciplines, including psychology, history, philosophy, statistics, anthropology, sociology, and political science. Although AERA is more than a century removed from its inception, the central mission of supporting, advancing, and disseminating education research to improve educational processes and influence public policy has remained the fundamental focus for over a century.

Structure and Function

The governance structure of AERA includes four main units: the council, executive board, standing committees, and annual committees. There are 12 divisions that represent various areas of educational research:

Division A: Administration, Organization, and Leadership

Division B: Curriculum Studies

Division C: Learning and Instruction

Division D: Measurement and Research Methodology

Division E: Counseling and Human Development

Division F: History and Historiography

Division G: Social Context of Education

Division H: Research, Evaluation, and Assessment in Schools

Division I: Education in the Professions

Division J: Postsecondary Education

Division K: Teaching and Teacher Education

Division L: Educational Policy and Politics

In addition, AERA has over 160 special interest groups that represent subfields within education research, with groups focusing on measurement and assessment in higher education and on leadership for social justice. Generally, members belong to one or two of the 12 divisions and a few special interest groups of their preference.

The association publishes six peer-reviewed journals including *Educational Researcher* and the *Journal of Educational and Behavioral Statistics*. AERA also issues a free monthly online newsletter named *AERA Highlights*, which keeps readers current with AERA-related news and initiatives related to education. Additional to the six journals and monthly newsletter, AERA publishes books on timely and prominent educational topics. Books published by AERA include *Standards for Educational and*

Psychological Testing and *Prevention of Bullying in Schools, Colleges, and Universities.*

To encourage scholarship and stimulate change in specific areas, AERA organizes targeted programs. These include the government relations program, which engages with federal agencies encouraging funding of education research, and the social justice program, which supports and disseminates scholarship on issues of social justice in education. AERA also takes a stand on social issues by releasing position statements. Some notable examples include position statements on the 2015 Charleston, South Carolina, church shootings and racism in the United States and on the use of value-added models to evaluate educators and educator preparation programs. Furthermore, the annual *Brown Lecture*, started in 2004 to commemorate the *Brown v. Board of Education* decision, highlights the importance of research in the pursuit of equality in education and demonstrates the organization's effort to take firm positions on various education-related issues.

Graduate Student Council

More than 28% of AERA's membership consists of students including 6,500 graduate students and 600 undergraduate students. As such, several resources devoted to student growth and development as well as numerous opportunities for student involvement. The GSC is a student-run council that facilitates and supports the development and transition from graduate student to professor or practitioner. By helping students navigate many obstacles and challenges of the academy, the GSC advocates for and serves the needs of students.

The GSC is made up of nine council members and 24 division representatives. The council's role is to support all students across the entire association, whereas the division representatives' role is to support the students within each of their respective divisions. The council has four elected positions including chair elect, secretary/historian, newsletter editor, and web secretary and two appointed positions including program chair and community leader. Each of the 12 divisions have two representatives, a junior and senior representative.

The GSC has five major responsibilities that consist of planning the annual meeting for students, advocating for student needs, disseminating information, community building, and self-governance. The GSC is governed entirely by students, who host 23 sessions at each annual meeting created for students. In addition, the GSC holds an annual community service project with an organization in the local community where the conference is held.

Annual Meeting

The annual AERA conference is a 5-day meeting held in either the United States or Canada. Approximately 14,000 researchers travel to the conference each year, attending hundreds of sessions dedicated to presenting the latest education research across various education disciplines. Invited presidential sessions on a current and major issue in education are typically given by prominent scholars or public figures. Respective divisions host several sessions in various formats that include paper symposiums, roundtable discussions, fireside chats, and poster sessions.

Prior to the annual meeting, various divisions host a preconference for graduate students and early career scholars, focusing on topics such as the job search, grant writing, and tenure review. For individuals interested in measurement and statistics, the annual meeting is held in accordance with National Council on Measurement in Education conference, and AERA members frequently attend both the conferences. The large variety and volume of topics and sessions offered at the annual conference provide several options for all AERA attendees.

Gabriel J. Merrin

See also American Evaluation Association; American Psychological Association; *Brown v. Board of Education*; Educational Researchers, Training of; National Council on Measurement in Education; Value-Added Models

Further Readings

American Educational Research Association. (n.d.). Graduate student council. Retrieved from www.aera.net/About-AERA/Member-Constituents/Graduate-Student-Council

American Educational Research Association. (n.d.).
    Featured education research jobs. Retrieved from
    careers.aera.net

Mershon, S., & Schlossman, S. (2008). Education,
    science, and the politics of knowledge: The American
    Educational Research Association, 1915–1940.
    American Journal of Education, 114(3), 307–340.

Websites

American Educational Research Association: www.aera.net

American Evaluation Association

The American Evaluation Association (AEA) is a
nonprofit international professional association
for evaluators. AEA's publications, conferences,
and topical interest groups (TIGs) deal with program evaluation, personnel evaluation, and other
forms of evaluation designed to assess the strengths
and weaknesses of programs, policies, personnel,
and organizations. As of January 2016, AEA com-
prised approximately 7,000 members from all
50 U.S. states and over 60 other countries. Members include evaluators, researchers, educators,
students, and stakeholders. This entry provides an
overview of AEA's creation and mission; organization; establishment of professional guidelines for
evaluators; and professional development opportunities, collaboration with other organizations,
and awards for members.

Creation and Mission

AEA was formed in 1986 as a result of the merger
between the Evaluation Research Society and
Evaluation Network. Its mission is "to improve
evaluation practices and methods, increase evaluation use, promote evaluation as a profession, and
support the contribution of evaluation to the generation of theory and knowledge about effective
human action" (AEA, n.d.).

AEA values high-quality, ethical, culturally
responsive evaluations that are intended to
improve the evaluated entities' effectiveness. It
seeks to develop an international, diverse, and
inclusive evaluation community in order to provide continual development opportunities for

evaluation professionals to deepen their understanding of evaluation practices and methodologies. To these ends, AEA's goals are to ensure that
evaluators have the skills necessary to be effective,
culturally competent, contextually sensitive, and
ethical; to provide a sense of professional affilia-
tion between evaluators; to increase evaluation's
visibility and perceived value as a field; to create
informed policy so that communities and organizations can participate in and learn from evaluation; and to ensure that members value their
membership.

Organization

AEA is led by a 13-member board of directors
responsible for programmatic decisions for the
association. Included on the board are four principal officers, namely, a president, a president-elect,
a past president/secretary, and a treasurer, who are
nominated from and elected by the membership.
Additionally, over 50 TIGs provide networking
opportunities and conference programming surrounding their particular interests.

As of January 2016, the five TIGs with the
most members were nonprofit and foundations
evaluation; independent consulting; organizational learning and evaluation capacity building;
collaborative, participatory, and empowerment
evaluation; and qualitative methods. A complete
list of TIGs can be found on the AEA website. In
addition to TIG membership, members can also
provide input by volunteering in a variety of
working groups that coordinate various aspects of
the association's activities. AEA also has numerous affiliated local and professional associations
recognized as having similar missions. AEA's
bylaws outline the organization's legal obligations
as a nonprofit entity. The most recent edition of
the bylaws as of January 2016 was the one that
took effect in January 2011.

Professional Guidelines for Evaluators

The Evaluation Research Society had adopted a
set of standards for program evaluation in 1982,
but no standards or guidelines were officially
adopted by AEA when it was formed. In 1992, a
task force was created to draft a set of guiding
principles for evaluators. This task force consisted

of William Shadish, Dianna Newman, Mary Ann Scheirer, and Christopher Wye. An initial draft was sent to all AEA members in 1993, and a final draft was approved in 1994, resulting in the *Guiding Principles for Evaluators*, a general set of principles to inform evaluators' practice in the field. The principles were reviewed and revised in a process throughout 2002 and 2003, and revisions were accepted by AEA membership in 2004.

As of January 2016, the 2004 version of the principles was the most recent. The AEA endorses five guiding principles: systematic inquiry, competence, integrity/honesty, respect for people, and responsibilities for general and public welfare. These principles are written as broad guidelines intended to guide evaluators' professional practice and apply to all types of evaluation, and they are not intended to serve as professional standards. Each of the overarching principles listed here has three to seven subprinciples. A complete listing of the principles can be found on the AEA website.

Activities

Since its inception in 1986, AEA has sponsored an annual conference called evaluation, which features presentations within various topical strands. It also offers a 3-day summer evaluation institute that provides professional development and training sessions. AEA publishes two journals: the *American Journal of Evaluation* and *New Directions for Evaluation*. Membership in AEA also includes access to *Evaluation Review* and *Evaluation and the Health Professions*.

AEA also maintains a blog with daily evaluation tips, a series of webinars that provide information on evaluation tools, virtual professional development courses, member discussion groups, and a newsletter. AEA contributes a representative to the Joint Committee on Standards for Educational Evaluation, which issues the *Educational Evaluation Standards*, the *Program Evaluation Standards*, and the *Personnel Evaluation Standards*. As of January 2016, AEA offers eight awards to recognize individuals in the categories of promising new evaluators, service, evaluation advocacy and use, evaluation practice, evaluation theory, outstanding evaluation, enhancing the public good, and research on evaluation. AEA also offers several fellowships for graduate students

and faculty members and has a program in which it collaborates with evaluation organizations in other countries.

Jennifer A. Brussow

See also Evaluation Capacity Building; Evaluation; Formative Evaluation; Personnel Evaluation; Program Evaluation; Summative Evaluation

Further Readings

American Evaluation Association. (n.d.). About AEA. Retrieved from http://www.eval.org/p/cm/ld/fid=4

Kingsbury, N. (1986). Coming together: Evaluation network and evaluation research society share common business agendas at Evaluation'85 leading to the American Evaluation Association. *American Journal of Evaluation, 7*(1), 107–110. doi:10.1177/109821408600700118

Yarbrough, D. B., Shulha, L. M., Hopson, R. K., & Caruthers, F. A. (2011). *The program evaluation standards: A guide for evaluators and evaluation users* (3rd ed.). Thousand Oaks, CA: Sage.

Websites

American Evaluation Association: www.eval.org

AMERICAN PSYCHOLOGICAL ASSOCIATION

The American Psychological Association (APA) is an organization dedicated to advancing the field of psychology and using psychology to contribute to a wide range of issues facing society. APA was founded in 1892 when psychology was just developing as a discipline, primarily as an outgrowth of philosophy. This entry discusses the activities and structure of APA and how it has contributed to the field of education, in particular, through its education directorate and collaborations with other organizations.

APA has grown from 31 members at its founding to over 117,500 members in 2016. APA members include psychology researchers, educators, clinicians, consultants, and students who span 54 different divisions of psychology. APA is divided into four directorates that each focus on a topic critical to APA's strategic plan: practice, public interest, science, and education.

The directorates engage in specific efforts toward research, advocacy, policy, and outreach that meet the various goals of each directorate. The practice directorate aims to increase awareness of and access to mental and behavioral health services in addition to developing and maintaining guidelines for practitioners and recipients of psychological services. The public interest directorate is focused on combating inequality and promoting social justice and human welfare. The science directorate seeks to support the discipline of psychology in a variety of ways, including providing training and funding for those studying or working in the field of psychology. Finally, the education directorate works both to improve psychology education and to apply valuable psychological research findings to educational practices.

Education at APA

The mission of the education directorate is to advance "the science and practice of psychology for the benefit of the public through educational institutions, programs, and initiatives" (APA, n.d.). It seeks to achieve this goal by supporting both education within psychology and the application of psychology to education. Regarding education within psychology, the directorate serves as the national accreditation organization for training in psychology through the APA Commission on Accreditation and promotes and monitors continuing education for psychologists. In addition, the directorate supports the teaching of psychology in high school through the Teachers of Psychology in Secondary Schools. Furthermore, the Center for Workforce Studies produces reports on the status of the psychology profession, including reports that provide data on the presence of psychologists in higher education.

Regarding the application of psychology to education, the directorate sponsors and conducts a range of activities, including the creation of resources and modules for teachers on topics such as student learning and diversity, the nature and enhancement of creativity, and student behavior and classroom management. One such resource is the Top 20 principles from psychology for PreK–12 teaching and learning, a report that describes 20 principles about teaching and learning drawn from the psychological research literature. The principles are organized into five categories including student thinking and learning; motivation; the relationship of social context, interpersonal relationships, and emotional well-being to learning; classroom management; and assessment. The Top 20 principles report has been translated into several languages and is used in both K–12 schools as a professional development resource and within college courses as a reading on advances in educational psychology.

Many of the education directorate's application-focused activities are products from the Center for Psychology in Schools and Education and special working groups such as the Coalition for Psychology in Schools and Education and the Coalition for High Performance. A mix of APA and external funding supports these groups.

Cutting across both areas of effort—psychology education and the application of psychology to education—the education directorate advocates for policy and funding for psychological science and education and maintains a robust outreach effort, including a strong social media presence.

However, not all education-related activities at APA occur within the education directorate, as other directorates and several APA divisions focus on education as well. In particular, Division 15 (Educational Psychology) has a strong K–12 focus, and to a lesser extent, Division 10 (Society for the Psychology of Aesthetics, Creativity, and the Arts) is involved in K–12 education. These and other divisions publish journals featuring education research, hold mini-conferences for researchers and practitioners, and provide resources for educators. Other organization-wide activities also have an impact on education, such as the development of an ethics program and corresponding educational programs and resources to help practitioners understand the ethical code of conduct.

Additionally, APA collaborates with other education-focused organizations, with a good example being the Standards for Educational and Psychological Testing, a project of the American Educational Research Association, APA, and National Council on Measurement in Education. The standards, which have been published jointly by these professional organizations since 1966, have become the professional standards for educational assessment and are used in several countries.

Jonathan A. Plucker and Lorraine Blatt

See also American Educational Research Association; *Standards for Educational and Psychological Testing*

Further Readings

American Educational Research Association, American Psychological Association, & National Council on Measurement in Education. (2014). *Standards for educational and psychological testing*. Washington, DC: American Educational Research Association.

American Psychological Association. (n.d.). Education Directorate. Retrieved from http://www.apa.org/ed/

Lucariello, J., Graham, S., Nastasi, B., Dwyer, C., Skiba, R., Plucker, J. A., . . . Lee, G. M. (2015). *Top 20 principles from psychology for preK–12 teaching and learning*. Washington, DC: American Psychological Association, Center for Psychology in Schools and Education.

AMERICANS WITH DISABILITIES ACT

The Americans with Disabilities Act of 1990 (ADA) is a civil rights law that prohibits discrimination against individuals with disabilities, including students in K–12 and higher education. The law is an extension of Section 504 of the Rehabilitation Act of 1973 (Section 504), which prohibits discrimination against those with disabilities in programs receiving federal funding. This entry first explains the ADA, then describes its impact on K–12 education, institutions of higher education, and standardized examination and high-stakes testing agencies.

To be eligible for protection under the ADA, an individual must have a physical or mental impairment that substantially limits a major life activity. In the years following the law's passage, several federal courts, including the U.S. Supreme Court, narrowly construed this definition of disability, resulting in limited coverage to individuals with disabilities. Congress responded by passing the Americans with Disabilities Act Amendments Act

of 2008 (ADAAA), which expanded the definition of disability to ensure broad coverage.

The ADAAA made clear that to be considered a substantial limitation, an impairment need not prevent or significantly restrict the ability to perform a major life activity. It also expanded the definition of major life activities, prohibited the consideration of ameliorative effects of mitigating measures when determining disability status (except for ordinary eyeglasses and contact lenses), and expanded the definition of auxiliary aids and services necessary to assist individuals with disabilities. The ADAAA states that individuals must be provided with reasonable accommodations or modifications to ensure participation in programs. However, an accommodation that results in a fundamental alteration of the program or undue burden is not considered reasonable.

Impact on K–12 Education

The ADA mandates protection against discrimination for students with disabilities in Grades K–12. While many K–12 students with disabilities are eligible for special education services under the Individuals with Disabilities Education Act (IDEA), the educational progress of other students with disabilities might not be impacted to a level that services are required under IDEA. However, these students are still eligible for protection from discrimination under the ADA and may be eligible for individually appropriate accommodations and auxiliary aids. Additionally, ADA regulations may provide services beyond what is required under IDEA. For example, the ADA standard concerning communication may require auxiliary aids for a deaf student beyond what is required under IDEA. It should be noted that a student who is eligible for services under the IDEA is also eligible for protection under the ADA and Section 504; however, as noted, not all students covered under the ADA and Section 504 are eligible for services under the IDEA.

The ADAAA legislation made clear that determination of coverage does not demand extensive analysis. A school should first evaluate whether the student requires special education services and then determine whether the student is entitled to reasonable modifications of policies, practices, or procedures even if special education services are not necessary. For example, a student with attention-deficit/hyperactivity disorder may require modification to length of homework assignments.

Students with disabilities may not be unnecessarily segregated from other students. Programs or services that segregate students must provide opportunities for integration with students without disabilities to the maximum extent appropriate. The ADA is not limited to educational activities but rather applies to all services, programs, and activities provided by the school district. Additionally, the ADA applies to private as well as public schools.

Institutions of Higher Education

Institutions of higher education are obligated to provide reasonable accommodations and auxiliary aids to ensure equal access to postsecondary education programs for students with disabilities. Unlike at the K–12 level, postsecondary students must self-report disability, provide documentation of disability, and request accommodations through the appropriate campus disability contact person. Accommodations are then determined by assessing the impact of the documented disability on the ability to participate in the educational program.

The ADAAA stipulates that reading, writing, thinking, speaking, concentrating, and communicating are major life activities and that previous academic achievement does not necessarily mean that a student does not experience substantial limitation of a major life activity. Instead, the condition, manner, or duration it takes an individual to perform an activity as compared to most people in the general population should be considered. For example, a person with a learning disability will often be substantially limited in learning, reading, and thinking as compared to most people.

Examples of reasonable accommodations include extra time on exams, screen readers, note takers, audio lecture recordings, and reduced course load. Because equal access to information is necessary to participate in postsecondary education, textbooks, readings, and website information must be available in formats that are compatible with common adaptive technology as higher education incorporates more online instruction and provision of course information. Accommodations that fundamentally alter essential academic requirements, impose an undue burden, or impose a direct threat to the health or safety of the student or others are not reasonable.

Standardized Examination and High-Stakes Testing Agencies

The ADA applies to agencies that provide standardized exams and high-stakes tests for applications, licensing, certification, or credentialing for secondary, postsecondary, professional, or trade purposes. These entities must provide accommodations and auxiliary aids to individuals with disabilities to best ensure results accurately reflect aptitude or achievement levels rather than an individual's impairment. Documentation required to obtain testing accommodations must be reasonable and limited to the need for requested accommodations.

Proof of past testing accommodations in similar test settings is generally sufficient to support current accommodations. A candidate should generally receive the same testing accommodations previously received under the IDEA or Section 504 in Grades K–12 or received in postsecondary education without requiring further documentation. An absence of prior formal testing accommodations does not preclude a candidate from receiving accommodations. Submission of documentation from qualified professionals based on evaluation and careful consideration should be sufficient documentation. Agencies must respond in a timely manner to requests for accommodations, and applicants should have a reasonable opportunity to provide additional documentation when needed. Annotating or "flagging" accommodated test scores is prohibited.

Joseph Madaus, Walter Keenan, and
Salome Heyward

See also Ability–Achievement Discrepancy; Accessibility of Assessment; Accommodations; Intellectual Disability and Postsecondary Education; Learning Disabilities; Special Education Identification; Special Education Law

Further Readings

Heyward, S. (2011). Legal challenges and opportunities. *New Directions for Higher Education, 154,* 55–64.

U.S. Department of Education—Office of Civil Rights. (2012). Questions and answers on the ADA amendments act of 2008 for students with disabilities attending public elementary and secondary schools. Retrieved January 10, 2016, from http://www2 .ed.gov/about/offices/list/ocr/docs/dcl-504faq-201109 .html

U.S. Department of Justice—Civil Rights Division— Disability Rights Section. (2009). *A guide to disability rights laws.* Retrieved January 10, 2016, from http:// www.ada.gov/cguide.htm

U.S. Department of Justice—Civil Rights Division— Disability Rights Section. (2014). *ADA requirements—Testing accommodations.* Retrieved January 10, 2016, from http://www.ada.gov.regs2014/ testing_accommodations.html

Legal Citations

Americans with Disabilities Act, 42 U.S.C. §§ 1210 1 *et seq.*
Individuals with Disabilities Education Act, 20 U.S.C. §§1400 *et seq.*

Amos

Amos is a computer program for performing structural equation modeling (SEM) and mean and covariance structure analysis. Its full name is IBM SPSS Amos, with Amos standing for "analysis of moment structures." It was developed by the Amos Development Corporation, which is now owned by the IBM SPSS Corporation. Because of its easy-to-use functions, it has become a popular SEM program. Many educational researchers use it to validate measures and test hypotheses. This entry describes the basic features and functions of Amos and illustrates its application in education research.

Features and Functions of Amos

Amos includes a graphical interface (Amos Graphics) and a nongraphical programmatic interface (Program Editor). While one can work directly on a path diagram in Amos Graphics, one can work directly on equation statements using syntax in Program Editor. Amos Graphics offers users a palette of tools and drop-down menus for analysis, while Program Editor provides a platform for analysis using VB.NET or C# scripts. The Amos package also includes a file manager, a seed manager for recording seed values in simulations of random sampling (e.g., bootstrapping), a data file viewer, and a text output viewer.

Amos is capable of performing confirmatory factor analysis (CFA), path analysis, multigroup analysis, multitrait–multimethod model, and multilevel analysis (e.g., latent growth curve model). In education research, Amos has commonly been used to (a) validate the factorial structure of an educational assessment instrument (single-group CFA), (b) test the measurement equivalence of a scale across different groups (multigroup CFA), (c) test a theoretical model (path analysis), and (d) examine the developmental trajectory of learning attributes (latent growth curve model).

Amos provides estimation with full information maximum likelihood to handle missing data, which is common in education research. Rather than imputing missing values, full information maximum likelihood estimates a likelihood function for each individual case based on the information from all the observed proportion of data. Full information maximum likelihood is theoretically robust and outperforms ad hoc methods such as listwise deletion, pairwise deletion, or mean imputation for addressing incomplete data. Besides conducting SEM with data that are measured on a continuous scale with multivariate normal distribution, Amos also provides Bayesian estimation to fit for ordered categorical data and allows users to conduct bootstrapping to tackle nonnormality.

With its graphic interface, Amos allows users who have little statistical knowledge of SEM to perform analysis efficiently. However, as researchers should take responsibility to conduct appropriate data analyses, it is highly recommended that they acquire an understanding of the corresponding concepts and practices of SEM. Amos can be purchased from the IBM SPSS website with its user's guide free to download.

Illustration of Amos Applications

To demonstrate the application of Amos, this section provides an example of the use of Amos Graphics to perform CFA. The goal of this analysis is to validate the factorial validity of a scale measuring family functioning, which is often linked to student well-being. In this scale, it is hypothesized that three components of family functioning—family mutuality, family conflict, and family communication—are assessed by 3 items, respectively. These three components are theoretically correlated with each other. A sample of 1,000 seventh graders was used. Usually, the procedure of SEM analysis includes five steps: (1) model specification, (2) data specification, (3) calculation of estimates, (4) model evaluation, and (5) model modification (if necessary).

Model Specification and Data Specification

The first step of CFA was to construct a hypothesized model and then read a data set. A CFA model was drawn by using Indicator icon to create three latent factors (indicators) with three observed variables each and Covariate icon to create three covariance paths between the latent factors. To meet the demand of identification of model that each indicator must have a scale, Amos creates an indicator model with one factor loading automatically set to be 1. Next, a data file was imported by clicking on Data icon. Amos reads data in several database formats, including

Microsoft Excel spreadsheets and SPSS databases, and text. Finally, the observed variables, factors, and measurement errors were labeled (Figure 1).

Calculation of Estimates

The maximum likelihood estimation approach was chosen in this case. Amos also offers users other approaches including unweighted least squares, generalized least squares, Browne's asymptotically distribution-free criterion, scale-free least squares, and Bayesian estimation. By clicking on the *Calculate Estimates* icon, the results were generated. The estimation results can be viewed in Amos Output while the estimates of parameters can be viewed on the screen by clicking on the *View Output Path Diagram* icon (Figure 2). The Amos Output shows three sets of information: model summary, model variables and parameters, and model evaluation.

Model Evaluation

Usually, a model will be evaluated based on the adequacy of the parameter estimates and the

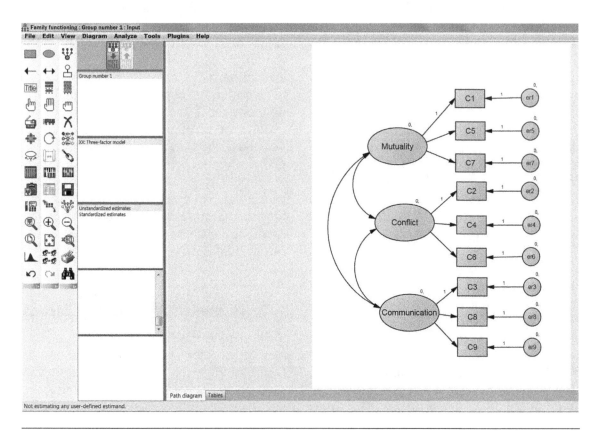

Figure 1 An illustration of the confirmatory factor analysis (CFA) path diagram

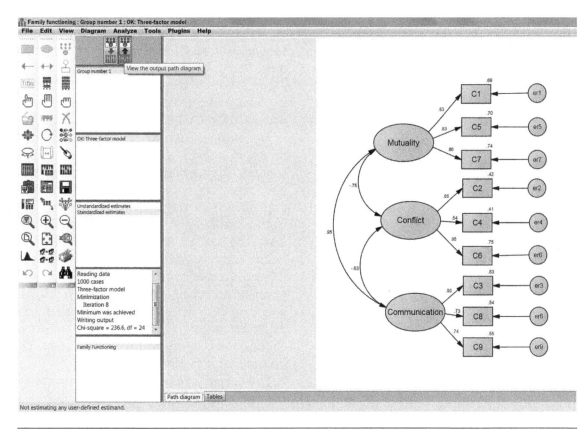

Figure 2 Standardized parameter estimates of the confirmatory factor analysis (CFA) model

model as a whole. First, parameter estimates were evaluated based on three criteria:

1. Feasibility of the parameter estimates: any incorrect sign or value?

2. Appropriateness of the standard errors: any error that is very small (i.e., close to zero) or very large?

3. Statistical significance of the parameter estimates: any statistically insignificant parameter estimate in regression weights, intercepts, covariances, and variances which may be regarded as unimportant?

There was no specific problem with the parameters of this example.

Next, goodness of fit between the hypothesized model and the sample data was evaluated by referring to the model fit indices. In Amos, model fit is reported for the hypothesized model, as well as two additional models: saturated model and independence model. The saturated model is the most general model without any constraints placed on the population moments. In contrast, the

independent model is the most restricted model with all the observed variables assumed to be uncorrelated with each other. An ordinary hypothesized model should lie in between these two models with better model fit. Amos provides eight groups of fit measures, as follows.

1. Minimum discrepancy between hypothesized model and sample data: for example, CMIN/DF (chi-square (*df*)), *p* (*p* value for chi-square test)

2. Measures based on the population discrepancy: for example, root mean square of error of approximation (RMSEA).

3. Incremental indices—comparative indices with comparison to a baseline model: for example, normed fit index, Tucker–Lewis index (TLI; i.e., nonnormed fit index), and comparative fit index (CFI).

4. Measures of parsimony—evaluating the simplicity of the model: for example, parsimony ratio.

5. Parsimony-adjusted measures: for example, parsimony-adjusted normed fit index

6. Information theoretic measures used for model comparison: for example, Akaike information criterion and Bayesian information criterion.

7. Goodness-of-fit index and related measures: for example, goodness-of-fit index and adjusted goodness-of-fit index.

8. Miscellaneous measures: for example, root mean square residual.

Conventionally reported fit measures include CMIN/DF ($\chi^2(df)$), CFI, TLI, and RMSEA. According to the rule of thumb, CMIN/DF > 2.00 represents a poor fit. For CFI and TLI, values > .90 represent an acceptable fit and > .95 a good fit. For RMSEA, values < .08 represent an acceptable fit and < .05 a good fit. Nonetheless, due to high sensitivity to large sample size, CMIN/DF is often used in model comparison rather than single-model evaluation. For the current example, results of the different indices are as follows: $\chi^2(24)$ = 9.860 (not good), CFI = .957 (good), TLI = .919 (acceptable), and RMSEA = .094 (not good). Further action can be taken to improve the model fit.

Model Modification

Amos provides modification indices (MIs) to detect model misspecification. MI represents the expected decrease in overall CMIN (χ^2) value if one certain parameter is to be freely estimated in a subsequent run. Users can decide whether they want to modify the model when an MI value is large. However, any modification should be theoretically justifiable. MI cannot be computed with missing data, which is an obvious limitation of Amos. Rerunning the program using a sample with expectation–maximization imputation for the missing data revealed that the largest MI value rested in the correlation between errors of Items 8 and 9, MI = 118.190. This result suggested that Item 8 and Item 9 measured an additional construct that was not represented by the latent factor—family communication. When the two errors were allowed to be correlated, the model fit increased: $\chi^2(23)$ = 4.123 (not good), CFI = .986 (good), TLI = .978 (good), and RMSEA = .056 (acceptable). Although correlating errors usually leads to improved fit, it is possibly at the cost of biased estimates of model.

Other Applications

In addition to CFA, Amos is capable of testing more complex models. When the covariances among latent factors are hypothesized to be explained by another factor, one can test a higher order CFA model. Daniel Tan-lei Shek and Lu Yu demonstrated how to test a second-order CFA model by assuming three latent factors (i.e., perception of program, perception of implementers, and perceived effectiveness of program) to be explained by a single higher order factor of subjective evaluation of program. They added a latent factor by using *Oval* icon, linked the first-order factor and second-order factor by adding a single-headed arrow from second-order factor to first-order factor (using *Path* icon), and finally, added a factor disturbance to each first-order factor by using *Error* icon, as the first-order factors become endogenous factors while the second-order factor becomes an exogenous factor.

In addition, Amos is often used to test factorial invariance of a measure. As illustrated by Yu and Shek, in 2014, full invariance includes configural invariance (i.e., invariance of factorial structure), structure invariance (i.e., invariance of factor covariance and factor variance), and measurement invariance (i.e., invariance of factor loadings, intercepts, and errors). To test the factorial invariance, users can use an important function of Amos—comparing nested models (i.e., a pair of models in which one can be obtained by constraining the parameters of the other). Users first need to create nested models using the function of "manage models," post constraints on the parameters in the constrained model via simple syntax, and finally compare the constrained model with the unconstrained model.

With the two models being estimated simultaneously, Amos provides comparison of model fit in terms of CMIN (χ^2), normed fit index, IFI, RFI, TLI, and χ^2 difference test, in which researchers often reply on χ^2 difference test for judgment. In their case, when the factor loadings of the subscale of perceived effectiveness of program were constrained to be equal across program implementers of three grades of secondary school, $\Delta\chi^2$ increased relative to that of the unconstrained model, but the increase is not statistically significant. This finding suggested that the subscale was metric invariant across the samples. If the constraints lead to a significant increase in χ^2, it would suggest that the constraints make the model fit worse, and thus, the invariance cannot be established.

Amos can also perform path analysis with or without latent factors. For example, in 2014, in Yu and Shek's illustration of path analysis, they tested a mediation model (i.e., family functioning predicts Internet addiction directly and via the effect of positive youth development) and compared it with several alternative models. For instance, in one alternative model, family functioning has an indirect effect on Internet addiction via positive youth development without a direct effect. Amos provides information on direct effects, indirect effects, and total effects in the output. The general procedure of path analysis is similar to that of CFA mentioned earlier, yet there are several issues worth noting. First, it is convenient to test alternative models with different relationship among variables in Amos, whereas the alternative models should be conceptually meaningful. Second, if latent factors are used, the measurement model of the latent factor should be tested (i.e., CFA) before performing path analysis. Third, Amos provides bootstrapping to confirm the mediation effect in the path analysis.

Daniel Tan-lei Shek and Li Lin

See also Bayesian Statistics; Bootstrapping; Confirmatory Factor Analysis; Measurement Invariance; Path Analysis; SPSS; Structural Equation Modeling

Further Readings

Arbuckle, J. (2013). *Amos 22.0 user's guide*. Chicago, IL: SPSS.

Blunch, N. J. (2008). *Introduction to structural equation modeling: Using SPSS and Amos*. Thousand Oaks, CA: Sage.

Byrne, B. M. (2001). Structural equation modeling with AMOS, EQS, and LISREL: Comparative approaches to testing for the factorial validity of a measuring instrument. *International Journal of Testing, 1*(1), 55–86.

Byrne, B. M. (2013). *Structural equation modeling with AMOS: Basic concepts, applications, and programing*. New York, NY: Routledge.

Kline, R. B. (2010). *Principles and practice of structural equation modeling* (3rd ed.). New York, NY: Guilford Press.

Shek, D. T. L., & Yu, L. (2014). Confirmatory factor analysis using AMOS: A demonstration. *International Journal on Disability and Human Development, 13*(2), 191–204.

Yu, L., & Shek, D. T. L. (2014a). Family functioning, positive youth development, and internet addiction in junior secondary school students: Structural equation modeling using AMOS. *International Journal on Disability and Human Development, 13*(2), 227–238.

Yu, L., & Shek, D. T. L. (2014b). Testing factorial invariance across groups: An illustration using AMOS. *International Journal on Disability and Human Development, 13*(2), 205–216.

Analysis of Covariance

Analysis of covariance (ANCOVA) is a statistical procedure that forms part of the general linear model. Indeed, it can be thought of as a combination of two other methods within this family of statistical models: analysis of variance (ANOVA) and linear regression. It represents the inclusion of a continuous predictor variable (covariate) within a standard ANOVA model, such that values on the outcome variable within the model are adjusted for values on the covariate. There are two main objectives of ANCOVA. First, it can be used in experimental designs to remove the effect of one or more confounding variables. Second, it serves to increase the sensitivity of a statistical test of the experimental factor in the statistical model. This entry discusses the form of the ANCOVA model, the functions of ANCOVA, assumptions of the analysis, using ANCOVA outside experimental contexts, and other considerations in the use of ANCOVA and alternative measures.

Form of the ANCOVA Model

The model for ANCOVA, in the case where there is just a single covariate, is:

$$y_{ij} = \mu + \tau_j + \beta z_{ij} + \varepsilon_{ij},$$

where y_{ij} is the outcome score for participant i in group j; μ is the overall mean score on the outcome variable in the study; τ_j is the effect of the experimental factor in group j; z_{ij} is the covariate score for participant i in group j; β is the regression coefficient for z (estimated from the sample data); and ε_{ij} is the residual for participant i in group j. Note that removing βz_{ij} would leave the basic ANOVA model. Normally, the term $(z_{ij} - \overline{z})$, where $\overline{z}$ is the overall mean covariate score within the study, is used rather than z_{ij} so that the constant term in the model is set at the overall mean for the outcome variable, giving this model:

$$y_{ij} = \mu + \tau_j + \beta(z_{ij} - \overline{z}) + \varepsilon_{ij}.$$

It follows that when ANCOVA is performed, each participant's score is adjusted in relation to the covariate—it is the "hypothetical" score the individual would have if all participants had the mean value of the covariate, $\overline{z}$. Accordingly, the mean for each group in the experiment is also an adjusted mean. The adjusted mean for group j is:

$$\overline{y}_j' = \overline{y}_j - \beta(\overline{z}_j - \overline{z}),$$

where $\overline{y}_j'$ and $\overline{y}_j$ are the adjusted and unadjusted means, respectively, for group j; $\overline{z}_j$ is the mean of the covariate for group j; and $\overline{z}$ is the overall covariate mean.

Functions of ANCOVA

Statistical Control

As noted earlier, ANCOVA can be used to remove the confounding effect of an extraneous variable in an experimental study. For example, a study might be set up to examine the effect of two methods of learning on test performance, in which students are randomized to the two methods of learning; the first method is mainly student-centered learning (SCL), whereas the second consists more of teacher-directed learning (TDL). If, however, age is also associated with test performance, and if there is additionally an imbalance in age across the two randomized groups, age is a potential confounding variable. Age would thereby provide an alternative explanation of any between-group difference in test performance that is observed, so that

this difference could not be confidently attributed to the different methods of learning. One cannot be sure that the groups would still have differed in terms of test performance if they had not also differed in terms of age. If, however, age is included as a covariate in the statistical model, the students' test scores would be adjusted for age, removing the confounding effect of this variable.

The precise effect of this adjustment will depend upon the magnitude and direction of the correlation between age and test scores and of the imbalance in age across the experimental groups. Suppose first that age is positively correlated with test score—*older* students tend to have *higher* scores, and also that the students in the SCL group are on average older than those in the TDL group. At the end of the study, if we took no account of age, the mean difference in test scores might favor the SCL group (i.e., this group had higher scores on average than the TDL group). However, because the students in this group were older than those in the TDL group, the apparent superior performance of the SCL group could be attributable in part to their age. The effect of the learning method has been confounded by the students' ages—their test scores have been biased upward. If we introduce age as a covariate, the mean age of the two experimental groups is statistically equalized. As the effect of age has been removed, the resulting mean difference will be adjusted downward, and this smaller difference will have a larger associated p value (and if the unadjusted mean difference had previously been statistically significant, it might no longer be so after this adjustment). Another way of looking at this is to think of students in the SCL group as having an unfair advantage because of their higher average age and thereby obtaining inflated test scores by comparison with the TDL group. The use of the covariate removes this bias.

Conversely, if the students in the SCL group were *younger* than those in the TDL group, the mean between-group difference in test scores would again be confounded if no account were taken of age. In this instance, however, the superiority of the SCL approach would be biased downward if not adjusted for age. The positive effect of the SCL method on test performance would be counteracted by a negative effect of the students' younger mean age in this group—their test scores would have been biased downward. In other words, instead of starting with an unfair advantage, they would start with an unfair disadvantage. Introducing age as a covariate would remove this bias. The mean between-group difference in test scores would be larger following adjustment and would have a smaller p value (and in the process may become statistically significant where it had not been prior to introduction of the covariate).

The process whereby covariates are selected for the purpose of statistical control should be specified in advance of the analysis. Otherwise, the analyst might be tempted to use as covariates, by trial and error, those variables that give the conclusion that the analyst wants. In addition, it should be remembered that steps can be taken at the design stage (e.g., matching or stratified randomization) to control for known potential confounding variables.

Statistical Power

The other primary objective of ANCOVA is to increase the precision of between-group estimates, thereby producing narrower confidence intervals around these estimates and increasing the sensitivity, or power, of a statistical test on the estimates. The p value in an ANCOVA model is derived from the F ratio and its associated degrees of freedom. The F ratio has, as its numerator, the variance in the outcome that is explained by the factor of interest in the experiment (in the current example, the methods of learning). The denominator for the F ratio is the unexplained variance in the outcome variable; this is the variance that is not attributable to the factor—the experimental error variance. The larger the ratio of explained to unexplained variance, the higher the value of F, and the lower the associated p value.

By introducing a covariate that is correlated with the outcome variable, some of the previously unexplained variance is now explained by the covariate and is thereby removed from the experimental error variance (the greater the correlation of the covariate with the outcome variable, the more variance is explained). As a result, the denominator of the F ratio is now smaller, the F ratio increases, and a smaller p value is produced. This will be achieved even if the groups do not differ on the covariate. So, in this example, even if students in the SCL groups had precisely the same

mean age as those in the TDL group, providing age is correlated with test performance, the sensitivity of the statistical test on the two methods of learning would increase following the introduction of age as a covariate.

A situation in which it is particularly helpful to use ANCOVA in this way is where there are pretest scores on the outcome variable. Pretest scores tend to have a fairly high correlation with posttest scores, and the proportion of variance in the outcome variable that is explained by the covariate is correspondingly large. For example, a correlation of 0.5 or greater between pretest and posttest scores is quite common, and in such a situation, owing to the increased power derived from using the pretest scores as a covariate, the required sample size can be expected to be about 25% lower than that required for an unadjusted analysis on the posttest scores.

The cost of adjusting for a covariate is a loss of one degree of freedom, but except in very small studies, and unless the covariate accounts for negligible variance, this is amply recompensed by the increased sensitivity of the statistical test.

Assumptions of the Analysis

The basic assumptions of ANCOVA are a combination of those for ANOVA and those for linear regression:

1. The level of measurement of both the outcome variable and the covariate is interval or ratio.

2. The predictive relationship between the covariate and the outcome variable is linear.

3. The covariate is a fixed variable and measured without error. Covariates are rarely fixed, but a covariate that is a random variable can normally be used provided that Assumption 7 in this list is satisfied.

4. The residuals are independent (i.e., the value of one residual does not influence, and is not influenced by, the value of any other residual).

5. The residuals have homogeneity of variance (homoscedasticity).

6. The residuals are (approximately) normally distributed—this assumption, which only applies to the residuals, not to the covariate, is required for hypothesis tests and confidence

intervals. With larger sample sizes, this assumption becomes less stringent.

7. The residuals are uncorrelated with the covariate.

There are two additional assumptions that are specific to ANCOVA. The first is that the regression slope, β, should be equal in the two groups (the homogeneity of regression slopes, or parallelism, assumption). In the present example, if the relationship between age and test performance (β) differs between the study groups, the degree of adjustment of test scores should also differ between the groups, requiring a differing value of β for each group. However, the adjustment carried out within the ANCOVA model is in terms of the overall regression slope for the whole sample, which would clearly be inappropriate if the group-specific slopes are different.

The assumption of homogeneous regression slopes can be tested by constructing a scatterplot of the covariate and the outcome variable and fitting separate regression lines for the groups; the extent to which these lines are parallel can be judged visually. In addition, the assumption can be tested statistically. This involves a test of the interaction between the covariate and the grouping variable, which will tell us whether the relationship between the covariate and the outcome variable differs significantly across groups. Accordingly, a statistical model is constructed with the outcome variable, the grouping variable, the covariate, and a term representing the interaction between the grouping variable and the covariate.

A nonsignificant interaction supports the assumption of parallel regression slopes—although it should be remembered that all statistical tests of model assumptions are sensitive to sample size, the results of the test should be interpreted alongside visual assessment of the scatterplot. If the assumption of parallel regression slopes is considered to be untenable, one possibility is to categorize the covariate and include it as a set of dummy variables. In the process, some information in the covariate will be lost, and it will perform less effectively as a control variable or as a means of increasing statistical power, but the requirement for homogeneous regression slopes will have been avoided.

The second assumption—which is more a design assumption than a strict statistical assumption—is

that the covariate should not be affected by the experimental factor. This normally has to do with the time at which a modifiable covariate is measured. Let us adapt the previous example, such that the covariate concerned is not age but anxiety. If we were to measure the students' anxiety after introducing the two methods of learning, it could be that these methods might differentially affect the students' anxiety (one method of learning might create greater self-confidence in a test situation and thus lower levels of anxiety in the group concerned). The implication of this is that the anxiety scores will contain within them part of the effect of the different methods of learning, so that when we adjust for anxiety we will at the same time adjust for the intervention effect. It is therefore important that any modifiable covariates are measured before the introduction of the experimental factor.

It should also be noted that issues of collinearity may arise if there are a number of covariates. With regard to its effect on p values, however, collinearity is often a less serious problem than in multiple linear regression, as the statistical significance of the covariates is not normally of interest when their function is simply that of statistical control.

Using ANCOVA Outside Experimental Contexts

The examples given earlier were from a randomized experiment. In a quasi-experimental design, the intervention groups are not formed by randomization but are preexisting, and often naturally occurring, groups. For example, a study might be based on testing two methods of instruction on male versus female students or on psychology versus sociology students. In this situation, the assumptions of ANCOVA need especially close attention (e.g., the homogeneity of regression slopes assumption may be more readily violated, and measurement error in the covariate may have more serious implications, than in a randomized experiment). Additionally, the results of the analysis should be interpreted carefully. For example, it might be argued that by adjusting the study groups in relation to a covariate, the "statistical" groups that are compared in the hypothesis test differ inappropriately from the "natural" groups on which the study was intended to be based. Additionally, the groups might be adjusted to an overall mean covariate score that would be unrepresentative of the individual groups if their mean scores on the covariate are at a considerable distance from the overall mean. It is helpful in such situations to present the results of an unadjusted analysis alongside those from the ANCOVA, as a sensitivity analysis.

Another issue that arises when employing ANCOVA with predetermined groups is closely linked to the earlier point about adjusting for an intervention effect in an experimental design. In an experiment, differences in covariate values between groups occur by chance in the process of randomization. In other instances, however, a chosen covariate may be intrinsically related to the factor that defines the groups to be compared. For example, a researcher intending to compare the academic performance of two group of students from different years—third grade and fourth grade, for example—might wish to adjust the comparison for age and sex. The adjustment for sex is probably appropriate, ensuring that differing proportions of boys and girls in the two groups do not confound the comparison of performance scores. However, age is likely to be correlated with many of the characteristics that distinguish third-grade students from fourth-grade students (e.g., age-related changes in problem solving, verbal reasoning, or abstract thinking), and an adjustment for age is likely to remove much of the difference between the two groups that the researcher wishes to test.

Other Considerations

ANCOVA employs a numerical (continuous or interval level) covariate. It is important to remember, however, that much the same effect, in terms of adjustment and/or statistical power, can be accomplished by introducing nominal or ordinal variables into the statistical model in a similar way. These might be thought of as also being covariates, although the term *ANCOVA* would only be used to describe the model when at least one such variable is numerical.

Another method that is sometimes used to control for pretest differences in an experimental study is the use of change (or gain) scores—that is, each participant's pretest score is subtracted from the participant's posttest score. However, this method is generally considered to be inferior to ANCOVA as a means of controlling for between-group differences in pretest scores because, unlike ANCOVA, it does not take into account the phenomenon of regression to the mean and may lead to biased estimates. Furthermore, the use of change scores will often lead to a less powerful statistical test than if ANCOVA were used.

ANCOVA provides an effective means of statistical adjustment for potential confounding factors—but it can only do so in respect of confounders that have been identified and measured by the investigator. Accordingly, ANCOVA is an adjunct to, not a substitute for, design features that control for confounding, in particular, randomization. Random allocation serves to balance all potential confounders across experimental groups, irrespective of whether they have been identified as confounders, irrespective of whether they have been measured, and irrespective of whether they are even measurable.

Julius Sim

See also Analysis of Variance; Gain Scores, Analysis of; Multicollinearity; Multiple Linear Regression; Simple Linear Regression

Further Readings

Egbewale, B. E., Lewis, M., Sim, J. (2014). Bias, precision and statistical power of analysis of covariance in the analysis of randomized trials with baseline imbalance: A simulation study. *BMC Medical Research Methodology 14*, 49.

Huitema, B. E. (2011). *The analysis of covariance and alternatives* (2nd ed.). Hoboken, NJ: Wiley.

Keppel, G., & Wickens, T. D. (2004). *Design and analysis: A researcher's handbook* (4th ed.). Upper Saddle River, NJ: Prentice Hall.

Maxwell, S. E., & Delaney, H. D. (2004). *Designing experiments and analyzing data: A model comparison perspective* (2nd ed.). Mahwah, NJ: Erlbaum.

Miller, G. A., & Chapman J. P. (2001). Misunderstanding analysis of covariance. *Journal of Abnormal Psychology, 110*, 40–48.

Milliken, G. A. (2002). *Analysis of messy data: Vol 3. Analysis of covariance*. Boca Raton, FL: Chapman & Hall.

Rutherford, A. (2011). *ANOVA and ANCOVA: A GLM approach* (2nd ed.). Hoboken, NJ: Wiley.

ANALYSIS OF VARIANCE

Often researchers are confronted with determining whether the means of two or more groups differ. The analysis of variance (ANOVA) technique is a parametric hypothesis test to answer this question. ANOVA seeks to partition the overall data into components that correspond to variance explained by the groupings and variance that is unexplained by the groupings. Often the groups are defined by which treatment has been given to each of the experimental units in the group. In cases where the experimental units are randomly assigned to the treatment groups, ANOVA can be used to show causation. This entry discusses the basic principles of ANOVA and its organization, extensions, its use in contrasts and post hoc tests, and its assumptions.

Basic Principles

The simplest case of ANOVA is the one-way ANOVA where the groups are varied across only one factor and each group has the same sample size. Suppose there are k groups and within each group there are n samples taken from each group for a total sample size of nk. For notation, let y_{ij} be the measurement of outcome of interest from the jth sample in the ith group. We let μ_i denote the population mean of group i. In this notation, the ANOVA null hypothesis is:

$$H_0 : \mu_1 = \mu_2 = L = \mu_k.$$

This hypothesis corresponds to the state where all of the means μ_i are equal to each other and hence do not differ. The alternative hypothesis in this case is:

$$H_A : \text{at least two } \mu_i \text{ differ.}$$

If the ANOVA test rejects H_0 in favor of H_A, this means there is enough evidence to conclude that the group means are truly different.

To accomplish this, ANOVA partitions the overall variance. The overall variance is simply the sample standard deviation squared of all of the data regardless of treatment group. In our notation, we would have:

$$S^2 = \frac{\sum_{i=1}^{k}\sum_{j=1}^{n}(y_{ij} - \overline{y}_{\bullet\bullet})^2}{nk-1},$$

where $\overline{y}_{\bullet\bullet} = \frac{1}{nk}\sum_{i=1}^{k}\sum_{j=1}^{n}y_{ij}$ is the overall mean. In our notation, $\overline{y}_{i\bullet} = \frac{1}{n}\sum_{j=1}^{n}y_{ij}$ is the sample mean for the ith group. Here, the denominator is not useful in partitioning the groups and will be discarded to create the sum of squares total, denoted by SS_{TO} and is given by:

$$SS_{TO} = \sum_{i=1}^{k}\sum_{j=1}^{n}(y_{ij} - \overline{y}_{\bullet\bullet})^2$$

By simply adding and subtracting the group sample mean in the SS_{TO} and doing some algebra (some algebra details have been omitted), one can obtain:

$$
\begin{aligned}
SS_{TO} &= \sum_{i=1}^{k}\sum_{j=1}^{n}(y_{ij} - \overline{y}_{i\bullet} + \overline{y}_{i\bullet} - \overline{y}_{\bullet\bullet})^2 \\
&= \sum_{i=1}^{k}\sum_{j=1}^{n}[(y_{ij} - \overline{y}_{i\bullet})^2 + 2(y_{ij} - \overline{y}_{i\bullet})(\overline{y}_{i\bullet} - \overline{y}_{\bullet\bullet}) \\
&\qquad\qquad + (\overline{y}_{i\bullet} - \overline{y}_{\bullet\bullet})^2] \\
&= \ldots \\
&= \underbrace{\sum_{i=1}^{k}\sum_{j=1}^{n}(y_{ij} - \overline{y}_{i\bullet})^2}_{\text{Error}} + \underbrace{\sum_{i=1}^{k}n(\overline{y}_{i\bullet} - \overline{y}_{\bullet\bullet})^2}_{\text{Treatment}} \\
&= SS_E + SS_T.
\end{aligned}
$$

Notice by doing this, the SS_{TO} can be expressed as the sum of a term associated with error and a term associated with the treatment group. This is the essence of ANOVA, partitioning the SS_{TO} into meaningful components. Furthermore, each of the components is itself a sum of items that are squared; hence, the names sum of squares error, SS_E, and sum of squares treatment, SS_T are often given to the components. Note that in this one-way ANOVA scenario, SS_T is often called the sum of squares between and the SS_E is often called the sum of squares within and are denoted by SS_B and SS_W, respectively.

Similarly, for the one-way ANOVA case with equal sample sizes, the total degrees of freedom, $df_{TO} = nk - 1$, associated with the SS_{TO} can also be partitioned into degrees of freedom error, $df_E = n(k-1)$, and degrees of freedom for treatment, $df_T = k - 1$. As with the sum of squares, the degrees of freedom also add together nicely $df_{TO} = df_E + df_T$.

Although all of this algebra may seem not to address the original answer, using the components above a signal-to-noise ratio can be created by:

$$F^* = \frac{SS_T / df_T}{SS_E / df_E}.$$

Notice that F^* is a fraction (ratio) with the observed "variance" associated with the treatment in the numerator and "variance" associated with the error in the denominator. Here, the $*$ in the superscript is to denote that this value is an observed value that is calculated from the data. As with all signal-to-noise ratios, if $F^* < 1$, then there is more noise than signal, and hence, there isn't much evidence for H_A. If $F^* \approx 1$, then there is about the same amount of signal as noise and again not much evidence for H_A. However, if F^* is much greater than 1, then there is a lot of signal and little noise giving evidence toward H_A. Often F^* is called the F-statistic to differentiate it from the F distribution.

The question then becomes how big does F^* need to be for there to be enough evidence toward H_A that one could consider it statistically significant? Fortunately, F^* has a probability distribution associated with it, namely the F distribution. Recall, the F distribution is defined by both its numerator and denominator degrees of freedom, denoted by df_{num} and df_{den}, respectively. In this case, df_{num} is simply df_T and df_{den} is df_E. For a hypothesis test of H_0 versus H_A with a Type I error rate α if the calculated F^* statistic is greater than the $100 \times (1 - \alpha)$ quantile of the F distribution with the associated degrees of freedom, then the F^* is deemed to be "big enough" to be considered statistically significant. Hence, if one rejects H_0, then

there are differences among the treatment groups. However, this test does give where the differences are, only if differences exist. To determine where the differences are a multiple comparison procedure would need to be performed after the ANOVA test.

Organization

Because there is a considerable amount of computation needed to calculate an ANOVA test, the intermediary calculations are typically organized into what is called an ANOVA table. Table 1 shows the structure of the one-way ANOVA table.

While in the one-way ANOVA case, the table seems simplistic and may not be clear why we would use this format; in the multiway ANOVA case, organization is paramount for both calculations and the ability to find the test one is looking for.

Extensions

One of the key advantages to the ANOVA approach is that it can be extended to more than a single treatment factor. The technique can be developed for two or more treatment factors where the individual treatments can be tested as well as the interactions between the treatments. For this work, only the two-way table will be presented with its corresponding formulae. Note that it is assumed that all treatments are considered fixed effects meaning that the levels of the treatments were not obtained at random but instead specified by the researcher before the experiment.

In the two-way ANOVA case, there are two treatments, Treatment A and Treatment B, where Treatment A has a treatment levels and Treatment B has b treatment levels. Here, each the treatment combinations are applied to experimental units. Furthermore, we will assume that each treatment

Table 1 Example of One-Way ANOVA Table Structure

Source	df	SS	MS	F	p Value
Treatment	$k-1$	SS_T	$MS_T = SS_T/(k-1)$	$F^* = MS_T/MS_E$	$p(F_{k-1,n-k} > F^*)$
Error	$n-k$	SS_E	$MS_E = SS_E/(n-k)$		
Total	$n-1$	SS_{TO}			

combination is applied to the same number, n, of experimental units. This is a balanced case where the formulae are much easier to write. Let y_{ijk}, denote the value of the kth observation in the ith factor level of Treatment A and the jth factor level of Treatment B. In this notation, the following means will be needed to partition the variation.

The overall mean: $\bar{y}_{...} = \dfrac{1}{abn}\sum\limits_{i=1}^{a}\sum\limits_{j=1}^{b}\sum\limits_{k=1}^{n} y_{ijk}$; the mean of treatment combination consisting of the ith factor level of Treatment A and the jth factor level of

Treatment B: $\bar{y}_{ij.} = \dfrac{1}{n}\sum\limits_{k=1}^{n} y_{ijk}$. There will be $a \times b$ of these; the mean of the ith factor level of Treatment

A: $\bar{y}_{i..} = \dfrac{1}{bn}\sum\limits_{j=1}^{b}\sum\limits_{k=1}^{n} y_{ijk}$. There will be a of these; the mean of the jth factor level of Treatment B:

$\bar{y}_{.j.} = \dfrac{1}{an}\sum\limits_{i=1}^{a}\sum\limits_{k=1}^{n} y_{ijk}$. There will be b of these.

As in the one-way ANOVA setting, the total variation, SS_{TO}, can be partitioned into variation associated with the treatments Treatment A, Treatment B, the interaction between treatments, and error, namely SS_A, SS_B, SS_{AB}, and SS_E, respectively.

$$SS_{TO} = \sum_{i=1}^{a}\sum_{j=1}^{b}\sum_{k=1}^{n}(y_{ijk} - \bar{y}_{...})^2$$

$$= nb\sum_{i=1}^{a}(\bar{y}_{i..} - \bar{y}_{...})^2 + na\sum_{j=1}^{b}(\bar{y}_{.j.} - \bar{y}_{...})^2$$

$$+ n\sum_{i=1}^{a}\sum_{j=1}^{b}(\bar{y}_{ij.} - \bar{y}_{i..} - \bar{y}_{.j.} - \bar{y}_{...})^2$$

$$+ \sum_{i=1}^{a}\sum_{i=1}^{b}\sum_{k=1}^{n}(y_{ijk} - \bar{y}_{ij.})^2$$

$$= SS_A + SS_B + SS_{AB} + SS_E.$$

For simplicity, the algebraic steps have been omitted. From the equations just presented, one can see that the computations for the two-way ANOVA setting are considerably more tedious than the one-way ANOVA setting as many items need to be kept track of.

Table 2 gives the ANOVA table for the two-way ANOVA setting. Notice that three tests are included in the table as given by the three p values on the right side of the table. In the two-way setting, the interaction term is considered first as it gives an indication of whether the two treatments act in conjunction with each other. If the treatments do interact, then the main effects tests do not accurately isolate the effect of the treatments.

Furthermore, ANOVA can be extended to any linear model setting, including linear regression, randomized complete block designs, fractional factorial designs, analysis of covariance, and repeated measures ANOVA. This flexible approach to partitioning the variance to determine which treatment factors may be significant is extremely useful and is readily available in statistical software packages such as SPSS, SAS, STATA, R, Minitab, and JMP. Most statistical software packages will provide the appropriate ANOVA table upon request.

Contrasts and Post Hoc Tests

Although ANOVA is extremely powerful for testing whether differences exist among the means, it does not identify where the differences in the group means are to be found. To determine which group means are different, one could employ either a contrast test or one of many post hoc tests. Contrast tests are specified before any experimentation begins and are used to test specific combinations of group means. Although contrast tests are far more powerful than post hoc tests, many researchers find them difficult to correctly specify the desired contrast test.

Post hoc tests ubiquitously used in research, despite the lack of power compared to contrast tests. There are many post hoc tests on the group means such as Fisher's least significant difference, Bonferroni correction, Tukey's honestly significant difference, Dunnett's test, and many others. These post hoc tests attempt to test a large number of differences between group means and are often called multiple comparison procedures. The fact that they are conducting multiple tests while attempting to control the Type I error rate is where these procedures lose statistical power compared to a predefined contrast test.

Table 2 Structure of a Two-Way ANOVA Table

Source	df	SS	MS	F	p Value
Treatment A	$a-1$	SS_A	$MS_A = SS_A/(a-1)$	$F_A^* = MS_A/MS_E$	$p(F_{a-1,n(a-1)(b-1)} > F_A^*)$
Treatment B	$b-1$	SS_B	$MS_B = SS_B/(b-1)$	$F_B^* = MS_B/MS_E$	$p(F_{b-1,n(a-1)(b-1)} > F_B^*)$
Interaction AB	$(a-1)(b-1)$	SS_{AB}	$MS_{AB} = SS_{AB}/[(a-1)(b-1)]$	$F_{AB}^* = MS_{AB}/MS_E$	$p(F_{(a-1)(b-1),n(a-1)(b-1)} > F_{AB}^*)$
Error	$n(a-1)(b-1)$	SS_E	$MS_E = SS_E/[n(a-1)(b-1)]$		
Total	$n-1$	SS_{TO}			

Assumptions

As with all statistical analyses, some assumptions are necessary and ANOVA is no different. Because ANOVA is a linear model, it has the same assumptions as regression analysis: normality, independence, and constant variance of residuals. Normality can easily be assessed using Q-Q plots and tested via tests such as Kolmogorov–Smirnov, Shapiro–Wilks, and Anderson–Darling. The normality assumption can be relaxed when the study is an experiment where random assignment to treatment group has been utilized. In this case, randomization theory can be used and normality is no longer a needed assumption.

Constant variance can be evaluated using side-by-side box plots of the residuals where each box plot corresponds to the residuals for a particular treatment combination and is tested via Levene's test, Bartlett's test, or Hartley's test. Independence is more difficult to assess and test as one would need to know the structure of the dependence such as temporal dependence or spatial dependence. Typically, the researcher should design the experiment in such a way that independence would be guaranteed by the experimental procedure versus testing for independence during the analysis. In cases where the assumptions are severely violated, the nonparametric alternative Kruskal–Wallis test may be employed which also results in a loss of statistical power.

Edward L. Boone

See also Analysis of Covariance; Bonferroni Procedure; Levene's Homogeneity of Variance Test; Multiple Linear Regression; Simple Linear Regression

Further Readings

Montgomery, D. (2012). *Design and analysis of experiments* (7th ed.). New York, NY: Wiley.

Ott, R. L., & Longnecker, M. (2015). *An introduction to statistical methods and data analysis* (7th ed.). Pacific Grove, CA: Brooks Cole.

Turner, J. R., & Thayer, J. (2001) *Introduction to analysis of variance.* Thousand Oaks, CA: Sage.

ANALYTIC SCORING

Analytic scoring is a method of evaluating student work that requires assigning a separate score for each dimension of a task. Often used with performance assessment tasks, analytic scoring rubrics specify the key dimensions of a task and define student performance relative to a set of criteria across performance levels for each dimension. For example, analytic rubrics used to evaluate student essay writing often include the following dimensions: development of ideas, organization, language use, vocabulary, grammar, spelling, and mechanics.

Analytic rubrics used to evaluate students' social studies reports might include the same dimensions but also dimensions specific to social studies: use of original source material, accuracy of information, quality of source material, and correct citations. The remainder of this entry describes the uses of analytic scoring in education and then looks at the benefits and challenges of this method.

Analytic scoring is used widely in education to evaluate students' performance in various subject areas (such as reading, writing, speaking, mathematics, the sciences, social studies, world languages, physical education, industrial technology, and the arts). It is also used to evaluate students studying for professional careers in various fields (such as engineering, nursing, business, and teaching). Analytic rubrics have been developed and used at all grade levels, including early childhood, elementary, secondary, undergraduate, graduate, and postgraduate.

Analytic scoring is most often used when there is a need to assess how well students perform on individual dimensions of whole product or performance. Teachers, students, and/or evaluators use analytic rubrics to review the product or performance and assign ratings for each dimension, resulting in a set of subscores that can be combined to generate an overall score. Each dimension can be weighted equally or the weights on dimensions can vary, depending on the importance of each dimension to the successful accomplishment of the task. It is important to note that the relative importance of each dimension and the definition of successful performance on each dimension may vary with the specific topic or task. Thus, analytic scoring rubrics need to be customized for each performance task.

In recent years, analytic scoring has also been used to develop automated essay scoring systems. Researchers use human analytic ratings on student writing to develop automated models of the key dimensions of writing and then to test the validity of the automated models.

Benefits

Because analytic scoring identifies the key dimensions of a performance task and defines performance along a developmental continuum for each dimension, it is an approach to evaluating student work that provides an effective mechanism for identifying students' strengths and weaknesses, more so than do alternate methods of scoring, such as holistic scoring. Holistic scoring involves examining multiple dimensions of students' performance and then assigning a single overall score to capture the level of that performance.

Holistic scoring is a very efficient way of identifying students at the upper end of the scale (who excel on most or all dimensions) and those at the lower end of the scale (who struggle on most or all

dimensions). However, for the majority of students who perform variably across dimensions, a single score is not very informative. Instead, the multiple dimension scores on analytic scoring rubrics provide students and teachers with specific information about students' performance that can be used to individualize students' learning plans and to monitor students' progress across time.

Research on the use of analytic scoring rubrics has found that they provide valid judgments of complex competencies and that the analytic domains capture meaningful variation in student performance. In addition, with proper rubric construction and training, experts can be trained to reach a high level of interrater agreement when using analytic scoring rubrics, and the multiple scores that result from using an analytic rubric positively contribute toward test reliability (more so than does a single holistic rating). There is some evidence that rating on multiple traits increases task generalizability, so that fewer performance tasks are needed on an assessment.

Moreover, the use of analytic scoring rubrics has been found to promote learning by (a) making expectations and criteria clear, (b) providing a common language for teachers and students to discuss the subject, (c) facilitating teacher feedback to students, and (d) supporting students' self-assessment. Students report that the feedbacks from analytic scoring rubrics are helpful.

Challenges

Some of the measurement challenges that surround the use of analytic scoring include concerns about whether unique information is provided by analytic scores. The dimensions defined by the rubric are often highly correlated and, thus, do not represent independent information about students' knowledge and/or skills. For example, in the evaluation of students' writing, the overall length of an essay correlates highly with many of the key dimensions of writing (such as the development of ideas, which requires a certain length of writing, and organization of ideas, which cannot be fully employed unless the essay has at least three paragraphs).

A related concern is the halo effect—when raters assign multiple analytic scores to a student performance or product, do they allow the rating of one dimension to influence their rating of the other dimensions? There is evidence to suggest that the analytic rating of student writing may be prone to the halo effect, so that the number of actual independent dimensions may be fewer than the number of dimensions on the rubric. To explore how well analytic scoring rubrics measure competencies across a number of dimensions, researchers recommend the use of factor analysis, which can provide rubric developers with valuable information so that each dimension on the rubric corresponds to one unique competency, enhancing the efficiency and effectiveness of the rubric.

Claudia A. Gentile

See also Holistic Scoring; Inter-Rater Reliability; Performance-Based Assessment; Reliability; Rubrics

Further Readings

Bennett, R. E. (2015, March). The changing nature of educational assessment. *Review of Research in Education, 39*(1), 370–407.

Hammond, L. D., & Adamson, F. (2014). *Beyond the bubble test: How performance assessments support 21st century learning.* San Francisco, CA: Jossey-Bass.

Lai, E. R., Wolfe, E. W., & Vickers, D. (2015, February). Differentiation of illusory and true halo in writing scores. *Educational and Psychological Measurement, 75*, 102–125.

McMillan, J. H. (2012). *SAGE handbook of research on classroom assessment.* Thousand Oaks, CA: Sage.

ANDRAGOGY

The term *andragogy* refers to a set of principles and assumptions about adult learners, the learning environment, and the learning process. Educational research, measurement, and evaluation require a firm understanding of the underlying instructional theories guiding best practices. This entry provides an overview of andragogy including its core assumptions of the learner and learning environment, key outcomes and criticism, and methods of assessment.

Originating from the Greek root *andra* (meaning adult) and *agogus* (meaning to lead), the concept of andragogy can be traced back to Alexander Kapp, a German educator, in the early 1800s; however, it was not until the late 1960s that andragogy was popularized by the work of American educator Malcolm Knowles. Although typically associated with adult learning, andragogy describes *adulthood* as a psychological, rather than a chronological, milestone in which the learner develops a self-concept striving toward independence.

Knowles defined andragogy as the "art and science of helping adults learn" (1980, p. 43). Central to andragogy are six core assumptions that adult learners:

(1) need to know the why, what, and how of the educational experience;

(2) strive toward a self-concept of independence, autonomy, and self-actualization;

(3) have invaluable resources from their previous experiences that can enrich their current educational endeavors;

(4) develop readiness to learn based upon the relevance of the current scenario to their current developmental tasks;

(5) have an orientation to learning that is grounded in real-world scenarios of personal importance; and

(6) are internally motivated by goal attainment and problem resolution.

Furthermore, andragogy outlines four assumptions about the learning environment. These assumptions are as follows:

(1) The teacher is a facilitator of a coconstructed experience of learning focused on self-directedness, autonomy, and self-actualization;

(2) Instructional methods such as experiential exercises, problem- and case-based learning, role-playing, simulations, Socratic questioning, and field experiences help students identify gaps between what they know, what they don't know, and strategies for how to fill in these gaps;

(3) Real-world scenarios are the organizing structure for the learning process; and

(4) Scenarios should be scaffolded according to the desired learning outcomes and current developmental level. Andragogical methods focus on the development of cognitive complexity and self-directed learning skills rather than the simple remembering of facts.

The evaluation of student learning outcomes when using instructional methods grounded in andragogy can be evaluated objectively through methods such as multiple choice exams but are best assessed using multiple strategies including portfolios, case presentations, role-playing, and clinical scenario exams. Andragogical methods are especially effective in increasing learners' situational interest, cognitive complexity, clinical reasoning, lifelong learning skills, satisfaction, long-term retention, performance on free-recall tasks, performance on short answer and essay tests, ratings by supervisors on clinical observations, and performance on clinical or case-based portions of exams. Andragogical methods may be less effective when the short-term recognition of facts and concepts is needed for multiple-choice and true–false portions of exams.

Eric T. Beeson

See also Instructional Theory; Learning Theories; Long-Term Memory; Portfolio Assessment; Self-Directed Learning; Short-Term Memory

Further Readings

Bolton, F. C. (2006). Rubrics and adult learners: Andragogy and assessment. *Assessment Update, 18*(3), 5–6.

Harden, R. M., & Davis, M. H. (1998). The continuum of problem-based learning. *Medical Teacher, 20*(4), 317–322.

Knowles, M. S. (1980). *The modern practice of adult education: From pedagogy to andragogy* (revised and updated). Englewood Cliffs, NJ: Cambridge Adult Education.

Knowles, M. S., Holton III, E. F., & Swanson, R. A. (2005). *Adult learner: The definitive classic in adult education and human resources development* (6th ed.). Burlington, MA: Elsevier.

St. Clair, R. (2002). *Andragogy revisited: Theory for the 21st century?* Retrieved from ERIC database. (ED468612)

Strobel, J., & van Barneveld, A. (2009). When is PBL more effective? A meta-synthesis of meta-analyses comparing PBL to conventional classrooms. *Interdisciplinary Journal of Problem-Based Learning, 3*(1). Retrieved from http://dx.doi.org/10.7771/1541-5015.1046

Taylor, B., & Kroth, M. (2009). Andragogy's transition into the future: Meta-analysis of andragogy and its search for a measurable instrument. *Journal of Adult Education, 38*(1), 1–11.

ANGOFF METHOD

This entry describes the Angoff method for setting standards on educational tests and how it can be used to set valid standards on educational tests. *Standard setting* refers to the process used to establish cut scores on educational tests that are used to classify test takers into categories such as "pass," "fail," "proficient," "advanced," and other categories generally referred to as achievement levels. Many educational tests, such as licensure tests professionals are required to pass to become licensed and high school graduation tests that students must pass to receive a high school diploma, require these standards.

Most people in modern society have taken tests based on which the standards are set. However, it is not widely known as to *how* those standards were set. The most popular method is the Angoff method and its variations.

In 1971, William Angoff wrote a seminal chapter called "Scales, Norms, and Equivalent Scores" in a book on educational measurement. In the chapter, he described how test developers transform students' responses to test items into standardized scores and how they maintain equivalence of these score scales over time.

In describing how to incorporate meaning into the score scale by setting "pass/fail" standards on the scale, Angoff described a method suggested by his colleague Ledyard Tucker. This process involved having subject matter experts (SMEs) think about the "minimally competent" test taker; that is, the test taker who "just barely" has the sufficient knowledge and skills required to pass the exam (sometimes referred to as the "borderline" candidate). The task for the SMEs was to review each test item and judge whether the minimally competent test taker would answer the item correctly. The passing score suggested by each SME is calculated by simply summing the number of items the SME predicted would be correctly answered by the minimally competent candidate and then averaging that score across the SMEs.

Angoff added a footnote to his description of Tucker's "yes/no" method and suggested instead of judging whether the minimally competent test taker would or would not correctly answer the item, the SMEs could estimate the *probability* the minimally competent test taker would correctly answer the item. Those probability ratings could then be summed, and averaged over SMEs, to derive the passing standard. The process he suggested in that footnote became known as the Angoff method and quickly became the most popular method for setting standards on educational tests.

Like all test-centered standard-setting methods (i.e., methods where SMEs review and rate test items), the Angoff method involves several steps. These steps include (a) discussing the knowledge and skills of the minimally competent test taker, (b) reviewing the test items, (c) providing a probability rating for each item, (d) discussing all or a subset of those ratings, and (e) revising the original ratings as the SMEs regard necessary. The final cut score is based on the revised ratings in Step (e).

As a simple illustration of the Angoff method, imagine a test with 100 items. If an SME reviewed each item and estimated the minimally competent test taker would have a 0.50 probability of answering each item correctly, the SME-suggested passing score would be 50 (i.e., 0.50×100 items). Of course, no SME would assign the same probability value to all items because items vary in their difficulty. Thus, our example is oversimplified to illustrate how the cut score is calculated for a single SME. The final cut score would be averaged over all SMEs.

The process described thus far refers to items that are scored dichotomously, which means 1 point for a correct answer and 0 for an incorrect answer. However, many educational tests use items that are scored on longer scales (e.g., an essay worth 6 points). Also, many educational tests, such as the National Assessment of Educational Progress in the United States, have more than two pass/fail standards. For these and other reasons, there have been many "modifications" of the Angoff method.

Modifications of the Angoff Method

Modified versions of the Angoff method have been introduced and widely used to (a) set standards on tests with polytomously scored items, (b) set standards on tests involving more than two standards (e.g., classifying students into categories such as "basic, "proficient," and "advanced"), and (c) increase the agreement among SMEs. The term *modified* indicates the original method has been altered for a specific application. In an extensive chapter on standard setting, Ronald Hambleton and Mary Pitoniak hypothesized there may be more than 100 variations of the Angoff method. The "traditional" Angoff method comprises five steps:

(1) train the SMEs on the process,

(2) facilitate a discussion of the minimally qualified (borderline) test taker,

(3) collect the first round of ratings of SMEs,

(4) SMEs discuss first round ratings, and

(5) SMEs revise their ratings based on the discussions.

In the case of polytomously scored items, rather than making a probability rating for each item, SMEs estimate the mean score they expect the borderline test taker to achieve on each item. For tests that involve more than two standards, modifications include having the SMEs make separate judgments for each item for each standard. To increase agreement among the SMEs, additional rounds of discussion are used.

A related modification is to give the SMEs statistics describing the difficulty levels of the items after they make their initial ratings. These statistics are thought to provide a "reality check" for the SMEs. For example, if an SME thought borderline candidates had a high probability of answering an item, but the item statistics suggested very few examinees answered the item correctly, the SME may take a deeper look at the item to understand why and possibly revise the rating.

Providing item statistics to SMEs is somewhat controversial. The Angoff method is intended to produce a content-based (criterion-referenced) standard, which is why SMEs who are familiar with the content being tested and the students being assessed are selected as judges. By relying on empirical information from test takers, the standard may become norm referenced. Studies have found that SMEs have a difficult time setting appropriate standards without empirical data, but critics counter item statistics can overly influence SMEs, leading to standards that are driven by item difficulty, rather than by SME judgment regarding what constitutes appropriate achievement.

Research has shown SMEs tend to make more inaccurate predictions of borderline test takers' performance on relatively easy or difficult items, when they are not provided empirical data in the form of item statistics. Some researchers point to this as an inherent problem in the Angoff method that reduces its utility as a standard-setting procedure.

Another modification of the Angoff method, and one that is not contentious, is facilitating several rounds of discussion among the SMEs. Such discussion allows SMEs to consider different viewpoints about what makes an item difficult and how the knowledge and skills of borderline test takers are exhibited in performance on an exam. Many studies have shown these discussions reduce variance (increase consensus) among SMEs. In fact, agreement among the SMEs is one of the criteria based on which standard-setting studies are evaluated. However, the type of feedback provided, and when it is provided, can impact how SMEs modify their ratings across rounds.

Evaluating and Validating Angoff Standard-Setting Studies

The validity of a standard-setting study is typically evaluated using procedural, internal, and external validity evidence. Procedural evidence refers to the quality of the standard-setting study, starting with recruiting qualified panelists and training them well, and proper execution of the study. Internal evidence focuses on the consistency of results, ideally estimating the variability in the standards set, if the study were replicated.

External evidence refers to the degree to which the classifications of examinees are consistent with other performance data. Examples of external validity evidence include classification consistency across different standard-setting methods, tests of mean differences across examinees classified in different achievement levels on other construct-relevant variables, and the degree to which external ratings of test takers' performance

are consistent with their test-based achievement-level classifications.

There are several actions standard setters can do to build validity into a standard-setting study, as opposed to evaluating the validity of the standard after it is set. One important consideration is the number and quality of the SMEs. Research suggests at least 10 SMEs be used but more is better to reduce the standard error of the (mean) cut score. Equally as important, if not more important, than the number of SMEs are their qualifications and representativeness. SMEs should be fully proficient in the knowledge and skill areas measured on the test, and they should represent the relevant population (e.g., students, teachers, licensed professionals) with respect to subdiscipline areas of expertise and demographic factors.

Another important consideration is the quality of the training. SMEs should be required to take at least some test items, without the answer keys, to get an appreciation of the difficulty of the exam. They should also practice rating items and discuss the items to make sure they are on task and they understand the notion of the minimally competent test taker.

After gathering initial Angoff ratings, validity can be built into the process by having SMEs discuss and review their ratings. These discussions often illuminate item features SMEs may have missed when initially rating the items and will correct any coding errors or other errors they may have made. Finally, surveys of SMEs during and at the conclusion of the study can help evaluate how well they understood their tasks and the factors they used in making their judgments.

The Influence of the Angoff Method

The Angoff method is not the only method for setting standards on educational tests, but it is often the method to which others are compared. The legacy of the Angoff method is that it illustrated how standards can be set on educational tests by aligning the standard to experts' judgments of what is considered to be "above standard" performance. Rather than awarding passing scores and other achievement levels based on how well test takers perform relative to one another, the Angoff method sets an "absolute" standard that all test takers can achieve.

By successfully implementing the Angoff method, standard setters can have confidence the standards they set will be valid. However, successful implementation of the method requires competent and representative SMEs who are carefully trained, who understand their tasks and the "minimally competent" test takers, and who can provide reliable and valid ratings. Surveys of SMEs, and comparing test takers' achievement-level classifications to their performance on other measures of their knowledge and skills, can help evaluate the quality of the results from an Angoff standard-setting study.

Stephen G. Sireci and Alejandra Garcia

See also Body of Work Method; Bookmark Method; Cut Scores; Ebel Method; Modified Angoff Method; National Assessment of Educational Progress; Standard Setting

Further Readings

American Educational Research Association, American Psychological Association, & National Council on Measurement in Education. (2014). *Standards for educational and psychological tests*. Washington, DC: American Educational Research Association.

Angoff, W. H. (1971). Scales, norms, and equivalent scores. In R. L. Thorndike (Ed.), *Educational measurement* (2nd ed.) (pp. 508–600). Washington, DC: American Council on Education.

Clauser, B. E., Mee, J., & Margolis, M. J. (2013). The effect of data format on integration of performance data into Angoff judgments. *International Journal of Testing, 13*, 65–85.

Hambleton, R. K., & Pitoniak, M. J. (2006). Setting performance standards. In R. L. Brennan (Ed.), *Educational measurement* (4th ed.). Westport, CT: American Council on Education/Praeger.

Kane, M. (1994). Validating the performance standards associated with passing scores. *Review of Educational Research, 64*, 425–461.

Raymond, M. R., & Reid, J. B. (2001). Who made thee a judge? Selecting and training participants for standard setting. In G. C. Cizek (Ed.), *Setting performance standards: Concepts, methods, and perspectives* (pp. 119–157). Mahwah, NJ: Erlbaum.

Sireci, S. G., Hauger, J. B, Wells, C. S., Shea, C., & Zenisky, A. L. (2009). Evaluation of the standard setting on the 2005 grade 12 National Assessment of Educational Progress mathematics test. *Applied Measurement in Education, 22*, 339–358.

ANXIETY

The two distinguishing hallmarks of anxiety disorders are an emotional state of fear and worry that result in diminished functioning. Fearfulness may be based on an actual experience or fostered by cognitive distortions that result in the misperception of a threat. Consequently, a physiological response occurs that ranges from disconcerting to debilitating and may result in aggressive or avoidant behaviors to escape the distress. The worry associated with anxiety creates a persistent state of angst or apprehension that is sustained over time. Without treatment, anxiety can negatively impact personal well-being, academic achievement, employment, and lifelong accomplishments. This entry discusses types of anxiety disorders as well as measurement options.

Anxiety Diagnosis

The *Diagnostic and Statistical Manual of Mental Disorders, Fifth Edition* delineates 11 disorders in the anxiety domain. All of the disorders share common features of fear and worry; however, they differ by the circumstance that triggers the anxiety, the type of response when anxious, and the thought distortions that maintain the anxiety.

Anxiety Onset in Early Childhood

Although there is variability in age of onset, two of these disorders are most likely to first occur during early childhood: separation anxiety disorder and selective mutism. The distinguishing feature for separation anxiety disorder is anxiety related to separation from individuals one has formed a deep emotional bond with (e.g., a parent). Symptoms may include fear about losing the primary caregiver or fear that grievous harm will occur to the caregiver. The resulting behaviors may include refusing to leave a caregiver, extreme distress when leaving home, and psychosomatic complaints. These behaviors can result in school absenteeism as well as a high incidence of school nurse visits for perceived physical complaints, thus missed instruction time and lower achievement.

Selective mutism has a pattern of only speaking in select social circumstances that are familiar and comfortable (e.g., at home) and only with certain individuals (e.g., parents, siblings). Children with selective mutism often avoid speaking at school, to teachers, and even to classmates. This behavior can result in limiting social skills development and also prohibit accurate classroom monitoring and assessment of skills.

Anxiety Onset in School-Age Children

Specific phobia and social phobia are anxiety disorders that most often occur among school-age children (i.e., those aged 7–15). Specific phobia involves a manifest significant fear of particular objects or circumstances, such as dogs, spiders, frogs, or high places (e.g., balconies). The level of fear accompanying exposure to the specific phobia may result in avoidant behaviors or hinder the individual from participating in activities. For example, a child afraid of heights may refuse to access a stairwell or elevator, thus mobility is compromised. For an adolescent with a fear of animals' participation in required science labs may be problematic.

A social phobia is characterized by fearfulness of social settings wherein individuals may be observed by others and there is a perception that they will be negatively evaluated by others. This apprehension results in significant discomfort and sometimes avoidance of the social interaction. Individuals with social phobia may avoid meeting new people or even quit talking in groups, which can narrow their social networks. The effects of social phobia can be particularly devastating when purposeful evaluation is expected (e.g., a student class presentation assignment).

Anxiety Onset in Early Adulthood

Panic disorder, agoraphobia, and generalized anxiety disorder diagnoses are most likely to be made during early adulthood (i.e., aged 20–35). Panic disorder involves unexplained and very sudden (i.e., within minutes), overwhelming fear arousal. A number of possible intense physiological reactions are present (e.g., racing heart rate, profuse sweating) and may give the individual an unwarranted sense of high alert or impending doom. Repeated panic episodes can result in individuals significantly restricting their own social opportunities and educational or career aspirations out of fear of inducing a panic attack.

Agoraphobia is characterized by significant fear of being trapped or unable to escape specific situations (e.g., confined space, bus). Individuals with agoraphobia may avoid public places and transportation, resulting in self-seclusion. Generalized anxiety disorder is characterized by broader multiple fears sometimes including aspects of daily life (e.g., work). Generalized anxiety disorder can result in disturbed sleep, tense muscles, and irritability and may lower overall quality of life.

Other Anxiety Disorders

The last four diagnoses do not have a dominant age of onset. Substance/medication-induced anxiety disorder occurs as a result of substance use or withdrawal. The particular anxiety symptoms and intensity will vary based on the type of substance (e.g., alcohol, cocaine) that has induced the effects. Anxiety disorder due to another medical condition is diagnosed when anxiety symptoms are present; however, they are better understood as a result of a medical condition (e.g., seizure disorder). Other specified anxiety disorder and unspecified anxiety disorder diagnoses are warranted when anxiety symptoms are present but not pervasive enough to meet the full criteria of another anxiety disorder. Additionally, several other mental health disorders outside of the *Diagnostic and Statistical Manual of Mental Disorders, Fifth Edition* anxiety disorders domain (e.g., obsessive-compulsive disorders) have anxiety-related symptomology.

Measurement for Anxiety

Measurement of anxiety symptoms is often accomplished through norm-referenced anxiety rating scales completed by teachers, parents, or self-report. These measures offer an objective comparison of frequency and intensity of specific symptoms. Interview methods also are helpful in identifying temporal sequence of symptom onset, specific triggers for anxiety, and thought patterns that may perpetuate worry. Observations afford the opportunity to understand anxiousness within a context and measure demonstrated behaviors.

Clinicians also may measure small changes in anxious feelings during counseling sessions through a self-reported Subjective Units of Distress Scale, a number scale created in collaboration with the patient that denotes level of stress. Additionally, the *Diagnostic and Statistical Manual of Mental Disorders, Fifth Edition* offers online symptom measures through the publisher's website. Together, these measures can inform treatment options and progression of symptoms.

Diana Joyce-Beaulieu

See also Asperger's Syndrome; Autism Spectrum Disorder; *Diagnostic and Statistical Manual of Mental Disorders*

Further Readings

American Psychiatric Association. (2013). *Diagnostic and statistical manual of mental disorders* (5th ed.). Arlington, VA: American Psychiatric Publishing.

Mash, E. J., & Barkley, R. A. (2014). *Child Psychopathology* (3rd ed.). New York, NY: Guilford Press.

Sattler, J. M. (2014). *Foundations of behavioral, social, and clinical assessment of children* (6th ed.). La Mesa, CA: Author.

APA

See American Psychological Association

APA FORMAT

The publication manual of the American Psychological Association (APA) sets the standard for writing in psychology and has also become the standard for writing in many other behavioral and social sciences disciplines such as education, nursing, and business. The sixth edition of the manual was published in 2009.

The guidelines set forth in the APA manual address how to communicate complex scientific writing, including writing style and the mechanics for formatting a paper. Writing in APA format involves two different tasks. The first of these is style, or the quality of the prose, and the second is the mechanics that includes requirements such as margin size, section headings, and how to give proper credit to others. This entry discusses APA guidelines for style and mechanics and lists other types of resources that can be used to understand APA format and other aspects of academic writing.

APA Writing Style: Writing Well

This entry gives only brief information about writing style, as there are many resources about how to improve writing style. Further, Chapters 3 and 4 of the APA manual detail how to write clearly (e.g., avoiding bias in language and writing in the active voice) as well as the expectations of grammar in scientific writing (e.g., using punctuation in text). Every manuscript is, of course, unique. However, in academic writing, certain conventions and elements are generally expected; these include that the manuscript has a thesis, that it be unified and coherent, and that it follow rules of grammar.

Thesis

A thesis, which is sometimes called a research question (though it is not written as a question but rather a statement) in an empirical paper, is the driving force behind any paper. A thesis, in general, is a clear statement of the paper's purpose. The thesis may be written in a way where it is implicit or explicit, but making a thesis explicit can help the author in writing the manuscript by creating a guide to what should be included.

Unity and Coherence

Once a paper has a clear thesis, the next step in writing is to make sure that the paper hangs together. Like any other paper, a manuscript written in APA format must have unity and coherence, which allows readers to remain focused on the relevant topic. Unity is when a paper logically flows from topic to topic throughout the manuscript, and each paragraph only contains a core idea. Specifically, the paper is united across all topics and each is linked to the thesis.

Coherence is when the ideas within a paragraph are presented in a rational order, and each is necessary in supporting the single idea presented in that paragraph. Thus, a paragraph should start with a topic sentence (that links to the thesis), include evidence supporting the topic, and then end with a concluding sentence that leads into the next paragraph. Papers include unity and coherence flow from the thesis to the conclusion, and this improves writing style and readability.

Grammar

Chapters 3 and 4 of the APA manual, as well as many other writing guides such as William Strunk Jr. and E. B. White's *The Elements of Style*, detail the requirements and expectations of proper grammar and writing with the style expected for scientific papers. Some of the concepts in Chapter 3 include organization, clarity, removing bias from language, and smoothness of expression. Chapter 3 ends with grammar and usage recommendations for scientific writing, such as avoiding the passive voice.

Chapter 4 of the APA manual is titled "The Mechanics of Style" and refers to "the rules or guidelines a publisher observes to ensure clear, consistent presentation in scholarly articles" (p. 87). This chapter describes many of the basic tools for writing, including punctuation marks and how to present statistics.

APA Format Mechanics

The mechanics of APA format are designed to improve the format, flow, and readability of review and empirical papers and to put those ideas into a format that a publisher may use for subsequent publication as necessary. These mechanics are somewhat different for empirical papers (those reporting findings of original research) and nonempirical papers. According to the APA manual, nonempirical work includes papers such as literature reviews, theoretical papers, and case studies.

There is little guidance in the APA manual regarding the overall flow of nonempirical papers. This is not surprising because the variety of topics

for nonempirical paper can vary considerably. On the other hand, a considerable proportion of the APA manual is devoted to writing empirical papers, where there are more consistent expectations for the order of the material presented (see Chapter 2 of the APA manual).

Empirical manuscripts, regardless of the content and audience, are for the most part designed to answer, in order, the following five questions:

(1) What did this project do? (Introduction)

(2) Why did this project do this? (Introduction)

(3) How did this project do this?

(4) What did this project find?

(5) What does it all mean?

Introduction

The first part of the introduction of an empirical paper typically answers the question *what did this project do?* The second, and often much more lengthy, part of the introduction section answers the question *why did this project do this?* To accomplish this, an introduction typically includes the following information: A brief summary that frames the project and explains why it is important, the thesis, a review of the past literature that has examined this issue, a logical explanation that explains the specific goals of the current project (usually also embedded in the relevant literature). Finally, a good place to end an introduction is with a brief paragraph that provides an overview of the method used to conduct the empirical study.

Method

Although there is some variability about the subsections that comprise a method section, the main point of the section is to explain the research process in enough detail so that another researcher may replicate the project. Thus, this section answers the question *how did this project do this?* The first part of this section should describe the design. This gives the readers a framework for understanding the remainder of the method section. After the design statement, the method section usually describes the sample for the project. The third part of the method section typically describes the materials (usually referring to things such as paper-and-pencil or online questionnaires) and/or apparatus (usually referring to physical materials, such as the type of computer and monitor). Finally, many studies end the method section with a description of the procedure, which is a step-by-step description of how the study occurred.

Results

The results section answers the question *what did this project find?* The purpose of this section is to explain just the facts with little to no interpretation. The goal for the results section is to explain the findings, including the descriptive information (e.g., themes if qualitative, or means if quantitative) as well as any relevant inferential statistics. Chapter 5 of the APA manual provides considerable detail about how to report numbers and statistics, including examples of tables and figures.

Discussion

The discussion section of a manuscript is where a researcher moves from the specific work in the study to some ideas to go beyond that study and answers the question *what does it all mean?* As in the introduction, the content in the discussion section varies from manuscript to manuscript. A discussion section can begin with a brief summary of what happened in the project (basically in one to three paragraphs restating what was stated in the results section). In short papers, this may seem redundant. Many papers, however, have multiple hypotheses and a short summary can help a reader better understand the disparate findings.

Next, the author should link the findings to past research. If the results, for the most part, support the hypotheses, this part of a manuscript may be a brief reiteration of the introduction. Most research, however, has at least some findings that are unexpected. In these cases, writing the discussion is often a more difficult process because it needs to explain why the findings occurred and, as in the introduction, ground that information in the past literature. This time, however, the explanations need to be based on new logic and literature. In this case, there are usually two major categories of explanations. The first category is methodological: That something about the method

turned out to be a poor test of the theories and ideas (e.g., the sample was inappropriate or too small). The second category is theoretical: The ideas captured in the introduction were not properly derived. A well-written discussion where some of the predictions are not supported should include information that covers both categories.

After explaining the results and linking them to past research, a discussion section should move beyond the findings. This can occur by recommending future research (to respond to methodological limitations and/or extend theory) as well as the real-life implications of the findings. An empirical manuscript then ends with a conclusion that ties the findings back to the initial thesis and, as in the beginning of the introduction, take the reader back to the overall importance of the findings.

Giving Credit

According to the APA manual (2009), "scientific knowledge represents the accomplishments of many researchers over time. A critical part of the writing process is helping readers place your contribution in context by citing the researchers who influenced you" (p. 169). There are two parts to giving credit: in-text citations and references. The in-text citations indicate where in a manuscript an author has discussed past work. A reference section appears toward the end of an manuscript written in APA style and lists the papers cited in the text; only the papers that are cited in the text should appear in the references (hence, the reference section is not a bibliography or listing of all resources). Chapter 6 of the APA manual discusses how to format in-text citations. In addition, the APA created an online source called APA Style that can help authors with formatting citations and references from Internet sources. Chapter 7 of the APA manual discusses how to format the reference section.

APA Format and Writing Resources

This entry provides a very brief explanation of APA format. There are many other resources to help authors, including, of course, the APA manual itself. Many templates, or sample papers, can be found online. These provide a detailed visual guide that an author can use in formatting a manuscript.

Some of the most popular templates and checklists are listed in the Further Readings section of this entry, along with summaries of the APA manual and other guides to academic writing.

Timothy Franz

See also Abstracts; American Psychological Association; Journal Articles; Literature Review; Methods Section; Results Section

Further Readings

American Psychological Association. (2016). *Sample one-experiment paper*. Retrieved June 26, 2016, from http://www.apastyle.org/manual/related/sample -experiment-paper-1.pdf

American Psychological Association. (2009). *Concise rules of APA style*. Washington, DC: Author.

American Psychological Association. (2009). *Publication manual of the American Psychological Association* (6th ed.). Washington, DC: Author.

Ashford University. (2013). *APA essay checklist for students*. Retrieved June 26, 2016, from https://awc .ashford.edu/cd-apa-checklist.html

Darley, J. M., Zanna, M. P., & Roediger III, H. L. (2004). *The compleat academic: A career guide* (2nd ed.). Washington, DC: American Psychological Association.

Hairston, M., Ruszkiewicz, J., & Friend, C. (2002). *The Scott, Foresman handbook for writers* (6th ed., pp. 791, 795, 801). New York, NY: Longman. Retrieved June 26, 2016, from https://www.slu.edu/Documents/ student_development/student_success_center/APA_ Format_Checklist_Handout.pdf

Houghton, P. M., & Houghton, T. J. (2009). *APA the easy way: A quick and simplified guide to the APA writing style* (2nd ed.). Ann Arbor, MI: XanEdu Publishing.

Off Campus Library Services, Indiana Wesleyan University. (2013). *APA style checklist*. Retrieved June 26, 2016, from http://www2.indwes.edu/apa/ apastylechecklist.pdf

Office of Research and Public Service, The University of Tennessee, Knoxville. (n.d.). *APA 6.0 templates for Microsoft Word*. Retrieved July 1, 2016, from https:// www.sworps.tennessee.edu/training/APA_6_0/ resources/apa_doc_templates.html

Purdue University Online Writing Lab. (n.d.). *Microsoft Word: Sample APA document*. Retrieved June 26, 2016, from https://owl.english.purdue.edu/media/ pdf/20090212013008_560.pdf

Rossiter, J. (2010). *The APA pocket handbook: Rules for format & documentation*. Port St. Lucie, FL: DW Publishing.

Schwartz, B. M., Landrum, R. E., & Gurung, R. A. R. (2016). *An easy guide to APA style* (3rd ed.). Thousand Oaks, CA: Sage.

Silva, P. (2007). *How to write a lot: A practical guide to productive academic writing*. Washington, DC: American Psychological Association.

Strunk, W., & White, E. B. (1999). *The elements of style* (4th ed.). Boston, MA: Allyn & Bacon.

Sword, H. (2012). *Stylish academic writing*. Cambridge, MA: Harvard University Press.

Websites

APA Style: www.apastyle.org

APPLIED BEHAVIOR ANALYSIS

Applied behavior analysis is a growing profession devoted to the application of basic learning principles to socially significant behavior occurring in many natural environments, including the home, school, workplace, and other public venues. Founded on well-documented learning processes, such as respondent and operant learning, applied behavior analysis involves direct observation and recording of relevant target behaviors, systematic and continuous data collection, and implementation of interventions designed to address behavioral deficiencies or excesses.

Behaviors targeted for intervention with applied behavior analysis are of practical, not theoretical, concern, and are usually identified by pertinent stakeholders, their teachers, parents, siblings, peers, coworkers, or the clients themselves. Applied behavior analysis has a significant track record of evidence-based treatments, especially in the domain of developmental disabilities. This entry discusses the history and development of applied behavior analysis, its major features, and areas where it is increasingly being used.

History and Development of Applied Behavior Analysis

Applied behavior analysis emerged in the 1960s as an extension of the laboratory science of behavior founded by B. F. Skinner in the late 1930s. Skinner's research on operant conditioning, which he termed the experimental analysis of behavior, identified foundational principles of learning, including reinforcement, extinction, punishment, and stimulus control (generalization and discrimination). Although primarily responsible for the development of the basic science, Skinner himself saw clear implications of operant principles for behavior in the real-world settings and, in the late 1950s, embarked on a program of research aimed at identifying more effective instructional tactics for professional educators. Being an amateur engineer, Skinner fashioned early teaching machines capable of systematically programming instructional contingencies to enhance student mastery of academic concepts. Skinner's laboratory analysis of behavior had revealed that any behavior could be conceptualized within the context of a three-term contingency, consisting of antecedent environmental events, the behavior of interest, and consequences that follow behavior.

In instructional design, academic materials, such as short written text or questions, served as antecedents, an active and objective response from the student served as behavior, and feedback regarding the accuracy of the student's response served as consequential stimulation. Using standardized programs, Skinner was able to show that students were able to efficiently master a number of academic skills, including math and science, rapidly and fluently as a result of the frequent active responding and immediate feedback characterizing such programmed instruction.

By the 1970s, considerable research had been conducted on programmed instruction and other behaviorally based instructional methods, including Fred Keller's personalized system of instruction. Meta-analyses of these research programs showed the instructional methods to be far more effective than traditional instructional methods, especially those dominated by instructor lectures. In fact, Project Follow Through, the largest educational experiment ever conducted, begun in 1967 as a part of President Johnson's War on Poverty, amassed strong evidence of the effectiveness of behaviorally oriented instruction. When pitted against nearly a dozen alternative educational tactics, methods of behavioral instruction developed at the University of Oregon and the University of Kansas produced substantially larger student gains in both basic academic skill development and affective measures, such as self-concept.

By the late 1960s, applications of basic learning principles to various target behaviors and settings had grown sufficiently to justify a specialized journal, and in 1968, the inaugural volume of *Journal of Applied Behavior Analysis* was published. To this day, *Journal of Applied Behavior Analysis* remains the preeminent outlet for research in the field. By the 1970s, applications of behavioral principles had become common, especially in the areas of developmental disabilities and autism.

Autism, characterized by severe deficiencies in language and social behavior and excessive stereotypic behavior and self-injury, had historically proven unresponsive to efforts at traditional therapy, and many individuals with this diagnosis lived most of their lives in institutions. During the late 1960s and early 1970s, however, behavioral psychologist O. Ivar Lovaas developed systematic programs for addressing both the behavioral deficits and excesses of children with autism, providing the first evidence that behavioral interventions could effectively enhance the independence and autonomy of such clients. In the ensuing decades, a significant database emerged replicating Lovaas's work and establishing applied behavior analysis as the only evidence-based treatment for autism, as acknowledged by both the surgeon general of the United States and the health and education departments in states including California, Maine, and New York.

Training in applied behavior analysis now occurs at hundreds of colleges and universities worldwide, and practicing behavior analysts must hold either a bachelor's or master's degree, have taken significant coursework, have practical experience at the undergraduate and/or graduate level, and possess certification from the Behavior Analyst Certification Board, founded in 1998. Demand for trained behavior analysts increased in response to an increased prevalence of autism diagnoses during the first decade of the 21st century.

Major Features of Applied Behavior Analysis

Regardless of the specific client, setting, or behavior being addressed, behavior analysts conceptualize and implement assessment and intervention protocols consistent with certain basic principles. Donald M. Baer, Montrose M. Wolf, and Todd R. Risley articulated the principal dimensions of applied behavior analysis in 1968, and they remain central attributes of the profession today: *applied, behavioral, analytic, technological, conceptual, effective,* and *generalizable.*

Applied

Although informed by the empirical data generated by a basic science of behavior, applied behavior analysts develop and deliver interventions for socially significant behavior occurring in natural settings. The range of behaviors to which basic principles have been applied, and the circumstances under which interventions have been delivered, is truly remarkable, running the gamut of human behavior. A very brief list of such applications would include the following:

Teaching academic skills to both normally developing and developmentally delayed students.

Reducing stereotypic and self-injurious behavior in individuals on the autism spectrum.

Teaching both verbal and nonverbal communication skills to noncommunicative clients.

Enhancing physical exercise or medical compliance in medical patients.

Teaching basic self-care skills (e.g., dressing, cooking, and cleaning) to developmentally disabled clients.

Teaching fire and gun safety to children.

Teaching children to respond effectively and assertively to potential abductors.

Teaching basic job skills, including interviewing, eye contact, and conversational skills.

Improving peer, sibling, and/or coworker interaction skills.

Teaching effective use of contemporary technology, such as tablets, computers, household appliances, and entertainment technology.

Behavioral

Applied behavior analysis primarily targets behavior that can be readily observed and measured, as opposed to such private activity as thinking, imagining, perceiving, and so on. Although

these "private events" can be conceptualized as behavior, actions that directly operate on the environment are both easier to observe systematically and more likely to have real-world, pragmatic value for the client. It is possible to devise observational and measurement tactics, for instance, for all of the behaviors that are part of the applications listed earlier, all of which can take on considerable social significance for the client. Direct measurement of behavior contributes importantly to the scientific status of applied behavior analysis and makes drawing inferences about intervention effectiveness more tenable.

Analytic

Behavior analysts deliver clearly articulated interventions to alter client behavior while simultaneously measuring target behavior in a continuous manner. By collecting data in real time, the behavior analyst is capable of identifying changes in behavior that are functionally related to the intervention. In order to establish that behavior change occurred in response to the treatment, and not some other variable, behavior analysts build multiple replications into treatment protocols, collecting relevant data systematically under all conditions. Replications can be carried out with the same client, sometimes across different settings or behaviors, and can also be carried out across multiple clients in order to establish the reliability of the functional relationship between interventions and behavior change.

Technological

In addition to collecting data systematically during behavioral interventions, behavior analysts describe their intervention tactics in clear and concise language and in a manner that could be readily carried out by others if necessary. Although many behavioral interventions are not carried out as part of a formal research process, behavior analysts do collect data throughout clinical protocols because making decisions about changes in treatment or about treatment effectiveness in the absence of supporting data is considered unethical. Because the actual behavior plans being implemented are described in significant detail, they can be replicated readily by other clinicians or researchers. This practice is characteristic of many mature sciences, especially those that have spawned applied technologies.

Conceptual

The interventions implemented by applied behavior analysts are not designed idiosyncratically by the individual clinician nor are they reflective of a commitment to an eclectic or generic behavioral science perspective. Instead, they are informed by a consistent dependence on the conceptual moorings of the basic science, the experimental analysis of behavior. This science, begun in the late 1930s, produced a cumulative database attesting to the role played by fundamental principles of behavior in natural settings. Such processes as reinforcement, punishment, extinction, generalization, and discrimination are known to underlie almost all adaptive behavior, both human and nonhuman. These foundational concepts subsequently define the parameters of the treatment plans developed and implemented by practicing behavior analysts.

Effective

As described in previous sections, ongoing data collection and analysis assist professional behavior analysts in determining whether interventions have produced effective outcomes for clients. In addition, behavior analysts purposefully seek out the opinions of important stakeholders, such as parents, siblings, peers, or coworkers, in evaluating client progress. The process of asking those who know the client best to offer feedback regarding the success of the behavior program is called social validation. This practice is important because these significant others will likely be substantial sources of reinforcement for the client, and reciprocal interactions between them and the client will have repercussions for the client's long-term behavior change.

Generalizable

It has long been known that the effects of therapeutic interventions delivered in highly specialized environments, for instance schools or hospitals, often fail to transfer outside the treatment environment. Behavior analysts are especially adept at

ensuring that such failures are minimized, as their professional skills include a working knowledge of tactics for enhancing stimulus control, including client generalization of learned skills across varying settings. Indeed, a behavioral intervention is not considered successful unless changes in client behavior have been formally assessed in a multitude of environments in which the behavior is likely to be important. Behavior analysts usually build into an intervention-specific tactics for ensuring generalization of client functioning in such environments.

Contemporary and Future Directions

Applied behavior analysis, initially incubated within the parent discipline of psychology, eventually emerged as a distinct profession. As is true of any relatively new profession, applied behavior analysis suffered early growing pains. National certification for professionals did not emerge until 2000, and although the Behavior Analyst Certification Board has now certified thousands of practitioners, the professional title is not yet familiar to others, including related professionals (e.g., psychologists, social workers, occupational and physical therapists) or the insurance companies responsible for remunerating most health-care professionals. This situation is changing and will no doubt continue to do so with the increasing number of certificants, national and international training programs, and states that have set up formal licensing boards to oversee the profession.

In addition to the basic growth of the profession, there has been a corresponding broadening of the kinds of behaviors, clients, and settings to which behavior analytic principles have been applied. The behavior principles targeted by applied behavior analysts are pervasive and influence nearly every action we take from the mundane to the profound. Consequently, applied behavior analysts have spread their professional wings in demonstrating the applicability of their principles to a variety of real-world circumstances, from weight loss to pet training.

In the area of education, contemporary behavior analysts can take advantage of the capabilities brought by the microcomputer and the Internet to use powerful sounds and graphics to reinforce academic responding. Computerized versions of

Keller's personalized system of instruction proved both easily adapted and successful in teaching college concepts and skills, including psychological principles and computer programming. In addition, preschoolers utilize behaviorally based computer reading programs. Effective academic contingencies, characterized by frequent active responding by the student, immediate and powerful feedback in real time, and nearly continuous assessment, are more realizable than ever before.

The use of basic behavior principles to encourage patients to adhere to medical regimens or exercise programs has long been a mainstay of applied behavior analysis. As in other behavioral domains, advances in technology have altered the landscape. In exergaming, for example, electronic games are designed to require high levels of physical exertion to make contact with the powerful reinforcers of the game environment. In studies of school-aged children, exergaming stations produced increased enthusiasm and higher levels of activity than stations employing more conventional physical education activities.

In addition, behavior analysts are leveraging the Internet, social media in particular, to create powerful support groups and social reinforcement for those facing a range of personal challenges, including medical treatments, substance abuse, weight loss, and gambling. In Europe, positive results were seen from a major effort at increasing schoolchildren's consumption of high-quality foods, utilizing personalized token systems. Technologies exist today that allow any individual to monitor a large array of health indicators, such as steps taken, calories consumed, and heart rate, and contingency management programs developed by behavior analysts have helped to put teeth into individual resolutions and self-improvement programs.

David Morgan

See also ABA Designs; Behaviorism; Experimental Designs; Generalizability; Learning Theories; Reinforcement; Response Rate; School-Wide Positive Behavioral Support; Single-Case Research; Time Series Analysis

Further Readings

Baer, D. M., Wolf, M. M., & Risley, T. R. (1968). Some current dimensions of applied behavior analysis. *Journal of Applied Behavior Analysis, 1*(1), 91–97.

Chance, P. (2006). *First course in applied behavior analysis.* Long Grove, IL: Waveland.

Cooper, J. O., Heron, T. E., & Heward, W. L. (2007). *Applied behavior analysis* (2nd ed.). Upper Saddle River, NJ: Pearson.

Fisher, W. W., Piazza, C. C., & Roane, H. S. (2011). *Handbook of applied behavior analysis.* New York, NY: Guilford.

Vargas, J. S. (2009). *Behavior analysis for effective teaching.* New York, NY: Routledge.

APPLIED RESEARCH

Applied research is an umbrella term that includes various kinds of systematic, empirical research that aims to solve particular problems. In the broad field of education, these problems are those that would arise not only in all aspects of teaching and learning across the lifespan but also from organizational and policy dimensions related to efforts to educate. Applied research seeks to ameliorate problems in education through collecting and analyzing data that directly inform organizational and institutional decision making.

As both public entities and private foundations devote increasing resources to educational programs, the evaluative role for applied research has grown, consistent with and at the same time as calls for accountability of schools and specific educational programs have increased. This entry presents research traditions that typically fall under the category of applied research, the relationship between applied and basic research, the methods and approaches used in applied research, the dissemination of applied research, and examples and criticisms of applied research.

Types of Applied Research

Many forms of research in education are within the purview of applied research. Evaluation studies are almost always applied research with the problem being to what extent a new or existing policy or program achieves intended goals (outcomes) and why (process). Researchers in educational measurement are frequently involved in applied research to develop measures of key constructs deemed important to the teaching and learning process while also investigating their validity and reliability, such as in the development of standardized testing instruments to measure learning in particular areas.

Paulo Freire popularized various forms of action research in education, including participatory action research. Community-based participatory research often are applied in their orientation, as well as design-based research (an early example is seen in education in Ann Brown's "design experiments") and the teacher (or educational practitioner) research movement highlighted by Joe Kincheloe, Marilyn Cochran-Smith, and Susan Lytle. An influential movement, recently spearheaded by Anthony Bryk and others, highlights the need for more "improvement science" that uses rapid, iterative cycles of Plan-Study-Do-Act to produce knowledge in naturalistic settings to enhance school efficacy in ways that can be used widely, that is, brought to scale. Knowledge produced through applied research in education may therefore be used to help develop new or revised products, strategies, procedures, or technologies.

Relationship Between Applied and Basic Research

The problem to be investigated in an applied research project could be selected by the researchers themselves or by nonresearcher stakeholders or clients. This can be compared to so-called pure or basic research in which the research problem is typically one that arises from a gap or contradiction identified in the existing research literature. Basic research always seeks to add to the theoretical research base, but applied research may not have that aim as a primary purpose.

Although the distinction between applied and basic research is useful in many ways, it is sometimes drawn too simplistically. In the process of solving problems and guiding decision making, applied research may also generate theoretical knowledge that is characteristic of basic research. It is also vital to understand the ways that these two forms of research have a reciprocal and iterative relationship over time within any particular field of education research. The design and development of an applied research project usually is supported at least in part by prior basic research results specifying key concepts and elaborating relationships between them, as well as pointing the way to appropriate research methods and designs.

Basic research, particularly in the field of education, often concludes with statements about the implications for practice of the research results, which often generates topics for applied research. In fact, many major funders of basic educational research, both government and private foundations alike, seek to improve "knowledge transfer" by requiring funded studies to consider implications for practice of the research, thus narrowing the distance from more theoretical, basic research to its application. In addition, there has been a reduction in the separation between the worlds of research and practice, such that practitioner-led applied research has become increasingly influential. Notions of reflective practice in education have come to include components of self-evaluation, such as a teacher systematically collecting and analyzing data on the effectiveness of a new way to teach a topic, that are in fact often small-scale examples of applied research. In short, just as the boundary between basic and applied research has blurred, understandings of who has the appropriate authority and expertise to conduct research, particularly applied, context-based research, has broadened.

Approaches and Research Methods

Applied research in education uses a range of approaches and research methods, employing various means to convey results to appropriate audiences. In solving a given problem, applied research can be exploratory, or it can aim to explain patterns (often with the aim of generating accurate predictions), or it can confirm an expected or intended result or prior finding. With the aim of finding a solution to a particular problem, applied research tends not to adhere to strong paradigmatic assumptions such as those outlined by Yvonna Lincoln and Egon Guba. Instead, the pragmatic imperative to solve the problem and guide decision making frames the work, leading some to call applied research "postparadigmatic."

Although often drawing on quantitative research methods, applied research can be purely qualitative or invoke mixed method approaches. The primary goal of applied research is not necessarily to generate generalizable results, but rather for evidence-based findings to be immediately applicable to a particular context. This is especially true when the problem has been selected by a group of stakeholders or clients based on their particular needs and circumstances.

Dissemination

To produce what some might call "actionable knowledge" applied in particular educational contexts, applied researchers need to pay special attention to the audience for their work and to the manner in which findings are conveyed. This may to some extent explain the preponderance of quantitative methods in action research, and it also suggests that much applied research is disseminated not through academic journals but through practitioner-oriented publications and magazines, think tank white papers, position papers by state/provincial departments of education, blogs, and the like.

Forums such as professional conferences and journals allow teachers, other educators, and administrators to disseminate results of practitioner-led applied research projects in order to share knowledge about how to solve common problems with their relevant professional communities. These venues may or may not conduct blinded peer-review of the research. In fact, to the extent that applied research is truly intended to solve a particular problem in a particular context, there may be no need to disseminate results at all beyond that setting. For example, a school district conducting applied research to solve a problem of low parental involvement may share results with district personnel only. Nevertheless, some peer-reviewed journals in education are especially known for publishing applied research, including the *Journal of Education for Students Placed at Risk* and the *Journal of Applied Research in Higher Education*.

Examples and Quality of Applied Research

In the U.S. context, some notable examples of applied research have been a series of reports on the impact of the early childhood education program Head Start, the Coleman report on the effects of racially segregated education, and studies of the effects of school voucher programs on outcomes for urban youth. Each of these represents an effort to delve into a politically sensitive and contentious issue. In judging the quality of applied research projects in these and other areas,

Alis Oancea and John Furlong have argued for a multidimensional framework, including not only quality in an epistemic sense common to all research, such as the use of ethical and robust research design and methods to produce trustworthy results, but also considering issues of value and capacity building. Quality applied research from this perspective is of value to users when it is responsive to their needs and contexts and is presented in an accessible manner.

To enable impact, applied researchers who are not themselves practitioners are wise to establish links with communities of practice early in the research process. Such a strategy is likely to enhance quality by improving the capacity building effect of the applied research, improving the receptiveness of researchers to take the complexity of practice into account, and allowing practitioners to incorporate lessons gleaned from applied research. Finally, the quality of applied research may also be judged by its value for money, that is, cost-effectiveness and transparent, rigorous accounting.

Concerns About Applied Research

Although applied research is widely embraced as a means for enhancing decision making, solving problems, and ultimately improving programs in education, some concerns do exist. Although the typical lack of paradigmatic grounding is not usually seen as an issue, the tendency for applied research to be atheoretical has been criticized in part because the lack of theory may produce a fragmented body of results. In quantitative applied research, the lack of theory to justify particular hypotheses can also lead to a higher likelihood of false-positive findings of statistical significance, for instance.

In an early statement of skepticism about applied research in education, David Cohen and Michael Garet challenged the tenet that applied social research, including applied research in education, provides authoritative knowledge on the costs and consequences of programs, noting that it, like basic research, does not typically reduce intellectual conflict about the value of one approach over another. Similarly, calls for applied research can sometimes be used to justify delays in program implementation. Finally, applied research sometimes functions to lend legitimacy to decisions that have already been made, following the decision making, rather than driving it.

Elizabeth H. McEneaney

See also Action Research; Data-Driven Decision Making; Design-Based Research; Improvement Science Research; Mixed Methods Research; Paradigm Shift

Further Readings

Brown, A. L. (1992). Design experiments: Theoretical and methodological challenges in creating complex interventions in classroom settings. *The Journal of the Learning Sciences, 2*(2), 141–178.

Bryk, A. S., Gomez, L. M., Grunow, A., & LeMahieu, P. G. (2015). *Learning to improve: How America's schools can get better at getting better.* Harvard Education Press.

Cochran-Smith, M., & Lytle, S. L. (Eds.). (1993). *Inside/ outside: Teacher research and knowledge.* Teachers College Press.

Cohen, D., & Garet, M. (1975). Reforming educational policy with applied social research. *Harvard Educational Review, 45*(1), 17–43.

Furlong, J., & Oancea, A. (Eds.). (2013). *Assessing quality in applied and practice-based research in education: Continuing the debate.* New York, NY: Routledge.

Greenwood, D. J., & Levin, M. (2006). *Introduction to action research: Social research for social change.* Sage.

Howell, W. G., & Peterson, P. E. (2006). *The education gap: Vouchers and urban schools.* Brookings Institution Press.

Kincheloe, J. L. (2012). *Teachers as researchers (classic ed.): Qualitative inquiry as a path to empowerment.* New York, NY: Routledge.

Schweinhart, L. J. (1993). Significant benefits: The high/ scope Perry Preschool Study through age 27. *Monographs of the High/Scope Educational Research Foundation* No. 10. Ypsilianti, MI: High/Scope Educational Research Foundation.

U.S. Department of Health and Human Services, Administration for Children and Families (January 2010). *Head Start Impact Study. Final Report.* Washington, DC.

APPRECIATIVE INQUIRY

Appreciative inquiry (AI) is an organizational development method grounded in social constructionist theory that engages stakeholders in an inquiry into their collective strengths, assets, and what is working as a precursor to identifying what they want more of and how to achieve that. It has proven to be a popular and successful transformational change approach. Some researchers advocate its use as a participatory evaluation method under certain conditions, particularly when there is a desire to improve a program or process. This entry describes first the theory and practice of AI and then its use as a method of evaluation.

AI Theory

AI was originally developed in the mid-1980s by David Cooperrider, Frank Barrett, Ron Fry, and Suresh Srivastva of the Organizational Behavior Department at Case Western Reserve University, in response to the dominant use of problem-solving in *action research*, a method of improving social systems by involving system members in self-study. They noted the lack of new theory generated by action research and argued that it engendered an unhelpful bias toward seeing organizations as problems to be solved. They argued that using positivistic, scientific assumptions and methods to improve groups and organizations made the mistake of treating people like simple stimulus–response mechanisms, ignoring how so much of collective life is based on sensemaking, narratives, and beliefs about the future.

Cooperrider, Barrett, Fry, and Srivastva described how assessing groups and organizations against predetermined models of health or dysfunction tended to create the very issues they were supposed to uncover and argued, instead, that there were no inherently correct ways to organize; our methods of organizing are limited only by human imagination and our collective agreements. A method of study that was interested in improving organizations, they argued, would have to lead stakeholders to produce new ideas grounded in their collective hopes and desires and that would most likely emerge if they first inquired, appreciatively, into what gave life and vitality to their organization.

After about 15 years of experimentation and study, a set of five principles of AI were developed that are now widely accepted:

The constructionist principle. What we believe determines what we do, and thought and action emerge out of relationships. People coconstruct the organizations they inhabit through conversations and day-to-day interactions. The purpose of inquiry is to stimulate new thoughts, stories, and beliefs that create new choices for decisions and actions.

The principle of simultaneity. As we inquire into human systems, we change them. The seeds of change, what is discovered and learned, are implicit in the very first questions asked. Questions are never neutral, and organizations move in the direction of the questions most persistently and passionately discussed.

The poetic principle. Organizational life is expressed through language and narratives, the story lines people use to make sense of what is taking place. Words are not passive transmitters of meaning. The words and topics chosen for inquiry have an impact far beyond just the words themselves; they evoke feelings, understandings, and worlds of meaning. Always use words that point to, enliven, and inspire the best in people.

The anticipatory principle. Choices made today are guided by beliefs about the future. The creation of positive imagery of a desirable future on a collective basis and the design of actions to take toward that future, refashions anticipatory reality.

The positive principle. Momentum and sustainable change require positive emotions and social bonding. Hope, excitement, inspiration, camaraderie, and joy increase openness to new ideas and different people, creativity, and cognitive flexibility. They also promote trust and good relationships between people, particularly between groups in conflict, required for collective inquiry and participatory change.

AI Method

During the 1990s, the creators of AI resisted developing formulas for how to do AI, instead of encouraging adoption of the principles and experimenting with ways to implement them in practice. As a result, AI is practiced in numerous ways. However, by 2000, Cooperrider and Diana Whitney developed the 4-D model, a set of four phases (discovery, dream, design, and destiny/deployment) that is now widely utilized, while Jane Magruder

Watkins and Bernard Mohr popularized a similar 4-I model that has been embraced by many using AI for evaluation. The model is as follows:

Initiate: Decide how and when to introduce AI. Determine the overall focus of the inquiry. Decide on the appropriate structure and leadership for the inquiry.

Inquire: Develop an interview guide and engage as many stakeholders as possible in a search for what is known about the program, process, group, or organization at its best.

Imagine: Work with the information collected during the interviews to catalyze conversations about collective aspirations for the program, process, group, or organization's future.

Innovate: Engage stakeholders in proposing activities and projects to move in the direction of those aspirations. Develop and implement processes to encourage taking action and embedding successful innovations.

Various architectures for engagement have been used, but most studies of transformational change report using some variation of the so-called AI Summit, in which a large group of stakeholders go through the 4-Ds (or inquire, imagine, and innovate) over 2–4 days. In an ideal AI process, all the stakeholders would gather to inquire into the best of what they know about the focal topic, understand and express their collective aspirations for the focal topic, foster the emergence of small groups of motivated people with common ideas and interests to develop proposals or plans for actions, and leave the summit with clear ideas about what they will do next. AI Summits with thousands of attendees have been successfully hosted.

Appreciative Interviews

A key innovation of AI is to gather stories about stakeholders' peak experiences at the beginning of interviews during the discovery or inquire phases. The generic AI interview asks, "Thinking about your history in this organization, please tell me the story about the time when you felt most alive, most involved, or most excited to be a part of this organization." The story is probed to understand what brings life and vitality to the organization. The rest of the interview guide asks what they most value about the organization, what their dreams or wishes for the future of the organization are, and what they think needs to happen for the organization to move in that direction.

AI interviews often focus on something specific the organization wants to improve, such as customer service, sustainability, or product innovation. The interview is then constructed similarly to a generic AI interview but refocused accordingly. In general, opening the interview by asking for a personally meaningful, "best of" story about the focus of the inquiry is considered essential for an AI.

Interviews can be done by an individual or small team, but studies have found that getting stakeholders to interview each other increases the amount of change produced by helping to build relationships and catalyze changes in conversations and narratives that occur after the interviews. Many research projects and evaluation studies, however, use just an individual or small group to do the interviews and don't actually do the other AI phases. Instead, they use the information collected as a qualitative data set that is analyzed using standard qualitative research methods. Most AI advocates believe these should not be called appreciative inquiries, but instead call them appreciative interviews.

Using AI for Evaluation

AI for evaluation has been used in a variety of situations, including to evaluate the effectiveness of foreign aid programs, social service program delivery, the effectiveness of training programs in corporations, audits for compliance with quality management system standards, and other organizational processes. There are many descriptions of the use of AI in educational settings, both from an evaluation perspective and from an organizational development perspective.

Proponents of the inclusion of AI as an evaluation method list it as a learning and development type of evaluation or within the category of participatory evaluation. At least five overall benefits have been advanced for using an appreciative approach to evaluation.

1. It generates information that has the maximum potential of being used. The inclusion of many stakeholders in conversations about what matters to them makes it more likely they will embrace the results of the evaluation and do something with it. The process itself can be motivating and energizing.

2. Better information can be gathered more quickly. Large group formats allow for the generation of large amounts of data in short time periods. Personal stories and scenarios provide very rich data for analysis. The collection of real stories from real users emphasizes what the users want as opposed to what designers believe they need.

3. It makes it more likely that groups in conflict or who do not trust each other, or do not trust the evaluators, will engage in the evaluation. By having people focus on what they like and want more of, people who might otherwise feel anxious or cautious about truthfully discussing problems and deficiencies are more likely to engage honestly.

4. For similar reasons to Number 3, it can be useful when there is a need to generate support for the evaluation, perhaps because of past evaluation failures, or fear or skepticism toward the evaluation. In situations where the group being evaluated has a history of oppression, asking for their stories of things at their best, and assessment of what works, is often experienced as being treated respectfully.

5. For any system that has democratic, pluralistic, and/or empowerment agendas, it is a more congruent evaluation approach. It can increase evaluation capacity of stakeholders and the system. AI's use of storytelling makes it particularly effective in cultures with oral history traditions.

Being a sociorationalist, postmodern approach that challenges the validity of scientific assumptions for studying people, AI does not fit well with traditional criteria for assessing evaluations such as independence, neutrality, and minimal bias. AI advocates argue that it is impossible for anyone to enter a social system from a neutral stance and that there is no such thing as independence; by their very presence, evaluators are influencing the social systems in which they enter. While concerns have been expressed that a focus on the positive may undermine the appearance of neutrality and, therefore, the collection of valid information, experience in the field suggests just the opposite—that people are willing to be more honest when asked about their opinions of what works than when asked about problems and failures.

Another concern is that with its focus on the positive, AI will miss seeing and reporting important problems. Researchers report, however, that asking questions such as "what is your wish for this project?" or "what is your dream for this organization?" or "how could we improve this process?" elicit all the same issues that asking directly about problems would surface but without feelings of rancor or recrimination.

All advocates emphasize the use of AI in specific circumstances and not in others. There is widespread agreement that AI is worth considering when it matches the values and culture of those who will use the evaluation and when the purpose of the evaluation is to develop and improve whatever is being evaluated. Conversely, AI is not likely to be a useful method when the values and culture of the target group do not favor a participatory approach, or there is a desire for mainly quantitative data, and/or when one of the aims of the evaluation is to terminate a process or program.

It has also been noted that successful use of AI requires specialized knowledge and skill sets not normally associated with evaluation training. Training in AI as a change method is available, but training in use of AI as an evaluation method is rare.

Gervase R. Bushe

See also Action Research; Collaborative Evaluation; Constructivist Approach; Democratic Evaluation; Evaluation Capacity Building; Narrative Research; Postpositivism

Further Readings

Barrett, F. J., & Fry, R. E. (2005). *Appreciative inquiry: A positive approach to building cooperative capacity.* Chagrin Falls, OH: Taos Institute.

Bushe, G. R. (2012). Appreciative inquiry: Theory and critique. In D. Boje, B. Burnes, & J. Hassard (Eds.), *The Routledge companion to organizational change* (pp. 87–103). Oxford, UK: Routledge.

Coghlan, A. T., Preskill, H., & Catsambas, T. T. (Guest Eds.). (2003, Winter). *New directions for evaluation, Vol. 100* (Special issue on appreciative inquiry in evaluation).

Cooperrider, D. L., Barrett, F., & Srivastva, S. (1995). Social construction and appreciative inquiry: A journey in organizational theory. In D. Hosking, P. Dachler, & K. Gergen (Eds.), *Management and organization: Relational alternatives to individualism* (pp. 157–200). Aldershot, UK: Avebury.

Cooperrider, D. L., & Srivastva, S. (1987). Appreciative inquiry in organizational life. In R. W. Woodman & W. A. Pasmore (Eds.), *Research in organizational change and development, Vol. 1* (pp. 129–169). Stamford, CT: JAI Press.

Cooperrider, D. L., Whitney, D., & Stavros, J. M. (2008). *Appreciative inquiry handbook* (2nd ed.). Brunswick, OH: Crown Custom.

Dunlap, C. A. (2008). Effective evaluation through appreciative inquiry. *Performance Improvement, 47*(2), 23–29. doi:10.1002/pfi.181

Ludema, J. D., Whitney, D., Mohr, B. J., & Griffen, T. J. (2003). *The appreciative inquiry summit.* San Francisco, CA: Berrett-Koehler.

Preskill, H. S., & Catsambas, T. T. (2006). *Reframing evaluation through appreciative inquiry.* Thousand Oaks, CA: Sage.

Watkins, J. M., Mohr, B. J., & Kelly, R. (2011). *Appreciative inquiry: Change at the speed of imagination* (2nd ed.). San Francisco, CA: Pfeiffer-Wiley.

APTITUDE TESTS

The term *aptitude*, according to most dictionaries, is derived from the Latin term *aptitudo*, meaning fitness. The psychological use of the term is similar in that it has traditionally referred to a potential for acquiring knowledge or skill. Traditionally, aptitudes are described as sets of characteristics that relate to an individual's ability to acquire knowledge or skills in the context of some training or educational program. There are two important aspects of aptitude to keep in mind. First, aptitudes are present conditions (i.e., existing at the time they are measured). Second, there is nothing inherent in the concept of aptitudes that says whether they are inherited or acquired or represent some combination of heredity and environmental influences. Also, aptitude tests do not directly assess an individual's future success; they are meant to assess aspects of the individual that are indicators of future success. That is, these measures are used to provide a probability estimate of an individual's success in a particular training or educational program. Although the meaning of *aptitude* is well delineated, there is much controversy over how to distinguish aptitude tests from other kinds of psychometric measures, specifically intelligence and achievement tests, partly because the major salient difference between intelligence, aptitude, and achievement tests has to do with the purpose of testing rather than with the content of the tests. What makes an assessment instrument an aptitude test rather than an intelligence or achievement test is mainly the future orientation of the predictions to be made from the test scores.

Historians generally date the movement of modern psychological testing from the 1905 work by Alfred Binet and Théodore Simon in developing a set of measures to assess intelligence. The Binet-Simon measures, and especially the English translation and refinement made by Lewis Terman in 1916, called the Stanford-Binet, are in widespread use even today. Few adults living in industrialized countries today have avoided taking at least one test of intelligence during their school years. Intelligence tests were designed with the goal of predicting school success. Thus, in terms of the definition of aptitude provided above, when the purpose of an intelligence test is prediction, then the intelligence test is essentially an aptitude test—although an aptitude test of general academic content (e.g., memory, reasoning, math, and verbal domains). Aptitude tests, however, sample a wider array of talents than those included in most general intelligence measures, especially in the occupational domain. By the late 1910s and early 1920s, dozens of different aptitude tests had been created for prediction of success in a variety of different occupations (e.g., auto mechanic, retail salesmen, waitress, telegrapher, clerk, Hollerith operator, musician, registered nurse).

It is important to distinguish between so-called trade tests and aptitude tests. The distinction rests more on the characteristics of the examinee population than on the content of the tests. That is, when all the examinees can be expected to have similar prior exposure to the knowledge and skills needed to perform well on the test, the test is essentially one of ability or aptitude. But when prior knowledge and skills have an important impact on the examinees' success on the test, it is essentially an achievement test, or a measure of learned knowledge or skills,

rather than an assessment of potential for acquiring such knowledge or skills. For psychologists who design aptitude tests, this is a critical concern. For example, the psychologist must be able to determine whether reading skills are an important determinant of test performance in order to present the test material in a paper-and-pencil format. Intelligence test developers assumed that individual differences in reading skills in young children were possible confounding influences, and so the developers created intelligence tests that did not require a child to know how to read or write. For assessing the aptitude of adults for an office clerk job, however, being able to read would be a prerequisite skill, so a paper-and-pencil aptitude test would certainly be appropriate.

Utility of Aptitude Tests

Aptitude tests are useful for the purpose of aiding educational or occupational selection when there are marked individual differences in the likelihood of success that are, in turn, determined by cognitive, perceptual, or physical abilities. The degree of utility of an aptitude test is determined by three major factors: (1) the cost of training or education, (2) the correlation between the aptitude test scores and success on the educational or occupational criterion, and (3) the ratio of the number of applicants to the number of places to be filled. When training is expensive, the cost to the organization of having trainees fail can be an important factor in adopting an aptitude testing program for screening applicants. When training is brief or inexpensive, such as for retail sales or other entry-level positions, the value of aptitude testing is diminished because the cost of accepting applicants who fail is not as burdensome for the organization. The correlation between aptitude test scores and success measures will determine how accurate the prediction of success or failure is. The larger the correlation, the more accurate the prediction. Finally, when there are many more applicants than spaces to be filled, the aptitude test will be more effective in maximizing the overall success rate. In contrast, when there are few applicants for each position, and thus nearly all applicants are accepted, the ranking of applicants by aptitude becomes largely irrelevant.

Two Types of Aptitude Tests

The aptitude tests developed over the past century have generally bifurcated into two different types: job-specific tests and multiaptitude batteries. Similar to the early aptitude tests described above, jobspecific aptitude tests are typically designed to determine which candidates are best suited to particular occupations. In theory, there can be as many different occupational aptitude tests as there are differentiable occupations. In practice, however, there are common aptitudes underlying many occupations. For example, different kinds of mechanical jobs (e.g., auto mechanic, electronics service repair, assembly worker) may all involve aptitudes for dexterity, fine motor coordination, visual perception, and so on. An organization that wishes to select employees for a particular occupational placement might attempt to identify (through job analysis) what particular aptitudes are needed for successful job performance. The organization, in order to select the applicants who are most likely to succeed in a training program, can then create an aptitude measure that samples these specific aptitudes. Alternatively, among the dozens of commercially available tests, the organization may find an off-the-shelf aptitude measure that covers the most important aptitudes for training success for the particular job.

The other kind of aptitude measure is the multiaptitude battery. These tests are used frequently in educational contexts, and some are used in large-scale employment testing situations. In the educational context, multiaptitude tests may be very general, such as the SAT, which was created in 1926 for selecting high school students for college and university placement. Today, the SAT is one of the most widely used aptitude test batteries in the United States and is administered to more than 1 million students each year. The original SAT assessed only two broad academic aptitudes: verbal and math. The most recent modification of the SAT also includes a writing component. Multiaptitude test batteries can also be designed to provide assessments across several different aptitudes. The first large-scale multiaptitude batteries for use in educational contexts were developed by Louis Leon Thurstone and Thelma Thurstone in the early 1940s and became known as the primary mental abilities battery. Another battery, the differential aptitude tests (DAT), was introduced and is still in use today. The DAT provides scores on eight different aptitudes (verbal, numerical, abstract reasoning, clerical speed and accuracy, mechanical reasoning, spatial relations, spelling, and language use).

There are many more such multiaptitude batteries that are administered in schools throughout the United States each year. Many of these tests do not have the term *aptitude* in their titles, but they are similar in content coverage and in the general purposes of testing. Such educational aptitude batteries are primarily used for counseling purposes. That is, the underlying premise for the utility of these tests is that they allow a parent or counselor to identify an individual student's aptitude strengths and weaknesses. Usually, the test information is presented as a profile, a set of bar graphs that show where the student stands in respect to some norming group on each of the different aptitudes. Counselors may use this information to help guide the student in a way that either builds on the student's strengths or attempts to remediate the student's weaknesses. In practice, however, many of the different aptitudes assessed with these measures are themselves substantially positively correlated because of shared variance with general intelligence. When that happens, it is more difficult to provide a reliable differentiation among the individual's strengths and weaknesses. This is one of the most intractable problems associated with the counseling use of multiaptitude test batteries.

Multiaptitude batteries for occupational selection tend to be somewhat more useful for selection and classification purposes. (Classification is the process of assigning particular individuals to specific jobs by matching the individual's profile of aptitude strengths and weaknesses to the job requirements.) The two largest occupational multiaptitude test batteries used in the United States are the Armed Services Vocational Aptitude Battery and the General Aptitude Test Battery. The Armed Services Vocational Aptitude Battery is used by the U.S. armed forces, and until recently, the General Aptitude Test Battery was used by federal and state employment agencies. In contrast to the multiaptitude batteries described above for educational contexts, these two tests are explicitly linked to a wide variety of specific occupations.

For example, when individuals complete the Armed Services Vocational Aptitude Battery, they are each provided with a set of scores that determines their suitability for all the different entry-level occupations within the military. With that information, they can be classified into the occupation in which they are most likely to succeed.

Concerns About Aptitude Tests

Although aptitude tests have been shown to be quite effective predictors of future academic and occupational performance, they have been somewhat controversial because of the meaning inherent in the assessment of potential and because of a wide variety of group differences in performance on standardized aptitude tests. Experience with the SAT, for example, has indicated marked mean score differences between male and female test takers; between Black, White, Hispanic, and Asian American test takers and between socioeconomic status groups. Because the SAT is not traditionally considered to be taken by a representative or random sample of 16- to 18- year- olds (because those students taking the test essentially are self-selected college-bound individuals), group differences on the SAT do not provide direct evidence for overall group differences in academic potential. However, the differences between group means are significant and sometimes substantial, which has led many commentators to question whether and how much the test is associated with prior educational background and other demographic variables. Much of the difficulty centers around the term *potential* associated with aptitude tests, in contrast with achievement measures. That is, if these different groups differ only in terms of academic achievement, there would be perhaps less controversy than there is if the groups are determined to differ in terms of academic potential. Many testing organizations have in fact revised the names of their aptitude tests to remove the term that is associated with potential (e.g., the Scholastic Aptitude Test became the Scholastic Assessment Test in the 1990s and later became known as simply the SAT). At one level, such a change may be cosmetic, but at another level, it does show that testing organizations have come to recognize that one does not need to imbue a test with the notion of potential in order to make predictions about future academic or occupational performance. That is, there is nothing inherently problematic in using an intelligence or achievement test for the same purpose as an aptitude test as long as it taps the same underlying knowledge and skills that are critical for performance on the predicted criterion measure. Given that intelligence, aptitude, and achievement tests assess only current performance, it is ultimately the prediction aspect of a test that makes it an aptitude test. Furthermore, it is fundamentally impossible to know what an individual's actual potential is for academic or occupational knowledge or skills because it is not possible to know what the universe of instructional or training programs may be. Should methods of instruction or training be improved at some time in the future, even those individuals with relatively lower aptitudes may show marked increases in performance. In that sense, the operational conceptualization of aptitude has to be in terms of whatever instructional or training methods are actually in use at any one time.

Over- and Underachievement

One aspect of aptitude tests that has been very much misunderstood is the notion of over- and underachievement. Typically, the term *overachiever* is given to individuals who have relatively higher scores on achievement tests than they do on aptitude tests, and the term *underachiever* is given to individuals who have relatively lower scores on achievement tests than on aptitude tests. However, given that both aptitude and achievement tests often assess the same underlying knowledge and skills, the choice of labeling one test or another an aptitude or achievement test is generally arbitrary. That means that one could just as easily assert that individuals have higher or lower aptitude in association with their achievement test performance, which makes little conceptual sense but is entirely consistent with the underlying properties of the tests. In fact, given the nature of statistical regression-to-the-mean phenomena, which are associated with taking the difference between any two measures, it is common for individuals with low scores on one test (e.g., aptitude) to have relatively higher scores on the other test (e.g., achievement), and similarly, individuals with higher than average scores on one test will have somewhat lower scores on the other test. The attribution that low-aptitude individuals are often overachievers and high-aptitude individuals are often underachievers is most often an artifact of this regression-to-the-mean phenomenon and thus does not provide any useful diagnostic information. Only extremely large differences between such scores (i.e., differences that significantly exceed the difference attributable to regression-to-the-mean effects) can provide any potential diagnostic information.

Phillip L. Ackerman

Note: Adapted from Ackerman, P. L. (2007). Aptitude Tests. In N. J. Salkind (Ed.), *Encyclopedia of measurement and statistics* (Vol. 1, pp. 39–43). Thousand Oaks, CA: SAGE.

See also Ability Tests; Achievement Tests; SAT; Stanford–Binet Intelligence Scales

Further Readings

Anastasi, A., & Urbina, S. (1997). *Psychological testing* (7th ed.). New York, NY: Prentice Hall.

Cronbach, L. J. (1990). *Essentials of psychological testing* (5th ed.). New York, NY: Harper & Row.

Thorndike, R. L. (1963). *The concepts of over- and underachievement.* New York, NY: Bureau of Publications, Teachers College, Columbia University.

APTITUDE-TREATMENT INTERACTION

Aptitude-treatment interaction (ATI), also known as attribute-treatment interaction or trait-treatment interaction, refers to the tenet that treatments or interventions that are well matched to learners' specific aptitudes, attributes, or traits are more effective in helping them to appropriate the object of learning, that is, what the learners are expected to learn. This entry further describes ATI and research in this area. It then details the evolution of ATI research, describes ATI research designs, and discusses implications for educational practice. Finally, it looks at future directions for ATI.

Early descriptions of ATI can be found in both Eastern and Western literature, such as in ancient Chinese and Hebrew writings, early Greek and Roman teachings, and early European philosophies. The basic premise of ATI in educational research is that no single treatment, which refers to any manipulable situational variable such as an instructional approach or a teaching resource, is best for every learner because differences in learners' aptitudes interact with the treatment, which in turn affects the treatment outcomes. In the presence of such an interaction effect, the research question, asking which treatment or intervention is better or more effective, becomes somewhat imprecise or unsophisticated. Instead, researchers in this area focus on which treatment is better or more effective for which group of learners and under what conditions and the underlying reasons or explanation for the existence of such relationships.

Research on ATI can help to determine whether and which particular treatments can be chosen or adapted to best fit specific groups of learners. The ultimate goal of ATI research is to identify and develop treatments that best match the aptitudes of different groups of learners to maximize their learning effectiveness. For instance, learners with high spatial aptitude learn better through an instructional approach that uses visual elaboration than one that uses textual materials only; conversely, learners with high verbal aptitude learn more effectively with an instructional approach that incorporates verbal elaboration than one that uses mainly visual aids. Alternatively, learners with high mathematical aptitude learn music composition more effectively when the instruction focuses on mathematical concepts (e.g., understand the rules for writing chords to create harmony), while learners with high kinesthetic aptitude profit more from actually singing the melody when they start to compose music.

An ATI effect is said to occur if the extent to which the outcomes for two or more treatments, or one treatment over two or more trials, shows a statistically significant difference for learners who differ on one or more of the aptitude variables under investigation. Therefore, adapting the instruction to correspond with the aptitude of learners is optimal in the sense that it can realize the learning potential of each group of learners and at the same time produce better learning outcomes for all of the learners involved.

Evolution of ATI Research

The development of ATI research can be traced back to the seminal work by Lee Cronbach and Richard Snow in which they investigated how differences in some individual aptitude variables might demonstrate strong interaction effects with particular interventions or treatments. Over the years, this research area has been in a state of flux, in which researchers have defined and characterized the notion of aptitude in different ways, devised different kinds of treatments, and made use of different methods to assess the interaction.

Aptitude

Early studies define aptitude as any personal characteristics that increase or decrease the probability of success of the learner who receives a particular treatment. Some further argue that those personal characteristics must be measurable and hypothesized as critical for eliciting a positive response to the treatment. Some researchers contend that these characteristics or aptitudes should not be confined to general intelligence or a fixed set of cognitive abilities but should include non-cognitive aptitudes such as personality, motivation, learning attitude, learning style, belief, self-regulation, self-efficacy, and emotion. Some recent studies posit that aptitude can be more content-specific, characterized by the learner's prior knowledge in relation to the object of learning. In other words, studies have shown that the effectiveness of treatments or interventions is influenced by how many and what critical aspects of the object of learning the learners have already discerned and focused upon.

The personal characteristics or aptitudes that may interact with the treatments are conceived to be many and varied, but not infinite. As learning is a highly complex phenomenon, there is a growing trend for researchers to conceptualize aptitude as a combination of multiple aptitude variables and to analyze the higher order interactions between them. The different combinations of aptitude variables, which are often called aptitude complexes, interact with the treatment and affect the treatment outcomes in different ways. For example, a 2003 study with college students and adults found that a combination of three aptitude variables—self-concept, interest, and motivation—was strongly correlated with domain knowledge and ability measures.

Aptitude is widely recognized as having multiple dimensions, including cognitive, conative, and affective domains. In the early stages, research in this area was more focused on cognitive aptitude, such as general intelligence and cognitive learning styles. Most of these studies aimed to examine whether and in what ways learning outcomes depend on the degree to which the treatments or instructional designs match the learner's specific cognitive aptitude. The most common and strongest ATI that emerged in early studies was related to general intelligence. Students with high general intelligence and who were relaxed and independent were found to benefit more from less structured learning environments, such as those using a student-centered instructional approach, inductive teaching methods, small group discussion, and discovery learning activities. The reverse was true for students with lower general intelligence and those with anxiety or a high need to conform. These students performed better in highly structured learning environments such as those using a teacher-centered instructional approach and didactic and lecture-based teaching methods.

However, ATIs are highly complex and context bound and can change rapidly, which is why they are so difficult to identify. In fact, no specific ATI effects have been sufficiently established to form the basis for designing instructional practices in the classroom on a large scale, which might be because some significant interactions remain unidentified. Some critics view students' learning outcomes as so dynamic that they cannot be based on cognitive aptitudes alone and argue that cognitive learning styles may vary within the individual when they attempt different tasks or encounter different situations.

Research has increasingly recognized the importance of elements of the conative domain (such as locus of control, self-regulation, and motivation) and affective domain (such as emotion, anxiety, and self-efficacy) for ATI and has explored the possible interactions of cognitive-conative-affective aptitude complexes with treatment effects. For instance, studies have attempted to investigate the power of emotions and intentions in guiding and managing cognitive processes and how they affect the treatment outcomes. Although the complex interplay between cognitive-conative-affective aptitudes is acknowledged by researchers, the growth and decline of cognitive abilities such as memory, attention, and so on, demonstrate an inverted U-shaped developmental trajectory across the life span in contrast to affect and conation. It is important to bear in mind that aptitudes should not be seen as fixed; they are dynamic in nature and represent the degree of readiness of the learner to learn and to perform well in a particular situation or in a fixed domain at a particular time and can be fostered and changed over time.

Treatment

In education, treatment always refers to the creation of the learning condition or environment in which the learners are situated. Researchers may introduce different instructional approaches or use different teaching resources to create different learning conditions for learners who have different aptitudes. They can then examine the interaction effect between the learning conditions and the aptitude of the learners in terms of the treatment outcomes, which are usually measured by pre-, post- and delayed posttests.

In terms of the types of treatments used, the most frequently manipulated treatment variables in earlier studies were structure and elaboration. The typical manipulation for structure involved providing one group with a more self-directed learning environment and another group with a more teacher-controlled, lecture-based learning environment. Elaboration was typically manipulated by providing one group with analogies or some other means of clarifying or elaborating the learning materials, while the other group typically received only the learning materials without any further elaboration. Other experimental manipulations included providing one group with deductive training and the other with inductive training or comparing a group of learners who engaged in learning primarily through a small group setting to another group who participated in a large group setting.

Recent ATI research has covered a broader range of treatments, including some innovative teaching strategies and curriculum designs. For instance, in one study, one group was provided with static pictures for recognizing rotated spatial structures, while the other group was offered animations. Another study examined the efficacy of a motivation-enhancing treatment, attributional retraining, to support students who were at risk because of a high failure-avoidance orientation (i.e., the tendency to maintain self-worth by avoiding failure).

Interaction

ATI occurs when the degree to which results for two or more treatments, or one treatment over two or more trials, shows a statistically significant difference for learners who also differ on one or more aptitude variables under investigation. Treatment-subgroup interactions may be assessed by either quantitative or qualitative methods. In earlier studies, most researchers made use of quantitative measures in which the direction of the difference between the treatment alternatives in terms of treatment effectiveness was the same for all subgroups, but they differed in the extent of the difference (see Figure 1); that is, the difference was only in magnitude.

Qualitative measures have become increasingly popular in recent years. The difference in treatment effectiveness may be in different directions for different subgroups. This is a statistical difference, as illustrated in the regression slopes in Figure 1. However, the qualitative treatment-subgroup interactions have greater practical value in suggesting the most appropriate treatments for different subgroups of learners for optimal treatment outcomes.

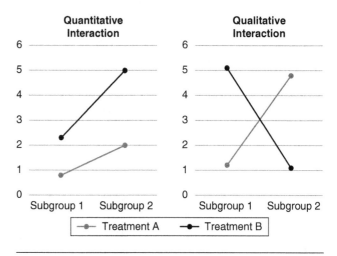

Figure 1   An example of quantitative and qualitative treatment-subgroup interactions

Source: Doove, Van Deun, Dusseldorp, and Van Mechelen (2015, p. 3).

Nevertheless, these early studies found no consistent ATIs in education and training, perhaps due to the small sample sizes in many of the studies. Some studies had further problems due to the large number of variables they measured and analyzed in an attempt to identify every main effect and interaction possible. The diversity of the treatments used, coupled with the relative lack of data points to detect any patterns of ATIs for many of the treatments, made it difficult to draw conclusions about the potential interactions with personal characteristics. With the advent of new methods of assessing ATIs and more robust research designs, it is encouraging that recent studies have found more support for ATIs.

ATI Research Designs

ATI research aims to identify and develop treatments that work best for particular groups of learners with certain aptitudes to optimize the treatment outcomes. For ATI research to be meaningful, it should be driven by plausible hypotheses rather than simply treating the study as a hit-or-miss exploration of statistical associations. The most commonly used research designs for ATI are (a) the standard experimental design, (b) the regression discontinuity design, and (c) the change curve (or growth curve) design.

The *standard experimental design* is the most common and comprises a simple, randomized, controlled experiment, in which two or more groups receive the same treatment and their learning outcomes are assessed with respect to different levels of the aptitude(s) under investigation. Figure 2 illustrates the ATI effect, in which treatment T_z is shown to be more effective than treatment T_y for persons with Aptitude A, but there is no difference between the two treatments for persons with Aptitude B.

The *regression discontinuity design* can be used when randomization cannot be carried out. In this design, learners are assigned to different treatments on the basis of a cutoff score on the aptitude(s) to be investigated. A treatment effect is observed if there is a discontinuity in the outcome measurement, as illustrated in Figure 3, where treatment T_X is more effective than the other treatments for learners above aptitude level A.

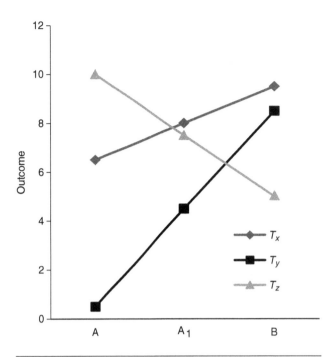

Figure 2 Standard ATI research design

Source: Adapted from Snow (1991, p. 208).

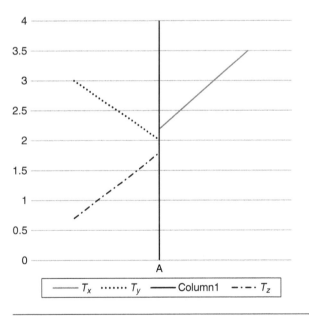

Figure 3 Regression discontinuity ATI research design

Source: Adapted from Snow (1991, p. 208).

In the *change (or growth) curve design*, the change in the outcome variable after learners receive the treatment is observed and analyzed over time, using a growth curve (see Figure 4). This design allows the data of individual learners

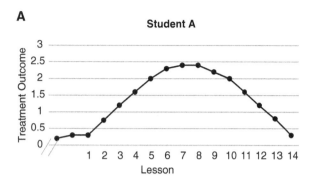

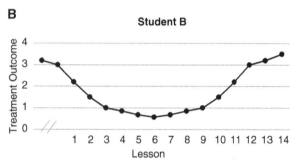

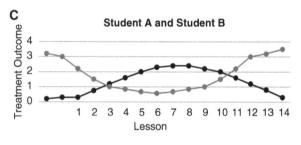

Figure 4   Change curve (or growth curve) ATI research design

to be shown and analyzed, and the design does not require a comparative trial control, which may not be feasible or ethical in some educational settings.

ATI designs require large sample sizes (i.e., at least 100 subjects per treatment) to ensure adequate statistical power to detect a moderately strong ATI with power of .90. In terms of treatment duration, longer interventions (i.e., at least 10 sessions or more) are recommended to obtain reliable results. Furthermore, to ensure adequate statistical power, it is advisable to have at least two different treatments, as interaction effects need to be shown to occur above and beyond the additive influence of the main effects. In terms of aptitude variables, the aptitude to be investigated should be strongly associated with the outcome for one intervention but not the others. It is important to note that studying one

aptitude at a time while disregarding other aptitudes may result in an unwarranted oversimplification. However, studying too many aptitudes or treatment components simultaneously may result in research findings that are infeasible, if not impossible, to interpret.

Implications for Educational Practice

ATI research has motivated a professional movement to introduce and promote differentiated curricula and differentiated instruction to cater for individual differences and learners' diversity in schools. The rationale behind differentiated curricula and instruction is that learners with different attributes or aptitudes benefit from different curriculum contents and/or instructional approaches, which is grounded in the ATI tenet. Teachers are recommended to design, customize, and adapt their curricula and instruction to match the different aptitudes and learning needs of different groups of learners in schools or classes.

Unlike ATI researchers, teachers may not have the time and expertise to design and administer rigorous diagnostic tests to identify and analyze the aptitude(s) of their students. Instead, they tend to ascertain and assess learners' aptitudes and learning needs based on informal classroom observations and analysis of student work samples and test performances. Insights from ATI research findings offer useful inputs and guidance to the teaching profession when devising plans and actions to provide pedagogical support for differentiation to their students.

Furthermore, a number of recent educational practices, such as learning progressions, response to intervention, and data-driven instructional decision making, were influenced by ATI research findings. Learning progressions involve learners progressing along a pathway of increasing proficiency or competency at their own pace. To help them master the target level of proficiency, teachers need to adjust and align their instruction and pace in accordance with the evolving progress of the learners at different points along the pathway.

In response to intervention, early intervention with customized support is given to those learners who are at risk of failing. An initial performance/capacity assessment is conducted to identify students who may encounter learning challenges.

These students are then given individualized pedagogical support, while the teacher closely monitors their progress. The tight coupling between the performance/capacity assessment and instruction forms a feedback loop, which follows the ATI principle of matching aptitude with appropriate instructional support in an optimal manner.

Data-driven instructional decision making is premised on the understanding that there is a genuine need to use various kinds of data to inform practice and continuously improve the quality of education. As with ATI research, the data can be from cognitive, conative, and affective domains. Teachers who obtain regular and frequent data related to the aptitudes of the learners are more likely to make well-informed pedagogical decisions and appropriately tailor their instruction to the aptitude profiles of the learners and thus realize the learning potential of every learner.

Future Directions

ATI theory has grown and evolved over the years. It remains the foundation for a broad range of research studies in learning and instruction and for a number of educational policies and practices around the world. The tenet of identifying the interaction between learners' aptitudes and alternative treatments or instructional interventions, and subsequently creating the learning conditions that match the aptitudes of the learners to achieve optimal learning outcomes, is well supported by different stakeholders in the educational arena.

With recent developments in educational neuroscience research, it is anticipated that new light will be shed on the underlying brain functions of learners with different aptitudes when engaged in the same or different treatments or interventions. This would make significant contributions to the field of ATI, both theoretically and practically.

Ming Fai Pang

See also Interaction; Regression Discontinuity Analysis; Two-Way Analysis of Variance

Further Readings

Caspi, O., & Bell, I. R. (2004). One size does not fit all: Aptitude × Treatment Interaction (ATI) as a conceptual framework for complementary and alternative medicine outcome research. Part II—research designs and their applications. *The Journal of Alternative and Complementary Medicine*, 10(4), 698–705.

Cronbach, L. J., & Snow, R. E. (1977). *Aptitudes and instructional methods*. New York, NY: Irvington.

Doove, L. L., Van Deun, K., Dusseldorp, E., & Van Mechelen, I. (2015). QUINT: A tool to detect qualitative treatment–subgroup interactions in randomized controlled trials. *Psychotherapy Research*, 1–11, 3.

Pang, M. F., & Marton, F. (2013). Interaction between the learners' initial grasp of the object of learning and the learning resources afforded. *Instructional Science*, 41(6), 1065–1082.

Snow, R. E. (1991). Aptitude-treatment interaction as a framework for research on individual differences in psychotherapy. *Journal of Consulting and Clinical Psychology*, 59, 205–216.

AREAS UNDER THE NORMAL CURVE

The normal distribution, also called the Gaussian distribution, is a probability distribution that arises in many different natural processes. For example, the height of adult organisms in most species follows a normal distribution. The normal distribution is important in statistics because many estimators have sampling distributions that are asymptotically normal; this includes means, medians, proportions, and all maximum likelihood estimators. This means that the null distribution for many hypothesis tests is a normal distribution and that the p value for these tests is given by the area under a normal curve.

This entry first discusses the general definition of probability as area, providing both a formal calculus-based definition and a less formal intuitive explanation. Then it discusses the relationship between the area under the normal curve and hypothesis testing.

Probability as Area

The normal distribution is characterized by its unimodal, symmetric "bell shape" and is defined by the density function:

$$f(x) = \frac{1}{\sigma\sqrt{2\pi}} e^{-(x-\mu)^2/2\sigma^2}$$

The probability that a particular event occurs is based on the area under this curve. Formally, the probability that a normally distributed random variable falls within a particular range is given by the integral of the density function over that range.

$$\text{Pr}n(a \leq X \leq b) = ab1\sigma^2\pi \, e - (x-\mu)22 \, \sigma^2 dx.$$

Intuition for this idea, which does not rely on calculus, can be developed through analogy to histograms: Consider an exam where the scores are normally distributed around 50 with a standard deviation of 10. Then if we administered the test to 100 people, we might see 29 scores between 35 and 45. This is shown as the shaded area in the left of Figure 1; the scores within this range represent 29% of the total area.

If we instead administered the test to 1,000 people, we might see 247 scores that fall between 35 and 45, and thus the shaded area in the center of Figure 1 is 24.7% of the total area in that histogram. If we could let the sample size go to infinity, and sample the entire population, then the proportion of scores within that range would be the area under the density curve, shown on the right of Figure 1, which is 24.2% of the total area under the curve.

Cumulative Distribution Functions

This definition of probability as the area under a curve holds in general. Other distributions (e.g., F distribution, chi-square distribution, and t distribution) have their own density functions, and the probability that an observation from one of these distributions would fall within a particular range corresponds to the area under the respective density curve. In general, the area under a density curve is expressed with a cumulative distribution function:

$$Fa = \text{Pr}\,(X \leq a) = -\infty af\,(x)dx.$$

Calculating the Area Under a Normal Curve

The integral for the area under the normal curve has no closed form (meaning there is no simpler way to write the formula), and therefore calculating probabilities without an aid is potentially quite time-consuming. Statistical software packages (such as R, SPSS, and SAS) have built-in functions to calculate probabilities from common distributions, including the normal distribution. Before the use of such software became widespread, it was common to look up the probabilities in a table. In the 2010s, tables of normal probabilities remain common primarily for pedagogical purposes in introductory courses.

On a normal curve, about 34% of scores will fall between the mean and 1 standard deviation above the mean, with another 34% between the mean and 1 standard deviation below the mean. Between 1 standard deviation and 2 standard deviations on either side of the mean, there is room for about 14% of scores. This leaves roughly

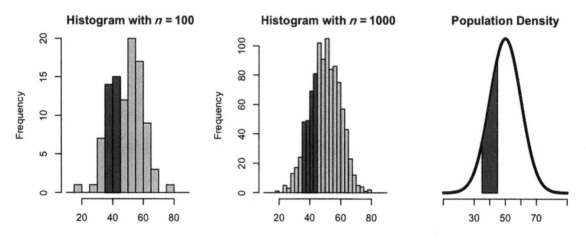

Figure 1   Probability and area

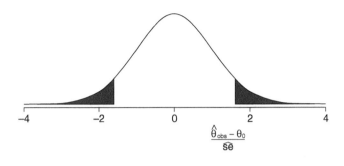

Figure 2   *p* Values and area

2% of scores farther than 2 standard deviations below and above the mean. These are roughly rounded off estimates (it is important to remember) because the normal curve is infinite and never quite touches the *x*-axis. There are tiny, but greater-than-zero probabilities of scores occurring as one moves farther and farther from the middle.

Relationship to Hypothesis Testing and *p*-Value Calculation

Many estimators for statistical parameters have asymptotically normal sampling distributions. For example, the sample mean *x* is normally distributed around the population mean (μ); and in linear regression, the estimated regression coefficients (β) are normally distributed around the "true" regression coefficients (β). This property is the critical component for many hypothesis tests, since this means that the null distribution for these estimators will be a normal distribution.

It is possible to build a Wald test for any estimator that is asymptotically normal, that is, whenever θ is an estimator of θ and $\frac{\theta - \theta_0}{se} \longrightarrow N(0,1)$. In general, a *p* value is the probability that the test statistic would be bigger than the observed value if the null hypothesis was true. In the Wald test for $\theta = \theta_0$, this is the probability $P\frac{\theta - \theta_0}{se} > \frac{\theta_{obs} - \theta_0}{se}$, where θ_{obs} is the observed value of the estimator, as shown in Figure 2.

Since the sampling distribution is normal, this probability is given by the area under the normal curve. Since all maximum likelihood estimators have normal sampling distributions, this Wald test (sometimes referred to as a *z* test) arises frequently.

April Galyardt

See also Central Limit Theorem; Distributions; Histograms; Hypothesis Testing; Maximum Likelihood Estimation; Normal Distribution; *p* Value; *t* Tests

Further Readings

Agresti, A., & Franklin, C. A. (2013). *Statistics: The art and science of learning from data* (3rd ed.). Upper Saddle River, NJ: Pearson.

Wasserman, L. (2004). *All of statistics*. New York, NY: Springer.

ASIAN AMERICANS AND TESTING

This entry examines the performance of Asian American students on tests and looks at the cultural traditions and other factors thought to be behind their generally strong academic performance. Asian Americans are Americans of Asian descent or the first-generation immigrants from Asia. Asian Americans, particularly children of those who immigrated to the United States after World War II, are perceived as high achievers in their scholarly work and are stereotyped as good test takers in U.S. schools.

Asians began coming to the United States in the early 19th century, but most have come since the passage of the Immigration Act of 1965, which eliminated the use of immigration quotas based on national origin. According to 2014 U.S. Census Bureau estimates, the total population of Asian Americans of 20 ethnic groups has reached 19 million, about 5.6% of the entire U.S. population. This percentage is up from less than 1% in 1965. The six largest groups of this population are Chinese (23%), Filipinos (20%), Indian (17%), Korean (10%), Vietnamese (10%), and Japanese (9%). Over 60% of Asian Americans are immigrants.

The most recent wave of Asian immigrants has been different from those who came in the 19th century escaping poverty to work as manual laborers on the transcontinental railroad. Many who have arrived since the 1980s, particularly those from China and India, have been immigrant investors or graduate students gaining entry to institutions for higher education. These Indians and

Chinese newcomers are on average well-educated and prosperous, whereas other Asian immigrants, especially those coming as refugees from Southeast Asia with limited English proficiency, often struggle to adapt their lives in the United States.

Academic Performance

On the whole, Asian Americans have relatively high levels of academic performance and educational attainment. As of 2015, 54% of Asian Americans had at least a bachelor's degree, compared to 33% of the general population of the United States. In addition, despite representing only 5.6% of the total population, Asian Americans receive 25–30% of the National Merit Scholarships and make up more than 30% of the math and physics Olympiad teams and Presidential scholars.

Relatively speaking, Asian Americans perform well on intelligence tests and standardized assessments. This population is seen as academic high achievers and industrious students who, on average, tend to outperform their White peers. Yet relatively high academic performance is by no means the norm for all Asian Americans. Many Asian immigrant students struggle in school and drop out at relatively high rate, particularly those from Southeast Asia.

Cultural Traditions and Social Context

Asian cultures tend to place high value on intellectual prowess as expressed on exams. Confucius, an ancient Chinese philosopher whose influence spread across Asia like that of Socrates and Plato in Europe, stressed that working with one's intellect was preferable to working with one's hands. The testing culture in China began during the Tang Dynasty (618–907), when imperial exams began to act as the gatekeeper to choose the best scholars for lucrative positions in the government and bureaucracy, the respected route for social upward mobility. This tradition of testing infiltrated other nearby societies, as the neighboring cultures of Korea, Japan, and Vietnam also began adopting such practices. In essence, ever since the first millennium, Asian cultures have viewed performance on tests as an important criterion of demonstrating competence.

There are three main schools of thought on the reasons for the superior academic performance of Asian American students. The first focuses on their families. There is evidence to suggest Asian families who immigrated to the United States tend to have attained higher levels of education, which may also lead to their marital stability and high incomes. These factors contribute to great family support for the academic achievement of Asian American youths. Considering children's accomplishment as parental success and family honor, Asian parents tend to put much of their resources and effort into their children's education and academic pursuits.

In addition, Asian students tend to have authoritarian parents who demand academic excellence and believe that great effort brings great success. These parents tend to push their children to work long hours, send them to tutoring programs and test–prep classes, establish community heritage schools for their children to study their home languages, and encourage their children to join chess clubs or participate in any activities that they consider would sharpen their children's minds and learning habits. With such familial support and motivation, Asian students come into school with a systemic foundation for scholastic achievement.

The second explanation of Asian academic performance involves intrinsic factors, such as motivation and self-control. Being from a culture that believes in sacrificing the present for the future and forgoing personal interest for family honors, Asian students are disciplined at a young age to fight against any distraction from their concentration on academic work. Studies have found that these internally oriented factors contribute to one's attentiveness to tasks, persistence to finish tasks, and patience for boring drills and memorization exercises. These abilities serve as major assets when taking exams, allowing great focus on the details of the questions asked and stamina throughout the duration of the exam. Such personality traits common among Asian American students contribute to strong performance on tests.

Asian Americans' academic effort may also be attributed to their immigrant status. There are several explanations for this "immigrant paradox." First, immigrants are self-selected for leaving their homeland for better opportunities and future success in their chosen host country. As newcomers devoid of much social or political capital, they may see education as the most efficient means for upward mobility in a foreign land.

Even without the guarantees of benefits of societal support, educational attainment may be seen as a path toward brighter futures. When nothing is guaranteed, Asian Americans may see education as an unbiased arbiter rewarding diligence and effort with a higher standard of living.

After a century of marginalization, Asian Americans, often seen as "foreigners" or "outsiders," have come not to expect anything, but to work hard to reach their goals. As indicated earlier, their collective history in the country began on the lower rungs of society, as largely invisible to the rest of society. To offset these barriers, Asians see academics and traversing the gatekeeper of exams as the best route to societal recognition.

Chief among these expectations is postsecondary education, as expectations for college entrance are markedly higher among Asian students as compared to their White peers. Standardized tests are the means to attain that goal, and so, Asian American families may expend more effort and capital in test preparation than other racial and ethnic groups. Asian students, as a result of this cultural and familial push, tend to see tests as more indicative of their worth and essential to their future success than do their White peers. As a result, they may strive harder to excel on these exams and take them more seriously than others. Compounded with the rich testing tradition, these factors compel and propel Asian test takers to outperform their counterparts.

Test-Driven Tradition and Its Drawbacks

Each Asian American ethnic group brings its unique characteristics and traditions to American society. Yet, all these ethnic groups seem to prioritize education and intellectual superiority, which may be seen as an assured guarantee of success. The Asian societies that best conform to the stereotype of superior test performance are Singapore, Hong Kong, Korea, Japan, Taiwan, and China. Three cultures, Singapore, Korea, and China, are highlighted in this section.

First, Singapore's entire educational system throughout the year is solely geared to the end of the year exams given throughout the country. Teachers mainly teach according to the textbooks, giving worksheets and drills to reinforce the material. Semantic memory of facts and specifics through sheer memorization and rehearsal are

prioritized. As such, all learning leads to eventual demonstration of taught knowledge on exams. This acclimates students to perform well on standardized exams.

As another example, South Korea also has had a long history of standardized examinations to assess student achievement. In fact, the nation utilizes one, standardized national exam for consideration for university admittance. This test prioritizes rote memorization and information recall and does not effectively gauge examinees' more fluid intelligences, such as creativity or analytical thinking. Also, because of these pressures from standardized achievement exams, most South Korean students (84%) attend extracurricular private educational academies to bolster their scores.

Finally, in China, standardized exams are also given much emphasis. Owing to its more direct Confucian roots and the perpetuation of well-established traditions of examination, Chinese students are also educated in a framework geared toward test performance. From elementary school onward, students are given unified competency exams to classify and rank students with classmates and compete with peers in the same province. There are entrance exams for middle and high school, and especially for college. College entrance exams are an entire family affair, as family members devote time and energy to provide the most conducive climate for achievement on these high-stakes exams. During the annual national college exam dates, some Chinese cities even limit traffic to ensure the proper conditions for students to take their exams.

Asian nations have developed as highly competitive test-driven societies. Responsible parents prepare their offspring to compete from the moment of their birth. As such, a large part of education in these Asian nations is on assisting in performance on these high-stakes tests. For example, Chinese parents are apt to spend exorbitant amounts of capital on test preparation services, which for the most part, teach tricks and guessing strategies to outsmart the test companies. In fact, test takers often have little to no idea what the questions are specifically asking but use test-taking and guessing strategies so adeptly as to approximate the correct answers. Test preparation and tutoring services have become one of the most lucrative businesses in China.

There are validity issues with standardized test performance after years of test-focused education.

First, these tests, rather than measuring the intended indices, may partly gauge students' test-taking abilities. Strategies such as how to memorize, formulate responses, and guess right answers on tests can improve scores dramatically without marked difference in intellect. Often those teachers who know how to guess the test items correctly are considered the most able teachers, and the test–prep cram schools are most favored when they can provide students with the practice exams that closely approximate testing items.

A second issue confounding validity is that of cheating. Giving the high stakes of test scores, cheating can be common in many Asian countries. For example, there are cases where test takers will memorize the entire standardized exam and print it in review books to assist future test takers. Specifically, in South Korea and China, cheating cases associated with standardized tests have caused cancellation and nullification of SAT scores by the Educational Testing Service or the College Board.

For many Asian American parents and students, the beliefs, expectations, and practices about academics common in their home cultures have carried over to their lives in the United States. Although high achievers who are seen as diligent and disciplined, Asian Americans are cast as great workers but face stereotypes that they lack the audacity, ingenuity, and other qualities of leaders. These stereotypes are believed to contribute to Asian Americans' underrepresentation in leadership positions in many areas of society. For instance, a 2015 report said that while Asian Americans make up 27% of the professional workforce in Silicon Valley technology companies, they comprise just 14% of executive positions.

Xiaodi Zhou and Danling Fu

See also Achievement Tests; African Americans and Testing; Cultural Competence; Culturally Responsive Evaluation; Gender and Testing; High-Stakes Tests; Intelligence Tests; Standardized Tests

Further Readings

Ghymn, E. M. (Ed.). (2000). *Asian American studies: Identities, images, issues past and present*. Peter Long International Academic Publishers.

Hsin, A., & Xie, Y. (2014). Explaining Asian Americans' academic advantage over whites. *Proceedings of National Academy of Science, 111*, 16–21.

Lee, J., & Zhou, M. (2015). *Asian American achievement paradox*. Russell Sage Foundation.

Ryan, C. L., & Bauman, K. (2016, March). *Educational attainment in the United States: 2015. Current population reports*. Washington, DC: U.S. Census Bureau.

Suárez-Orozco, C., Rhodes, J., & Millburn, M. (2009). Unraveling the immigrant paradox: Academic disengagement and engagement among recently arrived immigrant youth. *Youth Society, 41*, 151–185.

Zhang, Y. (2003). *Immigrant generational differences in academic achievement and its growth: The case of Asian American high school students*. Paper presented at the Annual Meeting of the American Educational Research Association, Chicago, IL.

ASPERGER'S SYNDROME

Asperger's syndrome is a neurodevelopmental disorder named after the Viennese pediatrician Hans Asperger. This entry first discusses the initial conceptualization of the disorder and more recent changes in how it is conceptualized. It then details the characteristics of the Asperger's syndrome, the tendency of children with the disorder to be teased and bullied, and the outcomes for those with the disorder as adults.

In the late 1930s, Hans Asperger, a Viennese pediatrician, noticed that some of the children referred to his clinic had a distinct and unusual profile of abilities. Despite having intellectual ability within the normal range, the children had a limited ability to have a reciprocal social interaction with peers and adults, difficulty reading body language, and conspicuous delays in social reasoning, as well as difficulties making and maintaining friendships. Other characteristics were an intense interest in a specific subject, difficulty coping with change, a tendency to impose routines and rituals, and extreme distress in response to specific sensory experiences. Asperger considered that the profile was an expression of autism, and we now conceptualize Asperger's syndrome as an autism spectrum disorder (ASD).

The term *Asperger's disorder* was first included in the fourth edition of the *Diagnostic and Statistical Manual of Mental Disorders (DSM)*, published in 1994. There has subsequently been a great deal of research defining the characteristics and evaluating intervention strategies for children at school and in the home and for adults at college and in the workplace. In May 2013, the American Psychiatric Association published the fifth edition of the *DSM* (*DSM-5*) and replaced the term *Asperger's disorder* with the diagnostic term *autism spectrum disorder level 1, without accompanying intellectual or language impairment*, a lengthier and more cumbersome term. The rationale is that ASD can be conceptualized as a dimensional rather than a categorical concept and that a single umbrella term of ASD, with specific information on the level of expression, is more accurate and consistent with the research literature and clinical experience. However, the term *Asperger's syndrome* is still used by clinicians, parents, teachers, therapists, and those with an ASD. The general public and media also continue to use the term. For simplicity and continuity, this entry uses the term *Asperger's syndrome*.

Key Characteristics

The *DSM-5* diagnostic criteria refer to persistent deficits in social communication and social interaction across multiple contexts, with deficits in social–emotional reciprocity, nonverbal communication, and the development, maintenance, and understanding of relationships. The underlying assumption is that someone who has Asperger's syndrome has difficulty "reading" social situations. The deficits in social–emotional reciprocity can be expressed by a tendency to be withdrawn, shy, and introspective in social situations, avoiding or minimizing participation or conversations; or, conversely, actively seeking social engagement and being conspicuously intrusive and intense, dominating the interaction and being unaware of social conventions such as acknowledging personal space. In each example, there is an imbalance in social reciprocity.

There is a third strategy for coping with difficulties with "reading" social situations and that is to avidly observe and intellectually analyze social behavior, subsequently achieving reciprocal social interaction by imitation and by using an observed and practiced social "script" based on intellectual analysis rather than intuition. This is a

compensatory mechanism often used by girls who have Asperger's syndrome, who are thus able to express superficial social abilities. In addition, adults who have Asperger's syndrome can gradually learn to read social cues and conventions, such that any deficits in social–emotional reciprocity may not be conspicuous during a brief social interaction.

One of the characteristics of Asperger's syndrome is a difficulty reading someone's body language, facial expressions, gestures, and voice to indicate their thoughts and feelings and then incorporating that information in the conversation or interaction. We conceptualize this difficulty as an expression of impaired theory of mind.

Asperger's syndrome is also associated with a signature language profile. This can include impaired pragmatic language abilities (i.e., the "art" of conversation) with a tendency to engage in monologues and a failure to follow conversational rules. There may also be literal interpretations, with a tendency for the person to become confused by idioms, figures of speech, and sarcasm. There may also be unusual prosody, for example, a child may consistently use an accent based on the voice of a television character or an adult may speak with an unusual tone, pitch, or rhythm. All these characteristics affect the reciprocity and quality of conversation.

Another diagnostic characteristic is restricted, repetitive patterns of behavior, interests, or activities. This can include insistence on sameness, inflexible routines, and the acquisition of information on a specific topic. Parents and teachers are often concerned that routines and rituals are imposed in daily life, with the child showing great agitation if prevented from completing a particular routine or ritual at home or in class. There is a determination to maintain consistency in daily events and high levels of anxiety if routines are changed.

The special interests, which can occur throughout both childhood and the adult years, often involve the acquisition of information and knowledge on a specific topic and are unusual in terms of intensity or focus. Each interest has a "use by date," ranging from hours to decades, and research has indicated that the interest has many functions, such as being a "'thought blocker" for anxiety, an energy restorative after the exhaustion of socializing, or an extremely enjoyable activity. Special interests can also create a sense of identity and achievement, as well as provide an opportunity for making like-minded friends who share the same interests. The sense of well-being associated with the interest can become almost addictive, such that the interest begins to dominate the person's time at home; this may lead to genuine concern that it is preventing engagement in any other activities.

The *DSM-5* includes reference to sensory sensitivity as one of the hallmark characteristics of ASD. This has been a characteristic of Asperger's syndrome that has been clearly and consistently described in autobiographies and recognized by parents and teachers. Sensory sensitivity can be a lifelong problem, with sensitivity to distinct sensory experiences that are not perceived as particularly aversive by peers. These can include specific sounds, especially "sharp" noises such as a dog barking or someone shouting; tactile sensitivity on a specific part of the body; and aversive reaction to specific aromas, light intensity, and other sensory experiences. In contrast, there can be a lack of sensitivity to some sensory experiences, such as pain and low or high temperatures. The child or adult can feel overwhelmed by the complex sensory experiences in particular situations, such as shopping malls, supermarkets, birthday parties, or the school playground. Sometimes, social withdrawal is not due simply to social confusion but to the need to avoid sensory experiences that are perceived as unbearably intense or overwhelming.

Additional Characteristics

Mood Disorders

While the child may have considerable intellectual ability and academic achievement, there is invariably confusion and immaturity with regard to understanding and expressing feelings and a vulnerability to developing signs of an anxiety disorder or depression. There may also be a need for guidance in the management and expression of anger and affection. The theoretical models of autism developed within cognitive psychology and research in neuropsychology and neuroimaging provide some explanation as to why children and adults with Asperger's syndrome are prone to secondary mood disorders.

The term *alexithymia* is used to describe a characteristic associated with Asperger's syndrome, namely an impaired ability to identify and describe feeling states. Children and adults with Asperger's syndrome often have a limited vocabulary of words to describe feeling states, especially the subtler or complex emotions, and will need education in perceiving and expressing emotions. Over the last decade, there has been the development and evaluation of a new range of cognitive behavior therapy programs for parents and teachers to help those who have Asperger's syndrome understand and express emotions at home and at school.

Cognitive Abilities

Children with Asperger's syndrome often have an unusual profile of cognitive abilities. Some young children may start school with academic abilities above their grade level, such as advanced literacy and numeracy that may have been self-taught through watching educational television programs, using educational computer programs, or avidly looking at books and reading about a special interest. Some young children with Asperger's syndrome appear to easily "crack the code" of reading, spelling, or numeracy; indeed, these subjects may become their special interest and a subsequent talent. In contrast, some children with Asperger's syndrome have considerable delay in these academic skills, and an assessment of their cognitive abilities suggests specific learning disorders, especially dyslexia. There are more children with Asperger's syndrome than one might expect at the extremes of cognitive and academic ability.

At school, teachers often recognize that the child has a distinctive learning style, often being talented in their understanding of the logical and physical world, as well as noticing details and remembering and arranging facts in a systematic fashion. However, the child can be easily distracted, especially by noises or social activity in the classroom, and when problem solving, appears to have a "one-track mind" and a fear of failure. As the child progresses through the school years, teachers may identify problems with organizational abilities, especially with regard to homework assignments and essays. They also note that the child appears to not follow advice, look to peers for guidance, or learn from mistakes. End-of-year school reports often describe a conspicuously uneven profile of academic achievement, with areas of excellence and areas that require remedial assistance.

The research on IQ profiles indicates that children with Asperger's syndrome tend to have good factual and lexical knowledge. Their highest scores are often on the subtests that measure vocabulary, general knowledge, and verbal problem solving. In the visual reasoning subtests, children with Asperger's syndrome can achieve relatively high scores on the Block Design and Matrices tests. However, the profile can also include slower processing speed and impaired auditory working memory.

Movement and Coordination

As much as children with Asperger's syndrome have a different way of thinking, they can also have a different way of moving. When walking or running, the child's coordination can be immature, sometimes with an idiosyncratic gait that lacks fluency and efficiency. On careful observation, there can be a lack of synchrony in the movement of the arms and legs, especially when the person is running. Parents often report that the young child needs considerable guidance in learning activities that require manual dexterity, such as tying shoe laces, dressing, and using eating utensils. The movement and coordination problems can be obvious to the physical education teacher and other children during PE classes and sports and in playground games that require ball skills. The child with Asperger's syndrome can be immature in the development of the ability to catch, throw, and kick a ball. One of the consequences of not being successful or popular at ball games is the exclusion of the child from some of the social games in the playground. Such children may choose to actively avoid these activities, knowing they are not as able as their peers.

Teachers and parents can become quite concerned about difficulties with handwriting. The individual letters can be poorly formed and the child may take too long to complete each letter, causing delay in completing written tasks. While other children in the class may have written several sentences, children with Asperger's syndrome are still deliberating over the first sentence, trying to write legibly, and becoming increasingly frustrated or embarrassed about their inability to write neatly and consistently.

Teasing and Bullying

Children who have Asperger's syndrome are frequently targets of teasing, bullying, rejection, and humiliation. This can have a devastating effect on self-esteem and is a major cause of depression in adolescence and a contributory factor for school refusal and school suspension for retaliation. Schools are becoming more aware of this problem and introducing programs to prevent teasing, bullying, and rejection specifically designed for children and adolescents who have Asperger's syndrome.

The Adult Years

The children who were diagnosed with Asperger's syndrome in the last 20 years are now becoming adults. Also, diagnosticians are increasingly receiving referrals for diagnostic assessments of mature adults who are the relatives of young children with Asperger's syndrome. Practitioners and researchers therefore are now exploring the challenges faced by adults in terms of tertiary education, employment, and relationships. There is a trend for the signs of Asperger's syndrome to become increasingly less conspicuous with maturity and support and the potential for the achievement of a successful career and a long-term relationship.

Tony Attwood

See also Anxiety; Autism Spectrum Disorder; *Diagnostic and Statistical Manual of Mental Disorders*

Further Readings

Attwood, T. (2007). *The complete guide to Asperger's syndrome.* London, UK: Jessica Kingsley Publishers.

ASSENT

Assent is an agreement to take part in research activities that may be given orally, in writing, or in the preferred communication medium of the participant. Assent to participate in research may be given following the provision of information about the project, or specific activity, but without the individual necessarily receiving a full disclosure about potential benefits, risks, and the procedures or activities of research participation, as would be the case for *informed consent*. In educational research, assent is most often discussed in relation to the involvement in research of children and young people (under 18 years old). A legal parent or guardian would typically be expected to provide fully informed consent before the child is approached for their assent. This entry describes the main principles and practices of assent and the different interpretations of the term in educational research.

Core Principles and Practices of Assent

Although there are differences of interpretation, there are some common core principles and practices of assent. Primarily, assent is understood to be an *agreement* to take part in a specific activity within a research project, such as an interview, group discussion, creative activities, being observed (e.g., in a classroom), or completing a questionnaire or test. The agreement to participate should be *voluntary and explicit*; nonrefusal or passive involvement are not typically accepted as indicators that a child has provided assent to take part in an activity. Participation should, therefore, be an *active choice*, which means that a child has to decide whether to participate or not. Choosing not to participate is usually called *dissent*, and children should be given clear opportunities to assent or dissent to their own research participation.

Researchers also need to respect the rights of children to be given the opportunity to assent or dissent and to respect their decision once made. To enable children to make a clear choice about research participation, they would usually be provided with information about specific project activities in an accessible way. This could be through the use of simplified text, pictures, photographs, or videos that may be accompanied by verbal explanations. This simplification of information is one of the features that distinguishes assent from informed consent.

Historical and Conceptual Development

The concept of assent emerged from developments in understanding children's status and agency as competent individuals, capable of making decisions and contributing their views. This *sociology of childhood* understands children as having unique and valuable perspectives on the world,

separate and distinct from adults. This perspective has been both strengthened by and reflected in a *rights-based approach* to children's participation, stimulated primarily by the United Nations Convention on the Rights of the Child (UNCRC) in 1989. The convention is aimed at supporting children's human rights internationally and has been ratified by 195 members of the United Nations, with the United States the only member state that had not ratified it as of 2016.

Among other things, the UNCRC stipulated the right of children to be heard in all matters affecting them, with due weight given to those views according to the age and maturity of the child (Article 12). According to the United Nations Children's Fund, this means that "when adults are making decisions that affect children, children have the right to say what they think should happen and have their opinions taken into account" (United Nations Children's Fund, n.p.). Article 12 of the UNCRC recognizes that children's ability to make decisions develops with age and so the views of teenagers, for example, would be given more weight than those of a very young child. Article 13 of the UNCRC accords children the right of freedom of expression, which means that (within the law) they can receive and share information in any way they choose, including talking, drawing, and writing. The principles of Articles 12 and 13 are relevant to assent because they recognize that children, depending on their age and maturity, may not be able to provide fully informed consent to take part in research. Children can, however, provide their assent or dissent based on specific information relating to specific activities, and their choice may be communicated in different ways.

Interpretations of Assent in Educational Research

There is not a consensus about what assent means in practice or in principle in educational research. Some researchers do not think that assent is a valid concept, partly because it implies that children are not competent or capable of giving their informed consent and that adults are always needed to provide an informed view. This stance critiques assent because it undermines the agency of children to make their own decisions.

There is also recognition that adults exert power over children's decision making in ways that make it difficult to dissent; for example, if a parent or teacher has already provided informed consent, then the child may not feel able to opt out. Assent is problematic when young people are involved in research about sensitive topics (e.g., teenage pregnancy, sexuality, illegal activities) where it could be detrimental (to the young person) to seek informed consent from parents or carers. By contrast, some researchers take a more pragmatic view, arguing that a child needs to understand and feel comfortable about what they are being asked to do, and a process of assent can enable this understanding. Within this context, there is an onus on researchers to be knowledgeable about, and sensitive to, the needs of the participants they want to include in their research. This means taking care to tailor the presentation and content of information in ways that will be accessible and meaningful for children and young people and revisiting assent throughout a project.

Sarah Parsons

See also Informed Consent; Institutional Review Boards; Qualitative Research Methods

Further Readings

Cocks, A. J. (2006). The ethical maze: Finding an inclusive path towards gaining children's agreement to research participation. *Childhood, 13*(2), 247–266.

Dockett, S., & Perry, B. (2011). Researching with young children: Seeking assent. *Child Indicators Research, 4*(2), 231–247.

Hammersley, M. (2015). Research ethics and the concept of children's rights. *Children & Society, 29*(6), 569–582.

Hurley, J. C., & Underwood, M. K. (2002). Children's understanding of their research rights before and after debriefing: Informed assent, confidentiality, and stopping participation. *Child Development, 73*(1), 132–143.

Parsons, S., Sherwood, G., & Abbott, C. (2016). Informed consent with children and young people in social research: Is there scope for innovation? *Children & Society, 30*(2), 132–145.

Renold, E., Holland, S., Ross, N. J., & Hillman, A. (2008). Becoming participant—Problematizing informed consent in participatory research with young people in care. *Qualitative Social Work, 7*(4), 427–447.

United Nations Children's Fund (n.d.). Fact sheet: A summary of the rights under the Convention on the Rights of the Child. Retrieved from http://www.unicef.org/crc/files/Rights_overview.pdf

ATLAS.ti

ATLAS.ti stands for *Archiv für Technik, Lebenswelt und Alltagssprache* (Archive for Technology, Lifeworld and Everyday Language.text interpretation) and is one of the several computer-assisted qualitative data analysis software (CAQDAS or more simply QDAS) packages that can be used to manage every phase of a qualitative research study. Other QDAS packages include QSR NVivo, MAXQDA, Dedoose, HyperResearch, QDA Miner, Quirkos, and Transana.

ATLAS.ti was developed from 1989 to 1992 as an interdisciplinary research project by scholars in psychology, educational science, and computer science at the Technical University of Berlin. In 1993, Scientific Software Development GmbH released the first commercial version. In 2013, Free iPad and Android apps were released, and in late 2014 a Mac-native version was released. Version 8 is scheduled for release in late 2016. Two ATLAS.ti user conferences were held in Berlin in 2013 and 2015, and the conference proceedings are available online.

QDAS packages can assist with the management and analysis of a wide variety of qualitative data useful for educational research, such as interviews, focus groups, recordings of classroom interactions and observational field notes, web pages, documents and records, social media conversations, images, videos, Google Earth maps, and responses to open-ended survey questions. This entry describes ways in which ATLAS.ti can be used to carry out a variety of analytic strategies, provides examples of how various components of the software can be used to do so, and recommends best practices for reporting the use of ATLAS.ti in research reports.

Analytic Activities

QDAS packages should not be confused with data analysis software such as SPSS, STATA, or SAS, which automatically analyze the data according to statistical formulas. Rather, ATLAS.ti is a platform, or workbench, in which researchers can choose how to organize, store, and structure their unstructured or semi-structured data in a systematic way that is aligned with their methodological approach. As described by the software manual, visualization, integration, serendipity, and exploration principles underlie its design. *Visualization* tools help researchers elicit meaning from the data; all project materials can be *integrated* within the software; browsing the data with the software encourages *serendipitous* findings; and the software supports an *exploratory* yet systematic approach to analysis.

Any qualitative methodological approach can be enacted in the software, be it thematic analysis, grounded theory analysis, discourse analysis, or ethnographic approaches to name a few. Christina Silver and Ann Lewins have suggested that there are five main categories of analytic activities that can be supported by ATLAS.ti and other QDAS packages: *integrating* data sources and analytic approaches; *exploring* the content and structure of the data; *organizing* materials and ideas; *reflecting* on data, interpretations, processes, and results; and *retrieving*, reviewing, and rethinking ideas about the data.

ATLAS.ti can be used to create what Zdeněk Konopásek called a textual laboratory to organize, store, and manage data sources alongside other project documents such as data collection instruments, ethics board approval forms, and even the research literature. Literature reviews require, in essence, a type of qualitative data analysis, and PDFs of articles can be uploaded into ATLAS.ti and the components used to analyze them in a systematic and visible way. With version 8, bibliographic data from reference management software such as Endnote, Zotero, and Mendeley can be imported into a project and triangulated with other data sources. Organizing the data in a project file makes the data portable, and annotating the data within the ATLAS.ti project file creates a visible audit trail. Both of these features support smooth collaboration across team members.

By taking a laptop or iPad into the field, researchers can easily type up field notes, take photos, record video and audio, and import relevant PDF documents into a project. The iPad data can then be uploaded to cloud-storage programs such as Dropbox and imported into the desktop version of the program for analysis. The iPad app does allow for direct coding or memoing of the files which can be useful for immediate analysis

and note taking that can be more fully developed upon return from the field.

ATLAS.ti supports the transcription of audio and video recordings as well as the association between the transcripts and the audio and video sources. Transcriptions can be done in ATLAS.ti with shortcut keys or by connecting a foot pedal to facilitate typing, and the resulting transcripts can be synchronized with the recordings. In this way, when the researcher clicks into the transcript, that part of the recording will be played, thus keeping the analyst closer to the source of the data. Audio and video files can also be coded directly without transcribing.

ATLAS.ti has some automated analysis tools such as text search tools, a word frequency count tool, and an auto-coding feature which allows the researcher to quickly find and label key words of interest. The various coding features allow the researcher to create and link analytically meaningful labels to various segments of the data, after which all labeled, and thus related, portions of the data can be retrieved at once. In this way, the researchers can review all related sections of the data together as they create the interpretations to answer the research questions. Data and initial interpretations can be graphically displayed for further exploration through visualization. All analytic work can be exported into text files or spreadsheets for further work outside of the software. ATLAS.ti provides writing tools in which reflective memos and notes, interpretations of the findings, team meeting notes, and other important decisions about the study can be documented.

Components of ATLAS.ti

Effective use of ATLAS.ti requires selecting and using software components in a way that will enact the desired analytic strategy. Nicholas Woolf and Christina Silver call this process Five-Level QDA, in which individual analytic tasks are matched to the underlying components of the software. They have organized ATLAS.ti's components into five major groups: components that support *providing* data, *segmenting* data, *conceptualizing* the segments, *writing*, and *interrogating* data and its analysis.

Providing data involves creating "primary documents" within the project file. These can be existing data sources (e.g., digital images or interview transcripts created outside of the software) or can be created internally to the software (e.g., by typing observational field notes directly into the software). Primary documents that are related in some way can be grouped and later interrogated for how the results of the analysis are distributed across any cases, participant groups, or other demographic characteristics of interest.

Segmenting data entails creating analytically meaningful units within the primary documents. These units are called "quotations" and can exist on their own (free quotations) or can be linked to other components—such as memos, codes, or other quotations. Quotations are the building blocks of the analysis, with all reports of the analysis organized by numbers of quotations, for instance, by numbers of quotations assigned to a certain code, numbers of coded quotations per primary document, or the co-occurrence of coded quotations across the data.

Conceptualizing segments refers to the process of creating analytic meaning from the data. "Codes" can be created and attached to quotations, codes that are related in some way can be organized into groups, and codes can be linked to other codes. ATLAS.ti has an "in vivo" coding feature where exact words of the participants become the code name. Codes can be organized by color or into hierarchies using prefixes or other naming conventions.

Writing is a fundamental practice of qualitative research. The "comment" component provides a space in which to capture important information about the primary document data sources, the meaning of codes, and reflections on individual quotations. A robust "memo" tool provides a flexible way to, for example, document the analytic approach being used, write up analytic insights and interpretations, capture team meeting notes, or pose questions that arise during the analysis. Memos that are related to each other in some way can be organized into groups.

The interrogating components of ATLAS.ti allow the researcher to ask questions of the data after quotations, memos, and codes have been created and/or linked. These include the ability to retrieve quotations that have been assigned to a certain code so that they can be viewed together; network views in which displays of linked components provide a visual representation of the analysis, and the co-occurrence explorer, which can retrieve quotations that have been coded with more than one code in order to display possible relationships between the codes.

Together, the components of ATLAS.ti provide a robust toolkit with which researchers can impose structure on the data in a way that is aligned with the methodological design of the study.

Best Practices in Reporting the Use of ATLAS.ti

Megan Woods, Trena Paulus, David Atkins, and Rob Macklin conducted a literature review of all peer-reviewed journal articles published from 1994 to 2013 that reported use of ATLAS.ti and QSR NVivo in order to investigate the prevalence of software use in qualitative research. Although the use of QDAS was found to be on the rise, most researchers are using it only for the data analysis phase of their studies and for traditional qualitative data sources (e.g., interviews, focus groups, documents, field notes, and open-ended survey questions).

Few researchers included details about how they used the software other than mentioning that they did so. Given the flexibility of the software, such lack of detail may perpetuate persistent misconceptions—that it can automatically analyze the data, for example, or that using QDAS inherently improves the study's rigor. Instead, researchers should report the following information when using QDAS in their studies: (a) Given that the components of QDAS change with each new version, identify the version that was used. (b) So as not to give the impression that the software, rather than the researcher, is doing the analysis, use active voice (the research team created quotations and assigned codes to the data) rather than passive voice (ATLAS.ti was used to analyze the data). (c) Provide a brief description of what the software is, what it is used for, why it was selected, and which components were used and how. If possible, include software outputs (e.g., code lists and definitions or network view graphical representations) as part of the data display and findings in order to retain the connection between the use of the software and the final researcher interpretations.

Trena M. Paulus

Further Readings

Friese, S. (2014). *Qualitative data analysis with ATLAS.ti 7* (2nd ed.). London, UK: Sage.

Gilbert, L. S., Jackson, K., & diGregorio, S. (2014). Tools for analyzing qualitative data: The history and relevance of qualitative data analysis software. In J. M. Spector, M. D. Merrill, J. Elen, & M. J. Bishop (Eds.), *Handbook of research on educational communications and technology* (4th ed., pp. 221–236). New York, NY: Springer.

Konopasek, Z. (2008). Making thinking visible with ATLAS.ti: Computer-assisted qualitative analysis as textual practices. *FORUM: Qualitative Social Research, 9*(2), Art. 12.

Paulus, T., & Bennett, A. (in press). Integrating ATLAS.ti into qualitative research methods courses: Beyond data analysis. *International Journal of Research and Method in Education.* Retrieved from http://dx.doi.org/10.1080/1743727X.2015.1056137

Paulus, T., & Lester, J. (2016). ATLAS.ti for conversation and discourse analysis. *International Journal of Social Research Methodology 19*(4), 405–428.

Paulus, T., Lester, J., & Dempster, P. (2014). *Digital tools for qualitative research.* London, UK: Sage.

Paulus, T., Woods, M., Atkins, D., & Macklin, R. (in press). The discourse of QDAS: Reporting practices of ATLAS.ti and NVivo users with implications for best practices. *International Journal of Social Research Methodology.* Retrieved from http://dx.doi.org/10.1080/13645579.2015.1102454

Pope, L. (2016). On conducting a literature review with ATLAS.ti. *ATLAS.ti Research Blog.* Retrieved from http://atlasti.com/2016/09/01/litreview/

Silver, C., & Lewins, A. (2014). *Using software in qualitative research: A step by step guide* (2nd ed.). London, UK: Sage.

Woolf, N., & Silver, C. (in press). *Qualitative analysis using ATLAS.ti: The five-level QDA method.* Routledge.

ATTENTION

The term *attention* refers to the way in which humans allocate limited cognitive resources to information processing. *Arousal, effort, mental effort, concentration, mental involvement*, and *engagement* are the terms that are usually used for defining attention. Selective attention, sustained attention, and divided attention are the issues of greatest concern in educational settings.

Due to the different definitions and issues emphasized in different disciplines such as cognitive psychology, clinical psychology, and neuropsychology, the assessment of attention involves different approaches with different instruments. The assessment of attention can reveal the individual differences in learning concentration and control strategies; therefore, it is important for studies in the science of learning, educational counseling, and individualized learning. This entry describes the definitions of attention from different perspectives and reviews the primary assessment approaches based on these perspectives. The entry concludes with an overview of the advantages and disadvantages of these evaluation approaches as well as a list of resources on the measurement of attention.

Issues of Attention

Multidimensional perspectives of attention have been addressed in various psychological disciplines since the 1950s when studies on cognitive process began to be increasingly emphasized. The foundation of attention in cognitive psychology is the capacity model, which argues that the total amount of cognitive resources for attention is limited. In the information processing model, attention is a process of information selection and filtering between the humans' sensory registers and working memory.

Selective attention can explain how students catch the main ideas in school lectures. *Effort* or *mental effort* is a term that is often used to indicate how much attention an individual puts into a task. *Mental involvement* and *mental engagement* are terms that are sometimes used to reveal different degrees of attention paid to processing specific learning materials. From the neuroscientific perspective, attention has been regarded as an *arousal* that is spontaneously activated by environmental stimulations or intentionally controlled for achieving specific goals. The manifestations of arousal include eye blink, pupil dilation, skin conduction, and brain wave.

Sustained attention indicates how individuals keep focused on a task. It is an important indicator for discriminating attention-deficit/hyperactivity disorder in clinics and special education. *Divided attention* refers to the divided allocations of attentional resources when an individual performs multiple tasks simultaneously. It is associated with the control and management of limited resources and plays an important role in the performance of multitasking. These attentional models serve as the theoretical foundations of the development of the multimedia learning theory and the cognitive load theory, the two primary guides for the contemporary design of instructional technology and digital learning.

Measurement of Attention

Generally, three primary approaches have been used for the assessment of attention: *reported scales*, *performance-based tests*, and *physiological measures*. Reported scales are the questionnaires or checklists to be checked by learners themselves or by others, such as teachers or parents. The attention assessed by a self-reported scale is often referred to as *perceived attention*. Sometimes, interviews are employed as complements of reported questionnaires. Performance-based tests are the most commonly used approach in lab-based experiments and clinical practice. For example, the continued performance test for sustained attention is commonly used for diagnosing attention-deficit/hyperactivity disorder in young children. Dual-task performance is an approach usually used to assess the attention one pays to the primary task by measuring the response time or error rate of the secondary task, which in turn reveals the cognitive load of the primary task indirectly. Reaction time or error rates are the measures often reported by performance-based tests.

Physiological measures are rooted in the significant correlations between the attentional features and physiological measures tracked by specific types of equipment. For example, *eye-tracking* systems can detect and track an individual's visual focus during a task and output various measures such as fixation-based, saccade-based, pupil-based, and eye-blinking measures. Analyses of these measures are usually used to reveal an individual's visual attention distributions and transfers on learning materials, which may imply the individual's mental workloads or learning motivation. An *electroencephalogram* can reveal an individual's wake–sleep state by detecting the brain waves of the α and θ signals. It is the most reliable tool to measure sustained attention. *Functional magnetic resonance imaging*, on the other hand,

can reveal the brain areas activated by specific cognitive functions.

Advantages and Disadvantages

Different advantages and disadvantages are associated with different evaluation methods for attention. Questionnaires are the most convenient instrument to use for conducting a large-scale survey. Well-developed scales or checklists are easy to use for preliminary diagnoses for attentional problems in educational settings or clinical institutes. Self-reported questionnaires are more reliable to use for adults than for young children.

Self-reported attention is sometimes referred to as perceived attention due to it being limited by self-awareness abilities. Performance-based tests are the most common tool used in laboratory-based experiments. With rigorous experimental controls, it is reliable to examine theoretical hypotheses via performance-based tests. However, the lab-based environments may sometimes restrict the generalizations of results into real and practical contexts.

Physiological measures are the most direct approach for the assessment of attention. Along with the rapid technological development in this area, an increasing amount of research has indicated that it is powerful to reveal humans' implicit behaviors through the assessment of physiological measures. These implicit behaviors include humans' visual attention, concentration, and metacognitive learning strategies. The traditional disadvantages of this method include the high costs of experimental equipment and could involve intrusive treatment. These problems may be changed by the rapid development of computer and image processing technology.

Finally, the three methods have different advantages and disadvantages. The selection of the methods depends on the purpose and the context of the problem to be resolved. Recently, researchers in technology-enhanced learning have begun to explore the potential of using the dynamic assessment of attention to provide personalized feedback for adapted learning.

Meng-Jung Tsai

See also Attention-Deficit/Hyperactivity Disorder; Cognitive Neuroscience; Information Processing Theory; Performance-Based Assessment; Self-Report Inventories; Working Memory

Further Readings

Mahone, E. M., & Schneider, H. E. (2012). Assessment of attention in preschoolers. *Neuropsychology Review, 22,* 361–383.

Oken, B. S., Salinsky, M. C., & Elsas, S. M. (2006). Vigilance, alertness, or sustained attention: Physiological basis and measurement. *Clinical Neurophysiology, 117,* 1885–1901.

Sternberg, R. J., & Sternberg, K. (2014). *Cognitive psychology.* Boston, MA: Cengage Learning.

Tsai, M. J., Huang, L. J., Hou, H. T., Hsu, C. Y., & Chiou, G. L. (2016). Visual behavior, flow and achievement in game-based learning. *Computers & Education, 98,* 115–129.

ATTENTION-DEFICIT/HYPERACTIVITY DISORDER

Attention-deficit/hyperactivity disorder (ADHD) is the term designated by the American Psychiatric Association in the fifth edition of its *Diagnostic and Statistical Manual of Mental Disorders* (*DSM-5*) to refer to the set of three core psychological symptoms—inattention, excessive activity, and impulsivity—when those symptoms begin by age 12, persist for at least 6 months, and interfere with individuals' development and ability to perform the tasks of everyday living. This entry further describes ADHD and discusses its prevalence, the development of the understanding of ADHD and diagnostic criteria for the disorder, risk and protective factors, treatments for ADHD, measurement issues in the evaluation of ADHD, and promising advances in diagnosis and treatment of ADHD from a neuroscience perspective.

For individuals with severe symptoms, the effects of ADHD can have lifelong negative effects on all aspects of cognitive, emotional, and social development, leading to difficulties in learning to read, poor memory, academic failure and dropping out of school, problems at work, alcohol and drug abuse, disruptive relationships with parents, friends, and coworkers, and criminal behavior. According to the Centers for Disease Control and Prevention, 6.4 million children aged between 4 and 17 years, or about 11% of children in that age range, had received a diagnosis of ADHD as of 2011. Centers for Disease Control and Prevention estimates show that boys are more than twice as likely as girls to have the diagnosis. The toll that ADHD can take on personal lives as well as its costs to the economy and society make this topic particularly relevant to the issues of research, measurement, and evaluation.

Effective identification, diagnosis, intervention, and prevention of ADHD remain a significant challenge and depend on the development of greater insights into the nature and progression of ADHD. To achieve this understanding, the development of reliable and valid measurement instruments and research to create powerful strategies for prevention and intervention for individuals with ADHD are needed.

The Concept and Diagnosis of ADHD

The three core symptoms of ADHD impact thinking, feelings, and behavior. Specifically, inattention refers to the inability to focus and sustain attention on relevant information. Typical indicators include making careless mistakes, frequent forgetting and losing of items, failing to complete assignments, and difficulties in organizing and planning. Hyperactivity/impulsivity refers to the inability to control one's thoughts, emotions, and behavior. Indicators include constantly moving and running around, fidgeting and squirming, and interrupting the activities and conversations of others.

ADHD is an incurable, chronic condition that varies in severity from mild to severe. Once considered primarily a childhood disorder due largely to the negative impact the three symptoms have on school performance, ADHD emerges as early as age 3 and continues into adulthood for about 50% of those diagnosed with ADHD as children. Although estimates of ADHD vary widely depending on access to caregivers, estimates of its prevalence range from about 5% to 7% of the world population.

The conception of ADHD has evolved over time as researchers, clinicians, and educators have contributed to the development of knowledge on the topic. Problematic behaviors in children involving their inability to focus and sustain attention and to control activity level and emotional and behavioral impulses when necessary became an issue of concern during the early 1900s with the introduction of universal education. During the 1930s and 1940s, emphasis was placed on the role of brain damage as the source of hyperactivity, but the lack of reliable and valid measures of that damage led to a change in focus. In 1980, in the *DSM-3*, the American Psychiatric Association introduced the term *attention deficit disorder* with and without hyperactivity, placing the emphasis on the attention deficit and impulsivity rather than hyperactivity.

In the *DSM-5*, published in 2013, three types of ADHD are described: inattentive, hyperactive/impulsive, and combined. Two other notable changes in the *DSM-5*, the most widely used manual for diagnosing ADHD, are the switching of ADHD from the category of disruptive behavior disorders to the category of neurodevelopmental disorders, reflecting the increasing evidence from neurological studies showing differences in brain structure and functioning in individuals with ADHD compared to individuals without ADHD and greater recognition of the developmental differences in the ADHD-related behaviors that distinguish ADHD in children from ADHD in adolescents and ADHD in adults.

Risk Factors

No single, definitive cause for ADHD has been identified, although genetic influences are important. Children with ADHD are more likely to have one or both parents and siblings with the condition than are children without ADHD. No single gene for ADHD has been found, although multiple genes have been identified that may interact with each other and the environment to influence the development of ADHD. In his book *What Causes ADHD? Understanding What Goes Wrong and Why*, Joel Nigg describes multiple factors that are involved in the development of ADHD and the need to develop a greater understanding of the interplay of these factors and the multiple pathways to ADHD.

Nigg emphasizes the complexities to consider in children's biological and psychological development as they are influenced by family, peers, and the school and community contexts over the course of development. Among the potential influences identified in research are, in particular, the

mother's behavior during pregnancy, including smoking, alcohol, and drug use, as well as stress. Exposure to toxins in the environment such as lead also places children at risk.

Children with severe ADHD are also at risk for other psychiatric problems. Although ADHD does not cause other mental disorders, the difficulties that individuals experience due to problems with inattention and hyperactivity/impulsivity can lead to learning disabilities, particularly in reading and mathematics, and to social problems that contribute to the development of anxiety and depression and in some instances to conduct disorders such as aggression and delinquency.

Protective Factors

Despite the difficulties that individuals with ADHD face, numerous positive influences can lessen the negative effects of the disorder. Characteristics of the individual can influence access to support in the environment. For example, the individual's attractiveness, intelligence, positive mood, problem-solving skills, and outgoing personality can elicit caring and support from parents, teachers, and peers.

Parents can offer crucial support for their children with ADHD. Examples include using a positive approach in helping children to create regular routines for daily activities; listening carefully and sensitively to their expressions of their needs; giving clear, brief, and reasonable directions to them; reducing distractions in the home; anticipating situations that will frustrate them; and preparing them for how they can manage those situations before they occur.

Similarly, educators can create school environments that provide accommodations for students with ADHD that enhance the focus and sustaining of attention, such as creating individually designed instruction to meet the students' special needs, helping students keep records of their academic performance daily so they can benefit from seeing their progress over time, assisting with organization and planning and management of time, providing work spaces that minimize distractions and extended time for assessments, and most importantly, designing instruction that is interesting and appropriate for the students' abilities. Similarly, strategies can be employed that enhance students' ability to calm and control their impulses, such as computer-enhanced instruction through games and simulations.

Because ADHD is considered a disability, children may qualify for special accommodations under Section 504 of the Rehabilitation Act of 1973. However, they are not eligible for special education accommodations under the Individuals with Disabilities Education Act if their grades are average but may qualify if it can be shown that they have an impairment that interferes with their learning.

Treatments for ADHD

Researchers, clinicians, and educators have identified a variety of approaches for helping individuals cope with their ADHD symptoms. Given the possibility of the lifelong duration of ADHD, a comprehensive approach that involves the patient and multiple caregivers (e.g., medical doctor, psychologist, teacher, and, if appropriate, social worker) working together to identify the most appropriate goals, measurements, and treatments to create the best possible outcomes is generally recommended. More specifically, research indicates that behavioral therapy and medication prescribed carefully to fit the specific needs of the patient are most likely to result in positive effects.

Medications

The medications used in the treatment of ADHD are not cures. They are stimulants that reduce symptoms, but when they are discontinued, the symptoms return. Even though stimulant medications have been used for over 50 years to treat the symptoms of inattention and hyperactivity, their effect on children's health and well-being have still not been adequately studied over the long term. Over the short term, combined with behavioral therapy, these drugs can be helpful in enabling students to improve their academic performance and reduce their hyperactivity and impulsiveness. Typically, side effects are minor (e.g., stomach aches, low appetite, disrupted sleep); however, in some cases, the adverse effects can be life-threatening (e.g., heart and liver problems and suicidal thoughts).

Behavioral Therapy

Extensive research has demonstrated that therapies that focus on helping individuals with ADHD increase their ability to focus, sustain their attention, and control their activity and impulses have a long history of success in the management of the classroom behavior of students with ADHD. These approaches use prompts to promote positive behaviors followed by immediate rewards to reinforce those behaviors. Similar successes have been reported when these approaches have been adapted to train parents to use these strategies with their children and to help adults with ADHD develop better self-regulation.

Measurement Issues in the Evaluation and Treatment of ADHD

The identification of children and adults with ADHD is typically based on clinical judgments from observations, interviews, physical exams, psychological tests, and behavioral rating scales completed by the person with ADHD, parents, and teachers. In addition to the subjectivity biases that can limit the reliability and validity of these judgments and perhaps contribute to the overdiagnosis of ADHD, the susceptibility of ADHD symptoms to variations in the environment, the idiosyncrasies of individuals, fluctuations with age, and confounding with coexisting conditions complicates the problem of obtaining accurate diagnoses. In general, these diagnoses are not connected directly to specific strategies for reducing the negative effects of the three ADHD symptoms. However, psychological assessments of specific cognitive impairments related to inability to focus attention, for example, could be tied to specific treatments to address those impairments. Extensive research and development of more objective measures linked to specific treatments designed to ameliorate such deficits are needed to help individuals learn to cope effectively with their ADHD symptoms.

Recent Advances in Diagnosis and Treatment of ADHD

Advances in technologies to study the human brain, such as functional MRIs, have the potential to offer new insights into the connections between structural and functional networks in the brain and the symptoms of ADHD. These advances promise greater specificity in identifying the neurological bases of ADHD symptoms and possibilities for more accurate diagnoses and effective treatments. However, caution is warranted in assessing the significance of research findings in the early stages of this research. Studies are often based on correlational analyses and small samples that do not support causal conclusions.

Patricia Teague Ashton

See also Anxiety; Attention; Developmental Disabilities; *Diagnostic and Statistical Manual of Mental Disorders*; Individuals with Disabilities Education Act; Learning Disabilities

Further Readings

Centers for Disease Control and Prevention (2017, February 14). Children with ADHD. Retrieved from https://www.cdc.gov/ncbddd/adhd/data.html

DuPaul, G. J., & Stoner, G, (2014). *ADHD in the schools. Assessment and intervention strategies* (3rd ed.). New York, NY: Guilford Press.

Gualtieri, C. T., & Johnson, L. G. (2005). ADHD: Is objective diagnosis possible? *Psychiatry*, 2(11), 44–53.

Lange, K. W., Reichl, S., Lange, K. M., Tucha, L., & Tucha, O. (2010). The history of attention deficit hyperactivity disorder. *Attention Deficit and Hyperactivity Disorders*, 2(4), 241–255.

Nigg, J. (2006). *What causes ADHD? Understanding what goes wrong and why*. New York, NY: Guilford Press.

Reynolds, C. R., Vannest, K. J., & Harrison, J. R. (2012). *The energetic brain: Understanding and managing ADHD*. San Francisco, CA: Jossey-Bass.

ATTENUATION, CORRECTION FOR

Charles Spearman noted that many variables, specifically those used in fields such as psychology and sociology, are measured using imperfect approximations. For example, a psychologist might be interested in understanding how cognitive ability is related to performance. The latent construct of cognitive ability could be measured in a number of different ways (e.g., Wonderlic Personnel Test; SAT). Likewise, the latent construct of performance could be measured in a number of different ways (e.g., the number of publications or patents generated by scientists, the overall GPA of undergraduate students). After selecting measurement devices and collecting data, the psychologist can correlate scores on the measure of ability (e.g., SAT) with scores on the measure of performance (e.g., GPA). However, because all measurement systems are subject to random measurement error, the correlation between observed measures will typically underestimate the "true" correlation between the latent constructs. The correction for attenuation is intended to estimate the value of this true correlation.

This entry first gives the formula for correction for attenuation, then discusses criticisms of the statistical procedure when it was first developed, and looks at the assumptions the procedure is subject to. Finally, it provides an example of the use of the procedure.

Formula

Spearman proffered a formula to estimate the true correlation as a function of the observed correlation and the reliability coefficients of each observed measure. Following the example in the previous section, where X = SAT scores and Y = GPA scores, the correction for attenuation is given by:

$$\rho_{xy}` = r_{xy} r_{xx} \times r_{yy},$$

where $\rho_{xy}`$ represents the estimate of the true correlation between X and Y, r_{xy} represents the observed correlation, and r_{xx} and r_{yy} represent the observed reliabilities of X and Y, respectively. The correction for attenuation provides an estimate of the correlation between X and Y in the absence of random measurement error (i.e., if there were a one-to-one correspondence between observed test scores and latent construct scores). Thus, the correction for attenuation is often interpreted as an estimate of the correlation, not between observed measures, but between the unobserved, latent constructs.

Spearman differentiated between attenuation (random or "accidental" error) and "systematic deviations" or errors related to unmeasured variables that bias scores in a particular direction (e.g., practice effects, fatigue). Although systematic deviations may increase or decrease the magnitude of a correlation coefficient, attenuation always decreases the magnitude, and therefore, assuming that unbiased and accurate estimates are available for the observed correlation and the reliabilities of X and Y, the estimated true correlation coefficient will always be equal to or greater than the observed correlation coefficient.

Criticisms

The correction for attenuation garnered immediate criticism from Karl Pearson who chided Spearman for not presenting algebraic proof of his formula and for presenting a formula which, in cases of extremely poor measurement, could result in a correlation coefficient exceeding unity. Spearman replied by providing the algebraic proof, emphasizing that error is rarely truly random, and agreeing that science should focus on developing measurement techniques accurate enough to eliminate the need for this formula.

Mathematically, the correction for attenuation cannot yield a true correlation coefficient exceeding unity except in cases where the observed correlation exceeds the observed reliability estimates. Because a correlation coefficient cannot theoretically exceed the magnitude of the reliability of either variable (i.e., X or Y), the correction for attenuation will only yield true correlation coefficients exceeding unity when the observed correlation or observed reliabilities have been misestimated. It is noteworthy that, at the time Spearman introduced the correction for attenuation, the only techniques available for estimating reliability were correlations between parallel forms, subsequent administrations, or multiple raters. Split-half correlations and internal consistency (e.g., Cronbach's α) coefficients did not exist at the time.

Lee Cronbach noted that different reliability coefficients estimate different aspects of a test (e.g., equivalence, stability). As a result, each reliability coefficient operationalizes error in a different way and, therefore, has different implications for use in the correction for attenuation. Cronbach also noted that the assumptions underlying the calculation of any given reliability coefficient are rarely met.

Assumptions

The correction for attenuation was derived using classical test theory and thus is subject to the same assumptions that underlie classical test theory. Specifically, true scores must be independent of errors and errors must be independent of one another. These assumptions ensure that the correlation between X and Y is not spurious (i.e., resulting from the relationship of both X and Y with a third variable) and that error is random as opposed to systematic. Because errors for X and Y are uncorrelated, the terms in the denominator (r_{xx} and r_{yy}) are considered independent. Thus, it is possible to correct for attenuation in either X or Y while ignoring attenuation caused by the other variable ($r_{xy}r_{xx}$ or $r_{xy}r_{yy}$).

The correction for attenuation is related to the Spearman-Brown prophecy formula, which estimates the expected increase in an observed reliability coefficient as a function of the number of parallel measurements added to the test. The true correlation coefficient estimated using the correction for attenuation represents the hypothetical value one might obtain if perfectly reliable measures of X and Y were available. One method of obtaining a perfectly reliable measure is to administer an infinite number of parallel measurements. In the Spearman-Brown prophesy formula, increasing the number of measurements by a factor of ∞ will increase all reliability coefficients (except .00) to 1.00. As a result, the correction for attenuation can yield an estimate of the correlation coefficient if it were computed using infinitely long measures of X and Y.

Example

In order to calculate the correction for attenuation, one must first calculate the observed correlation coefficient and estimates of reliability for the two variables (X and Y). Remember that correlations cannot theoretically exceed reliabilities. If the correlation coefficient is higher than either reliability estimate, at least one of these has been misestimated.

Observed correlation: .35

Reliability estimate for X: .72

Reliability estimate for Y: .89

Correlation corrected for attenuation in X only:
$r_{xy}r_{xx} = .35.72 = .35.85 = .41$.

Correlation corrected for attenuation in Y only:
$r_{xy}r_{yy} = .35.89 = .35.94 = .37$.

Correlation corrected for attenuation in X and Y:
$r_{xy}r_{xx} \times r_{yy} = .35.72 \times .89 = .35.64 = .35.80 = .44$.

Justin A. DeSimone and James M. LeBreton

See also Classical Test Theory; Correlation; Meta-Analysis; Reliability; Restriction of Range; Spearman-Brown Prophecy Formula; Validity Generalization

Further Readings

Cronbach, L. J. (1947). Test "reliability": Its meaning and determination. *Psychometrika, 12,* 1–16.

LeBreton, J. M., Scherer, K. T., & James, L. R. (2014). Corrections for criterion unreliability in validity generalization: A false prophet in a land of suspended judgment. *Industrial and Organizational Psychology: Perspectives on Science and Practice, 7,* 478–500.

Schmidt, F. L., & Hunter, J. E. (2015). *Methods of meta-analysis: Correcting error and bias in research findings* (3rd ed.). Thousand Oaks, CA: Sage.

Spearman, C. (1904). The proof and measurement of association between two things. *The American Journal of Psychology, 15,* 72–101.

Spearman, C. (1910). Correlation calculated from faulty data. *British Journal of Psychology, 3,* 271–295.

ATTITUDE SCALING

Attitudes represent people's overall evaluation of another person or object, which include cognitive and affective components. In general, attitudes vary in strength and lie on a continuum that ranges from unfavorable to favorable. Researchers cannot directly observe people's attitudes and thus need to infer them by observing behavior, or by direct or indirect measurement, as through attitude scales. This entry covers the history of attitude scaling, the aspects to consider when creating methodically strong attitude scales, and future directions in the area of attitude scaling.

The concept of attitudes was introduced in social psychology and continues to play a prominent role in a wide variety of fields today (e.g., public health, communication, marketing). Early scholars such as Gordon Allport helped define the concept of an attitude, while researchers such as Louis Thurstone and Charles Osgood pioneered attitude scaling techniques that laid the foundation for their scientific study.

Attitude scales measure participants' internal dispositions or attitudes toward a particular object or set of objects via self-report. For instance, if researchers are interested in measuring students' attitudes toward science, they might ask participants how much they disagree or agree with a series of statements about the various fields of science (see Figure 1).

Attitude Scales

Rating scales have been an important tool for measuring people's beliefs, opinions, and attitudes in the last century of social scientific research. Since Allport proposed the concept of attitudes over 100 years ago, researchers have devised many approaches for their measurement. This section outlines the original techniques (Thurstone's method of equal-appearing intervals and Guttman's scalogram) and those most commonly used now (Likert's method of summated ratings and Osgood's semantic differential). There is not necessarily one method that is best at achieving accurate results. Instead, researchers have a variety of tools to choose and must consider the appropriateness of each type for the specific context at hand.

Thurstone's Method of Equal-Appearing Intervals

In 1928, Thurstone developed the first systematic way to measure attitudes. The method of *equal-appearing intervals* involves four phases of scale construction. After the researcher decides what attitude is to be measured, the first phase involves generating many possible questions to cover all aspects of the construct of interest. In the second phase, a group of judges rates the items on

Method of Summated Ratings (Likert)				
1. I think science is a good field of study.				
strongly agree	agree	neutral	disagree	strongly disagree
(5)	(4)	(3)	(2)	(1)
2. I think science is an interesting field of study.				
strongly agree	agree	neutral	disagree	strongly disagree
(5)	(4)	(3)	(2)	(1)
3. I like science.				
strongly agree	agree	neutral	disagree	strongly disagree
(5)	(4)	(3)	(2)	(1)
4. I trust scientists.				
strongly agree	agree	neutral	disagree	strongly disagree
(5)	(4)	(3)	(2)	(1)
5. I think scientists are honest people.				
strongly agree	agree	neutral	disagree	strongly disagree
(5)	(4)	(3)	(2)	(1)

Figure 1   Example of Likert-type scale "Attitudes Toward Science"

their favorability, which allows researchers to assess the psychometric properties of the scale. In the third phase, researchers subject the judges' ratings to statistical analyses, using the results to choose 11–22 questions that constitute the final scale. The last phase is to administer the scale to participants who indicate whether they disagree or agree with each item. To get an overall idea of people's attitudes, their responses to all of the items are averaged—but counterintuitively, higher averages do not necessarily indicate more favorable attitudes toward the person or object under consideration.

Guttman's Scalogram

In 1944, Louis Guttman attempted to improve on Thurstone's method by developing a scaling method where participants with more favorable attitudes toward an object would, in fact, have higher total scores on the scale. Scores across items can be averaged to form a cumulative score

representing the favorability toward the object under investigation (see Table 1).

Using Guttman's method to create an attitude scale is very similar to Thurstone's technique—investigators create a large set of items that encompass the attitude under consideration. Next, a set of judges rates the items in terms of favorability in a yes or no manner; the judges' ratings are then tabulated hierarchically from items with the highest level of agreement to those with the lowest level of agreement. From this matrix, additional statistical analysis is conducted to finalize the scale. Lastly, the scale is administered to participants and their summed scale values represent their attitude toward the object. Due to the difficulties associated with item creation and selection, scholars today do not use either Thurstone's or Guttman's methods very frequently. Instead, researchers more often use the next two attitude scaling methods: Likert-type and semantic differential scales.

Table 1   Example of Guttman Scalogram for "Scale of Student Attitudes Toward Science"

Item #	Item	Yes	No
1	Science is a tolerable field of study.		
2	Science is a somewhat enjoyable field of study.		
3	Science is a highly enjoyable field of study.		
4	Science is a great field of study.		
5	Science is the best field of study.		

Likert's Method of Summated Ratings

Rensis Likert took the next step in attitude scaling in 1932, when he developed a method that was more efficient in time and resources and more effective than both Thurstone's and Guttman's methods. The two previous methods required participants to choose from just two options (e.g., yes or no, agree or disagree). Likert's new method used a multiple choice format in which people placed their response on a 5-point scale from *strongly disagree* to *strongly agree* with a *neutral or undecided* middle point. Each point along the scale would be given a value of 1 through 5, and participants' responses would be summed or averaged to indicate their overall attitude toward the person or object under investigation, as shown in Figure 1.

Only the initial process of the Likert's method resembles Thurstone's and Guttman's methods, as researchers develop a large potential set of questions. However, instead of finalizing a set of scale items that represent the attitude as a whole, in the Likert's method, researchers select items that are moderately favorable or moderately unfavorable with regard to the attitude object. As opposed to having a group of judges rate the items, the second phase in the Likert's method involves administering the set of items directly to respondents. A good rule of thumb is to multiply the number of questions to be administered by 10 to have an appropriate amount of respondents during this phase of the scale construction process. Once the responses have been collected, researchers apply statistical techniques such as factor analysis to the data to retain the items that will form the best final scale.

Likert's method advanced attitude scaling from Thurstone's and Guttman's methods; however, it shared in some of their liabilities—namely, that these three methods are relatively time and resource consuming, and new scales must be created every time a new attitude object is to be measured.

Osgood's Semantic Differential

In contrast to the three methods discussed to this point, in which people respond to statements about the concept under investigation, in 1952, Osgood proposed the semantic differential, in which people evaluate the person or attitude object directly using bipolar adjectives. For example, if researchers were investigating attitudes toward science, the concept of science is presented and then participants respond to a 5-point scale anchored by adjectives (e.g., good/bad, pleasant/unpleasant). These anchors can then be used for measuring different attitude objects without having to go through the time-consuming process of scale creation and validation as with the other three methods discussed. In comparison to Likert-type scales, semantic differential scales are shorter, easier to understand, can be completed more quickly, and are highly efficient in the scale creation process. Overall, this method is highly practical and efficient for researchers.

Attitude Scale Creation

When developing attitude scales, there are certain aspects to keep in mind, including question wording, response type, question ordering, and no opinion options. With a solid understanding of what constitutes a good scale, researchers can develop more accurate and efficient scales, saving both time and resources.

Wording Questions

There are two important issues that researchers should consider when deciding on how attitude questions should be worded. First, investigators must decide what they would like to know—questions meant to measure students' evaluation of science might be very different than those assessing academics' attitudes toward coffee. Additionally, researchers should take care to ask questions directly so that people are more likely to understand their true meaning. Similarly, researchers should use short, simple sentences that contain only one grammatical clause. When sentences contain more than one clause, these *double-barreled questions* can lead to ambiguity on the part of the respondent.

Question Ordering

A third issue that scale creators must consider is the order in which questions are presented. One important concern is that participants may be uncomfortable answering questions concerning their attitudes toward sensitive subjects (e.g., drug and alcohol use, sexual behavior, stereotypes). To account for this possibility, researchers should present the least threatening questions first and gradually work toward more sensitive material. Additionally, demographic questions (e.g., income, race/ethnicity) should be posed toward the end of the questionnaire because these too may be sensitive for participants.

Researchers must also consider the fact that when ordering questions, earlier questions and answers may affect later ones. For instance, investigators should be aware of priming effects and their ability to invoke a particular mind-set about framing and responding to questions. Counterbalancing or randomizing question order can help avoid any unintended ordering effects. When using written survey materials, the process of randomization can be time-consuming, so computer software can be highly effective at this task.

Dropout and the No-Opinion Response Format

Finally, researchers should attempt to limit participants from dropping out of the survey, as it may create problems for the generalizability of findings. When considering how to get participants to respond to all questions, researchers must consider

a "no-opinion" or "don't know" response option. Some questionnaires allow respondents to indicate a neutral response, while others force participants to indicate a preference on either side of the response continuum.

Researchers have investigated both response types for many years, and there are strong arguments for either the inclusion or exclusion of a neutral response option. Some scholars have suggested that providing a no-response option allows participants to avoid the cognitive work necessary to answer questions. Yet others indicate that having a no-response option may affect participants' interpretation of other response options. In general, the benefits of providing such an option seem to outweigh the negative aspects, and participants seem to prefer having such an option. One concern, however, is that even though they mean different things, participants often confuse "neutral," "not applicable," and "no opinion" response options. Thus, when a neutral response option is given, it is advisable to make clear to participants what such a response indicates.

Additional Considerations

Scale Length

When researchers first developed attitude measures, they used elaborate methods to create scales and they believed that large question sets were needed to accurately assess attitudes. However, these methods took great time and resources to both create and administer. Over time, due to a better methodological understanding of measurement scaling, researchers have concluded that shorter scales have clear advantages. Methodologically sound condensed scales can be just as reliable and accurate as longer scaling techniques. They also have the added benefit of taking less time for respondents to complete, thus limiting fatigue and potential for participants to drop out.

Monetary Consideration

Questionnaire design and assessment may have impositions based on monetary considerations. For instance, when conducting a national telephone survey, adding one or more questions will increase the time necessary for each telephone call. Even if 1 extra minute is added to each interaction, over thousands of calls, this extra cost multiplies quickly. While in some cases using multiple questions or scales to tap people's attitudes may be preferable, researchers sometimes may have to be content with shorter, more limited questionnaires.

Context

When people report their attitudes, the context of the situation needs to be taken into account because these reports may vary due to the context in which they were measured. For instance, if Americans were polled about their attitudes toward national security, these attitudes would likely vary if asked directly after a terrorist attack as opposed to being asked after years of relative calm. Additionally, if participants were to answer questions in the confines of a research lab, their responses may be different than in a "real-world" context. This may be due to participants in the lab wanting to be seen in a socially desirable way by the research team or perhaps the lab not providing the same real-world conditions as experienced in day-to-day life. As a result, an attitude measurement may only be useful in predicting future attitude in the environment in which it was measured.

Beyond Self-Report

Underlying all the measurement techniques discussed in this entry is a core concern—namely, that social context and social desirability can influence people's self-reported attitudes. Indeed, many times participants may fail to recognize the impact that their surroundings and/or internal motivations have on their reports about themselves. These biases can negatively affect the quality of the data the researchers gather; they can also lead to incorrect conclusions about people's attitudes and opinions.

In response to these realizations, scholars have developed measurement techniques for attitudes that do not rely on self-report—the so-called *implicit* measures, which assess attitudes indirectly (i.e., without directly asking people about them). These strategies for measuring attitudes disguise what attitude is actually being measured and may be effective at limiting the impact of participants wanting to be seen in a socially desirable light. Moreover, participants may fail to recognize the influence that their attitudes have on their behavior,

thus giving researchers a more "real-world" friendly measurement of attitudes.

Two key implicit measures have been developed. First, researchers can unobtrusively observe people's behavior; this technique has been widely used, including measuring helping behavior and social distance. In terms of indirectly measuring attitudes, techniques such as the implicit association test measure the strength of association between two concepts.

The implicit association test assesses the time it takes people to respond to different attitude objects in reference to negative or positive adjectives. If there is a bias toward one object over another (e.g., a preference for white faces over black faces), there will be a difference in the time it takes to respond to positive/negative words paired with the attitude object. This method is the most widely used implicit measure and has been used in a variety of domains including attitudes toward race, gender, and religion.

Future Directions

The number of online environments for completing attitudinal scales has been increasing in recent years. Sites such as Amazon's Mechanical Turk can be beneficial for data collection and analysis in numerous ways. For one, researchers conducting studies online can use myriad formats and types of attitude scales—even beyond the traditional ones covered in this entry. For instance, recent research examined the accuracy of sliding 100- or 250-point semantic differential scales in online samples. The use of online techniques to measure attitudes also offers the ability to collect vast amounts of data quickly—compared to administering traditional pen and paper scales, the collection of online data can take mere hours for hundreds or thousands of responses, which traditionally can take months or even years. The ability to gather data quickly and efficiently in this online environment enables researchers to more quickly create and validate new attitude scales.

Benjamin D. Rosenberg and Timothy C. Silva

See also Instrumentation; Rating Scales; Self-Report Inventories; Semantic Differential Scaling; Survey Methods; Surveys

Further Readings

Allport, G. W. (1935). Attitudes. In C. M. Murchison (Ed.), *Handbook of social psychology*. Winchester, MA: Clark University Press.

Buhrmester, M., Kwang, T., & Gosling, S. D. (2011). Amazon's Mechanical Turk: A new source of inexpensive, yet high-quality, data? *Perspectives on Psychological Science, 6*, 3–5.

Eagly, A. H., & Chaiken, S. (2005). *Attitude research in the 21st century: The current state of knowledge*. Mahwah, NJ: Erlbaum.

Krosnick, J. A, Judd, C. M., & Wittenbrink, B. (2005). The measurement of attitudes. In D. Albarracin, B. T. Johnson, & M. P. Zanna (Eds.), *Handbook of attitudes and attitude change*. Mahwah, NJ: Erlbaum.

Thurstone, L. L. (1928). Attitudes can be measured. *American Journal of Sociology, 33*, 529–554.

ATTRIBUTION THEORY

People share a great thirst to understand the causes of situations they encounter and often attempt to explain—to themselves or others—why a specific situation occurred. *Attribution theory* explains the connection between perceived causes of situations and the psychological consequences of these perceptions. The main idea of the theory is that all causes share three basic, underlying properties: locus, controllability, and stability; these properties determine the psychological consequences of perceived causes. Perceived causes have crucial emotional and behavioral consequences, including those related to the context of achievement motivation.

Much of the existing understanding of the process explained by attribution theory comes from research conducted in the context of school achievement. Individuals' attempt to understand the causes of their achievement in school often determines their reactions to these causes. This entry further explores the search for these causes and its psychological consequences, then looks at how the causes a person ascribes to events determines his or her psychological reality and how people use attribution theory in their dealings with others or to improve their performance.

Search for Causes of Events and Outcomes

People aspire to understand why different events and outcomes occur. This aspiration is motivated by humans' innate desire to both understand their environment and to use this understanding to effectively manage their lives. To this end, people often engage in attempts to explain to themselves and to others why an event or outcome came about.

Because the understanding of the reasons for an outcome or event helps people manage their lives, is has important emotional and behavioral consequences. For example, a student who failed an exam may come to the conclusion that this failure was caused by insufficient efforts to study for the exam. In consequence, the student may feel guilty and decide to invest more effort when studying for a future exam. By contrast, if the student thinks that the failure was caused by a lack of ability, this student is likely to feel shame and may decide to quit studies or move to a different field of study. As this example suggests, the cause the student attributes to the outcome determines which emotions are likely to arise and what type of behavior may result from it.

More generally, causal beliefs give rise to emotional reactions and to a variety of inferences, both in the actors who attribute their good or poor performance or situation to various causes and in the involved observers of this performance. Thus, it is not only students who may react to their poor outcome as a function of what they think caused the failure but also, for example, a teacher who also holds a certain belief about what caused this performance. If the teacher thinks that low effort caused the failure, the teacher may react with anger and punish the student. If, on the other hand, the failure is attributed to low ability, then the teacher is more likely to react with pity. This teacher may also infer that the student is lazy or unintelligent, as a function of each respective attribution. Thus, the way people explain events and outcomes determines how they respond to them. This is true for all domains of life, not only for achievements.

How Causes Determine Psychological Reality

A myriad of distinct possible causes can determine a given outcome, and there is an endless number of potential outcomes and events that can occur in different contexts. This makes it rather difficult to understand why a particular cause for a specific outcome leads to a specific consequence and not to another. Why is it the case that failure in an exam attributed to low ability leads to feelings of shame in the failing student? Why does the rejection of an invitation to a romantic date, attributed to appearance, also lead to shame?

One way to resolve the complexity of the connection between causes and consequences is by searching for a possible underlying structure of the main factor of interest, in this case, causes. By finding similarities and differences between different causes, one can reveal some underlying structure of causality. The next step would be to examine if and to what extent this underlying structure can explain the connection between causes and their consequences. This will enable the narrowing down of a rather complex phenomenon to a set of simpler unifying features that define it. Bernard Weiner's attribution theory, devised in 1985, does just that.

Attribution theory reveals the underlying structure of causality by describing the properties or dimensions that define all causes. Furthermore, it describes how dimensions of causes are related to specific types of psychological consequences. Thus, attribution theory is based on the understanding that all causes can be characterized according to three basic properties: labeled locus, controllability, and stability.

Locus refers to the location of a cause, that is, whether the cause is internal or external to the actor. For example, both low effort and low ability are likely to be perceived as internal to an actor; something that is associated with the actor rather than with the situation or someone else. On the other hand, a difficult or unfair exam as a cause for failure is associated with someone else—such as a teacher—and not with the actor.

Controllability refers to the degree to which the cause is subject to volitional change, that is, the extent to which the cause is controllable or uncontrollable. Thus, low effort is within the student's control because a student can decide how much effort to invest in studying for an exam. By contrast, low ability is more likely to be perceived as an uncontrollable factor, as a person cannot control the extent to which the person is endowed with skills or abilities. An unfair or difficult exam is also likely to be perceived as being within the teacher's control.

Stability pertains to the relative endurance of a cause over time. Whereas enduring causes are seen as stable, transitory ones are seen as unstable. In our examples, low effort is likely to be perceived as unstable as on a different occasion, in principle, the student may invest more effort in studying for an exam. Alternatively, low ability is stable because basic traits and skills are perceived as being unlikely to change much or at all over time.

These characteristics of causes are independent of one another such that the fact that a specific cause is characterized by a given location on one of the dimensions does not force any specific location on another dimension. In other words, causes can represent any combination of these dimensions. Furthermore, all causes can be seen as representing a combination of different locations within each of these dimensions. Thus, low effort as a cause for failure is likely to be perceived as internal to the actor, controllable, and unstable, whereas low ability is perceived as internal, uncontrollable, and stable.

Although the dimensional placement of a cause is a subjective reality—meaning, individuals may disagree with respect to a causal interpretation—there is a great deal of consistency concerning the characteristics of particular attributions. In other words, whereas most people may perceive luck, for example, as a cause of success that is external to the person, uncontrollable, and unstable, others may perceive luck as internal, uncontrollable, and stable. That is, instead of perceiving luck as representing a set of accidental circumstances unrelated to the intentional behavior of the actor, some may perceive luck as representing the property or trait of an individual, something this person is endowed with. What is common, however, is the dimensional structure of causes, as presented earlier, and the consequences of particular attributions as a function of their causal properties, as is described next.

As the examples given earlier clearly indicate, the perceived cause of a given event or outcome determines its emotional and behavioral consequences. The link between the perceived cause and its consequences is indirect, being mediated via the perceived dimensions of the cause. In other words, the perceived properties of a cause determine its consequences.

Each causal dimension has its unique psychological significance. The locus of a cause is linked to self-esteem and related emotions such as pride. Desirable outcomes attributed to internal causes lead to greater self-esteem and pride than the same outcomes attributed to external causes. By contrast, undesirable outcomes attributed to internal causes lead to lower self-esteem than the same outcomes when attributed to an external cause. For example, success in an exam attributed to high ability or to effort leads to increased self-esteem and pride. Success due to luck or an easy exam does not lead to the same consequences. Failure due to a lack of ability or low effort will lower the achiever's self-esteem. However, failure due to an unfair exam will not lower one's self-esteem.

The stability of a cause determines expectations about the future as well as the emotions and behaviors related to such expectations. When a given outcome or event is attributed to a stable cause, it is expected that the event or outcome will reoccur in the future. However, when the occurrence of an event or an outcome is attributed to an unstable cause, it is not necessarily expected that it will reoccur. For example, a failure attributed to low ability will lead to expectations of similar failures in the future because low ability is a stable cause. On the other hand, failure attributed to low effort is not necessarily expected to reoccur because low effort is unstable; that is, the situation can be changed by investing more effort.

Attribution of failure to low ability will also lead to hopelessness, because nothing much can be either done or hoped for, given the stable nature of the failure's cause. A change in behavior that better suits the abilities of the achiever may therefore be the result of this attribution. On the other hand, hope is a likely emotional consequence if the failure is attributed to low effort because the fact that the cause is changeable indicates the possibility that the undesirable outcome may also change.

Controllability of a cause determines inferences of responsibility as well as the emotions and behaviors related to it. A situation or event attributed to a controllable cause leads to the inference that the person who had control over the circumstances that brought it about is also responsible for the outcome. Alternatively, a situation or event attributed to an uncontrollable cause leads to an inference that the person of relevance is not responsible for it. For example, a student who failed an exam because of low effort is likely to take responsibility for the failure, as effort can be controlled. As a result, this student will feel guilty and may decide to invest more effort in the future. The same failure attributed to low ability, however, will lead to shame because the cause of the failure—the student's innate ability—is not controllable.

Judgments and emotions elicited as a result of the behavior of others also depend on attributions about responsibility for the behavior. For example, an observer is more likely to feel pity and offer to help a person encountering an undesirable situation if it is attributed to an uncontrollable cause, such as a disease caused by a genetic defect or an accident caused by the force of nature. Yet, if the same situation is attributed to a controllable cause—such as reckless behavior—anger and avoidance are more likely reactions.

To summarize, perceived causes of events and situations determine the related psychological consequences of these events and situations. The common underlying structure of causes determines their psychological consequences.

How People Use Attribution Theory

An important derivative of research in the context of attribution theory shows that people are aware of the links between specific causes, emotions, and behaviors as described by the theory. As such, they often use this knowledge to make sense of their social surroundings and ensure that their goals are fulfilled or to improve their performance. Hence, for example, witnessing a student expressing guilt in response to failing an exam, a teacher may understand that this student didn't invest sufficient effort in studying for the exam. This conclusion comes from the naive understanding that guilt reflects a sense of responsibility for the failure. Training people to replace undesirable attributions with desirable ones helps people improve their performance. For example, persuading students to take control over failures rather than blame them on uncontrollable causes improves their performance in school.

Shlomo Hareli

See also Educational Psychology; Emotional Intelligence; Motivation

Further Readings

Hareli, S. (2014). Making sense of the social world and influencing it by using a naïve attribution theory of emotions. *Emotion Review, 6*(4), 336–343. doi:10.1177/1754073914534501

Hareli, S., & Weiner, B. (2002). Social emotions and personality inferences: A scaffold for a new direction in the study of achievement motivation. *Educational Psychologist, 37*(3), 183–193. doi:10.1207/S15326985ep3703_4

Weiner, B. (1985). An attributional theory of achievement motivation and emotion. *Psychological Review, 92*(4), 548–573. doi:10.1037/0033–295X.92.4.548

Weiner, B. (1986). *An attributional theory of motivation and emotion.* New York, NY: Springer.

Weiner, B. (1987). The social psychology of emotion: Applications of a naive psychology. *Journal of Social and Clinical Psychology, 5*(4), 405–419. doi:10.1521/jscp.1987.5.4.405

Weiner, B. (1995). Judgements of responsibility: A foundation for a theory of social conduct. New York, NY: Guilford Press.

Weiner, B., Amirkhan, J., Folkes, V. S., & Verette, J. A. (1987). An attributional analysis of excuse giving: Studies of a naive theory of emotion. *Journal of Personality and Social Psychology, 52*(2), 316–324. Retrieved from http://dx.doi.org/10.1037/0022–3514.52.2.316

AUDITING

When referring to auditing within qualitative research, numerous definitions exist. In short, auditing refers to a transparent research process where each step of inquiry is clearly presented and analyzed. Auditing is often represented through an audit trail where the data are essentially tracked from the raw form to the ultimate finished product, which could range from a narrative of rich description to a more formalized research instrument or scale. The use of the term and process of auditing have similarities to the concepts of reliability, generalizability, and validity (what Steinar Kvale calls the "scientific holy trinity")—terms more popular in quantitative or postpositivist analysis arenas. This entry describes audit trails for qualitative inquiry and the debate over the use of auditing strategies in qualitative research.

Audit Trail

The trustworthiness of a qualitative research process is often shown through a transparent demonstration of the totality of the process of inquiry. In essence, the reader of the study can become immersed in each stage of the research and understand the decisions made at each stage. To some,

this increases the quality of the work and assures the results are not a result of deception, fraud, or manipulation. Yvonna Lincoln and Egon Guba are credited with the original conceptualization of an audit trail for qualitative inquiry where a third party could theoretically follow each step of the study and recreate, or confirm, the results. Lincoln and Guba argued for six categories of data that can help inform a proper audit trail:

1. raw data,

2. data reduction and analysis notes,

3. data reconstruction and synthesis products,

4. process notes,

5. materials related to intentions, and

6. preliminary developmental information.

Marian Carcary has further clarified that an audit trail can be "intellectual" or "physical." A physical audit trail deals with the "nuts and bolts" of the research process from the initial identification of the research problem to the resulting theory or instrument created as a result of the inquiry. The intellectual trail delves into decisions surrounding the internal thinking of the researcher throughout the process and the ways in which the researcher's own biases and dispositions influenced the procedure. In all, an audit trail serves as a way to enhance the trustworthiness and credibility of qualitative research.

An example of both trails can be found in Carcary's (2009) article. The author detailed her intellectual transition, describing how she questioned her traditional positivist beliefs and ultimately selected an adapted grounded theory approach. In the physical audit, the steps of the research process are clearly laid out with supporting information for each decision. For example, she describes her interview schedule:

> The semi-structured interview was the primary source of case-study evidence. Based on issues identified in the literature and in defining the research problem, an initial interview schedule was prepared. This was pre-tested in a number of pilot interviews in order to determine informants understanding of the questions and the depth of the research inquiry, and was subsequently refined. (p. 20)

Auditing Moving Forward

Considerable debate still exists over the best methods, if any, for measuring credibility, reliability, validity, and transferability in qualitative research. Many qualitative researchers have cautioned against the adoption of largely positivist ideas to "justify" or "give credibility to" qualitative work. Pierre Bourdieu has warned against a global audit culture where results and processes are scrutinized through a governance lens that ultimately influences the findings to a far greater degree than the types of audits previously discussed.

Other researchers have moved past the auditing terminology and rely on more constructivist terms such as *verification*. For example, Janice Morse and her colleagues argued for verification through (a) methodological coherence, (b) appropriate sampling, (c) collecting and analyzing data concurrently, (d) thinking theoretically, and (e) theory development. No matter what term is used, the debate about the use of auditing strategies in qualitative research likely will continue.

Jordan R. Bass

See also Grounded Theory; Mixed Methods Research; Qualitative Data Analysis; Qualitative Research Methods; Reliability; Validity

Further Readings

Carcary, M. (2009). The research audit trail—Enhancing trustworthiness in qualitative inquiry. *The Electronic Journal of Business Research Methods*, 7(1), 11–24.

Denzin, N. K. (2011). The politics of evidence. *The SAGE handbook of qualitative research* (pp. 645–658).

Lincoln, Y. S., & Guba, E. G. (1985). *Naturalistic inquiry* (Vol. 75). Thousand Oaks, CA: Sage.

Morse, J. M., Barrett, M., Mayan, M., Olson, K., & Spiers, J. (2002). Verification strategies for establishing reliability and validity in qualitative research. *International Journal of Qualitative Methods*, 1(2), 13–22.

AUTHENTIC ASSESSMENT

Authentic assessment is an approach to student assessment that involves the student deeply, is cognitively complex and intrinsically interesting, uses a format that is consistent with how ability is evaluated in the real-world, and evaluates skills and abilities that have value and meaning outside of the classroom or on the job. Educational scholar Grant Wiggins, who is credited with introducing the concept, describes authentic assessment as involving those activities or tasks that people actually do in the real-world. Indeed, *authentic* is often treated as a synonym for realistic. This entry further defines authentic assessment and discusses how it compares to traditional assessment.

Authentic assessment focuses on how students integrate and apply what they have learned through contextualized tasks. This form of assessment allows students to demonstrate learning individually or by working collaboratively with others to demonstrate competency in authentic settings. Authentic assessment usually describes classroom assessment, but the philosophy has been applied to standardized tests as well.

One goal of authentic assessment is to indicate the extent to which a student's knowledge and skills can be applied outside of the classroom. It might also be referred to as direct assessment as opposed to traditional formats (such as multiple-choice questions) that seldom require a direct demonstration of knowledge and skills. Because authentic assessment strategies do not focus entirely on recalling facts, students are required to integrate, apply, and self-assess skills and understanding. Student understanding of disciplinary content is desired, but it is also important for students to be able to use the acquired knowledge and skills in the world beyond their classes.

Assessments have to indicate whether students can apply what they have learned in authentic situations. When a student does well on a test of knowledge, this often infers that the student can also apply that knowledge, but that is indirect evidence. Knowledge tests can also provide evidence of knowledge about application, but again that is indirect.

Authentic assessments ask the student to use what the student has learned in a meaningful way. For example, it would not be possible to determine whether students can effectively debate a topic by listening and responding to contrasting views through multiple-choice questions or a description on a written test. Authentic assessment is designed to produce direct evidence in an authentic context. Similarly, authentic assessment can demonstrate whether students can interpret a current news story, calculate potential savings of a proposed budget, test a scientific hypothesis, play a musical instrument, converse in a foreign language, or apply other knowledge and skills they have learned.

Bruce Frey, Vicki Schmitt, and Justin Allen analyzed the concept of authentic as applied to assessment and identified nine dimensions of authenticity used in the literature. Researchers and teacher educators refer to an assessment as authentic when it has several of the following characteristics (Frey, Schmitt, & Allen, 2012, p. 5):

- the context of the assessment
  - realistic activity or context
  - the task is performance based
  - the task is cognitively complex
- the role of the student
  - a defense of the answer or product is required
  - the assessment is formative
  - students collaborate with each other or with the teacher
- the scoring
  - the scoring criteria are known or student developed
  - multiple indicators or portfolios are used for scoring
  - the performance expectation is *mastery*.

Authentic assessments nearly always are patterned after tasks that require performance of skills, supported by a foundation of required knowledge, at an achievement level at or beyond *what is expected* in the school classroom. A framework for authentic assessments begins the same way that curriculum for a program would be designed, by asking what students should be able to do as a result of what has been learned. Some examples of authentic assessments include simulations and role plays, lab experiments, budget proposals, application letters, and tasks that solve real-life problems. Students may also be asked to demonstrate learning by creating and producing a newscast, developing a museum exhibit on a specific topic, designing an efficient workflow for planning the prom, judging the efficiency of product manufacturing, carrying out pH tests of water samples, or carrying out similar tasks through which they will use acquired knowledge and skills.

Rubrics are often used to evaluate the quality of performance on tasks designated as authentic demonstrations of learning. This is consistent with performance assessments, but not all performance assessment is authentic. When the criteria for each achievement level is explicitly defined, the criteria will enable evaluation of student achievement for each learning category to be objective, consistent, and defensible. The intent of a rubric in authentic assessment is to guide students toward higher levels of achievement by providing these expectations as part of the instructions for the task.

Rubrics can also act as a guide to attain higher levels of achievement by engaging students in content and process, empowering task facilitation, contributing to synthesis of information to guide critical thinking and problem solving, and enabling the task to become a learning experience in and of itself. This also makes it likely that the assessment will be of increased interest for students, thus motivating higher levels of achievement.

Comparing Traditional to Authentic Assessment

Traditional assessment refers to forced-choice measures such as multiple-choice tests, fill in the blanks, and true-false tests for which students select an answer or recall information to complete the assessment. This type of assessment can be standardized or teacher created, administered locally or broadly. Traditional assessment often defines learning as recalling a body of knowledge and the demonstration of prescribed skills, such as working a mathematical problem without the students knowing where they could use it. These assessments are usually developed and administered to determine acquisition of knowledge as defined in a particular curriculum. Wiggins, the long-time advocate for authenticity in assessment, has emphasized, however, that traditional "inauthentic" assessment is not necessarily bad or invalid. As with all student assessment, any approach can work if there is consistency between objectives, instruction, and format.

As discussed earlier, authentic assessment requires students to synthesize and apply knowledge and skills through tasks that replicate, as close as possible, the challenges faced in real-life situations beyond the classroom. Student learning is assessed by the extent to which students demonstrate their mastery of knowledge and skill application through the particular authentic task. It is typical when authentic assessments are implemented, curriculum is designed around applied experiences with skills and knowledge taught and developed through a variety of tasks.

A teacher does not need to choose between authentic assessment and traditional assessment because they complement each other. Both types of assessment have various forms, and there is no bright line separating the two types, but traditional assessments tend to confirm recall, demonstration of skills, and connection between the two, while authentic assessment demonstrates the ways a student can apply the knowledge and skills while being assessed on attributes exhibited in the process and completion of a task.

The reason many teachers use authentic methods of assessment in addition to traditional means is because of two beliefs: That students must be prepared to do more than recall information; and the skills demonstrated in authentic assessment tasks will better prepare them for their future endeavors. Teachers also utilize authentic assessment methods because they enhance student engagement with the assessment process, engaging learners through active participation and interaction with the educational material, activities, and related community. Contemporary theories of learning suggest that when the activity in a learning environment is recognized by the students as worthwhile and meaningful, requires thoughtful creativity in solving a problem, and could have purposeful impact beyond the assignment, then the possibility of engagement with their learning is enhanced. These components are seen as strong characteristics of authentic assessment.

The judgment in scoring student learning in authentic assessment is defined through the descriptors in the scoring device based upon realistic expectations of process and product related to the designated task. Achievement expectations often allow for creativity and innovation in student response to a task, replicating or simulating the contexts in which the same proficiencies are demonstrated in one's workplace, community, or personal life. Assessment tasks should be designed to challenge students to efficiently and effectively use a variety of skills and draw from multidisciplinary knowledge to negotiate complex challenges. An important element of any assessment format, especially authentic assessment, is that students require appropriate opportunities to experience and practice a task, consult resources, and get feedback to refine their skills with whatever format of assessment is used. Poorly designed assessments may result in low achievement because of discomfort with the assessment format itself.

Authentic assessment tasks and the related scoring devices may require more time and effort on an instructor's part to develop. Such assessments are not necessarily more difficult to grade, but this is dependent upon the quality of the scoring device, often being a rubric. To confirm ease of grading for authentic assessments, descriptors of traits must be sufficiently specific to differentiate qualities of achievement criteria to be judged.

Scoring authentic performance through well-designed tasks does not automatically ensure that the result validly represents learning. A measure will not be valid if it does not effectively address the learning outcomes it was designed to assess. The foundation of any good assessment builds from meaningful learning outcomes and clear expectations defining the quality of student achievement. Alignment between learning outcomes and the scoring device is essential.

Authentic assessments build upon an understanding that students construct their own meaning using information taught and gathered from other experiences with the world. It is this belief that supports assessments beyond information recall. Authentic assessment tasks allow students to demonstrate the extent to which they accurately construct meaning about what they have been taught and provide them the opportunity to engage in further construction of meaning. They also provide multiple, sometimes alternative ways for students to demonstrate what they have learned. When blended with traditional assessments, the multiple perspectives of student learning create a far more complete understanding of what students know and can do and how they can apply their acquired skills and knowledge in authentic situations.

Frederick Burrack

See also Achievement Tests; Formative Assessment; Performance-Based Assessment; Rubrics; Standardized Tests; Standards-Based Assessment; Summative Assessment

Further Readings

Bransford, J. D., Brown, A. L., & Cocking, R. (Eds.). (2000). *How people learn: Brain, mind, experience and school* (Expanded ed.). Washington, DC: National Academy Press.

Frey, B. B., Schmitt, V. L., & Allen, J. P. (2012). Defining authentic classroom assessment. *Practical Assessment, Research & Evaluation, 17*(2), 2.

Guskey, T. R. (2003). How classroom assessments improve learning. *Educational Leadership, 60,* 6–11.

Marzano, R. J., Pickering, D. J., & Pollock, J. E. (2001). *Classroom instruction that works: Research-based strategies for increasing student achievement.* Alexandria, VA: ASCD.

Wiggins, G. (1998). Ensuring authentic performance. In *Educative assessment: Designing assessments to inform and improve student performance* (Chap. 2, pp. 21–42). San Francisco, CA: Jossey-Bass.

Wiggins, G. P. (1993). *Assessing student performance* (p. 229). San Francisco, CA: Jossey-Bass.

AUTHORSHIP

This entry discusses the guidelines and professional norms determining who is credited as an author for a piece of academic writing. Whether the manuscript produced is a book, conference paper, technical report, or research article, the names on the final product and their order should reflect the relative contribution of those involved.

Number of Authors

Different professional societies and publications have different guidelines for who should be considered an author, but in general, a person whose involvement was "substantial" is included as an author, in that the manuscript would not have been produced without the person's contribution. For example, conducting a literature search for related materials usually would not merit authorship, whereas writing the literature review would. Proofreading a manuscript before submission would not merit authorship, whereas making revisions based on reviewer recommendations would.

Products requiring extensive time or work, such as books, longitudinal studies, and lengthy reviews, may merit more authors. Some journals charge fees for number of pages published or open-access processing that can be several thousand dollars. Sometimes a large number of co-authors are included to share not only the publication credit but also the cost; however, it is considered inappropriate to recognize a person for authorship merely to defray the cost of publication.

Order of Authors

Authorship is the public affirmation of the relative contribution of those involved in the creation of the manuscript. In the social sciences, generally, the person doing most of the writing is listed as the first author regardless of other contributions. In some fields, such as some of the natural sciences, the last author is assumed to be the most important. The student is almost always the first author on any publications resulting from a dissertation. Involvement in the project and order of authorship should be discussed and established early. However, order of authorship may be modified as the project progresses and involvement shifts.

Issues in Authorship

Although sole and first authorship are usually valued most, inappropriate practices can be a concern. Sole authorships are thought to be more likely to be fraudulent. Some demand first authorship regardless of degree of involvement. Some demand authorship for sharing a database or a minor contribution even if they are not involved with the study or manuscript. Adding a department chair or committee chair as an author for a work he or she was not directly involved with is inappropriate. Authorship is not a gift; it is a valued recognition of scholarly work.

Gregory J. Marchant

See also APA Format; Literature Review

Further Readings

American Psychological Association. (n.d.). *Tips for determining authorship credit.* Retrieved from http://www.apa.org/science/leadership/students/authorship-paper.aspx

Eisner, R., Vasgird, D. R., & Hyman-Browne, E. (n.d.). *Responsible authorship and peer review* (course module). Columbia University Office for Responsible Conduct of Research. Retrieved from http://ccnmtl .columbia.edu/projects/rcr/rcr_authorship/

The Office of Research Integrity. (2013, October). *Authorship and publication* (ORI introduction to RCR: Chapter 9). Retrieved from http://ori.hhs.gov/ Chapter-9-Authorship-and-Publication-Introduction

AUTISM SPECTRUM DISORDER

Autism spectrum disorder (ASD) is a complex neurodevelopmental disorder, whose primary features are deficits in social communication and the presence of restricted interests and/or repetitive behaviors. In terms of social communication, individuals with ASD most commonly have difficulty with the pragmatic aspects of language, although some have difficulty using speech for communicative purposes (i.e., they are nonverbal or use few words). This entry further discusses the characteristics of individuals with ASD, the diagnostic standards for ASD and increased rates of diagnosis, the reasons why ASD is considered a complex disorder, and challenges with conducting and interpreting research on individuals with ASD.

The difficulties with the pragmatic aspects of language experienced by people with ASD involve the nonverbal cues present in language such as changes in pitch/tone that indicate emphasis or uncertainty on the part of the speaker. In addition, individuals with ASD have difficulty recognizing body language and facial expressions. These individuals may speak with a flattened aspect and tend to have difficulty understanding humor and sarcasm. They are often very literal in their use and comprehension of language. The difficulties with the pragmatic aspects of language lead to difficulties with peers, as individuals with ASD have difficulty engaging in social and play activities.

Additionally, these individuals often have a highly specialized area of interest. This restriction of interests can also interfere in their ability to develop and maintain peer relationships. Some individuals with ASD also engage in repetitive behaviors. One example is echolalia, which is the frequent repetition of vocalization for noncommunicative purposes. Some individuals will also engage in repetitive motor movements such as hand flapping, body rocking, or head banging. These verbal and motor stereotypies also interfere with these individuals ability to engage socially with others.

These behaviors can be detected as early as 18 months, and ASD is typically diagnosed in young children between the ages of 2 and 4 years. It affects approximately 1% of the population. However, recently more children have received the diagnosis. The screening and diagnostic standards have evolved and improved, which may explain increases in incidence in recent years. Many adolescents are being diagnosed, as they were not screened as children.

To complicate matters, the diagnostic standards for ASD have also shifted over time, which may explain increased rates of diagnosis. These increased rates may also reflect greater awareness and screening for the disorder in schools and medical settings. Previous clinical subtypes of the disorder (e.g., Asperger's syndrome) are no longer recognized by the current nosology (system for classifying psychiatric diagnoses). There are also many traits and behaviors that are associated features with ASD but are not diagnostic symptoms. These include behavioral challenges, heightened anxiety, and deficits in executive function. As noted, some individuals with ASD are also delayed and have resulting impairments in their language abilities. In addition, individuals with ASD may have poorly developed adaptive skills such as self-care, cooking, and personal finance to manage day-to-day life.

Complexity of ASD

ASD is a complex disorder of unknown etiology. Research involving genetic and environmental causes of the disorder is still ongoing and has yet to reach any significant findings. The neuropsychology of ASD is also still evolving, and as of 2016, many brain areas had been implicated as potential sources for the unique presentation of the disorder. However, no single brain area has been able to be isolated to explain the symptom presentation across the entire spectrum.

ASD is referred to as a spectrum because individual manifestation of the symptoms varies widely. Individuals range from those who do not communicate verbally and have significant intellectual limitations to individuals who have fully developed language and intellectual abilities. These individuals may have intense interests in a narrow area of focus as well as having difficulty with initiating and maintaining social relationships. Academic difficulties, repetitive behaviors, or sensory sensitivities may or may not be present.

The developmental trajectory of individuals with ASD also varies across the life span. Generally, symptoms become less severe as individuals age. However, greater difficulties during adolescence have been noted in some samples. Also, while the symptoms may reduce over time, the functional consequences of the remaining symptoms are often greater. In other words, while the symptoms may partially remit, the individual often experiences increasing social difficulties as the social expectations become greater as they age. These difficulties can lead to issues with anxiety, depression, and even social withdrawal. In addition, the adult outcomes for individuals with ASD across the spectrum are troubling as many individuals do not live independently and are not engaged in full-time employment.

Research Challenges

There are several challenges with conducting and interpreting research for individuals with ASD. The first challenge with ASD research is defining the population, as there are several issues to contend with in this area. The first is that ASD is defined differently in the medical system and in the education system. The second is that the conception of ASD including subtypes as previously noted has changed over time. The third issue in this area is how best to provide documentation of ASD for a sample.

In terms of the first issue, the medical world relies on diagnoses, whereas the education system has criteria that define a disability relative to educational performance. As such, some research conducted in education settings using special education students will have a different subset of the population. Simply put, some children who would qualify under the medical diagnosis may not qualify under the educational diagnosis and vice

versa. This means that there are differences in the populations that are studied. To further complicate matters, children with medical diagnoses of ASD may be classified under other education categories such as intellectual disability, multiply disabled, or other health impairment. In addition, some children with medical diagnoses of ASD will not qualify for special education services.

As mentioned, the second issue, comparing research on ASD over time, is due to the fact the diagnostic criteria have changed over time. While the criteria have evolved from the original concepts of Leo Kanner and Hans Asperger in the 1940s, the recent shifts are more germane to contemporary research. Under the previous nosology, autism used to be categorized as one of the pervasive developmental disorders and the term *autism* referred to more impacted individuals who demonstrated the unique signs of the disorder including language delays and repetitive behaviors (now often referred to as "classical autism").

Individuals with at least average intellectual ability and no history of language delays were classified as having Asperger's syndrome. These individuals also had to have evidence of a highly restricted area of interest. Mild symptom presentations were classified as pervasive developmental disorder, not otherwise specified. Other very rare subtypes such as childhood disintegrative disorder and Rett syndrome also had specific criteria. In the *Diagnostic and Statistical Manual of Mental Disorders, Fifth Edition* (DSM-5), published in 2013, the category of pervasive developmental disorder has been changed to ASD and the classification of subtypes has been altered. The diagnostic labels of Asperger's syndrome and pervasive developmental disorder, not otherwise specified have been removed, and the rare disorders are now considered special variants of ASD. Sensory sensitivities were also added as a diagnostic symptom under the new classification.

Beyond the differences between the medical and education criteria and the evolving diagnostic standards, the final related issue involves how studies confirm the diagnosis of ASD when defining their study population. Clinical judgment is considered the best tool for making the diagnosis, but the Autism Diagnostic Observation Schedule–Second Edition is the most common tool for gathering information on the presence of the disorder. The

Autism Diagnostic Observation Schedule–Second Edition is not a standardized instrument but is a structured observational tool that measures social communication and the presence of sensory interests and repetitive behaviors. There are several modules that are tailored with specific activities designed for specific ages and language abilities.

The Autism Diagnostic Interview Schedule–Revised is a structured interview for gathering information on the development of the individual. When used with the Autism Diagnostic Observation Schedule–Second Edition, this combination of assessments is considered the gold standard for documenting the presence of ASD, as this method has the most empirical support. Other rating scales are often used in the literature, but these rating scales can be best conceptualized as screeners as opposed to being diagnostic in nature.

Beyond the challenge of defining the ASD population in research, one of the further challenges for conducting and understanding research in this field is the heterogeneity of this population, as previously noted. This challenge cannot be understated, as individuals with ASD will vary from those who use augmentative communication to speak to those who were able to pursue advanced degrees.

Beyond having intellectual and communication differences, individuals with ASD will also vary in their skills in the areas of executive function, social skills, academic achievement, functional and adaptive abilities, anxiety, depression, and other psychiatric comorbidity. Further, individuals with ASD may also present with challenging behaviors such as verbal and physical aggression as well as passive noncompliance. These individuals will also have variety of strengths and interests that need to be considered when providing programming and interventions. This heterogeneity means that specifying the sample is critical in ASD research, as not all interventions will work for all individuals on the spectrum. In other words, having specific inclusion criteria (e.g., having ASD and concurrent anxiety) is important to match an intervention to the actual subpopulation of individuals with ASD on which it is expected to have an impact.

The final difficulty in conducting research on individuals with ASD is to gather large samples of these individuals. Part of this difficulty is due to the fact that there is often a need to specify a subset of the population and that ASD is a relatively low incidence disability. This can make it difficult to use traditional group-based research methods.

One way to continue to be able to use group-based methods is to limit the number of dependent variables and to tailor these variables to the intervention being conducted. Another approach is to use a class of research methods called single case designs in which one can use a small sample of individuals but utilize repeated measurement strategies. The conditions for the intervention and measurement are highly specified, and comparisons can be made across individuals or settings to demonstrate causal relationship (that the intervention is the only likely cause of the change in behavior).

Beyond the difficulties of defining and then recruiting samples, it is difficult to conduct research on individuals with ASD because they are a heterogeneous group and no one set of interventions or strategies works for all individuals on the spectrum. Nonetheless, research on individuals with ASD is growing at a rapid rate and further refinements to the disorder in terms of diagnostic and associated features are likely to evolve.

Nicholas W. Gelbar

See also Adaptive Behavior Assessments; Applied Behavior Analysis; Attention-Deficit/Hyperactivity Disorder; *Diagnostic and Statistical Manual of Mental Disorders*; Intellectual Disability and Postsecondary Education; Single-Case Research

Further Readings

American Psychiatric Association. (2013). *Diagnostic and statistical manual of mental disorders (DSM-5)* (5th ed.). Arlington, VA: American Psychiatric Publishing.

Autism and Developmental Disabilities Monitoring Network Surveillance Year 2010 Principal Investigators. (2014). Prevalence of autism spectrum disorder among children aged 8 years—Autism and developmental disabilities monitoring network, 11 sites, United States, 2010. *Morbidity and Mortality Weekly Report. Surveillance Summaries, 63*(2), 1.

Ch'ng, C., Kwok, W., Rogic, S., & Pavlidis, P. (2015). Meta-analysis of gene expression in autism spectrum disorder. *Autism Research, 8*(5), 593–608.

Lord, C., Rutter, M., DiLavore, P., Risi, S., Gotham, K., & Bishop, S. (2012). *Autism Diagnostic Observation*

Schedule, Second Edition (ADOS-2). Torrance, CA: Western Psychological Service.

Rutter, M., Le Couteur, A., & Lord, C. (2003). *Autism Diagnostic Interview Revised* (ADI-R). Los Angeles, CA: Western Psychological Services.

AUTOCORRELATION

Autocorrelation describes a set of data that is correlated with itself. When successive values ordered over time or space exhibit nonzero covariance, these data are said to be autocorrelated. Autocorrelation in time series data, often referred to as serial correlation, is frequently observed and has been widely studied and canonized. Examples are numerous: tomorrow's temperature is often predicted by temperature today, and a county's literacy rate next year will likely be well predicted by literacy this year.

While spatial autocorrelation remains an actively growing body of research, examples are also abundant: temperature in one county is often predicted by temperature in a neighboring county, and demographic makeup of a census block is likely similar to neighboring blocks. In both spatial and temporal data, autocorrelation has important implications for ordinary least squares regression, and other procedures that assume model errors are independent and uncorrelated. If not accounted for, the presence of autocorrelated errors can lead to misleading or invalid inference or imply model misspecification. Alternatively, autocorrelation can be marshaled for making predictions. In autocorrelated time series data, for example, future data points may be predictable because of their correlation with current and past values. This entry first explains how autocorrelation is quantified and discusses the importance of autocorrelation. It then looks at some of the nuances and implications of autocorrelation.

Quantifying Autocorrelation

Autocorrelation is easiest to demonstrate mathematically using time series data, where it is often represented in the form of a linear regression. The following equation shows the autoregressive (AR) model of autocorrelation, which shows the current observation (Y_t) as a linear function of previous observations plus a residual error:

$$Y_t = \beta_0 + \beta_1 Y_{t-1} + \beta_2 Y_{t-2} + \dots \beta_p Y_{t-p} + e_t.$$

Here is the familiar structure of an ordinary least squares regression with βs as constant coefficients, Y values at p previous intervals or *lags*, and a random error series e_t. This model assumes stationarity, such that the mean, variance, and covariance of the observations remain constant for all time periods. However, in many nonstationary cases, the residual error itself may be an autocorrelated series that requires more advanced AR moving average or AR integrated moving average models. First-order autocorrelation, in which an observation (Y_t) is correlated only with the observation immediately preceding it (Y_{t-1}), is commonly observed in time series data. Larger orders of autocorrelation include more lags and imply longer decays or greater inertia in temporal and spatial processes.

The most common way to measure the strength of autocorrelation is by computing the autocorrelation coefficient, symbolized as ρ. For the common case of the first-order autocorrelation, ρ is a two-variable correlation coefficient ranging between -1 and 1. Positive values of ρ are most frequently observed, indicating similarity between successive observations. Higher values of the coefficient indicate stronger dependency on previous values and milder decay. Although positive autocorrelation suggests that successive observations will move in the same direction, negative autocorrelation characterizes processes that oscillate in direction. A negative value of the autocorrelation coefficient can be exemplified by imagining the task of cutting equally sized pieces of ribbon into two unequal pieces. The smaller the first piece is cut, the larger the second piece will be. Thus, successive observations oscillate in size and are negatively correlated.

A sample first-order autocorrelation coefficient for time series data (r_t) can be calculated in similar fashion to a correlation coefficient, with N as the number of residuals in the time series data:

$$r_t = \frac{\sum_{t=2}^{N}(e_t)(e_{t-1})}{\sum_{t=1}^{N}e_t^2}.$$

As is clear from this equation, the total length of the time series is inconsequential, and only the *lag* between observations appears in this calculation. In addition to estimating the strength of correlation, this coefficient can be used as part of an inferential procedure to test the null hypothesis that there is no autocorrelation of residuals. In other words, the null hypothesis is that $\rho = 0$. For the first-order autocorrelation, the Durbin-Watson test is frequently employed for this purpose and generates a p value that can be used to determine whether the null hypothesis may be rejected or not.

A correlogram is often used to visually demonstrate and assess autocorrelation. The size of the autocorrelation coefficient is plotted on the vertical axis against increasing lag sizes on the horizontal axis. Autocorrelation coefficient values near zero on the correlogram indicate lag sizes at which correlation is weak, while large, distinct, or systematically occurring coefficient values occurring at one or more lag sizes suggest that there is dependency in the data.

Importance

Autocorrelation is a commonly occurring phenomenon, as many data change slowly over time and space. Data collection at small spatial or temporal intervals further increases the likelihood that successive observations will be correlated. Quantifying and parameterizing the strength and scope of autocorrelation as described earlier can be important in making predictions, and the aforementioned AR moving average and AR integrated moving average models excel in this regard. While the usefulness of autocorrelation in forecasting is clear, the importance of autocorrelation is more frequently framed around the problems of model inference and model specification.

Spatial and temporal data are often modeled using ordinary least squares regression or similar techniques that rely on the Gauss-Markov theorem assumption that error terms are uncorrelated. When autocorrelation is present in model residuals, this assumption is violated. Although parameter estimates remain unbiased, standard errors become biased—inflated when autocorrelation is positive and deflated when negative—and increase the chance of making Type I and Type II errors.

Additionally, results of t and f tests will be invalid and confidence intervals incorrect. The Durbin-Watson test for time series data and Moran's I for spatial data are the most common tests researchers conduct on residuals to evaluate whether autocorrelation has the potential to invalidate inference. If autocorrelation is found, it may be corrected by transforming the data using a generalized least squares or other approach.

The approach just described assumes that the model has been correctly specified and exhibits "pure" autocorrelation. However, a misspecified model can also produce autocorrelated residuals, regardless of autocorrelation in the data. This is common when a spatially or temporally dependent variable is excluded from a regression model, as those dependencies will now occur only in the error term of the model. Spatial and temporal lags of variables should be included to appropriately model these processes. Similarly common is the use of an incorrect functional form, such as using a linear model when a quadratic form is more appropriate, which often produces autocorrelated residuals.

Autocorrelation is thus common both as a real phenomenon and an artifact of modeling. Appropriate dynamic model specification is critical, and correctly dealing with autocorrelation allows for validity of inference, more appropriate analysis, and improved precision.

Additional Concepts

Research on autocorrelation is ongoing, and many nuances cannot be covered here. However, a few additional concepts deserve mention. Much of this entry describes the first-order autocorrelation. Although it is most common, higher order autocorrelation does occur, even when adjacent values show no relationship. Higher order correlation coefficients are represented as r_k, where k is the order of autocorrelation being assessed. Taken all together, the set of $(r_1, r_2, \ldots, r_k)$ coefficients is the autocorrelation function.

For stationary data, autocorrelation is likely to decay quickly, maintaining a consistent mean, variance, and covariance over time. However, if data are nonstationary, the effects of the past may accumulate rather than dissipate, maintaining long "memories." Integrated processes, including random walks, never discount the effects of stochasticity and may not ever return to a mean, while fractionally integrated processes decay very slowly. As a result, such processes can produce spurious inference if nonstationarity is not accounted for.

Finally as larger and larger data sets become available, an active area of research deals with the implications of autocorrelated data on sample size. Depending on the strength of autocorrelation, more data produced via sampling processes at a higher resolution do not necessarily mean more information. A tension thus exists between sample size, resolution, and the number of independent measurements. New methods for determining effective sample size and for conducting regressions between two autocorrelated data sets continue to be developed.

Alex McInturff

See also Correlation; Pearson Correlation Coefficient; Phi Correlation Coefficient

Further Readings

Box, G. E., & Jenkins, G. M. (1976). Time series analysis: forecasting and control (Rev. ed.). Holden-Day.

Clifford, P., Richardson, S., & Hemon, D. (1989). Assessing the significance of the correlation between two spatial processes. *Biometrics*, 123–134.

Diniz-Filho, J. A. F., Bini, L. M., & Hawkins, B. A. (2003). Spatial autocorrelation and red herrings in geographical ecology. *Global Ecology and Biogeography*, 12(1), 53–64.

Durbin, J., & Watson, G. S. (1950). Testing for serial correlation in least squares regression: I. *Biometrika*, 37(3/4), 409–428.

Enders, W. (2008). *Applied econometric time series.* Wiley.

Granger, C. W., & Newbold, P. (1974). Spurious regressions in econometrics. *Journal of econometrics,* 2(2), 111–120.

Legendre, P. (1993). Spatial autocorrelation: Trouble or new paradigm? *Ecology,* 74(6), 1659–1673.

Viladomat, J., Mazumder, R., McInturff, A., McCauley, D. J., & Hastie, T. (2014). Assessing the significance of global and local correlations under spatial autocorrelation: A nonparametric approach. *Biometrics,* 70(2), 409–418.

Automated Essay Evaluation

Automated essay evaluation (AEE) is the evaluation of written work through computer technology. AEE is an expansion of the earlier concepts of automated essay scoring (AES) and automated essay grading in that in addition to providing a numerical index of writing performance, the technology can provide qualitative feedback that can be used in formative writing applications. Although originally created for English, the technology has been expanded to other languages as well. This entry further describes AEE and how it is used in both summative and formative evaluations.

The web-based technology can be used in both summative and formative applications. AEE is used for both high-stakes tests and as part of an electronic portfolio system to facilitate the teaching of writing. AEE was originally developed by Ellis Page with the objective of making the grading of essays a bit easier by automating the evaluation of at least the mechanical aspects of writing. The hope is that, by reducing scoring costs, the technology can facilitate the writing performance items that are part of assessments created as a result of federal testing policies.

Numeric feedback, usually embedded in a rubric, is often given on a scale of 1–6 with 6 indicating *best performance* and a 1 indicating *poorest scorable performance.* In addition, the computer may be able to identify errors in grammar, mechanics, syntax, and organization and development. Some AEE programs can identify structure in narrative essays and can provide feedback along the lines of,

> The thesis of your paper appears to be that "democracy can only flourish when all citizens have the right to vote." You appear to be making three points—democracy is one five different forms of government, voting is a key element in the formation of a democracy, and governments have limited the rights of some individuals to vote. You have a lot of information about the first point but not too much information for the second and third points.

Note that the computer does not "understand" what is written; rather, scores and feedback are based on models of human rater performance. If humans reward a certain pattern of writing, then the program will attempt to apply the same reward to similar patterns of production. Additionally, the software programs can give an assessment of how "on topic" the writer is, can generally flag essays that include bizarre or threatening content, and can flag essays that are statistically unusual (e.g., very long essays).

Two types of model construction are employed for AEE—prompt-specific models and nonprompt-specific models. Prompt specific-models are used when the scoring of content plays an important role in the evaluation of the essay. As an example of the methods used to create and validate scoring algorithms, here are the procedures that might be used to create a model for the commonly used six writing trait rubric:

Six hundred essays are collected and scored by two human raters from a sample of examinees that are tested under conditions similar to the operational environment. Essay scores are typically sparse at the high score points and so training samples often have more essays at the lower score points and often very few essays at the upper score points (sometimes fewer than 20). Typically, a large proportion—66%—of the sample is used for model building, with the remainder held out as a separate cross-validation sample to evaluate model performance.

In the case of the 600 essays, 400 essays are randomly selected for model building. The essays are parsed and tagged, and variables (or consolidated meta-variables) classified by the parser are regressed against the scores of the human raters. Once the model is built and finalized, the remaining 33% (or 200 in this case) essays are scored by the model as part of a cross-validation procedure. The fit of the validation set is usually not as good as it was for the training set, as the models tend to overfit the training sample. Consequently, the regression weights associated with the model are adjusted to reflect the prediction inaccuracy on the validation set. Usually the adjustment is made by using all of the essays in the data set for forming the model.

Nonprompt-specific models evaluate good writing characteristics in an essay and not the content of what is written. These models are used when similar, but not the same, questions are asked of a narrowly stratified population (e.g., candidates taking a certification exam). The goal is to determine the writing ability of the individuals and not the mastery of a content domain. Model building is the same as for prompt-specific models except that the training and validation sets draw across multiple prompts.

An extension of the nonprompt-specific model is referred to as the "generic" model that is constructed when the goal is to evaluate across multiple prompts for one or more genre of writing. Again, the goal is to provide feedback on general writing characteristics. Generic models may be configured for a specific genre or developmental level of writing, but the attempt is to provide broader coverage than for other nonprompt-specific models. They are generally used for formative feedback because their estimates tend not to be as precise as for prompt-specific models. Model building is also generated from a much broader set of prompts within each genre.

Summative and Formative Use of AEE

AEE has been evaluated in both summative and formative contexts. The most comprehensive evaluation of the technology was part of a Hewlett Foundation–sponsored demonstration that contrasted the AES performance of eight commercial vendors and one university laboratory's performance on AES with that of human raters. That study employed eight different essay sets drawn from six states representing the Partnership for Assessment of Readiness for College and Careers and Smarter Balanced Assessment Consortium. Four of the essays were "source based." A student was asked to read an artifact and then respond with an essay. The remaining four essays reflected prompts of a more traditional variety (i.e., narrative, descriptive, persuasive).

Over 17,000 essays were randomly divided into two sets, a training set ($n = 13,336$) in which the vendors had 1 month to model the data and a test set for which they were required to make score predictions within a 2½-day period. The training set consisted of two human rater scores, the so-called resolved score, and the text of the essay. The resolved score reflected the final score assigned by the state. The test set consisted only of the text of the essay. Six of the eight essays were transcribed from handwritten documents using one of the two transcription services. Accuracy rates of transcription were estimated to be over 98%. The challenge to the nine teams was to predict scores based on essay performance that matched the ratings assigned as the resolved score.

Performance was evaluated on five different measures of a single evidentiary criterion—agreement with human raters. One set of measures focused on agreement at the distributional level and the other set on agreement at the individual response level. The individual-response-level measures included exact agreement, exact + adjacent agreement, κ, quadratic weighted κ, and the Pearson product–moment correlation. The AES engines performed well on the distributional measures. With a high degree of consistency, all nine demonstrators were able to replicate the means and standard deviations for the scores assigned by the states.

With regard to agreement measures, there was some variability, but the AES engines performed well on three of the five measures (exact + adjacent agreement, quadratic weighted κ, and correlation). On the two measures where the performance was not as high (exact agreement and κ), there was also high variability among the performance of operational human raters. In addition, scaling artifacts attributable to the way the state scores were adjudicated may have contributed to the relative lack of precision on predicted scores.

A follow-up study was performed as a competition with data scientists using the same (but anonymized) data sets. Over 200 competitors participated over a 3-month development period for a top prize of US$60,000. The course of the competition included a development forum in which participants helped one another by disseminating the results of their programming experiments. The top team came in with a quadratic weighted κ coefficient of .78.

Formative use of AEE has been in place for several years, but comprehensive evaluations of the technology are few. Mark Shermis, Jill Burstein, and Leonard Bliss looked at the impact of the Educational Testing Service product criterion in the writing outcomes of a 10th-grade English class at an urban high school in Miami, FL. After seven writing assignments, the researchers found that students produced fewer errors in writing and showed some evidence of growth.

A study on the use of AEE in a K–12 formative program showed performance across a range of grades within and across traits in a formative system. AEE was implemented in an online practice assessment program in a Southern state, using the CRASE platform, automated scoring proprietary software by Pacific Metrics Corporation. Responses were scored on a three-trait rubric (ideas, style, and conventions) with a score range of 1–4. The responses were scored by humans, and the CRASE engine was trained on these responses. The software program performed similar to humans across the grades and traits.

Averaged across the grades, mean scores were similar for CRASE and humans, with composite scores showing slightly larger, but still similar, differences. More important, though, are agreement rates. Exact agreements are influenced by score distributions and the rubric scale. Computer and humans agreed exactly 70–80% of the time with generally lower agreement rates on the conventions trait. Correlations between the software and manual scoring were around .70 for the traits and .80 for total scores.

There is more work to be done in the area of AEE, but the technology has demonstrated the capacity to accurately score in the contexts of formative and summative assessment. Predictions seem to be better for essays than for short-form constructed responses, but even with the latter, technology improvements are being made on a regular basis. Specific challenges for the technology include recognition and better assessments of arguments, making predictions about the reasonableness of conclusions and providing more targeted feedback on the nonmechanical aspects of writing.

Mark D. Shermis and Sue Lottridge

See also Formative Evaluation; Partnership for Assessment of Readiness for College and Careers; Smarter Balanced Assessment Consortium; Summative Evaluation

Further Readings

Shermis, M. D. (2014). State-of-the-art automated essay scoring: A United States demonstration and competition, results, and future directions. *Assessing Writing, 20*, 53–76.

Shermis, M. D. (2015). Contrasting state-of-the-art in the machine scoring of short-form constructed responses. *Educational Assessment, 20*(1), 46–65.

Shermis, M. D., & Burstein, J. (2003). *Automated essay scoring: A cross-disciplinary perspective* (pp. xvi–238). Mahwah, NJ: Erlbaum.

Shermis, M. D., Burstein, J., & Bliss, L. (2004). *The impact of automated essay scoring on high stakes writing assessments.* Paper presented at the annual meetings of the National Council on Measurement in Education, San Diego, CA.

Shermis, M. D., Burstein, J., & Bursky, S. A. (2013). Introduction to automated essay evaluation. In M. D. Shermis & J. Burstein (Eds.), *Handbook of automated essay evaluation: Current applications and new directions* (pp. 1–15). New York, NY: Routledge.

Shermis, M. D., Burstein, J. C., Elliot, N., Miel, S., & Foltz, P. W. (2015). Instructional applications for automated writing evaluation. In C. A. McArthur, S. Graham, & J. Fitzgerald (Eds.), *Handbook of writing research* (2nd ed., pp. 395–409). New York, NY: The Guilford Press.

Shermis, M. D., & Hamner, B. (2012). *Contrasting state-of-the-art automated scoring of essays: Analysis.*

Paper presented at the Annual National Council on Measurement in Education.

Shermis, M. D., & Hamner, B. (2013). Handbook of automated essay evaluation: Current applications and new directions. In M. D. Shermis & J. Burstein (Eds.), *Handbook of automated essay evaluation: Current applications and new directions* (pp. 313–346). New York, NY: Routledge.

Shermis, M. D., & Morgan, J. (2015). Using prizes to facilitate change in educational assessment. In F. Drasgow (Ed.), *Technology in testing: Measurement Issues* (pp. 323–338). New York, NY: Psychology Press.

Vantage Learning. (2001). *A preliminary study of the efficacy of IntelliMetric™ for use in scoring Hebrew assessments.* Newtown, PA: Author.

Williamson, D. M., Xi, X., & Breyer, F. J. (2012). A framework for the evaluation and use of automated essay scoring. *Educational Measurement: Issues and Practice, 31*(1), 2–13.

Wilson, J., & Andrada, G. N. (n.d.). Using automated feedback to improve writing quality. In Y. Rosen, S. Ferrara, & M. Mosharraf (Eds.), *Handbook of research on computational tools for real-world skill development* (pp. 678–703). Hershey, PA: Learning Disabilities: A Contemporary Journal.

b PARAMETER

Item response theory (IRT) uses several parameters. These parameters control the position and shape of IRT item characteristic curves (ICCs) that map the relationship between an examinee's ability, usually denoted by theta (θ), and the examinee's probability of making a particular item response (see Figure 1). The *b* parameter is present in all common IRT models. It is called the *difficulty* parameter, as it is the IRT analogy to traditional measures of item difficulty, such as *p* values. This entry first provides further context and discusses the importance of the *b* parameter. It then discusses unidimensional IRT models for dichotomous items and polytomous items, multidimensional IRT (MIRT) models, and the relationship between *p* values and IRT *b* parameters.

Context

IRT models the probability that an examinee will make a particular response to an item based on examinee's standing on the trait that a test measures. For a mathematics achievement test, IRT can model the probability that an examinee will earn a particular score on an item based on the examinee's achievement in math. For an instrument measuring extroversion, IRT can model the probability that an examinee will select the response *very accurate* for the statement *I make friends easily* based on the examinee's degree of extroversion. Virtually any type of instrument

(e.g., ability and achievement tests, personality and attitude assessments, and questionnaires and surveys) and any type of item (e.g., true or false, multiple choice, Likert) can be analyzed using IRT.

Importance of *b* Parameter

There are many practical benefits to the *b* parameter relative to classical measures of item difficulty. First, *b* parameters are not group dependent (provided the IRT model fits the data). Another advantage is that item difficulty, *b*, and examinee ability, θ, are on the same scale. This, combined with the fact that an item's maximum information occurs at or near the *b* parameter, means that inspection of the *b* parameters is helpful in the test construction process.

Unidimensional IRT Models for Dichotomous Items

The most common IRT models assume that (a) a single ability underlies the examinees' response processes and (b) items are dichotomously scored (e.g., right vs. wrong). The relationship between the probability of a correct response and examinee ability has a monotonically increasing ICC that is roughly *s* shaped, although it can be compressed and stretched at various points along the ability scale (see Figure 1).

The *b* parameter describes the ICC's location on the θ scale. Specifically, it shows where there is an inflection point on the θ scale (i.e., where the concavity of the curve changes) in the ICC.

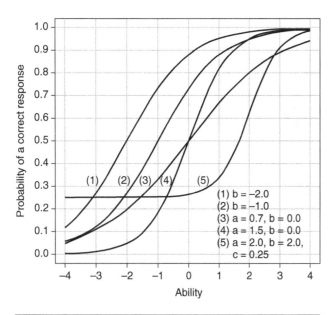

Figure 1 Item characteristic curves for five hypothetical items

The three-parameter logistic (3PL) model has:

(1) a discrimination parameter, denoted a, that controls the slope of the ICC;

(2) a pseudo-guessing parameter, denoted c, that represents the lower asymptote of the ICC; and

(3) a difficulty parameter, denoted b.

The two-parameter logistic (2PL) model does not have the pseudo-guessing parameter, c (or equivalently, one can consider $c = 0$). The one-parameter logistic (1PL) model also does not have the pseudo-guessing parameter, c, and all items are assigned a common slope, meaning items are modeled with only the b parameter.

In the 3PL model, the b parameter is located where the probability of a correct response is $(1 + c)/2$ on the θ scale. The 1PL model and 2PL model have no c parameter, so the b parameter's location on the θ scale is where the probability of a correct response is 1/2. Figure 1 illustrates ICCs for 2 1PL items, 2 2PL items, and 1 3PL item. The b parameters for Items 1–4 are at -2.0, -1.0, 0.0, and 0.0, respectively. The probability of a correct response for these items at those θ values is 0.50. Item 5, the 3PL item, has a probability of a correct response of $(1 + 0.25)/2 = 0.625$ at a θ of 2.0. Note that items with higher b parameters have ICCs that are shifted to the right along the θ scale.

Unidimensional IRT Models for Polytomous Items

Use is increasing for unidimensional IRT models for examinee response processes for items that are polytomously scored. The function of the b parameter depends on the exact polytomous model in question. The generalized partial credit model models response categories that are adjacent (e.g., 0 vs. 1, 1 vs. 2, 2 vs. 3). The b parameter represents the overall difficulty of the test item, and there are separate difficulties for each response category (denoted by d_s, where s is a particular item score). The graded response model models multiple dichotomous outcomes, where the examinee scores in a particular response category or any higher categories versus the examinee scoring in any lower response categories (e.g., 0 vs. 1, 2 and 3; 0 and 1 vs. 2 and 3; and 0, 1, and 2 vs. 3). Both the GPCM and GRM are used to show ordered response categories. The nominal model is used with unordered response categories, and it also has a difficulty parameter.

MIRT Models

The b parameter also occurs in MIRT. Although there are as many a parameters as there are dimensions of the MIRT model, there is only one b parameter, and the ICC becomes a surface instead of a curve. Strictly speaking, in MIRT models, the b parameter is related to the multidimensional difficulty of the item, which rescales the b parameter by dividing it by the square root of the sum of the squared a parameters.

Relationship Between *p* Values and IRT *b* Parameters

Allan Birnbaum and Frederic Lord noted that under certain conditions, an approximate relationship exists between the IRT b parameter and classical p values. The relationship is only approximate for b parameters under the 2PL model, so very little or no guessing by examinees should be expected. The 2PL b parameter is approximately equal to γ/r, where γ is the negation of the inverse cumulative normal distribution deviate corresponding to the item's p value and r_{biserial} is the item's biserial correlation.

Unlike p values, where lower values indicate harder items, b parameters that are higher in value indicate harder items that fewer examinees endorse or answer correctly. Only examinees high in ability will have a moderate to high probability of answering these items correctly. Lower b values indicate easier items that many examinees endorse or answer correctly. Whenever an examinee's ability equals an item's b parameter, the examinee will have 0.50 probability of answering the item correctly for 1PL and 2PL models.

Scott Bishop

See also a Parameter; c Parameter; Item Response Theory; p Value

Further Readings

Birnbaum, A. (1968). Some latent trait models and their use in inferring an examinee's ability. In F. M. Lord & M. R. Novick, *Statistical theories of mental test scores* (pp. 397–479). Reading, MA: Addison-Wesley.

Bock, R. D. (1972). Estimating item parameters and latent ability when responses are scored in two or more nominal categories. *Psychometrika, 37,* 29–51.

Lord, F. M. (1980). *Applications of item response theory to practical testing problems.* Hillsdale, NJ: Erlbaum.

Muraki, E. (1992). A generalized partial credit model: Application of an EM algorithm. *Applied Psychological Measurement, 16*(2), 159–176.

Samejima, F. (1969). *Estimation of ability using a response pattern of graded scores.* (Psychometrika Monograph, No. 17). Richmond, VA: Psychometric Society.

Backward Design

The term *backward design* refers to an approach to schooling, both at the system level and classroom level, predicated on a tight focus on achieving predetermined mission-related goals. Backward design for education was largely created and popularized by Grant Wiggins and Jay McTighe as an alternative to traditional design approaches wherein teachers typically began with content (such as textbooks, novels, or standards) and then created instruction around the ideas or questions that arose from selected materials. The backward design approach asks teachers and school leaders to determine skills, ideas, understandings, and dispositions most critical for students and then build learning experiences that ensure those outcomes. This entry discusses the application of backward design to curriculum design, schools and school systems, system-wide programming, and evaluation.

Although its applications are varied, backward design theory and technique is most typically used by teachers to develop lesson and unit plans and by educational leaders to improve system- or building-wide curricula. The most foundational principle of backward design is that educators must allow their work to be guided by jointly established goals (either for student understanding or for school/district improvement) and assessed using authentic performance assessments that generate acceptable evidence. The popularity of backward design increased dramatically through the first decade or so of the 21st century and it is commonly taught as part of educator preparation programs. Backward design is a valuable framework for educational evaluation, as it helps to operationalize key variables involved in school, program, or curriculum design.

Backward Curriculum Design

Backward curriculum design is sometimes also termed *understanding by design* after the book of the same name in which it is outlined in detail. It is not a prescriptive system of curriculum development, but rather is intended to be a way of thinking about instruction that keeps student understanding of essential concepts and ideas at the heart of schooling. Backward curriculum design may improve instruction by giving teachers a framework that encourages a focus on student growth rather than on the process of teaching and that avoids two common pitfalls of classroom instruction: teaching that is focused on activities or busy work and teaching that is focused on covering some quantity of content, such as a chapter in a textbook.

In the broadest terms, backward curriculum design is usually approached as a three-phase process. First, a teacher (or group of teachers) identifies desired results. Second, a determination is made about what will constitute acceptable evidence of learning. Third, the learning experience is planned in detail.

Identifying Desired Results

A frequently used analogy likens backward curriculum design to vacation planning; before planning the particulars of a trip (e.g., plane tickets, hotel bookings, excursions), a traveler must first decide on a destination. Similarly, when planning a learning experience, teachers who use backward design principles decide at the outset on what results they hope a lesson or unit will achieve. In other words, they decide what understandings, knowledge, and skills students will gain or enhance by participating in the experience.

Identifying such big ideas, however, can be challenging. Practitioners of backward curriculum design often begin by sorting their materials into three categories of importance: those ideas, facts, and skills that are essential, those that are important, and those that are worthwhile. Although the definitions of these categories are fluid and must be determined by each practitioner's assessment of learning needs of the practitioner's students, the basic guidelines are as follows:

Essential Ideas and Skills: Those enduring, transferable ideas and skills that are critical for navigating the world. These often require significant investments of time and effort.

Important Knowledge and Skills: Discrete facts, skills, and techniques that are broadly useful in school and in life, such as solving mathematical equations or crafting thesis statements. These can usually be learned with modest amounts of instruction and effort.

Worthwhile: Key dates, facts, figures, and terminology. These are often easily memorized facts that can be accessed through textbooks or ready reference sources such as printed or online encyclopedias.

Traditionally, schooling has focused on the latter two categories and given them priority over essential ideas and skills. Backward curriculum design, conversely, is driven by the first category and uses the important and worthwhile facts and skills in the service of those that are deemed essential.

Enduring Understandings and Essential Questions

Practitioners of backward design often frame their work by coupling enduring understandings with essential questions that are implied by the big ideas and skills that have been identified. Essential questions are those that inspire students to think about the big ideas that the teacher has determined to be critical. For example, the teacher whose students are studying the great depression might have posed the essential question, "What happens when a government's responsibilities to its individual people come into conflict with responsibilities to its industries?" Or, "Which group deserves more protection from the government: Individuals or industry?"

Essential questions are meant to provoke deeper thought, spark debate, and inspire more questions. They most often do not have "right" answers, but rather they can be approached from a variety of angles. They should intrigue students, they should be likely to have application outside the classroom, they should have relevance to core ideas inherent to the discipline, and they should help students make sense of abstract, multifaceted concepts. Furthermore, essential questions can be general, such as the two posed above, or content-specific, such as, "Were the government's actions during the Depression fair or unfair?"

Once determined, enduring understandings (there are typically at least two) serve as the "destination" or the desired result of the lesson to be designed. Everything that transpires through the course of a lesson or unit, including lecturing, activities, and reading, is done with the intention of helping students acquire or deepen those understandings. To some new practitioners of backward design, the focus on enduring understandings can be misunderstood as an eschewal of established curriculum frameworks or standards; however, this is not the case. State or national standards help to determine what content will be taught, whereas backward design helps teachers determine how content will be taught, and what broader understandings students will gain from the study of content.

Determining Evidence of Learning

Once enduring understandings are identified (along with key skills, terms, and knowledge), practitioners of backward curriculum design must determine what evidence will be sufficient to show that students have achieved the desired results. In other words, how will the instructor know that the desired understandings have been attained? Typically, backward design calls for multiple and varied assessments to occur throughout a unit or lesson and that ignorance (or lack of learning) should be assumed until evidence proves otherwise. Common types of assessments are informal checks for understanding, traditional tests or quizzes, open-ended academic prompts that are addressed orally or in writing, and authentic performance tasks that simulate (to the extent possible) the real-world problems or situations and which result in tangible products or polished performances.

Most often, authentic performance tasks are used as a unit's summative assessment (toward the end of the learning experience), whereas other types of assessment are used in a formative way (throughout the learning experience). Authentic performance tasks are intended to engage students in realistic questions or challenges that provide an opportunity to demonstrate the extent to which a student has grasped the intended enduring understanding. For example, students studying the Great Depression might be asked to look at a present-day issue that pits the rights of individuals against those of corporations and to make judgments about what should be done.

Planning the Learning Experience

Backward curriculum design is largely grounded in constructivist learning theory, and it asks practitioners to consider various elements of accepted pedagogical techniques when planning instruction. The following are the seven key considerations that must be present in the design of any lesson or unit:

- Do students know what they are learning and why it is important?
- Are students enticed to find the learning intriguing through some kind of initial hook?
- Throughout the lesson, are students provided with the necessary skills, knowledge, and experiences that will help them gain understanding and meet performance goals?
- Are students given opportunities throughout a learning experience to reflect on what they are learning, and revisit the big ideas of the lesson, and rethink their opinions?
- Are students given time to self-assess their learning and progress?
- Is the lesson differentiated to account for different learning needs and various levels of interest and readiness?
- Is the lesson organized in a way that makes understanding likely to happen (*vs.* being organized to ensure coverage of a topic)?

Although backward design requires teachers to spend time planning and organizing learning experiences, most practitioners see those prepared plans as flexible blueprints that are subject to change as rates of student learning become evident. Typically, instructional plans are designed with some flexibility to allow some students to move more quickly and possibly interact with more "important" and "worthwhile" knowledge and skills, whereas others remain focused on the essential components of the lesson. Determining what is essential, important, and worthwhile during the planning stage allows the instructor to make informed decisions about how to adapt the lesson while it is in progress.

Backward Design of Schools or School Systems

The same way of thinking that is used to plan individual lessons or units can be used to design system- or school-wide improvement. At base, the idea is simple and straightforward—all educators in a school or system decide together on what is most critical for students to know, understand, and be able to do by the end of their schooling and then educators work in a cohesive, coordinated way to ensure student success. However, this stands in contrast to many countries' deeply entrenched tradition of teacher isolation and autonomy, and it requires significant and sustained support on the part of school leaders. Schools that are using backward design as an improvement or reform strategy are guided by the following principles:

- Educators' job is to bring about student learning.
- All expectations for student learning should be clearly defined and regularly measured.
- When gaps are evident between what students are learning and what they are meant to be learning, it is the job of all educators to close such gaps.
- Schools must plan for reform with end results in mind.

Backward Design of System-Wide Programming

Schools using a backward design framework use their stated mission as a guide for all decisions and that mission reflects those big, cross-disciplinary ideas, understandings, and dispositions that should be reflected in every part of the curriculum. Those ideas then guide vertically coordinated teams of content-area specialists (e.g., arts, English, math) who determine which big ideas lie at the heart of their specific discipline, and thus which skills, dispositions, and understandings are the ultimate goals for student achievement. Those skills, dispositions, and understandings serve as the backbone of the curriculum, and they recur frequently as students move through their study of each discipline; content standards are also used in service to those larger goals but are not considered ends in themselves. Each course in a given discipline is designed to ensure student growth around that discipline's overarching goals; essential questions and enduring understandings that both fit with those goals, and with more content-specific goals, guide the instruction. Ten principles guide system-wide backward design curriculum work:

- A central goal of schooling is the ability learn knowledge, skills, and understandings that are highly flexible and can be adapted for use in various real-world situations.

- Students must understand the value of what they are learning so that they are motivated to undertake worthwhile challenges.
- Successful transfer of knowledge and skills requires that big ideas recur frequently throughout a curriculum.
- Enduring understandings cannot be "delivered" but must be uncovered so that student can make sense of the power of big ideas.
- All learners (children and adults) need clear guidance about what constitutes excellence in a given setting or assignment.
- All learners (children and adults) require timely, ongoing, specific feedback in order to improve.
- All learners (children and adults) require regular reflection in order to gain or deepen understanding.
- All learners (children and adults) must be encouraged to rethink and refine previously held beliefs.
- All learners (children and adults) need a safe and supportive environment in which to learn.
- Learning is most effective when it can be made personal and when it connects to or has application in the learner's everyday life.

District and school leaders should consider a three-phase approach to system-wide backward design. In the first phase, school and district leaders identify desired results, including long-term goals for what both students and teachers should know, understand, and be able to do. In the second phase, school leaders must determine how they will gauge success, that is, how they will know the extent to which goals are being achieved. In the third phase, leaders must plan for initial and ongoing actions toward achieving goals, carefully considering what types of support and resources teachers will need as changes are implemented. Six primary responsibilities fall to school leaders: helping to craft a mission, ensuring a coherent curriculum, identifying gaps between mission and reality, personnel management and development, effective policy creation and management of resources, and guidance of school culture.

A Backward Design Approach to Evaluation

Backward design may be of particular use to evaluators, as it is a framework against which to judge the quality of educational systems or programs. Using backward design, evaluators can operationalize key variables involved in school, program, or curriculum design.

Curriculum Mapping

Regardless of a school district's size, backward-designed evaluation of curriculum can help ensure that all students, regardless of which building they are housed in or which program of studies they choose to follow, are experiencing opportunities to engage with those ideas, dispositions, and skills that a district's educators have identified as the most essential. Critical to successful backward design of system-wide curricula is proper curriculum mapping. The purpose of curriculum mapping in a backward-design setting is not to guide pacing or lock-step instruction of content, but rather to ensure that big ideas—those central to the school, to the discipline, and to subdisciplines—are recurring throughout the curriculum in ways that are intellectually coherent.

Backward-designed evaluation also usually looks at indications of authentic performance tasks, analytic and longitudinal rubrics, examples of work, suggested resources, formative assessment strategies, suggestions for differentiation, and troubleshooting strategies. The job of curriculum auditors or evaluation teams using a backward-design framework is to predict and identify problems with existing curricula, to collect feedback about existing curricula from stakeholders, and to identify gaps between written, taught, and tested curricula. Furthermore, evaluators may examine the extent to which a curriculum adheres to the principles of understanding and knowledge transfer on which backward design is based.

Gap Analysis

Identifying gaps between mission (or goals) and reality (or results) is a core component of backward design, and one that is useful for educational evaluators. Gaps may be evidenced by quantitative data, such as test scores, graduation rates, absenteeism, grade distributions, or other observable indicators; gaps may also be evidenced by qualitative data such as school accreditation reports, surveys of constituent groups, or targeted interviews. The identification of such gaps is predicted on the clear articulation of the desired outcomes of any program or curriculum.

Usually, gap analysis is based on the goals of backward curriculum design. For example, a school might determine that one of its primary reform goals is to allow students regular opportunities to reflect on and revise their work based on feedback from teachers and peers. In that case, an evaluator (or team of evaluators) would collect data in order to determine the extent to which formative assessments are used to provide student feedback, the frequency with which students are asked to assess peers, and the frequency with which students are given the opportunity to revise their work.

Gap analysis may also be based on programming or school-wide goals grounded in a theory of action about improvement. For example, a school may determine that critical thinking is an important outcome goal for students and that high-quality questioning strategies is a key component involved in helping students develop that skill. Data must then be collected, usually through a process of observation-based, fine-grained evidence recording, to determine the extent to which such practices are at work in the school. Gap analysis is also helpful for evaluating school policies, procedures, and physical spaces. With clearly defined goals for understanding and dispositions, evaluators can examine the extent to which resource allocation, discipline policies, homework practices, and the layout of physical spaces supports or constrains student understanding of essential concepts.

Rebecca Mazur

See also Action Research; Authentic Assessment; Constructivist Approach; Curriculum; Curriculum Mapping; Formative Assessment; Zone of Proximal Development

Further Readings

Brooks, J. G., & Brooks, M. G. (2001). *In search of understanding: The case for constructivist classrooms.* Upper Saddle River, NJ: Merrill/Prentice Hall.

McTighe, J., & Wiggins, G. P. (2013). *Essential questions: Opening doors to student understanding.* Alexandria, VA: Association for Supervision and Curriculum Development.

Wiggins, G. P., & McTighe, J. (2005). *Understanding by design* (2nd ed.). Alexandria, VA: Association for Supervision and Curriculum Development.

Wiggins, G. P., & McTighe, J. (2007). *Schooling by design: Mission, action, and achievement.* Alexandria, VA: Association for Supervision and Curriculum Development.

Wiggins, G. P., & McTighe, J. (2012). *The understanding by design guide to advanced concepts in creating and reviewing units.* Alexandria, VA: Association for Supervision and Curriculum Development.

Zmuda, A., McTighe, J., Wiggins, G., & Brown, J. L. (2007). *Schooling by design: An ASCD action tool.* Alexandra, VA: Association for Supervision and Curriculum Development.

Bar Graphs

Bar graphs (also called *bar charts*) are a type of data visualization in which data points are represented by rectangular bars. Typically, the bars extend vertically from the bottom of the *x*-axis up to the data value, which is plotted along the *y*-axis; thus, the height of the bar (physical magnitude) is analogous to the numerical magnitude of the data point; bars may also be horizontal with length representing magnitude. Each data point is either labeled along the *x*-axis or referenced in a legend in a separate location near the graph. This entry discusses how bar graphs are used, factors that affect comprehension of bar graphs, and implications for educational research.

Bar graphs are often used to communicate scientific results, qualitative trends, and statistical analyses, such as main effects and interactions. Because data points are aligned along a common axis, bar graphs can facilitate comparison between individual data points; for instance, a user can quickly assess whether the data points are the same or different. Additionally, a user can easily compare differences between data points by judging the relative sizes of height gaps between bars. Global patterns, such as linear trends, are also

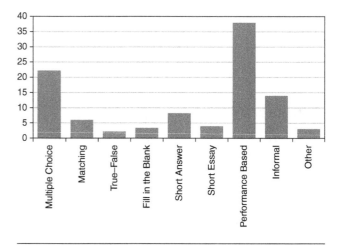

Figure 1 Percentage of times for different classroom assessment formats

salient in bar graphs. Thus, bar graphs are generally better for visualizing qualitative data patterns than exact values, which are more easily extracted from tables. In Figure 1, a simple bar chart shows the percentage of times different classroom assessment formats were used by a sample of teachers.

Factors That Affect Comprehension

The visual features of a bar graph, such how the bars are organized and how far apart the bars are from one another, can affect comprehension. Bar graph comprehension is often facilitated when the bars are grouped in various ways; for instance, bars that are clustered together along the *x*-axis or that have the same color are perceived as belonging to the same group and viewers are more likely to make comparisons within rather than across such groups. Additionally, larger effects (i.e., larger height differences between bars) are more salient and easier to perceive.

Because bars are usually spatially segregated in a bar graph, it is typically easier to compare discrete values than continuous values, for which line graphs are better suited. However, Jeff Zacks, Ellen Levy, Barbara Tversky, and Diane Schiano found that discrete height judgments of bars are subject to bias from neighboring elements in bar graphs (such as the presence and height ratio of nearby bars).

Additionally, the knowledge that the user brings to the graph can affect comprehension of bar graphs. One type of knowledge that affects comprehension is graphical literacy, which involves having basic knowledge about how graphs should look and what they are used for. Having graphical literacy would include, for example, knowing that independent or categorical variables are represented along the x-axis and/or legend, whereas the dependent variable is represented along the y-axis. Graph expertise is especially helpful because it can allow the user to compare data more efficiently through the use of mental manipulation and perceptual shortcuts.

Another type of knowledge that influences graph comprehension is familiarity with the content of the graph. Although content familiarity generally enhances understanding of a graph, it can also bias how the graph is interpreted if the user expects to see a specific effect in the data due to overinterpretation, exaggeration of effects, or overlooking some effects while emphasizing others.

Bar graph comprehension is also subject to certain processing constraints and individual differences. People do not extract information from graphs all at once but rather proceed through the different regions of a graph, often returning to look at the same region several times. Additionally, because the user must keep track of multiple elements, such as which bars to compare and how variables correspond to a legend, comprehension may be constrained by visuospatial skills and working memory capacity, which vary substantially across individuals.

Implications for Educational Research and Communication

Contrary to popular belief, bar graphs are not always intuitive, and the time it takes to comprehend a graph is more akin to the time it takes to read a paragraph than to perceive an image. Making inferences about data can be especially difficult for students. Additionally, Audrey Michal, Priti Shah, David Uttal, and Steven Franconeri used eye tracking to show that young children are more likely than adults to attend to bar graphs from left to right and that this left-first strategy was associated with inefficient graph comprehension. Finally, bar graphs may display several effects simultaneously, and it is not always clear which subset of the data are relevant.

Several design principles are thought to enhance the effectiveness of a bar graph as a communicative tool. Any significant differences between data points should be large enough to be discriminated visually. Relevant comparisons can be emphasized with visual cues (e.g., highlighting) or grouping cues, such as spatial proximity or similar color. The use of extraneous information should generally be limited because it can interfere with magnitude judgments and overload working memory. For instance, Zacks, Levy, Tversky, and Schiano showed that adding extraneous depth cues (i.e., 3-D information) to bar graphs lowered accuracy of magnitude judgments by a small amount. Additionally, Jennifer Kaminski and Vladimir Sloutsky found that adding extraneous visual information to bars in a graph, such as countable objects, interfered with young children's ability to compare the bars based on physical magnitude.

In educational settings, bar graphs are often used to report test scores, grades, and other evaluative information. Bar graphs are a useful format for score reporting because they can facilitate comparisons, such as between scores of different groups of students or between subscores for an individual student. However, bar graphs of score reports are subject to biases, such as overinterpretation of salient data (e.g., seemingly large effects), emphasizing relative versus absolute score differences, and oversimplifying results. These biases are particularly likely to occur when the user is unfamiliar with the content of the graph; thus, users should take caution when interpreting score reports.

Audrey Michal and Priti Shah

See also Data; Data Visualization Methods; Data-Driven Decision Making; Quantitative Literacy; Quantitative Research Methods; Scatterplots; Score Reporting

Further Readings

Hegarty, M. (2011). The cognitive science of visual-spatial displays: Implications for design. *Topics in Cognitive Science*, 3(3), 446–474.

Kosslyn, S. M. (2006). *Graph design for the eye and mind*. New York: Oxford University Press.

Shah, P., Freedman, E. G., & Vekiri, I. (2005). *The comprehension of quantitative information in graphical displays*. Cambridge, UK: Cambridge University Press.

BASAL LEVEL AND CEILING LEVEL

The basal level (also called the floor level) and the ceiling level are components of the termination criteria used in Binet-type individually administered adaptive tests that are used to measure IQ in educational and other settings. These tests are administered by psychologists or trained examiners and operate from a question/item bank that is organized into mental age levels. Mental age is defined for each test item as the average chronological age at which approximately 50% of the standardization examinees correctly answered the item.

The adaptive test is begun by the examiner by selecting a mental age level based on the examiner's knowledge of the child being tested. This information can simply be the child's chronological age or can be based on other information such as a teacher's statement about the child's probable IQ (e.g., she is an "above average" student or he is "below average" or "average"). Having selected a mental age level to begin the test, the examiner administers each item at that level and scores the result as correct or incorrect.

When all items at this entry level have been administered, the score for that level is tallied. If the child has answered all items at that level correctly, the examiner has identified the *basal level* for that test and has identified the upper limit of the portion of the item bank that is too easy for the child. If the basal level has not been identified, the examiner then has the option of moving to the next higher or lower mental age level and administering the items at that level. Again, the proportion correct is tallied and a decision is made based on that information. If the basal level had not yet been identified, the test can continue with items at

lower mental age levels until the child correctly answers all items at a given mental age level.

Alternatively, the examiner can first seek the *ceiling level* for that child—the mental age level at which all items are answered incorrectly, thus identifying the lower limit of the portion of the item bank that is too difficult for the child. Once both the basal level and the ceiling level have been identified, the test is terminated and the portion of the item bank that provides effective measurement for the child has been identified.

The IQ score that is computed from this procedure is based on a weighted function of the mental ages of the items answered correctly between the basal and ceiling levels. Because the items administered in the adaptive test are selected from the item bank based on the child's performance as the test is administered, the scores resulting from this type of test have greater measurement precision than those from tests in which all examinees receive the same set of items, many of which might not be appropriate for a given examinee.

David J. Weiss

See also Basal Level and Ceiling Level; Computerized Adaptive Testing; Intelligence Quotient; Intelligence Tests; Stanford–Binet Intelligence Scales

Further Readings

Weiss, D. J. (2011). Better data from better measurements using computerized adaptive testing. *Journal of Methods and Measurement in the Social Sciences*, 2(1), 1–27.

BAYESIAN STATISTICS

Bayesian statistics is a comprehensive and systematic interpretation of the field of statistics based on the quantification and manipulation of uncertainty in the form of probability distributions enabled by the Bayesian interpretation of probability laws. It is commonly considered a branch of statistics. This entry provides a basic description of Bayesian statistics. Although Bayesian statistics includes nonparametric approaches, the entry's scope is limited to the more common setting of parametric Bayesian inference.

Although the historical details surrounding the origins of Bayesian statistics are somewhat hazy, the broad strokes are well-documented. The basic theoretical machinery underpinning Bayesian statistics was established in the second half of the 18th century with the discovery of Bayes's theorem by Thomas Bayes, Richard Price, and, independently, Pierre-Simon Laplace. If beliefs concerning unknown quantities are represented with probability distributions, Bayes's theorem provides a mechanism to update the beliefs upon the arrival of new evidence, thus laying a foundation for scientific reasoning. This way of thinking became the de facto standard among statisticians from the time of its discovery until well into the 20th century under the name of *inverse probability*.

The modern term *Bayesian statistics* grew out of a great and divisive disagreement in the 20th century concerning the interpretation of probability as a contrast to the term *frequentist statistics*— statistics viewed from the perspective of the frequentist interpretation of probability. Although the frequentist methods of Ronald Fisher, Jerzy Neyman, and Egon Pearson dominated statistical thought for the majority of the 20th century, Bayesian methods did not achieve widespread use until the mid-to-late 20th century due to computational challenges of the paradigm. These challenges were significantly alleviated near the end of the 20th century due to the proliferation of the personal computer and advances in Monte Carlo algorithms.

By the late 20th century, Bayesian ideas had permeated virtually every area of statistical science. Now in the early 21st century, Bayesian methods continue to flourish and expand to larger audiences; however, frequentist methods are still more commonly used in practice and accepted by regulatory agencies. They also comprise virtually all introductory statistics education.

Introduction and Notation

The basic problem of statistical inference assumes that the observed data y_1, y_2, ..., y_n constitute a random sample from a population of interest represented by a probability distribution $p(y)$, which is either a probability mass function, if Y is a discrete variable, or a probability density function, if Y is a continuous variable. Although the exact distribution of Y is unknown, $p(y)$ is typically assumed to be one of a collection of possible distributions called a *statistical model M*, and the problem is to determine which distribution in the model represents the population, the true distribution of Y. In the common setting of parametric statistics, the distributions in the model are indexed by one or more quantities called parameters, collectively denoted θ, so that $M = \{p(y \mid \theta)\}_{\theta \in \Theta}$, where Θ is the set of indices called the parameter space. Under the assumption that $p(y)$ is one of the distributions in M, $p(y) = p(y \mid \theta^*)$ for some $\theta^* \in \Theta$, and the inference problem is reduced to estimating θ^* using the data. The estimator is commonly denoted $\hat{\theta}$; it is a function of the data so that $\hat{\theta} = \hat{\theta}(y_1, y_2, \cdots, y_n)$.

The field of statistics provides many methods to construct estimators of θ, regardless of the perspective one takes on how to interpret probability. One common way is maximum likelihood estimation (MLE). An MLE, $\hat{\theta}$, is an estimator that maximizes the likelihood function $I(\theta \mid y) = p(y \mid \theta)$, which has the same functional form as the distribution $p(y \mid \theta)$ but is considered a function of θ for a fixed value of the variable $Y = y$. The *likelihood principle*, a philosophical underpinning of statistical inference associated with the 20th-century statisticians Ronald Fisher and Allan Birnbaum, states that conclusions about θ drawn from the data ought only depend only the data through $I(\theta \mid y)$.

Flipping a coin provides a simple example of this to clarify notation. Suppose Y is a variable denoting the result of flipping a coin with $Y = 1$ if the coin flips heads and $Y = 0$ if tails. If the coin flips heads with probability θ, $P[Y = 1 \mid \theta] \theta$ and $P[Y = 0 \mid \theta] 1 - \theta$, so that $p(y \mid \theta) = P[Y = y \mid \theta] = \theta^y (1-\theta)^{1-y}$ for $y = 0$ or 1, and the model is $M = \{p(y \mid \theta)\}_{\theta \in \Theta} = \{P[Y = y \mid \theta]\}_{\theta \in \Theta} = \{\theta^y (1-\theta)^{1-y}\}_{\theta \in \Theta}$, where $\Theta = (0,1)$. If Y_1, Y_2, ..., Y_n denote n independent flips of the coin, the joint distribution of any sequence of flips is:

$$
\begin{aligned}
P[Y_1 &= y_1, ..., Y_n = y_n \mid \theta] \\
&= p(y_1, y_2, ..., y_n \mid \theta) \\
&= \prod_{i=1}^{n} p(y_i \mid \theta) = \theta^{\sum y_i} (1-\theta)^{\sum 1 - y_i}.
\end{aligned}
$$

For a given data set $y_1, y_2, ..., y_n$, this expression is the likelihood $\mathrm{I}(\theta \mid y_1, ..., y_n)$, and it can be shown that the MLE for θ is $\hat{\theta} = \dfrac{1}{n}\sum_{i=1}^{n} y_i = \bar{y}$, that is, the proportion of 1's in the observed data set. The Bayesian solution to this estimation problem is different and described later in this entry.

The Bayes's Theorem and Associated Distributions

Of fundamental importance to the Bayesian approach is the idea that all uncertainty is represented by probability distributions. Thus, in the Bayesian inferential setting, because the parameter θ is an unknown quantity (or quantities), it must be assigned a probability distribution that encodes all the uncertainty about θ—what values it is likely to be and what values it is unlikely to be. Because of this, it is often said that Bayesians treat parameters as random variables. This is only true in the sense that parameters are given distributions in the same way measured variables are; however, the quantities themselves (θ) are believed to be fixed, unknown quantities. Upon seeing data, the beliefs about θ change: They are updated in the light of the new evidence, the data.

The fundamental mechanism enabling the updating process is Bayes's theorem. In brief, Bayes's theorem is a mathematical result detailing how one can reverse the order of probabilistic conditioning. The probability density version of the result is introduced here for self-containment, although the result also applies in discrete and even more general settings. If $D = \{y_1, y_2, ..., y_n\}$ is the data, Bayes's theorem states:

$$p(\theta \mid D) = \frac{p(D \mid \theta)p(\theta)}{\int p(D \mid \theta)p(\theta)d\theta}$$

$$= \frac{\mathrm{I}(\theta \mid D)p(\theta)}{\int \mathrm{I}(\theta \mid D)p(\theta)d\theta}.$$

In this equation, $p(\theta)$ is known as the *prior distribution*; it represents the beliefs about θ before the data are gathered. It is a probability density function defined on the parameter space Θ. The quantity $\mathrm{I}\,p(\theta \mid D)$ is the likelihood of the data

previously described. The quantity on the left $p(\theta \mid D)$ is called the *posterior distribution* and represents the updated beliefs about the parameter θ after having seen the data D. The quantity in the denominator is the marginal probability of the data; it is a weighted average of the likelihood of the data over all the probability distributions in the model M and is equal to $p(D)$, while nevertheless still incorporating the modeling decisions of the functional form of $p(D|\theta)$ and the prior belief $p(\theta)$. This marginal distribution normalizes the product of the likelihood and the prior into a proper probability distribution. Considering the equation only as a function of the parameter(s) θ, the result is often written simply as:

$$p(\theta \mid D)\,\alpha\,\mathrm{I}(\theta \mid D)\,p(\theta).$$

The prior distribution $p(\theta)$ is often selected from a parametric family of probability distributions. When it is, it is commonly written in reference to the parameters that characterize it, $p(\theta|\eta)$; these parameters are referred to as *hyperparameters* and play an important role in Bayesian modeling.

The Bayesian approach also includes two *predictive* distributions that can be used at different stages of the inferential process to make predictions about the next observation of the variable Y. These distributions do not depend on the value of the parameter θ, as they eliminate it through the process of marginalization. The *prior predictive distribution* of the variable Y is the distribution $p(y) = \int p(y \mid \theta)\,p(\theta)\,d\theta$. It is the marginal distribution of the variable when the belief about the parameter is represented by the prior distribution $p(\theta)$, before data are collected. It can be used to predict the value of the variable using only the prior belief about the parameter.

The *posterior predictive distribution* of the variable is the distribution obtained when using the posterior distribution $p(\theta|D)$ instead of the prior distribution $p(\theta)$ to represent the belief about θ in the marginalization process: $p(y \mid D) = \int p(y \mid \theta)\,p(\theta \mid D)\,d\theta$. The posterior predictive distribution can be used to predict the value of a new observation Y having first had a belief about θ represented by the prior $p(\theta)$, seen data D, and updated one's belief according to Bayes's theorem.

Marginalization plays a key role throughout Bayesian statistics. In addition to the prior and posterior predictive distributions described earlier, marginalization can be used to systematically remove *nuisance parameters* from a model, parameters that affect the data but are not of interest. In the Bayesian setting, all parameters are endowed with a joint prior distribution that is updated through Bayes's theorem to a joint posterior distribution. Marginalizing this distribution over the nuisance parameters provides a posterior distribution over only the quantities of interest, eliminating the nuisance parameters entirely. The ability of Bayesian methods to systematically and easily deal with nuisance parameters is considered a great advantage of the Bayesian paradigm.

To continue the estimation of a population proportion example from the previous section, the prior distribution is often selected from the family of β distributions, so that $p(\theta \mid \eta) = p(\theta \mid \alpha, \beta) = \frac{1}{B(\alpha, \beta)} \theta^{\alpha-1} (1-\theta)^{\beta-1}$, where $B(\alpha, \beta)$ is the β function and the hyperparameter is the pair of β parameters α and β. The resulting posterior distribution $p(\theta|D, \eta)$ is also a β distribution; this property is described in the section on prior specification later in this entry. The prior predictive and posterior predictive distributions $p(y|\eta)$ and $p(y|\eta, D)$ are discrete distributions in the β-binomial family.

Bayesian Methods

Point Estimation

It is often desirable to have estimates of the unknown parameters θ. In a frequentist setting, maximum likelihood and the method of moments provide general strategies to construct estimators. In Bayesian statistics, after observing data, the belief about θ is completely described by the posterior distribution $p(\theta|D)$. If one is forced to reduce the posterior distribution into one parameter value, many options are available and routinely used in practice. All are summaries of the posterior distribution and referred to as Bayes's estimators. The most common is the posterior mean, but the median and mode of the posterior distribution are also routinely used. The latter method is referred to as *maximum a posteriori*

estimation and is equivalent to maximum likelihood with a constant (uniform) prior.

Credible Intervals

One of the most commonly used statistical procedures is that of probability intervals, such as the confidence intervals of frequentist statistics. Confidence intervals are collections of parameter values generated from the data that contain the true population parameter with a certain probability. One of the limitations of the frequentist approach to probability sets is that the frequentist interpretation of probability does not result in a natural interpretation of the confidence set. Where one wants to say, "the probability the parameter is in the set is $1 - \alpha$," this statement is not meaningful (or useful) in the frequentist interpretation of probability, and one is forced into the interpretation "the probability the set contains the parameter is $1 - \alpha$." The Bayesian approach to probability intervals, called *credible intervals* or *credible sets* for more than one parameter, alleviates this problem, because it is meaningful to refer to the probability that a fixed yet unknown quantity lies in a certain region of space.

There are many ways to create Bayesian credible intervals, and as with estimation, all depend on the posterior distribution $p(\theta|D)$. In the case of a single parameter, the most common credible interval is the *quantile interval*: One simply forms an interval from the $\alpha/2$ and $1 - \alpha/2$ quantiles of the posterior distribution $p(\theta|D)$; marginalization can be used to eliminate nuisance parameters. Although this method often allows for the easy computation of credible intervals, it does not always produce the smallest interval of a given probability $1 - \alpha$. This interval/set is called the *highest posterior density region*. A $(1 - \alpha)$ 100% highest posterior density region is the smallest region of the parameter space that contains $1 - \alpha$ probability. Although highest posterior density regions are small, they suffer from two disadvantages: They can be difficult to compute, and they may not be connected.

Bayesian Hypothesis Testing and Bayes's Factors

In frequentist statistics, one is often tasked with assessing a null hypothesis $H_0 : \theta \notin \Theta_0$ against an alternative hypothesis $H_1 : \theta \notin \Theta_0$, and decision rules are constructed based on Type I and Type II errors. Bayesian statistics treats this problem very differently, and indeed the term *hypothesis testing* is hardly ever used in Bayesian statistics. Bayesian statistics views the choice between two hypotheses, or more generally two models, as simply another application of Bayes's rule: Prior beliefs (often uniformly distributed) are updated, and decisions are based on posterior beliefs. Additionally, the Bayesian setting seamlessly accommodates several hypotheses/models in the same fashion. This is in stark contrast to the frequentist setting, where the selection of which hypothesis is the null, and the alternative is often chosen for mathematical convenience and yet has a dramatic effect on the result.

In the case of two competing models M_0 and M_1, where one or the other must be the case, a Bayesian analogue to frequentist hypothesis testing can be carried out with the use of Bayes's factors. It is easily shown using Bayes's theorem that

$$\frac{p(M_0 \mid D)}{p(M_1 \mid D)} = \frac{p(D \mid M_0) p(M_0)}{p(D \mid M_1) p(M_1)} = B \frac{p(M_0)}{p(M_1)}.$$

In words, the posterior odds of M_0 to M_1 is proportional to the prior odds with the constant of proportionality equal to $B = \dfrac{p(D \mid M_0)}{p(D \mid M_1)}$, a quantity called the *Bayes's factor* in favor of M_0. In basic cases, such as where the two models are representing different distributions in the same parametric family, the Bayes's factor simply reduces to the likelihood ratio, which is widely regarded as an evidentiary measure in support of M_0. In general, it indicates the extent to which the odds of M_0 have changed in light of the data. If $B > 1$, the data advocate in favor of M_0, and if $B > 1$ in favor of M_1, and the further they are from 1 indicates stronger evidence. Various scales have been suggested as to how to interpret the magnitude of B in terms of standards of evidence; however, these are outside the scope of this entry. In general, B is considered a suitable statistic for scientific reporting, provided it does not change substantially as the prior distributions used to compute B,

$$p(D \mid M_k) = \int p(D \mid \theta_k, M_k) p(\theta_k \mid M_k) d\theta_k \sqrt{2} \quad \text{for}$$

$k = 0, 1$, are changed. Note that in this description, M_0 and M_1 can be very different models; they can even have parameter spaces of different dimensions.

Hierarchical Models

One of the major advantages of Bayesian statistics is that the paradigm provides a natural and flexible modeling platform: Bayesian hierarchical models. A *Bayesian hierarchical model*, also known as a *multilevel model* or *Bayesian network*, is a statistical model with hyperparameters that are endowed with prior structure of their own. A hierarchical prior structure breaks apart uncertainty in a prior distribution into its constituent components, each of which are individually much more manageable. Prior structures on prior structures, often repeated several times, can yield very flexible and expressive models, especially when data are included as part of the prior structures.

Challenges of Bayesian Statistics

Computation

One of the chief challenges in the practical application of Bayesian methods, and one of the reasons they took so long to become widely used in practice, were computational challenges presented by the paradigm. Specifically, computing the marginal integral $\int p(y \mid \theta) p(\theta) d\theta$ in the denominator of Bayes's theorem is often incredibly difficult and almost always requires numerical quadrature (integration) methods.

The exception to this rule is found with a class of priors called conjugate priors. A prior $p(\theta)$ for θ is called a *conjugate prior* if it is a member of a parametric family $\{p(\theta \mid \eta)\}_{\eta \in H}$, and the posterior is also a member of the same family. In other words, both the prior distribution $p(\theta) = p(\theta \mid \eta)$ and the posterior distribution $p(\theta \mid D) = p(\theta \mid \eta')$ are members of the same family of distributions, so that the parameter of the posterior distribution η' is some (often simple) function of the prior parameter and the observed data, $\eta' = g(\eta, D)$. Most textbooks on Bayesian statistics contain tables of such priors, which list for a given statistical model (likelihood) the conjugate family and the function g. From an applied perspective, the chief advantage of using a conjugate prior is the alleviation of the computing problem, and this is the chief reason why conjugate priors are so often used.

Apart from the conjugacy setting, there are two main ways other than numerical quadrature that Bayesian inference is carried out: variational methods and Monte Carlo methods. Variational methods attempt to approximate the posterior distribution with a simpler distribution. For example, in many cases, the posterior distribution of the parameter converges to a multivariate normal distribution, as the sample size tends to infinity regardless of the prior used, a result known as the Bernstein–von Mises theorem. In these cases, it is often reasonable to approximate the posterior distribution with a surrogate multivariate normal distribution, which is very tractable, known as *Laplace approximation.*

More commonly used than variational methods are Monte Carlo methods, especially Markov chain Monte Carlo methods. Instead of computing the integral directly, the aim of Monte Carlo methods is to generate random samples from the posterior distribution, with the idea being that if one can sample from the distribution at will, one can compute any aspect of the distribution to an arbitrary degree of accuracy. Markov chain Monte Carlo methods are a class of sampling algorithms, including the Gibbs sampler and the Metropolis–Hastings algorithm, that involve a random walk whose stationary distribution is a probability distribution, here the posterior distribution. Markov chain Monte Carlo methods are typically the method of choice for most practicing Bayesian statisticians and are implemented as black boxes in the free software OpenBUGS, JAGS, and Stan.

Prior Specification

One of the most challenging components of a proper Bayesian analysis is the specification of the prior distribution $p(\theta)$, and there is a vast literature dedicated to this topic. There are a number of approaches taken with prior specification. The systematic quantification of belief is known as *prior elicitation* and has been a subject of statistical and psychological research since the middle of the 20th century. Because the prior tangibly affects the data analysis, one of the key considerations to take into account is how *informative* a prior is; this is loosely defined as how strong its beliefs are concerning the unknown parameter. Strongly informative priors can dominate the likelihood in Bayes's theorem, so that the posterior reflects almost entirely prior belief regardless of the data.

There are several terms used as opposites to informative: *non-* or *uninformative, reference, diffuse,* and in some cases *objective.* These are generally intended to represent vague or equal belief concerning the parameters. However, basic results demonstrate that no prior is truly uninformative, and priors that appear uninformative in one parameterization may be quite informative after transforming the parameter. This consideration led to the development of the *Jeffreys prior,* a prior distribution based on Fisher information invariant under transformations and widely regarded as having little influence on the posterior. Unfortunately, the method to construct a Jeffreys prior does not always result in a *proper prior* (one having total probability one), and consequently the posterior may also be improper, which is generally considered a bad thing. As a last alternative, upon selection of a prior family of distributions $\{p(\theta \mid \eta)\}_{\eta \in H}$, the *empirical Bayes's* strategy selects the prior parameter $\hat{\eta}$ based on the marginal distribution $p(y \mid \eta) = \int p(y \mid \theta) p(\theta \mid \eta) d\theta$, typically the MLE; however, this strategy is not considered "fully Bayesian."

However the prior is selected, varying the prior distribution and observing the effect on the posterior is generally considered good practice. This is known as a *sensitivity analysis.* If the posterior varies considerably when the prior is changed, further investigation is recommended.

David Kahle

See also Bayes's Theorem; Distributions; Prior Distribution

Further Readings

Berger, J. (1993). *Statistical decision theory and Bayesian analysis* (2nd ed.). New York, NY: Springer.

Christensen, R., Johnson, W., Branscum, A., & Hanson, T. E. *Bayesian ideas and data analysis: An introduction for scientists and statisticians.* Boca Raton, FL: CRC Press.

Fienberg, S. E. (2006). When did Bayesian inference become "Bayesian"? *Bayesian Analysis, 1*(1), 1–40.

Gelman, A., Carlin, J. B., Stern, H. S., Dunson, D. B., Vehtari, A., & Rubin, D. B. (2014). *Bayesian data analysis* (3rd ed.). Boca Raton, FL: CRC Press.

Gelman, A., & Hill, J. *Data analysis using regression and multilevel/hierarchical models.* New York, NY: Cambridge University Press.

Lindley, D. (2000). The philosophy of statistics. *Journal of the Royal Statistical Society: Series D (The Statistician), 49*(3), 293–337.

Lindley, D. (2013). *Understanding uncertainty* (2nd ed.). New York, NY: Wiley.

O'Hagan, A., Buck, C. E., Daneshkhah, A., Eiser, J. R., Garthwaite, P. H., Jenkinson, D. J., . . . Rakow, T. (2006). *Uncertain judgements: Eliciting experts' probabilities.* Chichester, England: Wiley.

Talbott, W. (2001). Bayesian epistemology. In E. N. Zalta (Ed.), *The Stanford encyclopedia of philosophy* (Summer 2015 ed.). Retrieved from http://plato.stanford.edu/archives/sum2015/entries/epistemology-bayesian/

Bayes's Theorem

Bayes's theorem is a way of estimating the likelihood of some event having occurred, or some condition being true, given some evidence that is related to the event or condition. This entry describes how Bayes's theorem is used, discusses three forms of the theorem, and provides detailed examples of the use of the theorem.

Throughout the sciences, we are faced with questions about how likely an event of interest is, given some information. For example,

How likely is a student to achieve at least a certain level of academic performance in the future, given the student's past performance?

What is the probability that a patient has a certain disease, given the patient's diagnostic test results and background health information?

How likely is it that a defendant is guilty of a certain crime, given all available evidence?

What is the probability that a coin would land heads at least 60 times in 100 tosses, given that the coin is fair?

How likely is a certain hypothesis, given the observed data?

These are all questions about *conditional probability*. Philosophical controversies have raged for centuries about exactly how to interpret probability, but conditional probability has a simple, uncontroversial definition: the probability of an event A, given an event B (with $P(B) > 0$), is

$$P(A|B) = \frac{P(A \text{ and } B)}{P(B)}$$

Swapping the roles of A and B, we have

$$P(B|A) = \frac{P(A \text{ and } B)}{P(A)}$$

Note that $P(A|B)$ is different from $P(B|A)$. Confusing $P(A|B)$ with $P(B|A)$ is a common—and commonly devastating—blunder, sometimes called the *prosecutor's fallacy* (though not all prosecutors commit this fallacy, nor is the fallacy exclusive to prosecutors).

This definition immediately yields two useful expressions for $P(A \text{ and } B)$:

$$P(A|B)P(B) = P(A \text{ and } B) = P(B|A)P(A),$$

for $P(B) > 0$. Dividing through by $P(B)$ gives a simple but powerful result that explains precisely how $P(A|B)$ and $P(B|A)$ are related. The next section gives several ways to express this relationship.

Three Forms of Bayes's Theorem

Basic Form

As explained earlier, a simple but fundamental consequence of the definition of conditional probability is the following theorem, which connects $P(A|B)$ to $P(B|A)$:

$$P(A|B) = \frac{P(B|A)P(A)}{P(B)}.$$

Here $P(A)$ is called the *prior* probability of A (it is the probability of A before we know whether B occurred), $P(A|B)$ is the *posterior* probability of A given B (it is the updated probability for A, in light of the information that B occurred), and $P(B)$ is the *marginal* or *unconditional* probability of B.

Remarkably, this theorem, whose proof is essentially just one line of algebra, has deep consequences throughout statistical theory and practice. Often $P(B|A)$ is easier to think about or compute directly than $p(A|B)$, or vice versa; Bayes's theorem enables working with whichever of these is easier to handle and then bridging to the other. For example, in a criminal trial, we may be especially interested in the probability that the defendant is innocent given the evidence, but it may be easier at first to consider the probability of the evidence given that the defendant is innocent.

Bayes's theorem is named after Reverend Thomas Bayes, due to his seminal paper *An Essay towards Solving a Problem in the Doctrine of Chances*, which was published posthumously in 1763 with help and edits from Bayes's friend Richard Price. Bayes's paper established conditional probability as a powerful framework for thinking about uncertainty and derived some important properties (including Bayes's theorem). Some historical controversies have arisen about whether anyone discovered Bayes's theorem earlier than Bayes, and how much of a role Price played.

The mathematician Pierre-Simon Laplace also played a crucial role in the early development of Bayes's theorem. He rediscovered the result (apparently unaware of Bayes's work), publishing it in a 1774 paper. A major part of Bayes's and Price's motivation was to provide ammunition for a theological debate with the philosopher David Hume; in contrast, Laplace showed that Bayes's theorem could be used to tackle scientific problems and make sense of data.

Odds Form

The *odds* of an event A are given by odds

$$(A) = \frac{P(A)}{1 - P(A)}.$$

For example, the odds of an event A with probability $1/4$ are $(1/4)/(3/4) = 1/3$; this is usually worded as "odds of 1 to 3 in favor of A" or "odds of 3 to 1 against A." Bayes's theorem has a very convenient formulation in terms of odds, which is especially useful when testing a hypothesis.

Let θ be a parameter of interest, and suppose there are only two possible values of θ: It is either θ_0 or θ_1. We wish to test the null hypothesis $\theta = \theta_0$ versus the alternative hypothesis $\theta = \theta_1$. We observe data $Y = y$. By Bayes's theorem,

$$\frac{P(\theta = \theta_1 \mid y)}{P(\theta = \theta_0 \mid y)} = \frac{P(\theta = \theta_1)}{P(\theta = \theta_0)} \frac{P(Y = y \mid \theta = \theta_1)}{P(Y = y \mid \theta = \theta_0)}.$$

Note that, conveniently, $P(Y = y)$ has canceled out in this expression. There are three key ingredients in this statement:

The ratio $P(\theta = \theta_1)/P(\theta = \theta_0)$ is the *prior odds* in favor of θ_1;

the ratio $P(\theta = \theta_1|y)/P(\theta = \theta_0|y)$, is the *posterior odds* in favor of θ_1;

the ratio $P(Y = y|\theta = \theta_1)/P(Y = y|\theta = \theta_0)$ is the *likelihood ratio*, which is the ratio of probabilities of the data that actually were observed, for the two different hypotheses. That is, Bayes's theorem says how to update our prior odds to get our posterior odds for a hypothesis of interest, given the observed data.

Density Form

Much of statistical inference focuses on estimating unknown parameters or predicting future observations, given what is known (the observed data).

Let θ be the unknown parameter of interest in some model, and suppose that we observe the data $Y = y$. We wish to find the *posterior distribution*: the distribution of the unknown (θ), given the known (y). However, statistical models are typically formulated by giving the distribution for Y given θ. For example, the binomial model with parameters n and p, with p unknown, is given by:

$$P(Y = y \mid p) = \binom{n}{y} p^y (1-p)^{n-y},$$

for $y = 0, 1, \ldots, n$. But Bayes's theorem lets us convert between these conditional probabilities: the posterior density of θ given the data y is:

$$g(\theta \mid y) = \frac{f(y \mid \theta)g(\theta)}{f(y)}.$$

Here $g(\theta)$ is the *prior* density for θ and $f(y)$ is the *marginal* (i.e., not conditioned on θ) density for y. The distribution of θ can be discrete or continuous and likewise for Y; we interpret "density" as a probability mass function in the discrete case and as a probability density function in the continuous case.

If θ and Y are both discrete, then this formulation of Bayes's theorem is exactly the same as the basic form, just with different notation. If one or both of θ and Y are continuous, it is completely analogous to the basic form, with probability density functions replacing probabilities when needed.

Among the most central concepts in statistical inference is the *likelihood function*, which is the function $f(y \mid \theta)$, when viewed as a function of θ, with y fixed at the observed value of Y. When treating y as fixed, the denominator $f(y)$ acts as a constant, making $g(\theta \mid y)$ sum or integrate to 1. Then Bayes's theorem has the following pithy summary: "Posterior is proportional to likelihood times prior."

Examples

This section provides several detailed examples of applications for Bayes's theorem.

Spam Filtering

Bayesian thinking suggests a way to build a spam filter for an e-mail system, using the fact that certain words appear much more frequently in spam (junk) e-mail than in legitimate e-mail. The goal is to determine in an automated way the probability that an e-mail message is spam, given information such as word frequencies in the e-mail.

Suppose that 80% of e-mail messages are spam. In 10% of the spam e-mails, the phrase "free money" is used, whereas this phrase is only used in 1% of nonspam e-mails. A new e-mail has just arrived, which does mention "free money." Given this information, what is the probability that it is spam? We can answer this question readily using Bayes's theorem.

Let S be the event that an e-mail is spam and F be the event that an e-mail has the "free money" phrase. By Bayes's theorem,

$$P(S \mid F) = \frac{P(F \mid S)P(s)}{P(F)}.$$

The quantities $P(F \mid S)$ and $P(S)$ were given in the problem, so we just need $P(F)$. For this, we use the law of total probability:

$$P(F) = P(F \mid S)P(S) + P(F \mid S^c)P(S^c),$$

where S^c denotes the complement of S (i.e., the event that the e-mail is legitimate). Thus,

$$P(S \mid F) = \frac{0.1 \cdot 0.8}{0.1 \cdot 0.8 + 0.01 \cdot 0.2}$$
$$= \frac{80}{82} \approx 0.976.$$

The strategy of using Bayes's theorem in tandem with the law of total probability, as just shown, is extremely useful in a wide variety of problems. The example just given is simplistic, as it uses only one bit of information: whether the new e-mail contains the phrase "free money." More realistically, suppose that we have created a list of, say, 100 key words that are much more likely to be used in spam than in nonspam. Let W_j be the event that an e-mail contains the jth word or phrase on the list. Let,

$$p = P(\text{spam}) \text{ and } p_j = P(W_j \mid \text{spam}),$$

where "spam" is shorthand for the event that the e-mail message is spam.

Let K be the observed evidence, specifying which of the key words appear and which do not appear. Then, Bayes's theorem looks the same as before, with K in place of F:

$$P(S \mid K) = \frac{P(K \mid S)P(S)}{P(K)}.$$

However, it may be challenging to compute or estimate $P(K \mid S)$. Under the assumption that $W_1, \ldots, W_{100}$ are conditionally independent given that the e-mail is spam, and also conditionally independent given that it is not spam, the problem becomes much easier. A method for classifying e-mails (or other objects) based on this kind of assumption is called a *naive Bayes classifier*. For example, this conditional independence assumption implies that:

$$P(W_1, W_2, W_3^c, W_4^c, ..., W_{100}^c \mid spam)$$
$$= p_1 p_2 (1 - p_3)(1 - p_4) ... (1 - p_{100}).$$

The conditional independence assumption may be plausible or naive, but either way we can use it together with Bayes's theorem to obtain a spam filter; later, we can directly evaluate the performance of the spam filter on a large sample of future e-mails.

Disease Testing

Suppose that a patient is being tested for a certain rare disease, afflicting 1% of the population. Let D be the indicator for the patient having the disease, defined to be 1 if the patient has the disease and 0 otherwise. Let Y be the indicator for the patient testing positive, so $Y = 1$ if the patient tests positive and $Y = 0$ otherwise. Suppose that $P(Y = 1 \mid D = 1) = 0.95$ and $P(Y = 0 \mid D = 0) = 0.95$. The quantity $P(Y = 1 \mid D = 1)$ is known as the *sensitivity* or *true positive rate* of the test, and $P(Y = 0 \mid D = 0)$ is known as the *specificity* or *true negative rate*.

The patient has just tested positive. How worried should he or she be? More precisely, what is the probability that the patient has the disease, given the positive test result? We know $P(Y = 1 \mid D = 1)$, but want $P(D = 1 \mid Y = 1)$; this calls for Bayes's theorem.

Note that this problem has the same structure as the first example (disease corresponds to spam, and testing positive corresponds to "free money" being mentioned). The corresponding calculation yields:

$$P(D = 1 \mid Y = 1) = \frac{P(Y = 1 \mid D = 1)P(D = 1)}{P(Y = 1)}$$
$$\approx 0.16.$$

So there is only a 16% chance of having the disease, given the test result. This seems surprising to

many people at first because the specificity and sensitivity values make it sound as though the test is highly accurate. But Bayes's theorem shows that there is a fundamental tradeoff between the accuracy of the test and the rarity of the disease. It is crucial to incorporate the prior information about the prevalence of the disease (the base rate) into our calculations, not just the information about the accuracy of the test.

Equivalently, we can work in terms of odds: posterior odds are prior odds times the likelihood ratio. Here, the prior odds are 99 to 1 against having the disease, but the likelihood ratio is $0.95/0.05 = 19$ to 1 in favor of having the disease, so the posterior odds are 19/99 in favor of having the disease. This corresponds to a probability of $19/(19 + 99) \approx 0.16$, in agreement with the previous calculation.

Normal–Normal Model

The *normal–normal model* is a widely used statistical model, in which both the data and the mean parameter for the data follow normal distributions.

Assume a scalar target μ is given that a priori follows a normal distribution,

$$\mu \sim N\left(\mu_0, \tau^2\right),$$

with μ_0 and τ both being known. Suppose that an unbiased estimate y of μ becomes available, normally distributed with mean μ and known variance $V = \tau^2$, that is,

$$y \mid \mu \sim N(\mu, V).$$

Then Bayes's theorem provides this normal distribution for μ given y:

$$\mu \mid y \sim N\left((1 - B)y + B\mu_0, V(1 - B)\right),$$

with

$$B \equiv V / \left(V + \tau^2\right).$$

The *shrinkage factor B* determines by how much the expected value of μ, given the data y, shrinks y toward the prior mean μ_0. The following example illustrates how this result about Bayes's theorem in the normal–normal model context can be applied.

Evaluating Educational Testing

The Educational Testing Service once conducted experiments in several schools to see how effective coaching for SAT tests might be. Students in the school that showed the greatest gain averaged $\bar{y} = 28$ points higher on their SAT, which had a standard deviation of 15 points. Because this extreme school has the largest estimate, we would expect that its true value μ is likely to be less than 28. We will use the normal–normal Bayesian model again to estimate this.

We need to establish a base rate for μ, and our choice will be based on seven other schools that also evaluated their coaching effects. These other schools had an average effect of 6 points and a (between groups) standard deviation of $\tau = 11$ points. We can summarize the normal–normal Bayesian model as follows:

$$\bar{y} \mid \mu \sim N\left(\mu, V = 15^2\right),$$

and

$$\mu \sim N\left(6, \tau^2 = 11^2\right).$$

The object is to determine the distribution of μ, the mean improvement at the extreme school, conditional on its observed $\bar{y} = 28$. The variance V is 15^2 and the shrinkage factor $B = V/(V + 11^2) = 0.65$. Bayes's theorem (as given in the example introducing the normal–normal model) says that, given $\bar{y} = 28$,

$$\mu \mid (\bar{y} = 28) \sim N\left(0.35 \cdots 28 + 0.65 \cdots 6, 15^2 \cdots 0.35\right).$$

So conditioning on sample and using base rate information, the true mean μ at School A has expectation 13.7 SAT points with a standard deviation of 8.9 SAT points. With this, and because μ has a normal distribution, we have that μ lies in the interval $13.7 \pm 1.96\ldots8.9$, that is, $-3.7 < \mu < 31.1$, with probability .95.

The extreme school had the largest effect, $\bar{y} = 28$ SAT points for the sample of students tested there. Even so, the base rate information suggests that its true coaching effect μ, if evaluated with many more of its students, probably lies much closer to the average of the other schools than to its own average, $\bar{y}$.

Conclusion

Along with the uses described in this entry, widespread Bayesian applications now exist that involve much more complicated data structures, enabled by high-speed computers and an ever-increasing array of efficient Monte Carlo techniques used to fit correspondingly complicated models. These advances emphasize the use of Bayesian hierarchical modeling, akin to but beyond the preceding normal–normal examples here. Readers especially interested in how these more advanced models apply to educational data are referred to *Hierarchical Linear Models: Applications and Data Analysis Methods*, by Stephen W. Raudenbush and Anthony S. Bryk.

Once the data (y) have been observed, as eventually happens with any application to real data, and given a prior distribution $g(\theta)$, Bayes's theorem allows statisticians to update their uncertainty about the unknown parameters (θ), given the known observed data (y). Intuitively, this is more meaningful than the frequency approach, which averages over values of y that might have occurred for the given data set but didn't.

Unfortunately, this advantage of the Bayesian approach is lessened because it requires a prior distribution $g(\theta)$ for θ, and how to make that choice has been the principal source of a long-standing philosophical controversy among statisticians. One widely used option is to choose a prior distribution g that provides little information, relative to the information in the given data. Then Bayes's theorem can be used to calculate a procedure for any y, so that the data, not the prior, dominate in determining the inference.

The Bayes's frequency controversy has diminished over the years. Now many thoughtful data analysts are able to develop approaches for their data from both perspectives. Indeed, there is little inherent conflict between Bayesian and frequentist approaches: Using Bayesian thinking to develop a procedure does not preclude using frequentist thinking to evaluate the procedure in repeated sampling.

Joseph K. Blitzstein and Carl N. Morris

See also Bayesian Statistics; Posterior Distribution; Prior Distribution

Further Readings

Bayes, T. (1683–1775). An essay towards solving a problem in the doctrine of chances. *Philosophical Transactions of the Royal Society, 53*(1763), 370–418.

Blitzstein, J., & Hwang, J. (2015). *Introduction to probability.* Boca Raton, FL: CRC Press.

Gelman, A., Carlin, J. B., Stern, H. S., Dunson, D. B., Vehtari, A., & Rubin, D. B. (2014). *Bayesian data analysis.* Boca Raton, FL: CRC Press.

Hoff, P. (2009). *A first course in Bayesian statistical methods.* New York, NY: Springer-Verlag.

Morris, C. N. (1987). Comment. *Journal of the American Statistical Association, 82*(397), 131–133.

Raudenbush, S., & Bryk, A. S. (2002). *Hierarchical linear models: Applications and data analysis methods: Vol. 1.* Thousand Oaks, CA: Sage.

Stigler, S. (1983). Who discovered Bayes's theorem? *The American Statistician, 37*(4), 290–296.

BAYLEY SCALES OF INFANT AND TODDLER DEVELOPMENT

Development is an umbrella term that encompasses language, cognitive, and motor as well as behavioral, social–emotional, and mental health domains. Screening, the process of testing infants and children to identify those needing further evaluation, is best conducted with standardized tests, which have a known rate of detection when administered correctly. The Bayley Scales of Infant and Toddler Development is one such direct assessment developmental screening measure. This entry describes developmental screening tests and then looks at the development and revision of the Bayley Scales of Infant and Toddler Development and the components, administration, scoring, and properties of the test.

The American Academy of Pediatrics recommends that all infants and young children be formally screened for developmental delay at periodic intervals and if concerns are raised by a parent or provider during routine developmental surveillance. It is estimated that 16% of children have a developmental and/or behavioral disorder. However, only 30% are identified before school entrance. Children with a disorder that is detected after school entrance miss the opportunity to participate in early intervention services. The primary goal of developmental surveillance and screening is early detection of developmental delays. Early detection by primary care providers results in early referral for diagnostic evaluation and early treatment, providing children with medical and ancillary support that is necessary to meet their full developmental potential.

Numerous tests exist that can be useful in screening delays in the five or so developmental domains: cognitive, gross and fine motor, speech and language, adaptive, and psychosocial. These clinician-administered, direct assessment screening tests have the benefit of direct assessment of skills and typically are used by pediatric health-care providers who have a particular interest in developmental problems. They may be used as the only screening test to complement the results of parent-report instruments or to explore an area of concern in greater depth (e.g., gross motor skills). Many health-care providers who use screening tests find that it enhances their relationship with the family and child and provides valuable information to make appropriate referrals. The Bayley Scales of Infant and Toddler Development is designed to assess the developmental functioning of infants and young children 1–42 months of age. It is used to identify suspected developmental delays in children and to provide information to plan and develop appropriate interventions.

Development and Revision of Bayley Scales

The Bayley Scales of Infant and Toddler Development is a standard series of measurements originally developed by psychologist Nancy Bayley used primarily to assess the developmental status of infants and toddlers, aged 1–42 months. This developmental measure consists of a series of play tasks and takes between 45 and 60 minutes to administer. Raw scores for successfully completed items are converted to scale scores and to composite scores. These scores are used to determine the child's performance compared with norms taken from typically developing children of their age (in months).

Both the Bayley Scales of Infant Development (BSID) and the BSID, Second Edition (BSID-II) have been used in the assessment of severely delayed individuals who are outside the age range for which the test was standardized. The Bayley Scales of Infant and Toddler Development, Third Edition (Bayley-III), published in 2006, is a revision of the BSID-II.

The Bayley-III now includes growth scores that can be calculated to monitor the individual's progress over time. The Bayley-III also can be used to obtain an estimate of developmental level when more age-appropriate measures cannot be used for older children or individuals with severe delays, such as those with profound mental retardation. The Bayley-III maintains the same types of tasks as those in previous editions, promoting task involvement through play-based activities for individuals with limited ability. The most significant revision to the Bayley-III is the development of five distinct scales (as compared to three scales in the BSID-II) to be consistent with the areas of appropriate developmental assessment for children from birth to age 3 years. Although the BSID-II provided Mental, Motor, and Behavior Scales, the Bayley-III revision includes Cognitive, Language, Motor, Social–Emotional, and Adaptive Behavior Scales.

The Bayley-III was standardized on a normative sample of 1,700 children aged between 16 days and 43 months and 15 days living in the United States in 2004. Stratification was based on age, gender, parent education level, ethnic background, and geographical area. Normative data for the Social–Emotional and Adaptive Behavior Scales followed the same stratification pattern but were derived from smaller groups (456 and 1,350 children, respectively).

The Bayley-III is a technically sound instrument, with strong internal consistency, as well as test–retest stability. The test was revised with the goal to update normative data, strengthen the psychometric quality, and improve clinical utility. The test is also revised to simplify administration procedures and instructions by reorganizing the manual. It now includes updated item administration by making the instructions more play

based, reducing the effect of receptive and expressive language on cognitive items, and allowing caregiver involvement providing administration procedures are followed. The test has updated stimulus materials to allow selection of materials that appeal to the child and to make materials more appealing but at the same time maintains basic qualities of the Bayley Scales. The Bayley-III shows scores that are consistent with other ability tests that have been revised in recent years and shows expected levels in various clinical groups.

Description

The Bayley-III is composed of five subscales:

a. Cognitive subscale assesses play skills, information processing (attention to novelty, habituation, memory, and problem-solving), counting, and number skills.

b. Language Scale assesses communication skills including language and gestures. It contains two subsets:
    i. Receptive Language subscale
    ii. Expressive Language subscale

c. Motor Scale is divided into two subsets:
    i. Fine Motor subscale
    ii. Gross Motor subscale

Two scales, the Social–Emotional Scale and the Adaptive Behavior Scale from the Social–Emotional and Adaptive Behavior Questionnaire, are completed by the parent or primary caregiver. The Social–Emotional Scale assesses emotional and social functioning as well as sensory processing. It is based on the *Greenspan Social–Emotional Growth Chart: A Screening Questionnaire for Infants and Young Children* (Greenspan, 2004). The Adaptive Behavior Scale assesses the attainment of practical skills necessary for a child to function independently and to meet environmental demands. It is based on the Adaptive Behavior Assessment System–Second Edition. The only modification to the Greenspan and Adaptive Behavior Assessment System–Second Edition in the Bayley-III is the use of scaled scores in addition to the originally provided cut scores, so that these measures may be more easily compared to the other Bayley-III subtest scores.

Test Administration and Scoring

Administration of each scale is started at a predetermined item based on the child's age. A child must achieve a score of 1 on the first three consecutive items at the predetermined start point to achieve the basal score. If not, administration begins at the start point for the next youngest age level (reversal rule). The reversal rule continues to apply until the child has achieved the first three consecutive items beginning at the determined start point. To complete testing and achieve the ceiling, a child must score 0 on 5 consecutive items. After having received these five consecutive 0 scores, no further items are administered (discontinue rule).

The Bayley-III provides norm-referenced scores. When scoring, each of the five subscales is given a raw score based on the number of items the child has achieved in addition to the number of items preceding the basal that were not administered. Higher scores indicate more mature development.

From these raw scores, scaled scores can be calculated for the Cognitive Scale and the two combined Language Scales and Motor Scales. These scores can then be used to determine composite scores, percentile ranks and confidence intervals, developmental age equivalents, and growth scores. Scores for the Cognitive, Language, and Motor Scales are provided in 10-day increments for children aged 16 days to 5 months and 15 days and in 1-month intervals for children over 5 months and 15 days. Scaled scores for the Social–Emotional Scale are reported according to the stages of social–emotional development. Scaled scores for the Adaptive Behavior Scale are reported in 1-month intervals for 0–11 months, 2-month interval for 12–23 months, and 3-month intervals for 24–42 months.

Total administration time ranges from 50 minutes for children younger than 12 months up to 90 minutes for children 13 months and older. The Bayley-III is intended to be administered by individuals who have training and experience in the administration and interpretation of comprehensive developmental assessments. Those administering the Bayley-III should have completed some formal graduate or professional training in individual assessment.

According to the technical manual for the Bayley-III, diagnosing developmental delay can be based on any one of the several criteria: 25% delay in functioning when compared to same age peers, 1.5 standard deviation units below the mean of the reference standard, and performance of a certain number of months below the child's chronological age. It cautions against the use of age equivalent scores as they are commonly misinterpreted and have psychometric limitations. It also states that scores on the Bayley-III should never be used as the sole criteria for diagnostic classification. It should also not be used to diagnose a specific disorder in any one area. Rather, poor performance in any particular area should be used as a measure to make recommendations or referrals for appropriate services.

Test Properties

Reliability

The Bayley-III has established reliability with internal consistency and shows reliability coefficients for the subscales and composite scores that range from 0.86 to 0.93. Reliability coefficients for the special groups assessed are similar to or higher than those of the normative sample, indicating that the Bayley-III is equally reliable for children with clinical diagnoses or risk factors as for the general population.

Test–retest reliability of the Cognitive, Language, and Motor Scales assessed on 197 children aged over 2–15 days shows correlation scores that range from 0.67 to 0.94 for the different subtests depending upon the children's ages. Test–retest reliability for the Adaptive Behavior Scale was calculated by asking 207 parents to rate their child twice over 2 days to 5 weeks. Reliability coefficients ranged from 0.71 to 0.92. Scores from the Greenspan Social–Emotional Growth Chart, which makes up the Social–Emotional Scale, indicate strong internal consistency with coefficients ranging from 0.76 to 0.94.

Validity

The Bayley-III has established convergent and divergent validity after correlating with other relevant instruments. It has shown good correlation with the Wechsler Preschool and Primary Scale of Intelligence, Third Edition (intelligence correlation score between 0.52 and 0.83), the Preschool Language Scale, Fourth Edition (language correlation score between 0.50 and 0.71), and Peabody Developmental Motor Scales, Second edition (motor skills correlation score between 0.55 and 0.59).

The validity of the Bayley-III in children with specific conditions or risk factors was also examined. These "special groups" included children with down syndrome, pervasive developmental disorder, cerebral palsy, specific or suspected language impairment, asphyxiation at birth, prenatal alcohol exposure; those who were small for gestational age, premature, or low birth weight; and other children at risk for developmental delay. Results indicate that the Bayley-III is sensitive to differences in performance of typical children and children at risk for developmental delay. There is no specific information provided regarding the validity of the Bayley-III Social–Emotional Scale, and there is moderate to low validity correlation of Bayley-III Adaptive Behavior Scale with other similar scales.

Shriniwas Chinta

See also Adaptive Behavior Assessments; Childhood; Cognitive Development, Theory of; Standardized Tests

Further Readings

Bayley, N. (2006). *Bayley Scales of Infant and Toddler Development* (3rd ed.). Administration Manual. San Antonio, TX: Harcourt Assessment.

Bayley, N. (2006). *Bayley Scales of Infant and Toddler Development* (3rd ed.). Technical Manual. San Antonio, TX: Harcourt Assessment.

Greenspan, S. I. (2004). *Greenspan social–emotional growth chart: A screening questionnaire for infants and young children.* San Antonio, TX: Harcourt Assessment.

Harrison, P. L., & Oakland, T. (2003). *Adaptive behavior assessment system* (2nd ed.). San Antonio, TX: The Psychological Corporation.

Beck Depression Inventory

The Beck Depression Inventory (BDI) was published by psychiatrist Aaron Beck in 1961, with the aim of better assessing depression severity and characterizing symptomatology. The author recognized the multidimensional nature of depression and need to quantify symptomatology for screening purposes. Questions center on the patient's thoughts, feelings, and how the patient thinks and views the world and self. For example, question content reflects cognitive distortions, negative thoughts, low self-esteem, and suicidal ideation as well as somatic/affective components (e.g., sleep or appetite disturbances and fatigue).

The strength and popularity of Beck's original inventory and subsequent revisions published in 1978 and 1996 in part reflects its ease of use, strong psychometric characteristics, and ecological validity. This entry discusses the characteristics of the original BDI and subsequent revisions, then looks at its validity and reliability, the normative sample used in developing it, and its clinical use, administration, and limitations.

Versions of the BDI

BDI-I

The original BDI measure consisted of 21 multiple-choice questions asking the patient to rate their feelings over the past week. Questions were ranked on a Likert-type severity scale from levels 0 to 3 (3 representing more intense or severe feelings). Respondents would be instructed to circle the number corresponding to the statement that was most accurate, and the responses were summed to yield a total score. Higher total scores indicated a more severe number of depressive symptoms.

Beck developed standard ranges and cutoffs for the scores, so that a clinical impression could be easily assessed from the total sum. Descriptors and ranges were minimal (0–9), mild (10–18), moderate (19–29), and severe (30–63).

BDI-IA

The BDI-IA was published in 1978 as an amended (revised) version of Beck's original questionnaire. Improvements included rewording and restructuring some items to remove the (a) and (b) choices to make the choices clearer for patients. In the original questionnaire, examinees were asked to answer questions based on their mood over the preceding week. This time frame was lengthened to 2 weeks on the BDI-IA so as to allow for a wider range of possible life events and emotions that might be tabulated.

Despite increased ease of administration and use in this version, the BDI-IA only addressed six of the nine *Diagnostic and Statistical Manual of Mental Disorders, Third edition (DSM-III)* symptom criteria for major depressive disorder. This flaw prompted the second revision of the BDI.

BDI-II

The second revision of the BDI occurred with the advent of the *DSM-IV* in 1996. This version, the most recent as of 2017, is one of the most widely used depression screening measures. The BDI-II retains a 21-question format, although 18 items were reworded to reflect new diagnostic criteria accompanying implementation of the *DSM-IV*. Questions pertaining to suicide, interest in sex, and feelings of punishment were not revised. Items referring to sleep and appetite were reworded to account for both increases and decreases in these domains as *DSM-IV* allowed for either direction of the disturbance to count as symptom criteria. Items assessing body image, hypochondriasis, and difficulty working were removed, as they no longer reflected diagnostic criteria.

Identical to the BDI-IA, the BDI-II asks individuals to choose their responses based on their thoughts or feelings over the most recent 2-week span. Respondents circle the number of the statement that most closely matched their feelings or thoughts, with 0 being the *least severe feeling* and 3 being the *most severe feeling*. All 21 items are tabulated, with higher total sums indicating a more severe number of depressive symptoms. BDI-II descriptors are minimal (0–13), mild (14–19), moderate (20–28), and severe (29–63).

Validity and Reliability

The BDI-II has strong internal validity, external reliability, and high test–retest reliability. Twenty-one items are highly intercorrelated, demonstrating strong internal reliability with a correlation of .92 in outpatients and .93 in college students. Test–retest reliability is strong (.93; $p < .001$), when the questionnaire is readministered 1 week after the first administration. Content validity of the BDI-II is higher than the BDI-I or BDI-A, which is thought to reflect updates to item content to more closely align with the *DSM-IV* diagnostic criteria. The BDI-II has been shown to be able to consistently differentiate between depressed and nondepressed patients when administered. BDI-II scores were on average 3 points higher than the BDI-IA scores.

Factor analysis of the BDI-II by Beck revealed two main types of factors of depression: somatic-affective and cognitive factors. While additional research has suggested that there may be additional factors or variations in factors that are indicated on the BDI, Beck continued to use the two-factor approach in revising the original BDI for subsequent versions. Questions pertaining to the somatic or physical components of depression as well as the cognitive or thought disturbance aspects of the disorder are thoroughly addressed throughout the 21-item questionnaire.

The BDI-II is highly correlated with the Beck Anxiety Inventory, a screening measure geared toward physiological symptoms of anxiety that was also developed by Beck. For this reason, pairing of these two questionnaires may be beneficial in screening both for symptoms of depression and for symptoms of anxiety.

Normative Sample

The normative sample for the BDI-II was made up of 500 psychiatric outpatients (63% female) from both rural and suburban areas from across the United States. Participants had been diagnosed with depression using either *DSM-III-R* or *DSM-IV* criteria. The mean age of the normative sample was about 37 years with an age range of 13–86 years. The racial makeup of the sample was lacking in diversity (91% White, 4% African American, 4% Asian American, and 1% Hispanic). Another, smaller sample of 120 Canadian college students served as a normal comparative group. Age range and racial data on this sample are not reported in the literature.

Clinical Use

The BDI-II is one of the most commonly used screening measures for depression because its inception into neuropsychological batteries in the early 1960s. It is suitable for clients who have reading and comprehension abilities of at least a fifth-grade level and who understand standard written English. There is also a Spanish version of the BDI-II that can be used in appropriate populations.

Because the BDI-II is meant to be used as a primary screening measure, it can be given to any individual who is experiencing symptoms that are similar to, or diagnostic of, depression, regardless of whether or not there is a prior or current diagnosis of depression. It is a useful tool in clinical practice to help characterize associated somatic and cognitive disturbances.

Administration

Ease and speed of administration makes this an ideal way to screen for depressive symptomatology and other mood and related cognitive disturbances. It is used in private practice, hospital settings, and other clinical situations, in which a quick and reliable measure is needed.

The BDI-II is a self-report questionnaire and is filled out independently of the examiner's assistance. Instructions are written at the top of the page and are also meant to be read aloud by the examiner to ensure comprehension. Instructions ask the examinee to carefully consider their feelings over the last 2 weeks. In order to obtain a total score, examinees are required to answer each item on the double-sided questionnaire. Examinees are instructed to choose a higher number (indicating greater severity) if they are torn between two response choices on an item. Administration is untimed but typically takes approximately 5 minutes.

Limitations

The BDI-II may not be an effective screening measure for elderly populations due to the mixed age range of the normative sample as well as potential variations in symptom manifestation across the life span. Additional research may be required to determine the clinical utility of the BDI-II in older adults, although it should be noted that the Geriatric Depression Rating Scale is the most widely used depression screening measure for the older adult population currently. Furthermore, the BDI-II is only normed for ages 13 and older and should not be used for children or young adolescents of any race or ethnicity, unless there is a clinically defensible reason for doing so.

Based on the homogeneity of races in the normative sample (i.e., 91% White), there is little research on the efficacy of the BDI-II in different populations and ethnic minorities. Future research is warranted in this area as well to better improve screening measures for depression in racial and ethnic minority populations. There is a Spanish translation of the Beck, although there are currently no other translations available. The Spanish BDI-II is available for appropriate populations, but lack of alternate translations should be considered when giving this form to nonnative English speakers. Cultural variations in how examinees experience depressive symptoms suggest that translation without adjustment to item content might not be adequate for generalizability.

Clinicians and researchers should also consider how the BDI-II aligns with the *DSM-5* published in 2013. Clinicians and researchers must determine whether any such differences are relevant to the purpose of a given administration (e.g., diagnosis vs. symptom characterization). Significant discrepancies may require selection of an alternative questionnaire or supplementation of additional content that is noted with appropriate documentation and consideration for potential compromises to validity.

Clinicians should not use the BDI-II as the primary measure of diagnosis, as it is not meant to serve alone as a diagnostic tool. The BDI-II should rather be used as a screening measure to inform treatment, guide interventions and assessments, and help the examinee gain insight into the type and severity of symptoms experienced.

Kimberly Ethridge, Kimberly Capp,
and Anthony Odland

See also Anxiety; *Diagnostic and Statistical Manual of Mental Disorders*; Minnesota Multiphasic Personality Inventory; Psychometrics; Screening Tests; Reliability; Test–Retest Reliability; Validity

Further Readings

American Psychiatric Association. (2013). *Diagnostic and Statistical Manual of Mental Disorders: DSM-5.* Washington, DC: Author.

Beck, A. T., Rial, W. Y., & Rickels, K. (1974). Short Form of Depression Inventory: Cross-Validation. *Psychological Reports.*

Beck, A. T., & Steer, R. A. (1984). Internal consistencies of the original and revised Beck Depression Inventory. *Journal of Clinical Psychology, 40*(6), 1365–1367.

Beck, A. T., Steer, R. A., & Brown, G. K. (1996). *Manual for the Beck Depression Inventory–II.* San Antonio, TX: Psychological Corporation.

Brown, M., Kaplan, C., & Jason, L. (2012). Factor analysis of the Beck Depression Inventory–II with patients with chronic fatigue syndrome. *Journal of Health Psychology, 17*(6), 799–808.

Conoley, C. W. (1987). Review of the Beck Depression Inventory (revised edition). In J. J. Kramer & J. C. Conoley (Eds.), *Mental measurements yearbook, 11th edition* (pp. 78–79). Lincoln: University of Nebraska Press.

Erbauch, J. (1961). An inventory for measuring depression. *Archives of General Psychiatry, 562*, 53–63.

Sharp, L. K., & Lipsky, M. S. (2002). Screening for depression across the lifespan: A review of measures for use in primary care settings. *American Family Physician, 66*(6), 1001–1008.

BEHAVIORISM

Behaviorism is a movement in psychology that focuses on the study of behaviors that can be objectively measured by a third party. Some behaviorists give little or no consideration to internal or mental events that cannot be measured, although others acknowledge the importance of internal events. This entry discusses the emergence of behaviorism, then describes methodological behaviorism and radical behaviorism, and then describes how these two strands have evolved.

Emergence of Behaviorism

Behaviorism was presented to the modern world by Johns Hopkins psychology professor John Broadus Watson (1878–1958) in an influential 1913 article *Psychology as the Behaviorist Views It.* Watson's behaviorism is based on two claims: First, that individuals' observations about their actions, motives, and mental processes are scientifically irrelevant. Second—and it almost follows from the first assumption—that the data of a scientific psychology must come from things that can be measured, and measured not by subject, but by a third party. As for theory, Watson didn't even mention it: "prediction and control" of behavior was his aim. And he recognized "no dividing line between man and brute [i.e., nonhuman animals]" (1913/1948, p. 457).

None of this was entirely new; other scientists had also rejected human consciousness as a means of explaining behavior. The process by which we see, recognize, and interpret the visual world is also hidden from consciousness. The German physicist, philosopher, and physician Hermann von Helmholtz (1821–1894) pointed out that perception operates by a sort of "unconscious inference." In 1934, an inventor, American ophthalmologist Adelbert Ames Jr. (1880–1955), built a special kind of room to illustrate the process of perceptual inference. Viewed through a peephole (i.e., from a fixed point of view), it looks like a regular room, with right-angle corners, and so on. But when a girl walks from one side of the room to the other, the girl seems to grow magically larger. The perception is wrong of course. The girl size has not changed. The reason the girl appears to grow is that the brain assumes—without the viewer's awareness—that the angles are all right angles and the floor is level, when neither is true.

Perception involves unconsciously using very partial data to call up a complete picture of whatever the individual (unconsciously) infers he or she is seeing. Visual illusions such as the Ames room show how this process can misfire. Other examples of unconscious processes include the "tip of the tongue" phenomenon: knowing the name of the old movie star on the screen but being unable to bring it to mind until suddenly it appears. Novelists frequently say that after a certain point, their characters seem to "write themselves." Mathematicians often say that proofs and theorems simply appear in their minds without any awareness of the complex calculations that must have been made to generate them.

If not conscious, these automatic processes must then be unconscious, yet Watson attacked the very idea of the unconscious. Behavior may be the product of unconscious processes, but what *are* they? On this, Watson's behaviorism was silent.

Methodological Behaviorism and Radical Behaviorism

Watson and other researchers of the early 20th century used rats and other animals to study learning. The dominant behaviorists of the time were Clark L. Hull (1884–1952) at Yale University; Edward Chace Tolman (1886–1959), a cognitive behaviorist at University of California, Berkeley; and, to a lesser degree, Edwin Guthrie (1886–1959) at the University of Washington. The dominant movement, Hullian, and then neo-Hullian, behaviorism, was relabeled by B. F. Skinner (1904–1990), as *methodological behaviorism*. Skinner contrasted methodological behaviorism to his own proposal, termed *radical behaviorism* and described in his 1938 book, *The Behavior of Organisms*, and many later works.

Methodological and radical behaviorism differ in several ways. The neo-Hullians were devoutly theoretical. They wanted to explain the process of learning, which seemed to require the between-subject method. To compare the effects of different experiences, a researcher cannot simply give the same animal the two experiences in succession because the animal is changed by the first experience. It's no longer "naive," so it may behave differently after Experience B if Experience A came first than it would have if Experience B came first. Given two identical animals, the researcher could give one the first experience, A, and the other the second, B, and look at the differences in behavior that result. But because no two animals are exactly the same, the researcher must settle for two groups, to which animals are randomly assigned: the *experimental* group, which gets the treatment being studied (A), and the *control* group, which gets no treatment (B). The average response of the groups must then be compared using a method called *null hypothesis statistical test*.

Skinner's method was quite different. He invented a simple method using the Skinner box, a device used for the animal to give a measureable response, such as pressing a lever or pecking a colored disk, that can be rewarded automatically in the presence of controllable stimuli, such as lights, colors, or patterns. The method generates quantitative data, initially in the form of a *cumulative record*, which is a graph that shows real time on the x-axis and cumulated responses on the y-axis. Skinner also discovered that animals—in his case, pigeons as well as rats—yield stable and reversible adaptations to a variety of *reinforcement schedules*, which are rules saying what the animal must do to get a bit of food—make 10 lever presses or wait 30 seconds, for example. Because the pattern of behavior produced by a given schedule is stable and can usually be recovered even after intervening experience with a different schedule, Skinner's method of what he termed *operant conditioning* allows the study of individual animals, which can be exposed successively, ABAB and so on, with the assurance that each exposure to A, say, will give the same result.

Both these approaches are flawed. The neo-Hullians developed theories based on the average behavior of groups and assumed that what was true of the group was true as well of the individual. Many theories attempted to explain the smooth learning curve typically found when a group of rats learns to choose the left versus the right arm of a T-maze. Yet each rat may in fact learn instantly, just with different delays for different rats. The average is smooth, but the individual is not. Indeed, Skinner famously published a cumulative record of a rat learning to bar press that shows just such sudden learning. But the neo-Hullians were undeterred and continued to deal entirely in group data.

Reliance on statistical testing of theoretical models has tended to deemphasize quantitative predictions in favor of simple binary tests. Theorists are often satisfied to show that A is greater (or less) than B, even if the actual quantitative difference may be very small. This is logically defensible, but in practice means that the theory being tested is weak, that it presents only a partial picture of the phenomenon under test.

Finally, a serious problem that affects many areas of social and biological science is the null hypothesis statistical test method. In recent years, problems with this method have been revealed as researchers have found that many experimental results in several areas, from social psychology to drug studies, have been impossible to replicate. An experimental result is accepted as fact if the chance of getting it by accident is less than 5%. The computation is based on assumptions about probability distributions that are often questionable. The single-subject method avoids the problems of the null hypothesis statistical test method but must cope with the fundamental irreversibility of the organism's state. The pigeon may behave in the same way on the second exposure to a given reinforcement schedule, but it is not the same pigeon. The only solution to this problem is *theory*. A theory about how exposure to one condition will affect behavior in another can be tested with individual subjects. The researcher may have an idea about how a sequence of conditions, say AB, will affect the organism's behavior in a new Condition C. For example, suppose the pigeon is trained with two choices: peck left or peck right. It is easy to show, with no statistics required, that if the pigeon is paid off for L for a few days then for R for a few days, then given nothing, it will try both L and R for a while before finally quitting. Conversely, another pigeon, equally naive at the beginning of the experiment, but rewarded only for pecking R, when reward ceases will peck L hardly at all. There are several theories that might explain this and other *transfer effects*.

Skinner, exponent of the single-subject method, ruled out theory, however. In an influential 1950 article entitled *Are Theories of Learning Necessary?* he answered emphatically "No!" and theories of learning languished among his followers. Watson also devalued theory, claiming that the objective of psychology should be to "predict and control" behavior rather than to understand it, even though the theory of evolution by natural selection shows that prediction is often impossible.

Behaviorism began to fragment in the 1930s and 1940s. The neo-Hullians, soon to become *associative learners*, were methodological behaviorists. They believe that psychology must restrict itself to third-party measureable data and not rely on private experience, that is, on introspection.

Experimental psychologists and most neuroscientists accept methodological behaviorism. But after about 1960, the methodological behaviorists began to call themselves cognitive psychologists and ceased to identify with behaviorism. The essentials of methodological behaviorism have been absorbed by empirical psychology of all types.

But radical behaviorism, based on Skinner's work, remains as a separate and vigorous movement. The reasons are partly practical. Skinner's emphasis on contingencies of reinforcement as the drivers of all operant (instrumental) behavior has allowed the development of effective techniques for managing autism and some other forms of mental illness. In *Verbal Behavior*, published in 1957, Skinner followed the same strategy with language as with the operant behavior of animals. He identified concepts such as *mand* and *tact* that he believed provided a way to understand how language is used, rather than what it is.

In animal learning, many Skinnerian terms already had widely used equivalents; for example, operant behavior was referred to as instrumental behavior, conditioned reinforcement as secondary reinforcement, and contingency as dependency. The concepts in *Verbal Behavior* appeared to many critics as much the same, a cumbersome reworking of traditional notions: *mand* to mean command and *tact* to mean describe or name. But Skinner was trying to understand the function of language in a way congenial to evolutionary psychology, later popularized by Richard Dawkins and many others. From an evolutionary point of view, language exists to control the behavior of other people. Skinner tried to apply what he knew of controlling the operant behavior of animals to the interaction between a human speaker and listener.

Linguists are interested in the structure of language, not its use as a tool of control. In a well-known 1959 critical review of *Verbal Behavior*, mathematical linguist Noam Chomsky discussed how behaviorism and reinforced learning cannot explain phenomena such as how children can combine words into sentences they haven't already heard. Although Skinner retained loyal followers, Chomsky's review effectively marginalized radical behaviorism.

Evolution of Behaviorism

In the 1960s, behaviorism was supplanted as the dominant movement in experimental psychology by the so-called cognitive revolution. Skinner's proscription of theory and the absorption of methodological behaviorism into general empirical psychology had left radical behaviorism no place to go. But some theory-friendly offshoots soon emerged. Skinner had always argued against the idea of *internal state*, the process that intervenes between stimulus and response. But he was not totally consistent about this. In the 1948 William James Lectures on which *Verbal Behavior* is based, Skinner referred to *latent* (verbal) *responses*. Because these by definition cannot be measured, they are clearly internal in some sense. Skinner had also argued that the *operant*, his behavioral unit, is defined by classes: a stimulus class and a response class defined by their orderly functional relation. Invoking the logic of historical systems, J. E. R. Staddon extended Skinner's definition to an organism's *history*, calling his modified view *theoretical behaviorism*. A class of past histories that are equivalent in terms of the organism's future behavior is termed an internal *state* but without any physical or physiological implications. Rather than having to list the effects of all possible histories on future behavior, they can be grouped into equivalence classes, states. A particular state is then a theory that describes the common effect of a set of histories.

A simple example of such a state is *hunger*. Many histories lead to a state of hunger, such as food deprivation, certain drugs, disease, and exercise. But all lead to much the same future behavior: seeking food and being rewarded by getting food. A state need not be motivational. Consider, for example, *habituation*, which is an almost universal learning effect. As a "neutral" stimulus is repeated, its effect diminishes—the dog pricks its ears and turns in response to a novel sound, but after a few repetitions—fewer the more closely spaced they are—the sound is ignored, the response extinguishes. Then, after some time with no sound, the response may recover again. But all extinctions are not equal: Habituation will take longer to dissipate if repetitions are spaced farther apart. A simple model with not one but two memory stores, one that dissipates rapidly and the other slowly, can capture this effect. It allows us to predict how long the animal will take to recover, to dishabituate, given any history, any sequence of stimuli. In such a model, at least two numbers— *state variables*—are needed to characterize *rate sensitivity* as this is called. Simply knowing that the response has extinguished, that its "strength" is zero, is not enough.

Regarding the rejection of introspection as an explanation for behavior, Skinner's view still prevails among radical behaviorists. Skinner denies introspection but does permit "internal stimulation," which he invokes to explain "feeling" and "thinking." For example, he writes in *About Behaviorism* that when we answer the question "What are you thinking? . . . it is . . . likely that we are describing private conditions associated with public behavior but not necessarily generated by it" (Skinner, 1976, pp. 30–31). What this seems to mean is that "we" are describing some internal state (but the word "state" is avoided). Skinner's alternative is "internal stimulation," although he does not specify what is stimulated by what. This poses the problem of how to deal scientifically with an internal stimulus that cannot be seen, measured, or postulated as part of a theory.

Methodological behaviorists, now become cognitive scientists, have not entirely avoided mentalistic explanations for behavior. Experimental psychologist David Premack (1925–2015), who performed research on both animals and human infants, began his career with a hypothesis about reinforcement of behavior (that a more frequent activity might reinforce a less frequent). But then, studying the behavior of monkeys and human infants, he proposed something called a *theory of mind* as an explanation for discriminations involving a third party. For example, a 3-year-old child is shown a Crayola box and, asked what it contains, answers "crayons." But then the child is shown that it really contains candles. Enter "Snoopy," a third party: "What does Snoopy think is in the Crayola box?" "Candles" says the 3-year-old. "Crayons" says a 5-year-old, with a developed theory of mind, apparently aware that Snoopy will not know the right answer. The different behavior of the 3-year-old and the 5-year-old can be explained in a variety of ways, some "cognitive" and others not. Research continues.

J. E. R. Staddon

See also ABA Designs; Applied Behavior Analysis; Cognitive Neuroscience; Replication

Further Readings

Pashler, H., & Wagenmakers, E.-J. (2012). Editors' introduction to the special section on replicability in psychological science: A crisis of confidence? *Perspectives in Psychological Science, 7*(6), 528–530.

Rachlin, H. (1991). *Introduction to modern behaviorism* (3rd ed.). New York, NY: Freeman.

Sidman, M. (1960). Tactics of scientific research: Evaluating experimental data in psychology. New York, NY: Basic Books.

Skinner, B. F. (1956 May). A case history in scientific method. *American Psychologist, 11*(5), 221–233.

Skinner, B. F. (1948). *Verbal behavior. William James lectures, Harvard University*. Retrieved from http://store.behavior.org/resources/595.pdf

Skinner, B. F. (1976). *About behaviorism*. New York, NY: Random House.

Staddon, J. E. R. (2014). *The new behaviorism* (2nd ed.). Philadelphia, PA: Psychology Press.

Staddon, J. E. R. (2016). *Adaptive behavior and learning* (2nd ed.). New York, NY: Cambridge University Press.

Watson, J. B. (1927, September). The myth of the unconscious: A behavioristic explanation. *Harper's Magazine*, pp. 502–508.

Watson, J. B. (1948). Psychology as the behaviorist views it. In W. Dennis (Ed.), *Readings in the history of psychology* (pp. 457–471). New York, NY: Appleton. (Original work published 1913)

BELMONT REPORT

The 1978 Belmont Report is a 5,000-word essay by the National Commission for the Protection of Human Subjects of Biomedical and Behavioral Research that outlines basic ethical principles for the protection of human subjects in research projects. The report, titled *The Belmont Report: Ethical Principles and Guidelines for the Protection of Human Subjects of Research*, has standardized the basis for decision making by institutional review boards in the United States and influenced similar bodies around the world. This entry discusses what led up to the report, the report's development, and the principles and guidelines found in the report.

History

The National Research Act of 1974 (U.S. Public Law 93-348) established and authorized the secretary of health, education, and welfare to appoint the National Commission for the Protection of Human Subjects of Biomedical and Behavioral Research, which was initially expected to complete its work in 2 years. The 11 members of the commission were charged with identifying basic ethical principles and guidelines for such research, considering the boundaries between research and the routine medical practice, the nature and definition of informed consent, the role of risk–benefit criteria in assessing human subjects research, and appropriate guidelines for selecting participants in such research.

The structure of institutional review boards was already in place at universities and biomedical organizations in the United States due to the 1966 Surgeon General's Directives on Human Experimentation, which mandated prior review by institutional committees of all research involving human subjects that was supported by the federal Public Health Service. The public disclosure and termination of the long-running Tuskegee syphilis experiment in 1972, which examined the course of syphilis in nearly 400 Black men without telling them of their diagnosis or providing penicillin, highlighted the need for stronger protections for human research subjects and precipitated the 1974 National Research Act.

The commission members were mostly university faculty in law, medicine, philosophy, and behavioral and life sciences. The group held many public meetings and a 4-day closed retreat in 1976 at the Belmont (MD) Conference Center, where the structure and core ideas of the report were developed. The report was issued in 1978 and published in the Federal Register in 1979.

Contents

The report is in three parts, beginning with distinguishing between research and practice; then outlining three fundamental ethical principles regarding the treatment of human subjects in research—respect for persons, beneficence, and justice; and finally elaborating on how the principles may be implemented. Research is defined as a departure from the practice of standard or accepted clinical therapy, designed to develop or contribute to generalizable knowledge, and usually described in a protocol that defines specific goals and procedures. Departures may be as simple as comparing the results of alternative prescriptions to different standard treatments. The report does not consider research in nonclinical fields, where this definition loses precision.

Each principle outlined in the report has two dimensions that are not entirely compatible. The principle of respect for persons focuses on self-determination or personal autonomy. The principle demands *both* that persons deemed routinely capable of self-determination enter research voluntarily and with adequate information, while those with diminished capacity for self-determination due to diverse conditions such as immaturity, disability, illness, or imprisonment be specially protected by bringing in third parties as decision makers.

The principle of beneficence is *not* to harm research subjects but to *minimize* harms while *maximizing* benefits. The admonition against direct harm is softened by permitting risk of harm, and benefits may be only to the greater good through enhanced societal knowledge.

The principle of justice refers to the fair distribution of burdens and benefits of research and a principle of equality but not absolute equality. Justice demands that the relative few who may be selected to carry the burdens of research (risks of harm) not be different as a demographic class from those who might benefit from the results. The authors cite as historical inequities the use of poor patients and of prisoners in experiments to develop therapies affordable mainly by wealthier patients or the free populace.

The authors recognize that these principles present challenges when balancing conflicting claims and making difficult choices. To assist, they elaborate on how the three principles may be implemented and certain issues resolved. The report discusses applying the principles through informed consent, risk/benefit assessment, and the selection of subjects of research.

Informed consent is the means through which respect for persons is implemented before and during research participation. Advance information about the research should include key points such as its purpose, procedures, risks, and benefits. The researcher must assure that the participant understands the information offered. Questions may be asked and must be answered truthfully. Some kinds of information may be withheld at the outset if the information would threaten the validity of the research but must be disclosed afterward. Agreement must be made free of overt or subtle coercion or undue influence (excessive or improper rewards). If participants have reduced capacity for comprehension or vulnerability to pressure, both the participant and a protective third party must give informed consent.

The principle of beneficence "requires that we protect against risk of harm to subjects and also that we be concerned about the loss of the substantial benefits that might be gained from research" (National Commission for the Protection of Human Subjects of Biomedical and Behavioral Research, 1979, n.p.). Review committees need to conduct a systematic, nonarbitrary analysis of the risks of harm as against the probability of benefits from the research. Finally, in accord with the principle of justice, there should be fair procedures and outcomes in the recruitment and selection of research subjects.

Dean R. Gerstein

See also 45 CFR Part 46; Human Subjects Protections; Human Subjects Research, Definition of; Institutional Review Boards; Nuremberg Code

Further Readings

The Advisory Committee on Human Radiation Experiments. (1995). The Development of Human Subject Research Policy at DHEW. In *The Final Report*. Retrieved May 20, 2016, from https://bioethicsarchive.georgetown.edu/achre/final/chap3_2.html

National Commission for the Protection of Human Subjects of Biomedical and Behavioral Research. (1979, April 18). *The Belmont Report: Ethical Principles and Guidelines for the Protection of Human Subjects of Research*. Retrieved May 15, 2016, from http://www.hhs.gov/ohrp/regulations-and-policy/belmont-report/index.html

William, H. S. (1966, February). Surgeon General, Public Health Service to the Heads of the Institutions Conducting Research with Public Health Service Grants, February 8, 1966 (Clinical research and investigation involving human beings) (ACHRE No. HHS-090794-A). Retrieved May 20, 2016, from http://history.nih.gov/research/downloads/Surgeongeneraldirective1966.pdf. Reprinted with addenda in Surgeon-General's Directives on Human Experimentation. (1967). *American Psychologist, 22*(5), 350–355. Retrieved from http://psycnet.apa.org/doi/10.1037/h0024885

BENCHMARK

A benchmark describes what a student should know and be able to do in a particular content area, grade level, or developmental level at a specified point in time. Generally, benchmarks represent shorter-term goals along a path toward mastery of content standards, learning objectives, or other longer-term educational outcomes.

Benchmarks can be used as a way to monitor student progress. At the individual level, monitoring students at various benchmarks can help students, educators, and parents make adjustments in order to help students stay on or get back on track. At an educational program level, monitoring aggregate student performance at various benchmarks can help organizations provide assistance to educators or schools in order to support student achievement.

Benchmarks can also show how much students have grown as they continue down the path toward mastery. For example, if a student is not meeting the standards at a particular benchmark but improves skills in order to meet the standards at the next benchmark, the student can be commended for showing good progress. Benchmarks can also help organizations determine program-wide progress toward goals and objectives.

To illustrate the use of benchmarks, imagine a fifth-grade student at the beginning of a school year. As the student proceeds through the math curriculum, the student's teacher evaluates the progress of the class every 9 weeks using short assessments aligned to the content standards. After interpreting a series of assessment score reports, as well as examples of the student's work, the teacher notices that the student is struggling to add and subtract fractions, a skill that should be mastered by that point in the school year. Noticing that a few other students were struggling in the same area, the teacher revisits adding and subtracting fractions with a subset of the class. With the extra help, the student does better on the next benchmark assessment, showing positive growth on the standards related to fractions. This positive growth is shared with the student and the student's parents at the next conference.

Continuing with the example, leadership in the student's district reviews the benchmark assessment results for fifth-grade math, districtwide, looking for patterns. Scores are analyzed at classroom and school levels, between schools, and even disaggregated by student characteristics. In particular, results are evaluated in the context of the district's annual goals, which included closing of achievement gaps between student groups. Noting the intermediate progress made in fifth-grade math so far this year by various student groups, the district reports the results to the local school board along with reports of other efforts to address student equity districtwide.

Gail Tiemann

See also Achievement Tests; Classroom Assessment; Formative Assessment; Progress Monitoring; Tests

Further Readings

Perie, M., Marion, S., & Gong, B. (2009). Moving towards a comprehensive assessment system: A framework for considering interim assessment. *Educational Measurement: Issues and Practice, 28*(3), 5–13.

Bernoulli Distribution

The Bernoulli distribution is the range of probabilities for two possible outcomes. It is a central statistical concept. This entry describes the Bernoulli distribution and Bernoulli random variables and explains the relationship between the Bernoulli distribution and the binomial distribution.

Suppose a random experiment has two possible outcomes, either success or failure, where the probability of success is p and probability of failure is $q = 1 - p$. Such an experiment is called a *Bernoulli experiment* or *Bernoulli trial*. For a Bernoulli experiment, define a real-valued random variable X which takes two values as: $X = 1$ if success and $X = 0$ if failure. Such a random variable X is called a *Bernoulli random variable*. The probability distribution of X is given by $Pr(X = 1) = p$ and $Pr(X = 0) = 1 - p$. This distribution is called a *Bernoulli distribution*, denoted by Bernoulli(p). It is named after Jacob Bernoulli, a Swiss mathematician of the 17th century.

The term *success* here means the outcome meets some special condition, and it is not based on a moral judgment. The following are some examples of Bernoulli random variables.

Toss a coin once. Two possible outcomes are "heads" and "tails." Suppose heads happens with probability p, while tails happens with probability $1 - p$. Let X be a random variable such that $X = 1$ if the outcome is heads, and $X = 0$ if the outcome is tails. Then X is a Bernoulli random variable and its distribution is Bernoulli(p). When a fair coin is tossed, we have $p = q = 0.5$.

Roll a die once. Let X be a random variable which takes two values: $X = 1$ if the Number 3 occurs, and $X = 0$ otherwise. Then X is a Bernoulli random variable. If the die is balanced, then the probability distribution of X is Bernoulli($1/6$).

In clinical trials, let X represent a patient's status after a certain treatment as, $X = 1$ if a patient survives, and $X = 0$ otherwise. Then X is a Bernoulli random variable.

Statistical Properties

Assume a random variable X follows a Bernoulli(p) distribution. Its probability mass function is given by $P(X = 1) = p$ and $P(X = 0) = 1 - p$. Equivalently, it is expressed as

$$P(X = x) = p^x (1-p)^{1-x}, \quad x = 0,1.$$

Its expectation is $E(X) = p$, variance is $\mathrm{Var}(X) = p(1 - p)$, and skewness is $\frac{1-2p}{\sqrt{pq}}$. The moment generating function is

$$M_X(t) = E(e^{Xt}) = 1 - p + pe^t.$$

The characteristic function is

$$\phi_X(t) = 1 - p + pe^{it}.$$

The family of Bernoulli distributions $\{$Bernoulli$(p), 0 \le p \le 1\}$ is an exponential family.

Estimation of p

Suppose we take a random sample of size n, $X_1, \cdots, X_n$, from Bernoulli(p). Then an estimator for p is given by the sample mean:

$$\bar{X} = \frac{1}{n} \sum_{i=1}^n X_i, \text{ i.e.,}$$

$$\hat{p} = \bar{X}.$$

Because the sample mean is unbiased for the population mean p, we have $E(\hat{p}) = p$. By the law of large numbers, $\hat{p}$ is also a consistent estimator for p. In other words, the sample proportion of successes from n experiments can consistently estimate the success probability p. The estimator $\hat{p}$ is also the maximum likelihood estimator.

Bernoulli Distribution Versus Binomial Distribution

If $X_1, \cdots, X_n$ are independent random variables, all following Bernoulli(p), then their sum $Y = \sum_{i=1}^n X_i$ follows a binomial distribution, denoted as Binomial(n, p). The probability mass function of Y is

$$P(Y = y) = \{n \setminus \text{choose } y\} p \wedge y (1-p) \wedge y,$$
$$\quad y = 0, 1, \ldots, n.$$

In other words, a sum of identical and independent Bernoulli(p) random variables is a Binomial(n, p) random variable. And a Bernoulli distribution is a special case of the binomial distribution, where $n = 1$. For example, if a coin is tossed n times, with probability p of getting a heads, then the total number of heads follows a Binomial(n, p).

Bernoulli Process

A Bernoulli process is a sequence of independent identically distributed Bernoulli trials. Formally, a {\it Bernoulli process} is a finite or infinite sequence of independent random variables $X_1, X_2, X_3,$ \ldots, where each X_i is a Bernoulli trial with success probability p.

For a Bernoulli process, because the trials are independent, the process is memoryless. In other words, when p is known, past outcomes do not provide any information on future outcomes.

Binary Logistic Regression

Regression analysis is a statistical technique for estimating the relationship between a dependent variable (response) and one or more independent variables (predictors). The goal of regression analysis is to estimate the conditional expectation of the dependent variable given the independent variables, which is called the regression function. When the response variable takes only two values, either 0 or 1, *binary logistic regression* is a major regression tool for estimating the probability of the response variable based on independent variables.

Generating Random Numbers From Bernoulli(p)

In R software, the function *rbinom*() can be used to generate random numbers from the Binomial(n, p) distribution. For example, rbinom(100, 1, 0.3) generates a random sample of size 100 from the Bernoulli$(p = .3)$ distribution. The functions *dbinom*(), *pbinom*(), and *qbinom*() can be used to compute the density function, distribution function, and quantile function for the binomial distribution, respectively.

Hao Helen Zhang

See also Binomial Test; Maximum Likelihood Estimation

Further Readings

Bertsekas, D., & John, N., Tsitsiklis, J. (2002). *Introduction to probability*. Belmont, MA: Athena Scientific.

Evans, M., Hastings, N., & Peacock, B. (2000). *Bernoulli distribution. Chapter 4 in Statistical Distributions* (3rd ed., pp. 31–33). New York, NY: Wiley.

Johnson N. L., Kotz, S., & Kemp, A. (1993). *Univariate discrete distributions* (2nd ed.). New York, NY: Wiley.

McCullagh, P., & Nelder, J. (1989). *Generalized linear models* (2nd ed.). Boca Raton, FL: Chapman and Hall.

Papoulis, A. (1989). *Bernoulli trials. Probability, random variables, and stochastic processes* (2nd ed.). New York, NY: McGraw-Hill.

BILINGUAL EDUCATION, RESEARCH ON

This entry first discusses the contexts of research on bilingual education, the development of bilingual education in the United States, and early research on bilingual education. It then looks at various types of research on bilingual education and research findings on the impact and effectiveness of bilingual education. Finally, the entry describes shifts in how bilingual education is conceptualized and in the ways it is researched.

Research on bilingual education, like bilingual education itself, is shaped by sociopolitical contexts, language ideologies, and communities in action. Diverse paradigms and perspectives found in qualitative, quantitative, and mixed-methods forms are used in research on bilingual education, which is any school setting where students' instruction and assessment takes place in more than one language. Research on bilingual education may highlight one or more educational programs that fall under the umbrella of bilingual education including dual language (one way and two way), heritage language, transitional bilingual, polydirectional bilingual, developmental bilingual, and maintenance bilingual education programs.

The majority of studies on bilingual education take place in U.S. schools, from preschool to Grade 12, as students learn in Spanish and English. Other studies look at U.S. bilingual education in languages including Mandarin, French, Haitian-Creole, Russian, Arabic, Korean, Yiddish, Hebrew, American Sign Language, or indigenous languages along with English. Policies on bilingual education can be vastly differ school to school and state to state, and research often focuses on individual schools, districts, or states for this reason.

Research in bilingual education also takes place in contexts beyond U.S. schools. Canadian French–English schools and multilingual European schools, such as those in the Basque country of Spain and in Alsace on the France–Germany border, have been the focus of research for their content and language integrated learning and developmental bilingual programs. Bilingual education in the form of heritage language or revitalization programs with indigenous languages and a colonial language (English, Spanish, or French) have been the subjects of research from the Maori schools in New Zealand to Mayan language education in Guatemalan schools.

Foundation of Bilingual Education

The historical events surrounding bilingual education set the stage for research about it and for it. In the midst of the civil rights movement, Title VII of the Elementary and Secondary Education Act of 1968, known as the Bilingual Education Act, was the first piece of federal legislation that recognized the academic needs of emergent bilinguals in schools. Prior to this recognition, students were being educated bilingually across the United States in Spanish–English and German–English classrooms. However, with World War II came the banning of German–English schooling, and except for a few strong programs in Miami and New York

City, Spanish–English programs were under attack, poorly financed, and rare. Research on the history of bilingual education focuses on early community efforts, seminal court cases such as *Lau v. Nichols* (1974), the impacts and intersections of immigrant action groups, and the events of 1968 as they shaped schooling and the lives of linguistically diverse students.

Early research conceptualized differences within bilingual education, especially considering the diverse learning contexts, schools, teachers, sociopolitical environments, and linguistic experiences for students. In 1974, Wallace Lambert described two types of bilingualism within schools—subtractive and additive. Subtractive bilingualism refers to educational approaches in which children's home language use or ability diminishes as they learn the dominant language of school. In opposition to this is additive bilingualism, occurring when a new language is added to the children's home language, which is maintained and even strengthened. Later research in bilingual education extends these ideas to reflect the reality for some emergent bilingual students of the in-between or border spaces. This can be an instance where a young person is neither monolingual nor biliterate and brings into the classroom complex language practices.

In the late 1970s and early 1980s, Stephen Krashen developed concepts in second-language acquisition that have been integral in shaping the groundwork of research in the fields of second-language acquisition and bilingual education. His concepts of the input hypothesis, affective filter, and the natural order hypothesis laid the foundation for how teachers, teacher–educators, linguists, and educational researchers would continue to conceptualize language and bilingual learning and teaching for decades to follow. Krashen also outlined essential components for success in bilingual education including content teaching in the home language, literacy development in the home language, and comprehensible input in English.

In 1979, James Cummins introduced the concepts of basic interpersonal communication skills and cognitive academic language proficiency (CALP) into the conversation and research on bilingual education. This paradigm of categorizing and understanding language learning has shaped many bilingual teacher education programs, and thus bilingual classrooms and students. By outlining specific benchmarks for learning both basic interpersonal communication skills and cognitive academic language proficiency in a new language, this research has also been the base for bilingual programming that maintains home language use for longer periods of time. Cummins's research continues to build on theories of language and power, promoting equity and social justice in and through bilingual education.

The National Association for Bilingual Education, founded in 1975, and other national and local organizations promote and support research on bilingual education through events and diverse opportunities. Here, communities of scholars, educators, families, and community activists are able to share their research, collaborate with colleagues, create spaces in the field of bilingual education, and build bridges to other fields.

Evaluating Impact and Effectiveness

Much of the research on bilingual education focuses on different programs' impacts on educational outcomes for emergent bilingual students. Related research looks at bilingual education's impact on, or intersection with, additional factors including students' social–emotional learning, teachers' and students' language use, relationships between language and culture, and family inclusion in schools. Other studies focus on an evaluation of bilingual pedagogy and assessments across multiple school districts, encompassing thousands of students, often as an experimental design. Numerous other studies focus on a single program in one school, often zeroing in on a particular classroom or even an individual teacher.

Most studies that seek to evaluate bilingual education or compare it with other forms of second-language learning have shown positive effects of bilingual approaches to teaching and learning. The conclusion of "positive effects" has a different definition and takes on a different meaning from study to study. Some of this research highlights the cognitive impact of bilingualism for young people, while others look at gains in language learning, students' linguistic complexity, or abilities in academic tasks. An additional body of work in this research on bilingual education sheds light on the positive impact of bilingual education on student identity, social–emotional well-being, and communities, including families' and students' cultural, linguistic, or religious communities.

Experimental studies place different types of bilingual education programs next to other approaches to second-language learning or, in other studies, compare one type of bilingual education to another. For example, some studies measure the effects of dual-language programs in comparison to transitional bilingual education. In these studies, which are often longitudinal studies, data are mostly drawn from student work products and assessments.

A 1997 study by Wayne Thomas and Virginia Collier, followed by a 2002 study by the same researchers, concluded that bilingual programs (specifically developmental bilingual or two-way bilingual immersion) that were strong in design and implementation had significant positive effects on students' academic achievement including English literacy, language, and content area classes. In this research, academic and linguistic outcomes for emergent bilinguals throughout five school districts were measured and analyzed in a variety of learning settings. These reports contain research that is continuously used in support of bilingual education, specifically dual-language or maintenance bilingual education, throughout the United States.

Meta-analyses analyzing numerous studies on the effectiveness of bilingual education also contribute to the body of research on bilingual education. The conclusions of multiple large-scale studies show small but favorable impacts of bilingual education on students' academic achievement. Some researchers have noted the importance of research design in the field of bilingual education, concluding that the more effective the experimental design, the more positive were the impacts of bilingual education.

Although research findings on bilingual education are generally supportive of multilingual pedagogical practices, some research does seek to challenge these practices. Researcher Christine Rossell has asserted that bilingual education is the least effective approach to educate immigrant children. However, many researchers have disputed this claim.

Shifts in Bilingual Education Conceptualization and Research

In a 2009 study, bilingual education as conceptualized by Ofelia García challenges traditional ideas of language learning in which bilinguals were thought to have two balanced language systems, supporting the separation of languages in schools and the notion that one language plus a second-language equals two separate languages. García calls for a reconceptualization of bilingual education to reflect bilinguals' fluid language practices. Her perspective emphasizes dynamic bilingualism and pedagogy reflective of students' multiple language practices in the classroom. Critical researchers in bilingual education are using this heteroglossic framework as a foundation to challenge power structures, oppression, and inequity in the schooling of emergent bilinguals.

Recent research on bilingual education often takes into account sociopolitical context, including the backdrops of high-stakes testing, the Common Core State Standards, and language policies, as well as rising tides of anti-immigration sentiments and neoliberalism. Participatory action research, in which research is done in collaboration with those affected by the issues being studied, has involved bilingual voices, putting the lived experiences and advocacy of emergent bilinguals in the foreground of the research.

Research in bilingual education faces new directions and new challenges as the field evolves. There has been a push to bridge theory and practice and also to bridge fields. This includes more research exploring intersections of bilingual education and special education, along with the development of anti-racist bilingual education and emphasis on community empowerment. Also, with increased attention in the education field to early childhood and initiatives such as the introduction of universal preschool in New York City, there is more demand for and more activity in research exploring bilingual education in early childhood education.

Heather H. Woodley

See also Cross-Cultural Research; Cultural Competence; Culturally Responsive Evaluation; English Language Proficiency Assessment; Second Language Learners, Assessment of

Further Readings

Baker, C. (2011). *Foundations of bilingual education and bilingualism* (5th ed.). Clevedon, UK: Multilingual Matters.

Cummins, J. (2000). *Language, power and pedagogy: Bilingual children in the crossfire.* Clevedon, UK: Multilingual Matters.

García, O. (2009). *Bilingual education in the 21st century. A global perspective.* Malden, MA: Wiley-Blackwell.

García, O., Zakharia, Z., & Otcu, B. (Eds.). (2013). *Bilingual community education and multilingualism: Beyond heritage languages in a global city.* Bristol, UK: Multilingual Matters.

Krashen, S. D. (1996). *Under attack: The case against bilingual education.* Culver City, CA: Language Education Associates.

Krashen, S., & McField, G. (2005, November/December). What works? Reviewing the latest evidence on bilingual education. *Language Learner, 1*(2), 7–10, 34.

Reyes, S. A., & Kleyn, T. (2010). *Teaching in two languages: A guide for K–12 educators.* Thousand Oaks, CA: Corwin Press.

Rossell, C. H., & Kuder, J. (2005). Meta-murky: A rebuttal to recent meta-analyses of bilingual education. In J. Söhn (Ed.), *The effectiveness of bilingual school programs for immigrant children* (pp. 43–76). Berlin, Germany: Programme on Intercultural Conflicts and Societal Integration (AKI) at the Social Science Research Center Berlin (WZB). Retrieved from https://www.bu.edu/polisci/files/2009/09/Meta-Murky-A-Rebuttal-to-Recent-Meta-Analyses-of-Bilingual-Education.pdf

Thomas, W., & Collier V. (2002). *A national study of school effectiveness for language minority students' long term academic achievement.* Santa Cruz, CA: Center for Research on Education, Diversity & Excellence (CREDE).

Willig, A. (1985). A meta-analysis of selected studies on the effectiveness of bilingual education. *Review of Educational Research, 55*, 269–317.

BILOG-MG

BILOG-MG is a software program for the development, analysis, scoring, and maintenance of educational and other measurement instruments within the statistical framework of item response theory (IRT). As a tool for applying IRT to practical testing problems, the program is concerned with estimating the characteristics of the items in an instrument (the item parameters) and the standing or position of respondents on the underlying attribute or latent trait the items are intended to measure (the person parameters or scale scores). The program is specifically designed for the analysis of item responses classified into two categories (i.e., dichotomously scored or binary items) and offers a wide range of options for fitting IRT models to item response data of that type. This entry describes the program's capabilities, the models and estimation procedures it implements, and the types of applications it accommodates.

Overview of the Program's Features and Capabilities

Housed within a Windows graphical point-and-click interface, BILOG-MG is designed for the IRT analysis of instruments comprising dichotomously scored sets or subsets of items intended to measure a single underlying attribute or latent dimension. As an extension of the BILOG program of Robert J. Mislevy and R. Darrell Bock to multiple groups of respondents, the program accommodates a broad range of practical applications that involve one or more than one group of respondents and one or more than one test form (version) of an instrument. The program offers an array of options for estimating the parameters of the items in an instrument, the scale scores of persons completing it, and the latent distributions of the groups or populations represented in the data. It also provides numerous indices and plots to inform and guide the development of instruments with good measurement properties.

Models for Dichotomously Scored Items

As a program specifically designed for the IRT analysis of dichotomously scored items, BILOG-MG relies on binary logistic functions to model the relationship between the characteristics of an item and the probability that a person with a given level of the underlying trait (typically denoted as θ) will respond to the item in one of two predefined categories. The categories may represent correct and incorrect responses to multiple-choice problems on

a test of educational achievement, the presence or absence of symptoms recorded on a checklist of characteristics associated with a particular medical condition, or some other binary classification of the responses to the items in an instrument. The latent trait measured with the items may be verbal proficiency, spatial ability, generalized anxiety, or any number of other underlying attributes that an individual may possess. In educational applications, the underlying trait often represents some form of cognitive proficiency measured by correct and incorrect responses to a set of multiple-choice or short-answer questions. The discussion that follows frames the program's features and models in those terms, referring to the underlying trait as proficiency and denoting the probability that a person with proficiency θ will respond to item j with a correct response $(xj = 1)$ as $P(xj = 1 \theta = Pj\theta)$.

BILOG-MG implements three binary logistic functions for the IRT analysis of dichotomously scored items, the one-, two-, and three-parameter models. The names indicate the number of item parameters in each model. The two-parameter model, for example, expresses the probability of a correct response to item j as a function of a person's proficiency and two parameters specific to item j that must be estimated from the data:

$$Pj\theta = 1(1 + e - aj\theta - bj).$$

The aj parameter represents the slope or discrimination power of the item. It indicates the extent to which an item discriminates among individuals with higher and lower levels of proficiency. Items with higher values of a are more effective in differentiating among individuals than items with lower values of a. The bj parameter represents the difficulty or threshold parameter of the item. It indicates the position or location of the item on the θ scale of proficiency. Items with higher positions on the scale are more difficult than items with lower positions on the scale. In the two-parameter model (as well as in the one-parameter model), the threshold parameter of an item is located at the point on the scale where a person with that scale score has a .5 probability of answering the item correctly.

The simplest of the three models, the one-parameter model, also known as the Rasch model, assumes that the items are equally discriminating.

In other words, the *a* parameter is the same for all items and a person's probability of answering an item correctly simply depends on the difficulty level of that item and person's level of proficiency. The least restrictive of the models, the three-parameter model, adds a parameter to the two-parameter model to take into account the effect of guessing on responses to an item. It is commonly used in the analysis of multiple-choice items where a respondent may answer an item correctly simply by chance.

Models for Multiple-Group and Multiple-Form Applications

By necessity or by design, measurement instruments often consist of more than a single test form. In educational applications, the forms might represent different versions of an instrument developed over time to prevent overexposure of the item content or to satisfy item disclosure requirements or correspond to age- or grade-specific versions of an instrument developed to monitor the educational achievement of children as they progress through school. In these cases, and whenever an instrument consists of more than one form, the forms must be equated for the scores to have the same meaning across forms. In IRT, it means placing the item parameter estimates from each form on a common scale. Various procedures that involve converting estimates from separate IRT analyses of the forms are used for that purpose.

Beyond simply carrying out a separate calibration of each form, BILOG-MG performs equivalent and nonequivalent groups equating in a single IRT analysis of the data from all test forms. When the groups completing each form are random samples of respondents from the same population (equivalent groups), it treats the forms as if they were one test administered to a single population and performs a conventional IRT analysis. When the groups completing each form are composed of respondents from different populations or from different subgroups within a population (nonequivalent groups), the program places the items on a common scale with a multiple-group model that takes into account differences among the latent distributions of the groups as it estimates the parameters of the items. The estimation

procedure allows for the simultaneous estimation of the latent distributions and the item parameters makes the program suitable for a wide range of practical applications that involve more than one group of respondents and one or more than one test form.

In estimating the item parameters of the one-, two-, and three-parameter models, the multiple-group models assume that the item response function for any given item is the same across all groups of respondents, except in applications of differential item functioning and item parameter drift over time. The differential item functioning and item parameter drift models allow the difficulty of the items to vary from group to group or from occasion to occasion to test for and identify Item × Subgroup interactions (differential item functioning) and Item × Time of Testing interactions (item parameter drift).

Estimation of the Item Parameters and Latent Distributions of Proficiency

To obtain estimates of the item parameters and the latent distributions of proficiency, BILOG-MG relies on the marginal maximum likelihood method proposed by Bock and Murray Aitkin and its extension to multiple groups of respondents detailed by Bock and Michele Zimowski. The procedure provides for the simultaneous estimation of the item parameters and the latent distribution or distributions of proficiency when there are multiple groups of respondents. Except in special situations, the marginal maximum likelihood procedure assumes that the response to a particular item is independent of the responses to other items in the test for all persons with the same level of proficiency (i.e., the assumption of conditional independence). The procedure also assumes that respondents in each group are drawn from some population in which the latent distribution of proficiency has a specified shape.

To start the estimation procedure, the user must specify the shape of the latent distribution of each group represented in the item response data. BILOG-MG offers several options for that purpose, including the program default of a normal distribution. When the assumption of a normal distribution seems untenable, the user has the option of specifying the shape of the distribution, keeping it fixed at its initial specification, or estimating it directly from the patterns of correct and incorrect responses along with the item parameters in the iterative estimation procedure.

In applications consisting of a single group of respondents, the program sets the mean and standard deviation of the latent distribution to zero and one to resolve the indeterminacy in the origin and unit of the latent distribution of proficiency. In applications involving more than one group of respondents, the user may choose to resolve the indeterminacy by setting the mean and standard deviation of the combined distributions of all groups to zero and one or by selecting one group as the reference group and setting the mean and standard deviation of its distribution to zero and one. Depending on the option selected, the means and standard deviations of the groups are set relative to the reference group or relative to the mean and standard deviation of the combined groups.

The estimation procedure generates marginal maximum likelihood estimates of the item parameters, except when the user chooses to impose prior distributions on the item parameters, in which case it generates marginal maximum a posteriori estimates. Depending on the model selected, the program generates estimates of the slope (a), threshold (b), intercept ($-a \times b$), lower asymptote (guessing parameter), and a one-factor item loading for each item included in the analysis, along with the respective standard errors. It also provides estimates of the means and standard deviations of the latent distributions of proficiency of the groups.

The program generates several indices for assessing the fit of a model to the item response data. When all or nearly all response patterns are present in the data, the program computes a likelihood ratio chi-square statistic for testing the overall Goodness-of-Fit of the model to the data. When that statistic is not available, the change in the negative of the marginal log likelihood between the one- and two-parameter models and the two- and three-parameter models can be used to assess whether adding parameters to the item response model improves fit. When a test consists of more than 20 items, the program generates an approximate chi-square test of item fit for each item in a test.

Estimating Scale Scores and Evaluating the Functioning of the Instrument

BILOG-MG computes three types of IRT scale scores or estimates of proficiency—maximum likelihood, Bayes's or expected a posteriori, and Bayes's modal or maximum a posteriori estimates. The user has the option of generating the estimates in the scale of the item parameters or rescaling them to another metric with a linear transformation or with respect to the location and scale of the scale score estimates in the sample. If expected a posteriori estimates are selected, the user also has the option of specifying the prior distribution to be used in their estimation and of rescaling the estimates with respect to the location and scale of the latent distribution.

For evaluating properties of the scale scores, the program computes the first four moments of the scale score distribution and an estimate of empirical reliability based on the IRT scale score variance and mean square error. For evaluating the properties of the individual items and the instrument as a whole, it plots item, test, and test-form information curves and computes theoretical reliabilities based on the item parameters, assuming normal latent distributions of proficiency.

Availability of the Program

BILOG-MG may be purchased from the website of Scientific Software International. SSI distributes the program electronically. For those who simply wish to examine the program, a free trial version is available for inspection for up to 15 days after the program is downloaded.

Michele F. Zimowski

See also Conditional Independence; Differential Item Functioning; Equating; Item Response Theory; Marginal Maximum Likelihood Estimation; Prior Distribution; Rasch Model

Further Readings

Bock, R. D., & Aitkin, M. (1981). Marginal maximum likelihood estimation of item parameters: Application of an EM algorithm. *Psychometrika*, 46(4), 443–459.

Bock, R. D., & Mislevy, R. J. (1982). Adaptive EAP estimation of ability in a microcomputer environment. *Applied Psychological Measurement, 6,* 431–444.

Bock, R. D., & Zimowski, M. F. (1997). Multiple group IRT. In W. J. van der Linden & R. K. Hambleton (Eds.), *Handbook of modern item response theory* (pp. 433–448). New York, NY: Springer.

du Toit, M. (Ed.). (2003). *IRT from SSI: BILOG-MG, MULTILOG, PARSCALE, TESTFACT.* Lincolnwood, IL: Scientific Software International.

Mislevy, R. J. (1984). Estimating latent distributions. *Psychometrika, 49,* 359–381.

Mislevy, R. J. (1986). Bayes modal estimation in item response models. *Psychometrika, 51,* 177–195.

Mislevy, R. J., & Stocking, M. L. (1989). A consumer's guide to LOGIST and BILOG. *Applied Psychological Measurement, 13,* 57–75.

Websites

Scientific Software International: http://www.ssicentral .com/

BINOMIAL TEST

Binomial experiments consist of a series of two or more independent trials, where each trial in the series results in one of two outcomes: a success or a failure. The purpose of the binomial test is to determine for such experiments whether the number of observed successes warrants rejection of an assumed probability of success, π. For example, a gambler may posit that the probability of getting a head in a flip of a coin is .5. A binomial test could be used to determine whether the number of heads observed in a series of independent flips warrants rejection of that hypothesis. This entry describes educational research applications, states the hypothesis and assumptions, defines and illustrates the exact probability computations, defines and illustrates the normal theory approximation, and discusses the consequences of violating the independence assumption.

Educational Research Applications

An educational researcher may believe that the probability of a child answering multiple-choice questions (with four options) correctly on a chemistry pretest is .25. That hypothesis could be tested using the binomial test, which would consider the number of successes (i.e., correctly answered questions) in a series of independently administered pretest questions. Another educational researcher may want to test the hypothesis that there is a .50 probability that an elementary school principal will support a newly proposed district policy. If so, principals could be independently sampled and interviewed to determine whether they supported the policy. A binomial test could be used to determine whether the number of successes (i.e., observed supporters) was (or was not) sufficient to reject the hypothesis that the probability of support was .50.

As a final example, consider an educational researcher who is interested in whether an intervention would increase the prosocial behavior of children with behavioral and emotional disturbances. The researcher could hypothesize that the probability of observing an increase in prosocial behavior for a child was .50. A binomial test could be used to determine whether the number of successes (i.e., number of children with observed improvements) in an independent sample was sufficient to reject the null hypothesis that the probability was .50. This final application of the binomial test would often be referred to as a sign test because it is based on counting up the number of positive and negative signed differences.

Hypothesis and Assumptions

The binomial test allows us to test the null hypothesis that the probability of success (π) is equal to some researcher specified value a. For a nondirectional test, the null hypothesis is H_0: $\pi = a$, and for a directional test, the null hypothesis is either H_0: $\pi \le a$ or H_0: $\pi \ge a$. The probability calculations, which are based on the binomial distribution, assume:

1. Observations are sampled from a binary population (i.e., there are only two possible values for each observation, a success or a failure).

2. Each observation is independent implying that it is not affected by any of the other observations.

3. The probability of a success is fixed for the population.

Binomial Probabilities

For a binomial experiment where the probability of success in any one trial is π, the probability that there will be r successes in n trials is computed as:

$$P(r) = {}_nC_r \times p^r \times (1-p)^{(n-r)},$$

where ${}_nC_r$ is the number of combinations of n things taking r at a time where ${}_nC_r = n! / (r!(n-r)!)$.

Illustration

Suppose a science education researcher is anticipating a student will not have the prerequisite knowledge to answer chemistry questions prior to instruction and thus expects that on a multiple-choice pretest the item responses from the student would be random guesses. For a pretest that consists of 5 multiple-choice items, each with 5 options, the researcher is hypothesizing that the probability of successfully answering a question is .20. To test the null hypothesis that H_0: $\pi = .20$ at an α level of .05, the researcher could first compute the probability that a student answers 0, 1, 2, 3, 4, or 5 questions successfully using the binomial probability formula.

$$p(0) = {}_nC_r \times p^r \times (1-p)^{(n-r)}$$
$$= 5! / (0! \times 5!) \times .20^0 \times .80^5$$
$$= .32768.$$

$$p(1) = {}_nC_r \times p^r * (1-p)^{(n-r)}$$
$$= 5! / (1! \times 4!) \times .20^1 \times .80^4 = .4096.$$

$$p(2) = {}_nC_r \times p^r \times (1-p)^{(n-r)}$$
$$= 5! / (2! \times 3!) \times .20^2 \times .80^3 = .2048.$$

$$p(3) = {}_nC_r \times p^r \times (1-p)^{(n-r)}$$
$$= 5! / (3! \times 2!) \times .20^3 \times .80^2 = .0512.$$

$$p(4) = {}_nC_r \times p^r \times (1-p)^{(n-r)}$$
$$= 5! / (4! \times 1!) \times .20^4 \times .80^1 = .0064.$$

$$p(5) = {}_nC_r \times p^r \times (1-p)^{(n-r)}$$
$$= 5! / (5! \times 0!) \times .20^5 \times .80^0 = .00032.$$

Note that if we sum these probabilities, we get 1.0 because the student had to answer 0, 1, 2, 3, 4, or 5 questions correctly. Next, to conduct the binomial test, we add the probability corresponding to the observed number of successes to all probabilities that correspond to numbers of successes that are as far or farther from what was hypothesized. If the student answered 4 items successfully, we would compute the probability of successfully answering four or more questions as .0064 + .00032 = .00672. Because this probability is less than our α of .05, we would reject the null hypothesis that $\pi = .20$, which in this context suggests that the student did not randomly guess but had some of the needed prerequisite knowledge.

Normal Distribution Approximation

When the number of trials is relatively small ($n < 25$), it is feasible to evaluate the exact binomial probability for each successful occasion. However, when there is a large number of trials, it could be tedious for researchers to compute the exact binomial probabilities for every possible number of success. With larger n, especially when the probability of success is close to 0.5, the binomial test could be alternatively conducted using the normal approximation approach. The normal probability approximation approach can be applied by simply evaluating the mean and standard deviation of the binomial distribution and then substituting these values into the Z score transformation formula. The computation of normal variate Z for the normal approximation is as follows:

$$Z = X - npnp(1-p),$$

where X is the number of success, np is the mean of the binomial probability distribution, and $np(1-p)$ is the standard deviation of the binomial probability distribution.

Because the binomial distribution is discrete and the normal distribution is a continuous distribution, a continuity adjustment can be applied as well.

$$Z = Xa - npnp(1-p),$$

where Xa is adjusted number of success for the discrete number of success X, such that $Xa = X - 0.5$ for a lower bound or $Xa = X + 0.5$ for an upper bound.

Note that with a large number of trials ($n > 25$), the Z is assumed to distribute as a normal distribution with 0 mean and 1 standard deviation (i.e., standard normal distribution). Once the Z score of the normal approximation for the binomial probability is computed, then the probability of X successes out of n trials can be calculated using the standard normal distribution probability. An illustration of the binomial test with the normal probability approximation is given next.

Continuing from the previous example, suppose that a pretest consists of 20 multiple-choice items, instead of 5 items, and each item has five options. The researcher anticipates that for students who did not have the prerequisite knowledge to answer the pretest, the probability of successfully answering a question correctly is still 0.2. To test the null hypothesis that H_0: $\pi = .20$ at an α level of .05, the researcher could compute the probability that the student answers 0, 1, 2, 3, and up to 20 questions successfully with the hypothesized probability 0.2 (or guessing probability). This computation with the binomial probability distribution can be time-consuming and tedious, but the normal approximation for the binomial distribution can be readily applied. If the student answered 8 items correctly, then the researcher would compute the probability of successfully answering 8 or more questions as follows.

$$Z = 8 - (20)(0.2)(20)(0.2)(0.8)$$

= 2.24 without correction for the continuity

or

$$Z = 7.5 - (20)(0.2)(20)(0.2)(0.8)$$

= 1.96 with correction for the continuity.

Note that Xa is $X - 0.5$ because the number of success is at least 8 for the discrete probability (binomial distribution), and thus the continuous probability (normal distribution) would include all values that would round to a value of 8 or higher. Then,

$$p(X > 8) =$$
$$p(Z > 2.24)$$
= .0127 without correction for the continuity.

or

$$p(X > 7.5)$$
$$= p(Z > 1.96)$$
= .0252 with correction for the continuity.

Because the probability is less than our α of .05, we would reject the null hypothesis that $\pi = .20$, which suggests that the student did not randomly guess but had prerequisite knowledge.

Consequences of Violations of the Independence Assumption

As noted previously, the binomial test is based on the assumption of independence. This entry next reviews a couple applications of the binomial test in educational research where independence could be questioned, and as a consequence, the validity of the binomial test could be challenged. In the context of analyzing single-case studies, researchers may estimate a trend line during the baseline phase and then compare the observations in the treatment phase to an extension of the baseline trend line. The binomial test was considered as a method of testing whether the proportion of observations in the intervention phase that exceeded the extrapolated baseline trend was greater than .50, which in turn would indicate a treatment effect. John Crosbie used simulations to show that the Type I error rate of the binomial test was substantially affected by autocorrelation (nonzero serial correlation), and thus the binomial test was not valid for this application.

Anthony Onwuegbuzie, Joel Levin, and John Ferron considered contexts where researchers examine differences between groups on a series of measures. A binomial test was considered as a method for testing whether the number of signed mean differences (e.g., $M_{Tx(i)} - M_{Control(i)}$ for variable i) was sufficient to reject the null hypothesis that the probability of the mean difference being positive was .50. They showed that when the variables being examined were correlated, the signed differences were not independent and that the binomial test failed to control the Type I error rate unless corrections were made for the dependency. In short, these studies show that when the trials in the binomial experiment are not independent of each other, the statistical validity of the binomial test is compromised.

John M. Ferron and Seang-Hwane Joo

See also Autocorrelation; Bernoulli Distribution; Maximum Likelihood Estimation; Normal Distribution; Single-Case Research; Type I Error

Further Readings

Crosbie, J. (1987). The inability of the binomial test to control Type I error with single-subject data. *Behavioral Assessment, 9,* 141–150.

Onwuegbuzie, A. J., Levin, J. R., & Ferron, J. M. (2011). A binomial test of group differences with correlated outcome measures. *Journal of Experimental Education, 79,* 127–142.

Ware, W. B., Ferron, J. M., & Miller, B. M. (2013). *Introductory statistics: A conceptual approach using R.* New York, NY: Routledge.

Bipolar Disorder

Bipolar disorders (formerly known as manic depressive illnesses) are a set of mood disorders in which patients experience phases or cycles of mood symptoms that create clinically significant impairment in daily functioning. Bipolar disorders are distinguished from unipolar depression by the inclusion of cycles that consist of unusually high, overly joyful, expansive, or irritable moods, denoted as manic episodes.

According to the *Diagnostic and Statistical Manual of Mental Disorders, Fifth Edition,* bipolar disorders were classified as bipolar I disorder, bipolar II disorder, cyclothymic disorder, substance/medication-induced bipolar disorder, and bipolar disorder due to another medical condition. The shared link of all of these disorders is the presence of episodes that include abnormally severe elevated and depressed moods. The primary difference between these specific disorders is the duration of episodes, timing, course, and etiology. The disorder, in all forms, is estimated to affect as much as 3.9% of the U.S. population.

In the early 20th century, German psychiatrist Emil Kraepelin studied the course of bipolar disorder and provide detailed descriptions of the condition in adults. Since that time, descriptions and conceptualizations have remained relatively consistent, and the focus of the disorder continues to be on adult-onset cases. Although the average age of onset for bipolar disorder is 18 years, symptom onset can vary and there has recently been an increased focus on adolescent- and childhood-onset forms.

Prevalence rates among adolescents are fairly similar to those observed among adults (1–2%), whereas prevalence rates among children are not well established. Despite increased attention to early-onset cases, common diagnostic criteria continue to focus on symptoms in adults. As a result, the diagnostic criteria are often challenging to apply to children. Strict adherence to the adult-based set of diagnostic criteria in children may miss some young individuals with bipolar disorder who have developmentally different symptoms, whereas extremely liberal application of the criteria may result in over diagnosing children with typical mood swings or other behavioral difficulties.

Due to episodic mood, behavior, energy, and sleep disturbances, there may be considerable social and educational challenges for children and adolescents who develop bipolar disorder with more significant impact with earlier onset. Due in part to the historic view of bipolar disorder as an adult disorder, treatment for bipolar disorders in youths has typically mirrored treatment for adults. Initial treatment is focused toward mood stabilization and behavior management. In addition, though, treatment often incorporates use of collaborative interventions that optimize family and educational strengths.

Students who have been diagnosed with bipolar disorder may qualify for special instruction and academic accommodations from an individualized education program or Section 504 plan, which allow for accommodations under the "emotional disability" or "other health-impaired" exceptionalities. With adequate supports at home and at school and from medical providers, many young people diagnosed with bipolar disorder may develop appropriate strategies to lead productive and educationally successful lives.

Ben P. Hunter, Ryan W. Schroeder,
and Kelli L. Netson

See also *Diagnostic and Statistical Manual of Mental Disorders*; Individualized Education Program; Self-Regulation

Further Readings

American Psychiatric Association. (2013). *Diagnostic and statistical manual of mental disorder* (5th ed.). Washington, DC: Author.

Goodwin, F. K., & Jamison, K. R. (2007). *Manic-depressive illness: Bipolar disorders and recurrent depression* (2nd ed.). New York, NY: Oxford University Press.

Grier, E. C., Wilkins, M. L., & Pender, C. A. S. (2007). Bipolar disorder: Educational implications for secondary student. *Principal Leadership, 7*(8), 12–15.

BLOOM'S TAXONOMY

Bloom's taxonomy is a multitiered model of classifying expected or intended educational learning objectives according to cognitive levels of complexity and mastery. Initially developed during the 1950s and later named after the American educational psychologist Benjamin S. Bloom, the model is concerned with the cognitive or thinking domain of learning. This entry describes both the original Bloom's taxonomy and the revised version, which also classifies learning objectives by the types of knowledge used in thinking. The entry discusses specific changes made in terminology, structure, and emphasis in the revised version of the taxonomy and discusses the practical application of the taxonomy to the educational setting.

Bloom sought to provide a logical, progressive model that identified and classified all cognitive educational outcomes from simple to complex. Recognized by educational researchers and practitioners alike as an effective empirical model for measuring the cognitive or thinking domain of learning, Bloom's taxonomy endures as a widely applied and taught framework across PreK–12 and higher education contexts.

Original Bloom's Taxonomy

Bloom initiated the idea of creating a theoretical model of learning that sought to identify and classify all educational objectives during discussions that took place at the 1948 Convention of the American Psychological Association. Intended for university academics, Bloom hoped that in doing this work he could aid academics in reducing duplicate or redundant test items measuring the same educational learning objectives. Eight years later, Bloom and his colleagues followed through on his initial idea, identifying three domains of educational learning:

Cognitive: knowledge or thinking

Affective: attitude or self

Psychomotor: manual or physical skills

First published in 1956 under the title *Taxonomy of Educational Objectives: The Classification of Educational Goals. Handbook I: Cognitive Domain,* the cognitive domain of learning was later renamed Bloom's taxonomy after Bloom as the model's primary developer. In education, the prime focus has been on Bloom's cognitive domain of learning.

Bloom's taxonomy is a hierarchical, six-tiered model of classifying thinking based on specific cognitive levels of complexity, starting from the simplest to most complex. The original six classification levels of the taxonomy are (1) *knowledge,* (2) *comprehension,* (3) *application,* (4) *analysis,* (5) *synthesis,* and (6) *evaluation.* The taxonomy was created to assist both educational researchers and practitioners to understand the fundamental, step-by-step process in which people develop and attain new knowledge and intellectual skills. In other words, the lower classification levels of the taxonomy must be

	Definition	**Example action verbs**
Evaluation	Make a judgment of the value of information for a given purpose using an external or self-selected criteria and rationale. As the highest level in the cognitive domain, it contains elements of all other classification levels	Justify, recommend, judge, defend, critique, predict, argue, appraise, consider, and evaluate
Synthesis	Mentally construct or put together information from a variety of sources to form a meaningful, integrated, and new complex idea	Hypothesize, plan, construct, create, invent, design, propose, formulate, integrate, and combine
Analysis	Deconstruct complex information into its constituent parts and interpret relationships and organization between these parts	Sequence, compare, contrast, categorize, analyze, survey, note causes/effects, classify, prioritize, and order
Application	Use or apply knowledge to new concrete situations	Research, apply, solve, organize, produce, generalize, perform, respond, use, and prepare
Comprehension	Understand and be aware of the literal meaning of the new information	Explain, restate, reference, retell, interpret, summarize, translate, give examples, paraphrase, and distinguish
Knowledge	Recall and recognize information as it was previously learned	List, memorize, label, describe, identify, define, recognize, select, reproduce, and locate

Figure 1   Bloom's taxonomy of educational learning objectives

understood and mastered before progressing to the next. Figure 1 presents the taxonomy with definitions and example action verbs for each classification level.

Bloom's levels define the steps in development of thought, and each level increases in cognitive difficulty. As such, educators often interpret the levels of the taxonomy as climbing a staircase of cognitive complexity, from lower to higher ordered thinking.

Revised Bloom's Taxonomy

In 1995, a former student of Bloom, Lorin W. Anderson, and David R. Krathwohl, a member of the academic team that developed the original Bloom's taxonomy, assembled and led a team of cognitive psychologists, teacher educators, curriculum specialists, and educational researchers in revising the taxonomy to more accurately represent 21st century teaching and learning. In 2001, Anderson and Krathwohl published their work titled *A Taxonomy for Learning, Teaching, and Assessing: A Revision of Bloom's Taxonomy of Educational Objectives*. Intentionally designed to assist educators in understanding and implementing standards-based curricula, the revised Bloom's taxonomy presents a two-dimensional model focused on both cognitive and knowledge processes. Figure 2 presents the revised Bloom's taxonomy in its most frequently depicted table or matrix form and includes the subcategories of levels for both cognitive and knowledge processes.

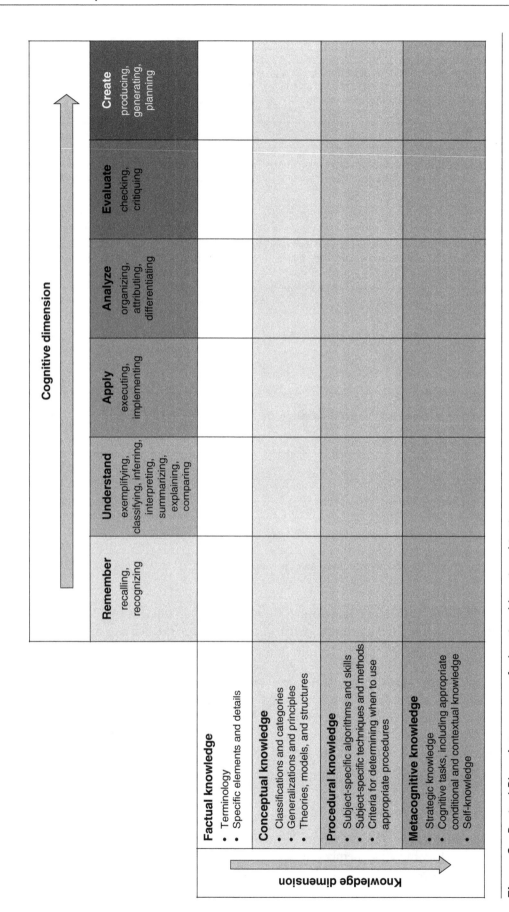

Figure 2   Revised Bloom's taxonomy of educational learning objectives

Source: Adapted from Tables 3.1 (p. 28), 3.2 (p. 29), and 3.3 (p. 31) and Figure 3.1 (p. 32), Anderson & Krathwohl (2001).

Specific Changes

When deciding on what changes should be made to the original taxonomy, Anderson and Krathwohl's team not only considered their own expertise but also considered the critiques and concerns expressed about the model by Bloom himself. The revised Bloom's taxonomy includes changes made to the terminology, structure, and emphasis as compared to the original taxonomy.

Terminology

Perhaps the most obvious differences between the two models are the changes in terminology. To reflect a more active form of thinking, the revised Bloom's taxonomy changed the names of the original six cognitive classification levels from noun to verb forms. Moreover, the lowest level of the original taxonomy, *knowledge*, was renamed to *remember* as were *comprehension* and *synthesis* renamed to *understand* and *create*.

Structure

In addition to making changes in terminology, Anderson and Krathwohl made alterations to its structure. The decision to switch the placement of the highest two levels of the taxonomy, *evaluation* (*evaluate*) and *synthesis* (*create*), represents the authors' assertion that learners' cognitive ability to evaluate came before their ability to synthesize or create. Additionally, they developed a separate *knowledge dimension* of the taxonomy that defined four classification levels of knowledge used in cognition. The levels of the *knowledge dimension* are (1) *factual*, (2) *conceptual*, (3) *procedural*, and (4) *metacognitive*. As such, the revised Bloom's structure is a two-dimensional model and is typically depicted in matrix form that identifies the types of knowledge to be learned (*knowledge dimension*) and the processes used to learn (*cognitive dimension*) these types of knowledge. Furthermore, the classification levels of both dimensions are also subdivided into either three or four categories in the *knowledge dimension* and three to eight categories in the *cognitive dimension*.

Emphasis

Finally, the revised taxonomy is intended for a much broader audience than the narrow higher education purpose of the original. Rather, these changes emphasize the revised model as a more useful and authentic tool to guide all educators in curriculum and assessment development and instructional planning and delivery. Additional emphasis placed on description and explanation of the dimensions' subcategories in the revised taxonomy aim to provide more coherence to the model.

Application of Bloom's Taxonomy to the Educational Setting

In both its original and revised forms, Bloom's taxonomy is used by educators across all levels and subjects to describe the degree to which they want students to know, understand, and use concepts. Bloom's taxonomy provides educators with a common vocabulary for developing comprehensive lists of educational learning objectives for classroom instruction representative of the breadth and depth of all cognitive and knowledge processes. In doing so, Bloom's taxonomy supports the alignment of student learning objectives with curriculum, instruction, and assessment. Applying the model can involve use of classification level verbs to plan and structure questions as part of daily lesson planning to promote higher order thinking in students. The model also can be used to create a table of specifications to design assessments in order to ensure a representative sample of assessment items across all levels of the thinking and knowledge dimensions.

Rachel Darley Gary

See also Backward Design; Critical Thinking; Goals and Objectives; Learning Theories; Metacognition; Zone of Proximal Development

Further Readings

Anderson, L. W., & Krathwohl, D. R. (Eds.). (2001). *A taxonomy for learning, teaching, and assessing: A revision of Bloom's taxonomy of educational objectives*. New York, NY: Longman.

Bloom, B. S. (Ed.). (1956). *Taxonomy of educational objectives: The classification of educational goals. Handbook I: Cognitive domain*. New York, NY: David McKay Company.

Hoy, A. W., Stinnett, A. M., Fernie, D. E., O'Sullivan, M., & Gabel, S. E. (2002). Revising Bloom's taxonomy. *Theory Into Practice, 41*(4), 212–218.

Body of Work Method

Body of work is a methodology used for standard setting. Broadly, standard setting is a process used to determine minimally acceptable scores of an assessment. Originally developed by Stuart Kahl, Timothy Crockett, Charles DePascale, and Sally Rindfleisch, the body of work method is generally used for setting standards for assessments that include, but are not limited to, constructed response tasks. Because examples of real student work are the heart of the body of work method, the process is considered an examinee-centered method rather than a test-centered method, which would focus more on the test items themselves. This entry discusses the work leading up to standard setting using the body of work method, what happens during the process, and the evidence that is collected to support the results generated by this method.

During the body of work process, panels of individuals with deep knowledge of the target content area convene to review examples of student work that have been previously scored. After training, the task of each panelist is to match the characteristics of that work to performance levels and extended descriptions of the student knowledge and skills required at each performance level. As panelists iteratively review the student work, sorting the work into performance levels, the scores that divide the performance levels, called cut scores, are determined.

Precursors to Standard Setting

Before standard setting, performance-level descriptors are written, describing what students should know and be able to do at different levels. A performance level could be labeled by a number or a phrase, such as Level 5, Level 4, or Level 3 or advanced, proficient, or needs improvement. The performance levels and descriptors themselves may be written by the governing body of the assessment (e.g., state education agency) along with the assessment developers and then reviewed and revised by content experts. One of the levels

may be deemed as the minimum "passing" level. For example, a Level 3 might be the level that a student must achieve to be "meeting the standards" in a particular content area.

Also prior to standard setting, the assessment is administered to students and the results analyzed and scored according to the guidelines established by the test developers. For the body of work method, actual examples of student responses at all possible score points are pulled from the entire population of completed tests. The samples of student work selected for standard setting may be double scored to ensure that the standard-setting event is based on reliable test results.

Preparation for Standard Setting

The general steps that lead up to a standard setting event involve recruiting subject matter experts to serve as panelists, arranging for panel facilitators, and preparing the materials needed during the meeting itself. Standard setting panelists should be subject matter experts in the content covered by the assessment and have experience with student work in the content area. Generally, panelists are selected to represent a wide variety of experiences, population characteristics, and geographical regions.

The facilitators have experience working with groups and are specifically trained in the body of work method. The facilitator's role is to guide panelists through the standard setting tasks, adhering precisely to the body of work procedure without directly or indirectly influencing the standard setting results in any manner. Additionally, the body of work method is material intensive. The iterative rounds of student work review require examples at all possible test score points. Examples of student work are organized into folders for each standard setting round: training, range-finding, and pinpointing.

During Standard Setting

Panelist Training

For optimal results, panelists must understand their responsibilities during each round of the standard setting process. Thoroughly reviewing examples of student work and sorting the work into performance categories is challenging yet important work, and each panelist should feel comfortable with the steps. Thus, several training activities are completed before the actual standard setting process begins.

First, it is common to ask participants to, on their own, respond to the same tasks that were required of the examinee on the assessment. The purpose of this activity is to familiarize the participant with the assessment tasks, the student performance required by the tasks, and the general difficulty of the tasks.

An additional step for panelist training involves deep review of the performance-level descriptors. Panelists may also consider what separates a student performing near the bottom of a performance level from a student performing near the middle. Considering the knowledge and skills of a student who is "just barely" in a category helps panelists focus on student performance that is near the cut score.

Finally, to prepare for the actual standard setting rounds, panelists complete a practice round. With body of work, panelists review a small group of student work samples (five–eight sets) representing a range of possible scores. Scores on each sample are hidden from the panelists but known to facilitators. Panelists proceed through the training examples, reviewing student responses and comparing each to statements found in the performance-level descriptors. After review, panelists place each response set into a performance category, anonymously marking their judgment on a rating sheet.

Once the rating sheets have been completed, facilitators compile the ratings for each response set and display the collective ratings so that panelists can see how they generally agreed or disagreed with each other. Panelists then discuss their ratings as a group, noting the particular characteristics of the task, the student responses, and/or the performance-level descriptors that contributed to their rating. Panelists may change their ratings based on discussion with peers; however, consensus is not a requirement of the body of work process.

Range-Finding

Once the training activities and practice round conclude, panelists begin the first body of work round known as the range-finding round. The purpose of the range-finding round is to make a first "rough cut" of the dividing point between performance levels.

Panelists begin by reviewing folders of student work that represent a range of possible assessment scores. Although the scores are still unknown to the panelists, the sets of student work are ordered within a range-finding folder by score. Once panelists have sorted the student work into different performance levels, facilitators record the ratings given to each student response set. Panelists may then discuss ratings as a group, reasoning for differences or similarities. Panelists may choose to change their own ratings based on discussion but do not have to do so.

At this point in the process, the cut score is the point where specific student response sets are clearly separated into different performance levels. However, if panelists disagree and there is overlap in the ratings of a particular response set, the overlap occurring near the cut score.

Pinpointing

Pinpointing folders allow panelists to view several examples of student work at particular score points in order to focus on a more precise location of a cut score. Pinpointing folders consist of several examples (about four to five) at every score point possible on the assessment. Before the standard setting meeting, the folders are prepopulated with example student responses to both constructed response and selected response items (where appropriate); however, the assessment scores remain hidden from panelists.

After reviewing the range-finding results and examining the overlap between the panelist ratings, facilitators select pinpointing folders that are near the cut scores. For example, if student work with scores between 16 and 18 was rated by panelists as both Level 4 and Level 3, but not Level 2, then pinpointing folders containing more examples of student work at scores of 16, 17, and 18 would be chosen for further review. The panelists then sort each work example into performance Level 4 or 3, again based on the statements in the performance-level descriptors.

Calculating the Cut Score

Once panelists have independently recorded their ratings of student work samples, facilitators take the data from the rating sheets and begin to calculate the cut scores. One method used to calculate cut scores is logistic regression. For the underlying variable test score, the cut score would be placed where the probability of a test score being assigned to a particular performance level is .5. An alternative method is to calculate a median score from panelist ratings on each side of two adjacent performance categories.

Evidence to Support Results

During and after standard setting, evidence should be gathered to support the reliability and generalizability of the body of work results. For example, panelists could be asked via survey to evaluate the overall standard setting process along indicators such as (a) clarity of instruction on the process, (b) level of understanding of the process, and (c) confidence in ratings and final cut scores. Additionally, standard errors of the cut scores that describe the variability in the cut scores among the participating panelists can be calculated. Interpretation of this standard error helps determine the extent to which panelists' placement of cut scores was consistent with each other. Additional evidence could be collected from replications of the body of work process in other locations or with other panelists, though these methods are logistically more complex.

Once the standard setting event concludes, the compiled cut score calculations and generalizability evidence are presented to the assessment's governing body for review, possible adjustment, and final approval.

Gail Tiemann

See also Achievement Tests; Angoff Method; Ebel Method; Psychometrics; Standard Setting; Tests

Further Readings

Kahl, S. R., Crockett, T. J., DePascale, C. A., & Rindfleisch, S. L. (1994, June). *Using actual student work to determine cut scores for proficiency levels: New methods for new tests.* Paper presented at the National Conference on Large-Scale Assessment, Albuquerque, NM.

Kahl, S. R., Crockett, T. J., DePascale, C. A., & Rindfleisch, S. L. (1995, June). *Setting standards for performance levels using the occupational tests.* Princeton, NJ: Educational Testing Service.

Kingston, N. M., & Tiemann, G. C. (2012). Setting performance standards on complex assessments: The body of work method. In G. J. Cizek (Ed.), *Setting performance standards: Foundations, methods, and innovations* (2nd ed.). New York, NY: Routledge.

BONFERRONI PROCEDURE

Researchers interested in determining differences between the means of groups often employ analysis of variance (ANOVA) as a first test to determine whether differences exist. When the ANOVA test indicates that differences do exist among the group means, the next step involved is identifying which group means differ. This is typically done using either contrast tests or post hoc tests on the mean. One popular post hoc test to determine which group means differ is the Bonferroni procedure, named for Carlo E. Bonferroni, the Italian statistician who popularized the approach in the early 20th century. This entry further describes the procedure and how it is used to deal with experiment-wise error rates and for multiple comparisons.

The Bonferroni procedure is a very important tool in statistical inference and is typically used in multiple comparison situations, which is applied to many areas where multiple tests need to be conducted while preserving an overall family-wise error rate (FWR). One of the beautiful aspects of the Bonferroni procedure is its simplicity and that the resulting multiple comparisons are easy to compute. The procedure is quite common in microarray and genomics studies where there are often hundreds, if not thousands, of comparisons to be made. In those cases, the Bonferroni procedure requires the difference between the means to be quite large to be declared significant.

On the spectrum of multiple comparison procedures, the Bonferroni procedure is considered a conservative approach. Procedures such as Fisher's least significant difference, Tukey's honestly significant difference, and Student–Newman–Keuls test are considered more liberal and Scheffé's method is considered more conservative. The conservative nature of the Bonferroni procedure is one of its assets, where if something is declared significant using the Bonferroni procedure, then one can be sure that the specified Type I error rate is truly preserved.

Experiment-Wise Error Rates

The main issue with comparing a large number of group means is being able to control the Type I error rate, in this case, falsely claiming two group means are different. Suppose a researcher is interested in k groups means: $\mu_1, \mu_2, \ldots, \mu_k$. To examine every possible difference between two means would result in $\frac{k(k-1)}{2}$ separate tests. If k is large, this could be a large number of tests each with its own Type I error rate of α. Using probability, we can find a lower bound for the Type I error rate for all comparisons, which is much higher than α. The Type I error rate across a family of comparisons or hypotheses is called the FWR, denoted α_F, and reflects the probability that one makes at least one Type I error among all comparisons. The individual Type I error rate is often called the *experiment-wise error rate*, denoted α_E, and is the probability of making a Type I error when considering a single comparison of two means. Using probability, we can obtain a lower bound for the experiment-wise error rate based on the number of comparisons and the comparison-wise error rate and assuming all Type I errors are independent.

$$\alpha_F = P(\text{at least one Type 1 error})$$
$$= 1 - P(\text{no Type 1 errors})$$
$$= 1 - P(\text{no Type 1 error on a single comparison})^{\frac{k(k-1)}{2}}$$
$$= 1 - \left[1 - P\binom{\text{Type 1 error on a single}}{\text{comparison}}\right]^{\frac{k(k-1)}{2}}$$
$$= 1 - (1 - \alpha_E)^{\frac{k(k-1)}{2}}.$$

Before going forward, it should be mentioned that the formula just shown works for any situation where the number of tests/comparisons, denoted h can be computed. Simply replace the

$\frac{k(k-1)}{2}$ with h. This can be useful for situations where one may not be interested in all possible paired comparisons. For example, one may be simply interested in whether a specific treatment-level group differs from the control group.

Table 1 shows the FWR, α_F, for various number of groups to be compared with $\alpha_E = .05$ and .01. Notice that even for a few number of groups to be compared that the number of actual paired comparisons, $\frac{k(k-1)}{2}$, is quite high. For example, consider the case when $k = 5$, the number of paired comparisons is 10 and the FWR is $\alpha_F = .401$ which means there is a 40.1% chance that a Type I error will be made on at least one of the paired comparisons. The problem gets worse for larger number of groups, say $k = 10$, the number of paired comparisons is 45 and the experiment-wise error rate is $\alpha_F = .901$, which means that there is a 90.1% chance that a Type I error will be made on at least one of the paired comparisons. Many researchers would consider the FWR to be unacceptably high in these cases.

Because the problem of high experiment-wise error rates is motivated by probability, the solution can be found there as well.

Using the Bonferroni inequality, we can obtain a correction for the significance level so that the resulting inferences will satisfy the FWR. Suppose

Table 1 Family-Wise Error Rates, α_E, Calculated for All Pairwise Comparisons for Various Number of Groups, k, and Experiment-Wise Error Rates, α_E

k	$\frac{k(k-1)}{2}$	α_E	α_F	α_E	α_F
3	3	.05	.143	.01	.030
4	6	.05	.265	.01	.059
5	10	.05	.401	.01	.096
6	15	.05	.537	.01	.140
7	21	.05	.659	.01	.190
8	28	.05	.762	.01	.245
9	36	.05	.842	.01	.304
10	45	.05	.901	.01	.364

we are testing h hypotheses, $H_1, H_2, \ldots, H_h$ (which could ccorresponding p values $p_1, p_2, \ldots, p_h$. Under the null hypothesis that all hypotheses are true, then the FWR is the probability we reject at least one of the hypotheses. This gives the following:

$$\alpha_F = \text{FWR} = P(p_1 \leq \alpha_E \text{ or } p_2 \leq \alpha_E \text{ or} \ldots p_h \leq \alpha_E).$$

This establishes that $\text{FWR} \leq h\alpha_E$. Hence, by simply setting a *Bonferroni corrected* significance level to $\alpha_E^* = \dfrac{\alpha_E}{h}$, one can guarantee that $\alpha_F \leq \alpha_E$. For the multiple pairwise comparison case, the corresponding Bonferroni corrected significance level would be $\alpha_E^* = \dfrac{2\alpha_E}{[k(k-1)]}$. Using α_E^*, the lower bound on the resulting experiment-wise error rate, α_F^* can be calculated by $1 - (1 - \alpha_E^*)^{\frac{k(k-1)}{2}}$.

Table 2 shows the number of groups, the number of pairwise comparisons, the associated Bonferroni corrected significance levels, and the resulting lower bound on the experiment-wise error rates. Notice that as the number of groups

increase the Bonferroni corrected significance levels, α_E^* decrease dramatically for both $\alpha_E = .05$ and .01. Also notice that the resulting lower bound on the experiment-wise error rate, α_F^*, remains constant and slightly below α_E.

Bonferroni Procedure for Multiple Comparisons

In a 1973 article, James M. Smith and Henryk Misiak attempted to determine whether the individuals' critical flicker frequency, or the frequency at which the person cannot distinguish a flickering light from a steady, nonflickering light, is related to their iris color. The critical flicker frequency is the highest frequency in which an individual can detect a flicker. This is important as the multiple screens in modern life have various refresh rates and both manufacturers and users want a visually smooth experience. The data from their experiment is given in Table 3 below. Notice that the data are unbalanced in the sense that there are not an equal number of observations in each group (iris color).

The first step in the Bonferroni procedure for multiple comparisons is to perform an ANOVA analysis to determine whether differences exist

Table 2 Bonferroni Corrected Significance Level,
$\alpha_E^* = \dfrac{2\alpha_E}{[k(k-1)]}$, Calculated for All Pairwise
Comparisons for Various Number of Groups, k,
and the Resulting Lower Bound on the
Experiment-Wise Error Rates,
$\alpha_F^* \geq 1 - (1 - \alpha_E^*)^{\frac{k(k-1)}{2}}$

k	$\dfrac{k(k-1)}{2}$	α_E	α_E^*	α_F^*	α_E	α_E^*	α_F^*
3	3	.05	.0167	.0492	.01	.0033	.00997
4	6	.05	.0083	.0490	.01	.0017	.00996
5	10	.05	.0050	.0489	.01	.0010	.00996
6	15	.05	.0033	.0489	.01	.0007	.00995
7	21	.05	.0024	.0488	.01	.0005	.00995
8	28	.05	.0018	.0488	.01	.0004	.00995
9	36	.05	.0014	.0488	.01	.0003	.00995
10	45	.05	.0011	.0488	.01	.0002	.00995

Table 3 Flicker Frequency Data With Sample Means and Standard Deviations

	Iris Color	
Brown	*Green*	*Blue*
26.8	26.4	25.7
27.9	24.2	27.2
23.7	28	29.9
25	26.9	28.5
26.3	29.1	29.4
24.8		28.3
25.7		
24.5		
$\bar{x}_1 = 25.588$	$\bar{x}_2 = 26.920$	$\bar{x}_3 = 28.167$
$S_1 = 1.365$	$S_2 = 1.843$	$S_3 = 1.528$

Source: Smith, J. M., & Misiak, H. (1973, p. 93).

and to obtain the mean square error and degrees of freedom for the error. In this example, a significance level of $\alpha = .05$ is employed. Table 4 shows the ANOVA table for the flicker frequency data. Notice that the p value for the overall test for group differences is .02325 which is below the chosen significance level of $\alpha = .05$ and indicates that significant difference exists among the mean flicker frequencies across eye color.

Because differences exist in the data, the Bonferroni procedure will be used to determine which means differ. Similar to Fisher's least significant difference procedure, the following formula is used to determine the minimum difference for two means to be significantly different:

$$B_{ij} = t^*_{\frac{a_E}{2}, n-k} \sqrt{MSE\left(\frac{1}{n_i} + \frac{1}{n_j}\right)},$$

where $t^*_{\frac{a_E}{2}, n-k}$ is the critical value for the t distribution with $n - k$ degrees of freedom and n_i and

n_j are the sample sizes of groups i and j, respectively. Notice that α^*_E is divided by 2 in the formula to reflect that a two-sided test is being performed. If the absolute difference between $\bar{x}_i$ and $\bar{x}_j$ is larger than B_{ij}, then the means are considered statistically significantly different. In the case of balanced data, B_{ij} will be a constant number across all pairwise comparisons. This is not the case in the flicker frequency data and B_{ij} will need to be calculated for each pairwise comparison.

In order to perform the multiple comparisons on the flicker frequency data, the critical value from the t distribution is needed and in this case is $t^*_{\frac{a_E}{2}, n-k} = t^*_{\frac{.0167}{2}, 16} = t^*_{.00835, 16} = 2.672$. From Table 4, the MSE is 2.3994 and $n_1 = 8$, $n_2 = 5$, and $n_1 = 6$. Table 5 shows the calculations for the absolute difference in means $|\bar{x}_i - \bar{x}_j|$, B_{ij}, and the determination of whether the difference is statistically significant or not. Notice that B_{ij} differs for each comparison due to the unbalanced nature of the data and that in the second case one would declare μ_1 and μ_3 as statistically different. The other two comparisons would not be considered statistically different.

An alternative approach (with less power) for determining whether the groups differ would be to perform all three pairwise t tests and evaluate the resulting p values with the $\frac{\alpha^*_E}{2} = .00835$ significance level. In the case of the flicker frequency data,

Table 4   ANOVA Table for the Flicker Frequency Data

Source	df	Sum Sq	Mean Sq	F Value	Pr(> F)
Color	2	22.997	11.4986	4.8023	.02325
Residuals	16	38.31	2.3944		
Total	18	61.307			

Note: ANOVA = analysis of variance.

Table 5   Calculations Illustrating Applying the Bonferroni Procedure to the Flicker Frequency Data

Means	$\left|\bar{x}_i - \bar{x}_j\right|$	B_{ij}	Significant?
μ_1, μ_2	1.332	$2.672\sqrt{2.3994\left(\frac{1}{8} + \frac{1}{5}\right)} = 2.357$	No
μ_1, μ_3	2.579	$2.672\sqrt{2.3994\left(\frac{1}{8} + \frac{1}{6}\right)} = 2.233$	Yes
μ_2, μ_3	1.247	$2.672\sqrt{2.3994\left(\frac{1}{5} + \frac{1}{6}\right)} = 2.503$	No

this approach would yield the same inferences as the approach presented earlier.

Edward L. Boone

See also Analysis of Variance; Experimental Designs; Post Hoc Analysis; Type I Error

Further Readings

Montgomery, D. (2012). *Design and analysis of experiments* (7th ed.). New York, NY: Wiley.

Ott, R. L., & Longnecker, M. (2015). *An introduction to statistical methods and data analysis* (7th ed.). Pacific Grove, CA: Brooks Cole.

Smith, J. M., & Misiak, H. (1973). The effect of iris color on critical flicker frequency (CFF). *The Journal of General Psychology, 89*, 91–95.

Turner, J. R., & Thayer, J. (2001). *Introduction to analysis of variance*. Los Angeles, CA: Sage.

BOOKMARK METHOD

The bookmark method is a standard setting method used to establish one or more cut scores associated with interpretable levels of performance on an assessment. In 1995, Daniel Lewis and Howard Mitzel developed the bookmark method that became widely used in the 2000s, with a majority of states employing it to meet the requirements of the No Child Left Behind Act (in particular, requirements associated with reporting test results in terms of achievement levels). This entry describes the technical foundations of the bookmark method and how it uniquely executes activities common to many standard setting procedures.

Standard setting is necessary to systematically set one or more cut scores that separate a test scale into two or more categorical levels of achievement such as "failing" and "passing." The bookmark method is differentiated from other standard setting methods by its use of item response theory and the ordered item booklet (OIB) as a foundation for key standard setting activities. The bookmark method continues to be widely used both internationally and for U.S. state summative

assessment programs. Variations of the bookmark method, such as the Mapmark method, have also emerged in practice.

Most standard setting methods assemble a qualified panel of subject-matter experts to participate in a standardized process that includes the following three key activities:

1. the orientation of panelists to the testing program and test of interest,

2. the training of panelists to make ratings that support cut score estimation, and

3. discussion and consensus building among panelists over multiple rounds of ratings.

The bookmark method's approach to these three standard setting activities uniquely defines the method. The primary bookmark method tool, the OIB, is assembled in print or digitally as an ordered set of scaled test items that is representative of the construct measured by the assessment of interest.

OIB items are displayed in ascending order, by difficulty, which is defined as scale location. The scale location of dichotomous item i is the score, S_i, such that an examinee with ability S_i has a specified probability of success, referred to as the response probability. The most common response probability employed in practice, and for discussion in this entry, is 2/3. Thus, a selected response item is located at the scale location where an examinee has a 2/3 probability of success.

Polytomous items are located at multiple scale locations, one for each positive score point. For example, a constructed response item with obtainable scores of 0, 1, and 2 is mapped on two locations—the scale scores where an examinee has a 2/3 probability of achieving at least a 1 and at least a 2, respectively. Thus, the OIB is a set of test items that represent the construct of interest, presented in order of difficulty, with dichotomous items intermingled with polytomous item score points. The OIB supports each of the three key standard setting activities listed earlier. For simplicity, let us assume panelists are setting a single "passing" cut score.

The first activity—the orientation of panelists to the testing program and test of interest—begins with training that is relatively undifferentiated among standard setting procedures including discussion of the nature and consequences of the testing program, the content standards, and scoring rubrics. However, training on the construct measured by the test is uniquely implemented under the bookmark method by a structured study of the items in the OIB. Panelists typically study the OIB in small groups by reviewing the test items in order, from easiest to hardest, and answering and discussing the following two questions for each item:

1. What does this item (score point) measure? That is, what do you know about a student who knows the correct response to this item (obtains at least the given score point)?

2. Why is this item (score point) more difficult than the previous items in the OIB?

This activity is intended to impart to panelists an integrated conceptualization of what the test measures.

The second activity—the training of panelists to make ratings that support cut score estimation—also utilizes the OIB. Panelists make their ratings, for say, the passing cut score by placing a bookmark at the first point in the OIB such that a student who has mastered the content reflected by the items prior to the bookmark has demonstrated a level of achievement sufficient to pass. By defining "mastered" as "having at least a 2/3 likelihood of success," a passing cut score can be associated with each bookmark using item response theory.

The third activity—discussion and consensus building—fosters communication among panelists to support their common understanding of the diverse perspectives reflected by panelists' varied bookmark placements. Panelists make their first ratings independently and without discussion. A second round of ratings occurs after discussion of the rationales that support panelists' different ratings. This substantive discussion is facilitated using a concrete, content-based representation of panelists' ratings by placing a bookmark in the OIB for each panelist's rating—all panelists' ratings are represented in each panelist's OIB. Discussion of panelist differences is based on a review of the items between the first and last of the panelists' bookmarks (which represent the lowest and

highest panelist expectations, respectively). This discussion requires panelists whose bookmarks differ to provide rationales for their inclusion or exclusion of items that students are expected to master to pass the test of interest.

During this process, consensus is *fostered* through discussion of differences but is not *required*. A "consensus" cut score is estimated, typically by taking the median rating, as the cut score recommended to the sponsoring agency.

Daniel Lewis

See also Angoff Method; Body of Work Method; Cut Scores; Ebel Method; Item Response Theory; Proficiency Levels in Language; Standard Setting

Further Readings

Karantonis, A., & Sireci, S. G. (2006). The bookmark standard setting method: A literature review. *Educational Measurement: Issues and Practice, 25*(1), 4–12.

Lewis, D., & Lord-Bessen, J. (2016). Standard setting. In W. J. van der Linden (Ed.), *Handbook of item response theory: Vol. 3. Applications.* Boca Raton, FL: Chapman & Hall/CRC.

Lewis, D. M., Mitzel, H. C., Mercado, R., & Schulz, M. (2012). The bookmark standard setting procedure. In G. J. Cizek (Ed.), *Setting performance standards: Concepts, methods, and perspectives* (2nd ed.). Mahwah, NJ: Erlbaum.

Mitzel, H. C., Lewis, D. M., Patz, R. J., & Green, D. R. (2000). The bookmark procedure: Cognitive perspectives on standard setting. In G. J. Cizek (Ed.), *Setting performance standards: Concepts, methods, and perspectives.* Mahwah, NJ: Erlbaum.

BOOTSTRAPPING

Bootstrapping, or the bootstrap, is a statistical methodology that is frequently used in situations where standard distributional assumptions, such as normality, do not hold. In addition, the bootstrap can be used to estimate standard errors and confidence intervals for parameter estimates. It is particularly useful where there is not a known sampling distribution for the statistic of interest, thereby making calculation of standard errors difficult or impossible. There are a number of variations in the bootstrap that make it useful in a wide variety of situations. Regardless of context or application, the bootstrap is based upon a basic framework of resampling with replacement from the original sample. This entry discusses the basic nonparametric bootstrap, bootstrap confidence intervals, variations in the bootstrap, and when to use the bootstrap.

Basic Nonparametric Bootstrap

As an example, we will consider the problem of estimating the standard error for the mean, x. This statistic can be calculated in a straightforward manner using the equation:

$$SE_x = S/\text{Square root}(N), \qquad (1)$$

where S is the standard deviation of the sample and N is the sample size.

Equation 1 is based upon an assumption that the population distribution underlying the variable x is normal. However, if this is not the case, then Equation 1 no longer yields the appropriate standard error estimate of x. The bootstrap offers an alternative approach for calculating the standard error. The basic nonparametric bootstrap operates using the following steps:

1. Calculate sample statistic of interest (e.g., x) for the original sample.

2. Randomly sample n individuals from the original sample of size n, with replacement; individuals can appear multiple times in the bootstrap sample, while others may not appear at all.

3. Calculate the mean, xB^*, for the bootstrap sample.

4. Repeat Steps 2 and 3 many times (e.g., $B = 10,000$) to create a sampling distribution for the statistic of interest.

5. Calculate the bootstrap standard error:
   $SB = 1\,BxB^* - x^*2B - 1.$

To illustrate the bootstrap, consider the following simple example involving a sample of five individuals with scores 8, 3, 6, 1, and 5. The mean of these values is 4.6, and the standard deviation is 2.7. Based on Equation 1, the standard error is $S_x = 2.75 = 1.2$. Now, let's draw five bootstrap samples (which would be far too few in practice but helps to illustrate how the bootstrap works) and calculate the mean for each. The samples appear below.

The standard deviation of the means for the five bootstrap samples is 0.68. Thus, based on these five samples, we would report that the bootstrap standard error of the mean is 0.68. In actual practice, we would use many more than five bootstrap samples, perhaps as many as 10,000. To finish this illustration of the basic bootstrap, a total of 1,000 bootstrap samples of the five data points were drawn using the software package SPSS, yielding a bootstrap standard error estimate of 1.06.

Bootstrap Confidence Intervals

Standard errors are frequently used to construct a confidence interval for the statistic of interest, in this case the mean. Confidence intervals reflect the neighborhood of values within which the population parameter is likely to reside. Using normal theory methods, the confidence interval for the mean is calculated as:

$$x \pm tcvsxn, \qquad (2)$$

where the terms in the equation are as defined earlier, with the addition of tcv, which is the critical value of the t distribution corresponding to the level of confidence that we would like for our interval (e.g., 95%). There are three common methods for constructing confidence intervals using the bootstrap. In the first of these, the bootstrap standard error approach, sx, in Equation 2 is replaced by SB leading to:

$$x \pm tcvsBn. \qquad (3)$$

The second method for constructing a confidence interval using the bootstrap is known as the percentile bootstrap method. It works by taking the bootstrap distribution of the mean and ordering the values from smallest to largest. The lower bound of a 95% confidence interval would

Table 1 Bootstrap Samples for the Illustrative Example

Sample 1	Sample 2	Sample 3	Sample 4	Sample 5
3	1	5	1	6
6	8	6	8	3
1	3	3	5	8
5	8	5	8	1
1	1	1	3	5
$\xi = 3.2$	$\xi = 4.2$	$\xi = 4.0$	$\xi = 5.0$	$\xi = 4.6$

correspond to the 2.5th percentile of this distribution, and the upper bound of the confidence interval would correspond to the 97.5th percentile.

The third approach for constructing the confidence interval of the mean using the bootstrap is called the bootstrap-t approach. With this method, the following value is calculated for each of the bootstrap samples:

$$t^* = xB^* - x^* SBn, \qquad (4)$$

where the terms are as defined previously. The confidence interval is then calculated as:

$$x \pm t95\text{th percetile}^* Sxn. \qquad (5)$$

The t95th percentile* is simply the bootstrap t value corresponding to the 95th percentile across the entire bootstrap t distribution.

Variations in the Bootstrap

The methodology described earlier represents the basic nonparametric bootstrap. There are, however, a wide variety of bootstrap algorithms available for use in specific situations. The parametric bootstrap is similar in spirit to the nonparametric approach, except that rather than draw samples from the data itself, bootstrap samples of size N are drawn from a known distribution, such as the normal. For example, a psychologist working with IQ scores may elect to draw bootstrap samples from the normal distribution with a mean of 100 and a standard deviation of 15, as these correspond to the population distribution of IQ scores. In so doing, the psychologist is making the tacit

assumption that the current sample comes from the population where the distribution of IQ scores matches that described earlier, and thus drawing from that distribution may yield somewhat more representative values than merely drawing from the current sample.

Another alternative bootstrap approach is known as the smooth bootstrap. This methodology is based upon the nonparametric bootstrap but adds a small random value to each of the data points drawn in the process of bootstrap resampling. Thus, in the illustration described in the previous section, each of the five values drawn for each bootstrap sample would have added to it a small random number drawn from, perhaps, the standard normal distribution. The reason for doing this is similar to that underlying the use of the parametric bootstrap, namely, to recognize that the current sample, while hopefully representative of the population, does not contain all possible values of the variable in the population. Thus, by adding a small random number to each sampled value, we increase the breadth of the bootstrap sample.

When the original data are sampled in a clustered fashion, such as students within schools, it is more beneficial to conduct the bootstrap resampling at the higher level of data (e.g., resampling schools rather than children). This approach is known as the block bootstrap. As an example, assume that an educational researcher has randomly sampled 100 schools within a state and that each child in each school is then included in the sample. The researcher would like to estimate a regression model relating academic motivation to academic achievement. Given the clustered nature of the data, the school that a child attends must be considered in any statistical modeling that is done. Thus, in the context of bootstrapping, the resampling will be done at the school level, so that schools are resampled with replacement, and all of the children within the selected schools for a given bootstrap sample are included in the subsequent analysis. In other respects, the block bootstrap works in much the same fashion as the nonparametric bootstrap described earlier, such that a large number of resamples are drawn, and the statistics of interest are calculated. The block bootstrap is the preferred method for bootstrapping clustered data and can also be applied to time series data, in which individuals are measured across time.

In the context of regression and other linear models, there are two additional bootstrapping algorithms that have proven to be useful. The first of these involves the resampling of model residuals rather than the actual sampled data. This approach works as follows:

1. Fit a regression model to the data, such as $y = b_0 + b_1 x$.

2. Calculate the residuals from this model, $e = y - y$ for each individual in the sample.

3. Add the residual to the observed dependent variable value for each individual: $y^* = y + e$.

4. Fit the regression model using y^* as the dependent variable rather than y.

5. Repeat Steps 3 and 4 a large number (e.g., 1,000) of times.

This approach to bootstrapping incorporates information about the regression relationship and thus has the advantage of leading to more accurate and representative models than does simply resampling the individual observations as in the standard bootstrap.

Another alternative to the bootstrap is the wild bootstrap, which is similar in spirit to the resampling of residuals approach. It is particularly useful when the regression model exhibits unequal variance. The wild bootstrap involves resampling residuals, and creating a y^* value, just as with the residual bootstrap. However, the residuals are adjusted by a multiplier, v: $y^* = y + ve$. The value v can come from the standard normal distribution or could come from another distribution as is described in the literature. The wild bootstrap has been shown to be particularly useful for the small samples with unequal error variance.

When to Use the Bootstrap

The bootstrap is applicable in a wide range of situations and for many different statistics. Earlier, the entry discussed the simple example of estimating the standard error of the mean and then constructing a confidence interval for the mean. However, the bootstrap can be used for hypothesis testing, estimating standard errors and confidence intervals for complex statistical models such as factor analysis and item response theory, and has application in multilevel modeling.

The bootstrap is an alternative both to standard data analytic techniques that are based on distributional assumptions, such as normal-based methods, and to traditional nonparametric approaches to data analysis that rely on ranks, or permutations of the data. In addition, when the mathematical function underlying a particular statistic or model is not well known or proves intractable to estimate, the bootstrap can serve to be a valuable tool for estimating standard errors and confidence intervals. The bootstrap is useful for work with small samples, particularly if the model is complex and difficult to estimate. Researchers should carefully consider the bootstrap as an alternative to more traditional methods of estimating standard errors and conducting hypothesis tests, particularly when sample sizes are small and data do not meet standard distributional assumptions.

The bootstrap can yield biased estimates, and the researcher should consider the bias corrected and accelerated approach to estimating standard errors and confidence intervals based on the bootstrap. In addition, if the sample itself is not representative of the population, then results from the bootstrap are no more generalizable than those from any other statistical procedure. In summary, the bootstrap is a useful tool for researchers to consider when the model to be fit is complex and the standard error does follow a standard form. It is not, however, a panacea and should be used thoughtfully and with care, just as is the case with any statistical model.

W. Holmes Finch

See also Confidence Interval; Random Assignment; Random Selection; Simple Random Sampling; Standard Error of Measurement

Further Readings

Efron, B., & Tibshirani, R. (1993). *An introduction to the bootstrap.* Boca Raton, FL: Chapman & Hall/CRC.

Davison, A. C., & Hinkley, D. V. (1997). *Bootstrap methods and their applications.* Cambridge, UK: Cambridge University Press.

Lunnebor, C. E. (2000). *Data analysis by resampling: Concepts and applications.* Pacific Grove, CA: Duxbury Press.

Wilcox, R. (2012). *Introduction to robust estimation and hypothesis testing.* Amsterdam, the Netherlands: Elsevier.

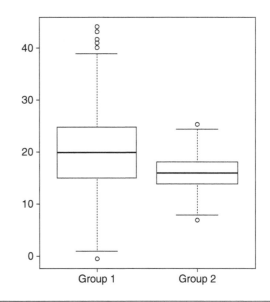

Figure I   Box plot with whiskers and outliers

Box Plot

Box plots (also called box-and-whisker diagrams) are a concise way of displaying the distributions of a group (or groups) of data in terms of its median and quartiles. This way of describing a data set is commonly called a *five-number summary*, where the five numbers are the minimum, first quartile, median, third quartile, and the maximum. While less informative than histograms, box plots are helpful for identifying outliers and comparing distributions between groups. Figure 1 provides an example of a box plot showing the distributions of data for two different groups. The whiskers are represented according to their most common method of calculation: the most extreme values falling within 1.5 times the interquartile range (sometimes abbreviated as IQR).

A box plot consists of a box whose upper bound represents the 75th percentile, or third quartile, and lower bound represents the 25th percentile, or first quartile. The boundaries of the box are sometimes called the *upper and lower hinges*, and the distance between the hinges is sometimes referred to as the H-spread. The median, or 50th percentile, is represented by a line bisecting the plot. The median is also referred to as the second quartile. The mean may also be displayed in a box plot by adding a cross or an "X"

to the plot. The range between the upper and lower bounds is called the interquartile range (sometimes abbreviated as IQR).

In some instances, "whiskers" are added to this box; the whiskers typically extend to the farthest points in the data that are still within 1.5 times the IQR from the lower and upper quartiles. The unit of 1.5 times the IQR was set by John Tukey when he created the box-and-whisker plot and is sometimes called a *step*. Values falling outside of the whiskers, yet within 3 times the IQR, are considered *outliers* and are represented on the plot with dots or asterisks. Values falling beyond 3 times the IQR are considered *extreme values* and may be denoted with a different type of marking than the outliers.

Box plots may be drawn horizontally or vertically, though the vertical format is most commonly encountered. Figure 2 provides an example of a horizontal box plot. Some simple box plots are constructed, so that the whiskers extend all the way to the minimum and maximum values of the data set; in this layout, there would be no outliers or extreme values displayed. Another variation sets the boundaries of the whiskers at 1 standard deviation above and below the mean of the data; still other variations set the boundaries at the ninth and 91st or second and 98th percentiles. When constructing a box plot, it is appropriate to include information regarding the conventions used in its construction in the caption.

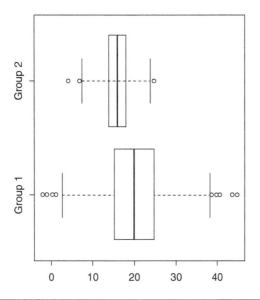

Figure 2   Horizontal box plot with whiskers and outliers

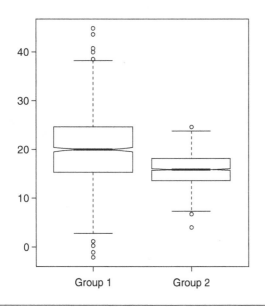

Figure 3   Box plot with whiskers, outliers, and notches

Another variation of the box plot includes notches around the median; the width of the notch is proportional to the IQR. Figure 3 shows an example of this variation. Notches are commonly used to offer information on the significance of the difference between medians. If the notches do not overlap, the difference between the medians is likely to be statistically significant.

Although box plots are less informative than histograms, they take up less space within a

document and allow the viewer to quickly contrast several groups of data. They also provide more information about the data set than simply reporting the mean and standard deviation for each group because these values can be misleading when dealing with nonnormal data and do not provide information regarding outliers. Box plots are an efficient way to visualize multiple groups of data while also providing information about skewness and outlying values.

Jennifer A. Brussow

See also Bar Graphs; Data Visualization Methods; Histograms; Interquartile Range; Quartile

Further Readings

McGill, R., Tukey, J. W., & Larsen, W. A. (1978). Variations of box plots. *The American Statistician, 32*(1), 12–16.
Tukey, J. W. (1977). Box-and-whisker plots. *Exploratory Data Analysis*, 39–43.

BROWN V. BOARD OF EDUCATION

This entry provides a brief historical overview of the U.S. Supreme Court's landmark decision in *Brown v. Board of Education of Topeka* and elaborates on how the process of achieving equal access to educational opportunities for all public school students has taken shape. It also discusses the role the *Brown* decision has played in educational assessment, research, and practice, with a focus on the sociopolitical aspects of these practices.

The 1954 decision in *Brown v. Board of Education* set forth an historical shift in the U.S. public educational system's responsibility to provide educational opportunities for all students, regardless of race. The case was filed on behalf of Oliver Brown, a parent of a Black child who was denied access to a segregated White school in Topeka, Kansas. Segregation can be understood as a practice that divides and orders individuals along racial lines.

Although the case falls under one single name, there were actually two decisions—namely, *Brown I* (1954) and *Brown II* (1955)—both of which were unanimous. *Brown I* put an end to the "separate but equal" doctrine, arguing that public schools that separate students into different facilities based on race are not equal nor can they be made equal, thereby marking them unconstitutional. The court unanimously held that the racial segregation of children and youth in public schools violates the Equal Protection Clause of the Fourteenth Amendment. This clause states that "no state shall make or enforce any law which shall . . . deny to any person within its jurisdiction the equal protection of the laws." Furthermore, the court asserted that the Fourteenth Amendment guarantees all children and youth access to an equal education, regardless of race. Prior to this decision, a state was allowed to divide people along racial lines, designating some schools Whites-only as long as it provided facilities and teachers that were of equal quality.

In the following year, the same court put forth a second decision referred to as *Brown II* that delegated responsibility to states and districts to implement the new Constitutional principles outlined in *Brown I* "with all deliberate speed." As part of this full compliance, localities were required to identify methods for addressing and assessing equal access to education among students in newly integrated school settings.

The *Brown* decision is relevant to the topics of education research, assessment, measurement, and evaluation in two meaningful ways: First, the decision helps to define parameters for understanding equal educational opportunity through a lens that focuses on the comparative differences among student subgroups (e.g., students of color vs. White students); and second, the decision advances the notion that school systems fail when they do not provide all students with equal opportunities to perform at the same levels. These two points of relevancy will inform the subsequent sections of this entry.

Assessment, Measurement, and Accountability to *Brown*

The *Brown* decision played an instrumental role in establishing a precedent on the importance of equalized access to educational opportunities among students of color that were not previously existent in the context of lawful segregation. Through a lens that views education as a great equalizer—where schools are viewed as a foundational institution for accessing opportunity—the *Brown v. Board of Education of Topeka* victory paved the way for students of color to have equal access to the same educational opportunities as their White peers. Equality and opportunity were to be defined in terms of buildings, curricula, educator qualifications, and teacher salaries; all of which are objective and measurable factors that place the onus of educational access in the hands of school systems.

As part of this framework's implementation, it became necessary to develop evaluation methods that demonstrated the extent to which state and districts were in compliance. Accordingly, cognitive tests were increasingly used to assess students.

Standardized tests are hailed as being a cost efficient form of evaluation that is capable of being administered in mass, and universally, to students in varied contexts. Such approaches are particularly appealing to fiscal decision makers who are primarily concerned with costs. Standardized assessments also allow for comparative analyses that reveal differences in performance levels among student subgroups. These analyses of comparative differences inspired the concept of the achievement gap, which remains a primary focal point in education today.

The achievement gap, or the observed, persistent disparity of educational performance between groups of students, is measured foremost by student performance on standardized testing and at times by other outcome measures such as graduation rates, dropout rates, or grade retention. The concept of the achievement gap brings into consciousness the idea that a student's ability, as demonstrated by performance on standardized metrics, is the central focal point for understanding access to an equal education. This framework places the onus on the recipient (i.e., students) rather than the institution (i.e., schools), thereby presenting a conceptual deviation from *Brown*'s focus on access to an equal education as a function of institutional availability to opportunities. The latter framing is understood in education as the "opportunity to learn," where disparities in a student's educational trajectory are understood through the gaps and differences embodied within and across schools.

With the rise of standards-based reform, which calls for clear, measurable academic standards that all students are required to master, test-based assessment became a common form of evaluation used to understand the access to equal education that schools are extending to all students. In some instances, standardized testing is used as a summative assessment method in tandem with formative and interim (e.g., daily interactions and observations) assessments that identify learning problems or inform instructional adjustments. These practices are referred to as low-stakes testing. At other times, standardized summative assessments are used to determine whether individual students have access to opportunities such as graduation and grade promotion—a practice that the field of education terms high-stakes testing. High-stakes testing is defined as using any test to make important decisions about students, educators, or schools.

High-stakes testing assessment practices have increasingly become the linchpin of larger state and federal accountability policies, such as the No Child Left Behind Act, that are premised on remedying the achievement gap and serve as a compliance mechanism for the larger mandates put forth in *Brown*. These systems are premised on the notion that equal access to educational opportunities can only be realized through a system that rewards progress toward that end goal and applies sanctions for failure to make progress or meet the goal. Accountability policies can be used in ways that punish or deny opportunities, such as retaining students in a grade, firing educators, or closing schools, or in ways that give rewards, such as providing access to higher level classes and providing salary increases or bonuses to educators.

High-stakes testing accountability policies that serve as methods for ensuring equal access to educational opportunities for all students operate on three notable assumptions: First, that standardized testing is an accurate measure of a student's knowledge of subject matter, quality of instruction, and the quality of the education a student has been afforded; second, that schools will be driven to use student-centered practices for improving access to educational quality for all students—regardless of characteristics such as race, socioeconomic status,

and gender—as a consequence of the rewards and punishments (sanctions) linked to performance measures; and finally, that students who share common characteristics are homogeneous, whereby one-size-fits-all remedies for extending quality education suffice. Consistent in these assumptions is a framing of students and their educability based upon standardized, test-based performance; this is simultaneously reinforced by a reward structure that labels schools and allocates resources accordingly.

Research and Practice

Today, many argue, schools are just as segregated as they were prior to the *Brown* decision. Notwithstanding persistent issues of race and integration that permeate public school institutions and society alike, assessment and evaluation policy approaches post-*Brown* have presented a disconnect between their premised theory of ensuring equal access to quality educational opportunities and the practice of using standardized performance measures that label and punish students and schools. The social construction of students and schools as "failing" based upon test-based performance measures emulates historical narratives of inferiority, a positioning that many scholars say can deflect from conversations related to resource allocations and relative student needs. Observing how states shift their policies and practices in response to the Every Student Succeeds Act, which was enacted in 2015 to replace the No Child Left Behind Act and changed how schools report performance and are identified for improvement, will be important to the broader conversations on assessment and equity.

Research and researchers play an important role in how the field of education understands access to equal educational opportunity among students of color in the context of post-*Brown* mandates. These different ways of knowing lead to divergent inferences—in some instances wedded to strict, disciplinary rules and parameters (e.g., theoretical frameworks, scope of research questions, or limits of research methodology). In other cases, analyses are interconnected to historical and sociopolitical understandings of education issues (or lack thereof).

In some cases, researchers contribute to, and participate in, discourses that operate within the failure and success dichotomy to discuss the extent to which students are achieving and schools are affording access to educational opportunities. These analyses often evaluate student test score data with an eye toward providing public disclosure of students' educational standings and equated to test-based measures. Proponents of this approach often argue that public transparency will motivate communities to take active roles in responding to undesirable results and subsequently hold their schools accountable.

One point of consideration related to this approach is that it can undermine the ability to obtain a global portrait of academic trajectories and comparisons. By extension, narrow evaluations and inferences contribute to actions such as shaming schools that can produce negative effects thereby ultimately blaming the victim (e.g., students and struggling schools). The focus on test-based measures also isolates symptoms associated with educational inequities devoid of an in-depth understanding of structural, root causes. Finally, a sole reliance on student test scores elevates the visibility and legitimacy of the achievement gap as a framework for understanding inequality and students' access to educational opportunities.

Understanding access to equal education through lenses that are inclusive of sociocultural aspects of education informs yet another approach taken by researchers. In particular, these analyses attend to issues of curriculum, instruction, and resource allocation as being interrelated to equal education. Examples and points of consideration related to this approach include the limits of understanding *Brown* and equal access through a Black–White paradigm that places a sole focus on racial comparisons. This focus alone can leave silent issues of socioeconomic status, gender, and language—all indicators that are similarly used to separate and provide differentiated access to quality instruction among students; and finally, the idea that sameness (i.e., equality) does not equate to fairness (i.e., equity). In particular, the argument that students have relative needs that must be considered when assessing and evaluating their access to equal education.

Finally, emerging research approaches an examination of *Brown* with a focus on sociopolitical factors. These approaches consist of structural and institutional analyses that evaluate decision-making processes, the ethics of measurement and the legitimacy of testing for addressing educational equality, and the political tensions involved in (re)distributing access to educational opportunities. Examples and points of consideration related to this approach include how assessment reconstitutes inequalities and hierarchies in a manner that makes them appear natural while still maintaining a larger system of merit that partly inspired the *Brown* case, and, finally, the role of special interests in using student assessment and the evaluation of schools as a mechanism to privatize education and offset the constitutional mandate to fund public schools.

Patricia D. López

See also Accountability; High-Stakes Tests; Minority Issues in Testing; Paradigm Shift; Policy Evaluation

Further Readings

Balkin, J. M. (2001). *What Brown v. Board of Education should have said: The national top legal experts rewrite America's landmark civil rights decision.* New York: New York University Press.

Bell, D. (2004). *Silent covenants: Brown v. board of education and unfilled hopes for racial reform.* New York, NY: Oxford Press.

Frankenberg, E., & DeBary, E. (2011). *Integrating schools in a changing society: New policies and legal options for a multiracial generation.* Chapel Hill: The University of North Carolina Press.

Haney, W. (1984). Testing reasoning and reasoning about testing. *Review of Educational Research, 54*(4), 597–654.

López, P. D. (2012). *The process of becoming: The political construction of Texas' lone STAAR system of accountability and college readiness* (Doctoral dissertation), University of Texas at Austin.

Nieto, S. (2004). Black, White, and US: The meaning of Brown v. Board of Education for Latinos. *Multicultural Perspectives, 6*(4), 22–25.

Scheurich, J. J., & Skrla, L. (2004). *Educational equity and accountability: Paradigms, policies and politics.* New York, NY: Routledge Press.

Legal Citations

Brown v. Board of Education of Topeka I, 347 U.S.483 (1954).

Brown v. Board of Education of Topeka II, 349 U.S. 294 (1955).

BUBBLE DRAWING

The bubble drawing is a type of projective or enabling technique for research use. It facilitates research participants in describing their thoughts and feelings in relation to a research question of interest. Its advantage is that it is a relatively quick and easy way of accessing and understanding the more emotional considerations in educational choices. This technique can be used in any type of research including educational research. This entry further describes the technique and how it is used.

The drawing is given to research participants (respondents) as a catalyst or stimuli to further discussion. Typically in the drawing, two people are talking to each other with speech bubbles coming out of their mouths and thought bubbles emerging from their heads (minds). The research question is encapsulated in the speech bubble of one of the people (or objects) in the drawings. The speech and thought bubbles of the other person are empty, and it is the job of the research participant to complete these in answer or response to what has been asked or said in the other speech bubble.

For example, if a university or college was researching its attractiveness to students, it may present research participants with a drawing of a building to represent the institution and a drawing of a person to represent the potential student. The university might be saying something like "Why not come and study here, we have a great reputation?" The research participant would be asked to complete, by writing within the bubbles, what the other person—in this case, a potential student—was saying and thinking.

In reply, the speech bubble would tend to contain answers that reflect the rational aspects of the choice of educational establishment. These answers would be more or less the same as would be gained from a similar question in a questionnaire. However, the thought bubble typically contains the underlying and/or emotional and otherwise rarely articulated concerns of the student regarding the particular university or college. This often provides valuable and informative insights.

Just as with other projective techniques, the advantage of the bubble drawing is that it depersonalizes the answers because the research participants are told to fill in the speech and thoughts of the other person in the drawing (not to answer on their own behalf). This depersonalizes the answer and thereby removes some of the potential sensitivity of the answers that are given. This in turn enables the researchers to get a deeper understanding of the "real" concerns of the research participants. This is because the research participants unself-consciously project their own thoughts, feelings, and concerns onto the person in the drawing.

The use of a bubble drawing in research is also assumed to stimulate the nonverbal, less rational, and more emotional parts of the brain, thus facilitating answers that may otherwise be difficult to obtain because they are less consciously considered by the research participant. For example, the bubble drawing technique could be useful in researching the emotional reasons for undergraduate withdrawal (C. R. Boddy, 2010)because it may otherwise be too sensitive for failing students to openly discuss their emotions concerning loneliness, isolation, and academic bewilderment. Their answers to more rational and direct investigations may be biased by social desirability bias—the tendency to give answers that are more socially acceptable or that portray the respondent in a better light.

Using the bubble drawing technique should give a fuller and more comprehensive understanding than that gained from direct questioning alone, because the indirectness of the approach helps to get around, and deactivate, the conscious defenses of research participants.

The bubble technique is also unusual from the research participants' point of view and can be seen as a nonthreatening and more interesting type of question, one that research participants find stimulating to engage with and even enjoyable to complete. This again puts the research participants more at ease and facilitates unguarded and open replies.

Similarly, instructors have used the bubble drawing technique to gain an understanding of their teaching style and effectiveness from the students' point of view. This research aimed to provide the lecturer with information from students in order to help develop student-centered learning and teaching opportunities. One issue uncovered related to the (quick) speed of delivery of lectures (to a largely international group of students). Peer observations of the same teaching (by native English speakers) had found that delivery was well timed rather than being too fast. This insight highlights the usefulness of a student-centric approach to research.

The bubble technique is often used in qualitative research, but it can also be incorporated into a quantitative questionnaire. The responses can then be coded and the themes and codes be analyzed statistically. In qualitative research, the research participants can be asked to discuss their answers to stimulate even further discussion and deeper understanding.

Clive R. Boddy

See also Collage Technique; Projective Tests; Qualitative Research Methods; Quantitative Research Methods

Further Readings

Boddy, C. R. (2004). From brand image research to teaching assessment: Using a projective technique borrowed from marketing research to aid an understanding of teaching effectiveness. *Journal of Quality Assurance in Education, 12*(2), 94–105.

Boddy, C. R. (2010). A paper proposing a projective technique to help understand the non-rational aspects of withdrawal and undergraduate attrition. *Ergo: The Journal of the Education Research Group of Adelaide, 1*(3), 11–20.

Buros Mental Measurements Yearbook

The Buros *Mental Measurements Yearbook* (MMY) is a comprehensive compilation of test reviews oriented to test consumers. It is published by the Buros Center for Testing, University of Nebraska–Lincoln within the Educational Psychology Department in the College of Education and Human Sciences. The first MMY was published in 1938; Volume 19 was published in 2014. The MMY is well respected across fields and is used to find tests appropriate for making decisions about employment, as a reference, for discussion within college courses related to psychological testing, and in the courts.

Reviewed tests within the MMY represent a variety of fields, including psychology (e.g., personality, intelligence, behavior), vocational, education, and the business community. To be reviewed in the MMY, each test must meet several criteria; specifically, they must be available commercially, published in English (although some Spanish tests have been reviewed in recent volumes), and new or revised, as well as widely used since the publication of the previous volume. Additionally, supporting documentation of the technical properties of the test has been required following publication of the 14th volume.

Two reviewers holding a doctorate and having psychometric training conducted most of the reviews in the MMY. A typical entry for each test consists of both a description and an evaluation of the instrument. The description section typically includes such information as the name, author, and publisher of the test; the publication date; the purpose and an overview of the test; a description of test materials; and scoring information.

The evaluation section comprises several different types of information. First, information is provided on the development of the test, including its underlying theories and/or assumptions as well as the process used to develop individual test items. Second, the psychometric properties of the test are reviewed, including information on the reliability and validity of the instrument as well as on the standardization of the test, in which information on the norm sample is discussed. Third, both an overall summary of the test, in which the strengths and weaknesses of the test are highlighted, and a conclusion on and recommendations about the test's quality are provided.

Each volume of the MMY is available in print, and after the Ninth Edition, online. If accessing the MMY online, a brief description of a selected test and publisher contact information is available for free, while a full review of the test may be purchased through the Buros Center for Testing website.

Stephanie Schmitz

See also Intelligence Tests; Personality Assessment; Psychometrics

Further Readings

Buros Center for Testing. (n.d.). *Information for reviewers*. Retrieved from http://buros.org/reviewers

Buros Center for Testing. (n.d.). *Mental measurements yearbook*. Retrieved from http://buros.org/mental-measurements-yearbook

Carter, N. F. (2011). Mental measurements yearbook. *Reference & User Services Quarterly, 41,* 181.

Plake, B. S., & Conoley, J. C. (1995). *Using Buros Institute of Mental Measurements materials in counseling and therapy* (ERIC Digest ED391987). Retrieved from http://files.eric.ed.gov/fulltext/ED391987.pdf

Szostek, J., & Hobson, C. J. (2011). Employment test evaluation made easy: Effective use of mental measurements yearbooks. *Employee Relations Law Journal, 37,* 67–74.

c PARAMETER

In item response theory (IRT), the *c* parameter is the lower asymptote of an item characteristic curve (ICC). It is used in the three-parameter logistic (3PL) IRT model, and it is often referred to as the *pseudo-guessing parameter*. In IRT, the probability that an examinee will make a particular response to a test item is modeled on the examinee's standing on the trait that the test measures. As an example, for a mathematics achievement test, IRT can model the probability that an examinee will earn a particular score on a mathematics test item based on the examinee's achievement in math. The ICC visually maps the relationship between an examinee's ability, usually denoted by θ, and the examinee's probability of making a particular item response (Figure 1).

Why Is the *c* Parameter Needed?

Selected-response item formats, such as multiple-choice and true–false items, are frequently used on assessments because of their efficiency; selected-response items can sample more of the content domain that a test covers, per unit of testing time, than other item formats. However, some examinees can answer these items correctly as a result of some degree of chance, perhaps depending on how many response options the examinee can accurately eliminate. Guessing is generally not a concern with constructed-response item types. The *c* parameter helps IRT account for an

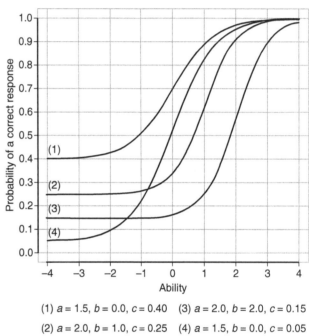

(1) *a* = 1.5, *b* = 0.0, *c* = 0.40 (3) *a* = 2.0, *b* = 2.0, *c* = 0.15
(2) *a* = 2.0, *b* = 1.0, *c* = 0.25 (4) *a* = 1.5, *b* = 0.0, *c* = 0.05

Figure 1 Item characteristic curves for four hypothetical items

examinee with extremely low ability correctly answering selected-response items.

Unidimensional IRT Models for Dichotomous Items

The most commonly used IRT models assume that (a) a single ability underlies an examinee's response process and (b) items are dichotomously scored (e.g., right *vs.* wrong). The relationship between the probability *p* of a correct response to a dichotomously scored item *i* and examinee ability θ has a monotonically increasing ICC that is roughly *s*-shaped, although it can be compressed and stretched at various points along the ability scale (see Figure 1). Several parameters are used within IRT to control the position and shape of the ICCs. The 3PL model has the following:

1. a discrimination parameter, denoted *a*, that controls the slope of the ICC;

2. the difficulty parameter, denoted *b*, that indicates the point on the θ scale where there is an inflection (i.e., where the concavity of the curve changes) in the ICC; and

3. a pseudo-guessing parameter, denoted *c*, that represents the lower asymptote of the ICC.

The probability of a correct response can then be calculated as:

$$P(\theta) = c + (1-c)\frac{1}{1+e^{-a(\theta-b)}}.$$

Figure 1 shows 3PL ICCs for four hypothetical items. All 4 items have *b* parameters that are fairly high in value to allow the lower asymptote to be visually prominent at the lowest θ values shown in this graph. Depending on any given item's *b* parameter value and the range of θs shown in the graph, the lower asymptote may not always be as distinct. As shown in Figure 1, the higher the value of *c*, the more likely it is that examinees with extremely low ability will answer the item correctly.

The theoretical value of the *c* parameter should be 1 divided by the number of response options for the item. For an item with two response options, like a true–false item, the theoretical value would be 1/2, for an item with three options, the suspected value would be 1/3, and so on. Although these theoretical expectations are reasonable, in reality, they do not hold in most cases. Very frequently, *c* is lower than the inverse of the number of response options. It is well-known that experienced item writers use common student misconceptions in the incorrect response options and that will make the empirical *c* value lower than the theoretical value. Of course, the empirical *c* value can also be higher than the theoretical value, perhaps when some misconceptions are not very common among students.

It can be informative to compare the 3PL to other univariate IRT models that do not include a *c* parameter. The two-parameter logistic model does not have the pseudo-guessing parameter (or equivalently, one can consider *c* = 0). The one-parameter logistic model also does not have the pseudo-guessing parameter, *c*, and all items are assigned a common slope, meaning items are modeled with only the *b* parameter. Inclusion of the *c* parameter generally results in improved data–model fit for selected-response items. However, IRT software can have difficulty estimating *c* in some cases, such as when there are a small number of test takers. In these cases, one can use a model without *c*, set a prior on *c*, or fix *c* to a specific value (perhaps to a value near to, or just under, the theoretical value). The *c* parameter also has an effect on where an item's maximum information occurs. In one-parameter and two-parameter logistic models, the maximum information occurs at the item's *b* parameter. However, the addition of the *c* parameter changes the location of maximum information, so that it is somewhat higher than the value of the *b* parameter.

Other IRT Models

There are unidimensional IRT models for examinee response processes regarding items that are polytomously scored, and their use is increasing. The most frequently used polytomous IRT models—the generalized partial credit model and the graded response model—do not include a *c* parameter. However, there is multidimensional IRT extension of the 3PL model. Although there are as many *a* parameters as there are dimensions of the multidimensional IRT model, there is only one *b* parameter and one *c* parameter.

Comparison to Classical Psychometrics

In traditional psychometrics, there are analogs to the IRT *a* and *b* parameters (e.g., biserial correlations and item means). However, there is no real-item statistic that compares to the IRT *c* parameter. At the test level, a correction for guessing can be applied to an examinee's total test scores, in which a fractional value for every incorrect answer is subtracted from the examinee's total raw score. For items that have five answer options, the fractional correction is one fourth of a point; for items that have four answer options, the fractional correction is one third of a point; and so on.

Scott Bishop

See also a Parameter; b Parameter; Item Response Theory

Further Readings

Muraki, E. (1992). A generalized partial credit model: Application of an EM algorithm. *Applied Psychological Measurement, 16*(2), 159–176. doi:10.1177/014662169201600206

Reckase, M. D. (1985). The difficulty of test items that measure more than one ability. *Applied Psychological Measurement, 9,* 401–412. doi:10.1177/014662168500900409

Samejima, F. (1969). *Estimation of ability using a response pattern of graded scores* (Psychometrika Monograph No. 17). Richmond, VA: Psychometric Society. Retrieved from http://www.psychometricsociety.org/sites/default/files/pdf/MN17.pdf

C Programming Languages

The family of C programming languages, consisting of C, C++, C#, and Objective-C, is a set of similar languages from different paradigms. The first of these languages, C, serves as the foundation for the set because its syntax, structure, and logic strongly influenced the development of the latter languages. Perhaps the most notable difference is that C# and Objective-C are object-oriented languages using classes that gain additional programming properties to build on the C language. The C++ language is inherently capable of object-oriented programming, but its flexibility also allows it to be programmed in the same paradigm as C. Due to the large number of similarities between them, a deeper understanding of C facilitates learning the other languages, as its programming principles can be generalized to the others. For that reason, this entry focuses on C, providing programming principles, sample code, compilation, and applications to educational research, measurement, and evaluation.

Programming Principles in C

Programming languages follow *paradigms* or ways of writing code at different levels of abstraction (i.e., how closely the language resembles the binary machine code of 0s and 1s). C follows an imperative (and more specifically, procedural) paradigm, which means that the code describes *how* to perform a task.

C code accomplishes tasks using *functions*, a term that bears similarity to the mathematical definition. Functions use input to produce output, although this is not always the case. Some functions perform tasks with no explicit input values required, and others use input to perform a task with no specific output values. The *main* function is a requirement in C code when it is compiled to produce an executable program.

A collection of functions written in a single file to be used across multiple programs is called a *library* (which may have a static library file extension, *.a or *.lib, or dynamic library file extension, *.so or *.dll). A library may contain header files (with the file extension *.h), which are preprocessing directives that are evaluated before source code (i.e., the program that a user writes). A primary example of this is the C Standard Library, and it contains a standardized set of header files that allows for basic commonly used functions to be used by programs. More specifically, a header file (e.g., <stdio.h>) contains the standard input/output functions that are not reserved words in the C language. Under the current C11 standard, there are 44 reserved words in C that cannot be used for naming variables or functions; for instance, a variable cannot be named *int* because the compiler understands that term to denote the integer data type. If the end goal is a user-written library, an executable program is not required because libraries typically do not have an execution thread of their own.

There are four basic data types that can be specified in C. First, arithmetic data types are used to store alphanumeric symbols in memory (i.e., *char, int, float,* and *double*). Second, type modifiers can be used to denote the possibility of negative values (i.e., *signed* vs. *unsigned*) or the amount of memory needed (e.g., the number of decimal places) for that particular value (i.e., *short* vs. *long*). Third, enumerated data types are useful for situations involving loops and discrete calculations, such as dummy codes and categorical indicators. Finally, void data types are null values that serve as a proxy for functions returning no values or for declaring pointers to variable locations in memory without specifying a particular data type. However, the classification of these data types could be conceptualized in multiple fashions. It is even possible to declare constants, as opposed to variables, for those values in memory that should not be changed during code execution. Declaring variables is technically separate from initialization. The former creates and names the variable, while the latter gives the variable a starting value.

Derived data types are possible as well. That is, there are more complex data types defined using the basic data types described earlier. As an illustration, an array is a collection of elements of the same type within a predetermined-sized range. Conceptually, this can be thought of as a table of values indexed (with the first value starting at an index of 0 as opposed to 1) by dimension using subsequent brackets (e.g., *data*[0][9] would access the value in the first row and 10th column of the two-dimensional array named *data*). A common example of an array is a string because it is a collection of individual characters. Another example of a derived data type is a pointer, which is a variable that holds the memory address of another variable. Furthermore, functions are derived data types because the return value must be a particular basic data type. All in all, there is static type-checking with all of these various data types. This means that the consistency of data types is checked whenever the program is compiled (i.e., created) as opposed to during run time of the program.

The functionality of the code tasks is further manipulated using control structures. These can route logic conditionally (e.g., *if-then-else* and *switch* statements) or iteratively (e.g., *for*, *while*, and *do-while* loops). Additionally, operators can be used inside or outside of control structures to perform actions with the variables in memory. Types of operators include arithmetic (e.g., $+, -, \times, /, \%$), comparison (e.g., $==, !=, <, >$), assignment (e.g., $=, +=, -=$), and logical (e.g., *true*, *false*, *not*, *and*). Furthermore, when multiple operators are used, the grouping of expressions and the order of their evaluation is affected by the precedence and associativity of the operators. For example, the use of parentheses around an expression could change the order in which a mathematical expression is computed: $2 \times 2 + 2$ versus $2 \times (2 + 2)$ results in 6 and 8, respectively. Reference tables have been created that describe the order of operator precedence.

Example Code

One of the most traditional code examples is writing a basic program that outputs "Hello World" to the terminal window. A variant of this common code is presented in Figure 1. The first line begins with code comments placed between /* and */ to denote the beginning and end of a comment, respectively. Text between these two placeholders can span multiple lines. The importance of commenting code cannot be emphasized enough, especially if code is shared with others or is to be revisited at a later date.

The code example continues with an *#include* preprocessor directive to tell the C compiler that the functions in the standard input/output header file (<stdio.h>) should be made available for the subsequent code to use. The third line begins the declaration of the *main* function, which returns an integer data type as the output. The *void* given to the function is not required technically but is shown here to illustrate an assumption that the compiler would otherwise make. The code within the function is indented for readability purposes. This is a very useful practice in programming because C compilers ignore such spacing.

```
/* Comments appear between these symbols */
#include <stdio.h>
int main(void)
{
    printf("Hello World\n");
    return 0;
}
```

Figure I   Example of C programming code

Within the curly braces on Line 5 of Figure 1, the *printf* function is used to send formatted output to the terminal window. The content inside the double quotes gets printed on the screen. Inside of the quotes, any character that immediately follows a backslash (the combination of which is known as an *escape sequence*) is ignored, so that the compiler can receive additional instructions. The \n tells the compiler to create a line break. The end of the statement ends with a semicolon, as all expression or declaration statements should. However, preprocessor directives (i.e., *#include*) and control structures (i.e., loops and conditional logic) do not require a semicolon, as evidenced in the example code. Finally, Line 6 returns the integer zero to the terminal to indicate that the program executed correctly. Typically, nonzero values are used by programmers to denote warning or error messages in more complex coding.

Code Compilation

In order to develop an executable program, one must use a compiler. The purpose of the compiler is to take source code (e.g., the C code written by the user) and translate it to the lowest level of software as a series of 0s and 1s (corresponding to the absence or presence of electrical activity in the central processing unit) that the machine hardware can understand directly. This process occurs through several intermediate steps.

Making the assumption that the code is free of compilation errors, both syntactical and logical in nature, the source code will first be modified by the preprocessor. The preprocessor is used to define constants used globally in the program, substitute macro functions in the code with those from library files, and provide directives that stipulate which libraries to include and which code should be compiled according to conditional logic. Following this, the compiler translates the preprocessed code into assembly code. It is similar to machine code but has mnemonics (simpler words, symbols, and numbers) to represent the binary code. Next, the assembler translates the assembly code directly into machine code. After this point, the linker links any libraries directly to the machine code. The final result is an executable binary file.

Using an integrated development environment is perhaps the simplest method for all of the preceding steps to be performed, as it contains a text editor, compiler, and linker. Although many compilers exist, a more commonly used one is the GNU (a recursive acronym for "GNU's not Unix") C Compiler. Windows users would use part of the GNU C Compiler known as Minimalist GNU for Windows (MinGW), Linux users typically have access to a GNU compiler that is included in the operating system distribution, and Mac users may use the Apple Developer Tools for compilation.

Applications in Educational Research, Measurement, and Evaluation

Although many software applications used by researchers, measurement practitioners, and evaluators are written in higher level languages, often with extensive graphical user interfaces, C code has an advantage of being very quick for statistical and psychometric calculations. As such, it is not unusual for other programming languages to call dynamic link libraries (*.dll) written in C to quickly and efficiently perform routine tasks. Fortunately, there are repositories of C code, available under open-source licensing conditions, related specifically to psychometric analyses.

One such repository is provided by the Center for Advanced Studies in Measurement and Assessment from the College of Education at the University of Iowa. On their website, there are multiple projects that contain C executable programs. In particular, the *Equating Recipes* project contains over 25,000 lines of C source code for users to use, or appropriately adapt, as needed. This resource provides excellent didactic examples and can feasibly be integrated into research projects and operational practices. Another library of functions, freely available for those interested in item response theory, is the *libirt* library. It contains functions for parameter estimation of parametric and nonparametric models for dichotomous and polytomous data. Multiple estimation algorithms are available for users to implement as well.

C undergirds major software systems and environments that are often used in application. Over half of the core functions in the R programming language and environment are underwritten using C. Because of the open-source nature of R, many of the C functions used for statistical/psychometric calculations can be viewed through the Comprehensive R Archive Network. While the previous examples have highlighted resources that are freely available, C is even used for commercial software. For example, SAS is written in the C language. More specifically, SAS *data* and *proc* steps are interpreted and correspond with C code that is executed incognito. Overall, both R and SAS can be used to call compiled C code, although this functionality extends to other statistical languages and environments as well.

Allison Jennifer Ames and
Jonathan D. Rollins III

See also Computer Programming in Quantitative Analysis; Quantitative Research Methods; R; SAS

Further Readings

Banahan, M., Brady, D., & Doran, M. (2007). *The C book* (2nd ed.). Retrieved from http://publications.gbdirect.co.uk/c_book (Originally published by Addison-Wesley, 1991).

Gookin, D. (2014). *Beginning programming with C for dummies*. Hoboken, NJ: For Dummies, a Wiley Brand.

International Organization for Standardization. (2011–2012). *ISO/IEC 9899:2011* (3rd ed.) [C11 Standard]. Geneva, Switzerland: Author.

Kernighan, B., & Ritchie, D. (1988). *The C programming language*. Englewood Cliffs, NJ: Prentice Hall.

McGrath, M. (2012). *C programming in easy steps* (4th ed.). Warwickshire, UK: In Easy Steps.

Zhang, T. (2000). *Sams teach yourself C in 24 hours* (2nd ed.). Indianapolis, IN: Sams.

Websites

Center for Advanced Studies in Measurement and Assessment (CASMA), College of Education, University of Iowa. Computer programs: http://education.uiowa.edu/centers/center-advanced-studies-measurement-and-assessment/computer-programs

Comprehensive R Archive Network: http://cran.r-project.org

libirt, Item Response Theory Library: http://psychometricon.net/libirt/

CANONICAL CORRELATION

Canonical correlation is a statistical measure for expressing the relationship between two sets of variables. Formally, given two random vectors $\mathbf{x} \in \mathbb{R}^{dx}$

and $\mathbf{y} \in \mathbb{R}^{dy}$ with some joint (unknown) distribution D, the canonical correlation analysis (CCA) seeks vectors $\mathbf{u} \in \mathbb{R}^{dx}$ and $\mathbf{v} \in \mathbb{R}^{dy}$, such that the random vectors when projected along these directions, that is, variables $u > x$ and $v > y$, are maximally correlated. Equivalently, we can write CCA as the following optimization problem: find $\mathbf{u} \in \mathbb{R}^{dx}$, $\mathbf{v} \in \mathbb{R}^{dy}$ that:

$$\text{Maximize}_{dx\,dy}\ \rho(u > x, v > y), \quad (1)$$
$$u \in \mathbb{R},\ v \in \mathbb{R}$$

where the correlation, $\rho(u > x, v > y)$, between two random variables, is defined as $\rho(u > x, v > y)$ $= \sqrt{\text{cov}(u > \sqrt{x}, v > y)}$. Assuming that vectors $\mathbf{x}$ and $\mathbf{y}$ are 0 mean, we can write CCA as the problem $\text{var}(u > x)\,\text{var}(u > x)$ of finding $u \in \mathbb{R}^{dx}$, $v \in \mathbb{R}^{dy}$ that:

$$(2)$$

Affine Invariance

A simple observation suggests that if we scale either u or v or both, the objective does not change. That is, if $u \mapsto \alpha u$ and/or $v \mapsto \beta v$, the objective does not change. This has a profound implication—canonical correlation is statistical measure that is invariant to affine transformations, unlike other measures, for instance, those optimized by principal component analysis and partial least squares.

CCA as a constrained optimization problem: Because the CCA objective is affine invariant, we might as well choose the scaling coefficients, α, $\beta \in \mathbb{R}$ such that:

$$\mathbb{E}[u^\top xx^\top u] = 1, \mathbb{E}[v^\top yy^\top v] = 1.$$

This yields an equivalent constrained optimization problem:

$$\text{maximize } \mathbb{E}(x,y)[u^\top xy^\top v],$$
$$u \in \mathbb{R}^{dx}, v \in \mathbb{R}^{dy} \quad (3)$$
$$\text{subject to } \mathbb{E}_x[u^\top xx^\top u] = 1, \mathbb{E}_y[v^\top yy^\top v] = 1.$$

CCA Solution

We can show, using the Lagrange multiplier's method, that the solution to the constrained optimization problem above is given by choosing u to be the top eigenvector of $C_{-xx1}C_{xy}C_{-yy1}C_{yx}$ and choosing $v = C-yy\sqrt{1}C_\lambda yxu$.

Simultaneous Solution to CCA

Subsequent CCA directions can be found by deflation by constraining them to be uncorrelated to previous ones. Alternatively, we can solve for to pk CCA dimensions simultaneously by solving for the following optimization problem:

Find $U \in \mathbb{R}^{d_x \times k}, V \in \mathbb{R}^{d_y \times k}$ that

maximize: $\mathbb{E}_{(x,y)\sim D}\left[\text{trace}\left(U^\top xy^\top V\right)\right]$

subject to: $\mathbb{E}\left[U^\top xx^\top U\right] = I_k, \mathbb{E}\left[V^\top yy^\top V\right] = I_k$.

In other words, CCA can be posed as the problem of finding the most correlated k-dimensional subspace of D and columns of U are given as the top-k eigenvectors of $C_{-xx1}C_{xy}C_{-yy1}C_{yx}$ 29th Conference on Neural Information Processing Systems (2016), Barcelona, Spain.

CCA as Minimizing Reconstruction Error

Given n data (x_i, y_i) in $R^{dx} \times R^{dy}$, from an unknown D, find $U \in R^{dx \times k}, V \in R^{dy \times k}$ that

minimize: $\mathbb{E}_{x,y\sim D} \| U^\top x - V^\top y \|_2^2,$

subject to: $U > C_{xx}U = I_k, V > C_{yy}V = I_k.$

Expand the objective:

$$\mathbb{E} \| U^T x - V^T y \|_2^2 \\ = \mathbb{E}\left[x^\top UU^\top x\right] - 2\mathbb{E}\left[x^\top UV^\top y\right] + \mathbb{E}\left[y^\top VV^\top y\right] \quad (4)$$

$$= E^b \text{trace} U^\top xx^\top U)] \\ - 2\mathbb{E}\left[\text{trace } U^\top xy^\top V\right] + E^b \text{trace } V^\top yy^\top V)].$$

History

CCA is a classical technique in multivariate statistics, proposed by Harold Hotelling in 1935, for measuring correlations between two

random vectors. Hotelling first studied this problem to predict success in college. In his 1935 article, titled *The Most Predictable Criterion,"* he argued that no single regression equation provides fully adequate solution and that regressing on the dependent variate with the largest multiple correlation with predictors yields best accuracy.

Applications

CCA is widely used in multivariate analysis, finance, management sciences, chemometrics, bioinformatics, and neuroscience. CCA has been successfully applied to various tasks in speech, natural language processing, and computer vision. CCA admits a nonstandard stochastic optimization problem where not only the objective but the constraints are stochastic or equivalently the objective is a ratio of two expectations rather than an expectation of a loss function. Consequently, the CCA objective does not decompose over the sample and designing stochastic approximation algorithms for CCA remains a challenging open problem.

Raman Arora

See also Correlation; Multivariate Analysis of Variance; Multiple Linear Regression; Part Correlations; Partial Correlations

Further Readings

Adrian, B., Raman, A., & Mark, D. (2016). Learning multiview embeddings of Twitter users. In *ACL*.

Aria, H., Percy, L., Taylor, B.-K., & Dan, K. (2008). Learning bilingual lexicons from monolingual corpora. In *ACL*.

Hotelling, H. (1935). The most predictable criterion. *Journal of Education Psychology, 26,* 139–142.

Hotelling, H. (1936). Relations between two sets of variates. *Biometrika, 28*(3/4), 321–377.

Hardoon, D. R., Szedmak, S., & Shawe-Taylor, J. (2004). Canonical correlation analysis: An overview with application to learning methods. *Neural Computation, 16*(12), 2639–2664.

Paramveer, D., Dean, P. F., & Lyle, H. U. (2011). Multiview learning of word embeddings via CCA. In *Advances in Neural Information Processing Systems* (pp. 199–207).

Raman, A., Andrew, C., Karen, L., & Nathan, S. (2012). Stochastic optimization for PCA and PLS. In *Allerton Conference* (pp. 861–868).

Raman, A., & Karen, L. (2012). Kernel CCA for multi-view learning of acoustic features using articulatory measurements. In *Proceedings of the MLSLP*.

Raman, A., & Karen, L. (2013). Multi-view CCA-based acoustic features for phonetic recognition across speakers and domains. In *Proceedings of the ICASSP*.

Sujeeth, B., Raman, A., Karen, L., & Mark, H.-J. (2008). Multiview acoustic feature learning using articulatory measurements. In M. B. Blaschko & C. H. Lampert (Eds.), *International Workshop on Statistical Machine Learning for Speech Recognition, 2012. Correlational spectral clustering.* In *CVPR*.

Weiran, W., Raman, A., Karen, L., & Jeff, B. (2015a). On deep multi-view representation learning. In *ICML*.

Weiran, W., Raman, A., Karen, L., & Jeff, A. B. (2015b). Unsupervised learning of acoustic features via deep canonical correlation analysis. In *ICASSP*.

Weiran, W., Raman, A., Nati, S., & Karen, L. (2015). Stochastic optimization for deep CCA via nonlinear orthogonal iterations. In *53nd Annual Allerton Conference on Communication, Control and Computing*.

Weiran, W., Raman, A., Karen, L., & Jeff, B. (2016). *On deep multi-view representation learning: Objectives and optimization.* Retrieved from arXiv preprint arXiv:1602.01024.

Case Study Method

A case study is an in-depth exploration from multiple perspectives of the richness and complexity of a particular social unit, system, or phenomenon. Its primary purpose is to generate understanding and insights in order to gain knowledge and inform professional practice, policy development, and community or social action. Case study research is typically extensive; it draws on multiple methods of data collection and involves multiple data sources. This method culminates in the production of a detailed description of a setting and its participants, accompanied by an analysis of the data for themes, patterns, and issues. A case study is therefore both a process of inquiry about the case at hand and the product of that inquiry. The case study method is employed across

disciplines, including education, health care, social work, history, sociology, management studies, and organizational studies. This entry outlines the defining characteristics of the case study method, provides types of case studies, and describes the role of the researcher.

Defining Characteristics of Case Studies

A review of case studies reported in the literature yields several defining characteristics:

- Clear boundaries—The researcher begins by identifying a specific case or set of cases to be studied. Each case is an entity that is described within certain parameters, such as a specific time frame, place, event, and process. Hence, the case becomes a *bounded system*. Typically, case study researchers analyze the real-life cases that are currently in progress so that they can gather accurate information that is not lost by time.

- Purposeful sampling—Selecting the case requires that the researcher define the unit of analysis and establish a rationale for why the particular case was selected in terms of purpose and intended use, why the specific boundaries were chosen to surround the case, and why specific categories of information were sought.

- Design flexibility—Reliance on a single source of data is typically not sufficient to develop the necessary in-depth understanding and insights. Many forms of qualitative data are therefore collected, including interview, direct observations, participant observation, and physical artifacts (audiovisual materials, documents, and archival records). In addition, some quantitative data, including survey and/or census information, may be collected to augment the qualitative data.

- Thick narrative description—Key to understanding the data is that the report provides thick narrative description of the case, including the current context, history, chronology of events, and a day-to-day rendering of the activities of the case. This description enables deeper understanding on the part of the reader.

- Thematic analysis—In addition to description, the researcher seeks to identify topics or issues that emanate from the findings and that shed light on understanding the complexity of the case. When multiple cases are selected, a typical format includes a detailed description of each case as well as reports of themes within each case (*within-case analysis*) followed by thematic analysis across cases (*cross-case analysis*). Themes aggregate information into larger clusters of ideas and illustrate similarities and differences. Themes can also be presented as a theoretical or conceptual model.

- Transferability—One myth about case study research is that findings cannot be applied beyond the cases studied. This viewpoint is based on statistical generalization, which relies on the use of representative random samples in order to extrapolate findings to a larger general population. Gaining a complex and rich understanding of the data through intense in-depth exploration means that the findings from just one case may hold a wealth of transferable information and knowledge that can be applied in other similar contexts, settings, and conditions. As such, transferability, rather than generalizability, becomes the goal of the case study method.

Types of Case Study Methodologies

Case Study Design

A single case can be selected for in-depth study, or several cases can be selected so that they can be compared. The intent or objective of conducting a case study plays an important role regarding the choice of research design, and there are three design variations: *intrinsic case study*, *instrumental case study*, and *collective* or *multiple case study*.

A single intrinsic case study can be conducted to illustrate a case that needs to be documented and described. The research focuses on the case itself to the extent that it represents a unique situation or holds intrinsic or unusual interest. Alternatively, the intent of the study may be to understand a specific issue, problem, or concern, and a case or cases would be selected as a vehicle to illustrate and better understand the underlying concern. This would be a single instrumental case study. Finally, if more than one case is involved, this would be a collective case study or multiple case study, with the intent to compare and contrast

perspectives regarding the same issue. The focus is on the analysis of diverse cases to determine how it confirms the findings within or between cases or if it calls the findings into question.

Case Study Research Approach

Depending on the researcher's methodological perspective and the overall research questions, there are several types of case study approaches:

- Exploratory—This type of case study is selected for its data gathering possibilities, and also for what it may reflect or represent regarding other similar cases. Pursuing an exploratory design allows the researcher to gain new insights based on the data, with the goal of generating specific ideas or theories that might be used to test ideas regarding similar cases.
- Descriptive—A descriptive case study is selected when the researcher seeks to portray the specifics of a social phenomenon or issue that is not well conceptualized or understood. The goal is to seek rich detail regarding the inner processes of the given case and to provide multiple ways of understanding the layers of meaning inherent in the case through various data-gathering techniques.
- Explanatory/causal—This type of case study is usually associated with a quantitatively driven case study design, in which the researcher begins with a specific agenda or set of hypotheses to test. A qualitative approach entails comparing and contrasting the data as well as seeking evidence of negative cases (data that do not fit with the hypotheses) as a way to build validity for the findings.

Analytic strategies are chosen according to the unique opportunities and challenges the case presents. The approach to data analysis also differs depending on the research design and the intent of the study. Some case studies report on the case in its entirety (holistic analysis), whereas others involve the analysis of specific aspects within the case (embedded analysis). When multiple cases are examined, the typical analytic strategy is to provide detailed descriptions of themes within each case (within-case analysis), followed by thematic analysis across cases (cross-case analysis). In the final interpretive phase of analysis, the researcher derives conclusions from the findings and analysis and discusses the underlying meaning behind the findings.

Role of the Researcher

At the outset, a researcher must determine whether the case study approach is appropriate for analyzing the chosen research problem. A case study is a suitable approach when the researcher has a clearly identifiable and bounded case or cases and seeks to achieve an in-depth understanding of the case context. Selecting a case to study requires that the researcher establish a rationale for a purposeful sampling strategy as well as clear indications regarding the boundaries of the case. In many instances, case studies may not have clear beginning and end points, and deciding on boundaries that adequately surround the case can be challenging.

In conducting case study research, identifying and describing contexts (which are typically complex, overlapping, and multidimensional) are vital to generate deep meaning and convey understanding. The case is investigated from different angles by gathering data on multiple dimensions, and methods are selected by the researcher based on their effectiveness in gathering data about key aspects of the case. Data collection methods can include interviews, oral history, critical incidents, ethnographic observation, and document analysis. Qualitative case study designs do not preclude the use of quantitative methods such as surveys, which can be used to gather information in a more standardized manner to achieve a more precise measure of particular factors that are part of the case. In selecting the set of data collection methods, the researcher should take into account the alignment between research questions and the type of data needed to address those questions.

The research is typically presented as a report that contains thick narrative description, and in the final interpretive phase of analysis, the researcher derives conclusions and explains the underlying meaning behind the findings. This phase constitutes the lessons learned from the case. Meaning comes from learning about the issue or concern (i.e., an instrumental case study) or learning about a unique or unusual situation (i.e., an intrinsic case study). The researcher's conclusions, recommendations, and personal reflection on conducting the study contribute to the reader's overall understanding of the case analyzed.

Given the interpretive nature of qualitative inquiry, rather than merely identifying and isolating a case, the researcher can reconstruct it. As a result, the academic discussion has departed from arguing the ability of the case study method to establish generalizations, instead becoming redirected toward *phronesis* (practical, contextualized knowledge that is responsive to its environment) and transferability; that is, how (if at all) the understanding and knowledge gained can be applied to similar contexts, settings, and conditions. Toward this end, the researcher attempts to address the issue of transferability by way of rich description that will provide the basis for a qualitative account's claim to relevance in some broader context.

Indeed, much of the discussion around case study research has concerned its value because its findings may be unable to be generalized beyond the case itself. In practical terms, this leads to the view that, rather than seeking guidance for practice from bodies of theory or generalized knowledge, the case study approach can offer ways of providing insights into social life based on *exemplary knowledge*—that is, by viewing and studying something in its completeness and richness and attempting to understand this. Through such exemplary knowledge, one can develop analytical insights and make connections with the experiences of others. The researcher therefore undertakes a case study to make the case understandable. This understanding may be what the reader learns from the case or its application to other similar cases, thereby constructing practical knowledge that is reflective of and responsive to its environment.

Linda Dale Bloomberg

See also Educational Research, History of; Generalizability; Qualitative Data Analysis; Qualitative Research Methods; Reliability; Representativeness; Sample Size

Further Readings

Creswell, J. W., & Poth, C. N. (2017). *Qualitative inquiry and research design: Choosing among five approaches* (4th ed.). Thousand Oaks, CA: Sage.

Flyvbjerg, B. (2011). Case study. In N. K. Denzin & Y. S. Lincoln (Eds.), *The SAGE handbook of qualitative* research (4th ed., pp. 301–316). Thousand Oaks, CA: Sage.

Hamilton, L., & Corbett-Whittier, C. (2013). *Using case study in education research*. Thousand Oaks, CA: Sage.

Stake, R. E. (1995). *The art of case study research*. Thousand Oaks, CA: Sage.

Thomas, G., & Myers, K. (2015). *The anatomy of the case study*. Thousand Oaks, CA: Sage.

Yin, R. (2017). *Case study research: Design and methods: Vol. 5. Applied social research methods* (6th ed.). Thousand Oaks, CA: Sage.

CATEGORICAL DATA ANALYSIS

Categorical data analysis is a field of statistical analysis devoted to the analysis of dependent variables that are categorical in nature. Development of analytic techniques for inference utilizing categorical random variables began around 1900 when Karl Pearson introduced the chi-square statistic (χ^2). From this first introduction of tests of two-way contingency tables, the field has developed to include not only analyses of contingency tables but also more sophisticated analytic techniques such as the generalized linear mixed model. This entry defines categorical variables, outlines the most frequently utilized probability distributions for categorical variables, describes the most commonly used statistical analyses in the field of categorical data analysis, and discusses estimation methods for parameter estimates.

Categorical Variables

Categorical variables are a class of random variables whose outcomes fall into discrete categories as opposed to a continuous range of numbers. Discrete categorical variables can be categorized based on their level of measurement, either nominal or ordinal. Nominal categorical variables contain categories of responses that have an arbitrary ordering. That is, variables measured on this scale cannot be ranked or ordered based on their observed outcomes. The categories are simply placeholders for the outcomes. As an example, gender is measured on a nominal scale, as the following two outcomes, male and female,

cannot be ordered in a meaningful way. Ordinal categorical variables, in contrast, contain categories of responses that have a natural ordering to them. The observed outcomes can be ranked or ordered based on this natural ordering, which provides meaning to the categories. As an example, age categories are measured using an ordinal scale, as the following two age categories, 20–29 and 30–39, have a meaningful order to them. The second category, 30–39, represents subjects who are older than those in the first category, 20–29.

Probability Distributions

The use of inferential statistics requires an assumption of the distributional properties of the variables of interest. The distributional assumption of the categorical dependent variable provides the theoretical distribution of responses in the population, which is the basis for the statistical analysis being performed. For categorical data, the four most common distributions utilized in inferential statistics are the binomial distribution, the multinomial distribution, the hypergeometric distribution, and the Poisson distribution.

Binomial Distribution

The binomial distribution for random variable X calculates the probability of observing the count, Y, of the number of successes in a fixed number of trials of a Bernoulli experiment. A Bernoulli experiment is a random event in which there are two outcomes that have a fixed probability of occurring. In a binomial distribution, one of those outcomes is deemed a "success." In a total of n trails, these successes are counted and the outcome X is the frequency of occurrence of a successful outcome. For example, if the Bernoulli experiment was flipping a coin, the outcome X could be the number of heads that occur in $n = 5$ trials (note that X ranges from 0 to n).

Multinomial Distribution

The multinomial distribution calculates the probability of observing the counts of each category when multiple outcomes are possible. The multinomial distribution is different from the binomial distribution in that there are three or more outcomes possible in each random experiment. Rather than utilizing the probability of a success, the probability of each outcome is calculated and creates a distribution of the counts of each outcome category. This is a multivariate distribution of all of the outcomes, where each individual outcome falls into a binomial distribution (that category vs. not in that category). The probabilities are calculated based on the occurrence of each category. For example, when asked to select a new drink, the options are "Drink A," "Drink B," and "Drink C." The multinomial distribution will look at the probability of the frequencies of the three outcomes simultaneously in a sample. One example would be the probability of observing the counts of 4, 3, and 3, respectively, in a sample of 10 subjects.

Hypergeometric Distribution

The hypergeometric distribution is similar to the binomial distribution in that it is looking at the count of events. The difference between the hypergeometric distribution and the binomial distribution is that the trials are not independent in the hypergeometric distribution as the subsequent trials occur without replacement. The resulting probability distribution of X will count the number of times a specific outcome occurs within a particular number of trials, where the number of outcomes available is fixed and the sampling of outcomes occurs without replacement. For example, in a box of 20 light bulbs, it is known that four of them do not work. One could calculate the probability that if one selects three light bulbs, X is the count of the number of working light bulbs. When sampling without replacement, the probabilities are not constant, as the current outcome affects the probability of any subsequent outcome. However, as a note, when the sample size is extremely large and the conditional probabilities do not change substantially, the hypergeometric distribution converges to the binomial distribution.

Poisson Distribution

The Poisson distribution for a random variable X calculates the probability of the number of times a particular event is observed. The Poisson is similar to the binomial distribution in that it is counting up the number of times an event is observed. However, the Poisson is different from the binomial in one important way: The exact probabilities are not known. In the Poisson distribution, probabilities are based on the observed frequencies, or the average outcomes observed within the data. The count of the number of outcomes within a specific unit of measurement (or number of trials) is calculated based on the average probability of occurrence. For example, in a Poisson distribution, one may count the number of phone calls, X, that is received in an hour if it is known that on average eight phone calls are received every 15 minutes (note that a trial can be thought of as a single minute).

Statistical Analyses

Contingency Tables

Analyses of frequencies of observed outcomes of categorical variables, or contingency tables, are the foundation of categorical data analysis. Analysis of a simple one-way contingency table, with one categorical variable, can test deviance from a theoretical frequency distribution. Analysis of a two-way contingency table, with two categorical variables, can test for dependence between two categorical variables (i.e., the extent to which the distribution of outcomes in a second variable deviate from those expected based on the distribution of outcomes in the first variable). Analysis of a three-way contingency table, with three categorical variables, allows for testing of interaction, or moderation effects, within the relationship of the variables.

The main statistical test for most contingency tables is that of the chi-square test. This test will look at the observed frequencies in the table as compared to the theoretical frequencies that are assumed under the null hypothesis. In a 2×2 contingency table, odds ratios and relative risk measures can be calculated and compared along with comparisons of proportions. A proportion measures the probability of a single outcome, the relative risk looks at the ratio of probabilities of two outcomes, while the odds ratio looks at the ratio of odds, or likelihood of occurrence, for two outcomes. What is consistent between these three is that they all can be used to evaluate probabilities of events in relation to a second outcome.

In very small samples, probabilities can be computed using Fisher's exact test. For larger two-way tables, tests of independence are typically calculated based on the analysis of conditional probabilities. If variables are ordinal rather than nominal, linear trends can be analyzed using a Spearman correlation and tested using the Cochran–Mantel–Haenszel statistic.

Three-way contingency tables allow the analysis of independence between each pair of variables as well as conditional associations among all three variables (i.e., whether the level of dependence between the first two variables differs based on the outcome of the third variable). Contingency tables themselves are the basis of almost all of the subsequent analyses discussed in this entry.

Generalized Linear Models

Although the general linear model assumes a normal distribution for the response variable, the class of models called the generalized linear model allows the response variable to follow a distribution other than the normal distribution. Generalized linear models must have the following components: (a) The response variable must be a random variable, (2) the relationship between the independent variables and the response variable must be linear in form, and (3) the model must contain a link function that brings Components 1 and 2 together. This link function reflects functional form of the probability distribution underlying the response variable, Y. Common link functions for dichotomous responses are (a) the linear probability model, which models the probability of a dichotomous response as a linear function, (b) the logit link, which models the probability of a dichotomous response as an exponential function, and (c) the probit link, which models the probability of a dichotomous response in relation to the standard normal distribution. The logit link is the most common link function that is applied to variables with multinomial outcomes. When looking at count data, the log link is the most common link function, which models probabilities along a logistic distribution. The fit of different generalized linear models is typically evaluated using the Wald statistic or by comparing likelihood ratio statistics.

Logistic Regression

Logistic regression is a special case of a generalized linear model that utilizes the logit link to model the probabilities of dichotomous outcomes. The logit link is defined as the natural logarithm of the odds ratio. Individual parameter estimates must be interpreted after conversion back to the scale of the dependent variable (i.e., reversing the logit link). In logistic regression, though the response variable must be dichotomous, the independent variables can represent any level of measurement. That is, they can be both continuous and categorical. Estimated probabilities are compared in relation to the independent variables. Interpretation of these effects will depend upon the level of measurement of the independent variable. For categorical independent variables, probability estimates can be compared for each of the dependent variable categories based on each level of the independent variable. For continuous independent variables, probability estimates are compared in relation to a change in the level of the independent variable. In multiple logistic regression, model fitting is important to obtain the most parsimonious model.

Multinomial Logistic Regression

Multinomial logistic regression is a special case of the generalized linear model as well. This model will analyze the probabilities of multiple response categories simultaneously. The multinomial logistic regression model also utilizes the logit link function. However, as the multinomial distribution is multivariate, the multinomial logistic regression model analyzes each adjacent category in the multinomial distribution simultaneously with individual logistic regression functions. That is, the log odds of each adjacent category can be analyzed simultaneously in a multinomial logistic regression. The probabilities of each category can then be evaluated in relation to the previous category. Interpretation of these model parameters is important with relation to the scale of measurement, as the previous category is arbitrary for nominal categories. The placement of nominal categories in the model will alter the parameter estimates. As this model is an extension of logistic regression, similar recommendations are given for the multiple multinomial logistic regression models with regard to the independent variables that can be utilized and model parsimony.

Log-Linear Models

Log-linear models are an extension of both generalized linear models and of the analysis described previously for contingency tables. Unlike the other generalized linear models, all variables in a log-linear model must be categorical in nature. The main distinction between log-linear models and analysis of a contingency table using a chi-square statistic is the distinction between an independent and dependent variable, as opposed to analyzing the association between two variables. Log-linear models aid in the interpretation of multiway contingency tables, as model estimates utilize the conditional distributions of the variables.

As in the assumption used for contingency tables, the main assumption under the null hypothesis in log-linear models is that of independence between the variables. Log-linear models utilize the logit function, which analyzes the log odds of moving between categories. If this assumption of independence does not hold and dependence is found, the parameters in the log-linear model allow analysts to more easily separate out the row effects from the column effects in the dependence. That is, how does the independent variable affect the probability of moving between two adjacent categories of the dependent variable. This is especially useful when three-way contingency tables are analyzed, as this model can distinguish between each marginal main effect, each pairwise conditional interaction effect, as well as analyzing a three-way interaction effect. Unlike analysis of variance models, the parameters in log-linear models do not reflect a hierarchy. In that sense, evaluating fit of the model to determine the most parsimonious and predictive model is important.

Generalized Linear Mixed Models

Generalized linear mixed models are yet another extension of generalized linear models. Generalized linear mixed models are appropriate when the categorical dependent is independently distributed (i.e., the responses are not clustered temporally, spatially, or in any other way, and errors are therefore uncorrelated). However, when this independence assumption is violated, standard errors are underestimated, the generalized linear mixed models must be used instead. Put differently, generalized linear mixed models accommodate one or more random effect, whereas generalized linear models only accommodate fixed effects. The difference between a random effect and fixed effect is the interpretation of the individual levels of the measure. When the individual levels of the variable are important, or they encompass all of the possible outcomes, then the independent variable is said to be a fixed effect. Gender is an example of a fixed effect. A random effect occurs when the individual values encompass a random selection of all of the possible outcomes of that variable. In education, teachers are typically assumed to be a random effect, as the teachers selected are a random sample of all teachers. That is, one do not need to measure differences between individual teachers (i.e., how much Mrs. A and Mrs. B differ), but the model will account for the differences that exist among all teachers as a collective.

The first application of these generalized linear mixed models was within item-response theory. For example, the Rasch model is a generalized linear mixed model using a logit link function with a dichotomous outcome of correct response on a test and a random independent variable which is the ability of the subject. Although differing link functions can also be used, the most common link is the logit link.

When a generalized linear mixed model contains two independent variables that are random effects, and these two variables are said to be nested within one other (e.g., students and teachers; students within a teacher's classroom), these can be analyzed within a multilevel modeling framework.

Other Models

As this is a brief description of categorical data analysis, not every analysis can be described in this entry. There are many additional methods that are included within the umbrella of categorical data analysis. A few of these methods include probit model, complementary log-log model, conditional logistic regression, inter-rater reliability analysis, latent class analysis, and cluster analysis.

Estimation of Models

The most common method for estimating the parameter estimates of models involving categorical data is through the use of maximum likelihood estimation. However, this method may not be the best when subject responses are not independent. In this instance, the generalized estimating equations control for nonindependence in its estimation and may therefore produce more robust parameter estimates. Since the 1960s, the use of Bayesian techniques for producing parameter estimates for categorical data analytic models has been well researched. Bayesian methods provide additional distributional information that is used to aid in the estimation of the final parameter estimates for these models. Most of the aforementioned methods have Bayesian analogs.

Many computer software programs that run statistical analysis have estimation procedures for categorical data analysis built into their systems. SAS, SPSS, R, S-PLUS, STATA, and SYSTAT all have the function to compute most, if not all, of the statistical analyses mentioned in this entry.

Sara Tomek

See also Bayesian Statistics; Bernoulli Distribution; Binomial Test; Chi-Square Test; Cluster Analysis; Inter-Rater Reliability; Item Response Theory; Latent Class Analysis; Levels of Measurement; Logistic Regression; Mann-Whitney Test; Mantel-Haenszel Test; Maximum Likelihood Estimation; McNemar Change Test; Nominal-Level Measurement; Odds Ratio; Ordinal-Level Measurement; Poisson Distribution; Probit Transformation; Rankings; Rasch Model; Spearman Correlation Coefficient; Two-Way Chi-Square

Further Readings

Agresti, A. (2012). *Categorical data analysis* (3rd ed.). Hoboken, NJ: Wiley.

Agresti, A. (2015). *Foundations of linear and generalized linear models*. Hoboken, NJ: Wiley.

Agresti, A., & Hitchcock, D. B. (2005). Bayesian inference for categorical data analysis. *Statistical Methods and Applications, 14*, 297–330.

Allison, P. D. (2012). *Logistic regression using SAS: Theory and application* (2nd ed.). Cary, NC: SAS Institute.

Azen, R., & Walker, C. M. (2010). *Categorical data analysis for the behavioral and social sciences*. New York, NY: Routledge.

Friendly, M., & Meyer, D. (2015). *Discrete data analysis with R: Visualization and modeling techniques for categorical and count data*. Boca Raton, FL: CRC Press.

Hosmer Jr., D. W., Lemeshow, S., & Sturdivant, R. X. (2013). *Applied logistic regression* (3rd ed.). Hoboken, NJ: Wiley.

Nussbaum, E. M. (2015). *Categorical and nonparametric data analysis: Choosing the best statistical technique*. New York, NY: Routledge.

Tang, W., He, H., & Tu, X. M. (2012). *Applied categorical and count data analysis*. Boca Raton, FL: CRC Press.

Tutz, G. (2011). *Regression for categorical data* (1st ed.). Cambridge, UK: Cambridge University Press.

van der Ark, L. A., Croon, M. A., & Sijtsma, K. (Eds.). (2005). *New developments in categorical data analysis for the social and behavioral sciences*. Mahwah, NJ: Erlbaum.

CATTELL–HORN–CARROLL THEORY OF INTELLIGENCE

The Cattell–Horn–Carroll (CHC) theory of intelligence is a psychometric taxonomy designed to explain how and why individuals differ in cognitive ability. It provides a common frame of reference and nomenclature to organize cognitive ability research. Its name comes from integrating Raymond Cattell and John Horn's subsequent occurrence theory with John Carroll's three-stratum theory, both of which are largely driven by factor analysis of psychometric measures of cognitive ability. This entry first looks at the historical antecedents of CHC theory, the development and purpose of the theory, and criticisms of the theory.

History

Although CHC theory can trace its heritage to the work of Francis Galton, Charles Spearman, Cyril Burt, Philip Vernon, and L. L. Thurstone, it largely begins with Raymond Cattell. Cattell studied with Spearman in the 1920s. At this time, Spearman was revising his notions about general intelligence (*g*), as it did not appear to be strongly related to scholastic tests or information retention. Cattell later expanded on this idea by noting that there were two abilities common to all measures of cognitive functioning: fluid intelligence (Gf) and crystallized intelligence (Gc) abilities.

Cattell defined Gf similarly to how Spearman defined *g*: a general ability to perceive the relations between the fundamental aspects of any problem. Likewise, he defined Gc as representing Spearman's ideas about tasks that were not good measures of *g*. He thought these tasks required habits established in a particular content area that originally required Gf but no longer need this type of reasoning for the successful completion of problems. In other words, Cattell believed that Gf "invests" in Gc; thus, both Gf and the environment in which a person operates determine the development of Gc.

At the same time, Cattell was developing his Gf-Gc theory, other scholars were finding different common abilities among groups of cognitive ability tests. Scholars came to realize that the number of common abilities that factor analysis could find was arbitrarily large, depending only on the number and similarity of the analyzed tests. Thus, factor analysts developed ways to factor analyze the common factors (i.e., hierarchical models).

The two most common hierarchical approaches were higher order and bifactor. Higher order models assume there are a small number of broad abilities that work through more primary abilities to influence differences in cognitive performance. They are developed by factor analyzing the correlations among primary factors. Bifactor models assume that all abilities directly influence

cognitive performance. They are developed by factor analyzing the residual correlations among cognitive performance tasks after extracting a general factor (i.e., the aspect that is in common with all analyzed tasks).

Using higher order models, Cattell and one of his students, John Horn, began significantly expanding Gf-Gc theory. They posited that there was a plethora of primary abilities common to any given set of cognitive tasks, but these primary abilities only influence a small aspect of cognitive functioning. The relations among these primary abilities could be further factor analyzed to find a smaller number of broad abilities. Although these broad abilities included both Gf and Gc, they included other abilities as well; eventually, the number of broad abilities came to a total of 10. All 10 broad abilities and their descriptions are given in Table 1.

Although there was a corpus of scholarship supporting Gf-Gc theory, there were many competing theories for how human cognitive ability was structured. To determine what theory had the most empirical support, in the early 1980s, John Carroll began reanalyzing all previously published cognitive ability data sets he could find. Eventually, he found over 460 data sets, all of which he submitted to a common method of exploratory factor extraction and rotation.

From his results, Carroll created a systematic framework for classifying human cognitive ability comprising three different strata. The strata represented his method for differentiating the abilities based on their abstractness. At the least abstract level (Stratum I) are many primary abilities (what he called narrow abilities). At Stratum II are eight broad abilities that he believed represented the basic cognitive characteristics of individuals. They are more abstract than those at Stratum I, and many are similar to the broad factors from Gf-Gc theory (see Table 1). At Stratum III is the most abstract factor: Spearman's *g*.

Although they have many similarities, there are some fundamental differences between the Gf-Gc and three-stratum theories. First, Gf-Gc theory does not include *g*, while *g* is central to the three-stratum theory. Second, each theory specifies a different number of broad and narrow abilities (see Table 1). Third, Gf-Gc theory posits that broad abilities are built upon narrow abilities;

Table I   Broad Abilities in the CHC, Gf-Gc, and Three-Stratum Theories

CHC Broad Ability	Gf-Gc	Three-Stratum	Description
General Intelligence (g)	No	Yes	Common aspect to all measures of cognitive ability
Auditory Processing (Ga)	Yes	Yes	Detect and process meaningful nonverbal information in sound
Comprehension-Knowledge (Gc)	Yes	Yes	Depth and breadth of knowledge and skills that are valued by a culture
Fluid Reasoning (Gf)	Yes	Yes	Operations used to solve a relatively novel task that cannot be performed automatically
Long-Term Storage and Retrieval (Glr)[a]	Yes	Yes	Store, consolidate, and retrieve information over longer periods of time than that required for Ga.
Processing speed (Gs)	Yes	Yes	Perform simple, repetitive cognitive tasks quickly and fluently
Reaction and Decision Speed (Gt)	Yes	Yes	Speed of making very simple decisions or judgments, typically measured through chronometric measures.
Short-Term Memory (Gsm)[a]	Yes	Yes	Encode, maintain, and manipulate information that is in immediate awareness
Visual Processing (Gv)	Yes	Yes	Use of mental imagery to solve problems
Quantitative Knowledge (Gq)	Yes	No, it was included as a narrow Gf ability	Depth and breadth of knowledge related to mathematics
Reading and Writing (Grw)	Yes	No, it was included as a narrow Gc ability	Depth and breadth of written language knowledge and skills
Domain-Specific Knowledge (Gkn)	No	No	Depth, breadth, and mastery of specialized knowledge
Kinesthetic abilities (Gk)	No	No	Detect and process meaningful information from limb position and movement sensations
Olfactory Abilities (Go)	No	No	Detect and process meaningful information in odors
Psychomotor Abilities (Gp)	No	No	Precision, coordination, or strength in performing physical body motor movements (e.g., fingers, legs)
Psychomotor Speed (Gps)	No	No	Speed and fluidity in making physical body movements
Tactile abilities (Gh)	No	No	Detect and process meaningful information from touch-related sensations

Note: Parenthetical terms are CHC abbreviations for the ability.
[a]There are noticeable differences in how this ability is defined across the three theories.

thus, broad abilities work through the narrow abilities and are not directly related to performance on cognitive tasks. The three-stratum theory, however, posits that all aspects of cognitive ability are independently operating within an individual and are directly related to any differences on cognitive tasks.

Development and Purpose of CHC Theory

Both Gf-Gc and three-stratum theory remained largely of theoretical interest until Richard Woodcock and Kevin McGrew began work on the revised edition of the Woodcock-Johnson Psycho-Educational Battery (WJ-R). They developed the instrument to map onto Gf-Gc theory by purposefully measuring the broad abilities. Moreover, as part of the WJ-R development of process, they invited Horn and Carroll to a series of meetings to discuss the structure of cognitive ability.

When Woodcock and McGrew started work on the third edition of the Woodcock-Johnson (WJ-III), they again invited Horn and Carroll to consult on the instrument. Between the development of the WJ-R and WJ-III, McGrew started integrating the Gf-Gc and three-stratum theories in order to have a single way to classify various measures of human cognitive ability. It was the publication of the WJ-III, however, that provided the first definition of CHC theory as an amalgamation of the Gf-Gc theory and the three-stratum theory.

Like the three-stratum theory, CHC comprises three strata, each of which represents abilities at different level of abstraction. Like the Gf-Gc theory, initially there were 10 broad abilities at Stratum II, although the number subsequently expanded to 16 abilities (see Table 1). Also like the Gf-Gc theory, most CHC-based factor analysis uses higher order models.

Unlike the Gf-Gc and three-stratum theories, the primary purpose of developing the CHC theory was for clinical purposes: to have a taxonomy to classify individual tests from different cognitive ability instruments as well as develop new instruments. Initially, the process of test classification was done through conducting confirmatory factor analysis of multiple large-scale cognitive ability instruments. This focused largely on classification of tests at the Stratum II level.

Classifications at Stratum I were usually made by finding the consensus classification from a select few scholars about what the tests measure. The major finding from the test classification studies was that no single instrument measured all the Stratum II abilities that CHC scholars thought were important to understand an individual's cognitive functioning. Moreover, the test an instrument used to measure a given Stratum II ability was not equivalent as some tests did a better job of measuring the constructs than others. This eventually gave birth to the cross-battery approach to cognitive assessment, which is a way to combine test scores from independent instruments for the purposes of a clinical evaluation.

Initially, the WJ-III was the only cognitive instrument whose development was based on CHC. As the theory gained in popularity, however, it began to be used by more test developers. By 2015, most new and revised popular intelligence instruments either are grounded explicitly in CHC theory or pay some form of implied allegiance to it.

Criticisms

Despite the popularity of the CHC theory, it has also been criticized. One major criticism is its lack of focus on g. Although most CHC factor models include g as a higher order factor, CHC applications typically eschew g in favor of the Stratum II abilities. Critics have noted that the prioritization of Stratum II abilities is typically inappropriate as g (or its manifestation in a global composite score) explains more variance in test scores and has better psychometric properties; moreover, Stratum II abilities seldom add any additional information in predicting external criteria beyond that provided by g.

A related CHC criticism is the number of Stratum II factors. As of 2015, CHC theory had 16 Stratum II abilities, compared to 10 in its original formation and only eight in the three-stratum theory. As is the case with narrow abilities, Stratum II factors can increase almost indefinitely by adding more measures of Stratum I factors in a given analysis. Critics argue that just because these factors can be extracted does not mean that they are clinically useful. Designing instruments to measure many Stratum II factors makes them longer and requires increased administration, scoring, and report writing time. This additional cost is not counterbalanced by the information gained from measuring the additional abilities, however, as there is little evidence that knowledge of levels of Stratum II abilities increases accuracy of diagnosis or intervention planning.

A. Alexander Beaujean

See also *g* Theory of Intelligence; Intelligence Quotient; Intelligence Tests; Multiple Intelligences, Theory of

Further Readings

Beaujean, A. A. (2015). John Carroll's views on intelligence: Bi-factor vs. higher-order models. *Journal of Intelligence, 3*, 121–136. doi:10.3390/jintelligence3040121

Carroll, J. B. (1993). *Human cognitive abilities: A survey of factor-analytic studies.* New York, NY: Cambridge University Press.

Frazier, T. W., & Youngstrom, E. A. (2007). Historical increase in the number of factors measured by commercial tests of cognitive ability: Are we overfactoring? *Intelligence, 35*, 169–182. doi:10.1016/j.intell.2006.07.002

Glutting, J. J., Watkins, M. W., & Youngstrom, E. A. (2003). Multifactored and cross battery ability assessments: Are they worth the effort? In C. R. Reynolds & R. W. Kamphaus (Eds.), *Handbook of psychological and educational assessment: Vol. 1. Intelligence and achievement* (2nd ed., pp. 343–373). New York, NY: Guilford Press.

Keith, T. Z., & Reynolds, M. R. (2010). Cattell–Horn–Carroll abilities and cognitive tests: What we've learned from 20 years of research. *Psychology in the Schools, 47*, 635–650. doi:10.1002/pits.20496

McGrew, K. S. (1997). Analysis of the major intelligence batteries according to a proposed comprehensive Gf-Gc framework. In D. P. Flanagan, J. L. Genshaft, & P. L. Harrison (Eds.), *Contemporary intellectual assessment* (pp. 151–179). New York, NY: Guilford Press.

McGrew, K. S. (2005). The Cattell–Horn–Carroll theory of cognitive abilities: Past, present and future. In D. P. Flanagan & P. L. Harrison (Eds.), *Contemporary intellectual assessment: Theories, tests and issues* (2nd ed., pp. 136–181). New York, NY: Guilford Press.

McGrew, K. S., & Woodcock, R. W. (2001). *Woodcock-Johnson III technical manual.* Itasca, IL: Riverside Publishing.

Schneider, W. J., & McGrew, K. S. (2012). The Cattell–Horn–Carroll model of intelligence. In D. P. Flanagan & P. L. Harrison (Eds.), *Contemporary intellectual assessment* (3rd ed., pp. 99–144). New York, NY: Guilford Press.

CAUSAL INFERENCE

Causal inference refers to the process of drawing a conclusion that a specific treatment (i.e., intervention) was the "cause" of the effect (or outcome) that was observed. A simple example is concluding that taking an aspirin caused your headache to go away. Inference for causal effects in education might include, for instance, aiming to select programs that improve educational outcomes or identifying events in childhood that explain developments in later life. This entry's examination of causal inference begins by first exploring the principles of randomized experiments, which are the bedrock for drawing causal inferences. The entry then reviews the design of causal studies, three distinct conceptual modes of causal inference, and complications that can arise that may prevent causal inference.

Basic Principles of Randomized Experiments

Randomized experiments are the gold standard for drawing causal inferences, but drawing such inferences from observational studies is often necessary and requires special care. Here, we use the Rubin causal model (RCM) framework, which begins by defining causal effects using potential outcomes, a formulation originally due to Jerzy Neyman in the context of randomization-based inference in randomized experiments. We use well-accepted statistical principles of design and analysis in experiments to connect to the design and analysis of observational studies.

Randomized controlled trials (RCTs) are commonly used to compare treatments (i.e., interventions). The simplest setting has two groups, with each unit (e.g., person, classroom) having a known probability of assignment into the active treatment or the control treatment, and the units are followed for a predefined period of time to observe outcome variables, generically denoted here by Y. An example would be a posttest score 1 year after randomization.

RCTs ideally have strictly developed protocols specified in advance of implementation. A critical feature of RCTs is that the active versus control treatment is randomly chosen for each unit; thus, in expectation, the treated group and the control group are balanced on measured and unmeasured covariates, where *balance* here means having the same expected distributions of all covariates. Covariates are variables, like age and baseline pretest scores, thought to be correlated with Y, but that differ from Y because their values are known to be the same for each unit whether the unit was assigned to the treatment or control group; examples include male–female, age, and educational history of parents. Observed covariates are denoted by X.

Assignment of Units in Randomized Experiments

An RCT is a special type of assignment mechanism. Let $W_i = 1$ if the ith unit ($i = 1, \ldots, N$) is assigned to receive the active treatment, and let $W_i = 0$ if the ith unit is assigned to receive the control treatment. In an RCT, the probability that the ith unit assigned active treatment is between 0 and 1; notationally,

$$0 < P(W_i = 1 \mid X_i) < 1, \tag{1}$$

where the vertical line indicates conditioning, and X_i indicates the values of all observed covariates for unit i; implicitly, the probability in expression (1) does not depend on any values of unobserved covariates or on any values of Y but can depend on X_i; this kind of assignment mechanism is called unconfounded.

Although it is common in RCTs with two treatment groups for each unit to have a 50% chance to be assigned to the active or control treatment, this is not required. For example, with an active treatment that is considered likely to be beneficial for older students, to encourage units to enroll in the RCT, investigators might choose to randomly place two thirds of older units into the active treatment group and one third in the control group, whereas younger students would be equally assigned to either treatment.

The causal effect of the active treatment relative to the control treatment for unit i is the comparison of the outcome that would be observed when unit i is assigned active treatment, referred to as $Y_i(1)$, to the outcome that would be observed when unit i is assigned the control treatment, referred to as $Y_i(0)$, with both measured the same length of time after the assignment. In any real-world setting, a unit can only be exposed to either the active treatment or the control treatment. Because we cannot go back in time to give the other treatment, we can only observe $Y_i(1)$ or $Y_i(0)$ for unit i, thus the primary problem facing causal inference is the problem of missing data. Consequently, although these causal effects are defined at the level of the individual unit, they cannot be directly measured.

The collections of observable values of X and $Y(1)$, $Y(0)$ under all possible assignments are called "the science." For the N units in the study, the science includes (a) the covariates X, a matrix with N rows, the ith row being, X_i; (b) the potential outcomes under treatment $Y(1)$, which is a matrix with N rows, the ith row being $Y_i(1)$, which gives values for the outcome variables when unit i is exposed to the active treatment; and (c) $Y(0)$, which is a matrix of the potential outcomes under the control treatment with N rows, the ith row being $Y_i(0)$, which gives the values of the outcome variables for unit i under the control treatment.

The science, the array $(X, Y(1), Y(0))$, represents all observable values of X and Y under the stable unit-treatment value assumption, which asserts that each potential outcome is a function only of the unit label, i, and the assigned treatment W_i. More precisely, for unit i, stable unit-treatment value assumption disallows (a) "hidden" treatments not represented by $W_i = 0$ or $W_i = 1$ as well as (b) interference between units; that is, the potential outcomes $(Y_i(1), Y_i(0))$ for unit i are not affected by the treatments assigned to any other units.

Formal Definition of the Assignment Mechanism

The assignment mechanism gives the probability of the N-component vector of treatment assignments $W = (W_1, W_2, \ldots, W_i, \ldots, W_N)^T$—(the superscript T denotes transpose, so that W is a column vector)—given the science, notationally,

$$P(W \mid X, Y(1), Y(0)). \tag{2}$$

This notation reveals the possible dependence of the assignment mechanism is not only on the covariates but also on the potential outcomes.

The possible dependence on the potential outcomes in Equation 2 is the bane of observational studies because, for example, teachers may assign the active treatment to students they think are more needy, based on unmeasured assessments, a feature that could violate the unconfounded assumption of Equation 1. RCTs are also probabilistic in the sense that every unit has a positive probability of being assigned either treatment. RCTs possess other advantageous features.

Sometimes the assignment mechanism can be written as proportional to the product of N propensity scores, $e(X_i) = P(W_i = 1|X_i)$, where $e(X_i)$ is the probability that unit i with covariate value X_i is assigned to be actively treated. In an RCT, the N propensity scores are known, whereas in an observational study, they must be estimated—a critical distinction affecting both design and analysis of observational studies.

Causal Estimands

Even though there is no way to calculate unit-level causal effects from observed data because at least one of the potential outcomes is missing, typical causal effects can be estimated. For example, a common estimand compares the average potential outcome under the active treatment with the average potential outcome under the control treatment, $\bar{Y}(1) - \bar{Y}(0)$, where $\bar{Y}(1)$ is the average value across all N units of the $Y_i(1)$, and analogously for $Y_i(0)$. Or the estimand could be the median individual causal effect, $\text{med}_i[Y_i(1) - Y_i(0)]$. Generally, causal estimands are a comparison of $Y_i(1)$ values and $Y_i(0)$ values on a common set of units.

RCTs can provide reliable answers to causal questions because we know the rule used to select the treated and control units, and each unit has a known chance to be in either group. More precisely, consider an RCT with each unit having an equal probability of being in the treatment or control group. The observed $Y_i(1)$ values are simply a random sample from all $Y_i(1)$ and so fairly represent all $Y_i(1)$; analogously, for the observed $Y_i(0)$ values, fairly representing all $Y_i(0)$. With nonrandomized studies, it is usually difficult to use the observed values of $Y_i(1)$ to estimate fairly the missing values of $Y_i(1)$, and analogously for the values $Y_i(0)$ because of possible baseline differences between observed and missing $Y_i(1)$ values, and between observed and missing $Y_i(0)$ values, as in the example of teachers who assign students they perceive as more needy at baseline (in unmeasured ways) to the active treatment.

Design of Causal Studies

The first task in the design of any causal study is to try to create, using only values of X, active and control groups that have nearly the same distributions of X. This task is easier when one can use randomization to assign treatments, and there is a vast literature on the design of RCTs. The literature on the proper design of observational studies is far more recent and often utilizes estimated propensity scores and associated diagnostics for assessing the balance in active and control X distributions.

Modes of Causal Inference from Data

There are three distinct conceptual modes of causal inference in RCTs: one due to Ronald Fisher, one due to Jerzy Neyman, and one due to Donald Rubin. These are extended to nonrandomized studies in the RCM.

The Fisherian approach is closely related to the mathematical idea of proof by contradiction and begins with a sharp null hypothesis, which is that the treatments have absolutely no effect on the potential outcomes. This null hypothesis is called "sharp" because under it, all potential outcomes are known from the actual observed values of the potential outcomes; for each unit, either $Y_i(1)$ or $Y_i(0)$ is observed, and by assumption they are equal. Under the null hypothesis, it follows that the value of any statistic such as the difference in the observed averages for units exposed to Treatment 1 and units exposed to Treatment 0, $\bar{y}_1 - \bar{y}_0$, is known, not only for the observed assignment but also for all possible assignments W. From this fact, we can calculate the significance level (or p value) of the observed $\bar{y}_1 - \bar{y}_0$. Neymanism randomization-based inference can be viewed as drawing inferences by evaluating the expectations of statistics over their distributions induced by the assignment mechanism to calculate a confidence interval (e.g., 95%) for the typical causal effect. This mode is currently dominant in educational investigations of causal effects.

The third mode of inference (Bayesian) for causal effects requires a probability model for the science, $P(X, Y(0), Y(1))$. A virtue of the RCM framework used here is that it separates the science and a model for it, from what we do to learn about the science—the assignment mechanism. This approach directly and explicitly confronts the missing potential outcomes by multiply imputing them. That is, the RCM perspective takes the specification for the assignment mechanism and the specification for the science and derives the conditional distribution, called the posterior predictive distribution (i.e., posterior because it conditions on all the observed data and predictive because it is based on predicting the missing potential outcomes), of the missing potential outcomes given all observed values (i.e., X, W, and the observed potential outcomes). This approach relies on current computational environments that rely on simulation, here the simulation of the missing potential outcomes.

Complications

Many complications may, and often do, occur in real-world studies for causal effects, many of which can be handled much more flexibly with the Bayesian approach than with randomization-based methods. Of course, the models for the science can be difficult to formulate in a practically reliable manner. In addition, Neymanian-style evaluations are still important. Fisherian p values are a special case of Bayesian posterior predictive p values. Thus, the wise investigator should understand all three modes.

Most of the field of classical experimental design is devoted to issues that arise with more than two treatment conditions and covariates that can define blocking structures. The common modes here are randomization based.

Missing data, due perhaps to unit dropout, can complicate analyses more than one would expect. Methods such as multiple imputation, the expectation–maximization algorithm, data augmentation, and the Gibbs sampler are more

compatible with the Bayesian approach to causal inference than the other modes.

Another common complication is noncompliance with assigned treatment, which is often unavoidable in education investigations. Further complications include partially defined outcomes, such as final exam scores that are only well defined for students who are still in school at the time of measurement. In the real world, complications typically do not appear simply one at a time. For example, an RCT can suffer from missing data in both covariates and longitudinal outcomes and also from noncompliance and partially defined outcomes. Many of the aforementioned complications can be viewed as special cases of principal stratification.

Donald B. Rubin and Elizabeth R. Zell

See also Bayesian Statistics; Compliance; Experimental Designs; Markov Chain Monte Carlo Methods; Missing Data Analysis; Outcomes; Propensity Scores; Random Assignment

Further Readings

Fairlie, T., Zell, E. R., & Schrag, S. (2013). Effectiveness of intrapartum antibiotic prophylaxis from prevention of early-onset group B streptococcal disease. *Obstetrics & Gynecology, 121,* 570–577.

Frangakis, C. E., & Rubin, D. B. (2002). Principal stratification in causal inference. *Biometrics, 58,* 21–29.

Imbens, G., & Rubin, D. B. (2015). *Causal inference in statistics, and in the social and biomedical sciences.* New York, NY: Cambridge University Press.

Little, R. J. A., & Rubin, D. B. (2002). *Statistical analysis with missing data* (2nd ed.). New York, NY: Wiley.

Rosenbaum, P. R., & Rubin, D. B. (1983). The central role of the propensity score in observational studies for causal effects. *Biometrika, 70,* 41–55.

Rubin, D. B. (1974). Estimating causal effects of treatments in randomized and non-randomized studies. *Journal of Educational Psychology, 66,* 688–701.

Rubin, D. B. (1978). Bayesian inference for causal effects: The role of randomization. *Annals of Statistics, 6,* 34–58.

Rubin, D. B. (1997). Estimating causal effects from large data sets using propensity scores. *Annals of Internal Medicine, 127,* 757–763.

Rubin, D. B. (2004). *Multiple imputation for nonresponse in surveys.* New York, NY: Wiley.

Rubin, D. B., & Zell, E. R. (2016). Causality in experiments and observational studies. In S. J. Henly (Ed.), *Routledge international handbook of advanced quantitative methods in nursing research* (Chapter 15). Oxford, UK: Routledge.

CAUSAL-COMPARATIVE RESEARCH

Causal-comparative research is a family of research designs used to examine potential causes for observed differences found among existing groups. Causal-comparative research is useful for the study of causes where experimental assignment or manipulation is infeasible, unethical, or in some way prohibited. It is frequently used with large-scale survey data such as Programme for International Student Assessment or National Assessment of Educational Progress but also common in smaller scale studies. It is similar to correlational research designs, except that the independent variable to be tested is categorical (e.g., school or class membership) and the analysis explicitly attempts to test causality. Although some scholars debate the conceptual distinction between causal-comparative and correlational designs in education research and recommend merging correlational and causal-comparative under the heading "nonexperimental quantitative research," the distinction is still present in many methods textbooks. This entry presents the basic principles of causal-comparative research and steps to conduct a causal-comparative study.

Basic Principles

Causal-comparative research begins with a known or expected outcome—a dependent variable that is the *effect*—and a group distinction to be compared as a possible *cause* for the effect. The researcher compares two or more *intact groups* to test the cause. When data on both the effect and the potential causes are already known by the researcher—hence the situation under study has already completely transpired—the study is retrospective. Retrospective causal-comparative studies are therefore *ex post facto*, or "after the fact" studies, because all data about group differences and about potential causes are obtained after both cause and effect have occurred. When the potential causes are studied contemporaneously before effects are observed, the study is a prospective one. Such cases are sometimes called *natural experiments*. However, regardless of whether retrospective or prospective, causal-comparative studies do not have experimental manipulation by a researcher and so technically cannot be classified as experimental research.

Alternative to Experimental Research

Causal-comparative research is an alternative to experimental and quasi-experimental designs, but the distinction with experimental research is an important one. In general, experimental designs involve some manipulation by the researcher of a causal intervention or treatment of some kind. For the so-called true experiments, the distinction with causal-comparative research is readily apparent: A true experiment has random assignment of participants to an experimental condition. The distinction with quasi-experimental research may be less obvious in certain cases. In some quasi-experimental studies, the researcher may work with intact groups just as in causal-comparative research, but a quasi-experiment would have a manipulation of some kind. By contrast, in causal-comparative research, the researcher does not control the study conditions.

Consider the following example: A researcher studying the potential causes for observed differences in elementary classes' average mathematics achievement chooses to focus on use of newer textbooks in some of the classes. In this example, the effect is the difference in mathematics achievement, and the potential cause is the use of the new textbook. The two groups to be compared are classes using the newer textbooks and classes using the older textbooks. In a true experiment, the researcher would form groups by randomly assigning students into classes using the new textbooks or an older textbook. In a quasi-experiment, the researcher would not be able to assign the students into classes randomly but may still be able to assign some classes to use the new textbook as a comparison with classes using the older textbook. In a causal-comparative study, the researcher does not assign students to classes and does not influence which textbooks are used. Instead, the researcher finds classes already using the new textbook and compares them with classes using the older textbook.

The lack of experimental manipulation makes causal-comparative research similar to correlational studies; it is often presented in methods textbooks in the same chapter with correlational designs. One important difference is that a causal-comparative study must involve two or more groups being compared with the intention of uncovering cause, whereas correlational designs typically focus on descriptive or trend analysis (whether within a single group or across groups) and need not assert that group differences are caused by the group membership variable in any way.

Causal-comparative research is particularly useful in situations where a researcher cannot influence either the group membership or the experiences of the groups. That is, situations where experimental manipulation is impossible or in contexts where group membership and the potential causes are limited due to feasibility, ethics, or legal reasons. For example, in a study of potential sex differences in reading ability, it is technically infeasible to "assign" students to be boys or girls. Likewise, any study of biological or social variables that cannot be manipulated must be causal–comparative—such as the effects of age, race, and ethnicity.

In other situations, it may be impractical or unethical to control assignment or to manipulate the environment. Consider a study of education interventions among incarcerated youth and the effect on the youths' recidivism, comparing different subgroups in the detention center or across different detention centers. Research in this context is restricted in group membership to incarcerated youth by definition. Practically, any one youth detention center may have one or few classes for a given age range, prohibiting multiple experimental groups. Policy may also prevent detention centers from implementing various interventions without some evidence of potential benefit of the new intervention. Furthermore,

ethically speaking, the youths may be in a vulnerable situation that would affect their ability to freely opt into or out of the study's experimental conditions. Causal-comparative research could be the only ethical and practical approach to study in such circumstances.

Limitations

There are two serious limitations in causal-comparative designs that researchers must recognize: the fallacy of homogeneity and the post hoc fallacy. The *fallacy of homogeneity* is an error of assuming groups are internally homogeneous. It arises when researchers assume that a demographic group (e.g., women, persons of color) is sufficiently internally similar to allow meaningful comparison with other groups, when in fact all groups are internally varied on some other variable that also influences the effect (e.g., socioeconomic status [SES]). The *post hoc fallacy* is an error in attributing causation where no cause can be established. It arises when researchers presume that an observed correlational relationship implies a causal relationship. Both fallacies cannot be eliminated—they can only be controlled through careful and thorough consideration of alternative explanations for an observed effect as discussed in the next section.

Conducting a Causal-Comparative Study

To conduct a causal-comparative study, a researcher must identify an effect and potential causes within a context and among groups. This order is not obligatory; a researcher is very likely to encounter a context and intact groups and then begin to consider potential causes for an observed effect. Then, the researcher must identify and attempt to eliminate alternative explanations for the findings. Finally, the researcher analyzes group differences to test the proposed causal relationship and alternative explanations.

Effects and Causes

The first step in causal–comparative is to identify the effect and propose a cause. For new studies, this may arise from practical experience with the context. For secondary analyses of large-scale data, this involves reading through the documentation on the survey measures. A researcher must provide a strong argument for the mechanism by which the proposed cause is expected to yield the effect, typically with a combination of the following: theoretical analysis of the context, the effect, and various causes; corroboration from other empirical research on causal relationships; and a clear and logical rationale. Without a strong logical, theoretical, and empirical argument, there would be little to demonstrate that the observed relationship is causal.

Identifying or Forming Groups

The next step is to identify or form groups for comparison of the potential cause. Group identification could follow from existing group information, such as in the example on textbook use—one group of students in classes using a newer textbook and one group of students in classes using an older textbook. But, it is also common that researchers identify groups using other data. Such groups could be formed based on organismal data (e.g., sex and age), other demographic data (e.g., gender, race, ethnicity, or religion), or constructed from other responses (e.g., based on a calculated SES index or performance on previous tests).

Group formation can be sensitive. Race, ethnicity, and gender identification can be complex and have multiple, competing interpretations in varied circumstances. In addition, comparing groups by race, ethnicity, or SES may be contentious in some research contexts or scholarly fields. Furthermore, a focus on one identified grouping variable (e.g., ethnicity) may mask other group differences (e.g., by SES) that could also be pertinent, giving rise to the fallacy of homogeneity. There may also be multivariate combinations, or intersections, of some grouping variables that warrant attention. For example, research on gender difference in undergraduate science majors may miss further differences for the subgroup of women from underrepresented minorities. Given the complexity and potential sensitivity, causal-comparative researchers need to exercise caution in the identification of groups for comparison. This further highlights the importance of a logical, theoretical, and empirical argument for the mechanism connecting cause and effect.

Identifying Alternative Explanations

The researcher next identifies alternative explanations for observed effects. The purpose is to recognize other possible explanations, so that they can be examined and potentially eliminated. Identifying alternative explanations is quite similar to the need to identify the causal mechanism—there is a combination of theory, empirical review, and logical argument. An effective approach is to conjecture what a reasonable and informed reader might suggest as a different cause for the effect or a different mechanism between proposed cause and observed effect. Failure to identify and account for alternative explanations may lead to *spurious causation*: when the proposed cause and observed effect actually result from a different cause that was not considered, a case of the post hoc fallacy.

Reconsider the earlier textbook adoption example and suppose that students in classes using the newer textbooks outperformed students using the old textbooks. Is this caused by the textbook? One alternative cause is that schools that have purchased newer textbooks may have more financial resources for book purchases because they are in wealthier neighborhoods and, thus, such students may perform better on tests. If that were the case, then the notion that textbooks caused differences in student performance would be spurious: both the observed textbook adoption and the differences in performance are evidence of a different cause that was not considered. One alternative mechanism is that teachers willingly using the new textbooks may be more knowledgeable or more open to teaching in new ways—so it is not the textbook adoption itself but the teachers' use of the new textbooks. Ultimately, researchers should look to competing theories or conceptual frameworks to identify the various possible causes for an effect. Then, the researcher must be sure to gather data on these alternatives to be considered during the analysis phase.

Analysis Approaches

Analyses for causal-comparative studies are varied, but analysis of covariance (ANCOVA) and multiple regression are most common. Both ANCOVA and multiple regression allow the researcher to consider alternative explanations while also testing the proposed causal variable by (a) including other grouping variables in addition to the proposed cause and (b) accounting for other covariates that may influence the relationship between proposed cause and the effect, such as preexisting differences on other measures. ANCOVA is somewhat more common where the proposed cause involves more than two groups, but this is also available in multiple regression using *dummy-coded variables*. Alternative explanations are eliminated by demonstrating they are statistically nonsignificant or that they have weaker relationship with the outcome than the proposed cause (for ANCOVA, using effect estimates like partial η^2; for multiple regression, using standardized coefficients or changes in R^2).

Advances in statistical techniques are also prompting changes in analyses in causal-comparative designs. Hierarchical linear modeling and structural equation modeling are increasingly used for causal-comparative studies, especially for studies of large-scale survey data, as these methods and appropriate software become more widespread in education research. These techniques can allow better estimates for standard errors in situations with nested data (such as students who are part of an intact class) or for testing competing causal relationships simultaneously.

Gavin W. Fulmer

See also Causal Inference; Correlation; Experimental Designs; Scientific Method

Further Readings

Bliss, S. L., Skinner, C. H., Hautau, B., & Carroll, E. E. (2008). Articles published in four school psychology journals from 2000 to 2005: An analysis of experimental/intervention research. *Psychology in the Schools*, 45(6), 483–498. doi:10.1002/pits.20318

Fraenkel, J. R., & Wallen, N. E. (2008). *How to design and evaluate research in education* (7th ed.). New York, NY: McGraw-Hill Education.

Gay, L. R., Mills, G. E., & Airasian, P. W. (2011). *Educational research: Competencies for analysis and applications* (10th ed.). Upper Saddle River, NJ: Pearson.

Johnson, R. B. (2001). Toward a new classification of nonexperimental quantitative research. *Educational Researcher*, 30(2), 3–13. Retrieved from https://doi.org/10.3102/0013189X030002003

Lee, J. (2008). Is test-driven external accountability effective? Synthesizing the evidence from cross-state causal-comparative and correlational studies. *Review of Educational Research*, 78 (3), 608–644. doi:10.3102/0034654308324427

Mertens, D. M. (2014). *Research and evaluation in education and psychology: Integrating diversity with quantitative, qualitative, and mixed methods.* Thousand Oaks, CA: Sage.

CEILING LEVEL

See Basal Level and Ceiling Level

CENTRAL LIMIT THEOREM

The central limit theorem is a fundamental theorem of statistics. It prescribes that the sum of a sufficiently large number of independent and identically distributed random variables approximately follows a normal distribution.

History of the Central Limit Theorem

The term *central limit theorem* most likely traces back to Georg Pólya. As he recapitulated at the beginning of an article published in 1920, it was *"generally known that the appearance of the Gaussian probability density* exp $(-x2)$" in a great many situations *"can be explained by one and the same limit theorem"* which plays *"a central role in probability theory."* Pierre-Simon Laplace had discovered the essentials of this fundamental theorem in 1810, and with the designation *central limit theorem of probability theory,* which was even emphasized in the article's title, Pólya gave it the name that has been in general use ever since.

In this article of 1820, Laplace starts by proving the central limit theorem for some certain probability distributions. He then continues with arbitrary discrete and continuous distributions. But a more general (and rigorous) proof should be attributed to Siméon Denis Poisson. He also intuited that a weaker version could easily be derived. As for Laplace, for Poisson the main purpose of that central limit theorem was to be a tool in calculations, not so much to be a mathematical theorem in itself. Therefore, neither Laplace nor Poisson explicitly formulate any conditions for the theorem to hold. The mathematical formulation of the theorem is attributed to the St. Petersburg School of probability, from 1870 until 1910, with Pafnuty Chebyshev, Andrey Markov, and Aleksandr Liapounov.

Mathematical Formulation

Let $X_1, X_2, ..., X_n$ be independent random variables that are identically distributed, with mean μ and finite variance σ^2. Let

$$\bar{X}_n = \frac{X_1 + ... + X_n}{n}$$

denote the empirical average, then from the law of large numbers $[\bar{X}_n - \mu]$ tends to 0 as n tends to infinity. The central limit theorem establishes that the distribution of $\sqrt{n}[\bar{X}_n - \mu]$ tends to a centered normal distribution when n goes to infinity. More specifically,

$$p\left(\sqrt{n}\frac{[\bar{X}_n - \mu]}{\sigma} \leq x\right) \to \Phi(x) = \int_{-\infty}^{x} \frac{1}{\sqrt{2\pi}} exp\left(-\frac{z^2}{2}\right) dz.$$

We can also write

$$\sqrt{n}\left(\frac{[\bar{X}_n - \mu]}{\sigma}\right) \xrightarrow{L} N(0,1)$$

or $\sqrt{n}(\bar{X}_n - \mu) \xrightarrow{L} N(0, \sigma^2)$ as $n \to \infty$.

A Limiting Result as an Approximation

This central limit theorem is used to approximate distributions derived from summing, or averaging, identical random variables.

Consider for instance a course where 7 students out of 8 pass. What is the probability that (at least) 4 failed in a class of 25 students. Let X be the dichotomous variable that describes failure: 1 if the student failed and 0 if the student passed. That random variable has a Bernoulli distribution with parameter $p = 1/8$ (with mean 1/8 and

variance 7/64). Consequently, if students' grades are independent, the sum $S_n = X_1 + \cdots + X_n$ follows a binomial distribution, with mean np and variance $P(1 - p)$, which can be approximated, by the central limit theorem, by a normal distribution with mean np and variance $np(1 - p)$. Here, $\mu = 3.125$ while $\sigma^2 = 2.734$. To compute $P(S_n \leq 4)$, we can use the cumulative probabilities of either the binomial distribution or the Gaussian approximation. In the first case, the probability is 80.47%,

$$\left(\frac{7}{8}\right)^{25} + 25\left(\frac{7}{8}\right)^{24}\left(\frac{1}{8}\right)$$
$$+ \frac{25 \cdot 24}{2}\left(\frac{7}{8}\right)^{23}\left(\frac{1}{8}\right)^2 +$$
$$\frac{25 \cdot 24 \cdot 23}{2 \cdot 3}\left(\frac{7}{8}\right)^{22}\left(\frac{1}{8}\right)^3$$
$$+ \frac{25 \cdot 24 \cdot 23 \cdot 22}{2 \cdot 3 \cdot 4}\left(\frac{7}{8}\right)^{21}\left(\frac{1}{8}\right)^4$$

In the second case, use a continuity correction and compute the probability that S_n is less than $4 + 1/2$. From the central limit theorem:

$$\sqrt{n}\frac{[\bar{X}_n - \mu]}{\sigma} = \sqrt{25}\frac{[4.5/25 - 1/8]}{\sqrt{7/64}} = 0.8315.$$

The probability that a standard Gaussian variable is less than this quantity is:

$$P(Z \leq 0.8315) = 79.72\% \text{ where } Z \sim N(0,1),$$

which can be compared with 80.47% obtained without the approximation (see Figure 1). Note that this approximation was obtained by Abraham De Moivre, in 1713, and is usually known as Bernoulli's law of large numbers.

Asymptotic Confidence Intervals

The intuition is that a confidence interval is an interval in which one may be confident that a parameter of interest lies. For instance, that some quantity is measured, but the measurement is subject to a normally distributed error, with known

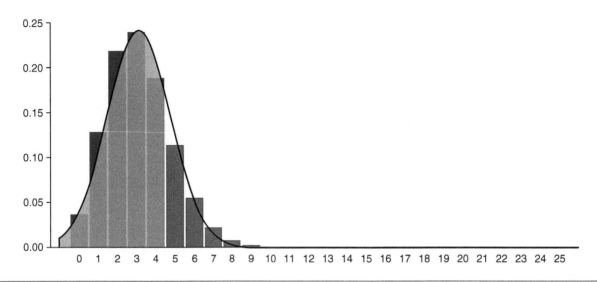

Figure 1   Gaussian approximation of the binomial distribution

variance σ^2. If X has a $N(\mu,\sigma^2)$ distribution, we know that:

$$P\left(\mu - 1.96 \cdot \sigma < X < \mu + 1.96 \cdot \sigma\right) = 95\%.$$

Equivalently, we could write:

$$P\left(X - 1.96 \cdot \sigma < \mu < X + 1.96 \cdot \sigma\right) = 95\%$$

or

$$P(\mu \in [X \pm 1.96 \cdot \sigma]) = 95\%.$$

Thus, if X is measured to be x, then the 95% confidence interval for μ is $[x \pm 1.96...\sigma]$.

In the context of Bernoulli trials (described earlier), the asymptotic 95% confidence interval for p is:

$$\left[\overline{x} \pm \frac{1.96}{\sqrt{\overline{x}(1-\overline{x})}} \cdot \frac{1}{\sqrt{n}}\right].$$

A popular rule of thumb can be derived when $p \sim 50\%$. In that context $1/\sqrt{p(1-p)}$ is close to 1.96 (or 2), and a 95% approximated confidence interval is then

$$\left[\overline{x} \pm \frac{1}{\sqrt{n}}\right]$$

(see Figure 2). If that confidence interval provides a good approximation for the 95% confidence interval when $p \sim 50\%$, it is an over-estimation when p is either much smaller, or much larger.

The Delta Method and Method of Moments

This method is used to approximate a general transformation of a parameter that is known to be asymptotically normal. Assume that:

$$\sqrt{n}\left(Z_n - \mu\right) \xrightarrow{L} N(0,\sigma^2) \quad \text{as } n \to \infty,$$

then

$$\sqrt{n}\left(h(Z_n) - h(\mu)\right) \xrightarrow{L} N\left(0, h'(\mu)^2 \cdot \sigma^2\right) \text{ as } n \to \infty.$$

For some continuous transformation h such that $h'\mu \neq 0$.

Consider now a parametric model, in the sense that $X_1, X_2, \ldots, X_n$ are independent random variables, with identical distribution F_θ (which can be a Weibull distribution to model a duration, a Pareto distribution to model the income or the wealth, etc.), with unknown parameter θ. The method of moments is a method of estimating parameters based on equating population and sample values of certain moments of the distribution. For instance, if $E[X] = \mu(\theta)$, then the

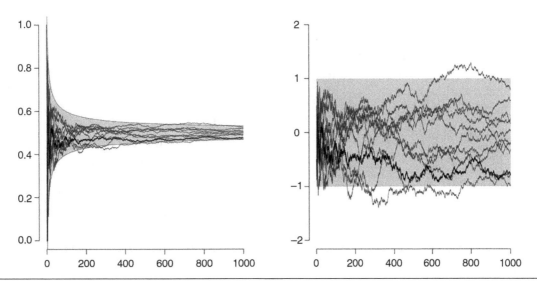

Figure 2   Law of large numbers on the left, with the convergence of $\bar{X}_n$ toward p as n increases, and central limit theorem on the right, with the convergence of $2\sqrt{n}[\bar{X}_n - p]$ towards a Gaussian distribution. The shaded area is the 95% confidence region.

estimator $\hat{\theta}$ of the unknown parameter is given by equation $\mu(\hat{\theta}_n) = \bar{x}$ or equivalently $\hat{\theta} = \mu^{-1}(\bar{x}_n)$. From the central limit theorem, we know that:

$$\sqrt{n}\left(\bar{X}_n - \mu\right) \xrightarrow{\ L\ } N(0, \sigma^2) \quad \text{as } n \infty$$

and applying the delta method with $h = \mu^{-1}$, then:

$$\sqrt{n}\left(\hat{\theta}_n - \theta\right) \xrightarrow{\ L\ } N\left(0, h'\left(h^{-1}(\theta)\right)^2 \cdot \sigma^2\right) \quad \text{as } n \to \infty$$

where a numerical approximation for the variance can be derived. This method has a long history, and has been intensively studied. Furthermore, this asymptotic normality can be used to compute a confidence interval, and also to derive an asymptotic testing procedure.

An Asymptotic Testing Procedure

Based on that asymptotic normality, it is possible to derive a simple testing procedure. Consider a test of the hypothesis H_0: $\theta = 0$ against H_1: $\theta \neq 0$, usually called a "significant" test for parameter θ (or significance of an explanatory variance in the context of regression model). Under the assumption that H_0 is valid, then $\sqrt{n}\hat{\theta} \xrightarrow{\ L\ } N(0, s^2)$ for some variance s^2, that can be computed using the

delta method. The p value associated with that test is:

$$p = P\left(|Z| > \left|\frac{\hat{\theta}_{obs}}{s}\right|\right)$$

where $\hat{\theta}_{\text{obs}}$ is the observed empirical estimator of the parameter and Z is a standard normal variable. Thus, the p-value can easily be computed using quantiles of the standard normal distribution. Here, the p-value is above 5% if:

$$-1.96 < \frac{\hat{\theta}_{obs}}{s} < 1.96.$$

Weaker Forms of the Central Limit Theorem

As stated by Laplace, the central limit theorem relies on strong assumption. Hopefully, most of them can be relaxed. In a first variant of the theorem, random variables have to be independent, but not necessarily identically distributed. If random variables X_i have averages μ_i and variances σ_i^2, then μ and σ_2 in the central limit theorem should be replaced by averages of μ_i and $\sigma_i^{2'}$s, with an additional technical assumption related to the existence of some higher moments (the so-called Lyapunov condition).

For a second variant of the theorem, random variables can be dependent, as in ergodic Markov chain, or in autoregressive time series. In that context, if $X_1, X_2, \ldots, X_n$ is a stationary time series, with mean μ, then define:

$$\sigma^2 = \lim_{n \to \infty} \frac{E[S_n^2]}{n}$$

and with that limit, the central limit theorem hold:

$$P\left(\sqrt{n} \frac{[\bar{X}_n - \mu]}{\sigma} \leq x\right) \to \Phi(x),$$

even if the variance term has here a different interpretation.

Finally, a third variant that can be mentioned is the one obtained by Paul Lévy about asymptotic properties of the empirical average, when the variance is not finite (actually, even when the first moment in not finite). In that case, the limiting distribution is no longer Gaussian.

Arthur Charpentier

See also Bernoulli Distribution; *F* Distribution; *t* Tests

Further Readings

Laplace, P.S. de (1810). Mémoire sur les approximations des formules qui sont fonctions de très grands nombres et sur leur application aux probabilités. Mémoires de l'Académie Royale des Sciences de Paris, 10. See http://www.cs.xu.edu/math/Sources/Laplace/approximations%20of%20formulas%201809.pdf

Le Cam, L. (1986). The central limit theorem around 1935. *Statistical Science* 1(1): 78–96.

Polyà, G. (1920). Ueber den zentralen Grenzwertsatz der Wahrscheinlichkeitsrechnung und das Momentproblem. *Mathematische Zeitschrift 8*, 171–181. See http://gdz.sub.uni-goettingen.de/dms/load/img/?PPN=PPN266833020_0008

CERTIFICATION

Educator certification is the process of documenting an individual's qualifications to practice teaching, administration, or special services in a public school. The standards and regulations of certification are dynamic and reflect the complex political and social issues that affect public education in the United States. The underlying purpose for certification is to ensure high-quality, competent educators.

In the 18th and 19th centuries, teachers were hired based on their ability to pass a locally accepted evaluation and the possession of "good moral character." Over time, states exerted more control over certification, and institutions of higher education developed pedagogy-based programs in efforts to boost professionalism. Typical requirements for new teachers in the 21st century include a minimum of a bachelor's degree, completion of an approved program of teacher preparation, passing scores on standardized certification exams, and a criminal background clearance. Most states also require recent knowledge or experience, referred to as recency, and there may be additional training mandated in topics such as first aid or identifying child abuse.

Traditional approved programs for teacher preparation consist of coursework in content and pedagogy, along with field experiences including a university-supervised student teaching experience. Alternative routes to certification come in many forms and typically allow a person with a prior bachelor's degree to start teaching full time while completing pedagogy courses or professional development in a state-approved program. In alternative programs, paid classroom experience replaces the supervised student teaching. These programs may be offered through a university, a school district, or a state agency.

An initial certification program provides the training for the main/first teaching certificate. Additional content areas may be added to the initial certificate in several ways as allowed by each state; options may include completing an additional approved program, passing a list of specific courses, or passing the appropriate state subject area exam. For example, in some states, a licensed elementary K–6 teacher might be allowed to add an endorsement in middle-level math 5–8 by passing a state subject exam.

Certification terminology varies state by state and country by country. Some states issue a *certificate* while others issue a *license*, and California issues a *credential*. Educators must file for a new certificate when they move to a new state. Reciprocity allows some states to issue a certificate if the applicant holds a similar certificate in another state based on comparable requirements.

There is no reliable centralized source for certification/licensure information across all 50 states. Information on requirements in each state can be obtained from local experts, including personnel at state agencies, certification officers at institutions of higher education, and human resources staff in local school districts.

Teacher salaries frequently constitute a major portion of the state's overall budget, so there are fiscal as well as qualitative reasons for certification. In most states, proper certification is required, so that educational personnel may be paid from the correct pool of money. Supply and demand may affect changes in certification requirements too, as states adapt in order to bring new candidates into the teaching ranks.

Alisa Palmer Branham

See also Common Core State Standards; Teachers' Associations

Further Readings

Angus, D. *Professionalism and the public good: A brief history of teacher certification*. Retrieved from https://edex.s3-us-west-2.amazonaws.com/publication/pdfs/angus_7.pdf

Ravitch, D. *A brief history of teacher professionalism*. Retrieved from http://www2.ed.gov/print/admins/tchrqual/learn/preparingteachersconference/ravitch.html

CHEATING

In general terms, cheating is an action taken by an individual to intentionally bias assessment results. The "individual" involved can be anyone with knowledge of or access to testing materials and/or the testing process: "testing materials" include test items, test booklets, scoring templates, answer sheets, score reports, or databases for item responses or test scores; and "testing processes" include test development, technical aspects of test delivery, test proctoring, test scoring, and test reporting. Cheating may involve one or more examinees, educators, third-party test preparation entities, testing staff, parents, or representatives of the testing company or its various partners and vendors. Although many actions may result in biased test scores, cheating requires that the actions are done with the goal of biasing the results. Similarly, whether the assessment results are actually biased, or biased in the intended direction, is irrelevant under this definition.

Cheating is important because it creates a fundamental fairness issue among examinees, and to the extent it allows individuals to acquire a license or credential to practice in a discipline for which they are unqualified may also present a possible threat to the health, safety, and well-being of the public. This entry begins by providing a general context for cheating and follows with discussions of preventing, deterring, and impeding cheating, detecting cheating, and deciding how to address cheating.

The Cheating Context

Although no compelling trend data exist to suggest that the overall prevalence of cheating has changed dramatically since the 1960s, since the start of the 21st century, the prevalence and magnitude of cheating have garnered more national and international media attention. Furthermore, the methods used for cheating have evolved as technology has evolved.

Cheating on assessments occurs across the globe and can involve individuals at any age and educational level. Individuals may feel more pressure to cheat when they perceive exam results will have a reputational, financial, or employment impact. The greater the impact of assessment results, whether positive or negative, the more likely individuals will be to engage in cheating. Because assessment results can significantly impact a variety of stakeholders, numerous individuals with access to testing materials or the assessment process may have an incentive to cheat.

Cheating can have measurement, societal, and financial consequences. Cheating on assessments can result in inaccurate data and invalid measurement results. When an individual cheats on a norm-referenced test, such as a classroom exam or an admissions/employment test, the cheater can gain an unfair advantage over others. When educators cheat, the conclusions drawn from invalid scores may result in a failure to provide students adequate instruction, inappropriate district-wide adjustments in curriculum and staffing, and skewed teacher evaluations or unwarranted salary adjustments. When examinees cheat to obtain professional credentials, individuals may be allowed to practice in an area that has direct impact on the health and safety of the public. Depending on the extent of cheating, society may determine legal consequences, such as civil or criminal liability, are appropriate. Tangible financial costs are associated with investigating cheating, invalidating scores, terminating testing staff, and engaging in administrative, civil, or criminal actions.

There are several common methods used to cheat on standardized exams, including copying, unauthorized use of exam aids (e.g., notes written on paper or clothing or answers stored or transmitted through digital means), use of a surrogate tester, examination preknowledge, and tampering. Examinees may attempt to gain access to secure test materials, including through theft of paper materials or digital hacking, in an attempt to gain knowledge of exam questions and answers prior to the exam administration. During administration, examinees may capture test content or answers with the intent of compromising score validity for subsequent administrations. Educators or training program employees may provide students with preknowledge by viewing the test in advance of the administration and teaching the questions and answers to students. Educators or test administrators may tamper with test results by coaching examinees during the test or changing responses after testing has concluded.

Left unchecked, cheating can become widespread. Thus, it is helpful for testing programs and score users, such as school districts, universities, credentialing programs, and employment entities, to have in place a holistic framework for addressing cheating, including steps to deter or prevent cheating, tools to detect potential cheating incidents, and processes to decide how to respond to incidents. Furthermore, because numerous individuals can engage in conduct that threatens valid assessment results, it is necessary to consider deterrence, detection, and decision-making across a broad range of actors.

Preventing, Deterring, and Impeding Cheating

The first line of defense against cheating is to attempt to prevent it entirely or, alternatively, to deter it from happening or impede its effectiveness in the event it does occur. Testing programs use multiple strategies to prevent, deter, and impede cheating on tests.

Test Design

Test developers have a range of tools available to make cheating more difficult and less likely to be successful. Different testing modalities pose different advantages and disadvantages with respect to cheating. Single-form, linear testing, in which all examinees see the same items in the same order, presents the greatest cheating risk because examinees who copy from neighboring examinees have a high probability of improving their performance, and examinees entering the testing room with prior information or preknowledge about operational test questions are guaranteed to see those items during the exam. Scrambling test items so they appear in different orders for different examinees may help prevent or reduce answer copying as well as reduce its negative impact. Using multiple equated test forms has many security advantages, including reducing the likelihood of neighboring examinees seeing the same items and reducing the likelihood examinees with preknowledge will be administered the compromised items. In addition, programs can ensure that retesting examinees are administered a different form of the test with limited content overlap.

Computerized adaptive testing (CAT), in which each examinee receives a tailored exam, optimized for the person's performance level, offers many security advantages over paper-based or computer-based linear testing. Answer copying is essentially eliminated in CAT; moreover, variable length CATs are inherently self-correcting for unusual responses, as might be the case for examinees with preknowledge of difficult items, provided there are no constraints on the length of the exam because in CAT, spuriously correct answers lead to more difficult questions for which the examinee's probability of correct response is lower. As a countermeasure against examinees entering with preknowledge, CATs often rely on several large, regularly rotated item pools and use a variety of methods to control the exposure rates of individual items.

Perhaps the most serious security vulnerability of computer-based tests is that to improve access and convenience, tests are often administered over extended periods, referred to as testing windows, ranging from several days to a few months. Although programs can implement security measures between testing windows, such as using entirely new item pools and limiting examinees to a single testing attempt per window, different examinees testing within a common window will often see a high degree of overlap in test content. Utilizing testing windows raises the risk of examinees entering with preknowledge obtained from an examinee who tested earlier in the window. Narrow testing windows can help reduce this type of cheating.

Communication and Contracting

To help deter cheating, testing programs should clearly communicate to examinees and testing staff what is considered appropriate (or prohibited) behavior and what materials are allowed (or not) in the testing room. Programs should also clearly denote copyrights and communicate potential consequences for violations of test security policies or agreements. Sanctions for cheating typically include outcomes ranging from score cancelation to legal action, including civil claims and criminal prosecution.

Information on cheating may be communicated to examinees through pretest instructions or in a contract agreed to at the time of registration or immediately prior to the test administration. It may also be communicated again following the exam to reinforce examinee obligations, including the obligation to maintain the confidentiality of exam content. In addition, testing program employees, test administration staff, and vendors are typically asked to sign confidentiality agreements, which require those individuals to maintain the security and confidentiality of the testing materials to which they have access.

Check-in

One of the most common and potentially successful cheating strategies is to access and utilize prohibited items during the exam, such as notes, the Internet, communication devices, or imaging equipment. Because detecting prohibited items during testing is difficult, it is common to take steps to locate and exclude them from the exam environment. Testing staff often require examinees to turn out their pockets to demonstrate they are empty, place hats, sunglasses, or other disallowed accessories in a storage locker outside the testing room, or submit suspicious outerwear, such as baggy sweatshirts or overcoats, to inspection prior to entering the testing room. Metal detection devices can be used to scan rooms or examinees for prohibited technology.

To address the risk of surrogate testing, examinees are commonly required to provide identification prior to entering the testing room, such as a government-issued photo ID, which can be cross-referenced by testing staff with the examinee's registration data to ensure physical likeness and identical matching of demographic data collected during the registration process. Many programs also use biometric data, such as palm vein scans or voice recognition, to authenticate candidates. Identification procedures are often used every time an examinee enters the testing room, including after scheduled and unscheduled breaks. Examinees without appropriate matching identification credentials are typically not allowed to test.

Test Administration and Proctoring

During group examinations, examinees are ideally randomly assigned seats by testing staff to deter collaboration among examinees. Seating examinees facing front with wide space between them makes answer copying or communication with other examinees more difficult.

Managing examinees during breaks is critical, especially during scheduled breaks, where all examinees are breaking simultaneously and communication between examinees is expected. Having a defined break area that restricts examinees' abilities to interact with individuals outside the testing center is common. Testing staff often remind examinees not to discuss test content or access technology or test materials during the break and monitor examinees for compliance.

Proctors should be free of conflicts of interest to help reduce the risk of cheating by the proctor.

Enough proctors should be used to adequately monitor testing activities and actively look for signs of cheating. Testing staff should be familiar with and adhere to the standardization protocol for each test administered. Ideally, staff should be able to identify and respond to a wide range of cheating behaviors and unusual situations (such as fire alarms) which could increase opportunities for cheating.

Detecting and Investigating Cheating

Despite testing programs' best efforts, prevention strategies are not always successful and examinees manage to successfully cheat on exams. Consequently, best practice is to also devote resources to detecting cheating after it happens. The late 20th and early 21st centuries have seen numerous advances in statistical methodologies designed explicitly for detecting different forms of test cheating. Figure 1 depicts the broad categories of statistical approaches and the types of cheating they are commonly used to detect.

Person-Fit

Cheating often produces response patterns that are not explained well by the psychometric models used to fit the data. Person-fit involves conducting a statistical test to identify nonmodel-fitting examinees. Many different person-fit measures exist, and in practice, testing for fit is often used as a

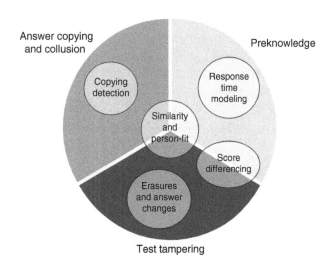

Figure 1   Statistical methodologies and common uses for detecting cheating

first step to reduce the pool of potential cheaters to a more reasonable number. However, because there are many legitimate reasons why an examinee may produce a nonfitting response pattern, such as time pressure, creative responding, carelessness, and unconventional instruction, person-fit measures often detect a lower proportion of actual cheaters than do other statistical methods.

Copying Detection and Similarity

Early work on cheating detection focused almost entirely on answer copying. With answer copying becoming less prevalent due to computerized testing, for many programs, focus has shifted to answer similarity. Copying and similarity indexes flag examinees who produce an observed number of answer matches that significantly exceeds the number of matches predicted under the model. Computationally, the difference between the two rests on the directionality of the index. With answer copying indexes, the expected number of matches is computed conditionally on the estimated trait level for the suspected copier and the answer string for the suspected source, thereby producing different index values depending on which examinee is evaluated as the copier. With similarity indexes, the expected number of matches is computed by finding the probability of matching on any of the item alternatives, conditioned on the trait levels for both examinees. The symmetry of similarity indexes allows them to be used to identify groups of examinees with similar responses; hence, they have proven useful for detecting other forms of cheating, such as preknowledge and test tampering. For both copying and similarity indexes, research has found that using all items, rather than only jointly incorrect items, results in the highest detection rates.

Score Differencing

Score differencing detects preknowledge by identifying examinees whose performance on a set of compromised items is significantly different than is expected based on their performance on secure items. Score differencing works best when it is known which items have been compromised, as might be the case when items are found on the Internet or examinees are found with printouts of live test content. However, when no known compromise exists, programs will often compare examinees' performances on pilot and operational items or on items with many exposures and items with few exposures. Because preknowledge usually results in inflated scores, it is typically easier to identify examinees with preknowledge when difficult items become compromised. However, in special cases where programs include items that are modified slightly from the compromised versions, blind reliance on preknowledge will lower the examinee's score and score differencing will work better if the modified items are easy.

Gain scores represent a special type of score differencing, in which an examinee's current test score is compared to a previous one. Retest candidates typically improve their performance; however, candidates who improve by more than the expected amount may be suspected of having preknowledge or having engaged in some other type of cheating. In educational accountability settings, students, classes, or districts that show unusual growth may be flagged for investigation into potential inappropriate coaching or educator tampering.

Erasures and Answer Changes

Research has found that examinees change their test answers infrequently; most estimates are that changes occur on approximately 2% of the items. Furthermore, when examinees do change their answers, approximately half the changes are expected to involve switching from a right to a wrong answer or from one wrong answer to another. Consequently, examinees with large numbers of answers that have been changed from wrong to right are suspicious and may indicate test tampering. Answer changing methods have most commonly been applied to K–12 accountability exams. The most frequently used answer change methods involve comparing the number or average number of wrong to right changes per student, often aggregated to the class, school, or district level. Although most of these methods have not been well researched and their effectiveness at detecting different amounts and magnitudes of tampering is not well understood, they have been used to help uncover many large-scale instances of educator cheating.

A second, newer class of answer change methodologies adopts a score differencing approach by comparing performance across those items for which the initial answer was changed with the expected score on those items based on the examinee's performance on all other items. Although the research on these methods is limited, they are theoretically preferable to count-based methods and appear to work quite well at detecting moderate-to-large amounts of tampering.

Response Time Methods

In computer-based testing, it is possible to collect data on the amount of time examinees spend answering each question. Response time has been shown to vary considerably across items, as a function of reading load, cognitive load, and the amount of computation, as well as intraindividual differences. Several response time models exist which predict the amount of time necessary to complete an item, based on both item and person characteristics. Irregular response time patterns—spending considerably more or less time than expected on certain items—can be useful for detecting examinees with preknowledge or attempting to steal exam content. Response time models are sensitive to examinees who answer many items very quickly, particularly if those items were largely answered correctly or were believed to be compromised. One unique feature of response time models is that multiple examinees producing both correct answers and unusually short response times on common items can help identify compromised items that had previously been believed to be secure.

Other Methods for Detecting Cheating

Cheating detection is not limited to statistical approaches. Although proctoring was discussed earlier as a deterrent to cheating, it is also one of the more common mechanisms for detecting cheating. Many programs establish an anonymous reporting service that enables individuals to report potential test security concerns through a secure hotline or webform. Frequent web monitoring can identify examinee attempts to hire surrogates or share live items. Use of nonscore-related data, such as examinee travel patterns or irregularity reports at test sites, can help identify or predict patterns of unusual behavior that can be used to trigger an investigation or increase monitoring.

Deciding How to Address Cheating

Once a potential cheating incident has been detected, several decisions are necessary. The first is whether and to what extent the potential incident will be investigated. There is professional debate concerning whether statistical evidence, standing alone, is sufficient to cancel scores. The traditional and conservative approach is to use statistical evidence to trigger an investigation. However, as methods have advanced, some programs are using results from statistical analyses to void or cancel scores.

If additional investigation is conducted, qualified and objective individuals ideally should conduct the investigation. The investigators may collect a wide range of evidence, such as interviews of examinees and testing staff, collection and evaluation of relevant materials, additional statistical analyses, and biometric data evaluation. Depending on who is implicated in the investigation, it may be necessary to include union or legal representatives in the investigation.

After the investigation concludes, the next decision is the appropriate body to evaluate the evidence and the process to be used for deciding consequences, if any. This may be impacted by state laws, agency regulations, local policies, and contract terms. Depending on the circumstances, the decision body may range from a teacher to an ethics committee, independent panel, or credentialing authority. Processes for deciding consequences may range from an informal meeting to a formal, recorded hearing and written decision by an administrative body. Typically, these bodies are asked to determine whether a score is invalid or whether cheating occurred by a preponderance of the evidence, and decisions rendered will be held to a reasonableness standard.

The next decision is what consequences to impose for individuals found to have engaged in cheating. Consequences will vary with the circumstances and evidentiary findings. For example, where cheating has impacted score validity, scores may be cancelled or voided at either an individual or group level and credentials may be revoked. Notice of the decision may be provided to third parties, such as school districts, colleges, employers, or law enforcement. Individuals found to have engaged in cheating may be required to undergo ethics training, be prohibited from retesting (or administering assessments, in the case of an educator or test administrator) for a period of time, be expelled from school, or have their credentials rescinded.

The final decision is whether, based on the investigative findings, steps can be taken to improve the assessment process. For example, in an effort to deter future misconduct, school districts or colleges and universities may decide to invest in additional staff training or create more messaging to students to ensure all stakeholders understand the consequences of cheating.

James Wollack and Rachel Watkins Schoenig

See also Test Security; Tests

Further Readings

Cizek, G. J. (1999). *Cheating on tests: How to do it, detect it, and prevent it.* Mahwah, NJ: Erlbaum.

Cizek, G. J., & Wollack, J. A. (Eds.). (2017). *Handbook of quantitative methods for detecting cheating on tests.* New York, NY: Routledge.

Josephson Institute. (2012). *2012 report card on the ethics of American youth.* Los Angeles, CA: Author.

Kingston, N. M., & Clark, A. K. (2014). *Test fraud: Statistical detection and methodology.* New York, NY: Routledge.

Lang, J. M. (2013). *Cheating lessons: Learning from academic dishonesty.* Cambridge, MA: President and Fellows of Harvard College.

National Council on Measurement in Education. (2012). *Testing and data integrity in the administration of statewide student assessment programs.* Madison, WI: Author.

Olson, J. F., & Fremer, J. J. (2013). *TILSA test security guidebook: Preventing, detecting, and investigating test security irregularities.* Washington, DC: Council of Chief State School Officers.

Wollack, J. A., & Case, S. M. (2016). Maintaining fairness through test administration. In N. J. Dorans & L. L. Cook (Eds.), *Fairness in educational assessment and measurement* (pp. 33–53). New York, NY: Routledge.

Wollack, J. A., & Cizek, G. J. (2017). Security issues in professional certification/licensure testing. In S.

Davis-Becker & C. Buckendahl (Eds.) *Testing in the professions* (pp. 178–209). New York, NY: Routledge.

Wollack, J. A., & Fremer, J. J. (Eds.). (2013). *Handbook of test security.* New York, NY: Routledge.

CHILDHOOD

Historically, childhood has been defined as the time period prior to adulthood or maturity. A more precise contemporary definition frames childhood as the period between the end of infancy and the beginning of adolescence or from approximately 2–12 years of age. The juvenile period of physical and cognitive immaturity is substantially longer relative to the overall life span for humans compared to other species. This lengthy period of immaturity is due to the complexity of the human brain.

Humans' lengthy childhood allows for substantial flexibility in development, such that individuals can adapt to a wide range of physical and cultural environments. Understanding of children and their development is critical to educational policy and practice. This entry discusses the history of the construct of childhood, methods for studying children and their development, and major domains of child development.

History

For much of history, children were viewed as the property of their parents (particularly their fathers), and the goal of child-rearing was to have children assume adult responsibilities as quickly as possible. It was common for children to work full days on farms or in factories. This version of childhood persists in many parts of the world. However, in developed countries, the view of children and childhood has changed substantially, such that children are generally protected from adult responsibilities such as paid work, and parents devote substantial time and resources to ensuring that their children are healthy and happy. A number of social, economic, and cultural factors contributed to these changes, including a move away from agrarian economies, increased availability of formal schooling, and decreased infant and child mortality rates.

Along with changes regarding children's value and roles, there have also been changes throughout history in views of the fundamental nature of children. For much of Western history, perceptions of children were shaped by the notion of "original sin"—a belief that people are born with an inclination toward evil and that children must be trained away from these tendencies by adults, often through the use of harsh discipline. In the 18th century, this view was called into question by the writings of two philosophers, Jean-Jacques Rousseau and John Locke.

Rousseau viewed children as "noble savages" who were born with an innate sense of right and wrong and were largely harmed, rather than helped, by adult intervention. Rousseau argued that the best outcomes would arise from allowing children to develop naturally, with minimal intervention from adults. Locke, in contrast, viewed the child as a blank slate, beginning from nothing and being shaped, either positively or negatively, by the actions of parents and other adults.

Both Locke and Rousseau argued that harsh treatment of children was not beneficial for their development. Their writings influenced the emerging field of developmental psychology in a variety of ways, including the examination of the roles of nature (innate characteristics, traits, and predispositions, such as those emphasized by Rousseau) and nurture (environmental influences, such as the actions of parents and teachers, as emphasized by Locke) in children's development.

Although philosophers and scholars have reflected on the nature of childhood and goals of child-rearing for centuries, the formal study of children's development has a relatively short history. The first careful observations of children's development we published in the mid-19th century included Charles Darwin's "baby biographies." Systematic theories and empirical study of child development emerged even later, with the work of early psychologists including Sigmund Freud, G. Stanley Hall, Melanie Klein, Jean Piaget, B. F. Skinner, Lev Vygotsky, and John Watson. These researchers sought to document and explain typical and atypical patterns of children's development and the factors that influenced development.

Methods for Studying Children

Researchers use a wide variety of methods for studying children's development. These methods include observations of behavior (both naturalistic and structured), interviews, surveys, case studies, and psychophysiological methods (measures of the physical manifestations of thoughts or emotions such as heart rate or brain activity).

In order to study the effects of age and development, researchers may use methods that examine children at different ages. Such studies might include longitudinal, cross-sectional, sequential, or microgenetic research designs. Longitudinal studies examine the same person at multiple points in time (e.g., assessing a group of children each year from ages 5 to 9). Cross-sectional studies, in contrast, examine children of different ages (e.g., 5-, 7-, and 9-year-olds) at the same point in time.

Sequential studies combine elements of cross-sectional and longitudinal designs, beginning with participants of different ages and following them over time. Microgenetic designs aim to examine children's behavior or cognition while it is changing; these designs assess children who are thought to be on the verge of an important developmental change by studying individuals at multiple time points over a fairly short span of time (typically several months to a year).

Stages

Childhood is frequently divided into three stages: early, middle, and late childhood. Early childhood spans the period from 2 to 5 or 6 years of age (the age at which children typically begin formal schooling). Middle childhood begins around age 6 and lasts until approximately age 10, roughly corresponding to the elementary or primary school years. Late childhood (sometimes referred to as preadolescence) spans approximately ages 10–12 years, at which point most children have begun puberty and thus entered adolescence. Preadolescents are sometimes informally referred to as "tweens," indicating their status as being in between childhood and adolescence.

Developmental Contexts

There are three developmental contexts that are viewed as most influential for children and thus most widely studied by researchers: the family, the school, and the peer group. Relationships and experiences within these contexts can have substantial influences on children's development. In addition, interactions of these contexts can have meaningful effects on the child. For example, parental involvement with schooling may promote children's academic achievement, whereas conflict between parents and teachers may have a negative impact on academic performance.

Developmental Tasks

Developmental tasks are the fundamental skills and abilities that must be acquired for optimal development at a given life stage. Accomplishment of these tasks provides a foundation for progress toward subsequent developmental stages. Key developmental tasks of childhood include developing a sense of personal identity, internalizing rules and moral standards for behavior, establishing peer relationships, managing emotions, learning to solve problems independently, and engaging with school.

Socialization

Socialization is the process by which an individual acquires the attitudes, knowledge, and skills needed to succeed within a particular social or cultural context. Socialization of the child is a primary goal of parents, teachers, and other adults who regularly interact with children. The goals of socialization will vary depending on the social and cultural context. For example, in individualistic cultures, there is typically a view that the child is born helpless and dependent, and a primary goal of socialization is to promote independence and self-reliance. In contrast, in collectivist cultures, the child is often viewed as having been born independent or separate from others, and a primary goal of socialization is to foster feelings of connection to family and community members. Cultures also vary widely in other aspects of socialization, such as flexibility of gender roles, tolerance of aggressive behavior, and the importance of deference to elders.

Goodness of Fit

One important aspect of promoting optimal child development is the goodness of fit between a child's developmental level and the environments the child experiences. For example, parents or teachers who have unrealistic expectations for children's abilities may become frustrated with a child's lack of performance and become harsh or rejecting with the child.

The educational construct of developmentally appropriate practice recognizes the importance of matching educational requirements to children's cognitive and socioemotional development. In some cases, researchers have criticized the educational system for the lack of attention to children's developmental needs. For example, when students transition from elementary to middle school, the environment often becomes more restrictive just as students are developmentally ready for greater autonomy; this lack of fit between students and their environment may decrease academic motivation and engagement.

Research on goodness of fit also emphasizes the importance of fit between a child's characteristics (such as temperament) and the child's environment. For example, a shy child who is born into an outgoing family may struggle with the expectations placed on her by her parents or siblings. Although goodness of fit is important throughout development, issues of fit may be especially important in childhood because children generally have less control and choice over their environments relative to adults (i.e., a child is less able than an adult to choose to leave a situation that is not a good fit).

Cognitive Development

Over the course of childhood, thought becomes increasingly logical and flexible. Executive function, the ability to monitor and regulate one's thinking and decision making, also increases over the course of childhood. As children move from early to middle childhood, their attention spans and memory capacities increase. Thus, children are increasingly able to understand and use deliberate learning strategies to retain information and accomplish academic tasks. Throughout the course of childhood, an environment that provides appropriate levels of cognitive stimulation (e.g., talking to children, reading to and with children, exploring nature) promotes cognitive growth and development.

Emotional Development

Basic emotions, such as anger, joy, and surprise, are present from infancy. Self-conscious emotions, such as guilt and pride, emerge in the early childhood years, once the child has developed a sense of self. Over the course of childhood, children become more skilled at recognizing emotions in themselves and others and at regulating and managing their own emotions.

By middle childhood, children have a range of emotion regulation strategies at their disposal, including cognitive reframing, emotion-centered coping (i.e., behavioral strategies intended to change one's emotional state, such as watching a funny movie), and problem-centered coping (i.e., behavioral strategies intended to change an upsetting situation, such as deciding to study harder next time after failing a test).

Identity Development

As children develop, their sense of self becomes more detailed and differentiated (moving from a generalized self-view to awareness of one's strengths and weaknesses in a variety of areas such as academic performance, physical skills, and relationships with peers). With development, self-views also become more accurate, as children become more aware of their own capabilities in comparison to peers and objective performance standards. Awareness of one's membership in important social categories (such as gender, race/ethnicity, and religion) increases across childhood; these social group memberships may play an important role in identity development.

Moral Development

Moral development includes multiple elements: moral reasoning (thinking about moral situations and actions), prosocial behavior (engaging in moral behaviors such as helping and sharing), moral emotions (such as feelings of guilt following a moral transgression), and development of conscience (a personal sense of right and wrong). Research indicates that allowing children ample opportunities for prosocial behavior, combined with the use of inductive discipline (which focuses on teaching children about the consequences of their behavior for self and others), is effective in promoting moral development.

Family Relationships

Relationships with parents and (for those children who have them) siblings are a major influence on children's development. Research indicates that the best outcomes occur when parents are warm and supportive toward their children while also setting clear limits for acceptable behavior. Parents should set clear rules, explain the reasons for these rules, and enforce appropriate consequences when rules are not followed. Optimal parenting also takes into account the child's developmental level and individual characteristics (e.g., a reserved child may need to be encouraged to take more risks, whereas a more adventurous child may need to be discouraged from doing so).

Peer Relationships

Friendships are important throughout childhood. Interactions with friends provide an opportunity to build social and cognitive skills, and positive relationships with friends can provide a buffer against negative experiences (such as bullying). As children grow older, friends become an increasingly important source of emotional support.

Conflicts among peers are relatively common. These conflicts can be learning experiences, encouraging children to think about events from another person's perspective. With increasing age, most children become less likely to resort to physical aggression during conflicts with peers, due to increasing ability to take others' perspectives and to use alternative strategies (such as verbal negotiation) to resolve conflicts. For children whose levels of aggression remain high, there is an increased risk of rejection by peers due to this aggressive behavior.

Risk and Resilience

There are a variety of risks or threats to optimal development that children may experience. These include physical or mental illness, exposure to environmental toxins, experience with trauma (such as physical or sexual abuse), and family conflict. Children whose families lack economic resources are more vulnerable to a variety of

threats, including poorer health, unsafe living conditions, and exposure to trauma.

Although exposure to these risk factors is generally associated with poorer developmental outcomes, many children express resilience or an ability to thrive despite negative experiences or difficult life circumstances. Factors that promote resilience include intelligence, high self-esteem, strong self-regulation abilities, and warm, supportive relationships with family members, peers, and teachers.

Meagan M. Patterson

See also Adolescence; Cognitive Development, Theory of; Erikson's Stages of Psychosocial Development; Kindergarten; Puberty; Resilience

Further Readings

American Academy of Pediatrics. (2014). *Caring for your baby and young child: Birth to age 5* (6th ed.). New York, NY: Bantam Books.

Berk, L. E. (2012). *Child development* (9th ed.). Upper Saddle River, NJ: Pearson.

Bjorklund, D. F. (1997). The role of immaturity in human development. *Psychological Bulletin, 122,* 153–169.

Bradley, R. H., & Corwyn, R. F. (2002). Socioeconomic status and child development. *Annual Review of Psychology, 53,* 371–399.

Hunt, M. (2007). The developmentalists. In *The story of psychology* (Rev. ed., pp. 401–458). New York, NY: Random House.

Lancy, D. F. (2015). *The anthropology of childhood: Cherubs, chattel, changelings* (2nd ed.). New York, NY: Cambridge University Press.

Masten, A. S., & Coatsworth, J. D. (1998). The development of competence in favorable and unfavorable environments: Lessons from research on successful children. *American Psychologist, 53,* 205–220.

CHI-SQUARE TEST

The chi-square test refers to a family of statistical tests that have been utilized to determine whether the observed (sampling) distribution or outcome differs significantly from an a priori or theoretically anticipated outcome or distribution. More simply stated, the test is formulated to determine whether the difference observed was due to a chance occurrence. This entry further describes the chi-square test and looks at its basic principles, applications, and limitations.

Although the most common chi-square test statistic is Pearson's chi-square test, there are other test statistics that exist with the same theoretical foundation including Yates's chi-square test, Tukey's test of additivity, Cochran–Mantel–Haenszel test, and likelihood ratio tests. Although the chi-square test has been applied to a plethora of statistical applications, the fundamental utilization has been as a goodness-of-fit statistic and difference test by comparing a hypothesized distribution to an observed distribution.

In 1900, Karl Pearson developed the chi-square test and published his work entitled "On the criterion that a given system of deviations from the probable in the case of a correlated system of variables is such that it can be reasonably supposed to have arisen from random sampling," where he outlined the limitations of related measures and the functional utility of the test he developed. While the idea of determining whether standard distributions gave acceptable fits to data sets was well established early in Pearson's career, detailed in his 1900 paper, he was determined to derive a test procedure that further advanced the problem of goodness of fit. As a result, the formulation of the chi-square statistic stands as one of the greatest statistical achievements of the 20th century.

Basic Principles and Applications

Generally speaking, a chi-square test (also commonly referred to as χ^2) refers to a bevy of statistical hypothesis tests where the objective is to compare a sample distribution to a theorized distribution to confirm (or refute) a null hypothesis. Two important conditions that must exist for the chi-square test are independence and sample size or distribution. For independence, each case that contributes to the overall count or data set must be independent of all other cases that make up the overall count. Second, each particular scenario must have a specified number of cases within the data set to perform the analysis. The literature points to a number of arbitrary cutoffs for the overall sample size.

The chi-square test has most often been utilized in two types of comparison situations: a test of goodness of fit or a test of independence. One of the most common uses of the chi-square test is to determine whether a frequency data set can be adequately represented by a specified distribution function. More clearly, a chi-square test is appropriate when you are trying to determine whether sample data are consistent with a hypothesized distribution. The test includes the following procedures: Compute the chi-square statistic, determine the degrees of freedom, select the desired confidence level or p value, compare the chi-square value to the critical value in a chi-square distribution table, and decide to accept or reject the null hypothesis on the basis that the observed distribution differs from the theoretical distribution based upon whether the chi-square value exceeds or is less than the critical value.

The chi-square test is also commonly used as a test of independence. By this, it is meant that two variables are compared in a contingency table to determine whether they are related. More generally speaking, the test of independence compares the distribution of categorical variables to see the degree to which they differ from one another. If the two distributions are identical, the chi-square statistic is 0. However, if there is a significant difference between distributions, the result will be a much higher number.

The basic formula for the chi-square statistic used in a chi-square test is as follows:

$$\chi_c^2 = \sum \frac{(O_i - E_i)^2}{E_i}.$$

In this particular formula, the subscript "c" denotes the degrees of freedom, whereas "O" is the observed value and "E" is the expected value. The summation symbol indicates that this calculation needs to be performed for every data point in your data set. The chi-square statistic is a single number that tells you how much difference exists between the observed and expected frequencies. The chi-square statistic can only be used on numbers and is not applicable to percentages, proportions, or medians, for example.

One of the most common ways to utilize the chi-square statistic is in hypothesis testing and involves the utilization of a chi-square table. After you have calculated the chi-square statistic and have the degrees of freedom, you can consult a chi-square distribution table to determine your p value, which will inform your decision to accept or reject the null hypothesis. Generally speaking, the smaller the p value, the higher the likelihood of rejecting the null hypothesis, as the likelihood for Type I error is minimal.

To better understand the utility of the chi-square test, a common example utilized is to examine the rolling patterns of two dice in a casino game. For any dice game, the odds that a specific number would come up when thrown should be 1 in 6. However, if we are looking to prove that the player is cheating and may be using "loaded" dice, we can use a chi-square test to determine whether certain numbers coming up more than others represents a meaningful difference or if it is by mere chance. The first step would involve establishing a hypothesis for how you believe the dice should act after a number of throws.

In the casino game example, if there are 60 throws, you would expect each number (1–6) to come up 10 times. Therefore, we could create a table that contains our expected frequency of each number to come up versus what we observe. Let's say over 60 throws of the dice, the following values come up: 1 = 5, 2 = 16, 3 = 17, 4 = 6, 5 = 7, and 6 = 9. It is important to remember that the expected number for each value is 10. Based on the frequency of certain numbers appearing more than others, it would lend credence to the idea that the die might be loaded to produce more 2s and 3s than the rest of the numbers. However, this could occur by chance as well.

A chi-square test can be used to determine whether the difference between the observed and the expected is meaningful and significant. By using the expected and the observed numbers as well as the number of observations, we can utilize the formula that was discussed earlier to derive our chi-square statistic. Once we have our chi-square statistic, we can consult the chi-square distribution table to determine our p value (ensuring also that we know the degrees of freedom). The significance level (remember, the smaller the p value, the more likely that we will reject the null hypothesis) provides guidance as to whether we want to reject or accept the null hypothesis (also informing us of the likelihood of committing a Type I or Type II error). The chi-square test

represents a family of statistical tools and has been used to develop other measures that can be utilized with other statistical tests. In this section, two such statistical methods are described: analysis of variance and structural equation modeling (SEM). In regression analysis, Tukey's test of additivity is a common statistical test that utilizes the principles of the chi-square test. Specifically, Tukey's test is commonly applied to a two-way analysis of variance. The overarching goal of Tukey's test is to test for interaction when a variable is added to the overall factorial model (typically referred to as an "additive" model). More clearly stated, if a researcher believes interaction (the effect of one variable differs depending on the level of another variable) is an issue, Tukey's test can be used to test the level of interaction effect with the variable added to the factor model.

In the realm of SEM, a chi-square statistic is a goodness-of-fit test and a common statistical tool used to measure the difference between observed and estimated covariance matrices. It is the only goodness-of-fit measure used for SEM that has a direct significance level attached to its testing and forms the basis of many other goodness-of-fit measures. Unlike how the chi-square test is interpreted in other statistical disciplines, for SEM, we actually desire a low chi-square value and in turn, the larger the p value, the better. The reason behind this is that the null hypothesis for SEM model testing is that the estimated covariance matrix and the observed matrix are equal. As a result, the smaller the difference between the estimated and observed covariance matrix, the better the hypothesized model fits the data.

Limitations

Although the chi-square test has formed the basis for numerous other statistical tests and represents a leap forward in the realm of statistics, its use comes with a number of limitations. First, it has been shown that a number of studies have incorrectly applied the chi-square test in a variety of research contexts. The most common sources of error were (a) the lack of independence among the measures/variables tested, (b) theoretical frequencies that are too small, (c) use of nonfrequency data, (d) incorrect determination of the number of degrees of freedom, and (e) failure to equalize the sum of observed frequencies and the sum of the theorized frequencies.

In the realm of SEM, the utilization of the chi-square statistic as the sole goodness-of-fit measure is problematic as well. The chi-square statistic is highly susceptible to being influenced by the overall sample size due to the fact that it is a mathematical function of N as well as the difference between the observed and estimated covariance matrix. As the sample size increases, so does the chi-square statistic, even if the differences in the matrices remain constant. Second, the number of observed variables also can influence it in that the more observed variables that are present in the SEM model, the higher the chi-square value will be. Although it is the only goodness-of-fit measure with a significance level attached to it, researchers must understand how this statistic is susceptible to the sample size and the number of observed variables in the model.

Brian S. Gordon

See also Analysis of Variance; Goodness-of-Fit Tests; Hypothesis Testing; Interaction; *p* Value; Sample Size; Structural Equation Modeling; Two-Way Chi-Square; Type I Error; Type II Error

Further Readings

Chernoff, H., & Lehmann, E. L. (1954). The use of maximum likelihood estimates in χ^2 tests for goodness of fit. *The Annals of Mathematical Statistics, 25*(3), 579–586.

Greenwood, P. E., & Nikulin, M. S. (1996). *A guide to chi-squared testing.* New York, NY: Wiley.

Lewis, D., & Burke, C. J. (1949). The use and misuse of the chi-square test. *Psychological Bulletin, 46*(6), 433–489.

Lorga, S., Lubin, L., & Parigi, P. (2003, April). About the chi-square test. Retrieved from http://ccnmtl. columbia.edu/projects/qmss/the_chisquare_test/about_ the_chisquare_test.html

Pearson, K. (1900). On the criterion that a given system of deviations from the probable in the case of a correlated system of variables is such that it can be reasonably supposed to have arisen from random sampling. *Philosophical Magazine, 50*(5), 157–175.

Pedhazur, E. J. (1997). *Multiple regression in behavioral research: Explanation and prediction* (3rd ed.). New York, NY: Wadsworth.

Plackett, R. L. (1983). Karl Pearson and the chi-squared test. *International Statistical Review, 51*(1), 59–72.

Satorra, A., & Bentler, P. M. (2001). A scaled difference chi-square test statistic for moment structural analysis. *Psychometrika, 66*(4), 507–514.

Tukey, J. (1949). One degree of freedom for non-additivity. *Biometrics, 5*(3), 232–242.

CIPP Evaluation Model

The CIPP model of evaluation developed by Daniel Stufflebeam is a decision-oriented evaluation approach designed to help those in charge of administering programs to make sound decisions. Designed as a multifaceted approach evaluation, the CIPP model provides a comprehensive framework for conducting both formative and summative evaluations of programs, projects, personnel, products, and organizations by focusing on context, input, process, and product.

Fundamental to the CIPP model is the belief that the most important purpose of evaluation is not to *prove* but rather to *improve*. In this manner, evaluation is viewed as a functional activity where the primary purpose is to strengthen and improve programs and provide a recursive approach to continuous program improvement. That is, evaluation is not seen as a time-limited activity but rather as an ongoing critical component of the programmatic enterprise. This entry describes the evaluation approaches that fall within the CIPP model and discusses how CIPP approaches can be part of the efforts to promote continuous quality improvement and enhancement.

CIPP Categories and Procedures

Consistent with an improvement focus, the CIPP model places a premium on guiding planning and implementation of development efforts. In doing so, the model's intent is to supply evaluators with timely and useful information for stakeholders, so that they may identify appropriate areas of development, form sound goals and activity plans, strengthen existing programs and services, determine whether and when goals and activity plans need to be altered, and develop plans for the dissemination of effective practices. The utility of the model is judged relative to the relevance, importance, timeliness, clarity, and credibility of findings rather than through common technical adequacy criteria as often found in requirements for internal and external validity.

The model itself comprises four different evaluation approaches that are designed to assist managers and administrators in responding to differing informational and decision-making needs. Although it is not required that each evaluation use each of the four techniques, programmatic enterprises could certainly make use of various components of all four in parallel as an integrated method of continuous program improvement. What follows is a discussion of each of the four separate subevaluation approaches relative to their objectives, methods, and uses. Brief descriptions of certain techniques that evaluators might find useful for conducting each type of evaluation are included.

Context Evaluation

The primary purposes of a context evaluation are to assess needs, problems, assets, and opportunities within a defined environment. *Needs* include those things that are necessary for an organization to fulfill its *defensible purpose*. *Problems* represent determents or impediments that must be overcome in order for the organization to successfully meet targeted needs. *Assets* include resources and expertise that are available and accessible that can be used to help fulfill the targeted purpose of the program. *Opportunities* represent resources and expertise that could possibly be used to support the efforts of the program in meeting its targeted needs and solving associated problems. *Defensible purposes* define what is to be achieved related to the organization's stated mission while adhering to ethical and legal standards. A context evaluation's main objectives are to:

set parameters and describe the setting for the intended service,

identify potential recipients, beneficiaries, and stakeholders of the intended service and assess their needs,

identify possible problems and barriers to meeting assessed needs,

identify relevant, accessible assets, and funding opportunities that could possibly be used to address the targeted needs,

provide a rationale and program theory for the program and develop improvement-oriented goals, and

establish a basis for judging outcomes and the worth or merit of targeted improvement and service efforts.

Context evaluations can occur any time during the delivery of a project, program, or intervention. The methodology of a context evaluation usually involves collecting a variety of types of information about members of the target population and their environment, with the goal of thoroughly understanding the context in which a program might be instituted. Information gathering techniques such as semi- and structured interviews, document reviews, demographic and performance data, hearings and community forums, and assessments are all examples of the wide range of activities that evaluators may use to assess the need, worth, and significance of a possible program or intervention.

Input Evaluation

An input evaluation's main objective is to develop a program or intervention that attends to the needs determined during the context evaluation. Included here is a critical examination of potentially relevant approaches that have been or are currently in use. The preliminary results of the input evaluation—what programmatic approaches were chosen and over what alternatives—are shared with primary stakeholders so that they may collaboratively share in the decision-making process. In doing so, a major purpose of the input evaluation is to identify and rate potential programmatic and intervention approaches and to assist decision makers in the deliberate examination of alternate strategies to address their targeted needs. In reviewing the state of practice in meeting identified needs and objectives, evaluators may use the following strategies:

review of the relevant empirical literature and assess the program's strategy for responsiveness to assessed needs and feasibility;

identify and investigate existing programs that could serve as a model for the contemplated program;

assess the program's strategy against pertinent research and extant literature base;

consultation with experts;

querying of pertinent information sources (e.g., those on the World Wide Web);

review of informational reports and available products and services;

assess the program's plan for sufficiency, feasibility, and political viability;

compile a draft input evaluation report and distribute to client and agreed upon stakeholders; and

discuss input evaluation findings with client and agreed upon stakeholders in a feedback workshop or strategy session.

The overall intent of the input evaluation is to assist the client and stakeholders in program planning efforts and to use input evaluation findings to devise a program strategy that is scientifically, economically, socially, politically, and technologically defensible. In using the results of input evaluations, clients and stakeholders must assure that the proposed program strategy is feasible for meeting the assessed needs of the targeted beneficiaries, can be supported within the budgeted amount for programmatic change, and is accountable with respect to the rationale for choosing the selected program strategy and has a defensible operational plan.

Process Evaluation

The process evaluation is a formative, ongoing assessment of the program plan or intervention's implementation as prescribed in the input evaluation and documentation of the fidelity and integrity of the program's specified procedures. A thorough process evaluation is facilitated by assigning an evaluation team member to monitor, observe, and provide a record of program implementation. Here, the main objective is to provide program staff and managers with formative feedback regarding the extent to which programmatic efforts are being carried out as planned in a timely

and efficient manner. Information gathered during the process evaluation may be used formatively to alter program plans in cases where initial decisions were unsound or not feasible. Moreover, another objective is to ensure that program staff members are delivering the program as intended and that they accept and can carry out their programmatic roles. Process evaluation may include activities such as:

choosing data collection sources/instruments, a schedule for data collection, and rules for collecting and processing information, including procedures for keeping it secure;

reporting specifications and schedule, including interim reports, and rules for communicating and disseminating findings;

in collaboration with program staff, maintaining a record of program events, problems, costs, and allocations;

periodically interviewing beneficiaries, program leaders, and staff to obtain their assessments of the program's progress;

periodically drafting written reports on process evaluation findings and providing the draft reports to the client and agreed upon stakeholders;

presenting and discussing process evaluation findings in feedback workshops to program leaders and staff; and

presenting a final process evaluation report (often incorporated into a larger evaluation report), so that clients and stakeholders can judge the effectiveness of a program relative to process efforts.

In turn, clients and stakeholders use the results of process evaluations to coordinate and strengthen staff activities and program design, to maintain a record of the program's progress and costs, and to report on the program's progress to interested parties such as financial sponsors, executive boards and committees, and other program developers.

Product Evaluation

The primary purpose of a product evaluation is to collect and interpret information and judge the worth or merit of a program relative to information gathered during the context, input, and process evaluations. Here, the main objective is to determine whether program outcomes met the preestablished criteria as defined by stakeholders and beneficiaries. Importantly, product evaluation decisions are made in light of both intended and unintended outcomes that influence both positive and negative outcomes. Product evaluations can be conducted using any one of a number or combination of evaluation approaches including objective oriented (e.g., evaluation of program theory, logic models), management oriented (e.g., Provus' discrepancy model, utilization-focused evaluation), or participant oriented (e.g., naturalistic evaluation, responsive evaluation, goal-free evaluation, empowerment evaluation).

By using a multifaceted approach, product evaluators can decide whether a given program, project, service, or other enterprise is worth continuing, repeating, or extending to other settings. Results should also provide information that evaluators find useful for modifying the program or replacing it so that the institution will more cost-effectively serve the needs of all stakeholders of a target audience and serve as an essential component of accountability in reporting.

As the CIPP model of evaluation has grown and adapted, product evaluations have been conceptualized and subdivided into four different types of product evaluation depending on the informational needs of program developers and evaluators.

Impact evaluations assess the extent to which a program demonstrated intended effects and served individuals and groups in a manner consistent with the program's intended beneficiaries. Moreover, results of impact evaluations allow stakeholders to make decisions regarding the extent to which the program reached and served the appropriate beneficiaries or community needs and whether the program's success was consistent with the program's intended purpose. That is, the resultant findings are consistent with program theory or they may be plausibly explained by other situational features. Consideration of such consistency is important if stakeholders and evaluators desire to consider other forms of product evaluation.

Effectiveness evaluations attempt to assess the quality and significance of program outcomes and whether they are consistent with designed program theory. Using a variety of methods as noted earlier, effectiveness evaluations attempt to ascertain the significance of the program's effects—positive and negative, and intended and unintended—and to obtain information on the nature, cost, and success of similar programs to make bottom-line assessments of a program's significance.

Sustainability evaluations attempt to assess the extent to which a program's contributions are institutionalized and successfully continued over time. Here, evaluators strive to understand and assess the program's provisions for continuation or lack thereof. Results of sustainability evaluations help decision makers understand whether stakeholders and beneficiaries favor program continuation and considerations for adaptation. In addition, findings from sustainability evaluations allow for decisions to be made regarding the continuing need or demand for continued program services. Lastly, sustainability evaluations assist program managers in setting long-term program goals and assigning authority and responsibility for program continuation.

Transportability evaluations assess the extent to which a program could successfully be adapted and applied elsewhere. By providing a description of the program and a summary of evaluation findings and quality, evaluators can assist other potential program adopters in judging the program's relevance to their situation and the likelihood of similar results and replicability across differing contexts.

CIPP as a Systems Approach to Continuous Quality Improvement

As a recursive model of program evaluation, CIPP approaches can be integrated into a system-wide approach to continuous quality improvement and enhancement. Within this view, program evaluation appropriately promotes the ongoing examination of program goals in a formative manner rather than a series of oblique one-off investigations. CIPP evaluation treats evaluation as a tool by which evaluators in concert with stakeholders can assist programs in promoting growth for their beneficiaries.

Applied correctly, CIPP evaluation represents a sustained, ongoing effort to help organizations organize and use information systematically to meet the needs and goals of a target audience in a respectful and dignified manner. At its core, the model is designed to promote growth and improvement. When used appropriately, the CIPP model of evaluation presents a sustained, ongoing effort to help an organization's leaders and decision makers organize and use information about the organization in a systematic manner to validate goals, meet the needs of stakeholders and target recipients, and provide an accountable approach to program delivery.

One of many approaches to program evaluation research and inquiry, the CIPP model views evaluation as a flexible approach to continuous program improvement and accountability. Notably, the approach is adaptable in the sense that it is responsive to the realities of applied social science endeavors in a manner not typically found with controlled, randomized experiments which are often narrowly focused on particular aspects of a program. While the goal of such latter approaches is often to "*prove*," the goal of CIPP evaluations is to "*improve*." As such, CIPP models of evaluation are designed specifically to allow users to conduct comprehensive and systematic evaluations of the programs that are delivered in real-world, organic settings, not the highly controlled conditions typically seen in experimental psychology where the goal is to minimize the influence of any extraneous variables. The CIPP model embraces such extraneous variables, as they likely represent the real-world conditions under which programs occur.

Lastly, at the larger level, the CIPP model views evaluation as an essential component of societal progress that can be used as an important piece of promoting the well-being of individuals and groups. The core of this belief rests on the contention that societal groups cannot make their programs or services better unless they critically examine both the strengths and weaknesses of what they are delivering. By carefully and continually examining and validating goals and assessing needs, program developers and service providers can plan effectively and invest their time and resources wisely in a manner that affects society at large.

John M. Hintze

See also Evaluation, History of; External Evaluation; Inputs; Logic Models; Program Evaluation; Program Theory of Change; Utilization-Focused Evaluation

Further Readings

Stufflebeam, D. L. (2001). Evaluation models. *New Directions for Evaluation* (89).

Stufflebeam, D. L. (2007). *CIPP evaluation model checklist* (2nd ed.). Retrieved from https://www.wmich.edu/sites/default/files/attachments/u350/2014/cippchecklist_mar07.pdf

Stufflebeam, D. L., & Shinkfield, A. J. (2014). *Evaluation theory, models, and applications* (2nd ed.). San Francisco, CA: Jossey-Bass.

CLASSICAL CONDITIONING

Classical conditioning is a simple associative learning process first systematically investigated by Ivan Pavlov (1849–1936). Pavlov was a Russian physiologist who studied the digestive processes in dogs and who incidentally noticed that dogs salivated not only to the presentation of food but also upon hearing the footsteps of the research assistant bringing the food. In follow-up laboratory studies of conditioning, Pavlov and his associates presented a neutral sound of a beating metronome (the conditioned stimulus [CS]) followed by the presentation of food (the unconditioned stimulus [UCS]), which elicited salivation (the unconditioned response [UCR]). After several CS-UCS pairings, the sound of the metronome began to elicit salivation (the conditioned responses [CR]), which it had never done before. The dog was classically conditioned to salivate to the metronome.

Since the time of Pavlov, classical conditioning has been extensively studied in a variety of lower animals as well as in humans. Of particular interest has been conditioning of emotional responses. This entry first looks at how classical conditioning has been studied in humans before discussing the studies of classical conditioning in animals, including research on the brain systems involved in conditioning.

Classical Conditioning in Humans

Emotions such as fear can be readily classically conditioned in both humans and lower animals. A common classical conditioning procedure with humans involves pairing a neutral CS such as a mild tone with an aversive UCS (e.g., moderately intense electric shock). The CR is usually measured by changes in autonomic responses such as heart rate and skin conductance following the CS. A conditioned emotional response can be established sometimes with only one pairing of the CS with the UCS. If the CS is subsequently presented a number of times without the UCS, the CR will gradually decline and completely vanish, a phenomenon known as extinction. However, in the absence of any extinction procedure, a CR may remain over time, even if the person realizes that the response no longer seems rational.

In order to ensure that the autonomic changes are truly conditioned to the CS, rather than general sensitization to all stimuli, it is common to randomly intermix presentation of two different CSs. Of the two CSs, only one, the CS+, is paired with the UCS, whereas the control CS, the CS−, is explicitly not paired with the UCS. Alternatively, the control CS can be randomly associated with the UCS in a separate control group. Evidence of successful conditioning is indicated by greater responding to the CS+ than the control CS.

Many individual differences in aversive conditioning have been reported, some of which are associated with the forms of psychopathology (mental illness). For example, a number of studies have found that psychopaths show impaired classical conditioning with aversive UCSs. This is particularly true for psychopaths with callousness and emotional detachment rather than simply antisocial behavior. Yu Gao and colleagues found that poor autonomic fear conditioning at age 3 was associated with criminal behavior at age 23. All in all, these results are consistent with the hypothesis that low fear of socializing punishments is associated with psychopathy. Classical conditioning is also thought to be the basis of many phobias, in which some originally neutral object (a dog, for instance, the CS) is paired with intense fear and pain (being bitten, the UCS), leading to fear of dogs (the CR). Ease of acquiring conditioned fear responses also may be related to anxiety disorders.

Another type of classical conditioning involves presenting a puff of air to the eye as the UCS and eyeblink as the response measure. Conditioning of the eyeblink response has been reliably demonstrated in both humans and lower animals. This appears to be a different type of conditioning than autonomic emotional conditioning because it occurs more slowly and requires a shorter interval between the onsets of the CS and UCS.

Other studies of human classical conditioning have employed brain imaging measures to determine the central nervous system mechanisms that mediate such conditioning. Activation of both the amygdala and frontal cortex has often been found to occur during fear conditioning. Studies of amygdala-damaged patients also indicate impaired autonomic aversive classical conditioning and this is consistent with studies of lower animals, as reviewed in the following section.

Classical Conditioning in Lower Animals

Fear conditioning in lower animals has been partly responsible for the renaissance of interest in emotion within neuroscience. Like the human conditioning paradigm, the prototypical paradigm is to present a tone to a rat followed by an electric shock. Following tone–shock pairings, a number of defensive behaviors (e.g., freezing), autonomic responses (heart rate), and endocrine responses (hormone release) will be elicited by the tone. Fear conditioning occurs in a wide variety of species.

A major advantage of studying conditioning in lower animals is that the effects of invasive brain lesions can be used to determine the areas essential for fear conditioning. Joseph LeDoux conducted a series of studies in rats during the 1980s and 1990s to trace the pathways in the brain involved in fear conditioning. LeDoux used lesions and chemical tracers beginning at the point at which the tone CS activates the auditory neocortex, then tracing the pathway backward to find the areas of the brain that the stimulus must reach to produce conditioning. On the basis of these studies, LeDoux and his colleagues found that the higher auditory neocortex was not necessary for fear conditioning. Instead, the critical point involved specific areas in the amygdala. Information can reach the critical amygdala areas via direct pathways from the thalamus (the low road) as well as by pathways from the thalamus through the cortex to the amygdala (the high road), but the critical point for forming the CS-UCS connection was in the amygdala.

Although the neocortex is not needed for simple conditioning with one CS, it may be necessary for more complex types of conditioning. Suppose that two auditory CSs are presented, a CS+ that is associated with the shock UCS and a CS– that is not. In this case, the animal must learn to discriminate the predictive meaning of two stimuli, and there is evidence that the neocortex is necessary for that discrimination learning. Studies of brain activity during discrimination fear conditioning in humans have also shown that in most circumstances, activity in the cortical areas, particularly the frontal lobes, is involved.

Michael E. Dawson and Anne M. Schell

See also Anxiety; Applied Behavior Analysis; Behaviorism; Educational Psychology; Punishment; Reinforcement; School-Wide Positive Behavioral Support

Further Readings

Gao, Y., Raine, A., Venables, P. H., Dawson, M. E., & Mednick, S. A. (2010). Association of poor childhood fear conditioning and adult crime. *American Journal of Psychiatry, 167,* 56–60.

LeDoux, J. (1996). *The emotional brain: The mysterious underpinnings of emotional life.* New York, NY: Simon & Schuster.

Pavlov, I. (1927). *Conditioned reflexes.* London, UK: Oxford.

Rescorla, R. A. (1988). Pavlovian conditioning: It's not what you think it is. *American Psychologist, 43,* 151–160.

CLASSICAL TEST THEORY

Classical test theory (CTT) is an approach to measurement that considers the relationship between the expected score (or "true" score) and observed score on any given assessment. The word *classical* is used in the sense that the theory is considered to be the first practical application of mathematics to describe this relationship. CTT offers a relatively parsimonious, elegant, and intuitive way to scale individuals according to some theorized latent construct. This entry further describes CTT and its basic principles and estimation procedures, then discusses its framework for determining a measure's proportion of true score variance, standard error of measurement, item analysis, and validity. Finally, it looks at the limitations to the theory.

Although more contemporary, model-based approaches to measurement, such as item response theory (IRT), have garnered more focus, CTT retains its relevance and importance for several reasons. First, CTT offers a relatively simple and intuitive analysis of response characteristics for an assessment. Even if the goal is to utilize more contemporary methods of measurement, CTT provides an initial framework of analyses to explore data; its relatively simple approach augments data diagnostic efforts. Second, CTT follows a less rigorous set of assumptions than the more complex IRT approach to measurement. It can be easily be applied to a wide variety of testing situations. Third, CTT requires fewer data demands for scaling procedures. Fourth, CTT extends from a framework of computations that are simpler in nature; variance, covariance, and correlation statistics lay the groundwork for CTT. Thus, almost any statistical software or data management program can be employed for most CTT analyses.

Basic Principles and Estimation Procedures

CTT was born out of the culmination of two particular advances in the field of measurement: first, the growing recognition of symmetrically distributed random errors in measurement (a concept that dates back to Galileo's masterpiece, *Dialogue on Two Main Systems of the Universe: Ptolemaic and Copernicus*). By the latter half of the 19th century, it was well accepted that experimental observations were jointly impacted by a stable, true score and an error in measurement defined as a random variable.

The advent of a metric to describe the degree of relationship between two variables provided the second groundwork for the CTT approach. Francis Galton derived the correlation statistic in 1886 to indicate the extent to which mean deviations in one variable reflect corresponding mean deviations in another variable. This metric laid the foundation for estimating the impact of random errors on the stability of a test score (reliability analysis).

Each of these motivations (randomly distributed error terms and correlation) was considered together in a landmark paper by Charles Spearman in 1904, in which he recognized that observed correlations between tests would be attenuated as a function of the amount of error measured with each test. By many accounts, this paper set the stage for the development of CTT as a proper measurement paradigm. Frederic Lord and Melvin Novick are credited with organizing the psychometric developments of the time into a cohesive framework in their 1968 book, *Statistical Theories of Mental Test Scores*.

Lord and Novick invoke the notion of randomly distributed error terms to develop the following formula, which forms the crux of CTT:

$$X = T + e.$$

Here, any observed score (X) is a result of the joint influence of a stable true score (T) and a random error term (e). Because the observed score is a function of a random variable (e), it itself can be considered a random variable.

To understand the error component in practical terms, it is helpful to distinguish random error from systematic error. In general, error represents the impact of all variables extrinsic to the trait of interest. Systematic error represents influences that bias the observed score in a consistent manner. For example, in a math ability assessment consisting of word problems, more linguistically demanding items may result in lower scores for nonnative speakers. Thus, linguistic ability, a variable extrinsic to the trait of interest, would influence scores in a consistent manner from one test administration to another.

Conversely, random error represents those influences extrinsic to the trait of interest that are not stable from one testing occasion to another. For example, distractions in the test environment, fatigue, and guessing may have differential effects on each test administration.

In the CTT model, true score is defined in purely statistical terms as the expected value of observed scores. Intuitively, the expected value can be thought of as a long run average of a series of observations. Computationally, it is defined as:

$$T_j = E = n = 1nXnpn.$$

Where T_j is the true score for subject j, X is the observed score for subject j, n corresponds to the particular testing occasion, and p corresponds to the probability of observing any particular score. If we assume that the frequency of observed scores is proportional to the probability mass function of random variable X, then the calculation simplifies to the arithmetic mean of observed scores. Thus:

$$T_j = EX = n = 1nXnpn = n = 1nXnN.$$

It extends from this definition that the expected value of the error is necessarily zero:

$$e = Xj - Tj$$
$$Ee = EXj - Tj = EXj - ETj.$$

And since $EXj = Tj$; then $Ee = Tj - Tj = 0$.

These definitions correspond to multiple testing occasions for a single subject. Invoking identical assumptions, it can be shown that the average true score for a population of subjects can be estimated from the average of all observed scores in a sample. Similarly, the average error term for a population of subjects can be estimated as the average of error terms for a sample; thus, population error = 0.

We might draw the practical conclusion that we can expect the average error over many testing occasions to approach zero. Practically speaking, we can expect random influences to positively impact the observed score just as often as we can expect them to depreciate it. Half the time, random error improves the observed score relative to the true score, and half the time, it decreases the observed score relative to the true score.

From this groundwork, a few additional corollaries can be derived:

(1) The correlation between true and error scores in a population is equal to zero (both within and across measures).

(2) The correlation between error scores on two separate measures is zero, assuming the observed scores are randomly drawn from independent distributions.

(3) The variance of the error term for a group of examinees is taken as the expected value of the within person score variance, over all n persons.

(4) Because we assume $CovT, e = 0$ (as referred to in no. 1), then necessarily the variance of the observed score in a population is the sum of the variance of true scores and error scores:

$$VarX = VarT + Vare + 2CovT, e$$
$$= VarT + Vare + 20$$
$$= VarT + Var(e).$$

At this point, it is important to emphasize a few notions regarding true scores in CTT. First, the true score in CTT is not defined by a particular physical, biological, or substantive indicator. Rather, the true score is defined according to the moment of an observed distribution of scores. Thus, the true score is dependent upon the measurement process itself. Importantly, this means that any consistent bias in measurement (systematic error) cannot be disentangled from the true score. That is, score variation due to systematic influences is absorbed into the true score estimate for persons. Second, neither term in the right side of the equation is directly observable. This means that the error is not a residual term in the traditional sense.

The assumption can be made that the expected value of the observed score is equal to zero, which fully constrains the error term to have an expected value of zero. Conversely, one can assume the error score has an expected value of zero, which sets the true score to the expected value of X. Thus, these terms derive wholly from the definitions applied. In this sense, error does not indicate lack of fit in the model, and falsification of CTT cannot be made a consideration.

Proportion of True Score Variance

The notion of an unpredictable error term impacting the observed score invites the question as to how stable a given measure is. In other words, how consistent would observed scores be from one measurement occasion to another with a particular assessment? This is the converse to asking the magnitude of random error influence. Essentially, for a given population, it is beneficial to decompose total score variance into true score variance and random error variance. Through this decomposition, the proportion of true score

variance is derived and can be used as a proxy for the stability of a measure. In CTT, this metric is referred to as the reliability of a measure.

$$\text{Reliability} = \sigma T \sigma T + \sigma e = \sigma T \sigma X.$$

Where σT is the variance of true scores in the population, σe is the variance of error scores in the population, and σX is the variance of observed scores in the population.

To arrive at this metric, it is necessary to consider the extent to which the true scores in a population covary with the observed scores. To the extent that the correlation between true score and observed score is greater, the error score variance is depreciated. In the extreme case of perfect collinearity with observed score and true score, the error score variance diminishes to zero.

Writing the true score/error score correlation (note: X and T are written as mean deviation values):

$$\rho XT = xtN\sigma T\sigma X = t + eDtN\sigma T\sigma X$$
$$= t2N\sigma T\sigma X + teDN\sigma T\sigma X.$$

Because the correlation between true and error scores is zero as defined previously:

$$\rho XT = t2N\sigma T\sigma X + 0 = t2N\sigma T\sigma X$$
$$= \sigma T2\sigma T\sigma X = \sigma T\sigma X.$$

Thus, we can interpret the correlation of true score to error score as the ratio of true score variance to total observed score variance. However, the true score is not directly observable. To circumvent this issue, it can be shown that the correlation between observed scores on parallel test forms is also equal to the proportion of true score variance:

$$\rho X1X2 = x1x2N\sigma X1\sigma X2 = \rho XT = \sigma T\sigma X.$$

However, a heavy constraint is placed upon this relationship. For this relation to hold, parallel test forms must satisfy the following conditions: (a) subjects earn the same true score on both measures and (b) there are equal error variances across the two measures. Therefore, much of the focus of CTT has been to develop strategies to develop parallel test forms. Four essential approaches to this end can be discussed:

(1) *Test–retest reliability* involves administering two identical assessments to examinees to ensure parallel forms. The time interval between assessments is selected partially based on the purpose of the test. For example, the authors of an occupational interest survey may be interested in the stability of test scores over a long interval (up to several years) and may space assessments accordingly. The reliability coefficient is calculated as the simple Pearson moment correlation between scores on the two assessments and is referred to as the coefficient of stability.

(2) *Alternate form reliability* involves constructing two different forms of an assessment that are thought to be equivalent in terms of item content and difficulty and administering them to a subject pool. Assessments are administered with as small a time interval as practical. This approach may reduce concerns of practice effects interfering with the reliability estimate. Additionally, this approach may be most appropriate when practical concerns require several distinct versions of an assessment to be administered (to reduce cheating or for test security reasons). The reliability coefficient is calculated as the simple Pearson moment correlation between scores on the two assessments and is referred to as the coefficient of equivalence.

(3) *Test–retest with alternate forms* combines the previous two approaches to arrive at a coefficient of stability and equivalence. Two equivalent forms of an assessment are administered to a subject pool after a particular time interval.

(4) *Internal consistency* considers parallel forms as being derived from two halves of a single assessment. Because only one assessment is administered, the derived reliability coefficient is not affected by maturational or practice effects. The simplest method to derive an internal consistency coefficient is to split the assessment into two halves and calculate the Pearson correlation coefficient between scores on each half. Several splitting methods exist: odd–even split, random assignment, and content matching. In the odd–even split, odd items comprise one half while even items comprise the second half. In random assignment, items are randomly selected to each half. In content matching, the test is split such that items have matching content across halves.

Regardless of the particular method chosen, it is important to recognize that by increasing the number of items in an assessment, the reliability generally increases. Thus, the split-half methods underestimate the reliability of an assessment because the coefficient is based on correlating only half of the test items. Therefore, a correction is usually applied to offer the expected, improved reliability coefficient for the full-length assessment. Several methods exist, but the procedure developed by both Spearman and Brown (identically, but independently) in 1910 gained the most traction. The final Spearman-Brown prophecy formula is defined as follows:

$$\rho_{composite} = 2\rho X1X21 + \rho X1X2.$$

Where $\rho_{composite}$ is the expected reliability of the composite, and $\rho X1X2$ is the observed correlation between the two halves. It should be noted that the Spearman-Brown prophecy formula is derived under the assumption of parallel test halves. To the extent that this assumption is not met, the corrected reliability coefficient is still likely to be an underestimate of the true value.

However, concern remained about the lack of a unique internal consistency estimate. That is, estimates were not invariant across different methods of test splitting. Three publications led to similar methods to address this issue. In 1937, G. Frederic Kuder and Marion Richardson developed the iconic KR 20 and KR 21 formulas, which offered procedures for developing a universal internal consistency metric. Later, Lee Cronbach developed what may be the most popular procedure to develop a universal internal consistency value:

$$\alpha = kk - 1(1 - \sigma i2\sigma X2).$$

Where k is the number of items on the assessment, $\sigma i2$ is the variance of item i, and $\sigma X2$ is the observed variance in total test score. This formula can accommodate both dichotomously and polytomously scored items.

Standard Error of Measurement

Extending the notions of true score variance and error score variance, a logical question to ask is how much error variability surrounds any given subject's true test score. Although this parameter is unknown at an individual level, it can be derived from the estimated true score variance. Conceptually speaking, one could administer a test iteratively to a single subject and obtain a distribution of scores. The mean of the distribution would represent the true score, while the standard deviation of the distribution would serve as an indication of the amount of error in measurement. The expected value of this standard deviation, taken over all subjects in the distribution, is the standard error of measurement. To derive this value, consider the CTT decomposition of observed variance into true score variance and error score variance:

$$\sigma X2 = \sigma T2 + \sigma E2.$$

And, dividing through by observed score variance:

$$1 = \sigma T2 \sigma X2 + \sigma E2 \sigma X2.$$

And because the ratio of true score variance to observed score variance defines the reliability coefficient, $\rho XX1$:

$$1 = \rho XX1 + \sigma E2 \sigma X2.$$

And, rearranging terms, we arrive at an estimate for the error variance around any given true score:

$$\sigma e2 = \sigma X1 - \rho XX1$$
$$= \text{Standard error of measurement.}$$

With the assumption of normally distributed error scores invoked, this statistic allows for calculation of a confidence interval (CI) around the true score:

$$CI = T \pm Z\alpha2 \times \sigma e2.$$

Item Analysis

Although CTT primarily focuses on psychometric properties at the global test level, a framework of item analysis statistics has been developed within the CTT paradigm. The goal of these statistics is ultimately to aid in selecting items that provide the most information regarding examinee performance and maximize reliability. To understand item selection procedures, it is first helpful to recall the variance of any composite score. If Y is a composite of n subcomponents, then:

$$\sigma Y2 = i = 1n\sigma i2 + 2\rho ij\sigma i\sigma j.$$

Where $i < j$. For dichotomously scored items, it is also true that the variance of a single item is equal to:

$$\sigma i2 = pi(1 - pi),$$

where p is the proportion of respondents answering item i correctly (also called item difficulty). Variance of scores for any item is maximized then when $pi = .5$. From this theorem, the following corollaries can be developed in relation to testing:

> Selecting items that exhibit high covariance values also maximizes test score variance.

> Selecting items with difficulty = .5 maximizes variance in respondent total score.

Thus, these items offer the most information for distinguishing examinees. Increased variance of scores also improves the stability and equivalence reliability coefficients because they are based on the correlation coefficient of scores between parallel forms. S. Henryssen recommends a general range of items with difficulty = .5.

The exception to selecting items with difficulty = .5 is when a specific cut score is to be used to distinguish groups of examinees. In these cases, *items with difficulty of .5 for only those examinees whose total score equals the cut score* should be included.

Item discrimination is another important variable to consider. In general, if an item is written well and relates to the trait of interest, individuals who pass the item should also obtain higher test scores. Conversely, those with a lower probability of answering an item should obtain lower test scores. One method to assess this property is to compute a biserial correlation between a single dichotomously scored item and the total test score for a group of subjects. The higher the observed biserial correlation, the better an item is able to distinguish high-performing subjects from low-performing subjects. Negative item total score correlations indicate a very poorly functioning item that is operating in the reverse (those with higher test scores respond incorrectly). It is important to note here that Cronbach's α metric for internal consistency will be maximized when the biserial correlations for all items are maximized.

Validity

The procedures reviewed earlier that describe the structural properties of a measure are helpful in determining the stability of measures and the extent to which items form a homogenous pool and elicit consistent responses from subjects. Validity concerns the inferences and applied utility of the measure. Validity is the extent to which interpretations and applications of test scores are appropriate. At a very basic level, if reliability informs the assessor regarding how consistent the test is, validity is concerned with what the test *actually* measures. Validity is not a property of the assessment itself but a collection of empirical findings and theoretical justifications pointing toward the suitability of the conclusions drawn from test scores. However, validity is partially a function of reliability; stability in test scores is a necessary, but not sufficient, criterion to establish the validity of test interpretation.

Traditionally, the psychometric community had defined validity in terms of several distinct types or aspects: content validity, criterion validity, and construct validity. Recently, however, there has been a growing trend to conceptualize any assessment as an indicator of a particular construct or domain and that multiple forms of evidence exist to establish convergence between test scores and the construct. The components of validity evidence recognized by the prevailing psychometric communities are content validity, response process evidence, internal structure, relationships to external variables, and consequences of test implementation.

Limitations

The weakness of CTT is threefold: First, CTT generally focuses on test-level statistics. Although an approach to item-level diagnostics exists in the CTT framework (as explicated previously), it is not elaborated as with the more contemporary IRT approaches. In CTT, no underlying model is specified to link specific item stimulus features to item difficulty or to the interaction with an examinee's latent trait in effecting a response outcome. Similarly, CTT generally assumes identically distributed error terms for each item. This assumption precludes a more discrete analysis where standard error of measure scores are estimated for each item separately. Generally speaking, the basis for scaling persons rests on the distance of an individual's true score from the true score of the norming population. Conversely, IRT approaches base person scaling on the location of a latent trait score on the item scale.

Second, CTT scaling is grounded on a circular dependency: Person observed scores are dependent upon the distribution of item statistics on the assessment, and the distribution of item statistics is dependent upon the distribution of observed scores. Thus, person true score estimates are not invariant across different item sets, and item property estimates are not invariant across different person samples. This imparts a particular difficulty in comparing true scores across different assessments. Although test equating techniques exist, considerable error can be introduced in the process. Generally speaking, this precludes the ability for CTT to be applied to adaptive testing procedures, where each examinee receives a different set of items conditional on the examinee's performance pattern.

As briefly discussed previously, another circular dependency exists in distinguishing error scores from true scores. True score and error score jointly define the observed score, but neither true score nor error score is directly observed. Thus, the main terms of CTT are defined by the particular assumptions of the theory. In this purest form of CTT, this precludes falsification of the model; it must be true by its own definition.

Despite these limitations, CTT continues to occupy an important place in the field of educational and psychological measurement. In fact, under certain conditions, CTT can return similar person ability estimates as the more computationally demanding and data-intensive IRT approach. Considered together with the benefits enumerated earlier, it behooves anyone involved in psychological or educational testing to have a basic understanding of the principles of CTT.

Clifford E. Hauenstein and
Susan E. Embretson

See also Correlation; Equating; Item Response Theory; Psychometrics; Reliability; Standard Error of Measurement; *Standards for Educational and Psychological Testing*; Validity; Validity Coefficients; Variance

Further Readings

American Educational Research Association, American Psychological Association, National Council on Measurement in Education. (2014). *Standards for educational and psychological testing*. Washington, DC: American Educational Research Association.

Anastasi, A. (1988). *Psychological testing*. New York, NY: MacMillan.

Crocker, L., & Algina, J. (1986). *Introduction to classical and modern test theory*. New York, NY: Holt, Rhinehart & Winston.

Embretson, S. (1996). The new rules of measurement. *Psychological Assessment, 8*(4), 341–349.

Jones, L., & Thissen, D. (2007). A history and overview of psychometrics. In C. R. Rao & S. Sinharay (Eds.), *Handbook of statistics: Vol. 26* (pp. 1–27). Amsterdam, the Netherlands: North-Holland.

Lord, F. M., Novick, M. R., & Birnbaum, A. (1968). *Statistical theories of mental test scores*. Reading, MA: Addison-Wesley.

Murphy, K. R., & Davidshofer, C. O. (1988). *Psychological testing: Principles and Applications*. Englewood Cliffs, NJ: Prentice Hall.

Novick, M. R. (1966). The axioms and principal results of classical test theory. *Journal of Mathematical Psychology, 3*(1), 1–18.

CLASSIFICATION

Classification refers to a broad set of statistical methods that arise in many different applications. In a classification problem, we have a categorical response variable that we wish to investigate in relationship to one or more input variables. Classification methods can be applied to problems in a wide variety of settings; applications in education include analyzing patterns of responses to standardized exams, inferring which middle school students will benefit from a drug prevention program, and predicting which graduating high school seniors will choose to attend a particular university if they are offered admission.

Common classification methods include logistic regression, support vector machines, decision trees, random forests, neural networks, and k-nearest neighbors. This entry discusses a few general issues in classification that should be considered when choosing a method and the differences between classification and the related problem of clustering.

General Issues in Classification

Classification problems include both *prediction* and *inference*. In an inference problem, the goal is to describe the relationship between the response variable and the explanatory variables, whereas in a prediction problem, the goal is to predict the value of an unobserved response variable for a new data point based on observed predictor variables. For example, if we wish to examine the relationship between a person's diet and whether the person later gets cancer, this is an inference problem because the question of which foods put a person at risk is of paramount importance. In contrast, if we wished to classify the content of an image based on features extracted from the digital representation of the image, this is a prediction problem because which features are useful for making the classification are not important.

Logistic regression and decision trees are examples of methods that are appropriate for inference because they provide easy to interpret information about the relationship between the response variable and the explanatory variables. Though, as with any statistical methodology, making causal claims based on the results from a classification analysis relies on proper experimental design. K-nearest neighbors, support vector machines, and random forests may provide accurate predictions, but can be more challenging to interpret, and are therefore more appropriate for prediction problems than inference problems.

Any problem with a categorical response variable may be deemed a classification problem, but methods differ based on how many levels the categorical response has. Logistic regression is most often used as a binomial method for a binary response variable; by contrast, multinomial logistic regression, k-nearest neighbors, and linear discriminant analysis can easily handle any number of classes.

Decision Boundaries

Decision boundaries separate the space of input variables into regions labeled according to classification. One of the key elements determining the complexity of a classification problem is the shape of these boundaries. Figure 1 shows two classification problems with two classes (Δ, +) and two predictor variables ($X1$, $X2$). The solid line shows the Bayes's optimal decision boundary, whereas the dotted line is the decision boundary estimated with logistic regression. Figure 1A shows a case where the Bayes's optimal decision boundary is linear, whereas in Figure 1B, the boundary is nonlinear. If the input variables describe a space best partitioned using a nonlinear decision boundary, it

is important to choose a method that can estimate such a boundary, particularly for inference problems.

Some of the most popular classification methods, including logistic regression, support vector machines, and linear discriminant analysis, will produce boundaries that are linear in the input space; in Figure 1, the dotted lines are the decision boundaries estimated using logistic regression. Other methods, such as k-nearest neighbors, decision trees, and random forests, can find decision boundaries that take more complex shapes.

Nonetheless, even when the optimal decision boundary is nonlinear, linear methods may still have very good *predictive* performance. In Figure 1B, the linear boundary is nonoptimal, but only a small percentage (4%) of points fall on the wrong side of the boundary. In general, this phenomenon is known as the *bias–variance trade-off* and is part of assessing model–data fit.

Relationship Between Classification and Clustering

Clustering is a closely related set of statistical methods. In both classification and clustering problems, we assume that the population consists of subgroups, so that the probability distribution

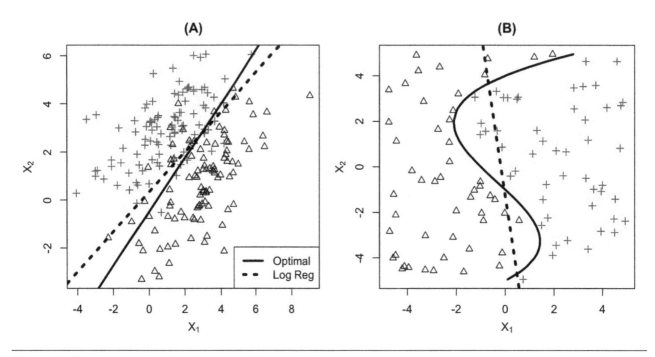

Figure I Two examples of classification problems

for the population can be expressed as a finite mixture model. The difference is that in classification, we observe the class labels for some or all of the data, whereas in clustering, we do not observe any group labels and must infer both what subgroups exist and which points belong to which group. Classification is part of a larger group of methods often called *supervised learning*, where the response variable is observed, whereas clustering is a subset of *unsupervised learning* methods where the investigator is looking for patterns in data but no specific response variable has been recorded.

In this sense, latent class analysis is a clustering method because the classes are latent and are to be inferred. Similarly, diagnostic classification models are unsupervised models; these models are used to infer which students are in a class possessing a particular set of skills, and the skill profile of each student is unobserved.

April Galyardt

See also Categorical Data Analysis; Cluster Analysis; Data Mining; Diagnostic Classification Models; Latent Class Analysis; Logistic Regression; Model–Data Fit

Further Readings

Agresti, A. (2013). *Categorical data analysis* (3rd ed.). Hoboken, NJ: Wiley.

Hastie, T., Tibshirani, R., & Friedman, J. (2009). *The elements of statistical learning: Data mining, inference, and prediction* (2nd ed.). New York, NY: Springer-Verlag.

Shmilovici, A. (2005). Support vector machines. In O. Maimon & L. Rokach (Eds.), *Data mining and knowledge discovery handbook*. (pp. 257–276). doi:10.1007/0-387-25465-X_12

Classroom Assessment

Classroom assessment refers to student assessments that teachers design and administer themselves. The term usually is distinct from the standardized tests that are given in schools such as intelligence tests or tests used in statewide testing systems. A more formal definition of classroom assessment would be the teacher-directed systematic collection of information about students' learning, traits, and abilities.

Classroom assessment can be used before, during, or after instruction and can be formal, with standardized procedures and predetermined scoring criteria, or informal, consisting of brief observations. This entry first describes the five basic approaches to classroom assessment. It then discusses the purposes of classroom assessment and how assessments are scored and interpreted.

Approaches to Classroom Assessment

There are five basic approaches to classroom assessment. Teachers choose an approach based on different philosophies, different reasons why the data are being collected, and how the data will be used. Different approaches differ in their purpose, in the nature of the data they produce, in their intended audience, and in some cases in the assumptions they make about children and about learning. The five approaches to classroom assessment are traditional paper-and-pencil, performance-based, formative, authentic, and universal design. For organizational purposes, this entry discusses these approaches as independent ways of treating assessment, but there is much overlap among the five approaches.

Paper-and-Pencil Assessment

Paper-and-pencil assessment is a familiar approach featuring items such as multiple-choice questions, matching items, true/false items, and fill-in-the-blank items. These types of tests are typically used for assessing knowledge and basic understanding. In many contexts, paper-and-pencil tests work the best to assess a large number of objectives quickly using a format with which students are familiar. There are traditionally two item formats for paper-and-pencil assessment: selection items and supply items. With selection items, the correct answer is there for students to select (e.g., a multiple-choice item). With supply items, the student must provide the answer, as with a fill-in-the-blank item or an open-ended, short-answer question.

Because paper-and-pencil assessments can be scored objectively without subjective evaluations, there is very little randomness in the scoring. Consequently, paper-and-pencil assessment is the most reliable of classroom assessment approaches. Whether these assessments are the most valid way to assess knowledge or understanding, however, is a different question. Often, approaches that explore understanding or ability more deeply do a better job of tapping into the constructs of interest.

Performance-Based Assessment

Thirty-five years ago, this approach was seen as newfangled, but now is so common Performance-based assessment gained popularity in the 1980s and 1990s and is now so common that many consider it as traditional as a multiple-choice test. The idea is to go beyond the measurement of low-level knowledge and understanding by asking students to perform a skill or create a product and assess student ability then assessing the performance or product. Performance assessment is typically used for assessing skill or ability and is the common approach in the areas of communication (e.g., writing and public speaking), mathematics, science, athletics and physical education, social skills, and the performing arts.

The performance-based assessment framework led by necessity to new scoring options, such as the creation of subjective scoring rubrics or guides that outline what teachers wish to measure, but can lead to scoring difficulties because of the judgments required. Scoring rubrics identify components or criteria of quality for an assignment or assessment and provide a range of scores for each piece. Often, rubrics provide descriptors for what each score along the range means. Assignments and classroom activities that are often scored with rubrics include:

group projects, in which students work together on a collaborative problem and can be assessed on their discussions or group presentations;

writing assignments, which require written description, analysis, explanation, or summary;

scientific experiments, which allow for observation of how well students can conduct scientific investigations;

demonstrations that students perform, showing their mastery of content or procedures; and

portfolios or collections of students' work. Typically, portfolios are used to evaluate students' development over time.

Formative Assessment

Data collection that occurs during instruction not only can guide the teacher on instructional effectiveness but also can let students know where they are and how they are doing. Formative assessment is typically used to give feedback to students and teachers about how things are going and does not affect grades. More importantly, providing frequent feedback directly to students so they can monitor and control their own learning is just about the only assessment approach that has been found to directly affect learning (and, of particular importance to administrators, to increase standardized test scores). Students who learn in a formative assessment environment become self-directed learners. Self-directed learners are self-managing (they make use of their own experiences), self-monitoring (they use metacognitive strategies), and self-modifying (they alter their approach to learning).

There are many ways that teachers use formative assessment in the classroom, including the following:

frequent quizzes or tests that do not affect grades but merely give feedback to students and teachers;

conferences in which work plans and strategies are discussed;

performance control charts on which students have a numeric criterion for success on an assignment; and

self-reflection work sheets to identify areas of difficulty or strength.

Authentic Assessment

A best practice in the modern classroom is to utilize assessment tasks that match the real-world expectations. Authentic assessment typically requires students to perform in ways that are valued outside the classroom. This approach may increase the meaningfulness of classroom assessment across all ages, preschool through graduate school. Understanding this approach to assessment has difficulties, though, because there is disagreement over what it means to say that an assessment is *authentic.*

The idea that assessment tasks should be intrinsically meaningful and motivating and require skills or knowledge that is valued in the world is a powerful one, though, and can produce powerful assessments. Authenticity in assessment has different meanings across different content areas and at different student ages. Common across these areas, though, are several dimensions that make classroom assessment authentic. Assessment is authentic when the context is realistic and cognitively complex, when students collaborate with each other and use feedback formatively, and when the scoring is interpreted under an expectation of mastery with multiple indicators combined.

Universal Test Design

Universal test design emphasizes accessibility and fairness for all children, regardless of gender, first language, ethnicity, or disability. Basic standards exist that can and should be applied to classroom assessment in all contexts and at all levels. Application of these standards can ensure that testing, whether teacher developed or state mandated, is inclusive and measures what it is supposed to.

Assessments following universal design principles are typically used when the classroom teacher is concerned that irrelevant student characteristics might affect performance. General guidelines for knowing whether the content of an assessment follows universal design principles and allows "access" to all students include making sure that all students would likely have the experiences and prior knowledge necessary to understand the question and that the vocabulary, sentence complexity, and required reasoning ability are appropriate for all students' developmental levels.

The wording used in assessments can affect accessibility. Sentences should be short, use the jargon of the field and instead of uncommon words, more common synonyms should be used. Finally, teachers should establish a consistency in format and style across assessments and within each assessment.

Choosing and Combining the Approaches

In the past, nearly all classroom assessment was traditional paper-and-pencil assessment with, especially in the last few decades, some performance-based assessment activity. More recently, the field has begun to recognize the value of modern approaches such as formative assessment, authentic assessment, and universal design of assessment. This is clear from a review of the scholarly literature on classroom assessment. Hundreds of studies have been published examining the effectiveness and usefulness of formative assessment, authentic assessment, and applications of universal design. The traditional multiple-choice test and performance assessment still predominate in the classroom, but these three modern approaches are now part of the conversation around classroom assessment.

The five approaches emphasized in this entry are derived from different theoretical frameworks, emphasizing different purposes of assessment, but they are not mutually exclusive. A teacher does not have to pick one theory or approach over another but can focus on the purpose for a particular assessment and choose different approaches that are consistent with that goal. A teacher can design a traditional paper-and-pencil test that follows universal accessibility guidelines. A single classroom assessment might be performance based, authentic, and formative. Most authentic assessments are probably performance based, but many performance-based assessments are not authentic. A formative assessment might inform both the teacher and the student and parents.

In general, teachers choose an assessment strategy using paper-and-pencil formats when they wish to measure basic knowledge that can be memorized and use performance-based formats when they wish to measure skill, ability, or deeper understanding of concepts. Formative assessment is used to give students and teachers feedback while learning is still happening. Authentic assessment following universal design principles is chosen when teachers wish to evaluate students using the real-world tactics that work equally well for all students.

Purposes of Classroom Assessment

Teachers can choose to use assessment for several different reasons, all of them important. Sometimes a combination of reasons is in play:

Assessment *for* learning: Teachers gather information about where students are "at" (what they know and can do) and how they are reacting to instruction. The purpose is to design and revise instruction, so that it is the most effective.

Assessment *as* learning: Data are gathered either *by* or *for* students to help them understand how they learn. This is the formative assessment approach. The purpose is that students develop learning skills and control their own learning.

Assessment *of* learning: Data are gathered to reach a conclusion about how much students have learned after instruction is done. Until recently, this was the only use of classroom assessment. The purpose is to share with the students and others how much they have achieved.

Scoring and Interpreting Classroom Assessment

The five approaches to classroom assessment consist of a set of three different formats or types of assessment designs (traditional, performance based, and authentic), a relatively new way of thinking about the purpose of assessment (formative), and an overall philosophy about the usefulness of a given assessment (universal test design) for all students. Whatever the format, classroom assessments can be scored and interpreted in two ways—norm-referenced and criterion-referenced.

Norm-referenced scoring means that performance is interpreted by comparing scores to each other; the information in a score comes from referencing what is normal. Criterion-referenced scoring applies external criteria that have nothing to do with how the average person performed.

Common criteria for classroom assessment score interpretation using this framework are grading scales that assign scores above 90% correct as an A, for example, or teachers concluding that instructional objectives have been met by applying a standard of mastery.

Classroom teachers use both criterion-referenced score interpretation and norm-referenced interpretations all the time. If everyone can get an A on a test or on a report card by meeting some set of standards, objectives, or criteria, then criterion-referenced interpretation is at work. If the grading is "on a curve" or individual scores have meaning only in comparison to how others performed, then norm-referenced interpretation is being used.

Norm-referenced evaluations are so common in education that one may not even realize that someone (a teacher, policy maker, administrator, and test developer) has chosen that approach over criterion-referenced interpretation. Criterion-referenced assessments are also common and just as much a part of the classroom culture as norm-referenced. The meaning of an assessment differs depending on which interpretation is applied.

Bruce B. Frey

Adapted from Frey, B. B. (2014). *Modern classroom assessment*. Thousand Oaks, CA: Sage.

See also Authentic Assessment; Formative Assessment; Paper-and-Pencil Assessment; Performance-Based Assessment; Universal Design of Assessment

Further Readings

Black, P. J., Buoncristiani, P., & Wiliam, D. (2014). *Inside the black box: Raising standards through classroom assessment*. Cheltenham, Australia: Hawker Brownlow Education.

Frey, B. B. (2014). *Modern classroom assessment*. Thousand Oaks, CA: Sage.

Frey, B. B., & Schmitt, V. L. (2007). Coming to terms with classroom assessment. *Journal of Advanced Academics, 18*(3), 402–423.

Mertler, C. A. (2016). *Classroom assessment: A practical guide for educators*. Abingdon, UK: Routledge.

CLASSROOM OBSERVATIONS

Classroom observation represents a measurement approach used to characterize teaching quality through the use of an observation protocol. This entry briefly reviews the history of how classroom observations have been used and then considers research that examines the design, reliability, and validity of classroom observations. This entry focuses on work that has been done in K–12 education only.

The History of Classroom Observations

Classroom observations have long been a primary component of teacher evaluation, a process that was intended to both support employment-related decisions and provide feedback to teachers to improve their instruction. Typically, principals or other school administrators would observe teachers once a year as they taught their class. Such observations were often required and specified by statute and/or labor contracts. The observer would usually make and record evaluative judgments using a form that listed a set of statements about teacher behaviors and classroom characteristics (e.g., *The teacher praised students*; *The students were well-behaved*). Based on the observations, principals would then provide an annual evaluation that included written and/or oral feedback.

Traditional observation approaches have been criticized as not being particularly useful in providing meaningful evaluative information in the majority of school contexts. In fact, the vast majority of teachers received the highest scores available across observation rating scales. Policy makers and many policy researchers have been dissatisfied with evaluations that did not effectively identify teachers who were weak performers. Educators were dissatisfied that evaluations were, in many cases, little more than a bureaucratic necessity that contributed little to the improvement of instruction.

This dissatisfaction with traditional observation methods, together with a significant research interest in understanding and characterizing teaching quality, has led to significant efforts in the design and study of classroom observations in order to assess, evaluate, and improve teaching.

The Structure and Process of Observation Protocols

A *protocol* includes a set of concepts, processes, and procedures that describes the design, training, implementation, scoring, and quality control of a classroom observation measurement system.

Observation systems require the application of a *scoring rubric* to a sample of teaching, typically a class lesson. A rubric typically consists of a set of *dimensions* that describe important aspects of teaching, such as classroom discourse, behavior management, and depth of content. Some protocols focus almost exclusively on teacher actions, while others focus on interactions between teachers and students in the classroom. Dimensions are often organized into *domains* that capture larger constructs of teaching, such as classroom environment and quality of instruction. Each dimension has a scale that includes categories describing different qualities of teaching. The number of points on the scale varies among rubrics. Rubric scales can be binary (i.e., a certain type of evidence is present or absent) or can differentiate performance levels, with between three and seven levels used most often.

Some protocols also include evidence and scales that address aspects of teaching beyond the observed lesson. For example, some protocols may include lesson plans, classroom artifacts such as instructional assignments, and teacher's oral or written reflections on the lesson.

Although the descriptions in the rubric are typically quite brief, many protocols also include detailed elaborations designed to help observers (and teachers) understand the intended meaning of each protocol dimension. Elaborations may include exemplars and explicit behavioral indicators that suggest different levels of teaching quality.

Protocols also differ in terms of their domain and age/grade specificity. Some of the most frequently used protocols in schools are designed to be applied across all K–12 classrooms by observers who may or may not have particular subject-matter expertise. Others are designed specifically to score observations in certain disciplines such as mathematics, science, or language arts. Domain-specific protocols provide greater detail about the nature of good teaching that is appropriate for a particular domain. For example, while a general protocol may include a dimension that values *analytic reasoning*, domain-specific protocols are more apt to detail the nature of such reasoning in the respective domain. Most often, domain-specific protocols have been used in research contexts.

The protocol design also specifies how teaching is *sampled* to create observation scores. In some protocols, the observer may watch an entire lesson before scoring the teaching. In other protocols, raters may observe lessons for some specified period, often referred to as a *segment* and lasting from 7 to 15 minutes, and then apply scores for the individual segment. Segment scores are then aggregated through averaging to create a lesson score.

Observers (or raters) learn to use the protocol through a *training* process that normally involves a review of each scoring dimension together with sample videos that exemplify different score points. Training includes instructions for taking notes that are thorough, descriptive, and nonevaluative during the observation segment. Once the segment is complete, raters review the notes and assign scores for each dimension. During training, scores are discussed, as the trainer attempts to ensure that observers have learned how to use the protocol to make valid judgments.

At the completion of training, raters typically take and need to pass a *certification* test. Such tests require candidates to assign scores to a small sample of selected video segments. Raters are certified if their assigned scores meet a threshold of agreement with the scores assigned by experts who have rated the videos previously.

Once raters are trained, the observation system may also include the *recalibration* of raters to ensure that they continue to apply the protocol dimensions as designed. Raters will be asked to score videos that have been assigned scores by experts. Raters may have to pass a recertification test and/or enter into discussion if their scores deviate substantially from the expert scores.

Conducting Observations

In educational practice, most observations are done with the observer physically present during the classroom lesson. The record of the observation consists of the observer's notes and scores. In research and assessment contexts, the classroom lesson is often captured using video camera technology. Raters judge the quality of teaching by watching the video and assigning scores as directed by the protocol. The training of observers can also vary and is increasingly being conducted using web-based training tools.

The scheduling of observations can also vary. In most cases, observations are scheduled in advance, but in some teacher evaluation systems, at least some observations are conducted without any prior notice to teachers. The number of times a teacher is observed for the purposes of an evaluation or assessment can vary substantially across and within systems. Within systems, the number of evaluations may depend on teacher seniority and prior evaluation scores. New teachers and those with weaker evaluation scores are observed more frequently in some systems.

In most evaluation systems, principals, assistant principals, and curriculum supervisors who have supervisory authority conduct the observations. After a short time following the observation, there is generally a feedback session in which the observer discusses the observation results with the teacher. Guidance to administrators about carrying out effective feedback sessions varies across protocols.

Research on Classroom Observations

Substantial research has been conducted on the reliability and validity of classroom observations. General patterns of research approaches and findings are described in this section.

Reliability

Reliability of observations considers the consistency of scores obtained under different conditions. Some variation, such as that which results from different raters judging the same lesson, represents measurement error. Other variation in scores, such as that which may be associated with different lessons, may be a function of actual differences in teaching performance. Researchers and evaluators often want to estimate a teacher's overall teaching effectiveness across different sources of variation. Thus, reliability analyses are used to determine how the number of observations and the conditions under which scores are produced affect the stability of an estimate of teaching quality for a given teacher.

Reliability of Raters

A key measurement issue concerns the degree to which different raters agree on the scores they give to an observation. Research studies often include observations that are independently scored by two raters. Agreement is sometimes indexed by exact agreement rates (i.e., both raters assign the same score), but better estimates that take into account the distribution of scores include κ and intraclass correlations.

Studies have also used generalizability designs to determine the proportion of score variance that is attributable to raters. Across studies, there is substantial error attributable to raters, implying that using multiple raters would improve the quality of scores. It is also more challenging to obtain reliable scores on some dimensions than others, suggesting that observers may have more idiosyncratic understandings of different aspects of teaching.

Reliability of Lessons

Scores vary substantially across individual lessons. Researchers have also found that the quality of lessons can vary substantially over the course of the school year. Thus, it is important not to characterize a teacher's overall performance on the basis of a single lesson or from only one part of the school year. In order to fairly evaluate teachers, it is important to observe teachers multiple times (research generally recommends four observations to obtain a reliable estimate of teaching quality) that occur at different points during the school year.

Reliability of Mode

Researchers have explored whether it matters if the observation occurs live, takes place with the observer in the classroom, or is video recorded and later scored by a rater who was not physically present during the lesson. Scores based on these two methods are correlated almost perfectly when the correlation is adjusted for measurement error.

Validity

Validity refers to the quality of evidence supporting the interpretation and use of observation scores. The majority of research has focused on the meaning of scores and their relationship to other measures associated with teaching quality.

The Meaning of Scores

A number of studies have examined evidence to support the dimensional and domain structure of observation protocols. Using factor analysis, research has examined whether patterns of scores are consistent with the theoretical structure built into the protocol design. The evidence is mixed. In general, dimensions within a protocol are highly correlated and dominated by one general factor. A number of studies, however, have found modest evidence in support of multiple factors. In general, to the extent that different factors are identified, they seem to be associated with instructional and classroom environment constructs.

Other studies have examined the distribution of scores across dimensions. This work has shown that scores for classroom management dimensions (e.g., behavior, on-task activity) are typically higher on their respective scales than they are for instructional dimensions (e.g., the quality of content and reasoning about subject matter). In fact, across protocols, average scores for instructional dimensions are usually described by lower scale points in the scoring rubric.

Relationships to Other Measures

One question is whether different observation protocols lead to different inferences about teacher quality. In general, relative rankings of teachers across different protocols are very similar. Although different protocols may emphasize different aspects of teaching, they will result in highly similar relative ranking of teachers.

A second question is the extent to which observation protocols are related to other measures of teacher quality. The most widely studied measures are those that estimate teachers' contributions to student learning (e.g., value-added methods). This work has found consistently significant but modest correlations between these measures. Studies have also explored relationships with other measures including teacher knowledge and student surveys. Findings are mixed, but even when correlations are significant, they tend to be low. Low correlations are, in part, due to the measurement error associated with each of the separate measures contributing to the correlation.

Classroom Observations in Practice

Classroom observations have been and are currently used as part of formal assessment and evaluation systems. They now play a major role in state teacher evaluation systems that have been guided by federal and state policy. They have also contributed to assessments that have been used to license and certify teachers.

Licensure and Certification

In the 1980s, efforts were made to assess teachers by examining actual samples of teaching and not simply relying on paper-and-pencil tests. The National Board for Professional Teaching Standards, as well as a number of state licensure systems, called for a teaching portfolio that would include one or two video segments of teaching. The video was only one part of a portfolio that contained extensive teacher reflection and other teaching artifacts. The portfolio was scored using standardized assessment practices with trained raters who also had subject-matter expertise related to the teaching they were scoring.

Teacher Evaluation

More recently, teacher evaluation has been a cornerstone of educational accountability, formally codified in the Race to the Top federal initiative. States were expected to develop teacher evaluation systems that included both student growth and classroom practice components. All state evaluation systems have relied on classroom observations as the sole or major contributor to the classroom practice component.

States and districts have adopted commercially available observation protocols, some of which have been part of the research described previously. Other states and districts have developed their own protocols, although they have a great deal in common with the commercial products.

Given the constraints and pressures faced by schools, it is not surprising that many research recommendations have not been heeded in practice. For example, training and certification testing is normally much less intensive than it is in research studies. Double scoring of given observations to evaluate reliability is rare. Raters often have limited knowledge of the subject matter that is being taught. Many teachers are observed for fewer lessons than is recommended by research. And perhaps most importantly, observers have a personal stake in and a relationship with the teachers they are observing, which is quite different from the conditions under which research study observations are made. Additionally, policies often specify that teachers receiving mediocre ratings are subject to some type of job-related actions up to and including termination over time.

Therefore, it is also not surprising that scores vary substantially from those found in research studies. Scores are substantially higher in practice than they are in research studies. In some schools, there may be no discrimination at all among teachers. Thus, the meaning of scores that has been considered in research studies is quite different from the scores that are generated by evaluation systems in practice. There are few published studies that examine the quality of scores produced in functioning teacher evaluation systems.

Drew Gitomer

See also Certification; Data-Driven Decision Making; Race to the Top; Teacher Evaluation; Teachers' Associations; Value-Added Models

Further Readings

Bell, C. A., Gitomer, D. H., McCaffrey, D., Hamre, B., Pianta, R., & Qi, Y. (2012). An argument approach to observation protocol validity. *Educational Assessment, 17*, 62–87. doi:10.1080/10627197.2012.715014

Bill and Melinda Gates Foundation. (2012). *Gathering feedback for teaching: Combining high-quality observations with student surveys and achievement gains*. Washington, DC: Author. Retrieved from http://eric.ed.gov/?id=ED540960

Gitomer, D. H., Bell, C. A., Qi, Y., McCaffrey, D. F., Hamre, B. K., & Pianta, R. C. (2014). The instructional challenge in improving teaching quality: Lessons from a classroom observation protocol. *Teachers College Record, 116*(6). Retrieved from http://www.tcrecord.org/Content .asp?ContentId=17460

Hill, H., & Grossman, P. (2013). Learning from teacher observations: Challenges and opportunities posed by new teacher evaluation systems. *Harvard Educational Review, 83*(2), 371–384. doi:10.17763/ haer.83.2.d11511403715u376

Pianta, R. C., & Hamre, B. K. (2009). Conceptualization, measurement, and improvement of classroom processes: Standardized observation can leverage capacity. *Educational Researcher, 38*(2), 109–119. doi:10.3102/0013189X09332374

Weisberg, D., Sexton, S., Mulhern, J., & Keeling, D. (2009). *The widget effect: Our national failure to acknowledge and act on differences in teacher effectiveness*. New York, NY: The New Teacher Project. Retrieved from http://widgeteffect.org/ downloads/TheWidgetEffect.pdf

CLUSTER ANALYSIS

Generally, cluster analysis refers to the goal of identifying or discovering groups within the data, in which the primary caveat is that the groups are not known *a priori*. Prior to discussing methods for identifying clusters, it is helpful to consider the fundamental question: What is a cluster? For an $N \times P$ data matrix $\mathbf{X}$, containing measurements on N observations across P variables, each observation can be thought of as a point in P dimensional space. Clusters then are groups of points in P dimensional space that are similar in some fashion. After furthering the introduction of clusters, this entry lists and then examines the seven steps of cluster analysis. Those steps include determining which observations are to be clustered, which variables are to be used, and whether those variables should be standardized. Subsequent steps include selecting an appropriate measurement, choosing the clustering method, and then determining the number of clusters. The final step focuses on interpreting, testing, and replicating the results of the cluster analysis.

In an early, and still excellent, review of the field of cluster analysis presented to the Royal Statistical Society, Richard Melville Cormack advanced the notion that clusters have to be externally isolated and internally cohesive. Geometrically, internal cohesion indicates that the observations within a cluster are "clumped" together in the multivariate P dimensional space, whereas externally isolated indicates that the observations are well separated from each other. Alternatively, this can be further thought of as regions of the multivariate space that are dense with spaces of "sparseness" separating them, leading to a natural conceptualization of clusters corresponding to multiple modes in the multivariate space. While attempting to capture this dual notion of isolation and cohesion, several different metrics of "clusteriness" and algorithms to uncover these notions have been developed.

The vast majority of methods, whether hierarchical or nonhierarchical, often have the goal of obtaining a clustering solution such that the clusters are mutually exclusive and collectively exhaustive; that is, that each observation is assigned to one and only one cluster and all observations are assigned to at least one cluster. Initially, it seems like the best approach would be to evaluate all possible cluster solutions (e.g., look at all possible assignments of observations to clusters); however, the number of possible solutions (e.g., partitions) is enormous. Specifically, for N observations and K clusters, the number of possible ways to assign the N observations to the K clusters is given by the Stirling number of the second kind:

$$S(N,K) = \frac{1}{K!} \sum_{i=0}^{K} (-1)^i \binom{K}{i} (K-i)^N ,$$

a quantity that can be approximated by $\frac{K^N}{K!}$,

which increases rapidly for increases in both N and K. For instance, the number of possible partitions of 20 observations into five clusters is 7.95×10^{11}; modestly increasing the sample size to

100 observations results in 6.27×10^{81}, resulting in a situation in which it is impossible to evaluate all possible partitions. As such, the goal has been to develop approaches that give good solutions without evaluating all possible partitions. Because all possible solutions are not being evaluated, the ability to definitively state that the best solution (often referred to as the globally optimal solution) has been found is lost. That is, these approaches are heuristic in nature in that a set of rules are established that defines how the approach identifies the resultant clusters and not all possible solutions are evaluating, so it is impossible to know whether the final set of clusters is the best possible of all the $S(N, K)$ partitions. Given the monumental task of selecting a candidate partition as "the best" of all the possibilities, it is necessary to have some guidelines about how to proceed.

Steps of Cluster Analysis

Conducting a cluster analysis requires many decision points. Over his career, Glenn Milligan established the following seven steps as the requisite components of conducting a competent cluster analysis:

1. Determine which observations are to be clustered.

2. Determine which variables should be used in the clustering.

3. Determine whether and how variable standardization should be implemented.

4. Select an appropriate measurement of (dis) similarity for assessing how similar observations are with each other.

5. Choose the clustering method/algorithm.

6. Choose the number of clusters.

7. Validate the cluster solution through interpretation, testing, and replication.

Determining the Observations to Be Clustered

The primary directive of choosing the observations to be clustered is to ensure that the observations should contain the underlying clusters or populations that are being sought. Simply put, the resultant clusters will reflect the cluster structure within the sample. Unlike many methods, cluster analysis is not wholly driven by statistical theory, and the sample size estimates and power analysis that are normally employed with many techniques (e.g., regression) are not available. Beyond making sure that the sample covers the groups being sought, one other concern when choosing the observations is whether a particular observation may or may not be an outlier. Unfortunately, this determination is complicated by the fact that outliers (e.g., an observation that is far from all other observations) could be (a) part of a small cluster if there are other "outliers" in the same vicinity or (b) the only point from a cluster that was undersampled in the original construction of the data set. As such, specific recommendations in the form of thresholds on a metric for determining an outlier are not available; rather, each situation must be evaluated based on the judgment of the analyst and subject matter experts.

Determining the Variables to Be Used

Many statistical methods are somewhat "robust" to the inclusion of irrelevant variables in the analysis. For example, in the case of multiple regression, if a predictor variable that is not related to the dependent variable is included in the regression model, it will appear as a nonsignificant predictor that can be removed on further refinement of the model. Often, users will carry over this logic to variable inclusion in cluster analysis and follow what is deemed as the "everything but the kitchen sink" approach; in other words, researchers often include all possible variables at their disposal in the cluster analysis. This approach is often used so as not to "lose" important information on any of the variables and is likely reinforced due to there being no inherent penalty in terms of algorithmic convergence or estimation by including a large number of variables. Unfortunately, cluster analysis is quite sensitive to the variables that are included. Specifically, each variable in the cluster analysis increases the dimensionality of the space in which the observations reside, and this increased dimensionality results in an overall *de facto* increase in the variation within the system. In the context of cluster analysis, variability can be thought of as good (e.g., originating as a by-product of a multimodal cluster structure in the multivariate space) or bad (e.g., originating as variability due to the nature of how the specific variables are measured and not related to the cluster structure being sought). In an idealized scenario, it would be possible to relate variable importance to the amount of multimodality exhibited by the marginal distribution of the variable; however, it is entirely possible that the multimodality (e.g., clusters) only manifest itself when certain variables are combined and examined jointly. Unfortunately, the inclusion of even one or two variables that comprise predominantly "bad" variability that never results in clusters being identified either in the full space or any of the possible reduced spaces can result in the complete inability to recover the true cluster structure present in the sample. As such, it is imperative that each variable is evaluated with regard to how it should theoretically contribute to uncovering the overall cluster structure being sought.

Determining Whether the Variables Should Be Standardized

One of the primary decisions that data analysts encounter in any analysis is the decision of whether to standardize the variables prior to analysis. Some type of standardization is usually recommended if variables are measured on different scales. Furthermore, the method of standardization that has become the *norm de rigueur* is the z score:

$$z_i = \frac{x_i - \bar{x}}{\sigma_X},$$

where $\bar{x}$ is the mean and σ_X is the standard deviation of the variable x, with such a standardization resulting in each variable having a mean of 0 and a standard deviation of 1. However, studies have shown that this is not the preferred method for standardization in the context of cluster analysis. Specifically, by setting all the variables to have a variance of 1, variables with cluster structure will be relatively down weighted and variables without cluster structure will be relatively up weighted.

An alternative method to the standard z score is standardizing by the range, given by the formula:

$$z_i^r = \frac{x_i}{\max(x) - \min(x)}.$$

This particular standardization seems to alleviate many of the problems related to standardization using z scores. Further, several studies have shown that clustering on range-standardized data generally leads to better recovery of cluster structure than clustering on raw data, whereas clustering z score standardized data can actually lead to worse recovery than clustering the raw, unstandardized data.

Selecting a Proximity Measure

To determine whether clusters are present within the data, it is necessary to define how similarities and differences between observations are measured. This is usually accomplished with some type of distance measurement, with the most common being Euclidean distance

$$d_{ij} = \sqrt{(x_{i1} - x_{j1})^2 + (x_{i2} - x_{j2})^2 + (x_{iP} - x_{jP})^2},$$

where x_{ip} is the measurement of the ith observation on the pth variable and d_{ij} represents the distance between the ith and jth observations. Some common alternative distance measures include the squared Euclidean distance (obtained by squaring the Euclidean distance) and the city-block distance (e.g., Manhattan or Taxi-Cab metric), which is obtained by taking the sum of absolute differences across all variables. Geometrically, the Euclidean distance is a straight-line distance between two observations in the multivariate space, while the city-block distance is the sum of the distances along each of the axes that define the multivariate space. The former is the most commonly used measure (and its squared counterpart), while the latter is used in situations where it is suspected that there may be outliers.

Although the aforementioned are the most common measures for continuous variables, there is a large suite of possible measures for binary data as well. In fact, the statistical computer package SPSS contains between 20 and 30 different measures of binary similarity. Although it is prohibitive to discuss each in detail, the measures are based on different formulations of four different quantities for each pair of observations: (1) the number of times that each observation exhibits a "1" on the same variable, (2) the number of times that the first observation exhibits a 1 on a variable and the second observation exhibits a "0" on the same variable, (3) the number of times that the first observation exhibits a 0 on a variable and the second observation exhibits a 1 on the same variable, and (4) the number of times both observations exhibit a 0 on the same variable. These four quantities lead to numerous proximity measures. For instance, the simple matching coefficient is $(a + d)/(a + b + c + d)$.

Choosing the Clustering Method/Algorithm

Traditionally, cluster analysis can be broken down into two different types of approaches: hierarchical and nonhierarchical. Although cluster analysis is an innate human process (e.g., assigning observations/items to groups), its formal representation as a mathematical algorithm extends back (at least) to the psychometrician Robert Thorndike (nonhierarchical clustering) and the biologists Robert Sokal and Peter Sneath (hierarchical clustering). Each of these approaches can be thought of as broad classes of approaches for finding clusters, with many variations within each class.

Hierarchical Clustering

Hierarchical clustering itself can be divided into two types: agglomerative and divisive. In the former, all observations begin in their own cluster and, as the algorithm proceeds, each observation is merged into clusters (either existing or creating a new cluster) until all observations are in the same cluster. The reverse is true for divisive clustering—all observations begin in one cluster and they are divided until each observation is in its own cluster. Of the two types, agglomerative is much more popular than divisive, so attention is focused there.

Within agglomerative hierarchical clustering, there are several different approaches for joining the observations, with the four most popular being single linkage, complete linkage, average linkage, and Ward's method. These techniques differ in how they define the similarity between pairs of observations, pairs of clusters, or an observation (e.g., a singleton cluster) and a cluster; however, the general structure of the agglomeration process is the same:

1. Begin with each observation in their own cluster.

2. Compute the distances between all pairs of clusters. Before any observations are merged into clusters, this is computing the pairwise distance between all observations. The closest pair is then merged together to begin the process—even though the algorithms discussed can lead to quite different results, the first merger is the same for all of them.

3. Merge the pair of clusters that are closest to each other.

4. Repeat Steps 2 and 3 until all observations belong to the same cluster.

As previously stated, the algorithms only differ in the definition of "close" in Step 3. *Single linkage* (e.g., nearest neighbor clustering) defines the distance between two clusters as the minimum distance between any pair of elements within the two clusters, resulting in clusters that can be long and straggly. *Complete linkage* (e.g., furthest neighbor clustering) defines the distance between two clusters as the maximum distance between any pair of elements within the two clusters, resulting in compact clusters of similar size. *Average linkage* defines the distance between two clusters as the average pairwise distance between the observations in one cluster with the observation in the second cluster. *Ward's method* merges observations such that the increase in the total variance of the clusters is a minimum at each step; as such, this is often done using squared Euclidean distance. Ward's method often results in spherical clusters of similar size.

Nonhierarchical Clustering

Rather than merging the observations in a sequence, nonhierarchical methods initialize their algorithm with some starting "seed" and then iterate through an estimation process until convergence has been reached. There are several nonhierarchical clustering algorithms of varying degrees of complexity, with the most popular being K-means clustering. While there are variations on the K-means algorithm, a general structure is the following alternating least-squares approach:

1. Randomly assign each observation to one of the K clusters.

2. Compute the mean of each cluster.

3. Compute the distance of each of the N observations to each of the K cluster means.

4. Assign observations to the cluster with the closest mean.

5. Repeat Steps 2–4 until no observation changes cluster membership.

The K-means clustering algorithm attempts to minimize within-cluster variability and can be thought of as the nonhierarchical counterpart to Ward's method. This type of algorithm (and nonhierarchical clustering in general) is prone to converging to a locally optimal solution, meaning that the final solution will depend heavily on the initialization in Step 1. As such, it is often recommended to initialize the K-means clustering algorithm several thousand times (say 5,000) and choose as the final solution the one with the smallest within-cluster variability. Other nonhierarchical clustering approaches include the P-median algorithm, swarm optimization approaches, and many more.

Choosing the Number of Clusters

Similar to all of the decisions in cluster analysis, there are numerous methods to choose the number of clusters; however, the favored technique is evaluating several different cluster solutions and comparing them with an index that takes into account the number of clusters being fit to the data. Although there are many, the most popular index that seems to compare favorably under many different scenarios is the Calinski–Harabasz index:

$$CH(K) = \frac{SSB / (K-1)}{SSW / (N-K)},$$

where SSB and SSW are the sum of squares between clusters and the sum of squares within clusters, respectively. The general approach is to fit estimate the number of clusters for several different values of K and then choose the solution that maximizes $CH(K)$. This index favors well-separated, compact clusters—and, all else being equal, a fewer number of clusters is better.

Interpreting, Testing, and Replicating

The final step in the cluster analysis is to assess the quality of the clustering solution. Interpreting the results relies on substantive knowledge about the content domain, and specific recommendations are not given beyond evaluating the means and variances of the clusters and determining how much they comport with theoretical expectations.

Statistical testing for cluster analysis is a little more delicate. Critically, tests to determine whether the clusters are significantly different from each other can only be conducted on variables that were not used to create the clusters in the first place. These tests are often conducted using analysis of variance in which the clusters serve as the groups. If the variables that were used to construct the clusters are tested, the results will almost always be significant; however, these results are invalid because the groups were designed to be maximally separate on those variables, and as such, any associated p values are meaningless. This type of analysis is analogous to externally validating the cluster structure.

Internal validation relies on replication, which is usually accomplished by splitting the sample into two (or more) subsamples and determining whether the same cluster structure is extracted from each subsample. The comparison of cluster structure can be done either informally by assessing whether the parameters (e.g., means and variances) are consistent across solutions or formally by comparing the solutions via an appropriate index (e.g., adjusted Rand index). Unfortunately, it is possible to consistently extract similar cluster structure from the data without actually proving that clusters truly exist. Even if that is the case, each of the decisions discussed in this entry can have a dramatic impact on the final solution, and being able to replicate that solution is required to have a semblance of confidence in the final result.

While replication is a necessary but not sufficient condition for determining whether true clusters have been identified, it is also the first step in determining whether a cluster structure exists.

Douglas Steinley

See also Cluster Sampling; Exploratory Factor Analysis

Further Readings

Cormack, R. M. (1971). A review of classification. *Journal of the Royal Statistical Society, A, 134,* 321–367.

Everitt, B. S., Landau, S., Leese, M., & Stahl, D. (2011). *Cluster analysis* (5th ed.). New York, NY: Wiley.

Milligan, G. W., & Cooper, M. C. (1985). An examination of procedures for determining the number of clusters in a data set. *Psychometrika, 50,* 159–179.

Sneath, P. H. A., & Sokal, R. R. (1973). *Numerical taxonomy.* San Francisco: W. H. Freeman.

Steinley, D. (2006). K-means clustering: A half-century synthesis. *British Journal of Mathematical and Statistical Psychology, 59,* 1–34.

CLUSTER SAMPLING

Cluster sampling is a probability sampling technique in which all population elements are categorized into mutually exclusive and exhaustive groups called clusters. Clusters are selected for sampling, and all or some elements from selected clusters comprise the sample. This method is typically used when natural groups exist in the population (e.g., schools or counties) or when obtaining a list of all population elements is impossible or impractically costly. As compared to simple random sampling, cluster sampling can reduce travel cost for in-person data collection by using geographically concentrated clusters. At the same time, cluster sampling is generally less precise than simple random or stratified sampling; therefore, it is typically used when it is economically justified (i.e., when a dispersed population would be expensive to survey). This entry discusses selecting clusters with equal and unequal probability and provides a comparison of cluster sampling to other sampling methods.

Selecting Clusters With Equal Probability

Cluster sampling can be applied in one or more stages but, regardless of the number of stages, the first step is to select the clusters (primary sampling units) from which sample elements (secondary sampling units) will be drawn. A basic one-stage design takes a simple random sample of clusters and selects for sampling all elements within those clusters, although this design is rarely used in practice. A researcher could select schools and collect data about every student in the selected schools. Because elements within a cluster are often similar—a phenomenon called a cluster effect—it may be redundant and inefficient to sample a large proportion of the elements within a cluster.

Large-scale studies typically use a multistage cluster sampling method. A basic implementation of this type of sample is a two-stage cluster sample selecting clusters via simple random sample and independently subsampling elements within each cluster, using the same sampling fraction across clusters. The downside of this simple approach is that it results in differing sample sizes per cluster, making it less attractive than other designs. Designs with more than two stages may also be useful; a three-stage statewide survey, for example, could sample school districts, then schools within selected districts, then teachers within selected schools.

In multistage sampling, the variance of the estimated quantities depends on within-cluster and between-cluster variance. Within-cluster variance is related to the intraclass correlation coefficient (ICC), which measures the degree of homogeneity of the variable of interest for elements within a cluster. ICC is typically interpreted as the correlation between the responses of individuals in the same cluster. Using schools as clusters and students' test scores as an outcome, an ICC of 0.2 would mean that 20% of the variation in the student test scores is accounted for by the school a student attends, and 80% is accounted for by variation across students within schools.

Selecting Clusters With Unequal Probability

Clusters may also be selected with probability proportional to size. This means that clusters containing a greater size measure (e.g., the number of population elements) are more likely to be included in the sample than clusters with fewer elements. Such a sampling scheme would, for instance, be more likely to select a college dormitory where 100 students live than one where 20 live. Specifically, the probability of selection for cluster c is $m \times N_cN$ where m clusters are selected from the population of clusters, N_c is the measure of size (e.g., the number of secondary sampling units) in cluster c, and N is the sum of the measure of size across all clusters (e.g., the number of elements in the population). If the cluster sample is stratified, then the numbers in this probability formula reflect those in a particular stratum. The second stage sample could select an equal number of elements from each cluster. This creates an equal workload in each cluster, which is preferable if data collection involves face-to-face communication, and in expectation results in a self-weighting sample. If the probability of selection within cluster c is nN_c, then the cumulative probability of selection for each secondary sampling unit reduces to mnN, a constant. The variance of an estimator of the population mean is a function of the number of clusters selected, the sample size within each cluster, and the ICC. Higher ICC values increase the variance for a given sample size, and increasing the ratio of the number of clusters selected to the sample size within a cluster reduces the overall variance and increases the precision of the final estimates.

Comparison to Other Sampling Methods

Cluster sampling has some parallels to stratified sampling, in that both divide the population into groups (clusters or strata) and make selections from those groups. However, cluster sampling samples elements from only selected clusters, where stratified sampling selects a sample of at least one element from every stratum. As a result, in cluster sampling, the selection process is subject to two levels of chance variation, one for the selection of clusters and one for the selection of elements within a cluster. In contrast, the stratified sampling process (and its simpler form as a simple random sample) is only subject to one level of chance from the selection of elements within each stratum, which will often improve the precision of an estimate made from the sample. There are

exceptions to this general rule depending on how the sample size is allocated across the strata to produce subgroup estimates. But stratified and simple random sampling, in general, produce a more precise estimate than cluster sampling for the same sample size.

Breanna A. Wakar and Dmitriy Poznyak

See also Representativeness; Sample Size; Simple Random Sampling; Stratified Random Sampling; Variance

Further Readings

Bethlehem, J. G. (2009). *Applied survey methods: A statistical perspective.* Hoboken, NJ: Wiley.

Kish, L. (1965). *Survey sampling.* New York, NY: Wiley.

Levy, P. S., & Lemeshow, S. (2008). *Sampling of populations: Methods and applications.* Hoboken, NJ: Wiley.

Lohr, S. L. (2010). *Sampling: Design and analysis* (2nd ed.). Boston, MA: Brooks/COLE.

Cochran *Q* Test

In conducting meta-analyses of estimates from a set of studies, researchers often use a statistic denoted by Q to assess the homogeneity of the estimates. When used as the basis of a formal statistical test of homogeneity, Q is commonly referred to a chi-square distribution, and the test is called the Cochran Q test. The name of the test, however, embodies a misunderstanding: Although William G. Cochran wrote about the statistic Q, he did not propose a test based on it. Also, the test generally uses an incorrect null distribution. This entry describes the Q statistic, examines its statistical behavior, and discusses implications for the heterogeneity measure I^2 and for a popular method of random-effects meta-analysis.

The *Q* Statistic

In the main paper in which Q appears, Cochran was concerned with combining estimates from k separate experiments. The types of experiments included determinations of a physical or astronomical constant, bioassays, and agricultural field experiments; typical estimates were a simple mean, a difference between two means, a median lethal dose, and a regression coefficient. Each experiment provided an estimate, y_i, and an estimate, s_i^2, of the variance of y_i. Also, each s_i^2 had a number of degrees of freedom, n_i, which would ordinarily come from a mean square (e.g., the sample variance or the residual mean square of a regression). Thus, the setting differed from most meta-analyses. Ideally, all experiments were estimating the same quantity, μ, but it could vary among experiments (i.e., the quantities could be μ_i instead of a single μ). Thus, Q summarized the variation among the estimates in the form of a weighted sum of the squared deviations of the y_i from the weighted mean $\bar{y}_w = \Sigma w_i y_i / \Sigma w_i$ with weights $w_i = 1/s_i^2$,

$$Q = \sum_{i=1}^{k} w_i (y_i - \bar{y}_w)^2.$$

A large value of Q indicates heterogeneity among the y_i. The degrees of freedom, n_i, are not used in calculating Q; but they do appear, for example, in an approximate formula for the standard error of $\bar{y}_w$.

When the degrees of freedom (n_i) are "large" and the μ_i are equal, the distribution of Q approaches the chi-square distribution on $k-1$ degrees of freedom. The literature, however, provides little information on a quantitative definition of "large."

In a meta-analysis, y_i is usually the estimate of the effect in Study i (e.g., the standardized mean difference or a difference of proportions), and s_i^2 is an estimate of its (within study) variance. The test of homogeneity refers Q to the chi-square distribution on $k-1$ degrees of freedom and rejects the null hypothesis if $p < .10$ (the criterion $p < .05$ is less common because the test is considered to have low power). Many authors routinely use chi-square on $k-1$ df as the null distribution. This procedure is understandable because the s_i^2 in a meta-analysis are rarely, if ever, accompanied by numbers of degrees of freedom. Indeed, some common measures of effect, such as a difference in proportions, do not have a natural way to define a number of df. When the n_i are available, they are often closely related to the total sample size of

the two groups in the study. In many meta-analyses, the total sample size is not "large," so the test of homogeneity is unreliable.

To illustrate the application of the Q statistic, Table 1 lists the values of the standardized mean difference, its estimated variance, and the corresponding weight for 19 studies of the effects of teacher expectancy on pupil IQ. These data yield $\bar{y}_w = 0.060$ and $Q = 35.83$. The usual test of homogeneity would have $p < .01$, but (as discussed in the next section) that test uses an incorrect null distribution. Also, a single number, such as Q (or, for that matter, $\bar{y}_w$), seldom gives an adequate summary of a set of data. Examination of the values of y_i in Table 1 provides an informal, but more useful, indication of possible heterogeneity. The bulk of the estimates range from about −0.3 to +0.3, and three high values stand out (1.18, 0.80, and 0.54). Thus, Studies 4, 10, and 11 would merit some scrutiny. Their relatively small weights suggest that those studies may have had relatively small samples, but they may have other distinctive characteristics. The authors who published the data in Table 1 used those data in a limited methodological example and did not discuss the studies' sample sizes or other characteristics.

A warning: Researchers sometimes choose between a fixed-effect meta-analysis and a random-effects meta-analysis on the basis of the test of homogeneity. That is a mistake. Even if the studies' sample sizes are "large" and the test uses the correct null distribution, the resulting two-step procedure has very little statistical support.

Statistical Behavior of Q

A key ingredient in the statistical behavior of Q (i.e., the distribution of Q in the presence of homogeneity or various patterns of heterogeneity) is the weights, w_i. If each weight was the reciprocal of the true within-study variance of y_i (i.e., $w_i = 1/\sigma_i^2$), straightforward applications of statistical theory would yield the null and non-null distributions of Q. The σ_i^2 are usually unknown, however, and that theoretical approach is not compatible with the actual weights in the definition of Q, $w_i = 1/s_i^2$. Many authors ignore this distinction, relying on s_i^2 to converge to σ_i^2 as the

Table 1   Effect, Estimated Variance, and Weight for 19 Studies of the Effects of Teacher Expectancy on Pupil IQ

Study	Effect (y_i)	Estimated Variance (s_i^2)	Weight ($w_i = 1/s_i^2$)
8	−0.32	0.04840	20.661
15	−0.18	0.02528	39.555
3	−0.14	0.02789	35.856
19	−0.07	0.03028	33.029
6	−0.06	0.01061	94.260
16	−0.06	0.02789	35.856
7	−0.02	0.01061	94.260
13	−0.02	0.08352	11.973
1	0.03	0.01563	64.000
18	0.07	0.00884	113.173
2	0.12	0.02161	46.277
12	0.18	0.04973	20.109
14	0.23	0.08410	11.891
5	0.26	0.13616	7.344
9	0.27	0.02690	37.180
17	0.30	0.01932	51.757
11	0.54	0.09120	10.964
10	0.80	0.06300	15.873
4	1.18	0.13913	7.188

Source: Shadish, W. R., & Haddock, C. K. (2009). Combining estimates of effect size. In H. Cooper, L. V. Hedges, & J. C. Valentine (Eds.), *The handbook of research synthesis and meta-analysis* (2nd ed., p. 264). New York, NY: Russell Sage Foundation.

sample size becomes large. Accurate estimate of a variance, however, can require surprisingly large samples.

In the setting discussed by Cochran, s_i^2 is usually statistically independent of y_i. For some measures of effect, however, s_i^2 and y_i are associated because of their relation to sample estimates. If y_i is the difference between the rates of an event in the two groups in Study i, $y_i = p_{i1} - p_{i2}$, and the groups' sample sizes are n_{i1} and n_{i2}, the usual estimate of the variance of y_i is $s_i^2 = [p_{i1}(1-p_{i1})/n_{i1}] + [p_{i2}(1-p_{i2})/n_{i2}]$.

Studies of the behavior of Q that take into account the variability of the s_i^2 and their relation to y_i involve substantial complexity; they generally use asymptotic expansions to obtain approximate formulas for the mean and variance of Q and then verify those formulas by simulation. The results for standardized mean difference, risk difference, and odds ratio yield three different null distributions for Q, none of which is the chi-square distribution on $k-1$ degrees of freedom. Thus, the usual test of homogeneity gives invalid p values.

Implications for I^2

The heterogeneity measure I^2 is usually calculated from Q:

$$I^2 = \max\left\{0, \frac{Q-(k-1)}{Q}\right\},$$

and interpreted as the proportion of total variation in the estimates of treatment effect that is due to heterogeneity between studies. The development of I^2 treated Q as having, in the absence of heterogeneity, the chi-square distribution on $k-1$ degrees of freedom. Thus, I^2 is positive when Q exceeds the mean of that distribution ($k-1$). Such a value of Q has a substantial probability: .392 when $k = 4$, increasing to .465 when $k = 30$ and approaching .5 as k becomes large. These probabilities are large enough to rule out interpreting I^2 as "the proportion of total variation in the estimates of treatment effect that is due to heterogeneity between studies," but they do not indicate the probability of larger values of I^2. The probability that $I^2 > 25\%$ decreases from .261 when $k = 4$ to .108 when $k = 30$, and the corresponding probabilities that $I^2 > 50\%$ are .112 and .001.

These probabilities are hypothetical because the null distribution of Q is generally not chi-square on $k-1$ degrees of freedom. If one wanted to continue using the mean of the null distribution as the threshold for positive values of I^2 (not necessarily a useful choice), the formula for that mean would depend on the measure of effect size and would generally have to be estimated from the data in each meta-analysis. These complications sharply limit the usefulness of I^2 as a measure of heterogeneity.

Role of Q in Random-Effects Meta-Analysis

The popular DerSimonian-Laird method for random-effects meta-analysis uses Q as the basis for its estimate of the between-study variance (i.e., the variance of the μ_i in the random-effects model). The method does not assume a particular distribution for Q, but it does use the s_i^2 as if they were the σ_i^2. The consequences include bias in estimating the between-study variance, bias in the overall estimate, and confidence intervals with inadequate coverage. The relation between y_i and $w_i = 1/s_i^2$ is an underappreciated source of bias.

David C. Hoaglin

See also Meta-Analysis; p Value; Power

Further Readings

Cochran, W. G. (1954). The combination of estimates from different experiments. *Biometrics, 10*, 101–129. doi:10.2307/3001666

DerSimonian, R., & Laird, N. (1986). Meta-analysis in clinical trials. *Controlled Clinical Trials, 7*, 177–188. doi:10.1016/0197-2456(86)90046-2

Higgins, J. P. T., & Thompson, S. G. (2002). Quantifying heterogeneity in a meta-analysis. *Statistics in Medicine, 21*, 1539–1558. doi:10.1002/sim.1186

Hoaglin, D. C. (2016). Misunderstandings about Q and "Cochran's Q test" in meta-analysis. *Statistics in Medicine, 35*, 485–495. doi:10.1002/sim.6632

Kulinskaya, E., & Dollinger, M. B. (2015). An accurate test for homogeneity of odds ratios based on Cochran's Q-statistic. *BMC Medical Research Methodology, 15*, 49. doi:10.1186/s12874 -015-0034-x

Kulinskaya, E., Dollinger, M. B., & Bjørkestøl, K. (2011). On the moments of Cochran's Q statistic under the null hypothesis, with application to the meta-analysis of risk difference. *Research Synthesis Methods, 2*, 254–270. doi:10.1002/jrsm.54

Kulinskaya, E., Dollinger, M. B., & Bjørkestøl, K. (2011). Testing for homogeneity in meta-analysis I. The one-parameter case: Standardized mean difference. *Biometrics, 67*, 203–212. doi:10.1111/j.1541 -0420.2010.01442.x

COEFFICIENT ALPHA

Social science measurement requires scores that are both valid and reliable. Reliability refers to the amount of random fluctuation in a set of scores. One of the most popular methods for estimating the reliability of test scores is coefficient α, which estimates the proportion of observed score variance that is due to true score variance. The coefficient α is widely used in the education and psychosocial literature as an index of reliability of test scores.

Coefficient α was first described by Lee Cronbach in 1951, so it is sometimes termed Cronbach's α. Coefficient α is used for establishing reliability of test scores from a single administration. However, in spite of the common use of coefficient α in the literature as an index of reliability of test scores, there is a lack of the proper use of coefficient α and its interpretation.

To achieve a greater understanding of coefficient α, this entry discusses these issues. First, the entry offers a more complete definition of reliability and then provides a detailed explanation of coefficient α. The entry then looks at assumptions of coefficient α as well as conceptual issues of this measure of reliability. Finally, the entry demonstrates when the use of alternative methods of reliability, such as ω, may be more appropriate.

Reliability

In 2011, in a study by Tavakol and Dennick, the reliability of a test is concerned with the capability of a test to consistently measure an attribute. A consistent test generates more or less the same results when administered on different occasions. Indeed, reliability refers to the trustworthiness of test scores (McDonald, 2014).

Reliability is based on the classical test theory model. Under the classical test theory model, the observed score is equal to the true score plus the error score (observed score = true score + error score). Researchers are interested in gaining knowledge about the true score and the discrepancy between an observed score and true score (i.e., how strongly the observed score is related to the true score). In other words, researchers want to know how much the differences in observed scores can be directly determined (explained) by the differences in true scores? By answering this question, researchers are in a position to identify the reliability index. Indeed, the reliability index is a correlation between the true score and the observed score (Raykov and Marcoulides, 2011). Given this, reliability is the ratio of the individual differences (variance or variability) of the true score to the individual differences of the observed score. Thus, the greater the ratio of the true score

differences to the observed score differences, the more reliable the test.

The Source of Measurement Error and Reliability

As previously pointed out, reliability is the ability of a test to consistently measure an attribute (e.g., students' competencies). For example, if a student is tested 1,000 times using the same assessment questions, these tests will likely have different scores. The mean of all 1,000 scores produces the true score of the student. However, practically researchers are unable to conduct that many tests in order to obtain the true score of the student. Using a single test administration, the observed score can be cofounded by random or systematic errors, as proposed by the classical test theory.

The random and systematic errors attached to the observed score decrease the function of a particular test. No test is immune from random or systematic errors. Indeed, reliability refers to the degree to which test results are free from random errors. Thus, if researchers minimize the measurement errors associated with the obtained scores in a test, the test scores will be more consistent, and researchers can have enough confidence to make a decision about the test results. In the following section, the association between reliability and the coefficient α is discussed.

What Is Coefficient α?

Error variance is an integral part of any measurement. If researchers are interested in measuring the error variance attached to the different items of a particular test, coefficient α is calculated to obtain the error variance that is due to the interaction between item scores and persons. The following formula is used for coefficient α:

$$\alpha = \left(\frac{n}{n-1}\right)\left(1 - \frac{\sum \sigma_j^2}{\sigma_x^2}\right),$$

in which n is the number of items in a test, $\sum \sigma_j^2$ is the sum of the variances of the individual items, and σ_x^2 is the variance of the whole test. Based on this formula, we need to have two or more items in a test to calculate coefficient α. Coefficient α is mainly affected by two factors: the number of test items and the correlation coefficients between items (the interrelatedness of the items in a test). As the number of items in a test increases, the value of coefficient α will increase. If the items within a test are highly correlated to each other, the coefficient α increases. Thus, to boost internal consistency of test scores, the test should include more items testing the same concept (Tavakol and Dennick, 2011a). It is also noteworthy to mention that coefficient α is not concerned with the reliability of a test itself. It is concerned with the reliability of the test scores from a specific sample of testees. Because the characteristics of the testees being assessed vary from one sample to another, coefficient α will vary from one cohort of testees to another. This suggests that the coefficient α should be calculated each time the test is administered. Coefficient α is addressed as a number between 0 (uncorrelated items) and 1 (perfectly correlated items). The closer the coefficient α value is to 1, the more reliable the test results are. If testees vary in relation to their performances, that is, when there is a wide dispersion of skills or performances, the coefficient α will approach 1.

If a test produces poorly reliable results (i.e., a low value of coefficient α), it is difficult to make fair assumptions on the test and its results. However, caution should be taken in interpreting the value of coefficient α, either high or low. For example, in educational assessments, students' abilities may be more or less the same (low variation in performance), or educators may be faced with a low value of coefficient α that is attributed to a low dispersion of scores on assessment questions. In addition, if a small sample of testees is selected for the test of interest, a low coefficient α may be produced. What is more, moderately difficult items (from 25% to 75% correct answers) that differentiate between who know the content and who do not contribute enormously to coefficient α values.

Given the Cronbach's α formula, if the items of a test are statistically independent (e.g., when items are randomly scored), σ_x^2 would be equal to $\sum \sigma_j^2$, then $\alpha = 0$. This indicates that if the test items are correlated to each other, the coefficient

of α is increased. If items in a test provide the same information (i.e., item responses of the test are the same), σ_x^2 is equal to $n^2 \sigma_j^2$, then $\alpha = 1$. This indicates that a very high value of α (e.g., greater than .90) does not necessarily mean you have better test scores. This may suggest redundancies and show the test length should be reduced by removing the items that repeat the information provided by other items. The generally acceptable value range for coefficient α is from .70 to .95. However, in educational research with groups, a coefficient α greater than .60 is allowable.

Robust Estimation of the Coefficient α

When it is stated that a test is reliable, it should be reliable for the bulk of the examinees. However, the traditional coefficient α does not reflect the bulk of examinees. It has been shown that test scores are often skewed with "very heavy tails." Because the coefficient α is based on the individual variances and total variance of test scores, a small departure from the normality of test scores can influence the variances, which in turn can provide a misleading value of the coefficient α. Consequently, it is necessary to have a coefficient α that is resistant to extremes. To overcome this issue and make a robust estimation of the coefficient α, the midvariance and midcovariance estimates are used instead of the variances and covariances in the coefficient α formula. Such a robust estimation of the coefficient α is resistant to extreme values (outliers) in a distribution of scores.

Assumptions of Coefficient α

Before data are subject to a particular statistical procedure, such as regression analysis, we check a number of assumptions about the data. If these assumptions are violated, our conclusions from the analysis of the data will be misleading. Similarly, before test items are subject to coefficient α, researchers need to assess the assumptions of coefficient α. If the assumptions are not satisfied, the coefficient α estimated results in a misleading estimate of reliability. Coefficient α is grounded in the *essentially tau-equivalent measurement model*, often referred to as the *true score equivalent model.* The essentially tau-equivalent measurement model assumes each test item measures the same latent variable on the same test. Put another way, the items of a test should be unidimensional (i.e., test items reflect one construct). Indeed, the factor loadings (i.e., correlations between items and the factors) under the framework of confirmatory factor analysis are identical in all items on a single-factor solution, but the error variances may differ. This suggests that items are homogenous in a test. It should be emphasized even if an item in a test does not measure the underlying construct equally like other items, the sensitivity of coefficient α may be significantly undermined.

It should also be emphasized that when test items are essential tau equivalent, the reliability is equivalent to coefficient α. To assess the assumption of essential tau equivalence on the reliability of test scores, the sample of test items is subject to confirmatory factor analysis. Under the confirmatory factor analysis approach, test items should be explained by the one-factor solution (the unidimensionality assumption) in order to use coefficient α. In addition, a broad difference in the standard deviations of item responses in a test may be an indication of the violation of the assumption of tau equivalence.

Conceptual Issues Surrounding Coefficient α

The reliability of test scores is equal to coefficient α if and only if all items are essentially equivalent, otherwise coefficient α does not equal the reliability of test scores. If one factor/trait does not underlie the items on a test, the assumption of the essentially tau-equivalent model is violated, and hence, coefficient α estimates a lower bound of the reliability of test scores. Stated another way, the calculated coefficient α in samples will be considerably below average for reliability in the population if the assumption of the essentially tau-equivalent model is not met. The greater the violation of the essentially tau-equivalent model, the more coefficient α underestimates the reliability of test scores. What is more is that it has been documented that when items measure an underlying single construct (i.e., a unidimensional test), the degree of the bias in coefficient α would be trivial. In addition to this, it has also been shown

that a well-constructed test with more than four items and a mean factor loading of .60 or higher is more likely to hold the assumption of essential tau equivalency and hence shows less bias.

It seems there is some confusion in the coefficient α literature on the use of the terms *internal consistency*, *homogeneity*, and *unidimensionality*, which are often used interchangeably. Having a clear understanding of these terms can help to improve the proper use of coefficient α. Internal consistency refers to the interrelatedness of a sample of test items, whereas homogeneity is concerned with the unidimensionality of a set of test items. Coefficient α is a function of internal consistency (the function of interrelatedness), that is, the average interitem correlation. This does not imply that the coefficient α equals the homogeneity or unidimensionality of a set of items. Both a unidimensional test and a multidimensional test can have a high or low value of coefficient α.

Mathematically speaking, the coefficient α is a function of the test length and the average interitem correlation. The coefficient α increases as the number of items in a test increases. A low coefficient α, therefore, may be due to a short test. Therefore, in order to improve the reliability of test scores of a shorter test, the length of the test should be increased. For example, a test of 40 items may have a better reliability compared with a test of 20 items. It should be emphasized that the reliability of test scores is inflated regardless of the consistency of items when large numbers of items are produced. Having a large number of items in a test is not "bad," but the coefficient α calculated should be cross-checked against other indices of internal consistency (e.g., the average interitem correlation). The higher the average of interitem correlation, the higher the coefficient α, and the more reliable the test scores. To calculate the average interitem correlation, all items that measure the same construct in a test are correlated to each other (i.e., correlation between each pair of items) and then the computed correlation coefficients are averaged. As a guideline, it has been recommended the average interitem correlation lies in a range of .15 – .50. A higher average interitem correlation is required if a test measures a narrower construct, such as "talkativeness."

Although the average interitem correlation is more suitable than the coefficient α, little attention has been paid to the average interitem correlation as an index of internal consistency. More importantly, if either the average interitem correlation or correlation between each pair of items is not presented, it is difficult to assess the coefficient α reported. In addition, the coefficient α is practically useless as an index of internal consistency when the number of items in a test is more than 40.

The Use of ω

Ignoring the fundamental assumptions of the coefficient ω can provide a misleading picture of the reliability of test scores. It has been well documented that these assumptions are hard to meet, such as, for example, the assumption of essential tau equivalence, which assumes all test items measure the same underlying construct (i.e., the test is unidimensional), or under factor analysis, all items have the same factor loadings. If these assumptions are violated, alternative reliability approaches to the coefficient α, such as ω (McDonald, 1999), should be used. ω has been strongly supported by the psychometric literature as an index of internal consistency, particularly as an alternative to α. Using the ω approach, the issues attached to the coefficient α, such as inflation or attenuation of internal consistency, are less likely to happen to a test.

Alternative Methods of Reliability

It has been argued that the coefficient α is not resistant to the resulting measures of reliability. Recommended robust alternatives approaches along with bootstrapping can better estimate the coefficient α. However, psychometricians believe that the coefficient α has been extensively misapplied. If the assumptions of the coefficient α are violated (e.g., the essentially tau-equivalent model), the resulting measures of reliability will be less decisive. Given the restriction assumptions that have been placed on the coefficient α (e.g., all items should have identical factor loadings), it is very likely that these assumptions are violated. If this is the case, the coefficient α should not be applied. Alternative approaches to the coefficient α, such as the ω approach, should be used.

The ω approach outperforms the coefficient α, if the assumptions of the coefficient α are violated.

However, the ω would perform the same as the coefficient α, if the assumptions of the coefficient α are met. By applying the ω approach along with bootstrapping, researchers can obtain a better estimation of the reliability of test scores.

Mohsen Tavakol

See also Omega; Reliability; Split-Half Reliability; Validity

Further Readings

Cronbach, L. (1951). Coefficient alpha and the internal structure of testes. *Psychometrika, 16,* 297–333.

Dunn, T., Baguley, T., & Brunsden, V. (2013). From alpha to omega: A pratical solution to the pervasive problem of internal consistency estimation. *British Journal of Psychology, 105,* 399–412.

Ebel, R. (1972). *Essentials of educational measurment.* London, England: Prentice-Hall International.

Graham, J. (2006). Congeneric and (Essentially) tau-equivalent estimates of score reliability. *Educational and Psychological Measurement, 66,* 930–944.

Lord, F., & Novick, M. (1968). *Statistical theories of mental test scores.* London, England: Addison-Wesley.

Nunnally, J., & Bernstein, I. (1994). *Psychometric theory.* New York, NY: McGraw-Hill Higher Education.

COGNITIVE DEVELOPMENT, THEORY OF

The theory of cognitive development developed by Swiss psychologist Jean Piaget (1896–1980) is one of the most influential theories in the fields of educational and developmental psychology. Piaget described his theoretical orientation as one of "genetic epistemology" focused on the emergence, growth, and evolution of knowledge. Piaget's theory of cognitive development is premised on the notion that thinking and learning are adaptive; our cognitions allow us to adapt to and function effectively within our environments.

Starting from this fundamental premise, Piaget explored the ways in which scientific thinking and reasoning develop, and how our interactions with the physical and social world shape our thinking. Piaget, along with other early psychologists such as William James and B. F. Skinner, contributed to the evolution of psychology as an empirical, rather than a purely theoretical, science. This entry discusses the development of Piaget's theory of cognitive development, its major constructs, the stages of cognitive development, and how the theory has been evaluated, applied in education, and built on by other researchers.

Piaget's theory is a general theory, based on the premise that disparate aspects of cognition develop together, undergoing similar changes. In his research, Piaget explored many aspects of children's thinking, including beliefs about the physical, biological, and social worlds. Piaget argued that cognitive development consists of a set of discrete stages and that thinking in different stages is qualitatively different. Piaget viewed cognitive development as driven by four critical factors: maturation, the physical environment, social interaction, and equilibration.

Piaget argued that children learn and understand through action. For young children, this action is generally physical (e.g., grasping and manipulating objects), whereas for older children, the action may be physical or mental (performing logical cognitive actions, termed operations). In contrast to earlier theorists who generally viewed children as relatively passive recipients of instruction, Piaget thought of children as "little scientists" who were constantly developing and testing hypotheses about the world around them. Piaget believed knowledge was a process and not a state and wanted to learn not just what children knew but how they knew it. Thus, he employed research methods that allowed him to study children's cognitive processes, including responses that might be considered incorrect or mistaken from an adult point of view.

Research Methods

Piaget used a variety of research methods in developing and testing his theory. One of the first methods he used was naturalistic observations of children (primarily his own children and the children of his friends). These observations were carefully recorded in diary entries, which included detailed descriptions of how the children interacted with the world around them. For example, in his book *The Construction of Reality in the Child*, Piaget describes an interaction with his 7-month-old son Laurent in which Laurent appears to lose interest in a desired object as soon as the object is hidden from view. Piaget used this interaction as support for his view that young infants lack an understanding of object permanence.

Piaget also frequently used clinical interviewing to study children's thinking and reasoning. These clinical interviews typically begin with the interviewer posing a question or problem for the child to address. The interviewer then observes the child's behavioral or verbal responses and asks follow-up questions to probe for additional information that elaborates on thought processes. For example, in *The Child's Conception of the World*, Piaget reports on clinical interviews conducted with a series of children that focused on what it means to be alive. In these interviews, Piaget would ask children whether various organisms and objects (e.g., trees, rivers, the sun) were alive and to explain the reasoning for their conclusions. Many children viewed motion or action as key elements of being alive (e.g., concluding that rivers are alive because the water in them moves from place to place). These responses contributed to Piaget's view of animism as a key component of young children's thinking. Clinical interviews sometimes included specially designed tasks, such as the "three mountains task" and conservation tasks described later in this entry.

Major Constructs

Piaget's theory was complex and far-reaching and evolved meaningfully over the course of Piaget's long scholarly career. Major constructs of his theory are a constructivist view of knowledge, schemas, equilibration, assimilation, accommodation, operations, décalage, and stages of cognitive development.

Construction of Knowledge

Piaget's theory of cognitive development is a constructivist theory, based on the belief that learners mentally construct an understanding of the world. These cognitive constructions are based on previous experiences as well as the learner's current level of cognitive development. In Piaget's view, children are not passive recipients of lessons from parents and teachers but active seekers of information and explanations for the phenomena that they observe.

Schemas

In Piaget's theory, schemas are the fundamental building blocks of knowledge. A schema is a basic cognitive structure, an organized way of making sense of experience. Schemas provide a general way of knowing the world used for processing information and analyzing experience. For example, the schema for "chair" would include what chairs generally look like (i.e., four legs, a seat, a back) and ways in which chairs can be used (i.e., for sitting, for standing on to reach things). Our knowledge of schemas underlies all of our behaviors.

Equilibration

Equilibration is the process by which learners create a stable understanding of a construct. The desire for cognitive equilibrium is an internal motivator that drives cognitive growth and change. Cognitive structures and abilities arise from the equilibration process and are the result of the learner's efforts to organize experiences into a coherent mental structure.

Equilibration involves movement between stages of equilibrium and disequilibrium. Typically, a learner begins in a state of equilibrium regarding a particular concept or schema. If the learner encounters new information that reveals that the learner's understanding is inadequate, this will push the learners into a state of disequilibrium. Eventually, the learner will revise the relevant schema to incorporate this new information and reach a new state of equilibrium.

Assimilation and Accommodation

Equilibration involves balancing assimilation and accommodation. The process of assimilation involves using existing schemas to interpret the external world, incorporating new objects or experiences into the existing schema. A child who sees a guinea pig for the first time and labels it "kitty" is using an assimilation process to fit this new animal into an existing cognitive structure. Piaget viewed play as a form of assimilation, in which the child engages in familiar actions or routines, using existing behavioral and cognitive schemas, and derives pleasure from this process. In contrast, accommodation involves making adjustments in one's cognitive organization of the world as a result of the demands of the world. In accommodation, the learner adjusts existing schemas or creates new ones when existing schemas do not capture the environment completely. The child who labels a guinea pig "kitty" is corrected, adds a new term to an existing understanding of animal categories, and is engaging in accommodation. When learners are in a state of equilibrium, they tend to assimilate more often than they accommodate, whereas when they are in a state of disequilibrium, accommodation tends to predominate.

Operations

Operations are mental representations of actions that are based on symbols and obey logical rules. With development, operations become more cognitive (less physically based) and more abstract. Operations exist in an organized mental structure in which all operations are linked together. All operations follow key logical principles, such as reversibility.

Décalage

In cognitive developmental theory, *décalage* refers to the invariant order in which cognitive skills develop. The theory differentiates between horizontal and vertical décalage. Horizontal décalage describes situations in which the child's thinking appears to be at different cognitive levels at a given point in time. Horizontal décalage is typically demonstrated through different tasks that tap the same underlying cognitive structure. For example, if a child displays conservation ability on tasks of conservation of number and volume, but not on tasks measuring conservation of mass, this would be an example of horizontal décalage. Horizontal décalage typically refers to the ordering of cognitive accomplishments within a given developmental stage.

Vertical décalage, in contrast to horizontal décalage, describes ways in which individuals approach the same task with increasingly complex approaches over the course of development. For example, a child may develop a sensorimotor knowledge of location (e.g., knowing how to move from one room in the house to another) long before a representational knowledge of location develops (e.g., being able to draw a map of the house or give verbal directions indicating how to get from one room to another). Vertical décalage typically refers to the ordering of cognitive accomplishments across developmental stages (i.e., how a given problem is approached and solved differently across stages).

Stages of Development

Piaget's cognitive developmental theory is a stage theory, in which the developing child progresses through multiple stages of cognitive development. Piaget proposed that these stages were universal and invariant (i.e., that one must move through each stage in order and that stages cannot be skipped) and that thinking was qualitatively different across stages. That is, it is not simply that thinking is faster, better, or more logical in later stages, but that learners in each stage approach, interact with, and conceptualize the world in meaningfully different ways. Thinking in each stage is characterized by certain cognitive accomplishments and limitations. Although Piaget indicated approximate age ranges for each stage, it is important to note that individuals of various ages may think in various ways, depending on factors such as environmental supports and task demands.

Sensorimotor Stage

In the sensorimotor stage, which lasts from birth to approximately 2 years of age, intelligence is expressed through sensory and motor capabilities. Thinking in this stage is limited, but over the course of the sensorimotor stage, children reach several key cognitive milestones. These include object permanence (the awareness that an object continues to exist even when it is not in view), the beginning of representational thought (the capacity to form mental images, as evidenced in the child's increasing language capabilities and capacity for deferred imitation), and understanding of causality.

The sensorimotor stage is divided into six substages. Movement through these substages is characterized by several overarching trends in development: movement from reflexes to goal-directed activity, transition from acting on the body to acting on the outside world, and increasing ability to coordinate multiple actions to achieve a goal. In substage 1, the infant's behaviors are limited to innate reflexes, such as sucking and grasping. In substage 2, the infant gains greater control over these reflex responses and engages in repeated physical actions (such as kicking the legs or sucking a thumb) for the enjoyment of these behaviors.

In substage 3, the infant moves beyond the bounds of the body and engages with objects in the environment. For example, a child in this substage might repeatedly bang a rattle against the floor to hear the sound that it makes. In substage 4, the infant is able to coordinate actions to reach a goal. For example, a child in this substage might crawl across a room, reach for and grasp a desired object, and use the arms and hands to place the object into the mouth. In substage 5, the infant begins to explore new possibilities with objects. In this substage, we begin to see the emergence of the "little scientist" who understands the world through trial and error. In the final substage, the beginnings of representational thought are evident. The child now has a basic understanding of using symbols (including words) to stand for objects.

Preoperational Stage

The preoperational stage, which Piaget posited as lasting from approximately 2 to 7 years of age, is characterized by increasing the use of mental representation (particularly in the realm of language) compared to the sensorimotor stage. The increasing capacity for mental representation at this stage also allows for thinking about the past and future and the development of pretend play. However, thinking in this stage tends to be rigid, inflexible, and illogical.

Preoperational stage children tend to be egocentric in their thinking (i.e., they have difficulty taking the perspective of others and often do not recognize that others do not necessarily see what they see or know what they know). Piaget demonstrated this egocentric thinking with the "three mountains task," in which children were seated on one side of a model landscape that included a variety of objects arranged around three central mountains. The mountains blocked certain objects from view, depending on one's location and visual perspective. Children in the preoperational stage tended to state that an experimenter seated opposite to them would see what they themselves saw, reflecting egocentric thinking. Piaget viewed this egocentrism as contributing to the lack of logical thinking at this stage—if one cannot take others' perspectives, one cannot use those perspectives to correct logical fallacies or otherwise revise one's reasoning.

Thinking in the preoperational stage also tends to be characterized by centration—a focus on one particular element of an object or situation and a tendency to ignore other relevant features. This cognitive centration is evident in children's performance on conservation tasks, which measure the ability to recognize that a quantity remains the same despite a change in appearance. For example, in a task intended to measure understanding of conservation of liquid volume, a child is first shown two short, wide glasses, each containing the same amount of water. The water from one glass is then poured into a taller, thinner glass. Children in the preoperational stage will often say that the thin glass now contains more water than the wide glass, because the level of liquid in the thin glass is higher. This reflects the fact that children's thinking was centered on one salient element (the level of the water) and did not include other relevant elements (e.g., the shapes of the two glasses).

Concrete Operational Stage

In the concrete operational stage, which includes children from approximately 7 to 11 years of age, thought is logical, flexible, and organized in its application to concrete information. Children are also able to cognitively manipulate their mental representations. Children in the concrete operational stage understand concepts such as identity, reversibility, and decentration, which allow them to perform successfully on conservation tasks. In relation to conservation tasks, identity refers to the idea that the appearance of an item can change without it changing the item's basic nature. Reversibility refers to the concept that the effects of actions can be reversed, whereas decentration refers to the idea that a change in one aspect of an item can compensate for a change in another aspect. However, the capacity for abstract thinking is not yet present. This means that children can solve a variety of logical problems, including conservation tasks, with reference to the real-world objects or situations, but are not able to solve the same types of problems in a purely logical or abstract context.

Formal Operational Stage

The last of Piaget's cognitive developmental stages is the formal operational stage, which begins around age 11–12 years and continues into adulthood (although it is important to note that most research on the formal operational stage was conducted with participants between the ages of 11 and 15 years). This stage is characterized by the capacity for abstract, scientific thinking. In this stage, individuals can engage in mental actions applied to hypothetical properties of objects or events. Achievements of this stage include hypothetical reasoning and logical, systematic hypothesis testing. Individuals in the formal operational stage are also able to reflect on their own thinking in a logical manner. Although Piaget generally viewed progress through the cognitive developmental stages as the result of biological maturation, he did acknowledge that formal education might be necessary in order to reach the formal operational stage.

Evaluation of Theory

Piaget's cognitive developmental theory has been influential due to a number of major strengths. First, Piaget's theory was one of the first theories of child development to focus on cognition and cognitive processes and to examine children's reasoning for its own sake. Piaget's view of the child as an active seeker of knowledge, rather than a passive recipient of environmental conditioning, was appealing and influential to many researchers and educators. Piaget's theory also had a wide scope, examining many important aspects of thinking and reasoning. Piaget also used ecologically valid methods, examining how children solved a variety of academic and social problems.

There are, however, meaningful critiques of Piaget's approach as well. The first is that Piaget's methods may have led to the underestimation of the capabilities of infants and young children. For example, to test for object permanence, Piaget required infants to reach for a hidden object. Later research that required only looking, rather than reaching, indicated that children may have a mental understanding of object permanence substantially earlier than Piaget's findings suggested. Similarly, Piaget's theory may have overestimated the cognitive abilities of those in the formal operational stage, particularly younger adolescents. Piaget's theory is also somewhat vague regarding the mechanisms of cognitive development (e.g., there is little discussion of what is happening in a child's mind during the process of equilibration). In addition, Piaget has been criticized for ignoring individual and cultural differences in development.

Educational Applications

The tenets of Piaget's theory have inspired a range of educational applications and practices. These include the use of developmentally appropriate practice, in which curriculum is tailored to students' level of cognitive and social development. Another application of Piagetian theory is the use of "hands-on" teaching methods, such as inquiry learning and the use of manipulatives.

As with Piaget's theory in general, there have been criticisms of attempts to apply cognitive developmental theory to educational practice. For example, educational psychologist Jerome Bruner opposed Piaget's notion of readiness. Bruner argued that teachers held students back by waiting for students to be cognitively ready for certain subject matter.

Neo-Piagetian Theories

A number of researchers have built on Piaget's foundations to advance research and theory in the field of cognitive development. These researchers have often integrated Piagetian theory and methods with constructs from other psychological theories, such as information processing theory or dynamic systems theory. Neo-Piagetians have built on cognitive developmental theory to explore areas such as the mechanisms of change within cognitive developmental stages. This includes research on how cognitive skills and capabilities such as working memory and executive function contribute to cognitive development. Neo-Piagetian researchers continued Piaget's tradition of exploring cognitive development across a range of domains, including thinking about the physical, biological, and social world.

Meagan M. Patterson

See also Active Learning; Adolescence; Childhood; Constructivist Approach; Educational Psychology; Kohlberg's Stages of Moral Development; Montessori Schools; Problem Solving

Further Readings

Beilin, H. (1992). Piaget's enduring contribution to developmental psychology. *Developmental Psychology, 28*, 191–204.

Birney, D. P., & Sternber, R. J. (2011). The development of cognitive abilities. In M. H. Bornstein & M. E. Lamb (Eds.), *Cognitive development: An advanced textbook* (pp. 369–404). New York, NY: Taylor & Francis.

Feldman, D. H. (2004). Piaget's stages: The unfinished symphony of cognitive development. *New Ideas in Psychology, 22*, 175–231.

Gruber, H. E., & Vonèche, J. J. (1995). *The essential Piaget: An interpretive reference and guide.* Northvale, NJ: Jason Aronson.

Inhelder, B., & Piaget, J. (1958). *The growth of logical thinking from childhood to adolescence: An essay on the construction of formal operational structures.* New York, NY: Psychology Press.

Lourenço, O. (2012). Piaget and Vygotsky: Many resemblances, and a crucial difference. *New Ideas in Psychology, 30*, 281–295.

Morra, S., Gobbo, G., Marini, Z., & Sheese, R. (2008). *Cognitive development: Neo-Piagetian perspectives.* New York, NY: Erlbaum.

Piaget, J. (1954). *The construction of reality in the child.* New York, NY: Routledge.

Piaget, J. (1959). *The language and thought of the child.* New York, NY: Psychology Press.

Smith, L. (1996). *Critical readings on Piaget.* New York, NY: Routledge.

COGNITIVE DIAGNOSIS

Cognitive diagnosis is a type of assessment or measurement used to identify the taxonomic group that an individual belongs to based on the individual's observed behaviors. In educational measurement (such as a test), an examinee's solutions to test problems are observed, and cognitive diagnosis provides assessment of the mastery status of the set of skills required by the test problems. This type of assessment or measurement is referred to as *diagnostic assessment* or *diagnostic measurement*. Instead of overall scores provided in traditional tests, cognitive diagnosis presents detailed assessments of the specific strengths and weaknesses in subcategory skills, based on which teachers may direct students to focused and effective future studies. After further explaining the basic concepts of cognitive diagnosis, this entry explores the components of diagnostic classification models (DCMs), examines two specific DCMs, and finally reviews empirical validation and construction of the Q matrix.

Concepts in Cognitive Diagnosis

There are several important concepts in cognitive diagnosis. The observed behaviors (for instance, solutions to exam problems) are often referred to as *responses* that are collected by instruments (exam problems). These instruments are called *items*. Responses to items depend either deterministically or statistically on certain characteristics of the individual (mastery status of various skills) that are often not observable. This dependence is the foundation based on which one assesses the unobserved characteristics through responses to items. The underlying characteristics are often referred to as *attributes*. These concepts are common for most measurement models such as classical test theory, item response theory, and so on.

There are several features that make cognitive diagnosis distinct from other measurements. Cognitive diagnosis features a set of discrete attributes for the diagnostic purpose. More precisely, each attribute has only finitely many possible states and in fact most of the time two states: "1" for *mastery of a skill* and "0" for *nonmastery*. In case of more than two states, it is often ordinal, such as, 0, 1, 2, . . . standing for different skill levels. The entire attribute profile is referred to as the *knowledge state*. Cognitive diagnosis measures the attributes by means of the responses to items and casts each individual onto a knowledge state according to the assessment of individual attributes. For instance, in an arithmetic test measuring two attributes, subtraction and multiplication, each of which has two states, there are potentially four knowledge states. Moreover, cognitive diagnosis aims to provide a fine-grained assessment of the subcategory skills instead of an overall score used to rank the students from the top to the bottom. There are multiple attributes associated with a set of items, and multidimensionality is another important feature of, though not unique to, cognitive diagnosis.

DCMs

The psychometrics models for cognitive diagnosis are referred to as DCMs. Their main task is to specify the relationship between the responses to J items denoted by $r = (r_1, \ldots, r_J)$ that are directly observed and the knowledge state α that is unobserved. The knowledge state is a multidimensional vector $\alpha = (\alpha_1, \ldots, \alpha_K)$. Each α_i is discrete and takes finitely many possible values. In educational measurement, each attribute α_i often corresponds to a subcategory skill. For instance, a list of skills measured by a test of fraction subtraction may contain converting a whole number to a fraction, separating a whole number from a fraction, simplifying before subtracting, finding a common denominator, borrowing from a whole number part, column borrowing to subtract the second numerator from the first, subtracting numerators, and reducing answers to simplest form.

The responses $r_1, \ldots, r_J$ connect to the knowledge state α through the so-called Q matrix. The Q matrix is a j by k matrix $Q = q_{jk}$. Each row corresponds to an item and each column corresponds to an attribute. Each entry q_{jk} takes two possible values: "1" means that *attribute k is associated to the response to Item j* and "0" *otherwise*. The following matrix is a simple and self-explanatory example of Q matrix for three arithmetic problems and two attributes.

	Subtraction	Multiplication
5 − 3	1	0
2 × 5	0	1
5 − 3 × 5	1	1

The Q matrix provides a qualitative description of the item–attribute relationship. The precise quantitative relationship depends on specific model parameterizations. DCMs are confirmatory in nature and the Q matrix specifies which items load onto which attributes.

Empirically, individuals admitting the same knowledge state may respond differently to items. Thus, the relationship between the item responses and the knowledge state is nondeterministic. DCMs specify a statistical relationship by characterizing the statistical law of the responses on each knowledge state. Technically, the model provides the conditional distribution fr α.

A measurement of the knowledge state α based on the response vector $\mathbf{r}$ is obtained by the posterior distribution of α given the observed r via the Bayes's rule. Measurement errors often exist due to the statistical relationship between the responses and the knowledge state and can be gradually removed as more responses are collected from the same individual.

Two DCMs

A variety of cognitive diagnostic models have been developed in the literature. The main variation among them lies in their loading structures. We present two such models and list the names of others.

Deterministic Inputs, Noisy "and" Gate (DINA) Model

The DINA model is one of the most popular DCMs, especially in educational measurement. It considers the simple case that both the responses and the attributes are binary. In particular, $r_j = 1$ represents the correct response to an exam problem and $\alpha_k = 1$ represents mastery of a skill. According to a Q matrix, suppose that Item j is associated to a number of attributes. Define the ideal response to Item j for a knowledge state α,

denoted by ξ_j, as whether α has all the required attributes, equivalently, $\xi_j = 1$ if $\alpha_k \geq q_{jk}$ for all $k = 1, \ldots, K$ and $\xi_j = 0$ otherwise. The ideal response labels whether an individual on knowledge state α is capable of solving a problem and it depends deterministically on the knowledge state. The ideal response does not necessarily equal the actual response in that students may not solve the problem correctly even if they are capable of doing so and vice versa. Therefore, two additional concepts are introduced, slipping and guessing. If $\xi_j = 1$, an individual responds correctly to Item j with probability $1 - s_j$ and thus s_j is the probability of slipping; if $\xi_j = 0$, the correct response probability is g_j and that is the guessing probability.

The DINA model assumes a conjunctive relationship among multiple attributes. One needs to master all required skills to correctly solve a problem. Such a situation frequently appears in educational testing.

DINO Model

The DINO model is mathematically considered as the dual of the DINA model. Its specification is very similar to the DINA model. The difference is that the ideal response is defined as $\xi_j = 1$ if $\alpha_k \geq q_{jk}$ for at least one $k = 1, \ldots, K$ and $\xi_j = 0$ otherwise. Thus, the ideal response is constructed based on a disjunctive relationship among the attributes. Given the ideal response, the response admits the same structure as that of the DINA model. The DINO model is mathematically equivalent to the DINA model if one applies the negation operator (in Boolean algebra) to both the responses and the attributes.

Other DCMs

There are several other DCMs. An incomplete list includes the noisy input, deterministic output "and" gate model, the noisy input, deterministic output "or" gate model, the reduced reparameterized unified model, the compensatory reparameterized unified model, the additive cognitive diagnostic model, the rule space method, the attribute hierarchy method, the nonparametric clustering method, the general diagnostic model, the log-linear cognitive diagnostic model, and the generalized-DINA model.

Empirical Validation and Construction of the *Q* Matrix

Cognitive diagnosis is confirmatory in nature. The *Q* matrix specifies the set of attributes each item measures. It is customary to have a prespecified *Q* matrix based on knowledge of the items and the attributes. For instance, a teacher specifies the set of skills tested by each problem in a test. In practice, such a subjective specification may not be entirely accurate. The misspecification of the *Q* matrix could possibly lead to inaccurate and biased assessments of the knowledge state and further misleading diagnostic results. Several methods have been developed in the literature to identify possible misspecifications in the *Q* matrix, to provide means for corrections, and to empirically reconstruct the *Q* matrix based on the responses alone. The results include fundamental theories, methods, and numerical algorithms.

Jingchen Liu and Gongjun Xu

See also Classical Test Theory; Classification; Computerized Adaptive Testing; Item Response Theory; Latent Class Analysis

Further Readings

Chen, P., Xin, T., Wang, C., & Chang, H.-H. (2012). Online calibration methods for the DINA model with independent attributes in CD-CAT. *Psychometrika, 77*(2), 201–222.

Chen, Y., Liu, J., Xu, G., & Ying, Z. (2015). Statistical analysis of Q-matrix based diagnostic classification models. *Journal of the American Statistical Association, 110,* 850–866.

Chen, Y., Liu, J., & Ying, Z. (2015). Online item calibration for Q-matrix in CD-CAT. *Applied Psychological Measurement, 39*(1), 5–15.

Chiu, C.-Y., Douglas, J. A., & Li, X. (2009). Cluster analysis for cognitive diagnosis: Theory and applications. *Psychometrika, 74,* 633–665.

de la Torre, J. (2011). The generalized DINA model framework. *Psychometrika, 76,* 179–199.

DiBello, L. V., Stout, W. F., & Roussos, L. A. (1995). Unified cognitive psychometric diagnostic assessment likelihood-based classification techniques. In P. D. Nichols, S. F. Chipman, & R. L. Brennan (Eds.), *Cognitively diagnostic assessment* (pp. 361–390). Hillsdale, NJ: Erlbaum.

Henson, R. A., Templin, J. L., & Willse, J. T. (2009). Defining a family of cognitive diagnosis models using log-linear models with latent variables. *Psychometrika, 74,* 191–210.

Junker, B. W., & Sijtsma, K. (2001). Cognitive assessment models with few assumptions, and connections with nonparametric item response theory. *Applied Psychological Measurement, 25,* 258–272.

Leighton, J. P., Gierl, M. J., & Hunka, S. M. (2004). The attribute hierarchy model for cognitive assessment: A variation on Tatsuoka's rule-space approach. *Journal of Educational Measurement, 41,* 205–237.

Liu, J., Xu, G., & Ying, Z. (2012). Data-driven learning of Q-Matrix. *Applied Psychological Measurement, 36,* 548–564.

Liu, J., Xu, G., & Ying, Z. (2013). Theory of self-learning Q-matrix. *Bernoulli, 19*(5A), 1790–1817.

Liu, J., Ying, Z., & Zhang, S. (2015). A rate function approach to computerized adaptive testing for cognitive diagnosis. *Psychometrika, 80*(2), 468–490.

Rupp, A. A., Templin, J. L., & Henson, R. A. (2010) *Diagnostic measurement: Theory, methods, and applications.* New York, NY: Guilford Press.

Tatsuoka, C., & Ferguson, T. (2003). Sequential classification on partially ordered sets. *Journal of the Royal Statistical Society: Series B (Statistical Methodology), 65*(1), 143–157.

Tatsuoka, K. K. (1985). A probabilistic model for diagnosing misconceptions in the pattern classification approach. *Journal of Educational Statistics, 12*(1), 55–73.

Tatsuoka, K. K. (2009). *Cognitive assessment: An introduction to the rule space method.* New York, NY: Routledge.

Templin, J. L., & Henson, R. A. (2006). Measurement of psychological disorders using cognitive diagnosis models. *Psychological Methods, 11,* 287–305.

von Davier, M. (2008). A general diagnostic model applied to language testing data. *British Journal of Mathematical and Statistical Psychology, 61,* 287–307.

Xu, G., & Zhang, S. (2015). Identifiability of diagnostic classification models. *Psychometrika.* doi:10.1007/s11336-015-9471-z

COGNITIVE NEUROSCIENCE

The advent of the ability to image the human brain has given rise to a new subdiscipline of cognitive neuroscience at the interface of neuroscience and psychology. Although neuroscience seeks to understand all brains and often chooses the simplest organism to gain the most general principles, cognitive neuroscience is centered on understanding the function of the human brain. Among the most important topics of the new field are attention, memory, and learning, all of obvious interest to the field of education.

Studies using the methods and theory of cognitive neuroscience applied to education have used various terms such as *educational neuroscience* or *brain and education*, and the journals *Mind, Brain, and Education* and *Trends in Neuroscience and Education* are central to the field. This entry outlines the methods used in cognitive neuroscience studies and gives some examples of the brain networks that have been examined and their application to education. It also examines new studies showing changes in the brain with development, looks at how exercises might enhance the brain, and considers individual differences in network efficiency.

Methods

The methods used by the field include those used to visualize the brain's activity. The most prominent are functional magnetic resonance imaging and electroencephalography and magnetoencephalography. Functional magnetic resonance imaging has been used to localize activity in brain areas and to trace connectivity between brain areas. Electroencephalography and magnetoencephalography can measure the time course of brain activity. Transcortical magnetic stimulation has been used to disrupt localized brain circuits. Direct current stimulation of frontal areas has been used in experiments designed to increase efficiency of new learning.

Methods that rely on changes in blood flow and oxygenation are best at localization of the activity of neurons within a cubic millimeter or so, however, this still involves many neurons. Methods that record electrical or magnetic signals from outside the brain are best for the study of temporal factors for which they may indicate changes in the range of a millisecond. Combining these methods results in moderately high levels of spatial and temporal accuracy, thus allowing us to trace the location of mental computations and their time of occurrence.

Brain stimulation by transcortical magnetic stimulation can be used to temporarily inhibit the activity of a particular area, which is valuable in determining whether that area is critical to achieving the expected performance. Recently, DC stimulation across the frontal lobes has been shown to enhance some forms of learning, but questions about the limits and safety of stimulation methods remain a subject of active investigation.

Brain Networks

A quarter century of work in neuroimaging has shown that brain networks involved in cognitive tasks must often involve a small number of brain areas restricted in size and often widely scattered over cortical and subcortical brain areas.

These active brain areas are connected by bundles of axons that form pathways between them forming a network. The brain areas in the network need to be orchestrated over a few hundred milliseconds to carry out such cognitive tasks as reading words or solving arithmetic problems. Networks studied by brain imaging related to cognitive, emotional, and social processes, along with subjects learned in school, include networks involving the following:

- Attention
- Autobiographical memory
- Facial recognition
- Fear
- Music
- Object perception
- Reading and listening
- Reward
- Self-reference
- Spatial navigation
- Working memory

Networks are thought to improve in the efficiency of activation with use, thus providing a source of change or plasticity with learning.

Enhanced Teaching

Applications of cognitive neuroscience to classroom instruction have been most obvious in the fields of early reading and arithmetic instruction. For example, imaging studies of word reading have provided evidence of two important regions of activation in posterior brain areas. The first, in the superior temporal lobe, appears to underlie the phonological interpretation of visual words and is obviously related to the problem of decoding. The second lies more fully in the visual system in the left fusiform gyrus and appears to relate to "chunking" of letters into a word. The first develops early in childhood with efforts to decode written words, whereas the second appears to develop slowly with exposure to visual words of one's language. There remains a lack of understanding of why successful decoding often fails to lead to fluent reading and debate continues within the education field over the effectiveness of phonological methods compared to the so-called look–say method of reading instruction. Understanding the brain systems involved may help teachers design an appropriate curriculum.

Imaging studies involving the processing of numbers are also important for early instruction. Studies have revealed a number line in the posterior part of the brain that allows even infants to appreciate the idea of quantity. The importance of the elaboration and connection of the number line to language and exact calculation systems provide goals for early instruction. As in reading, the brain imaging studies do not provide support for any particular curriculum, but knowledge of them may help the teacher in designing student learning.

Most of the cognitive neuroscience applications to education relate to elementary school learning. One approach to the study of higher level cognitive tasks learned in secondary school involves studies of high school algebra. Using principles of cognitive science, John Anderson and his colleagues have developed an intelligent tutoring system that has been used in 1,000 schools in the United States involving more than 500,000 students. They also conducted imaging studies to connect brain areas with some of the functions performed by the tutor.

In one study by Anderson and his colleagues, functional magnetic resonance imaging was used to study changes in brain areas following 6 days of training. The study examined six brain regions that previous studies identified as important in carrying out algebra problems. One of these areas was the anterior cingulate, which was found to be active early in problem solution and was identified as holding the subgoal used in solving the problem. The anterior cingulate operates in combination with the lateral prefrontal cortex in the storage and retrieval of declarative memories.

Thus imaging may be useful in understanding how intelligent tutoring changes brain activity.

More generally, the study of expertise within cognitive neuroscience can be applied to many advanced fields. Neuroimaging has also allowed us to understand mechanisms of expertise in particular domains. Some of these domains, such as perceiving faces, are common to most or all humans, whereas others, such as reading words, are of critical importance for school. Both of these skills depend, in part, on highly specialized mechanisms within the brain's visual system.

The efficient perception of faces depends on the right fusiform gyrus (fusiform face area). In the case of words, there is an important computation involved in word recognition that depends upon the left fusiform gyrus as was discussed earlier. The visual perception of words is clearly learned, and while face perception has innate components, there is evidence that face perception differs greatly with the familiarity of the face. Moreover, improved recognition due to expertise in birds or dogs appears to modify posterior visual brain areas used for faces. The involvement of posterior brain areas in high levels of expertise may underlie the observation that the experienced person perceives the world in a different way than the novice.

Brain Development

The use of magnetic resonance to image brain networks during the resting state has provided a new window on human brain development. Although it is difficult to design tasks that can be performed at all ages, it is possible to get people of all ages, even infants, to lie passively in a scanner. Brain scanning studies indicate that several brain networks are already present in infancy.

During the resting state, a default network not usually engaged in tasks alternates in activation with portions of the brain's attention system, which is engaged in most tasks. A protolanguage system in the left hemisphere is present even early in infancy, and the infants can show recognition of their own language and the phonemes that are constituents of all spoken languages, but in the month prior to the emergence of speech, the phonemes of the language(s) the infants hear become stronger and those of other languages weaker.

Network and State Training

Of importance to education are the claims that special kinds of training can improve brain function at all ages. The training often involves specific networks, for example, working memory, activated by cognitive tasks or computer games. No one doubts that the trained network can improve in efficiency, but the degree of transfer to other tasks is less clear. The utility of these methods may rest on better cognitive theory, which could help specify what set of tasks might help a child or adult to improve performance in daily life.

State training involves the use of very general practices such as physical exercise, mindfulness meditation, or exposure to nature that may allow a person to achieve a better overall physical and mental state that could improve performance in many situations. Certainly, physical exercise has the largest and most consistent evidence, but meditation has also been shown to produce improved attention and mood and can be applied in the school setting.

Individuality

While much of cognitive neuroscience deals with brain networks common to humans, there is recognition that individuals differ in the efficiency of these networks. Some teachers have applied the theory of multiple intelligences to deal with individual differences in the classroom. Cognitive neuroscience studies have revealed some of the mechanisms behind various form of intelligence. However, there is also evidence of brain structures that appear to underlie general intelligence, which is common among linguistic, musical, mathematical, and other forms of more specific ability.

Longitudinal studies have shown the importance of effortful control as measured from questionnaires in early childhood on the success of adults in measures of well-being, including health, income, and social interactions. Brain scanning studies have provided some evidence on the role of brain structures involved in effortful control. Moreover, exercises of the type discussed in the previous section have sometimes been useful in improving these networks, but how lasting the changes are and whether they effect daily life remains unknown. Considering the importance of temperamental characteristics such as effortful control on later life, teachers would be well advised to keep abreast of developments to better understand and help students improve effortful control.

Temperament can change in development but it is relatively fixed compared to attitudes. Research shows the importance of attitudes in school achievement. Brief interventions to make students understand that school performance depends on hard work, and not on some immutable innate ability, have been shown to improve school performance. It is important for teachers to know that mind-set or attitudes toward the educational experience can be critical in fostering achievement.

Michael I. Posner

See also *g* Theory of Intelligence; Multiple Intelligences, Theory of; Reading Comprehension

Further Readings

Anderson, J. R. (2007). *How can the human mind occur in the physical universe?* New York, NY: Oxford University Press.

Lambertz-Dehaene, G., & Spelke, E. (2015). The infancy of the human brain. *Neuron, 88*, 93–109.

Marceschal, D., Butetrworth, B., & Tomie, A. (2014). *Educational neuroscience.* Oxford, UK: Wiley Blackwell.

Paunesku, D., Walton, G., Romero, R., Smith, E., Yeager, D., & Dweck, C.S. (2015). Mindset interventions are a scalable treatment for academic underachievement. *Psychological Science.* doi:10.1177/0956797615571017

Poldrack, R. A., & Farah, M. J. (2015). Progress and challenges in probing the human brain. *Nature, 526*, 371–379.

Posner, M. I., & Rothbart, M. K. (2014). Attention to learning of school subjects. *Trends in Neuroscience and Education.* 3(1), 14–17. doi:10.1016/j. tine.2014.02.003

Rothbart, M. K. (2011). *Becoming who we are.* New York, NY: Guilford.

Tang, Y. Y, & Posner, M. I. (2014). Training brain networks and states. *Trends in Cognitive Science, 18*(7), 345–350. Retrieved from http://dx.org/10.1016/j.tics.2014.04.002

Tokuhama-Esponosa, T. (2014). *Making classrooms better.* New York, NY: Norton.

COLEMAN REPORT

The *Equality of Educational Opportunity* (EEO) report, known as "the Coleman report" after principal investigator James S. Coleman, is widely seen as one of the most significant contributions of the 20th century to education policy and research as well as the field of sociology. The national study, commissioned by Congress under a provision in the Civil Rights Act of 1964, documented school inequality on an unprecedented scale. Attempting to survey every principal, student, and teacher in a nationally representative sample of 4,000 schools, the EEO represented a historic data collection effort in American education. The project collected cross-sectional survey and test score data from approximately 600,000 students and 50,000 teachers. This entry further discusses how the researchers conducted the study and their findings. It then looks at critiques of the study and at research that reexamined its findings.

The report sought to assess the quality of educational opportunities available to racial and ethnic student subgroups across the nation. In defining school quality, Coleman and his colleagues measured school resources such as the number of textbooks and laboratories available, curricular offerings, and academic practices such as tracking systems. Authors also took into account student and teacher characteristics. Student characteristics included measures of socioeconomic status, parent education, and peer attitudes and aspirations, while teachers were evaluated on their education, experience, salary, attitudes, and aptitude.

Student achievement measures were constructed using scores on standardized tests of pupils' verbal and nonverbal skills at the end of Grades 1, 3, 6, 9, and 12 as well as results of more traditional achievement tests in reading and mathematics at Grades 3, 6, 9, and 12 and tests of students' command of science, social studies, and other general information administered at Grades 9 and 12.

Coleman and colleagues demonstrated that American public schools remained highly racially segregated 12 years after *Brown v. Board of Education*. Further, they documented large racial achievement inequalities among U.S. public school students. The Coleman study found that the Black–White test score gap among first graders was equivalent to approximately one grade level. By the time students reached 12th grade, this achievement gap had widened to 3.5 grade levels. However, after accounting for regional differences in educational resources, Coleman showed that racial gaps in school resources were relatively small. Further, and perhaps most notably, the Coleman report cast new doubts on the extent to which schools contribute to educational inequality, showing that within-school variation in achievement was larger than between-school variation. In short, students' achievement was impacted far more by their out-of-school experiences than the instructional practices and policies of their schools.

The Coleman study found that family background played a large role in student achievement while school practices such as per pupil expenditures and teacher quality had little effect. Summarizing these findings, the report goes on to say:

> One implication stands out above all: That schools bring little influence to bear on a child's achievement that is independent of his background and general social context; and that this very lack of an independent effect means that the inequalities imposed on children by their home, neighborhood, and peer environment are carried along to become the inequalities with which they confront adult life at the end of school (Coleman et al., 1966, p. 325).

Consistent with this interpretation, recent research on summer learning loss such as that by Allison Atteberry and Andrew McEachin indicates that class inequalities narrow during the months in which schools are in session and broaden during the summer months. The Coleman report is often credited with directing educational researchers' attention toward achievement inequalities that exist among youth prior to school entry as well as the role of family practices and resources in producing educational inequality. However, evidence is mixed regarding summer learning loss and the role of schools in producing Black–White achievement gaps. Further, several studies indicate that highly effective schools can have large enough effects on student achievement to offset achievement gaps.

Reexamining the Coleman Findings

Despite its considerable influence on the field of educational research, the Coleman report remains controversial, and its findings have been closely scrutinized. Scholars have raised questions about the extent to which survey nonresponse undermined the reports' claim to having assembled nationally representative data as well as the adequacy of the report's regression-based methods to identify the unique consequences of educational resources. However, reanalyses largely replicate the report's major findings.

Geoffrey Borman and Maritza Dowling reanalyzed the report's data using multilevel modeling; they found approximately 40% of achievement variation is between schools (net of student controls), which is 3–4 times higher than the variation that Coleman and colleagues reported. This is largely because Coleman and colleagues did all analyses within individual regions and thus failed to recognize remarkably large differences between schools in different regions and particularly low performance in the South. This finding suggests bigger school effects than the report originally found. However, consistent with the report's main finding, the Borman and Dowling reanalysis indicates that neither equalizing the school resources to which students of color are exposed nor desegregating schools are sufficient to erase Black–White test score gaps.

Other critiques focus less on the study's analytic techniques than its interpretation. Because Coleman and colleagues collected observational data at one time point, the report's findings are purely correlational. As such, it is impossible to separate the effects of the school resources at the center of the report's analyses from the potentially confounding effects of student characteristics that are associated with these resources.

Because the report focuses primarily on between-school educational inequalities, it provides limited information on the extent to which educational resources are allocated unequally within schools and the extent to which these resource inequalities matter for student achievement. In particular, although Coleman and colleagues found that teachers were the most influential school input on student achievement, recent work suggests that they underestimate the magnitude of teacher effects. The study measured teacher quality in terms of teacher education and experience—two factors that loosely correlate with value-added measures—and failed to capture the sizeable degree of variation in teacher quality within schools.

These critiques notwithstanding, more than 50 years after its publication, the Coleman report remains a central touchstone in American educational research.

Brittany Murray, Thurston A. Domina,
and Andrew McEachin

See also Achievement Tests; African Americans and Testing; Applied Research; *Brown v. Board of Education*

Further Readings

Atteberry, A., & McEachin, A. (2016). School's out: Summer learning loss across grade levels and school contexts in the U.S. today. In Alexander, K., Pitcock, S., & Boulay, M. (Eds.), *The summer slide: What we know and can do about summer learning loss.* New York, NY: Teachers College Press.

Borman, G. D., & Dowling, M. (2010). Schools and inequality: A multilevel analysis of Coleman's Equality of Educational Opportunity data. *Teacher's College Record, 112*(5), 1201–1247.

Bowles, S., & Levin, H. M. (1968). The determinants of scholastic achievement—An appraisal of some recent evidence. *Journal of Human Resources, 3*(1), 3–24.

Coleman, J., Campbell, E., Hobson, C., McPartland, J., Mood, A., Weinfeld, F., & York, R. L. (1966). *Equality of educational opportunity.* Washington, DC: U.S. Government Printing Offices. (ERIC No. ED012275)

Downey, D. B., & Condron, D. J. (2016). Fifty years since the Coleman report: Rethinking the relationship between schools and inequality. *Sociology of Education, 89*(3), 207–220.

Hoxby, C. (2016). The immensity of the Coleman data project. *Education Next, 16*(2). Retrieved from http://educationnext.org/the-immensity-of-the-coleman-data-project/

Jencks, C., Smith, M., Acland, H., Bane, M. J., Cohen, D., Gintis, H., . . . , & Michelson, S. (1972). *Inequality: A reassessment of the effect of family and schooling in America.* New York, NY: Harper & Row.

Mosteller, F., Moynihan, D. P., & Harvard University. (1972). In F. Mosteller & D. P. Moynihan (Eds.), *On equality of educational opportunity: Papers deriving from the Harvard University faculty seminar on the Coleman report*. New York, NY: Random House.

COLLABORATION, EVALUATION OF

Organizational collaboration is embraced across all sectors of society as a primary strategy for cultivating innovation, conserving economic resources, building relationships, addressing complex problems, and reaching essential outcomes. It is through collaboration that PK–12 educators address issues of teaching and student learning and accomplish organizational goals that fall outside the grasp of any individual teacher, principal, or school working independently. Although educational collaboration is widely recognized as having the capacity to connect fragmented educational systems and cultivate instructional innovation, effective collaboration does not emerge spontaneously and cannot be sustained without thoughtful attention to its development. The systematic examination and improvement of interorganizational and professional collaboration in educational settings has become imperative. This entry begins by providing a clear explanation of the two primary types of collaboration in an educational setting: interorganizational and professional. Next, the need for researchers to operationalize the concept of collaboration is discussed. Finally, the entry examines five approaches to evaluating collaboration.

What Is Collaboration?

Collaboration has become a fundamental school improvement strategy that denotes two or more people, groups, or organizations working together to reach goals that could not be accomplished by individual entities working independently. To attain essential educational outcomes, schools and school personnel increasingly work in strategic partnership with one another and with people and organizations from across all sectors of society. Interorganizational collaboration entails partnerships among schools and between schools and

other agencies. An example of federally sponsored school-based interorganizational collaboration is the Safe Schools/Health Students (SS/HS) initiative. The SS/HS initiative was launched through the joint efforts of the U.S. Departments of Education, Justice, and Health and Human Services. The SS/HS initiative is based on evidence that an integrated, community-wide, collaborative approach is the most effective way to promote healthy childhood development and to address the problems of school violence and alcohol and other drug abuse. Through the SS/HS initiative, more than $2 billion in resources have been allocated to 365 communities in nearly all 50 U.S. states.

Professional collaboration, on the other hand, generally refers to the work of a single group of individuals such as a grade-level or subject-area team made up of individual teachers or other educators. These teams or groups are often referred to as professional learning communities (PLCs). PLCs have gained widespread popularity among educators over the past decade and have taken root in schools across the country because their benefits are numerous and profound. Studies show that PLCs enhance everything from teacher satisfaction to student achievement, positively impact school culture, improve teacher self-efficacy, reduce teacher isolation, boost an organization's overall capacity, and build a shared culture of high-quality instructional practice. Collaboration, whether interorganizational or professional, is widely considered the lever through which student-, school-, and community-level outcomes will be obtained. Significant sums of federal, state, and foundation money are allocated to support the development of both interorganizational and professional collaboration. Hence, measuring, assessing, and evaluating the quality, value, and impact of organizational collaboration have become imperative.

Operationalizing the Construct of Collaboration

Although the literature in support of organizational collaboration is vast, cross-sectoral, and replete with case studies, collaboration persists as an underempiricized, misunderstood construct. Hence, evaluators who seek to examine organizational collaboration as a dependent and/or independent variable will confront the need to operationalize the concept. Take, for example, the following evaluation research questions:

- Do increases in collaboration between the county's early intervention program and the nurse home visitation program lead to reductions in referrals to special education?
- To what extent does collaboration between teachers and school psychologists lead to better instruction and improved outcomes for student learning?
- What is the optimal level of linkage between regional educational collaboratives?
- What is the relationship between teacher collaboration, instructional quality, and student achievement?

The construct of collaboration is the central evaluand in each of the previous questions; it must be operationalized so that its development, quantity, quality, and/or effects can be measured and observed.

A synthesis of systems theory and organizational learning literature suggests that there are several observable attributes through which the construct of collaboration can be operationalized. These attributes include: (a) the *sine qua non* of collaboration is a shared purpose, partnerships form in order to improve a shared practice and to address a shared problem or issue; (b) collaboration is a nested phenomenon that takes place within complex open systems, people collaborate within teams, within organizations, and across organizational boundaries; (c) collaboration is developmental and evolves in stages over time, groups form, storm, norm, and perform; (d) collaboration within and between organizations will vary by level of integration, "more" collaboration is not necessarily better; and (e) the process of professional collaboration entails cycles of inquiry, team members dialogue, make decisions, take action, and evaluate their actions.

These five principles can be used to operationalize the construct of collaboration and guide methodological approaches in what and how to evaluate collaboration. Obtaining a clear and theoretically grounded understanding of organizational collaboration can help researchers, evaluators, and practitioners to determine and isolate the most appropriate variables and phenomena to study related to the process and outcomes of educational collaboration.

Methods of Evaluating Collaboration

The following sections will highlight five important approaches that researchers and practitioners can take to examine and improve interorganizational and professional collaboration in education.

Approach 1: Inventory and Map Teams Within a School and/or That Link the School and Its Partner Organizations

Because teams are the predominant unit for decision making in any organization, it is important to ascertain a clear and accurate picture of all the groups at work within an educational alliance. In this approach, evaluators seek answers to the following questions: What teams/groups exist in this school/organization? Who is on each team? For what purpose do the teams meet? How often and with what frequency do the teams meet?

Data about who works with whom on what in an educational setting/partnership can be gathered through a review of archival data/organizational charts, interviews with key personnel, and/or survey methods. Regardless of whether the data are collected and analyzed using simple spreadsheets and pictures or through more complex mathematical processes such as social network analyses, a systematic and thorough inventory of groups within an organization is essential and the foundation for future steps in the evaluation of collaboration. The inventory and mapping process will reveal patterns of interactions between educators within and between organizations. Findings can then be used to determine which individuals or groups might be over- and/or underextended and which teams might be too big or too small and how to target next steps in the collaboration evaluation process.

Importantly, a thorough team identification and mapping process will bring to the surface high-leverage teams (i.e., those groups that appear to focus on substantive issues related to the central goals of the partnership with the greatest capacity to precipitate positive educational change). Educational leaders can use these findings to make informed and strategic decisions about where to channel resources and offer targeted support for collaboration within schools. When conducted over time, inventory and mapping data can be correlated with other measures to determine what patterns of collaboration yield the essential outcomes. For example, inventory data can be compared to longitudinal measures of teacher retention, school climate, and/or student learning.

Approach 2: Monitor Stages of Development

A key attribute of organizational collaboration is that it will go through the predictable stages of development: educators and their partners assemble to form groups, they work to set working norms and establish order, enact activities and perform their shared tasks, and will transform (or adjourn) their group as team goals are met and/or new members or leaders come on board. One stage may go by faster than another, a group may find itself stuck in a stage for a long time, or a team may find itself moving in and out of more than one phase at a time—but inevitably, collaboration requires its members to navigate and emerge from each stage of development in order to successfully implement tasks and reach educational outcomes.

Monitoring collaboration can stimulate groups' successful movement through the stages of development and will promote organizational performance. One effective monitoring strategy is to conduct interviews with members of high-leverage teams that have been identified through the inventory and mapping process in Approach 1. Interviews can be used to identify issues about collaboration quality related to each stage of development to be isolated for special attention, constructive criticism, and improvement. In the formation stage, team members might be asked to discuss their level of shared clarity about the purpose, structures, strategies, leadership, and key tasks of their interorganizational and/or professional collaboration. In transitioning from ordering to performing, evaluators could ask stakeholders how they will move from safeguarding resources and activities from external interference to strengthening the group's creative energy in pursuit of the accomplishment of its goals.

Approach 3: Assess Levels of Integration

One of the operational principles of collaboration is that there are levels of integration that can exist between and within organizations. More integration between organizations is not necessarily better—levels of integration between school and partner agencies should vary according to the purpose of their partnership. If the purpose is to share relatively simple or routine information with one another, then a fairly low level of organizational integration is necessary. On the other hand, if groups want to pool financial resources to create a new and semiautonomous organization to address a complex problem, a high degree of integration is warranted. Data about degrees of integration between organizations can inform decisions about what's working and the appropriate allocation of resources.

Evaluators can use a rubric or survey instrument to generate data about the degree of organizations' shared purposes, integrated leadership structures, and intensity of communications. Instruments such as the Levels of Organizational Integration Rubric or the Levels of Collaboration Survey describe multiple levels of organizational integration and the purposes, strategies/tasks, leadership/decision making, and communication characteristics that tend to be present at each level of integration. Evaluators can use tools such as these to facilitate a process (e.g., online and in person) through which partnership members discuss, determine, and record current and ideal levels of integration. This process can be repeated and data can be collected over time. Longitudinal data about levels of integration can be correlated with other important outcome measures such as school safety, school climate, and student learning.

Approach 4: Assess Quality of Team Process

Evaluating quality of collaboration within group such as PK–12 PLCs is paramount to their success. The instructional improvement process necessitates successful teacher team movement through a series of stages, including recognizing reality, owning the problem, determining a solution, implementing actions, and monitoring the outcomes of those actions. Assessment of teacher team cycles of inquiry can generate findings that can be used to increase team efficacy, efficiency, and effectiveness. Evaluation of professional collaboration can help educators avoid "collaboration lite," make meetings more meaningful, strengthen the collaboration skills of group members, and maximize group performance. Unless the scale and scope of a particular partnership is very limited, it is usually not feasible to evaluate the quality of collaboration in every team within or across a school or educational partnership.

Evaluators can use the inventory results (generated through Approach 1) to make decisions about which groups are high leverage and warrant an in-depth examination of their cycles of inquiry. Educational researchers and practitioners can evaluate the quality of team functioning through interviews and/or through the use of rubrics and survey tools that measure the behavioral and observable attributes of rigorous school-based educator teams. One such instrument is the Teacher Collaboration Assessment Survey, which explicates the characteristics of dialogue, decision making, action, and evaluation at three levels of quality. The Teacher Collaboration Assessment Survey and other valid and reliable measurement instruments for assessing the effectiveness of PLCs can be found through the Center for Effective School Practices at Rutgers University's forthcoming searchable online database.

Approach 5: Measure Outcomes of Collaboration

Educational researchers can employ a range of qualitative and/or quantitative methods to investigate the extent to which or ways in which interorganizational or professional collaboration leads to substantive improvements in teaching and learning and/or the attainment of school goals. For example, correlational and multiple regression analyses could be used to investigate the relationship between the quality of collaboration, changes in teachers' instructional practice, and student achievement on annual standardized assessments. In-depth case studies could be used to examine how community partnerships influence the social–emotional and behavioral health of children. Social network analyses could be used to ascertain how strength of ties between administrators affect school level of implementation of a district-wide curricular initiative.

Educational collaboration has emerged as one of the nation's most widely implemented strategies for improving instruction and PK–12 student learning outcomes. Studies suggest that effective interorganizational and professional collaboration can enhance everything from school safety and teacher satisfaction to student engagement and performance. Hence, the systematic examination of educational collaboration is an important undertaking for educational researchers and practitioners.

Rebecca H. Woodland

See also Applied Research; Surveys

Further Readings

Carolan, B. V. (2014). *Social network analysis and education.* Thousand Oaks, CA: Sage.

Daly, A. J. (Ed.) (2010). *Social network theory and educational change.* Cambridge, MA: Harvard Education Press.

Frey, B., Lohmeier, J., Lee, S. W., & Tollefson, N. (2006). Measuring collaboration among grant partners. *American Journal of Evaluation, 27*(3), 383–392.

Gajda, R., & Koliba, C. (2007). Evaluating the imperative of inter-personal collaboration: A school improvement perspective. *American Journal of Evaluation, 28*(1), 26–44.

Gajda, R., & Koliba, C. (2008). Evaluating and improving the quality of teacher collaboration: A field-tested framework for school leaders. *NASSP Bulletin, 92*(2), 133–154.

Woodland, R. H. (2016). Evaluating PK-12 professional learning communities: An improvement science perspective. *American Journal of Evaluation, 37*(4), 505–521.

Woodland, R., & Hutton, M. (2012). Evaluating organizational collaborations: Suggested entry points and strategies. *American Journal of Evaluation, 33*(3), 366–383.

COLLABORATIVE EVALUATION

Collaborative evaluation is a type of evaluation in which there is a substantial degree of collaboration between evaluators and stakeholders in the evaluation process to the extent that they are willing to be and capable of being involved. Collaborative evaluators are in charge of the evaluation, and they create an ongoing engagement between evaluators and stakeholders, contributing to stronger evaluation designs, enhanced data collection and analysis, and results that stakeholders understand and use. This entry further defines collaborative evaluation, presents a model for collaborative evaluations (MCEs), and discusses considerations when performing collaborative evaluation.

Collaborative evaluation is an approach that offers many advantages, including access to information, quality of information gathered, opportunities for creative problem solving, receptivity to findings, and the use of evaluation results. From a broad perspective, collaborative evaluation belongs to the *use* branch of the evaluation theory tree described by Marvin Alkin, concerned with enhancing evaluation use through stakeholder involvement. Through collaborative evaluation, it is possible to achieve a holistic learning environment by understanding and creating collaborative opportunities. In such an environment, stakeholders better understand the evaluation process and are therefore more likely to use its findings.

Collaborative evaluation has grown in popularity, bringing together evaluators and stakeholders from different sectors, disciplines, and cultures to exchange knowledge on how collaboration can be used as a strategic tool for fostering and strengthening evaluation practice. The literature about collaborative evaluation has increased in both quantity and quality, providing an opportunity for others to gain insights about this approach. One of the first related journal articles was "Researcher as Participant: Collaborative Evaluation in a Primary School" by Edward Booth, published in 1987. At the time, this entry was written, databases key word search with "collaborative evaluation," either in the title or in the abstract of the journal article, yielded a wide variety of titles appearing in evaluation journals, such as the *American Journal of Evaluation, International Journal of Assessment and Evaluation, Journal of Evaluation and Program Planning, Journal of MultiDisciplinary Evaluation, New Directions for Evaluation,* and *Studies in Educational Evaluation.* In addition, a number of books have made original contributions to the development of collaborative evaluations; some of these are listed in the Further Readings section at the end of this entry.

The steady maturation of collaborative evaluation has been shown as well by the contributions of national and international evaluation associations. For example, in 1995, the American Evaluation Association created the Collaborative, Participatory, and Empowerment Topical Interest Group. Since then, interest in collaborative evaluation has grown, as evidenced by the increasing number of presentations made every year at the American Evaluation Association conference. There has also been an increase in collaborative evaluation presentations at conferences around the world. This evaluation approach also has a growing number of supporters and has benefited immensely from feedback.

In an effort to facilitate understanding of this approach, some authors have structured a collection of comprehensive frameworks that outline the elements of collaborative evaluation while being grounded in the American Evaluation Association's *Guiding Principles for Evaluators* and within the evaluation literature. These conceptual frameworks have emerged from those authors' working experience and have been especially useful for novice evaluation practitioners in trying to understand how others view and apply collaborative efforts in a variety of settings.

MCEs

The MCEs, created by Liliana Rodríguez-Campos and Rigoberto Rincones-Gómez, revolves around a set of six interactive components specific to conducting a collaborative evaluation. Additionally, each of the MCE subcomponents includes a set of 10 steps suggested to support the proper understanding and use of the model (e.g., when and how the various elements need to be used). Even though the MCE could create an expectation of a sequential process, it is a system that incorporates continuous feedback for redefinition and improvement in which changes in one element affect other parts of the model.

The six MCE components are (1) identify the situation (the combination of formal and informal circumstances determined by the relationships that surround the evaluation), (2) clarify the expectations (the assumption, belief, or idea about the evaluation and the people involved), (3) establish a collective commitment (compromise to jointly meet the evaluation obligations without continuous external supervision), (4) ensure open communication (process of social interaction used to convey information and exchange ideas to influence specific evaluation actions), (5) encourage effective practices (sound established procedures or systems for producing a desired effect in the evaluation), and (6) follow specific guidelines (principles that direct the design, use, and assessment of the evaluation, evaluators, and collaborators). The MCE has contributed to greater conceptual clarity of the collaborative evaluation approach and has been used as a part of a wide variety of efforts, both in single- and mutiple-site evaluations, across several sectors, and for both formative and summative purposes.

Considerations When Using Collaborative Evaluation

The optimal use of collaborative evaluation requires awareness of its strengths and weaknesses and any potential opportunities and threats along the path of implementation.

The objectivity of collaborative evaluation and other stakeholder approaches has occasionally been questioned because evaluators and stakeholders bring their own experiences and views, which may affect the evaluation, and because some individuals could potentially bias findings in order to secure positive (or negative) evaluation results. In order to protect the credibility of the evaluation, care must be taken when determining what role everyone will play in the effort. In any case, the benefits gained (e.g., in staff cooperation, quality of information gathered, and receptivity to findings) can outweigh the potential difficulties that may ensue.

Individuals usually assume responsibility only for the distinct part of a project on which they work. However, effective groups assume responsibility for the entire project and develop an appreciation of the nuances in all aspects of their work. With a collaborative approach, evaluators can help understand and account for the nature of the work and the full range of stakeholders in the evaluation process.

A collaborative evaluation facilitates the engagement of key stakeholders and improves the odds

that the evaluation results will provide a useful basis for guiding a decision-making process that takes into account the evaluand and its interactions within its total system. Thus, the evaluation results are able to provide a useful basis for guiding the decision-making process because people work collaboratively while respecting the evaluand and its interactions within its total system. Collaborative evaluation can lead to an increased quality of information and receptivity to findings.

Liliana Rodríguez-Campos and Rigoberto Rincones-Gómez

See also Action Research; Collaborative Evaluation; Data; Data Mining; Evaluation; Focus Groups; Interviews; Member Check; Participatory Evaluation; Qualitative Data Analysis; Qualitative Research Methods; Quantitative Research Methods; Trustworthiness; Validity

Further Readings

Alkin, M. (2012). *Evaluation roots: A wider perspective of theorists' views and influences.* (2nd ed.). Thousand Oaks, CA: Sage.

Arnold, M. E. (2006). Developing evaluation capacity in extension 4-H field faculty: A framework for success. *American Journal of Evaluation, 27,* 257–269.

Bledsoe, K. L., & Graham, J. A. (2005). The use of multiple evaluation approaches in program evaluation. *American Journal of Evaluation, 26,* 302–319.

Cousins, J. B., Donohue, J. J., & Bloom, G. A. (1996). Collaborative evaluation in North America: Evaluator's self-reported opinions, practices, and consequences. *Evaluation Practice, 17*(3), 207–226.

Cousins, J. B., Whitmore, E., & Shulha, L. (2013). Arguments for a common set of principles for collaborative inquiry in evaluation. *American Journal of Evaluation, 34,* 7–22.

Davies, A., Cameron, C., Politano, C., & Gregory, K. (1992). *Together is better: Collaborative assessment, evaluation & reporting.* Winnipeg, CA: Peguis.

Fetterman, D. M., Rodríguez-Campos, L., Wandersman, A., & O'Sullivan, R. (2014). Collaborative, participatory and empowerment evaluation: Building a strong conceptual foundation for stakeholder involvement approaches to evaluation. *American Journal of Evaluation, 35*(1), 144–148.

Fetterman, D. M., & Wandersman, A. (2007). Empowerment evaluation: Yesterday, today, and tomorrow. *American Journal of Evaluation, 28,* 179–198.

Gajda, R. (2004). Utilizing collaboration theory to evaluate strategic alliances. *American Journal of Evaluation, 25,* 65–77.

Gibson, J. L., Ivancevich, J. M., & Donnelly, J. H. (2008). *Organizations: Behavior, structure, processes* (13th ed.). Burr Ridge, IL: McGraw-Hill.

Green, B. L., Mulvey, L., Fisher, H. A., & Woratschek, F. (1996). Integrating program and evaluation values: A family support approach to program evaluation. *American Journal of Evaluation, 17,* 261–272.

Jurmo, P., & Folinsbee, S. (1994). *Collaborative evaluation: A handbook for workplace development planners.* Don Mills, CA: ABC Canada.

Morabito, S. M. (2002). Evaluator roles and strategies for expanding evaluation process influence. *American Journal of Evaluation, 23,* 321–330.

O'Sullivan, R. G. (2004). Practicing evaluation: A collaborative approach. Thousand Oaks, CA: Sage.

Preskill, H., & Boyle, S. (2008). A multidisciplinary model of evaluation capacity building. *American Journal of Evaluation, 29,* 443–459.

Rodríguez-Campos, L. (2005). *Collaborative evaluations: A step-by-step model for the evaluator.* Tamarac, FL: Llumina Press.

Rodríguez-Campos, L. (2008). *Evaluaciones colaborativas: Un modelo paso a paso para el evaluador* [Collaborative evaluations: A step-by-step model for the evaluator]. Tamarac, FL: Llumina Press.

Rodríguez-Campos, L. (2012a). Advances in collaborative evaluations. *Journal of Evaluation and Program Planning, 35*(4), 523–528.

Rodríguez-Campos, L. (2012b). Stakeholder involvement in evaluation: Three decades of the *American Journal of Evaluation. Journal of MultiDisciplinary Evaluation, 8*(17), 57–79.

Rodríguez-Campos, L. (2015). *Collaborative evaluations in practice: Insights from business, nonprofit, and education sectors.* Scottsdale, AZ: Information Age.

Rodríguez-Campos, L., & O'Sullivan, R. (2010, November). *Collaborative evaluation Essentials: Highlighting the essential features of collaborative evaluation.* Paper presented at the American Evaluation Association Conference, San Antonio, TX.

Rodríguez-Campos, L., & Rincones-Gómez, R. (2013). *Collaborative evaluations: Step-by-step* (2nd ed.). Stanford, CA: Stanford University Press.

Ryan, K., Greene, J., Lincoln, Y., Mathison, S., & Mertens, D. M. (1998). Advantages and challenges of using inclusive evaluation approaches in evaluation practice. *American Journal of Evaluation, 19,* 101–122.

Sanders, J. (2005). *Foreword.* In L. Rodríguez-Campos (2005). *Collaborative evaluations: A step-by-step model for the evaluator.* Tamarac, FL: Llumina Press.

Stufflebeam, D. L., & Shinkfield, A. J. (2007). *Evaluation theory, models, and applications.* San Francisco, CA: Wiley.

Veale, J., Morley, R., & Erickson, C. (2001). *Practical evaluation for collaborative services: Goals, processes, tools, and reporting systems for school-based programs.* Thousand Oaks, CA: Corwin Press.

Yeh, S. S. (2000). Improving educational and social programs: A planned variation cross-validation model. *American Journal of Evaluation, 21,* 171–184.

COLLAGE TECHNIQUE

In art, a collage is a collection or combination of artwork. In research, the generation of a collage is used as an enabling or projective technique to facilitate the discussion of, and therefore the understanding of, a research topic. Collage construction has also been used as a teaching technique in order to teach the organizational culture topic to business students.

When the technique is used in research, participants would typically be asked to think about a topic prior to an interview or focus group discussion and to collect images or objects that express their feelings and attitudes toward the topic of discussion. Participants bring these images to the research exercise and use them to form a collage that is then discussed. Research participants come to the research with considered opinions because they have been thinking about the topic beforehand in their collection of visual stimuli. This facilitates discussion.

Alternatively, research participants can be given a set of magazines and newspapers when they arrive at the research exercise and then be asked to look through them to choose images or articles that correspond with how they view or understand a topic. Research participants could also be shown previously made collages and asked to what extent the images still represented their understanding of the topic under research.

The advantage of the collage technique is that it stimulates the nonrational areas of the brains of research participants because it entails the use of visual and often emotionally meaningful imagery. The technique is thought to access a deeper and broader understanding than rational questions alone would generate.

Furthermore, the use of exciting visual imagery can be different and enjoyable for research participants, and so can stimulate more animated and insightful discussion than might otherwise occur. For example, if an educational institution wanted to discern how its alumni viewed it, then previous students of the institution could be asked to attend a research session and to bring any pictures they found in magazines or newspapers that exemplify how they feel about the institution. For some establishments, the images collected may be of warmth (open fires), friendliness (smiling people), and enjoyment. For other institutions, the images presented may be of coldness (fridges, icebergs), avariciousness (open, empty wallets), and indifference. The researcher would use the images as a stimulus to generating discussion about the institution concerned and what the images collected meant to the research participants.

Clive R. Boddy

See also Bubble Drawing

Further Readings

Boddy, C. R. (2005). Projective techniques in market research: Valueless subjectivity or insightful reality? A look at the evidence for the usefulness, reliability and validity of projective techniques in market research. *International Journal of Market Research, 47*(3), 239–254.

Colakoglu, S., & Littlefield, J. (2011). Teaching organizational culture using a projective technique: Collage construction. *Journal of Management Education, 35*(4), 564–585.

Haire, M. (1950). Projective techniques in marketing research. *Journal of Marketing, 14*(5), 649–656.

Malchiodi, C. A. (Ed.). (2011). *Handbook of art therapy.* New York, NY: Guilford Press.

Powell, L., & Faherty, S. L. (1990). Treating sexually abused latency aged girls: A 20 session treatment plan utilizing group process and the creative arts therapies. *The Arts in Psychotherapy, 17,* 35–47.

White, M., & Epston, D. (1990). *Narrative means to therapeutic ends* (1st ed.). New York, NY: Norton.

COLLEGE SUCCESS

Factors such as retention, persistence, degree attainment, and grade point average are common measures of college success; however, in the field of higher education, there exists ambiguity regarding the meaning and definition of college success and how to operationalize and measure college success. There exists a lack of a standard and clear definition of college success in higher education because the research on college students is principally an amalgamation of scholarship across several fields, such as education, psychology, and other social sciences. Many theoretical perspectives, frameworks, and conceptualizations have contributed to present-day notions of college success. This entry describes the conceptualization of college success and the outcomes that have traditionally been considered to represent college success. It also describes the factors that higher education professionals, faculty, and researchers have typically contended are predictors of college success.

Conceptualization of College Success

The ways that student success have been conceptualized and measured have varied across higher education, however higher education professionals and scholars have largely focused on persistence and retention. Higher education scholars, faculty, and professionals utilize a wide variety and combination of measures to assess college success and the choice of a measure typically is at the discretion of the researcher. For instance, some studies may simply examine students who return for their second year of college as a proxy for student success. Degree attainment is commonly utilized as another measure to assess student success. Finally, academic grades (i.e., grade point averages) are typically considered to be a suitable measure of college success.

College success is often associated with retention and persistence from the first year to the second and subsequently to the fourth (or sixth) year of college. There are several seminal theories related to how and why students persist in college. Vincent Tinto theorized that students who socially integrate into the campus community become more committed to the institution and are more likely to graduate. Tinto's student integration model indicates that students' background characteristics are associated with their capacity to be socially or academically integrated into (or engaged with) their institution's environment and culture. Other models, such as John Bean's model of attrition and Alexander Astin's framework of involvement, are similar to prior notions of persistence but also account for matters such as the influence of the campus environment and peer interactions.

The first year of college serves as a critical transition period for college students. Many in the higher education field consider this to be a pivotal time for students transitioning from secondary schooling to advanced forms of learning. Intellectual and cognitive developments are critical elements of this period in their college experience. Additionally, success during students' first year functions as a crucial indicator of their ensuring college career. Therefore, many in higher education utilize first-year retention as a measure of college success.

Academic performance during college, as measured by cumulative grade point average, traditionally serves as a representation of college student success. College grades are usually correlated with retention and subsequent degree completion. Academic performance is also recognized as a proxy for college success because grade point average has been positively linked to postcollege outcomes, such as increased aspirations to obtain an advanced degree and academic achievement in graduate and professional programs. Grades during the latter years of college serve as a predictor of college success.

Student success may represent all of the other experiences that students have in college as well as the skills and competencies that students attain on campus that positively impact students' postcollege existence. Student success represents the collegiate experiences and competencies that subsequently can influence students' career and professional decisions. It also represents the experiences that students encounter in college that might influence nonacademic or career outcomes, such as civic engagement or volunteerism. Some of these skills and competencies might be participation in internship programs, publication of articles through undergraduate institutional research programs, completion of supplemental and voluntary certificates, or participation in cultural or leadership programs.

Predictors of College Success

Grade point average and scores on standardized tests such as the ACT and SAT during high school or during the early years of college historically have been deemed to be strong predictors of student success, primarily regarding early performance. High school grade point average has, however, been considered to be an inadequate predictor of college success because of disparate grading systems across secondary schools. The differing characteristics of high schools make it problematic to compare students from varying high schools, and thus grade point average is an ineffectual predictor of subsequent college success. There also has been criticism of the notion that grade point averages during the first or second year of college are a predictor of subsequent college success because of potential grading differences by faculty in individual courses and the differences in grading practices across institutions of higher education.

Student success is associated with students' academic and social integration while in college. There are psychological and behavioral factors that promote student success in college. Often, the psychological factors embody constructs such as students' self-reported satisfaction, motivation, self-confidence, and stress management. Students also demonstrate behavioral attributes that can impact their college success. These behavioral aspects are represented by students' academic and social engagements such as setting aside time to study, joining student organizations and clubs, attending cultural workshops, or participating in institutional programs and activities. While there is mixed evidence for most of these predictors of student success, effective time engagement has been shown to be positively associated with college success.

Demographic characteristics and personal and family background have traditionally been an area of focus for higher education professionals and researchers regarding college success. Factors such as race, gender, socioeconomic status, and first generation status are often considered to be significant influences on the capacity of students to persist, attain a degree, or have higher academic outcomes. Typically, these factors are suitable because of the availability of data. For instance, student affairs professionals can utilize data from students' admissions applications that represent race or gender to examine the association between demographic characteristics and college success.

Conversely, what to do with the information and results can be a challenge for college administrators primarily because they have little or no control of students' precollege and background characteristics that might consequently affect college success. For instance, college administrators sometimes consider the link between students' socioeconomic status and college access and academic preparedness. Yet, there exists a modest body of research that focuses on the specific experiences that promote college success for this particular group of students. Higher education professionals can only influence the college experiences of these students, not their socioeconomic status.

The organizational and institutional contexts are noteworthy themes regarding student success. Environmental conditions are important considerations regarding students' academic achievement, persistence, and subsequent degree completion. The organizational context comprises the practices, polices, and inherent structure of students' respective institutions. Elements of the organization or environmental context might be key organizational characteristics (e.g., prestige, size, or geographical location) or institutional resources (e.g., availability and allocation of financial support). These elements of the institution might influence students' success.

Related to the organizational context, perspective is the notion that student engagement and activities are predictors of college success. These types of experiences can involve opportunities for peer and faculty interaction, mentoring, fraternities and sororities, and study abroad. Generally, involvement in cocurricular activities is positively correlated with college success. College student engagement also embodies academic activities such as interactions within the classroom and nonclassroom experiences that are related to the curriculum or learning growth. Some examples of these activities are speaker series, workshops, and specialized training opportunities.

The research is largely inconclusive regarding the validity of any of these predictors as true indicators of eventual college success. Scholarship focusing on what determines college success is a large, mixed, and disparate amalgamation of research studies with varying evidence about what predicts college success. This is perhaps a result of the indistinct meaning and conceptualization of the term. Still, some higher education professionals and scholars contend that higher levels of predictors, such as student engagement or academic excellence, are positively associated with higher levels of college success.

Eugene T. Parker

See also ACT; Admissions Tests; SAT

Further Readings

Bean, J. P. (1980). Dropouts and turnover: The synthesis and test of a causal model of student attrition. *Research in Higher Education, 12,* 155–187.

Krumrei-Mancuso, E. J., Newton, F. B., Kim, E., & Wilcox, D. (2013). Psychosocial factors predicting first-year college student success. *Journal of College Student Development, 54*(3), 247–266.

Pascarella, E. T., Pierson, C. T., Wolniak, G. C., & Terenzini, P. T. (2004). First-generation college students: Additional evidence on college experiences and outcomes. *Journal of Higher Education, 75*(3), 249–284.

Pascarella, E. T., & Terenzini, P. T. (2005). How college affects students. In K. A. Feldman (Ed.) (Vol. 2). San Francisco, CA: Jossey-Bass.

Reason, R. D., Terenzini, P. T., & Domingo, R. J. (2006). First things first: Developing academic competence in the first year of college. *Research in Higher Education, 47*(2), 149–175.

Robbins, S. B., Lauver, K., Le, H., Davis, D., Langley, R., & Carlstrom, A. (2004). Dopsychosocial and study factors predict college outcomes? A meta-analysis. *Psychological Bulletin, 130,* 261–288.

COMMON CORE STATE STANDARDS

The Common Core State Standards (CCSS) were developed in 2010 to provide a set of consistent targets across the United States for English language arts (ELA) and mathematics learning for public school students in Grades K–12. Described as college- and career-ready standards, they represented a shift from previous individual state-defined content standards that were often deemed to be low-level standards that did not meet the needs of students in a global economy. This entry provides an overview of the development of the CCSS and then describes the ELA and the mathematics standards. It details the history of adoption and rejection of the standards by states. In addition, the assessments developed to measure achievement of the CCSS are described.

Development of the CCSS

The CCSS, developed with leadership from the Council of Chief State School Officers and the National Governors Association, were promoted as being (a) research and evidence based, (b) aligned with college and work expectations, (c) rigorous in content and application of knowledge through higher order thinking skills, and (d) internationally benchmarked. They were also described as "fewer, clearer, higher" standards that were built on the strengths and lessons of existing state standards and that could provide a roadmap for K–12 curriculum, instruction, and assessment.

Standards-based education reform began in the early 1990s, spurred by models of reform that rested on a clear designation of what students needed to know and be able to do. Driven by a quest for an education system that promoted both equity and excellence, the assumption was that all students should be taught the same content and be held to the same performance standards. States were to define the content and performance standards and then develop assessments to evaluate how students were doing in relation to the standards.

The need for something other than content standards of ELA and math defined by individual states grew out of numerous discussions among states and national organizations. The reasons behind the push for new standards were numerous. A primary concern was that the United States was falling behind other countries in terms of the knowledge and skills demonstrated by students on international assessments such as the Programme for International Student Assessment developed

by the Organisation for Economic Co-operation and Development. On the 2009 Programme for International Student Assessment, 15-year-olds in more than 30 countries outperformed 15-year-olds in the United States. Beyond that was the finding that many students entering postsecondary institutions had to take remedial classes because they had not obtained the skills that they needed, even though they had earned a high school diploma. Supporters of the need for new standards cited the finding that 20% of students entering 4-year colleges and 40% of students entering 2-year community colleges had to take remedial courses.

Another reason frequently cited was that each state had set different criteria for what students needed to know and be able to do, and when students moved from one state to another, they were suddenly either way behind or way ahead of where they needed to be. Evidence of the differences across states was the performance of students in Grades 4 and 8 on the National Assessment of Educational Progress, the one measure used across all of the states. Further, states' content standards were often deemed to represent minimal skills inconsistent with the skills that would be needed in jobs of the future, where individuals would need more than basic math and ELA skills, such as communication, technical reading and writing, literacy across disciplines, and more complex mathematics.

The push for new, more rigorous standards was realized in 2010 when the Council of Chief State School Officers and National Governors Association assembled experts and practitioners in mathematics and ELA to generate a set of common standards. Development teams worked quickly to produce a set of standards that were different in many ways from the standards for mathematics and ELA that states had at that time. Rounds of feedback on the standards were conducted, and a validation team was formed to confirm that the standards were evidence based.

In the introductory materials to both the ELA and the mathematics standards, several points were made about what the standards were not intended to do. For example, it was clarified that the standards were about what students were expected to know and be able to do and not about how teachers should teach. Further, the standards did not indicate how to support students who are well below or well above grade-level expectations. Similarly, they did not define the supports appropriate for English language learners or students with disabilities, although the introductory materials made clear that the same high standards must be met by these students so that they are ready for college and careers. In addition, the standards were described as being what was most essential, not all that could or should be taught. Further, it was recognized that students needed many other skills besides ELA and mathematics skills to be ready for college and career. These other skills included, to name a few, social, emotional, and physical development, as well as strong approaches to learning.

The CCSS were portrayed from the beginning as being for all students in U.S. schools. Attention was given to both students with disabilities and English language learners, two groups that advocates had suggested may not have been considered when states developed their own standards. It was recognized that these students and likely others as well would need instructional supports to ensure that they were appropriately held to the same standards. Nevertheless, there was a commitment to the importance of these students having the opportunity to learn and meet the same high standards as other students, so that they also could access the knowledge and skills needed for their post-school lives.

CCSS of ELA

The CCSS for ELA addressed reading, writing, speaking, and listening. The change in emphasis of these standards from a narrow focus on fiction and writing about personal experiences was reflected in the title of the standards—*Common Core State Standards for English Language Arts and Literacy in History/Social Studies, Science, and Technical Subjects.*

When describing these standards, most professionals and teachers noted that they reflected three major instructional shifts. One shift was the inclusion of greater focus on nonfiction. The new standards represented a balance of literary and informational texts in Grades K–5 and more emphasis on nonfiction and social studies and science content in the texts in Grades 6–12. Another shift was the broadened focus on writing and

speaking as well as reading. Students were expected to use evidence from one or multiple texts to support their responses in writing or verbally. The third major shift was to more complex texts and academic language from a variety of content areas.

The ELA standards were organized to reflect an interdisciplinary approach. They were presented by grade level for grades K–8 and then in grade bands for Grades 9–10 and 11–12. Further, they were divided into strands for reading, writing, speaking and listening, and language. The focus of the reading strand was on text complexity and the growth of comprehension. The focus of the writing strand was on text types, responding to reading, and research. The focus of the speaking and listening strand was on flexible communication and collaboration. The focus of the language strand was on conventions, effective use, and vocabulary. The 10 standards are (CCSI, English language arts standards, n.d., n.p.):

Standard 1: Read closely to determine what the text says explicitly and to make logical inferences from it; cite specific textual evidence when writing or speaking to support conclusion drawn from text.

Standard 2: Determine central ideas or themes of a text and analyze their development; summarize the key supporting details and ideas.

Standard 3: Analyze how and why individuals, events, or ideas develop and interact over the course of a text.

Standard 4: Interpret words and phrases as they are used in a text, including determining technical, connotative, and figurative meanings, and analyze how specific word choices shape meaning or tone.

Standard 5: Analyze the structure of texts, including how specific sentences, paragraphs, and larger portions of the text (e.g., a section, chapter, scene, or stanza) relate to each other and the whole.

Standard 6: Assess how point of view or purpose shapes the content and style of a text.

Standard 7: Integrate and evaluate content presented in diverse media and formats, including visually and quantitatively, as well as in words.

Standard 8: Delineate and evaluate the argument and specific claims in a text, including the validity of the reasoning as well as the relevance and sufficiency of the evidence.

Standard 9: Analyze how two or more texts address similar themes or topics in order to build knowledge or to compare the approaches the authors take.

Standard 10: Read and comprehend complex literary and informational texts independently and proficiently.

Research and media use skills were embedded throughout the standards.

The ELA standards for Grades 6–12 were further divided into two sections to reflect the roles of educators in secondary settings. One section was for ELA and the other was for history/social studies, science, and technical subjects. The history/social studies, science, and technical subjects' standards were not intended to replace the content standards in those areas but rather to support ELA skills related to those content areas.

The ELA standards also described the characteristics of the "literate individual" who had mastered the CCSS in reading, writing, speaking, listening, and language. These characteristics were demonstrating independence; building strong content knowledge; responding to varying demands of audience, task, purpose, and discipline; comprehending as well as critiquing; valuing evidence; using technology and digital media strategically and capably; and coming to understand other perspectives and cultures.

CCSS of Mathematics

Standards for mathematics addressed both content and practices. Three major shifts also were identified for mathematics by professionals and practitioners. A first shift was to narrow and deepen the focus in each grade to ensure that students gained conceptual understanding, skills, and fluency in procedures, and were able to apply their understanding to a wide range of problems. For example, the major focus for each grade or grade band prior to high school was as follows (CCSI, Key shifts in mathematics, n.d., n.p.):

K–2: Concepts, skills, and problem solving related to addition and subtraction.

3–5: Concepts, skills, and problem solving related to multiplication and division of whole numbers and fractions.

6: Ratios and proportional relationships and early algebraic expressions and equations.

7: Ratios and proportional relationships and arithmetic of rational numbers.

8: Linear algebra and linear functions.

In high school (Grades 9–12), the standards were presented by conceptual categories rather than by grades. The conceptual categories included number and quantity, algebra, functions, modeling, geometry, and statistics and probability. According to the standards document, these categories crossed typical high school course boundaries.

The second major shift was to emphasize the need to connect learning within and across grades, so that students build on information from previous years without repeating all the instruction from the previous grade. The third shift was to increase rigor to emphasize conceptual understanding, procedural skills and fluency, and application.

The mathematics standards included a set of eight standards for mathematical practice followed by grade-specific standards from kindergarten through eighth grade and then for high school overall by topic (number and quantity, algebra, functions, modeling, geometry, and statistics and probability). The eight practice standards were (CCSI, Standards for mathematical practice, n.d., n.p.):

(1) make sense of problems and persevere in solving them;

(2) reason abstractly and quantitatively;

(3) construct viable arguments and critique the reasoning of others;

(4) model with mathematics;

(5) use appropriate tools strategically;

(6) attend to precision;

(7) look for and make use of structure; and

(8) look for and express regularity in repeated reasoning.

Connecting the mathematical practices to the mathematical content standards was presented as a goal for curricula, assessments, and professional development. The introduction to the mathematical standards suggested that the expectations that began with the word "understand" provided the opportunity to connect the practices to the content.

History of Adoption of the CCSS

Chief state school officers adopted the CCSS relatively quickly. By January 2011, fewer than 10 of the 50 states had not yet adopted the standards. In addition, several of the U.S. territories had signed on to the standards, including the District of Columbia and the U.S. Virgin Islands. By 2012, only five states had not adopted both the ELA and mathematics CCSS (Alaska, Minnesota, Nebraska, Texas, and Virginia).

The rapid adoption of the CCSS was prompted, in part, by the incentive to do so provided by a U.S. Department of Education grant program known as Race to the Top. It made available $4.3 billion in grants to states that had adopted standards that were internationally benchmarked and that prepared students for college and careers. The funds were to be used by states to transform instructional practices in line with the more rigorous college- and career-ready standards, to support teachers and leaders, to leverage data systems, and to turn around the lowest performing schools. Over time, however, with changes in chief state school officers and the intervention of state legislatures, the CCSS were rejected in several of the states that had previously adopted them. They were replaced by the states' own standards for ELA and mathematics, albeit standards that were deemed to be consistent with college and career readiness.

Assessments of the CCSS

States that adopted the CCSS had to develop new assessments based on those standards. In another effort to provide funds to support rapid changes in the ways that states would assess the new, more rigorous standards, the U.S. Department of Education provided grants to consortia of states that would work together to develop common innovative, technology-based assessments. Two consortia of states received funds to develop comprehensive assessment systems. One consortium was called the Partnership for the Assessment of Readiness for College and Careers and the other was called the Smarter Balanced Assessment Consortium (Smarter Balanced).

With the realization that these two consortia did not cover all the assessments taken by students in a comprehensive assessment system, additional funding was provided to support other consortia. First, the U.S. Department of Education provided funds for consortia of states to develop alternate assessments based on alternate achievement standards. The two funded alternate assessment consortia were the Dynamic Learning Maps Alternate Assessment Consortium and the National Center and State Collaborative. These consortia developed assessments for students with the most significant cognitive disabilities.

Additional funding was made available to support English language proficiency assessments that were aligned to the CCSS. Two consortia received these funds: Assessment Services Supporting ELs through Technology Systems and English Language Proficiency for the 21st Century. These consortia based their assessments on standards for English language development that were aligned to the CCSS.

All of the assessments that were developed to be aligned to the CCSS were technology-based assessments that used innovative item types. Some also included classroom-based performance assessments. These new assessments were regarded by many as being more rigorous than previous state assessments, yet many of the states that initially planned to use assessments developed by one of the assessment consortia ultimately rejected them. Only 20 states and the District of Columbia planned to administer Partnership for the Assessment of Readiness for College and Careers or Smarter Balanced tests in 2016–2017, the same number as during the previous year, according to *Education Week*.

CCSS Into the Future

Despite the ups and downs of adoption and rejection of both the CCSS and the assessments based on them, these standards have had a considerable impact on U.S. public schools. When the Elementary and Secondary Education Act was reauthorized in 2015, an emphasis on college- and career-ready standards was evident. States had to adopt academic standards for mathematics, reading or language arts, and science that were aligned with entrance requirements for credit-bearing coursework in each state's higher education system and with relevant career and technical education standards. Consistent with this emphasis, national organizations pushed for high school graduation diplomas to be based on rigorous college- and career-ready standards rather than the minimal standards that had been used in the past. The CCSS continued to influence standards even in states that avoided using the name in referring to their standards.

Martha L. Thurlow

See also Achievement Tests; Every Student Succeeds Act; Formative Assessment; Partnership for Assessment of Readiness for College and Careers; Smarter Balanced Assessment Consortium; Summative Assessment

Further Readings

Calfee, R. C., & Wilson, K. M. (2016). *Assessing the common core: What's gone wrong—and how to get back on track*. New York, NY: Guilford.

Common Core State Standards Initiative. (n.d.). English language arts standards » anchor standards » college and career readiness anchor standards for reading. Retrieved from http://www.corestandards.org/ELA-Literacy/CCRA/R/

Common Core State Standards Initiative. (n.d.). Key shifts in mathematics. Retrieved from http://www.corestandards.org/other-resources/key-shifts-in-mathematics/

Common Core State Standards Initiative. (n.d.). Standards for mathematical practice. Retrieved from http://www.corestandards.org/Math/Practice/

Gewertz, C. (2017, February 15). National testing landscape continues to shift. *Education Week*. Retrieved from http://www.edweek.org/ew/articles/2017/02/15/state-solidarity-still-eroding-on-common-core-tests.html

Hess, F. M., & McShane, M. Q. (2014). *Common core meets education reform: What it means for politics, policy, and the future of education*. New York, NY: Teachers College Press.

Rothman, R. (2011). *Something in common: The common core standards and the next chapter in American education*. Cambridge, MA: Harvard University Press.

Thurlow, M. L. (2012, summer). Common Core State Standards: The promise and the peril for students with disabilities. *The Special Edge, 25*(3), 1, 6–8.

U.S. Department of Education. (2015). *Fundamental change: Innovation in America's schools under Race to the Top*. Washington, DC: Author.

COMPLIANCE

Compliance refers to investigators' obligation to abide by federal, state, and local requirements when seeking approval to conduct research with human subjects and when conducting research. Investigators are accountable to ensure that all applicable laws and regulations are adhered to, so that participants and the institution are protected from harm. Failure to comply with the terms and conditions of an approved protocol can result in the suspension of the investigator's research and possibly the suspension of all human subjects research at the investigator's institution.

Federal regulations require that federally funded research involving human subjects undergo a review for ethical propriety by an institutional review board (IRB). Most institutions where research is conducted require that all human subjects research be reviewed by an IRB, whether or not it is federally funded. An investigator is required to provide complete and accurate information regarding the study's aims, the proposed methodology, and any potential risks to participants. The investigator's qualifications are submitted as truthful evidence to conduct the research. When the IRB approves the protocol, the investigator agrees to comply with federal and IRB conditions.

Data collection cannot begin until the IRB has approved the research. Even if the research qualifies for an exemption because it involves certain categories of people (e.g., political officials), it must still be reviewed and approved by the IRB. Once the research has been approved, investigators agree to several stipulations. For example, they agree to obtain and maintain informed consent from all participants.

Consent may be provided on paper or in an electronic format and must be available for inspection by the institution or by federal regulatory agencies. In addition, investigators agree to conduct the research as proposed and to not change anything without IRB review and approval. Changes to an approved protocol require that the investigator submit a request for an amendment or modification to the study, and when the request has been evaluated and approved by the IRB, changes may be made.

During the course of the research, investigators agree to provide progress reports to the IRB and to submit periodic (typically annual) applications to obtain renewed approval for the study. If adverse events occur, such as participant injury or a breach of security or confidentiality, investigators should report the event to the IRB immediately. The IRB then evaluates the event to decide if adjustments to the protocol must be made or if the research must be suspended or ended. The investigator agrees to comply with all IRB decisions in this regard. Finally, the investigator agrees to cease data collection when the approved period for data collection has expired.

Failure to comply with any of these requirements may result in a suspension of the investigator's authorization to conduct future research with human subjects. Because the consequences of noncompliance are serious and potentially severe, it behooves investigators to understand and comply with all research regulations.

Robert D. Ridge

See also Belmont Report; Ethical Issues in Educational Research; 45 CFR Part 46; Human Subjects Protections; Human Subjects Research, Definition of; Institutional Review Boards

Further Readings

American Psychological Association. (2010). *Ethical principles of psychologists and code of conduct, including 2010 amendments*. Retrieved July 11, 2016, from http://www.apa.org/ethics/code/index.aspx

Code of Federal Regulations, Title 45, Part 46: Protection of Human Subjects. Retrieved July 11, 2016, from http://www.hhs.gov/ohrp/regulations-and-policy/regulations/45-cfr-46/

COMPUTER PROGRAMMING IN QUANTITATIVE ANALYSIS

Computer programming in quantitative analysis refers to the process of creating computer "code"— or instructions that a computer can interpret—to automate quantitative summaries of data. Due to the advent of powerful personal computers, high-level programming languages, and the increasing availability of high-performance computing clusters, such programming is becoming increasingly used and important in both publicly funded research and private and commercial settings. Such computer programming may take many different forms depending on the purpose of the quantitative analysis. This entry provides an overview of particular use cases for computer programming—progressing from the most basic to the most complex—integrated with the introduction of programming concepts.

Basic Use Cases

Applications of computer programming vary widely depending on the purpose of the analyses and on the experience of the programmer. Writing or recording the code used for quantitative analyses can be important for the ability to reproduce an analysis, automate a series of analyses or a simulation study, or develop and test a new quantitative analysis technique.

Reproducible Analyses

Suppose a researcher generates histograms for each of two variables (X and Y) and performs a regression analysis (Y regressed on X). If questions arise about the analysis, the researcher may not always remember the bin size used to construct the histograms, whether the predictor variable was standardized when they performed the regression analysis, and so on. A record of the analysis will make it possible to recall exactly how the analysis was conducted without relying on fallible human memory. Analyses that are recorded are called *reproducible analyses.*

Statistical software designed for novice analysts, typically operated by a point-and-click user interface, do not necessarily retain an exact record of the analyses performed. However, it is often possible to persuade such software to produce the underlying code. For example, SPSS can produce "syntax," which consists of code that can be saved as a plain text file record. This record allows one to see exactly which options were enabled or selected when the analyses were run, even if not immediately discernible to the untrained eye. The act of creating a record of instructions that can be replayed is a rudimentary example of programming. Once an analysis script is available, it is a small step for the user to edit this code by copying and pasting or changing a few variable names. Other popular all-purpose statistical packages, such as R, SAS, and STATA, are also sometimes capable of generating an analysis script from a point-and-click interface.

A typical next step is to copy results into a manuscript or report. Although the user may copy software output manually, it is increasingly possible to integrate the analysis code and narrative text. This approach is known as *literate programming* and has long been advocated by Donald Knuth, an early computer science visionary. For example, suppose the results of the aforementioned regression analysis are to become part of a publication. With authoring formats such as R Markdown or packages such as knitr, it is possible to combine the R code and manuscript text in the same file. Within an R editor such as Rstudio, a button click will run the R code, combine it with the narrative text, and generate a report that automatically displays the output of the R code and can automate generation of tables, figures, and so on. Reports can be generated in a wide variety of formats including portable document format (in conjunction with LaTeX), Microsoft Word, presentations (e.g., with Beamer), and web pages (HTML). Use of such an approach can reduce transcription errors and mislabeling of output and avoid loss of documentation regarding how the results for a figure or table were generated. The code used to run analyses resides in the same place as the text of the report, and the owner of

the file can see exactly what code generated each table, figure, or other in-text values reported, while optionally hiding such code from the report for esthetic reasons. Preparation of such integrated documents requires programming investment but pays off by resulting in reproducible analysis code.

Basic Programming Concepts

At a bare minimum, writing code may require understanding how to use *variables*, *functions*, and sometimes *loops*. Although there are many different terms for these concepts, usually they exist in some form regardless of the software or programming language.

Conceptually, a *variable* is a container that can store some type of data or intermediate result. For instance, a variable may contain an integer (5), some text ("Yay for statistics!"), or something more complex such as the data set that the researcher wishes to analyze or the results of a statistical analysis. The types of variables that software or a programming language can support generally depend on the allowable data types and data structures.

A *function* (or *macro* or *subroutine*) performs a specific task. The user gives the function some input, it does something with the input, and then gives back some output. Functions generally are written for performing complex tasks that would usually take many lines of code to write, and the output of a function can be stored in a variable. It is usually good practice to write functions in as general a way as possible such that the code may be reused.

More complex use cases may require a greater level of automation. For example, suppose that the researcher wishes to perform the exact same regression analysis, but for 100 different data sets. One option would be to copy/paste existing code 100 times, each time changing the name of the data set or to use the graphical interface to painstakingly perform all 100 analyses. Such an approach is not scalable to situations in which many data sets are to be analyzed. If the researcher has carefully named the variables ($X1$, $X2$, and Y within all data sets) and carefully named the data sets (e.g., *data001.txt*, *data002.txt*, through *data100.txt*), it is possible to write a program to perform the same task 100 times, each time changing the name of the data set and saving the result. This task is often accomplished by writing a *loop* and can usually be done in a compact and concise way with only a few lines of code.

Finally, basic code writing may at least entail use of a style guide and the ability to *debug*. A style guide is a series of conventions that dictates how the programmer should format code, name variables or functions, and provide comments or documentation such that others can more easily understand it. If multiple programmers follow similar conventions, it facilitates the ability to quickly read another person's code. The ability to debug is also useful for fixing mistakes or "bugs" in code. Put simply, debugging approaches let a programmer see what happens inside a function or help the programmer narrow down the various possible causes to an anomalous result.

Software Ownership, Source Code, and Programming Languages

One consideration relevant to reproducibility and more advanced use cases is the continuously evolving nature of statistical software and the software ecosystem on which it is built. New versions of software usually maintain backward compatibility, meaning that analysis scripts created with an older version of the software will continue to work properly with the new version. Occasionally, recorded analysis scripts that are intended to reproduce an analysis fail because of changes to the software ecosystem. When discrepancies arise across programs or across versions of the same program, ownership and accessibility to the source code can be important to allow the user to diagnose the cause of the discrepancy.

One approach to software stewardship is corporate ownership. For example, SPSS, SAS, and STATA are owned by corporations that exercise complete control over how the software evolves, including maintenance of compatibility. Another approach to software stewardship is known as copyleft, in which no group of people exercise exclusive control. Copyleft is a legal license that leverages copyright law to ensure that users can run, copy, distribute, study, change, and improve software themselves. For example, The

R Foundation is a steward for the R statistical software but has no special legally enforceable rights over the R software. In addition to these two approaches to software ownership, there is a middle approach known as open-source software that can often be regarded as a compromise between copyleft and corporate ownership. The differences among software ownership models and which is ideal for any given situation is a controversial topic.

In theory, the ability to reproduce an analysis is facilitated by copyleft or open-source software models, as users have access to the underlying code and may pinpoint the cause of a discrepancy or determine how to implement the same analysis using a different programming language or software. On the other hand, adaptation to breaks in compatibility may require expertise that is out of the reach of novice users. Commercial software developers may be more vigilant about maintaining compatibility because of paid support contracts. However, backward compatibility is not necessarily guaranteed regardless of the ownership model.

A variety of software and programming languages, each with a particular software ownership model, can be used to conduct programming in quantitative analysis. All-purpose statistical packages such as R, SAS, SPSS, and STATA offer their own idiomatic language to create macros or programs. All of these constitute high-level languages that make it relatively easy to write programs but may result in programs that do not run particularly fast. For example, although core R functions are written in C/C++ (fast, low-level languages), any new functions or code that a user types is interpreted by R rather than compiled into machine code. Low-level programming languages such as C/C++, Fortran, and Rust are typically compiled and may run faster but can require much more programming effort compared to high-level languages. Other programming languages include Java, Python, Perl, and GAUSS. It is increasingly possible for different programming languages or software to work together, such as using C/C++ or Fortran to implement functions to call from within R, execute R code from a proprietary program such as SAS or SPSS, or run and process output from proprietary programs using R.

Advanced Use Cases

Implementation of a Statistical Method

Sometimes the analysis that a researcher wishes to perform is not readily available in existing software. This happens frequently among those inventing new statistical methods but can also happen when methodological researchers publish the mathematical details of a new statistical method but do not provide suitable code. It is possible for the researcher to write code to perform the statistical analysis.

An interesting challenge can arise because of differences in the typical presentation of display mathematics in scientific papers and efficient implementation of the same mathematical idea. For example, in display mathematics, it is typical to represent a permutation using a permutation matrix:

$$a\ b\ c\ d \begin{matrix} 0100 \\ 1000 \\ 0001 \\ 0010 \end{matrix} = (b\ a\ d\ c)$$

However, matrix multiplication is not the best way to implement this idea in a computer, as it requires operations proportional to the square of the number of items to be permuted. The same permutation can be accomplished in linear time using a mapping (old position → new position). Programmers tasked with implementing mathematical algorithms are advised to become familiar with opportunities to reorganize equations such as the commutative and associative laws.

In other cases, a researcher uses a different programming language to implement a method in existing software. There are trade-offs to building such work on either commercial or copyleft licensed software. For example, it is possible to investigate the source code for copyleft licensed software to determine exactly what the program is doing. Such source code is typically not available for commercial software and it is not possible to directly inspect the accuracy of the mathematical formulae. On the other hand, inspecting source code is a difficult task and some may place more confidence in the correctness of particular software based on the track record or reputation of a particular developer/company or the resources that a company has for technical development and programming. Regardless, there is a potential for mistakes to be present in any software, and one should be more confident in replicating a method when independently developed programs converge on the same result.

Monte Carlo Studies and Parallel Computing

Researchers who study advanced statistical methods often do so through Monte Carlo simulation studies. For example, if data violate one of the regression analysis assumptions (e.g., the residuals are not normally distributed), it is possible to investigate the consequences of this through a simulation study. The researcher may write a program that generates a large number of data sets from a specified population with nonnormally distributed residuals, analyze each data set, and then save the results. In its simplest form, such programming may entail little more than writing a loop. In its more complex form, the researcher may study what happens under different sample sizes, different techniques for appropriately handling nonnormal data, different true regression coefficients in the population, and so on.

If many conditions are chosen in such a factorial design and the number of replications is large, or the type of analysis is computationally intensive, additional work may be required such that the simulations can be completed in a reasonable amount of time. This may entail writing some of the code in a faster, but lower level programming language, or use of parallel computing or a computing cluster. Modern computers often have central processing units that have more than one processing core. Separate processing cores can execute instructions at the same time. High-performance computing clusters may have hundreds or thousands of computing nodes, each with multiple cores. *Parallel computing* refers to creating the computer program so that it can utilize multiple processing cores to complete the analyses in a fraction of the time it would take if only one core were used. Such computing is also useful when only a small number of analyses are to be conducted, but using a computationally intensive technique. Although parallel computing may allow fast completion of analyses, developing the code involves additional complexity.

Collaboration and Best Practices

Making newly invented statistical methods available to applied researchers generally entails a complex programming task and sometimes collaboration among many researchers or programmers. For instance, SPSS, SAS, STATA, and R (and its many R packages) were programmed by many people over many years. In addition, programs such as Mplus and flexMIRT are specialized packages that are the result of fewer researcher programmers but are at the cutting edge of latent variable modeling and measurement research in the social sciences. Copyleft-licensed software, such as R, generally welcome contributions from any researchers interested in getting involved in development. In contrast, commercial software is developed mainly by paid employees of the company that sells the software as a product. In any case, such complex programming endeavors can get unwieldy without good design of the program and some best practices that standardize how programming and tests are conducted and how documentation and changes are tracked.

Deciding on a software ownership model and clear conceptual design is essential before embarking on a large-scale or complex programming problem. A conceptual design may consist of a list of stories that describe the different functions that the program is to perform (and their desired input and output) and its data structures such that the programmers will understand how the different pieces are supposed to work together. Each component of the project can then be tackled in small, manageable pieces. When the software is developed in a tightly integrated way, it can be very costly in terms of time and effort to change the original conceptual design. For example, a software package that is designed to address statistical questions using maximum likelihood may not be easily changed to address statistical questions with a Bayesian mean posterior approach. However, a modular design can help, which entails careful separation of the program into independent modules with well-defined interfaces. Changes to one module do not typically affect other modules, provided that the input/output format remains the same.

Sometimes the first draft of code for a function or component of a project is done so that it just "works," but is not particularly efficient or modular. *Refactoring*, or the process of rewriting or restructuring code, is essential for the long-term manageability of the program. The goal of refactoring is to clean up the underlying code without adversely impacting its functionality or behavior. That is, a user's reproducible analyses should continue to reproduce the same analysis results, while refactoring makes the underlying code more concise, easier to understand, or perform the task faster. In computer science, *technical debt* describes approximately how urgently refactoring is needed. With copyleft-licensed software, the level of technical debt can be evaluated and paid down by developers familiar with the code. In contrast, technical debt in commercial software exists in a quantity only known to the steward of that software and must be paid down by its own developers before it grows out of control. If too much technical debt accumulates, then it can be easier to start rebuilding a software product from scratch.

One way to cope with the challenge of ensuring reproducible analysis scripts is to invest in regression tests. In software engineering, regression is used to indicate something that broke that was previously working. A regression test checks whether an analysis script obtains the same answer that it did originally. For example, the correlation between two variables might have originally been computed as .4. With the release of a new version, the correlation may be computed as −.3. The analysis is no longer reproducible and a suitable regression test will alert the researcher that something is broken. Writing tests are a helpful way to discover lapses in compatibility. Often, these lapses in compatibility can be repaired by examining the release notes for suggestions or by utilization of a software support communications channel.

A final problem involves tracking changes to the underlying code and the ability for all those involved to readily access the latest version. For example, consider the confusion that may arise if a programmer found a mistake in a function, but the fix was not shared with all those involved or was overwritten by another programmer's changes to the function. Modern version control systems (e.g., git or subversion) are often used by programmers to track changes to the underlying code, and storage of code in a repository can ensure that everyone involved has access to the latest version. Although such systems can handle very complex collaborative projects, they may also be used by individual researchers who wish to document changes to their own code.

Carl Francis Falk and Joshua N. Pritikin

See also BILOG-MG; C Programming Languages; EQS; flexMIRT; HLM; IRTPRO; LISREL; Monte Carlo Simulation Studies; PARSCALE; R; SAS; SPSS; STATA

Further Readings

Eddelbuettel, D. (2013). *Seamless R and C++ integration with Rcpp*. New York, NY: Springer.

Gandrud, C. (2015). *Reproducible research with R and RStudio* (2nd ed.). Boca Raton, FL: CRC Press.

Knuth, D. E. (2011). *The art of computer programming: Vols. 1–4A*. Reading, MA: Addison-Wesley.

Loeliger, J., & McCullough, M. (2012). *Version control with Git* (2nd ed.). Sebastopol, CA: O'Reilly Media.

Matloff, N. (2011). *The art of R programming*. San Francisco, CA: No Starch.

Matloff, N. (2016). *Parallel computing for data science: With examples in R, C++, and CUDA*. Boca Raton, FL: CRC Press.

Press, W. H., Teukolsky, S. A., Vetterling, W. T., & Flannery, B. P. (2007). *Numerical Recipes: The art of scientific computing* (3rd ed.). UK: Cambridge University Press.

Wicklin, R. (2010). *Statistical programming with SAS/IML software*. Cary, NC: SAS Institute.

Zuur, A. F., Ieno, E. N., & Meesters, E. H. W. G. (2009). *A beginner's guide to R*. New York, NY: Springer.

COMPUTER-BASED TESTING

In computer-based testing (CBT), computer technology is used in the administration of achievement or ability test items. Such assessments have been gradually supplanting paper-and-pencil tests in educational assessment since their introduction in the 1970s. The attractiveness of CBT lies in its potential to expand, in multiple ways, the way educational assessment is conducted. This entry provides a brief history of its development, as well as an assessment of the advantages and limitations of CBT.

A Brief History

As the capability and preponderance of computers evolved during the latter part of the 20th century and into the 21st century, so has the nature and impact of CBT evolved. In the early 1970s, computerized testing was primarily found in university research institutions, using CBT delivered through mainframe computers. In the late 1970s, advances in item response theory (IRT) led to the first research on computerized adaptive test (CAT), a particular type of CBT that is highly interactive, conducted primarily at the University of Minnesota and Educational Testing Service.

The 1980s and 1990s saw the emergence of the first operational computer-based tests. Most notably, in the 1980s, the U.S. Department of Defense developed the CAT version of the Armed Services Vocational Aptitude Battery and the Northwest Evaluation Association introduced the first adaptive testing program for U.S. school children, Measures of Academic Progress. In the early 1990s, Educational Testing Service began offering CBT versions of the Graduate Record Exam. This time period also saw the development of numerous smaller scale computer-based tests in educational settings, most of which were computerized versions of preexisting paper-and-pencil tests. The 1990s also saw the first major advances in innovative item development, as researchers began to more fully exploit the capabilities of CBT.

In the early 21st century, CBT became more common in education, as computer technology gained increasing sophistication and the availability of computers in schools increased. Moreover, the emergence of the Internet brought with it increasing expectations that CBT would be delivered online. As of 2015, CBT was successfully being used in the majority of U.S. statewide K–12 testing programs, although online large-scale CBT showed uneven reliability.

Advantages

CBT offers a set of important advantages over paper-and-pencil tests. Some of these advantages influence the quality of measurement, while others favorably influence the costs and logistics of test administration.

Innovative Item Types

CBT enables the administration of innovative item types, which have been defined as those that depart from the traditional text-based, multiple-choice format. This is a broad definition whose meaning has expanded over time, as computer technology has evolved and researchers have increasingly understood the role that computers can play in testing. Innovative items can potentially improve measurement in several ways over traditional items. First, innovative items can provide a more direct measurement of some knowledge or skill. As an example, using CBT, a test taker might be asked to identify and correct grammatical errors in a paragraph—a task that would be awkward to do using text-based, multiple-choice items. Second, innovative items can allow measurement of important parts of a content domain that would be logistically very challenging to measure at all using traditional text-based items. For instance, a test taker might listen to a piece of music and be asked to identify its tempo. Both of these examples illustrate how both the types of cognitive skills that can be measured and the ways they are measured can be enhanced when CBT is used.

Innovative items in CBT can be classified along several dimensions. One dimension is *item format*, which refers to the response possibilities of the test taker. Item formats can range from selected response (in which the test taker chooses among a set of highly defined options) to constructed-response formats (in which test takers construct their own answers). There are, however, numerous possibilities in between. For example, a test taker might be asked to drag a number of historical events steps into chronological order—which is a task that could be administered very efficiently using CBT. Another dimension is *response action*, which represents the physical actions a test taker must perform to answer an item. Response actions that have been used include radio buttons or pull-down menus, typed-in responses, joysticks, use of touchscreens, spoken responses, or answers specified through mouse clicks. However, an endless array of options is possible, constrained only by the creativity of the test developer and the capability of the computer hardware. A third dimension is *media inclusion*, which refers to the degree to which innovative CBT items incorporate multimedia elements, such as graphics, sounds, video, or animations. A fourth dimension is the *level of interactivity* between the test and the test taker. Traditional test items are completely noninteractive; the test taker provides a response action, and the item is complete. In CBT, however, the testing software can interact with the test taker by responding to the test taker entered response in some way, such as giving feedback, branching to particular follow-up items, or performing a simulation based on information specified by the test taker. Collectively, the four dimensions could define a virtually unbounded number of innovative item types that can provide tests involving a wide array of task complexity.

Adaptive Testing

Unlike a traditional test, in which a group of test takers all receive a common predetermined set of test items, a CAT selects items individually for each test taker based on the test taker responses to previous items. As a result, each test taker in a group may receive a unique set of items drawn from a larger item pool. Lower achieving test takers will receive less difficult items, while higher achievers will receive more difficult items. This raises the psychometric issue of how to compare the achievement levels of a set of students if they all take tests of different average difficulty. This is accomplished using IRT, which provides the psychometric basis for scoring a CAT. In IRT, a test taker's score is a function of both the characteristics (e.g., difficulty) of the items administered and how the test taker did on those items. Of particular importance to a CAT is the IRT principle of item invariance, which states that a test taker's expected score would be invariant across any subset of items administered from a larger set. This implies that the scores of different test takers on a CAT can be compared because they are on the same measurement scale.

Selection of items on a CAT depends on two other features of IRT. First, both the difficulty of test items and the achievement levels of test takers are represented on the same scale. Second, the closer an item's difficulty lies to a test taker's achievement level, the more informative it is in measuring that individual. The psychometric goal of a CAT item selection is to match item difficulty to a test taker whose achievement level is initially unknown. It accomplishes this task by calculating a provisional achievement level estimate after each scoring item response and then selecting and administering an item well matched to that provisional estimate.

The use of a CAT has two favorable outcomes. First, testing becomes materially more efficient because test takers have administered items that are tailored to their achievement levels. As a result, a general rule of thumb is that a CAT can attain measurement precision equivalent to a fixed-item test in about half as many items. Put another way, within a given testing time, a CAT can yield scores that are much more precise than those from fixed-item tests. A second outcome is that a CAT can yield scores of similar precision for all test takers. This contrasts with fixed-item tests, for which test takers in the extremes of a test taker achievement distribution are typically measured less precisely than those in the middle.

Several variations in the basic CAT model have been proposed. Notable among them are multi-stage tests, in which the testing algorithm adapts after item sets rather than after single items, computerized classification tests, which are designed to classify test takers into proficiency categories, and self-adapted tests, in which test takers are permitted to select the difficulty level of each item they receive.

Enhanced Administration Control and Data Collection

It is desirable to exert control over the administration of test items because it helps standardize a test event and reduces the likelihood of construct-irrelevant factors affecting the validity of inferences made on the basis of test scores. In paper-and-pencil testing, a substantial amount of standardization is possible; test instructions, timing, and the physical environment are all under the control of the test administrator. Some aspects of testing, however, are usually not controllable. Test takers can choose how they take the test by skipping items, omitting answers, reviewing items, and possibly changing previously entered answers. Such test-taking behavior is an essentially uncontrollable consequence of the use of group-based paper-and-pencil testing. With CBT, in contrast, much more administrative control is possible, and test givers can decide the degree to which they will allow test takers to control the way they answer the items. For example, it is not uncommon for CBT to require a test taker to answer an item before the user moves on to the next item or to not allow item review. Such a degree of control may or may not be desirable, however, as some test givers prefer highly controlled test administration, while others prefer to provide test takers the same

amount of control as with paper-and-pencil tests (particularly if both CBT and paper-and-pencil versions of the same test are being used).

One advantage of CBT is its ability to collect more information about a test event than is available with paper-and-pencil testing. One important example is CBT's capability to record how long test takers spend responding to individual items. Item response time has been found to be related to a test taker's achievement level, cognitive processing speed, and test-taking engagement. Information about other behaviors such as whether test takers review their answers and how often answers were changed can provide useful insights about how people take tests, which can guide test development. Numerous other types of measures of test takers are potentially available when CBT is used, including eye tracking (which may indicate degree of test taker engagement) or biometric data (which can be useful in measuring test anxiety).

Accessibility Features

Testing software can provide a variety of accessibility features for test takers with disabilities. Moreover, many of these features can be provided in CBT with less variability than those provided by human educators. Such features include screen magnification/enlargement, text-to-speech, answer masking, and line readers.

Logistical Issues

Use of CBT can provide a number of logistical benefits to a testing program. When objective test formats are used, CBT can immediately score a test. While this capability is necessary for adaptive testing, the ability to provide immediate scoring is desirable in all types of CBT. Whenever test takers and educators can be provided immediate feedback about test performance, instructional information becomes much more timely and actionable than is typically the case with paper-and-pencil tests. In addition, the use of CBT allows more flexibility in test administration. Standardized test administration can be maintained while testing students at different times, in different locations, and on a variety of computers/devices. Moreover, online (i.e., Internet-based) tests allow test taking to occur at home or at other locations outside of school.

A number of security concerns associated with paper-and-pencil tests are alleviated with CBT. There are no test booklets that must be kept secure and accounted for at all times by test givers. Similarly, there are no concerns about the reliability of shipping test forms. It should be noted, however, that CBT is not inherently a more secure way to test, as CBT brings with it a new set of security concerns.

Limitations

The powerful advantages of CBT should be considered relative to its limitations. In general, CBT requires more planning and resources than paper-and-pencil tests. In addition, its use can threaten the validity of inferences made on the basis of test scores by the introduction of new construct-irrelevant factors.

Higher Costs and Logistical Demands

Relative to paper-and-pencil testing, considerable up-front resources are required to develop and implement a computerized testing program. Software for administering CBT must be developed or purchased, and computerized versions of items must be developed, along with scoring capabilities. For CAT programs, the item needs are usually sizable, as a large IRT-calibrated item pool will be needed for the CAT to operate effectively. There will be an accompanying need for adequate computer hardware for administering CBT. It is likely that computers will need to be purchased, and additional hardware will be needed for connectivity if online testing is used.

After CBT has been developed, there will be an additional set of ongoing challenges associated with maintaining the program. School computer resources typically vary in terms of type of computers (or other computer device), processing speed and memory, operating systems (both in type and version), connectivity, and Internet browser type and version. Although the test giver may be able to specify some minimum necessary hardware and software requirements needed for delivery of the computer-based test, it will typically be the case that such a test will need to be capable of running on a variety of computer configurations. Moreover, these configurations will continue to evolve over time as newer versions of operating systems and browsers are released.

Administration of CBT brings with it a set of logistical challenges. It will often be the case that the number of students to be tested far exceeds the number of available computers, resulting in multiple testing sessions being needed throughout a testing window. This raises additional security concerns, as students already tested may pass information on to students yet to be tested. In addition, when online testing is used, testing capability is dependent on the quality of the Internet connections. These connections can be slowed or disrupted, resulting in online testing typically having an element of risk that is not present in paper-and-pencil testing.

Comparability Issues

Whenever a test is administered in different modalities, it is important that it yield scores with comparable meaning across modality. In the context of CBT, there are several types of comparability that may need to be considered, including across delivery modes (i.e., CBT vs. paper-and-pencil), as well as across different operating systems, browser types, or computer/device types. The general concern is that the way test takers interact with their test items in CBT can be affected by a variety of factors such as screen size, screen resolution, font type and size, and item display time. Different modalities can vary on these factors, and if comparability is not present, test score validity can be threatened.

Comparability poses a continual challenge for CBT programs, which have a responsibility for evaluating and ensuring comparability. Because there are many types of comparability to consider, test givers have to devote substantial attention and resources to the issue. Moreover, the compatibility issue continues to pose an ongoing challenge throughout the life of a CBT program, as new types of devices, operating systems, and connectivity continue to emerge and require new comparability studies.

Construct-Irrelevant Factors

CBT is potentially vulnerable to several additional construct-irrelevant factors that do not affect paper-and-pencil testing. Test takers with limited experience using computers at home may be at a disadvantage when taking a computer-based test. Some test takers may experience anxiety when using computers. Others may have difficulty understanding how to use the features of the computer testing software. Each of these factors may degrade test takers' ability to demonstrate what they know and can do.

Steven L. Wise

See also Achievement Tests; Computerized Adaptive Testing; Diagnostic Tests; Item Banking; Performance-Based Assessment; Technology in Classroom Assessment; Technology-Enhanced Items; Test Security; Validity

Further Readings

Bennett, R. E. (2003, October). *Online assessment and the comparability of score meaning.* Paper presented at the International Association for Educational Assessment Annual conference, Manchester, UK.

Bunderson, C. V., Inouye, D. K., & Olsen, J. B. (1989). The four generations of computerized educational measurement. In R. L. Linn (Ed.), *Educational Measurement* (3rd ed., pp. 367–407). New York, NY: American Council on Education.

Drasgow, F., Luecht, R. M., & Bennett, R. (2006). Technology and testing. In R. L. Brennan (Ed.), *Educational measurement* (4th ed., pp. 471–515). Washington, DC: American Council on Education.

Drasgow, F., & Olson-Buchanan, J. B. (Eds.). (1999). *Innovations in computerized assessment.* Mahwah, NJ: Erlbaum.

Huff, K. L., & Sireci, S. G. (2001). Validity issues in computer-based testing. *Educational Measurement: Issues and Practice, 20(3),* 16–25.

Mills, C. N., Potenza, M. T., Fremer, J. J., & Ward, W. C. (2002). *Computer-based testing: Building the foundation for future assessments.* Mahwah, NJ: Erlbaum.

Parshall, C. G., Spray, J. A., Kalohn, J. C., & Davey, T. (2002). *Practical considerations in computer-based testing.* New York, NY: Springer-Verlag.

Scalise, K., & Gifford, B. (2006). Computer-based assessment in E-learning: A framework for constructing "intermediate constraint" questions and tasks for technology platforms. *The Journal of Technology, Learning and Assessment, 4(6).*

Thurlow, M., Lazarus, S. S., Albus, D., & Hodgson, J. (2010). *Computer-based testing: Practices and considerations* (Synthesis Report 78). Minneapolis, MN: University of Minnesota, National Center on Educational Outcomes.

Wise, S. L., & Kingsbury, G. G. (2000). Practical issues in developing and maintaining a computerized adaptive testing program. *Psicológica, 21,* 135–155.

COMPUTERIZED ADAPTIVE TESTING

Computerized adaptive testing (CAT) is a method of sequentially selecting test items or larger test units in real time so that the final difficulty of each test form is optimally matched to the proficiency of each examinee. This tailoring of a test form by difficulty to each examinee's proficiency helps ensure an accurate final score using as few test items as possible. The statistical efficiency of a CAT is therefore realized by reduced test lengths and less testing time and/or improved score accuracy relative to a fixed-test form where every examinee is administered the same items.

Various applications of adaptive testing are found in educational achievement testing, placement, and college readiness, for a variety of psychological tests and aptitude tests, and in many types of employment and certification/licensure tests. This entry provides an overview of the assessment technologies underlying CAT as well as discussing different varieties of adaptive testing.

Key Features of Computerized Adaptive Tests

Most paper-and-pencil test forms comprise a fixed number of test items. These fixed test forms are typically constructed by test developers to meet a set of specifications comprising a content *blueprint* that indicates the proportional representation of content on each test form and statistical requirements such as the target test difficulty and minimum reliability (e.g., minimum score precision per form). All examinees assigned to a particular test form see exactly the same test items—usually in the same position.

CAT replaces the paradigm of using *fixed* test forms with one using *variable* test forms that are uniquely customized for each examinee.

Theoretically, under CAT, every individual can receive a test form uniquely designed to match his or her proficiency. One of the earliest adaptive testing paradigms was proposed in 1971 by Frederic Lord, who investigated flexilevel testing as a precursor to CAT. Fixed test booklets contained items arranged in order of difficulty. An examinee would start the flexilevel test in the midrange of difficulty and take easier items each time the examinee answered the current item incorrectly, or conversely, a more difficult item for each correct answer. This same principle underlies most CATs in operational use, today. Figure 1 provides an overview of a slightly more sophisticated (and modern) CAT algorithm.

As shown in Figure 1, the CAT is typically initiated by selecting and administering a small number of preselected test items to provide a preliminary estimate of the examinee's proficiency score. That preliminary proficiency score is then used to select easier or more difficult test items, similar to the logic of a flexilevel test. (The actual maximum information criterion used for optimally selecting the next item is discussed later in this entry.) The selected item is then administered, a new provisional proficiency score is estimated, and another item is selected. The process continues until a fixed test length or some other designated stopping criterion has been reached—a criterion usually related to decision accuracy or to the precision of the estimated proficiency score.

Despite the seeming simplicity of the CAT algorithm shown in Figure 1, it is important to understand that the phrase *computerized adaptive testing* actually refers to many different types of computer-based test (CBT) delivery models and technologies. Two factors tend to distinguish most types of adaptive test: (1) the size and nature of the test units selected and (2) the actual test unit selection/test form assembly and scoring mechanisms employed. In addition, there are a number of subtle variations on the theme of item-level CAT, such as Wim van der Linden's *shadow testing*, a method of ensuring extended control over the content balance and quality of each customized test form, and *stratified CAT*, a method that attempts to buffer the overexposure of "statistically popular" items in the item bank.

Nature of the Test Units

CBT delivery and modern high-speed, high-bandwidth digital data transmission capabilities have greatly expanded the potential repertoire of item types that can be administered—going beyond multiple-choice, short-answer, and constructed response essays typically encountered on paper-and-pencil test forms. Exploiting the

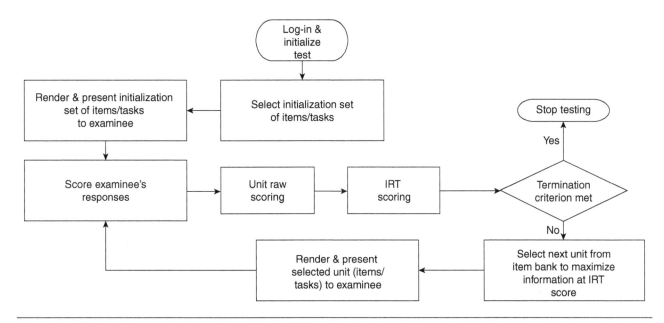

Figure 1   A basic computerized adaptive testing (CAT) algorithm

sophistication of modern graphical computer interfaces, multiple input devices (keyboard, mouse, touch screen, and voice recognition), and new response-capturing capabilities, a vast array of CBT item types is possible. This array includes multiple-choice and similar selected response item types, problem-based item sets, various technology-enhanced item types such as "hot spot" and "drag-and-drop" items, open-ended constructed response item types that collect text-based inputs or specific outputs such as the graph of a mathematical function, and complex work simulations involving highly interactive software applications containing drawing tools, programming and design interfaces, spreadsheets, calculators, and search engines.

In addition, almost any of these item discrete types can be combined and preassembled with additional stimulus materials and auxiliary software components to present to each examinee with larger, intact units. For example, two or more items can refer to a reading passage, a graphic or another type of stimulus material. These self-contained units are usually called *testlets*. When the testlets are adaptively selected, they can be called *testlet-based CATs*. Items and CBT performance tasks can be further combined using detailed content and statistical specifications to form preassembled modules that differ in overall difficulty—and that possibly differ in content, as well. The modules are then preassigned as self-adaptive test units called *panels*.

Adaptive Test Assembly and Scoring

As noted earlier, CAT assembles a customized test form for every examinee in real time. The items or tasks are selected from a database called an *item bank*. The item bank typically contains five types of data about each item: (1) the item text and other rendering data that is used by the testing software (called the *CBT driver*) to present the item to the test takers and capture their response; (2) the answer keys or other response scoring mechanisms; (3) item content codes, cognitive codes, and other nonpsychometric data used by the test assembly algorithm; (4) item response theory (IRT) item parameter estimates; and (5) item exposure control parameters or constraints.

The test assembly can occur in real time—that is, while the examinee is actually taking the test—or at least partially in advance of testing where preconstructed testlets or modules are prepared by the test developers and administered in the real time as larger, intact units. An adaptive test is basically an iterative three-step process (see Figure 1). First, an item (or larger test unit) is selected by an assembly algorithm. Second, the item is administered. Third, the examinee's responses are scored and the new provisional score is used to select the next item or test unit. Key to both adaptive test assembly and scoring is an underlying metric or scale that can link the statistical difficulty and other psychometric characteristics of all of the items to the apparent performance and ultimate scoring of the examinees. That is where IRT comes into play.

Most multiple-choice or selected response items are dichotomously scored (i.e., scored correct or incorrect) and employ the one-, two-, or three-parameter logistic IRT models—often abbreviated as 1PL, 2PL, or 3PL models. These IRT models make it possible for the statistical characteristics of the items such as item difficulty to be calibrated relative to a common scale called theta (and typically represented by the Greek letter θ). For example, the more general 3PL model mathematically expresses the probability of a correct response to an item as:

$$Pr(u_i = 1 \mid \theta; a_i, b, c_i) \equiv P_i(\theta) = c_i$$
$$+ (1 - c_i)\{1 - \exp[-a_i(\theta - b)]\}^{-1}, \quad (1)$$

where $u_i = 1$ is a correct binary scored item response, θ is the proficiency scale, a_i is a discrimination parameter that denotes the sensitivity of each item to the proficiency scale, b_i is the item difficulty parameter that locates each item along the proficiency scale, and c_i is a pseudo-guessing parameter that helps fit inconsistent or noisy response patterns near the lower regions of the θ. That is, the lower asymptote of the IRT probability function is governed by c_i. As the examinee's proficiency, θ, increases, the probability of a correct response, $P_i(\theta)$, increases, approaching 1.0 for examinees with very high proficiency scores. The actual item parameters are estimated using IRT calibration software. More complex IRT models are also available for item types that use polytomous scoring such as integers 0, 1, 2, . . . , or for testlets.

Once the items are calibrated using IRT, examinees can all be scored on the common θ scale regardless of whether they were administered an easy, moderately difficult, or difficult test form. As noted earlier, this is an essential component of any adaptive test: the capability to actually score the examinees on a common scale regardless of the difficulty of their test form. IRT conveniently provides that capability.

If the 3PL IRT model is used, the item bank will contain a_i, b_i, and, c_i parameter estimates for all $i = 1, . . . , I$ items in the bank. If the 2PL model is used, only the a_i and b_i parameter estimates are stored (i.e., $c_i = 0.0$ for all items). The most simplistic 1PL model only uses the b_i parameter because $a_i = 1.0$ and $c_i = 0.0$ for all items. In addition to the IRT parameter estimates, the item bank may also contain item exposure control parameters that are used to restrict the overexposure of the best items, as well as various content and other coded item attributes that may be used by the CAT item selection algorithm.

In order to understand how the actual adaptive test assembly takes place, we first need to understand IRT scoring. There are three types of IRT scores: (1) maximum likelihood (ML) scores; (2) Bayes mean scores—often called *expected a posteriori* scores; and (3) Bayes modal scores—usually called modal *a posteriori* scores. For example, modal a posteriori scores can be estimated as:

$$\hat{\theta}_{u_{i_1},...,u_{i_{k-1}}} \equiv \max_{\theta}\left\{g\left(\theta \mid u_{i_1},...,u_{i_{k-1}}\right) : \theta \in (-\infty,\infty)\right\}, (2)$$

where the value of θ at maximum of the posterior likelihood function, $g\left(\theta \mid u_{i_1},...,u_{i_{k-1}}\right)$, is the model estimate of θ.

Classification-based scores (e.g., nonmaster/ master) can also be computed under certain types of IRT latent class models. A comprehensive discussion of classification scoring methods, maximum likelihood, expected a posteriori, and modal a posteriori scores, is beyond the scope of this entry. Suffice to say, as long as the IRT item parameter estimates used for scoring are calibrated to a common scale, the ensuing estimates of θ for all examinees will be on the same scale, as well.

An adaptive test assembly or item selection algorithm uses the provisional proficiency estimate of θ as the basis for locating the optimal next item to administer to the current examinee. That is, if we let $\hat{\theta}_{u_{i_1},...,u_{i_{k-1}}}$ denoted the provisional proficiency score estimate based on accumulated responses for $k - 1$ items administered up to that point in the test (i.e., for raw-scored item responses $u_{i_1},...,u_{i_{k-1}}$), then the next item or test unit is then selected from the unused segment of the item bank, R_k, to satisfy the function:

$$i_k \equiv \max_{j}\left\{I_{u_j}\left(\hat{\theta}_{u_{i_1},...,u_{i_{k}}}\right) : j \in R_k\right\}. \quad (3)$$

Equation 3 chooses the next item with the maximum information at the provisional θ estimate. To accomplish that, we need *an item information function*. The concept of an item information function was introduced by Allan Birnbaum in 1968 and relates to the precision that each item provides with response to a given scoring function. For the 1PL, 2PL, and 3PL IRT models described earlier, the item information function can be written as:

$$I_i(\theta) = \left\{P_i(\theta)\left[1 - P_i(\theta)\right]\right\}^{-1}\left[\partial P_i(\theta)/\partial\theta\right]^2, \quad (4)$$

where ∂ denotes the first partial derivative of the IRT probability function, $P_i(\theta)$—see Equation 1. The probability function and associated first derivative terms change for each of the IRT models. For example, the 3PL item information function can be written as:

$$I_i(\theta) = \left\{a_i^2\left[1 - P_i(\theta)\right]\left[P_i(\theta) - c\right]^2\right\}\left[P_i(\theta)(1-c)^2\right]^{-1}, \quad (5)$$

(also see Equation 1), with obvious simplifications for the 2PL and 1PL models. Equation 3, which chooses the (unselected) item from the item bank with the maximum information at the provisional estimate of θ, can therefore be implemented by inserting into Equation 5 the requisite item parameter estimates and score estimate.

Consider the item information functions for four sample items shown in Figure 2. The associated 3PL item parameters are $a_1 = 1.1$, $b_1 = -1.5$, $c_1 = 0.12$ for Item 1; $a_2 = 0.9$, $b_2 = -0.5$, $c_2 = 0.12$ for Item 2; $a_3 = 0.8$, $b_3 = 0.5$, $c_3 = 0.12$ for Item 3; and $a_4 = 1.3$, $b_4 = 1.5$, $c_4 = 0.12$ for Item 4.

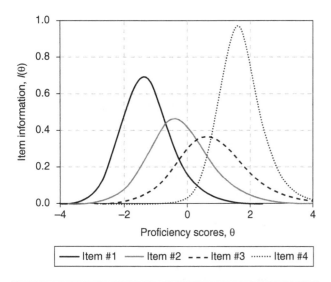

Figure 2 Item response theory (IRT) item information functions for 4 items

Based on the maximum information criterion for adaptive selection, we can visually confirm that Item 1 would most likely be chosen as most informative for examinees with proficiency scores below −0.67. Item 2 would be chosen for examinees with provisional proficiency scores falling within the interval −0.67 ≤ θ < 0.33, Item 3 would be selected for examinees with scores in the interval 0.33 ≤ θ < 0.8, and Item 4 would be selected for examinees demonstrating proficiency at or above 0.8.

Another interesting implication of Figure 2 is the relatively small range of θ where information is maximal for Items 2 and 3. In both cases, the lower *a* parameters (0.9 and 0.8, respectively) reduce the effective range of adaptive utility for those 2 items. Conversely, Items 1 and 4 are more informative over a wide range of the proficiency scale. However, the increased utility of those 2 items also increases their likely exposure (overuse) within the examinee population. This point is briefly addressed in the following.

The test unit size being selected does not alter the basic adaptive algorithm shown earlier in Figure 1 because the item information (Equations 4 and 5) is additive across items or test units. That is, if we create a new test unit as a collection of 5 items, the information for those 5 items can be summed and used for selection.

IRT item information functions directly contribute to the overall precision of the θ score estimates. That is, under IRT, the conditional measurement error variance of estimated proficiency scores is inversely proportional to the test information function (TIF) which is the sum of the item information functions. That is, the error variance of estimate of the proficiency scores is inversely proportional to the TIF:

$$\sigma^2(\hat{\theta} \mid \theta) = \left[\sum_{i=1}^{n} I_i(\theta) \right]^{-1}, \qquad (6)$$

where $I_i(\theta)$ is the item information function at some estimate $\hat{\theta}$ of the proficiency score of interest. As noted earlier, the exact mathematical form of the information function varies by IRT model (e.g., see Equation 5 for the 3PL item information function). Each item adds some information to the TIF. The more item information we add to each examinee's adaptive test, the smaller we force the error variance to be. This reduction in the error variance is the ultimate goal of most adaptive test algorithms.

Figure 3 shows what happens to the provisional proficiency scores and associated standard errors (the square root of the error variance from Equation 3) for five hypothetical examinees each taking a sequence of 100 adaptively administered items. These hypothetical examinees are each at a

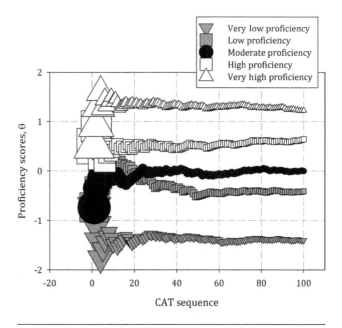

Figure 3 Expected *a posteriori* (EAP) θ score estimates for five examinees each taking a 100-item computerized adaptive testing (CAT)

different level of proficiency (*very low* θ, *low* θ, *moderate* θ, *high* θ, and *very high* θ). Because of their proficiency differences, each examinee saw a different sequence of 100 items. For example, the very low proficiency examinee saw an easier set of items than the low proficiency examinees. The very high proficiency examinee saw the most difficult set of items. Note that the plotted estimated θ scores are IRT expected a posteriori scores mentioned earlier.

The item pool used for this example comprises 600 items. The proficiency scale is shown as the vertical axis (−2.0 to +2.0). The sequence of 100 adaptively administered items is shown on the horizontal scale. Each plotted symbol is located at the current, provisional estimated θ. The size of each symbols is directly proportional to the standard error of estimate—that is, the square root of the TIF-based error variance from Equation 6. The standard errors are extremely large early in the CAT sequences, but eventually become quite small as more items are administered. All five examinees start with proficiency score estimates near zero, but then, the provisional estimates tend to fluctuate quite a bit. The trajectories of the estimated proficiency scores soon begin to separate for the five examinees after approximately 15 items are administered and tend to fully stabilize at 50–60 items. The standard errors continue to decrease in magnitude for the entire CAT sequence, as evidenced by the decreasing symbol sizes.

In practice, an adaptive test can achieve maximum test information (and minimum standard errors of estimate) in two ways. One way is to choose highly discriminating items that provide maximum item information within particular regions of the proficiency scale or at specific proficiency scores (e.g., see Figure 2). Or, we can merely continue adding items to increment the amount of information until a desired level of precision is achieved. Maximizing the test information at each examinee's score is tantamount to choosing a customized, optimally reliable test for each examinee.

However, maximizing the information may overexpose certain items within the examinee population. This is especially serious for testing programs that use the same item bank over extended periods of time. Overexposure of test items implies that some portion of items in the item bank are administered too often and can be easily be memorized and shared with examines testing at some later date. Almost any type of high-stakes use of test scores (e.g., granting entrance into graduate school, awarding scholarships, providing access to a highly coveted course placement, getting a high-paying or prestigious job, obtaining a professional license or certificate) must consider the possibility that there could be a group of cheaters intent on beating the odds (of random chance or luck) by employing well-thought-out strategies that provide them with any possible advantage of even slightly raising their scores. One of the most common security risks in high-stakes CAT involves groups of examinees collaborating to memorize and share items, especially when the same item database is active over a long period of time, and testing is nearly continuous during that time period.

There are methods of mitigating the overexposure risks. One approach is to increase the size of the active item database to reduce the likelihood of selecting a particular item. A second approach is to build different versions of the item bank that can be rotated in and out of active use over time. The third approach involves a modification to the CAT item selection algorithm. Extensive simulations are used to estimate item control parameters for all items in the bank. Those item control parameters are then used with a relatively simple probabilistic mechanism to buffer the likelihood of always choosing the most informative items. A more extensive discussion of item exposure controls is beyond the scope of this entry.

Concluding Comments

As presented in this entry, CAT is far more than a simple test delivery algorithm—it is a multifaceted collection of algorithms, test designs, and technologies for creating more efficiency tests. There is no single CAT delivery model or framework that universally works "best" for every application. But, CAT is continually evolving to incorporate new assessment applications or purposes and to take advantage of new CBT and psychometric technologies.

Richard M. Luecht

See also Cheating; Computer-Based Testing; Item Banking; Item Information Function; Testlet Response Theory

Further Readings

Birnbaum, A. (1968). Estimation of an ability. In F. M. Lord & M. R. Novick (Eds.), *Statistical theories of mental test scores* (pp. 423–479). Reading, MA: Addison-Wesley.

Drasgow, F. (Ed.). (2016). *Technology and testing: Improving educational and psychological measurement.* New York, NY: Routledge.

Drasgow, F., Luecht, R. M., & Bennett, R. (2006). Technology and testing. In R. L. Brennan (Ed.), *Educational measurement* (4th ed., pp. 471–515). Washington, DC: American Council on Education/Praeger Publishers.

Hambleton, R. K., & Swaminathan, H. R. (1985). *Item response theory: Principles and applications.* Hingham, MA: Kluwer.

Lord, F. M. (1980). *Applications of item response theory to practical testing problems.* Hillsdale, NJ: Erlbaum.

Luecht, R. M. (2014). Computerized adaptive multistage design considerations and operational issues. In D. Yan, A. A. von Davier, & C. Lewis (Eds.), *Computerized multistage testing: Theory and applications* (pp. 69–83). New York, NY: Taylor & Francis.

Luecht, R. M., & Sireci, S. G. (2011). *A review of models for computer-based testing.* New York, NY: The College Board (Research Report, 2011–2012).

Mislevy, R. J. (1986). Bayesian modal estimation in item response models. *Psychometrika, 86,* 177–195.

Parshall, C. G., Spray, J. A., Kalohn, J. C., & Davey, T. (2002). *Practical considerations in computer-based testing.* New York, NY: Springer.

Sands, W. A., Waters, B. K., & McBride, J. R. (Eds.). (1997). *Computerized adaptive testing: From inquiry to operation.* Washington, DC: American Psychological Association.

Segall, D. O. (2010). Principles of multidimensional adaptive testing. In W. J. van der Linden & C. A. W. Glas (Eds.), *Elements of adaptive testing* (pp. 57–76). New York, NY: Springer.

van der Linden, W. J., & Glas, C. E. W. (2010). *Elements of adaptive testing.* New York, NY: Springer.

Yan, D., von Davier, A. A., & Lewis, C. (Eds.). *Computerized multistage testing: Theory and applications.* London, UK: CRC Press.

Concept Mapping

Concept maps are node-and-link diagrams that represent the key terms and relations among terms within a set of materials. *Concept mapping* refers to the activity of creating a concept map. There are a variety of ways to create concept maps, but all share common elements: People construct concept maps by identifying key terms or ideas, placing those key terms in nodes, drawing lines that link related terms, and writing a description of the nature of the relation along the link. Figure 1 shows an example of a concept map created by a college student while they read a text about the composition of blood. No sophisticated tools are needed to create concept maps—pencil and paper will suffice—but several computer programs have been developed to aid in the creation of concept maps. Concept mapping is done in educational settings in a variety of ways, from students creating concept maps as they study on their own (e.g., while they read a textbook) to teachers and students constructing maps as a collaborative classroom activity. Concept mapping may be used for a wide variety of purposes, including creative brainstorming, note-taking, outlining, and—the focus of this entry—as an activity intended to promote learning. Concept mapping enjoys widespread popularity in educational settings and among the general public.

Concept Mapping and Related Techniques

Concept maps bear a surface resemblance to semantic networks developed in cognitive psychology in the early 1970s. Such network models depict semantic knowledge as a set of interconnected nodes and assume that when one idea or concept is activated, the activation spreads throughout the network to other related notes. In the late 1970s, Joseph Novak developed concept mapping as a pedagogical tool. The original intent of concept mapping was to track students' conceptual change over time. For example, a student's knowledge about the composition of blood may change over the course of a semester-long anatomy

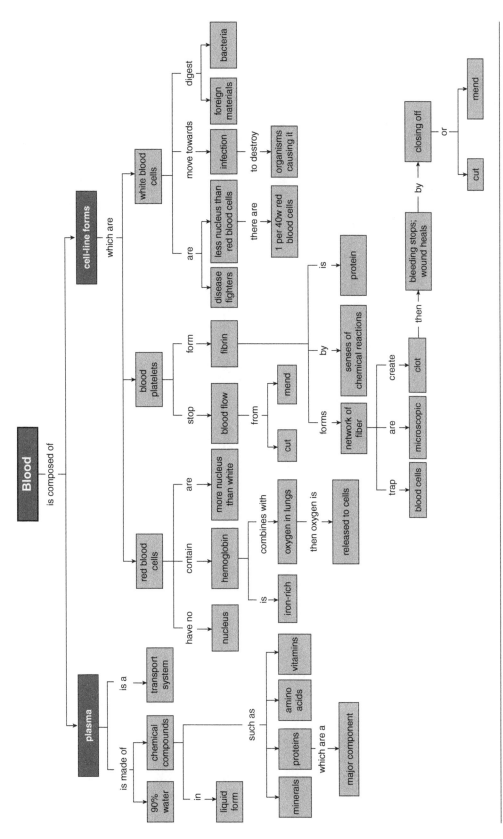

Figure I Example of a concept map created by a student in an experiment by Karpicke and Blunt (2011)

class, and such changes would be reflected in the changing organization of concept maps produced by the student at different points in the semester. An assumption behind concept mapping is that when learners express their knowledge on a concept map, they express more, or express knowledge differently, relative to what they would express on a different assessment.

Concept mapping shares similarities with other mapping techniques, all of which can be considered types of *graphic organizers*. In a technique known as *knowledge mapping*, students create node-and-link diagrams, just as they do in concept mapping, but must use a predefined set of relations to do so (e.g., "part," "type," "example"). There is no universal agreement about whether concept maps and knowledge maps are functionally similar activities, and no direct comparisons exist in the literature. *Mind mapping* is another technique that also involves representing knowledge in a node-and-link diagram, but mind maps typically center on a single concept (node) with several associated images and ideas radiating from this central node. Likewise, causal maps and flowcharts represent knowledge in node-and-link diagrams. While concept maps may represent cause-and-effect relations, concept mapping is generally considered to be different from mind maps, causal maps, and flowcharts.

Evaluating Concept Maps

A great deal of debate has focused on the most meaningful and informative ways to evaluate students' concept maps. Perhaps the most straightforward way to assess a concept map is to tally the number of *idea units* represented on the map, whereby an idea unit is a proposition that expresses an idea or concept. For example, in the map in Figure 1, "blood is composed of plasma" was scored as one correct idea unit. Evaluations of concept maps can become considerably more sophisticated than this simple example, when one begins to consider the number of nodes, the number of links, and the overall organizational structure of links on a map. In a map like the one in Figure 1, nodes exist in different levels of a hierarchy, and students may identify *cross-links*, where a node in one section or level of a map is linked to a node in a different section or level. The presence

of cross-links on a student's map is thought to represent relatively deeper knowledge and insight about a domain.

Claims About Concept Mapping

The chief claim about concept mapping is that concept maps improve learning, but many additional claims about concept mapping have appeared in the literature and popular media. Concept mapping has been proposed to stimulate brainstorming and the generation of new ideas, aid in creativity, improve metacognitive monitoring (the self-assessment of one's own knowledge), enhance critical thinking, and serve as an effective note-taking technique. Many of these claims have not been thoroughly examined in experimental or quasi-experimental research, for instance, by comparing a concept map condition to a plausible control condition and determining whether concept mapping improves the outcome of interest (e.g., idea generation or metacognitive accuracy). All of the claims mentioned here are plausible and perhaps true; but without more thorough research, no firm conclusions can be drawn.

One claim that has been examined in experimental research is that concept mapping improves students' affect, self-efficacy, and motivation. A 2006 meta-analysis of concept mapping research identified six papers that examined these outcomes, all of which reported positive effects of concept mapping. This represents promising support for the effectiveness of concept mapping in promoting students' affect, self-efficacy, and motivation, but given the relatively small number of studies in the literature, further exploration is warranted.

Mechanisms of Concept Mapping: Why Should Concept Mapping Promote Learning?

It is worth considering why concept mapping should be expected to promote learning. Although there is a fairly extensive research base on concept mapping, few studies have targeted the underlying cognitive processes that learners might engage in when they create concept maps. In the basic cognitive science literature, it is well established that a combination of *relational* and *item-specific processing* supports effective and durable encoding. Relational processing refers to tasks in which learners consider how items are similar to one another, whereas item-specific processing refers to tasks that emphasize how items are distinctive, unique, or different from one another. When trying to learn new information, engaging in both relational and item-specific encoding is a recipe for a robust mental model of the material.

Concept mapping would seem to emphasize relational processing by focusing on how terms are similar to one another and how ideas fit together within an organizational structure. The concept map shown in Figure 1 appears to provide a clear depiction of the overall relational structure of the text. It is possible that concept mapping also promotes distinctive or item-specific processing; perhaps this would be especially true when learners create cross-links or links that emphasize the distinctiveness of terms within categories. However, the literature is sparse when it comes to discussion of possible encoding mechanisms that concept mapping might afford.

One recent study, reported in 2015, examined the effects of concept mapping on relational and item-specific knowledge and suggested that some concept mapping activities may be detrimental to item-specific encoding. Standard concept mapping instructions emphasize that learners should form many relations among items. As a consequence, learners may create overloaded categories in which too many terms become linked to higher level category nodes. Ultimately, the creation of overloaded categories hurts learning performance relative to other study strategies that also encouraged organizational or distinctive processing.

Does Concept Mapping Promote Learning?

The simple question of whether concept mapping promotes learning is not so simple after all because concept mapping is not a single prescribed activity. Concept mapping can be done in a variety of ways. For example, students might study a concept map as an advance organizer before a lesson, perhaps one created by a teacher or one that accompanies a text. Students might create maps while reading, or they might create them after they have read something (as a retrieval practice activity). Students might create maps on their own or in collaboration with other learners. And students might engage in concept mapping activities that offer varying degrees of support. For example, they might have access to a "node bank" that contains the key terms to be used on a map, they might be given a portion of a map and asked to fill out the remainder, or they may engage with an adaptive computer program that assists learners as they build concept maps (e.g., the Betty's Brain intelligent tutoring system).

The most extensive analysis of the effectiveness of concept mapping was a 2006 meta-analysis that identified 55 experimental and quasi-experimental studies of concept mapping and knowledge mapping. In general, concept mapping produced positive effects on measures of student learning. The largest effects were observed in studies that compared concept mapping to relatively passive control conditions, like listening to material in lecture format. Studying concept maps produced small but positive effects on learning relative to studying by reading texts or outlines. In studies that compared concept mapping to other active control conditions (e.g., creating an outline rather than simply reading an outline), concept mapping showed even smaller but, nonetheless, positive effects on learning. In short, concept mapping tends to benefit learning, but the size of the effect depends on whether concept mapping is compared against passive or more active control conditions.

Future Directions

As noted earlier, concept mapping remains very popular in a range of educational and applied settings. However, many of the central claims about concept mapping require further research and investigation. Many studies have shown positive effects of concept mapping on learning, but there is a continuing need to identify the most effective ways to structure concept map activities to support effective encoding and promote learning.

Jeffrey D. Karpicke

Further Readings

Biswas, G., Segedy, J. R., & Bunchongchit, K. (2015). From design to implementation to practice a learning by teaching system: Betty's Brain. *International Journal of Artificial Intelligence in Education*.

Blunt, J. R., & Karpicke, J. D. (2014). Learning with retrieval-based concept mapping. *Journal of Educational Psychology, 106*(3), 849–858. doi:10.1037/a0035934

Collins, A. M., & Loftus, E. F. (1975). A spreading-activation theory of semantic processing. *Psychological Review, 82*(6), 407–428. doi:10.1037/0033-295x.82.6.407

Grimaldi, P. J., Poston, L., & Karpicke, J. D. (2015). How does creating a concept map affect item-specific encoding? *Journal of Experimental Psychology: Learning, Memory, and Cognition, 41*(4), 1049–1061. doi:10.1037/xlm0000076

Hunt, R. R. (2012). Distinctive processing: The co-action of similarity and difference in memory. In B. H. Ross (Ed.), *The psychology of learning and motivation* (Vol. 56, pp. 1–46). San Diego, CA: Elsevier Academic Press.

Karpicke, J. D., & Blunt, J. R. (2011). Retrieval practice produces more learning than elaborative studying with concept mapping. *Science, 331*(6018), 772–775. doi:10.1126/science.1199327

Nesbit, J. C., & Adesope, O. O. (2006). Learning with concept and knowledge maps: A meta-analysis. *Review of Educational Research, 76*(3), 413–448. doi:10.3102/00346543076003413

Novak, J. D., & Cañas, A. J. (2006). *The theory underlying concept maps and how to construct and use them* (Technical Report). Pensacola, FL: Institute for Human and Machine Cognition.

Ruiz-Primo, M. A., & Shavelson, R. J. (1996). Problems and issues in the use of concept maps in science assessment. *Journal of Research in Science Teaching, 33*(6), 569–600. doi:10.1002/(sici)1098-2736

CONCEPTUAL FRAMEWORK

A conceptual framework provides a map of the world a researcher intends to study. It captures what researchers see and how they make sense of what they are exploring. *Concept* means ideas, perceived facts, beliefs, mental pictures, perceptions, and theories. *Framework* indicates basic structure or underlying organizational elements.

Drawing on these definitions, a conceptual framework is an organizing structure or scaffold that integrates related ideas, mental images, other research, and theories to provide focus and direction to the inquiry. It defines the "what"—the substantive focus—of the study and thus serves to guide and direct the on-going decision making required in any research endeavor. Ultimately, the conceptual framework puts forward an argument and establishes the significance of the study. After reviewing the elements that make up conceptual frameworks, this entry explains how to successfully build and then use conceptual frameworks.

Elements

Conceptual frameworks consist of three elements: the researcher's personal experience and viewpoints, existing information and knowledge of the phenomenon under study, and relevant theoretical positions regarding the phenomenon. A clear, well-developed conceptual framework functions as an integrated system that discloses these perspectives, illustrates interrelationships, and establishes boundaries. Any argument or thesis that drives a study emerges from the conceptual framework, and tools for analysis and interpretation are embedded within the framework.

Building a Conceptual Framework

The first element in a conceptual framework for any study begins with the researcher—the researcher's knowledge, experiences, and interests related to the phenomenon. As thinking beings, researchers bring to the topic their interests, preferences, and interpretations. Systematic and rigorous inquiry requires that researchers make these central assumptions or claims explicit: Why have they chosen this topic? Why do they consider it important? What do they know about it already? What attitudes and opinions do the researchers hold regarding the topic? The answers help identify *sensitizing concepts* and *orienting perspectives* that suggest areas for focus, aspects and relationships to explore, possible ways to organize including boundaries to set, as well as *currents of thought* that can inform the inquiry.

The second element in the conceptual system is these currents of thought (i.e., relevant bodies of literature and the existing knowledge) about the phenomenon of interest. Recognizing these extant bodies or currents allows researchers to ground their work in scholarly and public discourse concerning what is already known about the phenomenon. Through the literature, researchers connect their particular interest to a larger, more general interest. Whatever the topic, someone has questioned, researched, or written about the general phenomena under consideration, so researchers critically read research studies, policy writings, reports about practice, evaluations, essays and opinion pieces, newspaper editorials and articles, and even popular communication on the topic. They ask: *What have scholars or "experts" said about this topic? What is the discourse in the public domain? What questions have already been raised or explored? What previous research can be built upon?* Relevant information and knowledge is woven into the framework to ground the study in what is already known, provide substantiation for points, clarify logic, define concepts, and suggest relevant theories.

Finally, the conceptual framework has a theoretical base that further connects the researcher's perspectives, the specific study focus, and the larger scholarly or public conversations about aspects of the phenomenon. A researcher asks: *What theoretical positions have informed my perspectives? What theories might usefully provide insights or direction for the inquiry project?* A theory is a set of propositions that describe, explain, and predict phenomena; it models some aspect of reality. Theory with a capital T consists of what Peter Burke calls an accepted and coherent set of statements, assumptions, or axioms that have been tested and accepted as explanations for particular phenomena. These Theories carry labels (e.g., self-efficacy) and are often attributed to an individual or group of individuals (e.g., Thomas Kuhn's *Structure of Scientific Revolutions*). In addition, many references to theory imply hunches or intuitive propositions believed to guide actions. As Carol Weiss has noted, a theory does not have to be universally accepted or correct; theory can be viewed as a set of working understandings or hypotheses that underlie action and guide analysis and interpretation. Researchers bring *theories* to their studies, and they find *Theories* among the scholarly discourse. Both enlighten and broaden researchers'

perspectives, offer explanations, suggest patterns, and contribute to a generative foundational (i.e., based in theory) conceptual framework.

Using the Conceptual Framework

As previously stated, the conceptual framework defines "what" is to be studied. Specifically, the researcher uses the conceptual framework to

- describe and explain the phenomenon,
- embed the phenomenon in a context,
- construct an argument that articulates perspective,
- generate questions or hypotheses,
- sharpen the focus,
- propose strategies for action,
- provide categories for analysis, and
- link the questions to larger theoretical constructs and policy discussions.

The process of developing the framework is both inductive and deductive. It forces researchers to be explicit about their thinking and intended actions and to integrate their ideas with other research and theory. The framework becomes a selection tool that facilitates a coherent study, that is, a researcher uses it constantly to decide what is important, to explicate rationale and significance, to frame research questions, to choose the "how" (design and method), to choose which data to gather, to provide direction for analysis, and to interpret findings. The process also serves as a catalyst that raises the researchers' thinking from the particular and descriptive to contribute to some larger body of ideas contained in the research, writings, and experiences of others.

Sharon F. Rallis

See also Concept Mapping; Literature Review; Logic Models; Program Theory of Change

Further Readings

Blumer, H. (1954). What's wrong with social theory? *American Sociological Review, 19*(1), 3–10.

Bowen, G. A. (2006). Grounded theory and sensitizing concepts. *International Journal of Qualitative Methods, 5*(3), 2–9.

Burke, P. J. (2009). *The elements of inquiry: A guide for consumers and producers of research* (p. 62). Glendale, CA: Pyrczak.

Leshem, S., & Trafford, V. (2007). Overlooking the conceptual framework. *Innovations in Education and Teaching International, 44*(1), 93–105.

Rallis, S. F., & Rossman, G. B. (2012). *The research journey: Introduction to inquiry* (pp. 85–110). New York, NY: Guilford.

Schram, T. H. (2006). *Conceptualizing and proposing qualitative research* (2nd ed., p. 58). Upper Saddle River, NJ: Pearson Merrill.

Weiss, C. H. (1998). *Evaluation: Methods for studying programs and policies* (2nd ed., p. 55). Upper Saddle River, NJ: Prentice Hall.

Williams, B., & Hummelbrunner, R. (2011). *Systems concepts in action: A practitioner's toolkit* (pp. 18–23). Stanford, CA: Stanford University Press.

CONCURRENT VALIDITY

Concurrent validity refers to the extent to which the results of a measure correlate with the results of an established measure of the same or a related underlying construct assessed within a similar time frame. This entry considers how concurrent validity fits within both the classical framework of validity and Samuel Messick's unitary view of validity and provides examples of its importance and application within educational research.

Place in Validity Framework

In classical views of validity, concurrent validity is a type of criterion validity, which concerns the correlation between a measure and a standard regarded as a representative of the construct under consideration. If the measure is correlated with a future assessment, this is termed *predictive validity*. If the measure is correlated with an assessment in the same general time frame, this is termed *concurrent validity*. Conversely, poor correlation of the measures where correlation would be expected provides evidence against concurrent validity.

This validity concept aligns well with Messick's commonly held unitary view of validity, in which concurrent validity is an example of validity evidence provided by relations to other variables. This type of validity is supported when two measures of the same construct correlate well with one another and called into question when such correlation is not seen.

Importance and Examples Within Educational Research

Understanding correlations among measures of specific constructs is of great importance in educational research. Two examples will illustrate these concepts. First, a criterion standard test of medical knowledge might involve hundreds of examination items administered over many hours. A shorter medical knowledge assessment's concurrent validity could be assessed by evaluating the correlation of results from the shorter examination with results from the criterion standard administered shortly before or after the abbreviated test. A strong correlation would provide evidence of concurrent validity which could then be supplemented by evaluations of other elements of validity. If little correlation was found, however, concurrent validity of the shorter measure would not be supported.

Second, an established instrument for depression diagnosis among medical students might be compared with results from a concurrent assessment of burnout. Strong observed correlation between these two measures would support concurrent validity of the burnout measure with the established depression measure. On the other hand, lack of correlation between the two measures would represent evidence against concurrent validity of the burnout measure in the evaluation of depression.

Colin P. West and Thomas J. Beckman

See also Correlation; Criterion-Based Validity Evidence; Internal Validity; Predictive Validity; Tests; Unitary View of Validity; Validity

Further Readings

American Educational Research Association, American Psychological Association, National Council on Measurement in Education (1999). *Standards for educational and psychological testing.* Washington, DC: American Educational Research Association.

Cook, D. A., & Beckman, T. J. (2006). Current concepts in validity and reliability for psychometric instruments: Theory and application. *American Journal of Medicine, 119*, 166e7–166e16. doi:10.1016/j.amjmed.2005.10.036

Messick, S. (1989). Validity. In R. L. Linn (Ed.), *Educational measurement* (3rd ed.). New York, NY: American Council on Education and Macmillan.

CONDITIONAL INDEPENDENCE

Statistical independence and conditional independence (CI) are important concepts in statistics, artificial intelligence, and related fields. Let X, Y, and Z denote three sets of random variables, and let P denote their probability distribution or density functions. X and Y are conditionally independent given Z, denoted by $X \perp Y \mid Z$, if and only if $P(X, Y \mid Z) = P(X \mid Z)P(Y \mid Z)$. It reflects the fact that given the values of Z, further knowing the values of X does not provide any additional information about Y. Generally speaking, such a CI relationship allows us to drop X when constructing a probabilistic model for Y with (X, Z), resulting in a parsimonious representation. Moreover, independence and CI play a central role in Bayesian network learning and causal discovery, which aims at recovering the underlying causal model from purely observational data.

A direct way to assess if $X \perp Y \mid Z$ is to estimate the involved probability density or distribution functions and then check on whether the definition is satisfied. However, density estimation in high dimensions is known to be difficult: In nonparametric joint or conditional density estimation, due to the curse of dimensionality, to achieve the same accuracy, the number of required data points grows exponentially in the data dimension.

Testing for CI is much more difficult than that for unconditional independence. For CI tests, traditional methods either focus on the discrete case, in which the chi-square test can be used, or impose simplifying assumptions to deal with the continuous case. In particular, the variables are often assumed to have linear relations with additive Gaussian errors. In that case, $X \perp Y \mid Z$ reduces to zero partial correlation or zero conditional correlation between X and Y given Z, which can be easily tested. However, nonlinearity and non-Gaussian noise are frequently encountered in practice and, accordingly, the partial correlation test may lead to incorrect conclusions.

CI is just one particular property associated with the distributions; to test for it, it is possible to avoid explicitly estimating the densities. There exist some ways to characterize the CI relation that do not explicitly involve the densities, and they inspired more efficient methods for CI testing. Note that when (X, Y, Z) is jointly Gaussian, $X \perp Y \mid Z$ is equivalent to the vanishing of the partial correlation coefficient between X and Y given Z. As its generalization, J. J. Daudin showed that in the general case, $X \perp Y \mid Z$ if and only if $f(X, Z) - E[f \mid Z]$ is always uncorrelated with $g(Y) - E[g \mid Z]$ for any square-integrable functions f and g. Here, $E[f \mid Z]$ denotes the conditional mean of $f(X, Z)$ given Z. In this way, CI is characterized by the uncorrelatedness of functions in suitable spaces. Kenji Fukumizu and others showed that one can use the reproducing kernel Hilbert spaces corresponding to the so-called characteristic kernels (e.g., the Gaussian kernel) instead of the square-integrable spaces and proposed a measure of conditional dependence. Kun Zhang and others further developed a kernel-based CI test. Such a nonparametric conditional dependence measure and CI test have received many applications in machine learning, statistics, and artificial intelligence.

Kun Zhang

See also Bayes's Theorem; Bayesian Statistics; Partial Correlations

Further Readings

Daudin, J. J. (1980). Partial association measures and an application to qualitative regression. *Biometrika, 67*, 581–590.

Dawid, A. P. (1979). Conditional independence in statistical theory. *Journal of the Royal Statistical Society. Series B, 41*, 1–31.

Fukumizu, K., Gretton, A., Sun, X., & Schölkopf, B. (2008). Kernel measures of conditional dependence. In J. C. Platt, D. Koller, Y. Singer, & S. Roweis (Eds.),

Advances in neural information processing systems 20 (pp. 489–496). Cambridge, MA: MIT Press.

Gretton, A., Fukumizu, K., Teo, C. H., Song, L., Schölkopf, B., & Smola, A. J. (2008). A kernel statistical test of independence. In *NIPS 20* (pp. 585–592). Cambridge, MA: MIT Press.

Zhang, K., Peters, J., Janzing, D., & Schölkopf, B. (2011). Kernel-based conditional independence test and application in causal discovery. In *Proceedings of the 27th Conference on Uncertainty in Artificial Intelligence (UAI 2011), Barcelona, Spain.*

CONDITIONAL STANDARD ERROR OF MEASUREMENT

It is often assumed that classical test theory requires the standard errors of measurement to be constant for all examinees. This is not true. Rather standard errors of measurement can and do vary for examinees with different true scores. A conditional standard error of measurement (CSEM) is a measure of the variation of observed scores for an individual examinee with a particular true score. Measurement is more precise for examinees with small CSEMs.

In 1955, Frederic Lord developed the best known CSEM for number-correct scores. Its estimator is $x_p(k - x_p)/(k - 1)$, where x_p is the number of correct dichotomously scored items for examinee p, and k is the total number of items in a test. Subsequently, in 1984, Leonard Feldt extended Lord's method to tests in which items are nested within strata, such as fixed categories in a table of specifications. The Lord and Feldt formulas apply only to relatively simple tests with dichotomously scored items. In 1998, using the principles of generalizability (G) theory, Robert Brennan extended CSEMs to any type of raw scores obtained from many different test designs.

In most testing contexts, the scores reported to examinees are not raw scores; rather, the reported scores are transformed raw scores, called scale scores. For linear transformations, the previously mentioned methods can be used with simple adjustments. Usually scale–score transformations are nonlinear, however. If so, obtaining estimated CSEMs is almost always more complicated. Many methods for nonlinear transformations are developed in the 1990s. Item response theory can also be used to obtain estimated CSEMs for nonlinear transformations, although the theoretical basis for doing so is quite different from other methods.

Differentiating between CSEMs for raw and scale scores can have very important implications. For example, for raw scores, CSEMs are often considerably *larger* in the middle of the score distribution than in the ends. By contrast, for many nonlinear scale–score transformations, CSEMs are considerably *smaller* in the middle of the score distribution than in the ends. This is particularly likely for CSEMs obtained using IRT.

Robert L. Brennan

See also Item Response Theory; Generalizability Theory; True Score; Reliability; Standard Error of Measurement

Further Readings

Brennan, R. L. (1998). Raw-score conditional standard errors of measurement in generalizability theory. *Applied Psychological Measurement, 22,* 307–331.

Brennan, R. L., & Lee, W. (1999). Conditional scale-score standard errors of measurement under binomial and compound binomial assumptions. *Educational and Psychological Measurement, 59,* 5–24.

Feldt, L. S. (1984). Some relationships between the binomial error model and classical test theory. *Educational and Psychological Measurement, 44,* 883–891.

Haertel, E. H. (2006). Reliability. In R. L. Brennan (Ed.), *Educational measurement* (4th ed., pp. 65–110). Westport, CT: American Council on Education/ Praeger.

Kolen, M. J., Hanson, B. A., & Brennan, R. L. (1992). Conditional standard errors of measurement for scale scores. *Journal of Educational Measurement, 29,* 285–307.

Lee, W., Brennan, R. L., & Kolen, M. J. (2000). Estimators of conditional scale-score standard errors of measurement: A simulation study. *Journal of Educational Measurement, 37,* 1–20.

CONFIDENCE INTERVAL

The term *confidence interval* refers to an interval estimate that provides information about the uncertainty or the precision of estimation for some population parameter of interest. In statistical inference, confidence intervals are one method of interval estimation, and they are widely used in frequentist statistics. There are several ways to calculate confidence intervals. This entry first emphasizes the importance of confidence intervals by distinguishing interval estimation from point estimation. It then introduces a brief history of confidence intervals. The essentials of constructing confidence intervals are discussed, followed by a brief introduction to other types of intervals in the literature. Confidence intervals have been emphasized in the social and behavioral sciences, but they are often misinterpreted in statistical practice. Thus, the entry concludes with a discussion of common misunderstandings and misinterpretations of confidence intervals.

Interval Estimation Versus Point Estimation

The purpose of inferential statistics is to infer properties about an unknown population parameter using data collected from samples. This is usually done by point estimation, one of the most common forms of statistical inference. Using sample data, point estimation involves the calculation of a single value, which serves as a best guess or best estimate of the unknown population parameter that is of interest.

Instead of a single value, an interval estimate specifies a range within which the parameter is likely to lie. It provides a measure of accuracy of that single value. In frequentist statistics, confidence intervals are the most widely used method for providing information on location and precision of the population parameter, and they can be directly used to infer significance levels. Confidence intervals can have a one-sided or two-sided confidence bound. They are numerical intervals constructed around the estimate of the unknown population parameter. Such an interval does not directly infer a property of the parameter; instead, it indicates a property of the procedure, as is typical for a frequentist statistical procedure.

The American Psychological Association's *Publication Manual* strongly recommends the use of confidence intervals for reporting statistical analysis results. In fact, in the literature, it has been concluded that confidence intervals and null hypothesis significance testing are two approaches to answer the same research question. They give

accessible and comprehensive point and interval information to support substantive understanding and interpretation. As George Casella and Roger L. Berger pointed out, in general, every confidence interval corresponds to a hypothesis testing and vice versa. Whenever possible, researchers should base discussion and interpretation of results on both point and interval estimates whenever possible.

Brief History of Confidence Intervals

In the early 19th century, Pierre-Simon Laplace and Carl Friedrich Gauss had already recognized the need for interval estimation to provide information about measures of accuracy. However, the term *confidence intervals* was not used until Jerzy Neyman's presentation before the Royal Statistical Society in 1934. In the appendix of this paper entitled "On the Two Different Aspects of the Representative Method," Neyman proposed a straightforward way to create an interval estimate and to determine how accurate the estimate is based on sample data. He called this new procedure *confidence intervals* and the ends of the confidence intervals *confidence bounds*. Also, the arbitrarily defined values termed *confidence coefficients* indicated how frequently the observed interval obtained from sample data contains the true population parameter if the experiment is repeated. Nowadays, a confidence coefficient is often referred to as a *confidence level* for its relation to null hypothesis significance testing. Neyman finally addressed the theory of confidence intervals extensively in 1937 in "Outline of a Theory of Statistical Estimation Based on the Classical Theory of Probability." In this paper, the mathematical assumptions, derivations, and proofs provided the philosophical and statistical foundation for confidence intervals.

Construction of Confidence Intervals

There are several approaches to the construction of confidence intervals. The approaches discussed in this entry are commonly used in psychological and educational testing, and they differ in the way of obtaining the standard error (SE) of the sampling distribution for the parameter of interest. The most common, standard procedure is to invert a test statistic as Casella and Berger demonstrated in their textbook *Statistical Inference*. What follows exemplifies the construction of confidence intervals for a population mean μ.

After data are observed, the sample mean $\bar{X}$ may or may not be close to μ and the distance, $\bar{X} - \mu$, is the estimation error and is different for every sample. The margin of error (MOE) is defined as the largest likely estimation error and a confidence interval has this general form, $[\bar{X} - MOE, \bar{X} + MOE]$. For the cases with a "likely" confidence coefficient of .95, we say about 95% of the values from the sampling distribution of the mean falls within MOE, which is 1.96 times the SE of the sampling distribution. By virtue of central limit theorem, the value 1.96, denoted $z_{.95}$, is the critical value of a standard normal distribution. The SE is computed in two ways, depending on whether the population standard deviation σ is known. For a known population standard deviation, the SE is $\sigma / \sqrt{N}$, where N is the sample size. The 95% confidence interval of the population mean is $[\bar{X} - z_{.95} \times \sigma / \sqrt{N}, \bar{X} + z_{.95} \times \sigma / \sqrt{N}]$. When the sample standard deviation s is used as an estimate of σ, the critical value comes from a t distribution associated with the proper degree of freedom. That is, the 95% confidence interval for μ is $[\bar{X} - t_{.95}(N-1) \times s / \sqrt{N}, \bar{X} + t_{.95}(N-1) \times s / \sqrt{N}]$.

Compared to the procedure just shown, a more general approach to constructing a confidence interval is done under the likelihood theory. When estimates are constructed using the maximum likelihood principle, the technique of forming confidence intervals is called the asymptotic normal approximation, which works for a wide variety of statistical models. The SE is computed by $1 / \sqrt{-l''(\hat{\theta})}$, where $-l''(\hat{\theta})$ is the second derivative of the log likelihood function with respect to θ, evaluated at $\theta = \hat{\theta}$, the maximum likelihood estimate of the parameter of interest.

For resampling methods, Thomas J. DiCiccio and Bradley Efron provided a heuristic overview of various bootstrapping confidence intervals that can be routinely constructed even for parameters of a complicated statistical model. A bootstrapping procedure yields a certain number of samples such that the bootstrapping SE is obtained for computing the MOE. This MOE value, together with the average of all bootstrapping sample estimates and a given confidence coefficient for

obtaining a critical value from the z table, one can derive the bootstrapping confidence interval to depict the precision or stability of the estimator of interest. As DiCiccio and Efron showed, asymptotically, bootstrapping confidence intervals are not only good approximate confidence intervals, but more accurate than confidence intervals derived from standard procedures using sample variance and normality assumptions.

Confidence Intervals Versus Other Types of Interval Estimation

Several interval estimation approaches exist in addition to confidence intervals. This entry discusses three such intervals: prediction intervals, tolerance intervals, and Bayesian credible intervals.

Prediction Intervals

A prediction interval specifies the boundaries between which future observations fall. Prediction intervals are often used in regression analysis, where the predicted value for the parameter of interest is obtained, given what has already been observed. The interpretation of prediction intervals is similar to that of confidence intervals. Assuming a confidence coefficient of .95, we can say that the probability that a regression method produces an interval that contains the value of a future observation is 95%.

The difference between prediction intervals and confidence intervals is that the SE used in prediction intervals has to take into account the variability from the difference between the least-square solutions and the true regression as well as the variability of the future response variable. Thus, prediction intervals are always wider than confidence intervals.

Tolerance Intervals

A tolerance interval is an interval to cover a specified proportion of a population distribution with a given confidence for the purpose of predicting a range of likely outcomes. This statistical procedure is often used for quality control in manufacturing. To specify a tolerance interval, both the proportion of the population and a specified confidence level are required. This confidence level is the likelihood that the interval covers the specified, desired proportion of the population.

The width of tolerance intervals differs from that of confidence intervals. The width of a confidence interval, which approaches zero when the sample approaches the entire population, is solely due to sampling error. In contrast, the width of a tolerance interval is affected by not only sampling error but the variance in population.

Bayesian Credible Intervals

In Bayesian statistics, population parameters are random variables rather than fixed values as they are in frequentist statistics. The properties of a population parameter are inferred from the posterior distribution. For example, a 95% credible interval is the 2.5th and 97.5th percentiles of a unimodal posterior distribution.

In general, Bayesian credible intervals differ from frequentists' confidence intervals in some aspects. Credible intervals incorporate information from the prior distribution and the observed data, whereas confidence intervals are solely based on the data. Also, credible intervals and confidence intervals treat nuisance parameters in different ways. Simply put, Bayesian credible intervals treat the parameter being estimated as a random variable, and the resulting interval bounds as fixed values once the posterior distribution of the parameter is found. In contrast, in confidence intervals, the parameter is treated as a fixed value and the bounds are viewed as random variables that depend upon the observed data and can take different values. Prediction intervals mentioned earlier are also used in Bayesian statistics. Again, they are for predicting the distribution of individual future points, whereas Bayesian credible intervals are for predicting the distribution of estimates of the true population parameter that cannot be observed.

Common Misunderstandings and Misinterpretations of Confidence Intervals

There is much confusion about how to interpret a confidence interval. It is important to keep in mind that the interval, not the parameter, is the random quantity. Confidence intervals are probability statements of the procedure but not the probability of the parameter itself. For decades, people argued that confidence intervals were misleading; some even accused Neyman of being unclear about what that probability referred to. In fact, in his paper in 1935, Neyman explicitly displayed the whole concept of confidence intervals. In particular, in one of his formulas, a conclusive probability statement has conveyed all important concepts regarding confidence intervals; that is,

$$\sum_{n=1}^{\infty} p\{x = x_n\} p\{\theta_1(n) \le \theta \le \theta_2(n) \big| (x = x_n)\} = \alpha.$$ Let us assume α is 95%. The probability statement says if we were able to take repeated samples, based on the sample data observed, 95% of our intervals would contain the population parameter (i.e., $\theta_1(n) \le \theta \le \theta_2(n)$). It is hoped that for researchers this clarification of the definition is helpful to prevent from misunderstandings and misinterpretations of confidence intervals.

Conclusion

Confidence intervals are probability statements that combine a point estimate with the precision of that estimate and are commonly reported in tables or graphs in scientific writing. Confidence intervals do not allow for probability statements about the true population parameter as the parameters are fixed values in frequentist statistics. Instead, confidence intervals provide for probability statements about the performance of the procedure of constructing such intervals assuming we were able to do so repeatedly.

Researchers sometimes interpret confidence intervals as if they were Bayesian credible intervals, in which the probability statement is about the true parameter itself. The true parameter is unknown. Once data are observed, a confidence interval either contains the true parameter or not. Thus, for confidence intervals, it is false to say that there is a 95% probability that the true parameter lies in the calculated confidence bounds. Such statements and similar arguments should always be avoided.

Yi-Fang Wu

See also Bayesian Statistics; Central Limit Theorem; Inferential Statistics; Interval-Level Measurement; Standard Error of Measurement

Further Readings

Belia, S., Fidler, F., Williams, J., & Cumming, G. (2005). Researchers misunderstand confidence intervals and standard error bars. *Psychological Methods, 10,* 389–396.

Casella, G., & Berger, R. L. (2002). *Statistical inference* (2nd ed.). Australia: Thomson Learning.

DiCiccio, T. J., & Efron, B. (1996). Bootstrap confidence intervals (with discussion). *Statistical Science, 11,* 189–228.

Howe, W. G. (1969). Two-sided tolerance limits for normal populations—some improvements. *Journal of the American Statistical Association, 64,* 610–620.

Neyman, J. (1934). On the two different aspects of the representative method: The method of stratified sampling and the method of purposive selection. *Journal of the Royal Statistical Society, 97*(4), 558–625.

Neyman, J. (1935). On the problem of confidence intervals. *The Annals of Mathematical Statistics, 6,* 111–116.

Neyman, J. (1937). Outline of a theory of statistical estimation based on the classical theory of probability. *Philosophical Transactions of the Royal Society of London, Series A, Mathematical and Physical Sciences, 236*(767), 333–380.

CONFIDENTIALITY

It is customary to identify *confidentiality* as a property of information that is obtained on an identifiable individual or an entity. In education research, the information may take the form of a written hard document or digitized record, a video or audio recording, or an oral report on an observation from the researcher's memory. A *confidentiality assurance* to an individual or an entity entails a promise that, to the extent possible, the information on identifiable individuals or entities will not be disclosed outside the research context in which it is generated and for which it is used. Such an assurance is common in many social research sectors, including education. This entry further defines confidentiality and discusses how it relates to public information, private information, and professional codes of ethics. It then looks at approaches that reduce or obviate the need for confidentiality and the relationship of confidentiality to research that involves linking records over time or linking records from multiple sources.

Confidentiality is distinguished from and related to *privacy*, which is a property of the individual on whom information is obtained. One may assure an individual or a group that whatever information they provide will remain confidential, though the information's provision can be construed in a narrow sense as a reduction in privacy. Assurance then constitutes a limit on any further reduction of privacy.

Security is distinguishable from both confidentiality and privacy. It usually refers to the conditions under which information is maintained and used. Physical locks and electronic encryption schemes are examples of security measures.

Public Versus Private Information

At one extreme, much information on identifiable individuals is public. In the United States, for instance, administrative records on public school teachers are collected and maintained by state education agencies. That information—on teacher identity, teaching or administrative assignments, and other data—is, at times, publicly accessible on state data systems websites and is used in education research. In such records, and in other public systems on parole officers or nurses or others employed by government, salaries and other information on individuals are disclosed.

At the other extreme, law and regulation can restrict access to information and, in doing so, actualize an assurance of confidentiality. For example, records on students in education institutions, whether the institutions are public or private, are covered in the United States by the Family Educational Rights and Privacy Act. Such records cannot be disclosed to anyone who is not associated with the school unless certain conditions are met. One such condition involves asking the students to agree in advance to the disclosure of their records for research purposes, as is the case for some massive online open-access course data systems.

Between these two extremes, there is considerable variation in the factors that influence, or are influenced by, assurances of confidentiality. The World Wide Web, generally, and social media initiatives, in particular, engender far more complicated issues.

Professional Codes of Ethics and Confidentiality

Many professional associations have developed codes of ethics that attend to confidentiality in the context of educational and social research. Section 12 of the American Educational Research Association Code of Ethics published in 2011, for instance, considers the topic in detail. Among other things, it tells its members that "confidential information is protected," that "educational researchers take reasonable precautions to protect the confidentiality of information related to research participants. . . . (and) do not allow information gained in confidence to be used in ways would unfairly compromise research participants, students, employees, clients, or others" (p. 149). Other organizations that have addressed confidentiality issues, and to which education research is at times relevant, include the American Psychological Association, American Criminological Society, and American Sociological Association.

Obviating or Reducing the Need for Confidentiality Assurance

When education research relies solely on public records, as suggested earlier, it obviates the need to assure any person or entity of confidentiality. Although useful for many research purposes, however, public records are of limited use for many others. A controlled trial on approaches to reducing teacher turnover, for instance, might reasonably rely on public records on public school teachers to determine their positions over time. A similar study on teachers in the context of private schools would have to rely on surveys or other special arrangements to access institutional records because the records are not public.

Different approaches to assuring confidentiality, when confidentiality must be assured, can be classified as procedural, statistical, and legal. For instance, eliciting anonymous responses is a useful and common procedural approach in cross-sectional surveys. Anonymous responses are useless in longitudinal research unless one can rely on respondent-created aliases and consistent use of the aliases over time or on probabilistic matching algorithms. The anonymity is limited in that deductive disclosure of the identities of supposedly anonymous respondents can be accomplished at times though this might take considerable effort and skill. A survey of graduates of a university school of nursing in the United States at a point in time, for instance, may involve one male graduate whose responses to the survey can easily be coupled to auxiliary information on graduates to learn who the anonymous respondent is and to learn more about him.

Statistical approaches to assuring confidentiality in personal interviews and surveys involving identifiable people that deal with sensitive topics are underused in education and related research. Using these methods, the researcher can elicit sensitive information from identifiable individuals in a way that assures that the response cannot be tied directly to the status of the respondent. Some of the methods fall under the rubric of "randomized response."

Statutory approaches to assuring confidentiality of information on an identifiable participant in research are at hand. Census bureaus in developed countries for instance, including the United States, Canada, United Kingdom, Sweden, Germany, and others, are governed by laws that prevent redisclosure of the information obtained by the census worker or the census agency. More to the point of education related research, several U.S. laws provide the researcher with protection from being compelled to disclose involuntarily the respondent's confidential information to nonresearch entities such as a court or prosecuting office. These education-related sectors deal with adolescent use of controlled substances, criminal disorder, and mental and physical health, among others. The relevant legal protection, Certificates of Confidentiality, and conditions for them and limits on them can be found at the National Institutes of Health website.

Record Linkage and Integrated Data Systems in Education Research

Longitudinal research on children requires unique identifiers so as to link records over time. More generally, integrating or linking records from different sources has become important in the social and education sciences. One learns about the correlation between children's early exposure to lead and their subsequent academic achievement only by linking their education records with, for instance, other records on their housing or health. The different record systems are in most countries governed by different government agencies. Each agency may have its own rules on the confidentiality of their records on identifiable individuals. Consequently, linkage agreements and agreement on principles of linkage can be complex.

The Organisation for Economic Co-operation and Development and the American Educational Research Association have initiated efforts to understand how productive record linkages across agencies within countries can be accomplished without compromising confidentiality assurances made to the people on whom records are kept. The specific context has been longitudinal information systems, but this work has larger implications. The Organisation for Economic Co-operation and Development–American Educational Research Association meetings in 2015 aimed to develop basic principles that would be acceptable to people in the countries involved (Ireland, the United Kingdom, the United States, Russia, the Slovak Republic, Norway, and others). One of the lessons of this and related meetings is that the benefits of linking records have to be documented well in any effort to balance the privacy values of the individuals on whom records are kept against the societal and scientific value of the research. The confidentiality of the records is a critical ingredient in this balance.

Robert Boruch

See also Family Educational Rights and Privacy Act; Health Insurance Portability and Accountability Act; Institutional Review Boards; Qualitative Research Methods

Further Readings

American Educational Research Association. (2011). Code of ethics. *Educational Researcher, 40*(3), 145–156. doi:10.3102/0013189X11410403

Boruch, R. F., & Cecil, J. S. (1979). *Assuring the confidentiality of social research data*. Philadelphia: University of Pennsylvania Press.

Bouza, C. N., Herra, C., & Mitra, P. (2010). A review of randomized response procedures: The qualitative variable case. *Revista Investigacion Operacional, 31*(3), 240–247.

Lensvelt-Mulders, G., Hox, J., van der Heijden, P., & Maas, C. (2005). Meta-analysis of randomized response research: Thirty-five years of validation. *Sociological Methods and Research, 33*(3), 319–348.

National Institutes of Health. (2016, May 18). Certificates of Confidentiality (CoC). Retrieved from https://humansubjects.nih.gov/coc/index

Palys, T., & Lowman, J. (2014). *Protecting research confidentiality*. Toronto, Canada: James Larimore and Company.

CONFIRMATORY FACTOR ANALYSIS

Confirmatory factor analysis (CFA) is a specific type of factor analysis that allows one to determine the extent of the hypothesized relationship between observed indicators and factors (underlying latent variables). CFA, unlike path analysis, allows the distinction between latent variables (referred to as factors) and the indicators (variables) used to measure these latent variables. With CFA models, the factors are assumed to cause the variation and covariation between the observed indicators which are fit to a correlation matrix. This assumption is the primary distinction between CFA and exploratory factor analysis models in which no hypothesis about the number of factors and the relationship between those factors and the indicators is proposed. Thus, CFA can be used for psychometric evaluation, construct validation, and testing measurement invariance. This entry begins with a discussion of the model specification followed by model identification, estimation, evaluation of model fit, and advanced applications of CFA.

CFA models have three primary characteristics:

1. Indicators are continuous variables with two components: (1) one underlying factor that is measured by the indicator and (2) and everything else which is referred to as error.

2. Measurement errors must be independent of each other and the factors.

3. The associations between the factors are not analyzed.

The basic steps in SEM are represented in Figure 1.

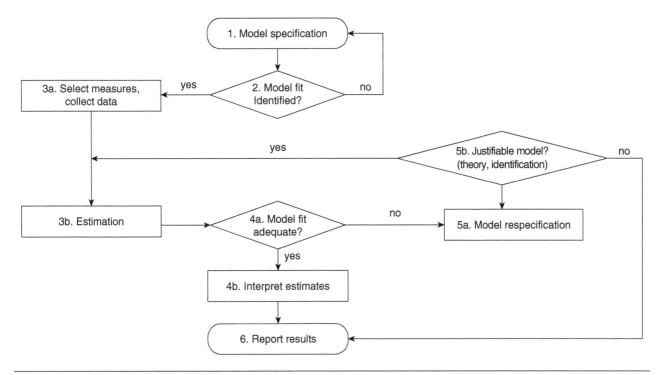

Figure 1   Steps in SEM implication framework

Within a structural equation modeling framework, CFA models serve two purposes: (1) to obtain parameter estimates for both the factor (i.e. the factor loadings, the variances, and covariances) and the indicator variables (i.e. residual error variances) and (2) to evaluate the extent to which the model fits the data.

Model Specification

Specification is defined as the representation of a hypothesis in the form of a structural equation model. Specification can take place either before or after data are collected. A CFA model can be defined using various models such as the linear structural relations model (LISREL), the covariance structure analysis model, Bentler-Weeks model, and/or reticular action model (RAM). Provided here are the best known models for continuous observable variables, LISREL and RAM. Figure 2 provides a visual representation of examples of a CFA model with two factors and six indicators.

In Figure 2, squares (or rectangles) and circles (or ellipses) represent observed variables and latent variables, respectively. Also, lines with a single arrowhead and a curved line with two

arrowheads reflect hypothesized causal directions and covariances, respectively. This model has seven linear regression equations underlying it, a single structural equation, and six measurement equations. We write the LISREL with matrix notation as:

$$y = \Lambda_y \eta + \varepsilon$$

$$x = \Lambda_x \xi + \delta$$

$$\eta = B\eta + \Gamma\xi + \zeta,$$

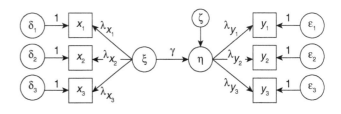

Figure 2   Graphical presentation of an example of a CFA model using LISREL symbols. CFA = confirmatory factor analysis; LISREL = linear structural relations model.

where x, y: exogenous and endogenous variable vectors;

$\Lambda_x \Lambda_y$: factor loading matrices;

ε, δ: uniqueness vectors;

η, ξ: endogenous and exogenous latent variable vectors;

B: regression coefficient matrix relating the latent endogenous variables to each other;

Γ: regression coefficients matrix relating endogenous variables to exogenous variables; and

ζ: structural disturbance vector.

A general covariance matrix for y and x can be written as:

$$\Sigma \begin{bmatrix} \Sigma_{yy} & \Sigma_{yx} \\ \Sigma_{xy} & \Sigma_{xx} \end{bmatrix}$$
$$= \begin{bmatrix} \Lambda_y(I-B)^{-1}(\Gamma\Phi\Gamma' + \Psi)(I-B)^{-1}\Lambda_y' + \Theta_s & \Lambda_y(I-B)^{-1}\Gamma\Phi\Lambda_x' \\ \Lambda_x\Phi\Gamma'(I-B)^{-1} & \Lambda_x\Phi\Lambda_x' + \Theta_\varsigma \end{bmatrix},$$

where Φ: the variance–covariance matrix of the exogenous latent variables;

Ψ: the variance–covariance matrix of the disturbance terms; and

Θ_s, Θ_δ: the variance–covariance matrices of the measurement errors ε and ς.

In terms of the parameter vector Ω, we have $\Omega = (\Lambda_x, \Lambda_y, \Theta_s, \Theta_\delta, \Phi, B, \Gamma, \Psi)$.

Unlike with LISREL, the RAM, observable or unobservable, endogenous, exogenous variables are generally labelled as $v_1, v_2, ..., v_n$. Thus, only one residual variance–covariance matrix of all variables is specified. We write the RAM with matrix notation as:

$$v = Av + u,$$

where A: coefficient matrix;

v: latent and observed variable vector; and

u: residual vector.

To express the covariance matrix of LISREL as a RAM, we write:

$$\Sigma \begin{bmatrix} \Sigma_{yy} & \Sigma_{yx} \\ \Sigma_{xy} & \Sigma_{xx} \end{bmatrix}$$
$$= \begin{bmatrix} I & 0 & 0 & 0 \\ (I-B)^{-1}\Gamma & (1-B)^{-1} & 0 & 0 \\ \Lambda_x & 0 & I & 0 \\ \Lambda_y(I-B)^{-1}\Gamma & \Lambda_y(I-B)^{-1} & 0 & I \end{bmatrix}.$$

If response variables are ordered categorical or dichotomous data, latent continuous response variables, z^*, can be used for the CFA model. For the ordered categorical case, observed variables can be defined as:

$$z = c, \text{ if } \tau_c < z^* < \tau_{c+1},$$

where z^*: underlying continuous variable;

τ_c: thresholds as parameters for the categories $c = 0, 1, 2, ..., C-1$, for a variable with C categories, and where $\tau_0 = -\infty$, $\tau_c = -\infty$.

Also, the linear "inner" model describes the relationship for a set of p latent response variables y^* and a set of q latent response variables x^*,

$$y^* = v_y + \Lambda_y \eta + \varepsilon$$

$$x^* = v_x + \Lambda_x \xi + \delta,$$

where v_x, v_y: parameter vector of intercepts. Modeling follows the same general structure as when testing a CFA with continuous indicators:

$$\Sigma^* = \Lambda^* \Phi^* \Lambda^{*'} + \Theta^*,$$

where Σ^*: the variance–covariance matrix for modeling relationship between latent response variables;

Λ^*: the factor loading matrix;

Φ^*: the latent variance–covariance matrix among one or more latent variables; and

Θ_s: the variance–covariance matrices of the measurement errors.

Identification

Identification is a key concern in model specification. Parameters to be estimated in a model are identified if a unique set for them can be obtained given the model. When every parameter in a model is identified, the model as a whole is identified. The minimum condition of identifiability is that there should be at least as much known information as unknown information (i.e., number of free parameters). The degrees of freedom for a model typically equal the difference between the known and unknown information. Ideally, prior to estimation, the identification of all parameters would be verified. However, in practice, identification is linked to (re)specification.

Estimation

Estimation is the process of finding values for the unknown parameters that minimize the discrepancy between the observed covariance matrix and the estimated (or implied) covariance matrix given the model and the data. For example, in Figure 2, CFA obtains simultaneous estimates of the population coefficients for the seven equations as well as parameters including factor variances, covariances, and error variances using estimation methods. The most commonly used method of estimation is maximum likelihood (ML), which analyzes the covariance matrix of data. The estimates are the ones that maximize the likelihood that data were drawn from the population of interest.

The statistical assumptions of ML estimation include multivariate normality for the joint population distribution of the endogenous variables (which implies that they are continuous), independence of observations, exogenous variables and disturbances, unstandardized observations, and large samples (e.g. $N = 200$, but $N \geq 200$ needed when analyzing a complex model or outcomes with nonnormal distributions and using an estimation method other than ML). When analyzing categorical variables with asymmetrical distributions, the ML method is probably not appropriate. For categorical indicators, a full information version of

ML method can be used. Full information version of ML also directly analyzes the raw data using methods for numerical integration to estimate response probabilities in joint multivariate distributions of the latent response variables, which is the underlying continuous and normally distributed continuum. One alternative method is the fully weighted least square (WLS) method, which does not assume particular distributional form and thus can be applied to continuous or categorical variables.

To reduce the computation complexity of the fully WLS, robust WLS estimation can be used. Robust WLS methods use only the diagonal elements in the weight matrix from full WLS estimation. In the Mplus program, mean-adjusted least squares and mean- and variance-adjusted weighted least squares options are available. Values of the same fit indices can differ over these two methods due to different chi-square and degrees of freedom values. Simulation studies generally favor the mean- and variance-adjusted WLS method over the mean-adjusted WLS. If these estimation methods are applied to data that violate the underlying statistical assumptions of each method, misleading results may be obtained.

Model Fit

Evaluation of model fit concerns whether the specified model explains the data or should be rejected or respecified. Also, if we wish to choose among multiple competing models, fit indices can be used to compare these models. To compare nested models, most of the practical fit indices include the chi-square statistic, which tests the exact-fit hypothesis that there is no difference between the predicted covariance matrix and the population covariance matrix. The chi-square statistic is regarded as undesirable because the chi-square test is quite sensitive to sample size. To overcome this problem, other approximate fit indices have been developed. Indeed, there are more than 50 fit indices introduced in published entries. Here, we summarize the most popular indices.

Alternative fit indices can be classified under absolute and relative (comparative, incremental) fit indices. Absolute fit indices are functions of the discrepancies and include "goodness-of-fit index"

(GFI), adjusted GFI, root mean square error approximation, and standardized root mean square residual. Relative indices reflect increments in fit of the researcher's model over a null model and include incremental fit index, normed fit index, comparative fit index, relative noncentrality index, and Tucker–Lewis index (also called nonnormed fit index). It is customary to report the model chi-square with its degrees of freedom (df) and p value, root mean square error approximation with its 90% confidence interval, comparative fit index, and standardized root mean square residual as a minimum set of fit indices. Commonly reported alternative fit indices and related information are represented in Table 1.

F_{ML} = discrepancy function for the ML estimation procedure; χ^2_{SB} = Satorra-Bentler scaled chi-square; c = scaling correction factor; 0 = baseline model; 1 = hypothesized model; r^2_{jk} = standardized residual from a covariance matrix with j rows and k columns; p^* = the number of nonduplicated elements in the covariance matrix.

Also it can exceed 1, which indicates an extremely well-fitting model.

In Table 1, indices are classified into GFIs where larger values indicate better fit; or conversely, "badness-of-fit" indices in which smaller values indicate improving fit. All relative fit indices are GFIs; absolute fit indices can be either of two types of indices. Also, while sample-bases indices reflect the discrepancy between the model-implied covariance matrix and the sample covariance matrix, population-based fit indices estimate the discrepancy between the reproduced covariance matrix by the model and the population covariance matrix. For some fit indices, they are adjusted depending on their model complexity. Suggested cutoff criteria are not universal for every situation, and so residuals and modification indices should also be investigated for model evaluation. For CFA with categorical data, χ^2_{SB} can be used instead of chi-square. For evaluating nonnested models, Akaike information criterion, consistent information criterion, Bayesian information criterion, cross-validation index, and expected cross-validation index have been proposed.

Although these fit indices provide helpful information for evaluating models, it is most important that the choice between alternative models should be decided based on theoretical rather than statistical considerations as fit measures are not based on meaningful theories but only average or overall model–data correspondence.

Cautions

Researchers and/or practitioners interested in applying factor analytic models with their own data should be mindful of three cautions. First, incorrect model specifications (based on either bad theory or hypotheses) may lead to false conclusions. Moreover, as the CFA model is meant as a test of the measuring instrument as a whole, limited feedback can be provided to the researcher with respect to individual items. Readers should refer to models based in item response theory for drawing such conclusions. Finally, the impact/role of sample size in factor analytic models is considerable. For example, relatively large sample sizes are required to obtain reliable estimates particularly when there are a large number of variables.

Jennifer Randall and Hyun Joo Jung

See also Exploratory Factor Analysis; Path Analysis; Structural Equation Modeling

Further Readings

Akaike, H. (1973). Information theory as an extension of the maximum likelihood principle. In B. N. Petrov & F. Csaki (Eds.), *Second International Symposium on Information Theory* (pp. 267–281). Budapest, Hungary: Akademiai Kiado.

Bentler, P. M. (1990). Comparative fit indexes in structural models. *Psychological Bulletin, 107,* 238–246.

Bentler, P. M. (1995). *EQS: Structural equations program manual.* Encino, CA: Multivariate Software.

Bollen, K. A. (1989). *Structural equations with latent variables.* New York, NY: Wiley.

Hoyle, R. H. (2012). Introduction and overview. In R. H. Hoyle (Ed.), *Handbook of structural equation modeling* (pp. 3–16). New York, NY: Guilford Press.

Hu, L.-T., & Bentler, P. M. (1999). Cutoff criteria for fit indexes in covariance structure analysis: Conventional criteria versus new alternatives. *Structural Equation Modeling, 6,* 1–55.

Jöreskog. K. G. (1970). A general method for the analysis of covariance structures. *Biometrika, 57,* 239–251.

Table 1 Fit Indices for Nested Models

Absolute or Relative	Fit Index	Goodness or Badness	Sample Based or Population Based	Adjustment for Parsimony	Theoretical Range	Cutoff Criterion
Absolute	$\chi^2 = (N-1)F_{ML}$ or $\chi^2 = NF_{ML}$	Badness	Sample based	x	≥ 0	$p < .05$
	$\chi^2_{SB} = \dfrac{\chi^2}{c}$	Badness	Sample based	x	≥ 0	$p < .05$
	$RMSEA = \sqrt{\dfrac{\max(\chi^2_1 - df_{1,0})}{df_1(N-1)}}$	Badness	Population based	O	> 0	$< .06$
	$SRMR = \sqrt{\dfrac{\sum_j \sum_{k \leq j} r^2_{jk}}{p^*}}$	Badness	Sample based	x	> 0	$< .08$
Relative	$CFI = 1 - \dfrac{\max(\chi^2_1 - df_{1,0})}{\max(\chi^2_0 - df_{0,0})}$	Goodness	Population based	x	$0\sim1^a$	$> .95$
	$TLI = \dfrac{\dfrac{\chi^2_0}{df_0} - \dfrac{\chi^2_1}{df_1}}{\dfrac{\chi^2_0}{df_0} - 1}$	Goodness	Sample based	x	$0\sim1$	$> .95$

[a]Tucker–Lewis index can have a negative value, which indicates an extremely misspecified model.

Kline, R. (2016). *Principles and practice of structural equation modeling* (4th ed.). New York, NY: The Guilford Press.

Muthén, B. (1983). Latent variable structural equation modeling with categorical data. *Journal of Econometrics, 22,* 43–65.

CONFLICT OF INTEREST

In the area of research, conflict of interest usually involves researchers being in a position to personally benefit from particular information generated in the research or personally benefiting directly or indirectly as a consequence of engaging in the research. Typically, though not exclusively, conflict of interest involves financial gain for oneself, one's family or friends, or one's business associates. The information of typical concern is what one learns about the opportunity for personal gain that is incidental to the declared purpose of the research and that may undermine the confidentiality assurances or understandings that the research engenders.

The Singapore Statement on Research Integrity, developed in 2002 at the Second World Congress on Research Integrity, gives a succinct definition and directive on conflict of interest as part of its list of 14 responsibilities for researchers: "9. Conflict of Interest: Researchers should disclose financial and other conflicts that could compromise the trustworthiness of their work in research proposals, publications, and public communications as well as in all review activities." This entry discusses how the topic of conflict of interest is handled in professional codes of ethics, how it comes into play in research and advisory work, and the consequences of failure to disclose actual or potential conflicts of interest.

In developed countries, the codes of ethics of professional organizations attend in detail to the topic of conflict of interest in research. The codes issued and revised periodically by the American Educational Research Association (AERA), American Sociological Association, and American Psychological Association are among the most explicit in dealing with the subject. The AERA Code, for example, provides guidance on potential conflicts in direct research, in the workplace, and outside the workplace.

Section 10 of the AERA's Code of Ethics, adopted in 2011, declares that researchers must disclose:

> Relevant sources of financial support and relevant personal or professional relationships that may have the appearance of or potential for a conflict of interest to an employer or client, to the sponsors of their professional work, and to the public in written and verbal reports. (p. 148)

In research on the use of beer or wine by adolescents, for example, the receipt of a research from a brewery must be disclosed partly because the research results (finding that wine drinkers are more polite and achieve higher test scores than beer drinkers) can be influenced by the sponsorship.

Further, the AERA code declares that the researcher must not seek to gain from confidential or proprietary information that they obtain as part of their employment or relationship with a client unless they have permission from the employer or client. Research on students who invent robotic devices, for example, can generate information on the device or on the student's need for capital investment in production, information that could be exploited unfairly by the researcher.

Some publishers of education research require that authors disclose potential conflicts when they have a journal article accepted for publication. These conflicts can include forms of financial support or financial interests related to the research.

In the research work environment, potential or actual conflict of interest is sometimes less clear, but nonetheless important. A university researcher, for instance, may choose to be first author on a report for which junior colleagues developed new ideas and did most of the research work. Sexual exploitation of vulnerable colleagues (student researchers or research staff) is also a type of actual conflict of interest though it may not be labeled as such.

Research intensive universities formally explicate conflict of interest policies that relevant faculty and research personnel must abide by. For example, Stanford University's detailed policy emphasizes financial gain issues and informs readers of ways to mitigate conflicts. The list of Further Readings at the end of this entry includes

Stanford's policy and other examples of institutional and organizational policy statements that address conflict of interest.

Education researchers, at times, serve on boards of trustees for foundations or on the boards of directors of nonprofit organizations or boards of for-profit corporations. These researchers are not directly involved in research in these contexts, but nonetheless may have potential conflicts of interest. The National Council of Nonprofits in the United States has issued policy guidance on conflicts of interest so as to inform the ways that board members think about the topic. The guidance includes recommendations that board members disclose potential conflicts of interest and that members abstain from votes and decisions that may involve a conflict of interest. Some research-focused organizations require board members to submit detailed statements listing potential conflicts of interest involving their employment, business ownership and involvement, investments and financial interests, and gifts and gratuities.

Peer review of proposals to support research may engender conflicts of interest. The U.S. Institute of Education Sciences, for instance, requires that reviewers recuse themselves from participating in a review panel in several different circumstances, including when they "have professional differences that could reasonably be viewed as affecting the objectivity of their review" (2006, p. 6) or have a financial interest in a for-profit organization that has an application before the panel.

People can go to prison for failure to disclose conflicts of interest when it is clear that they make personal gain despite their conflict. It is easy to find recurrent episodes of the so-called insider trading in the commercial sector, some of which have resulted in legal sanctions. There is no evidence of any such sanctions in education or other social research sectors.

Even when legal sanctions do not apply or are not pursued, however, social sanctions may apply when academic researchers are careless about conflicts of interest. For instance, in 2013, two economists who published evaluation research on the effectiveness of private prison programs initially failed to disclose that they had been financially supported by private prison services corporations for the research. A complaint alleged the failure to disclose the information violated policies of the economists' university. The complaint and the university's response received wide coverage in the news media.

Robert Boruch

See also American Educational Research Association; American Psychological Association; Ethical Issues in Educational Research; Institutional Review Boards; Interviewer Bias

Further Readings

American Economic Association. (n.d.). Disclosure policy. Retrieved from https://www.aeaweb.org/journals/policies/disclosure-policy

American Educational Research Association. (n.d.). Professional ethics. Retrieved from http://www.aera.net/AboutAERA/AERARulesPolicies/CodeofEthics/tabid/10200/Default.aspx

American Institutes for Research. (n.d.). Code of conduct. Retrieved from http://www.air.org/page/code-conduct

Institute of Education Sciences. (2006, January 24). Procedures for peer review of grant applications. Retrieved from http://www2.ed.gov/policy/rschstat/guid/ies/peerreviewgrants.pdf

National Council of Nonprofits. (n.d.). Tools & resources: Conflict. Retrieved from https://www.councilofnonprofits.org/tools-resources/conflict

Singapore Statement on Research Integrity. (2010, September 22). Retrieved from http://www.singaporestatement.org/statement.html

Stanford University. (n.d.). Research & scholarship: Conflicts of interest. Retrieved from https://doresearch.stanford.edu/research-scholarship/conflicts-interest

University of Oxford. (8 April, 2011). Illustrative examples of conflict of interest. Retrieved from https://www.admin.ox.ac.uk/researchsupport/integrity/conflict/policy/illustrativeexamples

CONSEQUENTIAL VALIDITY EVIDENCE

Consequential validity evidence provides information about the social consequences that result from using a test for a particular purpose. Various types of evidence can be presented to provide information about a test's consequential validity; these types of evidence include subgroup scores, results of test-based classification decisions (e.g., instructional or curricular differences, negative social consequences within a peer group, differences in opportunity), and errors in test use. Evidence supporting consequential validity is typically used to demonstrate how intended outcomes have been achieved, a lack of differential impact across subgroups, and the presence of positive and absence of negative systemic effects resulting from the testing program.

In 1989, Samuel Messick introduced the idea of a consequential basis for validity; since that time, there has been a great deal of scholarship produced regarding whether consequential validity evidence is needed to support the interpretation of a test's results. Some scholars argue that since consequential evidence deals with ethical rather than measurement considerations, it should not be considered as part of the validity argument. Others argue that ethical issues should be included in the scope of validity, and consideration of the social consequences resulting from a test's interpretation is an important ethical consideration when constructing a validity argument. The following sections of this entry outline some possible types of consequential validity evidence, then explore the main arguments forwarded by scholars in favor of including consequential validity evidence in the validity argument and by scholars in favor of considering consequences outside of the framework of validity.

Although scholarship continues to be published on both sides of this debate, in 2008, Gregory Cizek and colleagues found that just 2.5% of the 283 tests they reviewed provided this type of evidence in their validity arguments. Although consequential validity evidence has been indicated as a source of validity evidence in the *Standards for Educational and Psychological Testing*, these results clearly show that it has failed to gain traction as an important source of validity evidence.

Types of Consequential Validity Evidence

One of the most commonly reported types of consequential validity is differences in subgroup scores. Psychometric analyses that detect differential item functioning or differential test functioning can provide information on whether certain subgroups—especially protected subgroups—are consistently performing lower than reference groups. This type of bias both suggests that the test may suffer from excessive construct-irrelevant variance and indicates that consequences resulting from test classification decisions may differentially impact different subgroups.

A related source of consequential validity evidence is a description of the results of test-based classification decisions. For example, students classified into different proficiency bands as a result of their scores on an academic achievement test may receive different instruction and/or curriculum as a result of their performance. In some instances, decisions about students' placement in special education programs, more intensive supports, or alternative settings can be influenced by test scores. Lower-performing students may also experience fewer opportunities to succeed as a result of their low test scores. Additionally, low test scores can result in negative social consequences within students' peer groups; lower-performing students are sometimes ostracized as a result of their lower academic achievement.

Evidence regarding the interpretation of test results should ideally include information about consequences resulting from the recommended interpretation of test results as well as any interpretations that may extend beyond the recommendations of the test developer. Although assembling evidence for the consequences of the test's interpretations outside of the recommended interpretations may be challenging, there are several avenues that test developers can pursue. Consequential validity evidence for a new test can attempt to anticipate and describe these possibilities. Established tests' consequential validity evidence can collect evidence from the populations who are impacted by test classification decisions to provide concrete statistics regarding these consequences.

Some of the test's uses and/or interpretations extending beyond the test developer's intentions may constitute errors in test use. Scholars disagree on whether consequential validity evidence should be provided to describe the consequences of erroneous test uses, although most agree that erroneous test use does not need to be considered within the validity argument.

The Case for Consequential Validity Evidence

Messick's 1989 validity framework presented validity as a unitary yet multifaceted concept that required many types of evidence to be adequately supported. Within this framework, construct validity was presented as the unifying force under which the rest of the validity framework resides. To argue for construct validity, many types of validity evidence must be brought to bear as part of the validity argument. To illustrate this idea, this work included a diagram that Messick termed the "progressive matrix," which was intended to illustrate the way that types of validity evidence stood in relation to each other. This matrix included social consequences in its fourth and final cell, which represented the intersection between test use and a consequential basis. The other three cells included construct validity, construct validity plus relevance/utility, and value implications. In later works, Messick specified six types of evidence to support a validity argument: content, substantive, structural, generalizability, external, and consequential. All of these types of evidence were presented as aspects of construct validity.

Throughout his scholarship, Messick has argued that the social consequences of test use are an ethical matter that must be taken into consideration to argue for an interpretation of a test as valid. Messick argues that anticipated consequences of legitimate test use constitute part of the nomological network that provides the framework for construct theory and are therefore part of the unifying construct validity argument. Because these consequences are part of the nomological network, the consequences of a test's use and interpretation must necessarily be sources of evidence for construct validity and, therefore, for the test's value and worth.

Additionally, the social consequences of specific score interpretations contribute to score meaning and are therefore also part of the overarching validity argument, especially because their value implications may not line up with the construct's implications for relative levels of the trait in question. Messick, Michael Kane, and other scholars have argued that negative consequences from a test's uses can render a score use unacceptable and

therefore invalid. Consequential validity evidence is especially important, given that test scores are typically used to make decision inferences about individuals at different score levels, and these decision inferences are at least partially based on the score users' assumptions about the consequences resulting from different decisions. If decisions result in adverse conditions or negative systemic effects for all or most of the populations, the decision rules and therefore the test's interpretation should be rejected as invalid. Kane proposes three major categories of outcomes that should be considered when assembling consequential validity evidence:

1. the extent to which the intended outcomes are achieved,

2. differential impact on groups (particularly adverse effect on legally protected groups), and

3. positive and negative systemic effects (particularly in education).

Both positive and negative as well as intended and unintended consequences resulting from the testing program should be considered when assembling consequential validity evidence as part of a validity argument.

The Case Against Consequential Validity Evidence

Although some scholars support the inclusion of consequential validity evidence in a validity argument, other scholars argue that consequential evidence, while important for consideration, should not be considered under the umbrella of validity evidence. Scholars arguing against the use of consequential validity evidence in the validity argument—such as James Popham, Lorrie Shepard, and others—assert that inserting social consequences into the concept of validity leads to further confusion surrounding the issue. The concept of validity has already undergone several transformations throughout its history, and many practitioners are currently unclear about its definition. Common misconceptions include reference to different types of validity rather than different types of validity evidence and statements about the validity of tests rather than the validity of score interpretations. Including social consequences as a required part of a validity argument may sacrifice the clarity of the definition of validity set forth in the 1985 *Standards for Educational and Psychological Testing*, which defined validity as "the degree to which th[e] evidence supports the inferences that are made from [test] scores" (p. 9).

A similar argument is that while consequences of test use and interpretation should be addressed by test developers and policy makers, this evidence should not be considered as part of the validity argument. By including consequential validity evidence, the validity argument is incorrectly expanded to include considerations of possible consequences that are outside of the scope of test development. While the test development process can assemble validity evidence showing that the test adequately and accurately measures the construct, thereby yielding accurate inferences about examinees' proficiency levels, policy decisions that are made regarding the consequences of those inferences cannot be rightly considered as part of the validity evidence for the test's interpretation and use. If consequences resulting from test scores are unreasonable, that does not necessarily impact the validity of test-based inferences about examinees' proficiency.

In fact, inclusion of consequential validity evidence can result in test misuse in terms of errors in procedure and/or policy and can detract from the validity of correct, legitimate use of the test.

An argument taking a different view of adverse consequences of test use posits that observed adverse consequences of test use only indicate a lack of validity if they are traceable to a gap in some other part of the validity argument such as construct underrepresentation or construct-irrelevant variance. These are both aspects of construct validity evidence that must be considered in a validity argument. This position argues that while consequences should be considered, consequential validity evidence should not be included in the validity argument; instead, sources of invalidity that lead to adverse consequences should be identified and accounted for using the other types of validity evidence outlined in Messick's framework or the 2014 *Standards for Educational and Psychological Testing*. By viewing challenges to the validity argument in terms of the other types

of validity evidence, the issue of validity remains a question of scientific measurement rather than of ethics.

Jennifer A. Brussow

See also Construct-Related Validity Evidence; Content-Related Validity Evidence; Criterion-Based Validity Evidence; Unitary View of Validity; Validity; Validity, History of

Further Readings

American Educational Research Association, American Psychological Association, & National Council on Measurement in Education. (1985). *Standards for educational and psychological testing*. Washington, DC: American Educational Research Association.

Kane, M. T. (2013). Validating the interpretations and uses of test scores. *Journal of Educational Measurement*, 50(1), 1–73.

Messick, S. (1989). Validity. In R. L. Linn (Ed.), *Educational measurement* (3rd ed., pp. 13–103). Washington, DC: American Council on Education & National Council on Measurement in Education.

Newton, P., & Shaw, S. (2014). *Validity in educational and psychological assessment*. Thousand Oaks, CA: Sage.

Popham, W. J. (1997). Consequential validity: Right concern-wrong concept. *Educational Measurement: Issues and Practice*, 16(2), 9–13.

Shepard, L. A. (1997). The centrality of test use and consequences for test validity. *Educational Measurement: Issues and Practice*, 16(2), 5–24.

CONSTRUCT IRRELEVANCE

Construct irrelevance, as the name might suggest, refers to measuring phenomena that are not included in the definition of the construct. This is generally considered to be one of the two biggest threats to the validity of an assessment, along with construct underrepresentation. Although construct underrepresentation involves an assessment not adequately measuring all aspects of the construct of interest, construct irrelevance (sometimes referred to as construct irrelevant variance) occurs when an assessment is measuring more than just the construct of interest. This entry examines how construct irrelevance occurs and its implications and then provides illustrative examples of construct irrelevance.

Construct Irrelevance in Practice

The underlying assumption of all assessments is that the score that is produced reflects a test taker's ability on the construct of interest. In an educational setting, this construct is often an educational content area. For example, if a student takes a math assessment, we assume that the score that student receives represents, and is an accurate measure of, his math ability.

As noted previously, construct irrelevance occurs when the score produced by the assessment is dependent on more than just the construct of interest. Continuing with the example of the math assessment, suppose that some of the questions were word problems. These word problems will require some level of reading and comprehension ability in order to understand the question and respond appropriately. This is construct irrelevance. We are not interested in measuring a student's reading ability with this assessment. That is, reading ability is irrelevant to math ability, as we have defined the construct.

The implication of including these items on the assessment is that a student's score may not accurately reflect that student's ability on the construct of interest. Suppose a student with poor reading ability but high math ability took the assessment previously described. This student might be fully capable of performing the math necessary to correctly answer the word problems, but because of her poor reading ability, she doesn't understand the question and gets the item wrong.

As this type of construct irrelevant error variance accumulates over many word problems, the student's math ability score is going to be biased down. The student will get many questions wrong that someone with a high level of math ability should get correct, due simply to her reading ability. Thus, the score she receives is not an accurate representation of her true math ability. This can in turn influence which performance levels students are placed in, which then has implications for many of the decisions in educational settings that are based on student test scores.

This example clearly demonstrates the importance of construct irrelevance to the overall validity argument of an assessment. If an assessment contains variance that is irrelevant to the construct, the scores will be biased, and thus it becomes extremely difficult to justify using those scores to make decisions. Therefore, it is important to ensure that sources of construct irrelevance are minimized as much as possible to safeguard the validity of the scores and their intended uses. Common sources of construct irrelevance and methods used to detect some of these sources are discussed in the following section.

Examples of Construct Irrelevance

In operational psychometrics, construct irrelevance is most commonly associated with differential item functioning (DIF) and differential test functioning. This is because at their core, both DIF and differential test functioning represent construct irrelevance. Thus, possible sources of DIF are also possible sources of construct irrelevance. If performance on an item can be predicted by group membership after accounting for ability level on the construct on interest, then construct irrelevance is present. Most commonly, the groups of interest in these analyses are gender, ethnic, and socioeconomic groups.

When a reading assessment is administered, there is no intention for that assessment to also measure a student's gender or race. Thus, if one group (e.g., females) is favored over another (e.g., males) after accounting for ability level, construct irrelevant variance is introduced into the scores. Similarly, if an item or the assessment overall favors a particular racial or socioeconomic group after accounting for ability, then the assessment is not only measuring the construct of interest, but also the racial or socioeconomic group membership.

Construct irrelevance is not limited to group membership, however. For example, individuals' performance on an assessment may be influenced by their motivation or their preconceived notions about how they will perform (e.g., stereotype threat). Thus, the assessment would be measuring not only the construct of interest but also the individual's motivation.

This can also be true of tests that are overly long. If individuals get tired at the end of a long assessment, then the assessment now measures exhaustion in addition to the construct of interest. When providing scores, only the construct of interest should be included. Therefore, it is of the utmost importance construct irrelevance is considered throughout the assessment development from item writing (to lower the chance of construct irrelevance through DIF) to the blueprint of assessment (to avoid test designs that may invite additional sources of error).

W. Jake Thompson

See also Construct-Related Validity Evidence; Construct Underrepresentation; Differential Item Functioning; Threats to Research Validity; Validity

Further Readings

Downing, S. M. (2002). Threats to the validity of locally developed multiple-choice tests in medical education: Construct-irrelevant variance and construct underrepresentation. *Advances in Health Sciences Education, 7,* 235–241.

Haladyna, T. M., & Downing, S. M. (2005). Construct-irrelevant variance in high-stakes testing. *Educational Measurement: Issues and Practice,* 23(1), 17–27.

Messick, S. (1994). The interplay of evidence and consequences in the validation of performance assessments. *Educational Researcher,* 23(2), 13–23.

Messick, S. (1995). Validity of psychological assessment: Validation of inferences from persons' responses and performances as scientific inquiry into score meaning. *American Psychologist,* 50(9), 741–749.

CONSTRUCT UNDERREPRESENTATION

Construct underrepresentation occurs when a test does not adequately measure all aspects of the construct of interest. There are various sources of construct underrepresentation. This entry first discusses the sources of construct underrepresentation, the effects of construct underrepresentation on test use and score interpretation, and how to minimize construct underrepresentation. It then looks at specific ways of dealing with potential sources of construct underrepresentation in different types of assessment.

For a construct having multiple facets, when one of the facets is not tapped in the measurement, the construct is underrepresented. For example, if a particular test intended as a comprehensive measure of anxiety measures only psychological reactions and not emotional, cognitive, or situational components, it might underrepresent the intended construct. In addition, covering only trivial content in the curriculum will create construct underrepresentation.

Other times, construct underrepresentation is due to inadequate use of test questions. For example, a test of reading comprehension intended to measure children's ability to read and interpret stories might not contain a sufficient variety of reading passages or might ignore a common type of reading material. An examination of sufficient length will be a fairer, more accurate, and reliable sample of important knowledge. Maldistribution of examination items leads to oversampling of some content areas and undersampling of others; too few test questions results in failure to adequately sample the learning content in the achievement domain desired. Consequently, the reliability of the examination suffers.

From the perspective of test development, multiple-choice tests are designed to measure skills ranging from lower order (e.g., recognition, recall) to higher order (e.g., reason, synthesis, application, evaluation) skills. However, it takes time, energy, and expertise to create multiple-choice items that tap higher order thinking skills; therefore, many multiple-choice tests overrepresent lower order skills and underrepresent higher order skills. If the test purporting to measure a broad range of cognitive skills employs few items assessing evaluation and application, its scores will be invalid because they underrepresent higher order thinking in the domain.

Construct underrepresentation also occurs when assessment objectives are deficiently considered. Items at a low level of cognitive function require only rote memorization to recall isolated facts that may not reflect the integrated knowledge to support critical thinking or problem-solving ability for real-world situations. A test full of this type of questions underrepresents the construct. Also, teaching to the test leads to scores that are an inaccurate reflection of the knowledge domain and leaving out items that require higher order cognition and problem-solving skills. When teaching to the tests, teachers focus on some subjects at the expense of others, some aspects of a subject at the expense of others, and some students at the expense of others. Consequently, learning becomes narrow, shallow, and transient as a result of construct underrepresentation.

Effects on Test Use and Score Interpretation

In education, test scores are interpreted, acted upon, and used as the basis for inferences and decision making. The extent to which these consequences are aligned with intended purposes and are appropriate and meaningful, given the available sample and data, is the scope of validity. Construct validity is about the meaning of the scores. Evidence is gathered to support the argument for solid validity in the measured construct that renders meaning for the scores. Construct underrepresentation occurs when important elements of the construct are missing from the measurement instrument and it cannot be eliminated but only minimized.

As a source of invalidity, construct underrepresentation negatively affects the soundness of score meaning, relevancy, and value implications. When construct representation is found to contribute to social consequences, the construct and/or the measure needs to be adapted in keeping with such a finding. For example, in cross-cultural comparisons, it is crucial to ask whether a less studied cultural group conceives of or values the construct in the same manner as the most often studied group upon which the construct and the measure were developed. The answer to this question reveals how much the obtained scores reflect construct underrepresentation and/or construct irrelevancy. The presence of construct underrepresentation cautions against direct test use for that group because the intended meanings of the scores may have been contaminated by the factors within the context.

How to Minimize Construct Underrepresentation

The breadth of content specifications for a test should reflect the breadth of the construct invoked in score interpretation. Equally important is for measurement research in general and construct validation in particular to entail multiple measures of each construct under investigation. Critically, test developers and users must be conscious of the relationship between score meaning and social consequences. Samuel Messick argued that if social consequences occur that are traceable to construct underrepresentation and/or construct-irrelevant variance, the construct and/or measure need to be modified to incorporate these findings; if they are not, then they are not part of validity.

During the process of validation, empirical evidence and a compelling argument are presented to support the intended inference and to show that alternative or competing inferences are not more viable. In particular, the degree to which construct underrepresentation and construct-irrelevant variance are problems needs to be analyzed. Validation puts both the test and the theory under scrutiny; and if research findings obtained from test scores and the theory disagree, then this discrepancy must be resolved by drafting a new test or postulating a new theory or both.

Because invalidity threats like construct underrepresentation can happen to both the test and the explanatory theory, validation as an ongoing process needs to account for both dimensions. Threats to the interpretability of obtained scores from construct underrepresentation can be minimized by clearly defining how particular psychological or educational tests are to be used. When constrained with a single test score, a strategy can be employed to triangulate on the referent construct by incorporating multiple formats of items or tasks in a composite total score. Messick pointed out the potential role of social consequences in expounding the values and meanings of test score and test use. Therefore, considering values and social consequences in the validation process and minding potential impacts from legitimate/illegitimate use and interpretation of test scores is a way of minimizing construct underrepresentation.

When developing a criterion-based assessment, construct representation must be well reflected in test specifications, often created with the help of an in-depth needs analysis of the requirements from the test users and the skills and ability certain levels of obtained scores should possess. For higher level constructs, use of multiple-choice items can be limited and constructed-response question formats used more often. Test and item specifications can be further developed following field tests and feedback from stakeholders. Follow-up studies, as part of the validation process, are necessary for maintaining construct representation.

Rasch analysis is a powerful tool for evaluating construct validity. The Rasch model assumes a hypothetical unidimensional line along which persons and items are located according to their ability and difficulty magnitude. The items that fall close enough to the hypothetical line contribute to the measurement of the single dimension defined in the construct theory. Long distances between the items on the line indicate that there are big differences between item difficulties, so people who fall in ability close to this part of the line are not as precisely measured by means of the test. Gaps along the unidimensional continuum are indications of construct underrepresentation.

Dealing With Sources of Construct Underrepresentation

This section gives a few examples how the issue of construct underrepresentation is handled to illustrate the issues discussed previously.

Test Accommodation

Construct underrepresentation endangers validity of test accommodation. For example, if speed is part of the intended construct, it is inappropriate to allow for extra time, a common accommodation, in the test administration. Because speed will not be part of the construct measured by the extended-time test, scores obtained on the test with extended administration time may underrepresent the construct measured with the strictly timed test. Similarly, it would be inappropriate to translate a reading comprehension test used for selection into an organization's training program if reading comprehension in English is important to successful participation in the program.

Valid test accommodations avoid creating construct underrepresentation; those that reduce construct representation are invalid. Valid accommodations include offering an example in a reading comprehension test, enlarging the text print, or allowing the use of eyeglasses; invalid accommodations may include reading the text to a person who is visually impaired because doing so reduces construct representation by removing the element of text decoding.

Computer-Based Testing (CBT)

How test questions are developed, selected, and calibrated within a CBT can impact representation of the construct measured. Typical procedures adopted by CBT such as algorithmic item writing, computerized-adaptive testing (CAT), and unidimensional item calibration can potentially cause construct underrepresentation. First, the item selection algorithms used in adaptive testing can possibly lead to construct underrepresentation. In many CATs, an algorithm is used to select items or testlets to be administered to an examinee. The typical algorithm attempts to align item difficulty with estimated proficiency and limits how frequently a specific question can be administered. These activities can reduce content coverage (and thus construct representation) at the test score level for a particular examinee.

Although CAT algorithms include content constraints to ensure content coverage of items, it is important to evaluate the content quality of CATs administered to specific individuals and acknowledge that content quality and construct representation are continuous qualities, which are unlikely to be guaranteed within an item selection algorithm that is inherently binary. Therefore, we need evidence that construct representation does not differ across levels of proficiency and the CATs given are roughly parallel forms.

Second, with automatic item generation, which CBT uses to develop a test, it is possible that parallel items have differing statistical and substantive properties. Comprehensive field testing of generated items may circumvent this problem, but methods to determine or predict item properties need to be further developed in order to ensure that algorithm-produced items have desirable and expected psychometric properties. The validity of the resulting measurement will be undermined if the predicted item parameters do not adequately represent the true attributes of the generated item.

Third, construct underrepresentation in CBT can also stem from the use of an item calibration model that puts statistical criteria ahead of qualitative criteria, such as construct representation. For example, with a unidimensional item response theory model, construct-relevant items that do not fit the model may be eliminated and might result in a particular substantive area insufficiently represented and a poorly represented construct.

Language Use in Science Assessments

The absence of linguistic complexity from content area tests in text structures, genres, or styles of rhetorical organization common in the scientific discipline can potentially cause construct underrepresentation. In science learning, students are often expected to produce and comprehend explicit procedure recounts and/or research articles, arguments with claim and evidence, explanations, and comparisons. Therefore, if students are not expected to make meaning from argumentation and explanation texts on science tests, this may suggest that these assessments suffer from construct underrepresentation; that is, the inclusion or exclusion of specific text structures may pose a threat to the validity of these tests.

For test developers, because specific linguistic knowledge is a component of content area mastery and linguistic features are part of the target construct on content area tests, definitions of the science achievement construct used in assessment design should explicitly include a description of the linguistic features that are necessary for participation in grade-level written and oral discourse.

Both lexical and grammatical elements of language and text-level organizing structures (rhetorical organization and cohesion) should be analyzed. Work is needed to investigate the styles of rhetorical organization used in these assessments and to match this organization to that common in the measured domain. If text-level styles of organization such as argumentation are central to the domain but absent from content area tests, this may suggest language-related construct underrepresentation.

Game-Based Assessments and Simulation-Based Assessments

In game-based assessments use cases, construct-representation evidence for validity is found from domain analysis research. The evidence-centered assessment design framework includes elements and processes that embody this research. Failure to evoke aspects of the targeted capabilities constitutes construct underrepresentation. Construct representation may be improved by including interaction, an array of actions and representations, and open-ended spaces for assembling and carrying out strategies.

Simulation-based assessments are often used in medical fields, where validity research helps determine whether limitations in the simulation model led to construct underrepresentation. Only part of the real-world tasks can be simulated seamlessly with high fidelity. For example, the use of standardized patients—laypeople trained to portray real patients—provides a potentially valuable means for assessing skills such as the ability to collect a patient history and the ability to communicate with the patient. With standardized patients, it is difficult, however, to simulate abnormal physical findings. This limitation restricts the range of problems that can be presented, which in turn may reduce the likelihood that the examinee will check for abnormal findings—even though the examinee would have in the real world—and it also may lead examinees to record that those findings were absent despite the fact that they did not check for them.

The complexity of the problem of developing tasks and creating variables makes it clear that a lengthy program of test development and refinement is likely to be necessary before optimal solutions can be found for the problem of variable identification. Currently, answers remain context specific.

Yi-Hsin Chen, Isaac Y. Li, and Walter Chason

See also Construct Irrelevance; Construct-Related Validity Evidence; Cross-Cultural Research

Further Readings

American Educational Research Association, American Psychological Association, National Council on Measurement in Education, Joint Committee on Standards for Educational & Psychological Testing (US). (2014). *Standards for educational and psychological testing*. American Educational Research Association.

Drasgow, F. (Ed.). (2016). *Technology and testing: Improving educational and psychological measurement.* New York, NY: Routledge.

Huff, K. L., & Sireci, S. G. (2001). Validity issues in computer-based testing. *Educational Measurement: Issues and Practice, 20*(3), 16–25.

Messick, S. (1989). Validity. In R. L. Linn (Ed.), *Educational measurement* (3rd ed., pp. 13–103). New York, NY: Macmillan.

Zumbo, B. D. (2007). Validity: Foundational issues and statistical methodology. In C. R. Rao & S. Sinharay (Eds.), *Handbook of statistics, Vol. 26: Psychometrics* (pp. 45–79). Amsterdam, the Netherlands: Elsevier Science B.V.

CONSTRUCTED-RESPONSE ITEMS

Constructed-response items refer to a wide range of test items that require examinees to produce answers in various formats; they are often contrasted or compared to multiple-choice (or selected-response) items in which examinees are required to select one or multiple appropriate options out of a given list. In practice, any items that do not take the selected response item format (e.g., multiple-choice or true/false items) can be referred to as constructed-response items. The term itself does not refer to a single format of items but implies flexibility in item formats. Because of this flexibility, "items" can be extended to "tasks" or "exercises" that are included not only in a written test but also in a performance test. The *Standards for Educational and Psychological Testing* defines constructed-response items, tasks, or exercises as follows:

> Items, tasks, or exercises for which test takers must create their own responses or products rather than choose a response from a specified set. Short-answer items require a few words or a number as an answer; extended-response items require at least a few sentences and may include diagram, mathematical proofs, essay, or problem solutions such as network repairs or other work products. (pp. 217–218)

In large-scale assessments and formative assessments, the constructed-response item format is primarily used to measure a complex set of skills or composition of knowledge that cannot be easily summarized in a short list of response options. Due to the complexity in the skill sets to be measured, writing items as well as grading and analyzing item responses are inevitably accompanied by a certain level of complexity (e.g., nature of multidimensional latent traits or skills). This entry reviews various formats for constructed-response items within different contexts and addresses the issues in developing, grading, and analyzing constructed-response items for educational assessments.

Item Formats for Constructed-Responses

The constructed-response item format exhibits great diversity, reflecting distinct characteristics of the content domain (e.g., language arts, mathematics, science, social studies, or computer science) and cognitive demand (e.g., knowledge, skill, or ability) to be measured. The taxonomy of constructed-response item format has been developed with contributions made by many researchers. With some variabilities, all taxonomies include a common dichotomy: whether an item requires open-ended or closed-ended response. Here, the distinction between open-ended or closed-ended lies on the existence of a well-defined (or constrained) scope for the set of skills or ability to be measured. In the meantime, the taxonomy developed by Steven Osterlind and William Merz includes reasoning competency (predictive, analytical, and interpretive reasoning, and factual recall) and cognitive continuum (convergent vs. divergent thinking), while Thomas Haladyna's taxonomy includes scoring (objective vs. subjective) and outcome dimensions (product vs. performance). Extant studies identified the following numerous constructed-response item formats: anecdotal, cloze (embedded answers), demonstration, discussion, essay, exhibition, experiment, fill in the blank, grid in response, interview, observation, oral report, performance, portfolio, project, research paper, review, self/peer test, short answer, writing sample, and video-based task.

While the constructed-response item can take various formats, the most commonly used item formats in large-scale assessments (e.g., National

Assessment of Educational Progress or Programme for International Student Assessment) are arguably limited to cloze, fill in the blank, grid in response, and short answer for all content domains. In addition, essay writing and oral exams (e.g., the speaking section in the TOEFL, a test of English as a foreign language) are used to measure language competency. Finally, it should be noted that the item formats and taxonomy for constructed-response items need to be and will be even more varied and extended as modern technology (e.g., computers, tablets, or motion-detection devices) plays a more significant role in the educational learning and assessment environment.

Developing Constructed-Response Items

The general standard procedure of item writing can be routinely applied to develop constructed-response items; in addition to that, specific recommendations and guidelines for developing constructed-response items have been offered in multiple resources as well. Drew Gitomer emphasized the coherence among task, rubric, and scoring apparatus that are built on well-defined constructs. Haladyna listed four categories of concerns that need to be addressed in writing constructed-response items—content, formatting/style, writing directions/stimulus, and context—and provided detailed guidance within each category. As can be seen from most of the literature on constructed-response items, a clear definition of the knowledge domain and skills to be measured, and an appropriateness of the item format is the key in writing constructed-response items. Both ensuring a precise mapping of items on the test blueprint with clear domain definitions and avoiding construct-irrelevant features are closely related to content or construct validity of test scores. In addition, the most distinctive and important aspect of writing constructed-response items is that the item writing cannot be separated from the concerns in scoring. Thomas Horgan and Gavin Murphy found more than 75% of textbooks recommend anonymous scoring, scoring one item at a time, and using a rubric or an ideal answer. Haladyna also suggests that item writers should "provide information about scoring criteria." The following section addresses some methodological issues and practices in scoring constructed responses.

Issues in Scoring Constructed Responses

To analyze item response data for assessing quality of items (e.g., to obtain item difficulty and discrimination information), it is necessary to transform various forms of constructed responses (either product or performance) into numeric data. The assignment of numeric values to constructed responses can be achieved by using a rubric (or scoring guide) that can be holistic, analytical, or developmental. While a holistic rubric can be efficient in that it describes the overall quality of a product or performance in a single rating number (e.g., SAT writing), a drawback of the holistic rubric is that it does not provide precise and useful information. Accordingly, holistic rubrics are more appropriate for summative assessment rather than formative assessment in which explicit feedback is crucial to diagnose. On the other hand, an analytical rubric details characteristics of a product or performance with respect to each analytical category, so that multiple subrating numbers are included in the final rating. Assuming that the analytical rubric is well constructed with clearly distinctive categories and characteristics, using analytical rubrics can provide more explicit feedback. A developmental rubric describes the developmental characteristics of a product or performance either holistically or analytically.

Regardless of the type of rubric being used, multiple raters are typically involved to secure fairness and objectiveness in scoring; therefore, ensuring an appropriate level of interrater reliability through developing rubrics and training raters is critical. Agreement among raters can be quantified by using various coefficients. For dichotomously scored data, κ coefficients, intraclass correlation, or tetrachoric correlation are often used. For polytomous data, weighted κ, intraclass correlation, or polychoric correlation can be calculated. These approaches are, however, limited in that the analysis is somewhat post hoc and definitive. Furthermore, other reliability coefficients such as internal consistency or test–retest reliability are often calculated separately after a satisfactory level of interrater reliability is established.

Researchers can also apply the generalizability theory to investigate the reliability of constructed-response items in a more comprehensive and systematic fashion. In particular, when scoring constructed responses is involved in multiple facets of the measurement structure (e.g., multiple raters, multiple tasks, and multiple occasions), generalizability theory provides a theoretical and analytical framework that enables researchers to specify sources of measurement error and to gauge how much variability in scores can be attributed to different sources of error. A typical generalizability theory application is composed of two studies: a G study in which a variance component for each facet is estimated and a D study in which an optimal measurement structure to ensure a certain level of reliability can be determined given the variance components estimated in the G study. Through the D study, researchers can make decisions on how many raters, occasions, or items are needed to ensure a desired level of reliability considering cost efficiency.

With advances in technology, automated scoring has become an alternative approach to score constructed responses, particularly for large-scale assessment to save time and reduce the cost of resources while ensuring scoring consistency. A few large testing companies (e.g., Educational Testing Service, Pearson, Pacific Metrics) have developed computer programs for scoring essays, contents, and math. To ensure the quality of scoring, an automated scoring system is often adopted through a carefully composed protocol with excessive caution. Usually, it serves as a cross validation for human scoring at the beginning and is gradually extended to a substitution of human scoring after eliminating systematic errors in an iterative process. However, caution should be taken if human scoring is to be completely substituted by automated scoring because many large-scale assessments or standardized tests are used to make high-stakes decisions.

Analysis of Constructed-Response Item Data

Once scoring constructed responses is completed by raters, the next step is to evaluate the psychometric properties of the items using the scored item responses. Measurement theories such as classical test theory or item response theory provide analytical tools for assessing items.

Within the classical test theory framework, the item discrimination can be calculated as the correlation between item scores and total scores for both dichotomously and polytomously scored item responses. The item difficulty (also sometimes referred as item easiness) for a dichotomously scored item is defined as the percentage of examinees who answer to the item correctly. However, the possible rubric scores for constructed-response items often exhibit more than two categories; therefore, the ratio of the weighted sum scores to theoretically possible maximum sum scores across examinees can be alternatively used. For example, let there be 1, 2, and 3 rubric scores for an item, and observed numbers of examinees for a corresponding rubric category are 25, 5, and 20 for Item A and 15, 15, and 20 for Item B. The difficulty parameters for these two items can be calculated as follows:

$$1 \times 25 + 2 \times 5 + 3 \times 203 \times (25 + 5 + 20) = 0.63,$$

$$1 \times 15 + 2 \times 15 + 3 \times 203 \times 15 + 15 + 20 = 0.70.$$

While these numbers reveal that Item A is more difficult than Item B, 0.63 and 0.70 do not provide further information for each specific score category.

In contrast, item response theory defines item discrimination and difficulty as parameters to model the relation between item responses and a latent trait or ability. Among various item response models, Fumiko Samejima's graded response model, Erling Andersen's rating scale model, and Geoff Masters' partial credit model are often used for polytomously scored item responses. In case the order of rubric categories is not predetermined, R. Darrell Bock's nominal categories model can be utilized to determine which category requires a higher level of latent trait or ability to order the categories. These aforementioned models extract different information from item responses based on different assumptions. For example, both rating scale and partial credit models are extended from Georg Rasch's model that assumes the same discrimination parameters across items. On the other hand, nominal categories and graded response models allow varying discrimination across items. If there is a theoretical or empirical rationale for a categorized latent trait rather than a continuous latent trait, various cognitive diagnosis models can be also used for item analysis.

Another issue in analyzing constructed response item data is multidimensionality of latent traits because an item often taps on multiple skills or cognitive domains. With advances in multidimensional item response theory or item factor analysis, the measurement models become more flexible so that researchers can model more complex relations among latent traits.

Constructed-Response Items Versus Multiple-Choice Items

Because constructed-response items require more resources in scoring relative to cost-efficient multiple-choice items, there have been multiple studies to compare utility of the two types of items in large-scale assessment settings. However, consensus has not been made among researchers in educational testing because previous studies vary in terms of methods that include samples, subjects, and contexts. For example, while the scores on constructed-response items and multiple-choice items are highly correlated among the same group of examinees, gender is a factor that might be related to responses to different item formats according to Mark Pomplun and Nita Sundbye. Some also argue that carefully developed multiple-choices items can serve as a substitute for some short-answer items, particularly in large-scale assessments. Therefore, using constructed-response items in large-scale assessments is incorporated not because the constructed-response item formats are exclusively appropriate to measure the skill or domains but because using only multiple-choice items in assessments could introduce a less desirable phenomenon such as excessive focus on testing skills for multiple-choice items.

Ji Seung Yang, Monica Morell, and Yang Liu

See also Automated Essay Evaluation; Classical Test Theory; Cognitive Diagnosis; Difficulty Index; Discrimination Index; Generalizability Theory; Inter-Rater Reliability; Item Response Theory; Multiple-Choice Items; Performance-Based Assessment; Portfolio Assessment; Reliability; Rubrics; Scales; Tests; True Score; True-False Items; Validity

Further Readings

American Educational Research Association, American Psychological Association, & National Council on Measurement in Education (2014). *Standards for Educational and Psychological Testing*. Washington, DC: American Educational Research Association.

Gitomer, D. H. (2007). *Teacher quality in a changing policy landscape: Improvements in the teacher pool*. Princeton, NJ: Educational Testing Service.

Haladyna, T. M., & Rodriguez, M. C. (2013). *Developing and validating test items*. New York, NY: Taylor & Francis.

Hogan, T. P., & Murphy G. (2007). Recommendations for preparing and scoring constructed-response items: What the experts say. *Applied Measurement in Education, 20(4)*, 427–441.

Liu, O. L., Brew, C., Blackmore, J., Gerard, L., Madhok, J., & Linn, M. C. (2014). Automated scoring of constructed-response science items: Prospects and obstacles. *Educational Measurement: Issues and Practice, 33(2)*, 19–28.

Osterlind, S. J., & Merz, W. R. (1994). Building a taxonomy for constructed-response test items. *Educational Assessment, 2(2)*, 133–147.

Pomplun, M., & Sundbye, N. (1999). Gender differences in constructed response reading items. *Applied Measurement in Education, 12(1)*, 95–109.

Van Der Linden, W. J., & Hambleton, R. K. (1997). Item response theory: Brief history, common models, and extensions. *Handbook of Modern Item Response Theory*, 29–164.

CONSTRUCTIVIST APPROACH

Constructivism is the epistemological idea that we construct our knowledge by linking new information to what we already know, rather than simply being passive recipients of knowledge. Thus, a *constructivist approach to education* is one in which educators encourage students to solve problems by actively engaging in tasks that require the learners to create an interpretation of the outside world in order to construct their own new knowledge rather than relying on instructor driven didactic methods only. In addition to being at odds with a more didactic approach to education, constructivism is a cognitive learning theory, in which active cognitive processing is a fundamental element of learning.

The emphasis on the learner's active cognitive processes in constructivism is generally considered to be at odds with a behaviorist approach to learning and instruction, which in its simplest form suggests that learning occurs as a result of conditioning and can be measured by changes in behaviors. While behavior changes may occur as a result of learning with a constructivist approach, the focus for both the instructor and the learner is more on the cognitive processes and newly constructed knowledge used to solve problems and less on the behaviors that occur as a result of that learning. This entry describes the history of the constructivist philosophy, beginning with Lev Vygotsky and John Dewey. An explanation of constructivist learning philosophy, constructivist approaches to education, examples of constructivist activities, and criticism of constructivism are also included.

History of Constructivism

The constructivist approach has received much attention in the 21st century; however, constructivism was first formally discussed in early 20th century in Russia by Vygotsky, in the United States by Dewey, and later by Jean Piaget of Switzerland. Although Vygotsky and Dewey wrote about educational practice during the same era, it is unlikely that the two truly discussed their ideas due the political climate of the time. It is also unclear as to how familiar they were with each other's work because Vygotsky's work was not widely published until the 1970s, almost 40 years after his early death due to tuberculosis. Even so, both Vygotsky and Dewey encouraged educational practices in which the learners are engaged in thinking about practical, everyday, real problems rather than simply memorizing rote facts. Both Vygotsky and Dewey were concerned with creating good citizens through education, thus they believed that helping students become thinking

adults who could solve novel problems was more important than simply telling students exactly what they should know.

Following Dewey's work in the United States, in mid-20th century in Switzerland, Jean Piaget emerged as an advocate for constructivist approaches to education based on his studies of human development. Although Piaget's theories primarily focused on developmental stages, his theories about learning included the ideas of assimilation and accommodation, which are constructivist in nature. Assimilation occurs when a child encounters something new and in order to understand it, the children incorporates it into the knowledge the child already has. Accommodation is an opposite approach to the construction of knowledge in which a learner modifies the learner's interpretation of the world when encountering new information that does not fit into the knowledge base that the child already has. A simple example of these concepts is when a child encounters a dog that the child has never seen, the child may be told that it is a dog and add that to the child's category of dogs. If the child encounters a coyote, thinks it is a dog, and then is told that it is actually a coyote, the child must add the category of coyotes to the child's knowledge base. In both cases, the child is constructing the child's own knowledge by linking the new information to the child's own interpretation and understanding of the world.

Years before Vygotsky or Dewey began touting the virtues of active learning through practical problem solving, several other famous educators also integrated elements of what might be defined as a constructivist approach into their educational practice. Both the German Friedrich Froebel (the father of kindergarten) and the Italian Maria Montessori began suggesting the importance of active learning and problem solving for children in the 19th century. Their ideas, which included allowing children to work together to solve practical problems both indoors and outdoors through play and "work," are consistent with the basic tenets of constructivism. Montessori's philosophy of teaching was also child centered, such that children were encouraged to be active learners, presented with appropriate learning materials, so that they might fully explore and understand concepts as well as learn important life lessons.

Twenty-first-Century Constructivism

In the beginning of the 21st century, constructivism started becoming a catch phrase in educational theory, practice, and research. Educators and policy makers began to emphasize the importance of learning the so-called 21st-century skills, and there was increasing concern about the abilities of students to solve real-world problems. Although an emphasis on educational testing also became prevalent in the United States during this time, it was often at odds with educational researchers' and philosophers' consideration of using constructivist methods in order to increase students' engagement and abilities to solve novel real-world problems. Although many administrators and thus teachers began emphasizing more instructor centered approaches focused on the content on standardized tests, constructivist instruction remained student centered, with the instructor more often acting as a guide or facilitator, rather than the authoritative driver of the lessons.

In constructivist-based lessons, students are given real-world problems to solve and are expected to begin by creating connections from the knowledge they have to new information, so that they might construct the knowledge they need to fully answer the problems. The connections formed between what they already know and the new information include their interpretations of the new ideas and experiences. The learners often need to find additional sources of information through this process. This is where the guide (or teacher) can be most useful. By guiding the discovery, the teacher can scaffold or start where the student's knowledge level is and build from that level of knowledge. Using guided instruction, the teacher can also be sure that the students learn (or construct) the knowledge they need for a lesson.

Constructivist-based lessons are most often used in science classrooms, where students may be allowed to explore scientific concepts through the scientific method as well as through shared learning experiences with other students. Perhaps constructivism has become most popular in science classrooms because the materials lend themselves well to exploration and active learning.

Constructivism is sometimes considered "hands-on" learning and is often confused with active learning. Although active learning is an essential element in constructivist learning, the activity must occur foremost within the learners in their thoughts. Although it is easy to see engagement when learners are physically actively involved in the learning process, physical activity is not always essential for knowledge construction. A constructivist-based classroom is often filled with both physically and mentally active students. The learning process is expected to be interactive and dynamic, with students coming together to discuss and solve problems. New challenges and problems often emerge through the process. The constructivist approach relies on the process of evolving problem solving to create critical thinking skills as part of the newly constructed knowledge set.

Constructivist Lesson Plan Example

A teacher beginning a lesson in a constructivist classroom generally begins with a big picture concept. A high school science teacher or college professor might begin by talking about a concept such as sea level rise. After explaining the general idea of sea level rise, the instructor might ask the students to "pair and share" what they know about and wonder about sea level rise. The instructor might then ask them to work in small groups to come up with three questions they would like to know the answers about sea level rise. At that point, the instructor might ask the students to create a hypothesis about one of those questions and what might contribute to sea level rise. Then they might be asked to conduct an experiment in which they test that hypothesis in a laboratory setting.

Following the experiment, the students might be asked to find information that supports their findings. The students might then spend time discussing the question in the classroom, do Internet research on the topic, and write a response to the question. Following this work, the instructor might bring all of the groups together to discuss all of their findings and how they fit together. They then could have a classroom discussion about the scientific causes of sea level rise, the global causes of current sea level rise, and the potential impacts of sea level rise on different countries.

The constructivist approach suggests that the learners in this lesson would take knowledge that they had before the lesson about water, the sea, and other related issues and use it to interpret their findings and construct new knowledge about sea level rise and all of the connected issues that emerged during the lessons, the experiments, the presentations, and the discussions. This constructivist approach is in sharp contrast to a didactic lesson in which the teacher presents a lecture about sea level rise and its causes and impacts and then gives the students an in-class exam to assess learning.

Criticism of Constructivism

Constructivist approaches to education have been criticized for forcing learners to "reinvent the wheel." Critics have suggested that it is often more efficient to simply tell learners how things are rather than force them to discover what has already been discovered. For example, critics of constructivism might suggest that it is a waste of a student's time to expect them to rediscover Newton's laws, when an instructor can more simply explain the laws in lectures.

It is likely that constructivists would argue that they do not expect students to discover every fact on their own but expect that their need for that knowledge will arise from their attempts to solve real-world problems. When the students arrive at a point where they need to understand Newton's laws, then an instructor can serve as a guide and help them find the material that presents these ideas. The instructor can then allow the students to discuss and work together to construct their own interpretation and understanding of these laws.

Jill Hendrickson Lohmeier

See also Active Learning; Critical Thinking; Epistemologies, Teacher and Student; Learning Theories; Montessori Schools; Social Cognitive Theory

Further Readings

Dewey, J. (1966). *Democracy and education.* New York, NY: Free Press.

Fosnot, C. T. (2013). *Constructivism: Theory, perspectives, and practice.* Teachers College Press.

Glasersfeld, E. v. (1995). *Radical constructivism: A way of knowing and learning.* Washington, DC: Falmer.

Gunstone, P. J. F. R. F. (2013). *The content of science: A constructivist approach to its teaching and learning.* Routledge.

Steffe, L. P., & Gale, J. E. (Eds.). (1995). *Constructivism in education.* Hillsdale, NJ: Erlbaum.

Ultanir, E. (2012). An epistemological glance at the constructivist approach: Constructivist learning in Dewey, Piaget, and Montessori. *International Journal of Instruction, 5*(2), 195–212.

CONSTRUCT-RELATED VALIDITY EVIDENCE

Construct-related validity evidence demonstrates whether a test measures its intended construct, where a construct can be defined as a conceptual abstraction used to understand the unobservable latent variable that is responsible for scores on a given measure. Constructs are said to be situated within the nomological network, which was originally proposed by Lee Cronbach and Paul Meehl in 1955. *Nomologic* refers to rules of nature, and the nomological network situates a construct in terms of its relationship to other, known constructs and behaviors in order to provide a theoretical context for the construct. This theoretical context in turn suggests avenues through which construct-related validity evidence can be provided, for example, in terms of its relationship to other constructs or traits.

According to our current understanding of validity, construct validity is the only type of validity, and thus, construct-related validity evidence encompasses all possible types of validity evidence. Samuel Messick's 1989 framework redefined validity as a unified concept by defining all validity as construct validity; this definition effectively subsumes all possible types of validity evidence into the larger category of construct validity evidence. However, the term *construct validity evidence* is also sometimes used to refer to specific sources of validity evidence; this sense of the term recalls the historical definition of construct validity as a specific type of validity. In earlier decades when validity was conceptualized as having multiple types, construct validity frequently appeared alongside content validity and criterion-related validity as one of the main types of validity, and construct validity had its own sources of validity evidence. Although this conceptualization of types of validity is not the modern view, construct-related validity evidence is still discussed in the literature. The following sections outline the sources of construct-related validity evidence, provide an overview of the historical definition of construct validity as a type of validity, and provide an overview of our current understanding of construct validity as the sole type of validity in the unified theory.

Sources of Construct-Related Validity Evidence

Construct-related validity evidence supporting an item's nomological validity attempts to provide quantitative evidence to position the construct within the nomological network. In order to assemble nomological validity evidence, it is useful to consider both convergent and discriminant validity evidence. Convergent validity evidence rests on the assumption that constructs that are closely related in the theoretical framework of the nomological network should also be correlated when measured in reality. Convergent validity evidence can be provided in terms of a measure's correlation with other measures with strong validity arguments that assess theoretically related constructs. For example, if the construct of intelligence is thought to be closely related to working memory, then examinees' results on a test thought to measure intelligence should be highly correlated with their results on a measure of working memory.

Discriminant validity evidence is the counterpart of convergent validity evidence. This type of validity evidence is used to demonstrate that constructs that have no relationship or an inverse relationship in the nomological net are also not correlated in reality. Discriminant validity evidence can consist of a measure's low or negative correlation with other measures assessing theoretically opposed concepts. For example, if extraversion and introversion are assumed to lie at opposite ends of a spectrum, then examinees' results on a measure of extraversion should negatively correlate with their results on a measure of introversion.

In order to provide an approach to assessing the construct validity of a measure or set of measures, Campbell and Fiske developed the multitrait–multimethod matrix (commonly referred to as MTMM) in 1959. The multitrait–multimethod matrix provides a way to track correlations across multiple measures, measuring the same construct via different methods and different constructs by the same method. Through this process, both convergent and discriminant validity evidence is collected.

Another method of collecting construct-related validity evidence is to observe the effect of experimental variables on test scores. For example, if a test is designed to measure participants' skill in two-digit addition problems, one would expect that practice in solving these types of problems would improve test scores. By collecting data from the measure before and after participants take a practice session, the researcher can assess whether the practice impacts test scores. If practice on the skill in question fails to improve test scores, the measure may not actually be assessing the construct in question. Of course, this example would not hold true for measures of constructs that would not be expected to change with practice, such as most personality traits. In this case, evidence that practice fails to affect participants' scores would constitute validity evidence supporting the construct.

Other commonly used sources of construct-related validity evidence include statistical analyses such as factor analysis and structural equation modeling. By conducting a factor analysis to determine how much of the variance a factor accounts for, the researchers can provide evidence to support the presence of their construct and the adequacy of their measure. Such empirical data have been frequently used in validity arguments for decades and continue to be a popular source of validity evidence.

If content-related validity evidence turns out to yield negative findings that disconfirm the hypothesis, the researcher must consider the possible implications of this finding. Either the construct is improperly defined within the nomological network, the construct is well defined but the measure either assesses a different construct or is overly subject to construct-irrelevant variance, or the construct is poorly defined and the measure assesses a different construct. Negative construct-related validity evidence should always prompt researchers to more closely examine the construct and measure for which they are seeking to construct a validity argument.

Historical Definition

The idea of construct validity was formulated by Cronbach and Meehl for the first edition of the *Standards for Educational and Psychological Testing*, which was published in 1954. The idea of construct validity was more abstract than previous ideas about validity types and was motivated at least partially in order to deal with the perplexing issue of validating personality tests, which criterion and content validity were ill-equipped to handle. This initial definition called for both logical and empirical evidence to justify the inference of an underlying construct given test performance. However, construct validity itself was poorly defined, and it was presented as a fallback option of sorts. According to this initial edition of the *Standards*, logical approaches to validation were suitable for achievement or proficiency tests, empirical approaches were suitable for tests of aptitude or disorder, and both approaches were to be employed for tests of more nebulous concepts like personality—hence, construct validity. By using both logical and empirical approaches, researchers could attempt to simultaneously validate the test and its underlying theory.

Cronbach and Meehl's 1955 paper attempted to more clearly define the idea of construct validity and the processes for collecting construct-related validity evidence. This landmark publication introduced the idea of the nomological network and suggested several different sources of construct validity evidence. These sources included group differences in test scores, relationships between test scores as expressed by correlations and factor analyses, item correlations within tests, performance stability over time, and analysis of cognitive processes underlying test performance. These types of validity evidence are still important to include when constructing validity arguments. Indeed, Cronbach and Meehl also put forth guidelines for what to include in a validity argument. In order to construct a validity argument, researchers

were to explain the proposed interpretation of test scores in terms of the construct and its theoretical surroundings in the nomological net, express how adequate they believed the validity argument substantiated these claims, and detail the evidence and logical reasoning that supported the validity claims.

Current Definition

Messick's 1989 chapter on validity marked the field's move away from an understanding of types of validity. Instead, Messick's unifying theory of validity promoted construct validity to the encompassing idea that all types of validity evidence support. With this understanding of validity as a unitary concept, all validity evidence can be said to be construct validity evidence. In the years since Messick's publication, many scholars have debated the nature of construct validity, and several positions regarding construct validity theory have emerged. Brief summaries of several recent papers typifying some of these positions will follow.

Robert Lissitz and Karen Samuelson argue against the need for nomological networks, claiming instead that construct definition can take place without the need for the theory building originally envisioned by Cronbach and Meehl. Especially in the case of academic achievement tests, it is possible for the construct test measures to be logically extrapolated from its content rather than positioned in an external theoretical environment. A similar yet diverging viewpoint has been expressed by scholars such as Susan Embretson, James Pellegrino, and Joanna Gorin, who believe that while theory continues to be critical to construct validity evidence, the theories underlying constructs could best be understood in terms of internal underlying processes such as cognitive processes, skills, and knowledge. This understanding of constructs in terms of their internal processes also negates the need for the nomological network.

Another challenge to the nomological network—and to the definition of validity more generally—came from Denny Boorsboom, Gideon Mellenbergh, and Jaap van Heerden in 2004. These researchers contended that while our current understanding considers validity to be an epistemological matter, it should more accurately be considered an ontological concern. That is, instead of being concerned with how we know things, validity should be concerned with how things actually are. If an ontological definition of validity is accepted, then only two conditions must be met in order for a test to be considered valid. The construct in question must exist, and variation in test scores must be caused by that construct. This definition greatly reduces the scope of validity as a concept, sidestepping many of the concerns about inclusion of social issues in validity arguments.

This brief summary of several positions on validity from the 2000s and 2010s illustrates how construct validity continues to be a contentious issue within validity scholarship. From the foundational idea of the nomological net through the more recent subsummation of all other types of validity into the overarching idea of construct validity, all of the assumptions underlying construct validity are being challenged in the literature. Indeed, because all validity is construct validity under the current unified understanding of validity theory, construct validity and its sources of evidence will likely continue to evolve through time.

Jennifer A. Brussow

See also Consequential Validity Evidence; Content-Related Validity Evidence; Criterion-Based Validity Evidence; Multitrait–Multimethod Matrix; Unitary View of Validity; Validity; Validity, History of

Further Readings

Borsboom, D., Mellenbergh, G. J., & van Heerden, J. (2004). The concept of validity. *Psychological Review*, *111*(4), 1061–1071.

Cronbach, L. J., & Meehl, P. E. (1955). Construct validity in psychological tests. *Psychological Bulletin*, *52*(4), 281–302.

Lissitz, R. W., & Samuelsen, K. (2007). A suggested change in terminology and emphasis regarding validity and education. *Educational Researcher*, *36*(8), 437–448.

Messick, S. (1989). Validity. In R. L. Linn (Ed.), *Educational measurement* (3rd ed., pp. 13–103). Washington, DC: American Council on Education & National Council on Measurement in Education.

Newton, P., & Shaw, S. (2014). *Validity in educational and psychological assessment*. Thousand Oaks, CA: Sage.

CONSUMER-ORIENTED EVALUATION APPROACH

The consumer-oriented approach to evaluation is the evaluation orientation advocated by evaluation expert and philosopher Michael Scriven. The approach stems from the belief that evaluation ought to serve the consumer, that is, the ultimate end user of the particular object under evaluation, the evaluand—be it a program, a curriculum, a policy, a product, or a service. This entry first discusses the history and the key aspects of the consumer-oriented evaluation approach, including the centrality of the consumer, the goal of the evaluation, and the role of the evaluation and the evaluator. It then looks at the techniques used in consumer-oriented evaluation, the checklist developed by Scriven for this evaluation approach, and the advantages and challenges of the approach.

The consumer-oriented evaluation approach arose in the 1960s in reaction to the then-prevailing stances that saw evaluation as an exercise in value-free measurement of whether program goals were achieved. The consumer-oriented evaluation approach reminds evaluators, and those who commission and use evaluation, that an evaluation ought to produce a determination about the merit, worth, and/or significance of the evaluand and that the basis of evaluation ought to be referenced to the needs of consumers.

Centrality of the Consumer

At the core of the consumer-oriented evaluation approach is the stance that evaluation should be oriented toward the needs of the consumer. Scriven argues that an evaluation's task and goal should be directed toward the consumer (end user) primarily and, to a much lesser extent, the program developers and other stakeholders. Scriven recognizes that consumers' values may not always align with the values of developers, funders, or even the delivery partners. The author also observes that the consumer is not necessarily concerned with goals that program developers set out to achieve with an evaluand nor should they have to contend with what developers' intentions are. Rather, what truly matters to consumers is that an object has value, that is, merit, worth, and/or significance.

Goal of Evaluation

The significance of the consumer-oriented evaluation approach is best understood in context of the historical confluences that gave rise to it. One major source has been the limitations and flaws associated with objective-oriented approaches to evaluation or what has sometimes been referred to as Tylerian approach to evaluation. Proponents of Ralph Tyler's approach to evaluation see it as the determination of whether objectives have been achieved or not.

Scriven's critique of Tyler's approach is that conceptualizing evaluation in a goal-oriented way is narrow, for goals, as prescribed by program developers, can be flawed, incomplete, unrealistic, or inadequate in addressing the social ills that prompted the creation of the intervention in the first place. Evaluating in this fashion ignores the true needs of the consumer. This stance is echoed in contemporary discourse that emphasizes the importance of placing the learner first.

The methodological implication is that evaluation is not merely a technical exercise in measurement between what was set out and what was the case in reality, as is the case with evaluation conducted in the Tylerian tradition, but in bringing evidence to bear in reaching an informed judgment about an object's value independent of what developers set out to do. Scriven implores evaluators to understand all effects of an intervention, unconstrained by what developers had sought to achieve, and assess the needs of the users. On the bases of these two assessments, the evaluator advances a judgment concerning the value of the object. The determination of merit, worth, and significance of an evaluand is the singular goal of evaluation.

Role of Evaluation

Scriven further distinguishes the goal of evaluation from the role of evaluation. The author identifies two legitimate roles of evaluation, that of summative and formative evaluation. Summative evaluation advances a summary judgment concerning the overall value of the evaluand. For practical reasons, a summative evaluation is performed when the object is ready to be evaluated summatively, that is, when the evaluand has developed fully and when the evaluand is operating with sufficient regularities in its operation and is producing stable effects. To help program developers ready an evaluand for summative evaluation, an evaluation may be conducted formatively to identify shortcomings and deficiencies.

In either formative or summative evaluation, the evaluation activities are not materially different; the two only differ in purpose. Put simply, when the customer tastes the soup, it is summative evaluation. When the chef tastes the soup just before serving it, it is formative evaluation. In this way, summative evaluation constitutes the core of the role of evaluation in the consumer-oriented approach to evaluation.

Role of the Evaluator

Scriven sees that evaluation—and by extension, the evaluator—carries the ethical and moral imperative to determine whether an object contributes to the welfare of consumers. To that end, Scriven sees the proper role of the evaluator to be that of "enlightened surrogate consumer"; the evaluator discharges such responsibility by making informed judgments on consumer's behalf. In his writing, Scriven often cites the magazine *Consumer Reports* as illustrative of the consumer-oriented approach to evaluation.

Techniques

To aid in putting the consumer-oriented approach to evaluation in practice, Scriven advances several techniques.

Goal-Free Evaluation

Scriven advances the notion of a goal-free evaluation in an attempt to offer an alternative to goal-based approaches to evaluation. In a goal-free evaluation, the evaluator ignores the stated program goals on purpose. Instead, the evaluator investigates all possible outcomes—both anticipated and unanticipated—of a program. According to Scriven, advantages of goal-free evaluation "are that it is less intrusive than goal-based evaluation; more adaptable to mainstream goal shifts; better at finding side effects; less prone to social, perceptual, and cognitive bias; more professionally challenging; and more equitable in taking a wide range of values into account" (cited in Stufflebeam & Shrinkfield, 2007, p. 374).

Needs and Needs Assessment

One of the advantages to adopting program developers' goals in an evaluation is that assumptions about what constitutes valuable or meaningful outcomes have been made ahead of time. In the absence of adopting developers' goals in a goal-free evaluation, the quandary arises of whose values ought to be represented in an evaluation and by what means they could be established. Scriven resolves this issue by placing the onus upon the evaluator to explicate the needs of the consumer through a needs assessment.

Scriven is specific in how he defines a need. Consistent with the author's stance on orienting the evaluation toward the consumer, the author defines a need as "anything essential for a satisfactory mode of existence, anything without which that mode of existence of level of performance would fall below a satisfactory level" (cited in Stufflebeam & Shrinkfield, 2007, p. 375). A need defined in this way carries the notion of what is essential or necessary to the consumer. An example of such a need would be functional literacy. The findings of a needs assessment provide the basis to compare against observed outcomes in an evaluation.

Key Evaluation Checklist

Another major contribution Scriven has made to advance the approach is the creation of the Key Evaluation Checklist. The Key Evaluation Checklist draws together a comprehensive list of considerations and action items that the author views to be essential to conducting evaluation in ways consistent with the consumer-oriented approach. The checklist is organized into four sections and comprises 18 checkpoints. The remainder of this section summarizes each of the major sections.

Section A: Preliminaries

The first section of the checklist invites the evaluator to consider those issues that would have bearing on the design, execution, and reporting of the evaluation itself. Three checkpoints are identified: creating an executive summary of the most pertinent information concerning the evaluation itself; clarifying the intended audience of the evaluation, the role of the evaluator, stakeholders of the program, and the questions the evaluation is to answer; and, finally, the design and methods that would be employed to answer those questions.

Part B: Foundations

The second section invites the evaluator to establish a detailed description of the evaluand. Five checkpoints comprise this section: establishing the background and context surrounding the evaluand; defining and describing the evaluand and its composition; identifying the consumers or what Scriven sometimes refers to as "impactees"; uncovering what resources are made available to enable operation; and, finally, what values (needs) ought to be used in the evaluation of the evaluand.

Part C: Subevaluations

The third section concerns the processes of constructing evaluative claims. Five checkpoints comprise the section: establishing program processes, specifically around the means by which the evaluand achieves intended goals; establishing outcomes; establishing the costs associated with operating the evaluand (which can manifest in different forms, from monetary, nonmonetary, and nonmonetizable costs to direct, indirect, maintenance, and residual costs); comparing observations made of the evaluand to the needs and expectations put forth by consumers; and finally, establishing the extent to which claims can be generalized.

Part D: Synthesis

The last section concerns the construction of evaluative conclusions and implications stemming from the evaluation inquiry. Five checkpoints comprise the section: advancing a synthesis claim into the overall value of the evaluand; advancing recommendations, explanations, predictions, and redesigns, if appropriate; concerning the evaluand; reporting on the evaluation; and finally, subjecting the evaluation itself to scrutiny by engaging in a meta-evaluation process.

In sum, the four sections of the checklist advance a methodology for conducting a consumer-oriented program. The document that discusses the Key Evaluation Checklist is comprehensive and is freely distributed via the Evaluation Checklist website hosted by Western Michigan University.

Advantages and Challenges

The primary advantage of the consumer-oriented approach to evaluation is that it produces a comprehensive account and assessment concerning the value of an evaluand. The findings from such evaluations serve an important function in protecting consumer interest, a laudable goal. The benefit of the consumer-oriented evaluation comes from the systematic and comprehensive nature of the approach, which itself is grounded in philosophical arguments concerning the fundamental goal and role of evaluation. The comprehensive nature of the consumer-oriented approach to evaluation also imposes challenges in its execution. Satisfying the approach fully requires a highly competent evaluator and sufficient resources.

Chi Yan Lam

See also Formative Evaluation; Goal-Free Evaluation; Program Evaluation; Summative Evaluation

Further Readings

Scriven, M. (2003). Evaluation theory and metatheory. In T. Kellaghan, D. L. Stufflebeam, & L. A. Wingate (Eds.), *International handbook of educational evaluation* (pp. 15–30). New York, NY: Springer.

Scriven, M. (2013, March 22). *Key evaluation checklist* [Draft; latest version]. Retrieved from http://www.michaelscriven.info/images/KEC_3.22.2013.pdf

Shadish, W. R., Jr., Cook, T. D., & Leviton, L. C. (1991). *Foundations of program evaluation: Theories of practice*. Thousand Oaks, CA: Sage.

Stufflebeam, D. L., & Shrinkfield, A. (2007). *Evaluation theory, models, and application*. San Francisco, CA: Jossey-Bass.

CONTENT ANALYSIS

Content analysis is an analytic method used in either quantitative or qualitative research for the systematic reduction and interpretation of text or video data. Data can be generated from a variety of sources including (a) individual or focus group interviews; (b) responses to open-ended survey items; (c) text from social media; (d) printed materials such as research articles, newspapers, or books; (e) video-taped simulations; or (f) naturally occurring conversational events. It is also used in case study research. The aim of content analysis is to describe data as an abstract interpretation.

Use of content analysis as a research technique dates to the 1900s when it was used in communication research primarily to describe the quantity (frequency) rather than quality (meaning) of content contained in textual data. Since this early use, qualitative content analysis has gained popularity as a means to interpret data by identifying codes and common themes (manifest content) and then constructing underlying meanings (latent content). Content analysis is estimated to have been used as a qualitative analytic method in more than 3,000 research studies between 2005 and 2015 in such diverse fields as education, business, economics, social work, social science, and health sciences, including nursing, psychology, medicine, rehabilitation, gerontology, and public, environmental, and occupational health.

At least three distinct approaches to content analysis have emerged. These approaches differ in terms of study design, sampling decisions, and analytic strategies used, particularly how coding schemes are developed. The selection of approaches to content analysis largely depends on the research purpose and the availability of existing knowledge in the area of interest, particularly related models or theories. When existing knowledge around a phenomenon of interest is largely absent and the purpose of a study is to create knowledge, an *inductive approach* or *conventional qualitative content analysis* is appropriate where codes and themes are generated directly from the data.

When prior research or theory exists and the purpose of the research is to confirm, expand, or refine this existing understanding of a phenomenon, a more *deductive approach* or *directed qualitative content analysis* is appropriate using existing knowledge or theory to build the initial coding structure. When quantification of a specific content is desired, a summative content analysis approach is appropriate to identify and tally keywords or concepts.

As with any research method, sampling decisions are critical to meet study goals when using content analysis. Generally, sampling in a qualitative design seeks to maximize diversity of data around the phenomena of interest. Sample sizes may vary considerably when using content analysis depending on the research question. To understand a complex emotional event, researchers might conduct in-depth interviews with a small number of participants, while to understand what terms are used to describe a physical symptom, researchers might analyze written responses to an open-ended survey item from hundreds of participants. Using a directed content analysis approach, a researcher might purposively sample a particular group to refine or extend existing knowledge or theory about a particular phenomenon to a new population.

The development of the initial coding scheme and overall approach to coding differs depending on the specific content analysis approach chosen. With a directed content analysis approach, the researcher develops an initial coding scheme from existing theory or knowledge, using the data to modify or expand these codes. In a conventional content analysis approach, the initial coding scheme emerges from the data. With either approach, generally, it is helpful to first immerse oneself in the data to obtain a sense of the whole. Then data are coded through an iterative process. It is important to identify a consistent unit of coding, which might range from a single word to short paragraphs. Coding serves to reduce and condense the data based on its content and meaning. Finally, the relationships between codes are constructed by arranging them within categories and themes.

The process of abstraction from the raw data to meaningful themes requires establishing trustworthiness through strategies to ensure credibility, transferability, dependability, confirmability, and authenticity. A checklist for each phase of data analysis is helpful. In the data preparation phase, data collection methods, sampling strategies, and selection of units of analysis should be reviewed for trustworthiness. In the data organization phase, trustworthiness issues relate to categorization and abstraction, interpretation, and representativeness of results. Assessment of intercoder reliability is important in content analysis to establish credibility of the analytic process and findings.

Results of content analyses are presented through descriptive writing but should be complemented with figures and tables as appropriate. Examples include conceptual diagrams showing the relationships between codes and themes or tables showing codes in rank order of use, potentially for different groups of study participants. Although direct data quotes are used to illustrate findings, interpretation and presentation of the findings is essential. Commercial qualitative research software options are increasing that assist with managing data coding. These programs are helpful for handling large amounts of data and recognizing subtle patterns, but they are not substitutes for actual data analysis.

Qualitative content analysis has been criticized for lacking depth in abstraction. It is also of limited use for developing theory, in contrast to grounded theory methodology. Content analysis has several distinct advantages, however: (a) the analytic approach to data is unobtrusive and nonreactive, (b) novice researchers can learn basic techniques quickly, in contrast to other qualitative methodologies such as phenomenology where deep understanding is sought, and (c) it is more time efficient than methods such as ethnography where sustained immersion in the field is required. When choosing content analysis as an analytic approach, researchers should clarify which approach matches their research question, goal, and overall purpose. Content analysis remains one of the most widely used research strategies because it is fast and effective for finding patterns within multiple types of qualitative data.

Hsiu-Fang Hsieh and Sarah Shannon

See also Case Study Method; Qualitative Data Analysis; Qualitative Research Methods; Quantitative Research Methods; Trustworthiness

Further Readings

Burla, L., Knierim, B., Barth, J., Liewald, K., Duetz, M., & Abel, T. (2008). From text to codings: Intercoder reliability assessment in qualitative content analysis. *Nursing Research, 57*(2), 113–117. doi:10.1097/01.NNR.0000313482.33917.7d

Graneheim, U. H., & Lundman, B. (2004). Qualitative content analysis in nursing research: Concepts, procedures and measures to achieve trustworthiness. *Nurse Education Today, 24*(2), 105–112. doi:http://dx.doi.org/10.1016/j.nedt.2003.10.001

Hsieh, H. F., & Shannon, S. E. (2005). Three approaches to qualitative content analysis. *Qualitative Health Research, 15*(9), 1277–1288. doi:10.1177/1049732305276687

Kohlbacher, F. (2006). The use of qualitative content analysis in case study research. *Forum: Qualitative Social Research, 7*(1). Retrieved from http://www.qualitative-research.net/index.php/fqs/article/view/75/153

Mayring, P. (2000). Qualitative content analysis. *Forum: Qualitative Social Research, 1*(2). Retrieved from http://www.qualitative-research.net/index.php/fqs/article/view/1089/2385

Morgan, D. L. (1993). Qualitative content analysis: A guide to paths not taken. *Qualitative Health Research, 3*(1), 112–121.

CONTENT STANDARD

A content standard is a general statement that describes what students should know and be able to do following their participation in educational programming. Content standards are developed to offer consistency and coherence to educational programming, to eliminate redundancy in content covered over time, and to provide a foundation for the development of effective instructional and assessment programs. In contrast to achievement standards and/or performance standards, which describe the specific level at which students are expected to perform, content standards describe more generally what students are expected to learn. Within K–12 educational settings, content standards are typically developed to be grade level and discipline specific and are organized in a way that reflects a logical progression of essential knowledge and skills within a given content area.

An example of a first-grade English language arts content standard from the Common Core State Standards is: "Ask and answer questions about key details in a text." An example of an eighth-grade English language arts content standard is: "Cite the textual evidence that most strongly supports an analysis of what the text says explicitly as well as inferences drawn from the text." The current entry describes recent trends in the development of content standards that correspond to the standards-based reform movement, considerations for diverse learners, and ongoing tensions in the development and use of content standards in K–12 school settings. Although content standards may be developed for a variety of educational programs (e.g., early education, adult education, graduate education), across a variety of countries, and by a variety of organizations, the focus of the current entry is on content standards as they relate to K–12 education in the United States.

Standards-Based Reform and the Development of Content Standards

During the 1980s and 1990s, widespread concern with the status of U.S. public education relative to other countries ushered in educational reform efforts, with the intent to improve teaching and learning. At the core of these efforts was the standards-based reform movement. According to standards-based reform, student achievement will rise when (a) high expectations for student learning are clearly articulated, (b) assessment programs are designed to measure student progress toward those expectations, and (c) consequences are attached to student achievement, as measured by the assessment programs. The 2001 reauthorization of the Elementary and Secondary Education Act, namely, the No Child Left Behind Act of 2001, correspondingly required states to develop challenging academic content standards in English/language arts, math, and science, along with assessment programs that measured student progress toward those standards. Schools and teachers were offered flexibility in how they taught, but all students were expected to learn, at a minimum, the content articulated in the standards. Various consequences were applied to schools that did not demonstrate appropriate adequate yearly progress. In addition to the federally required content standards, some states and districts developed content standards in disciplines outside of those mentioned in the No Child Left Behind Act, such as health, fine arts, social studies, and citizenship.

Given a growing concern that states had disparate content standards and achievement standards at each grade level, the Council of Chief State School Officers and National Governors Association Center for Best Practices collaborated in 2009 to develop and validate a common set of standards. The Common Core State Standards were designed by a team of teachers, school administrators, and other experts in education from 48 different states. In the 2015reauthorization of Elementary and Secondary Education Act, namely, the Every Student Succeeds Act of 2015, an emphasis on state approval of content standards was maintained, along with the requirement for assessment programs to be developed and implemented to monitor student progress toward those standards.

Considerations for Diverse Learners

In the United States, federal law has required that all students, including those with disabilities, have access to learning and assessment according to the same grade-level content standards. This requirement was intended to ensure that all students experience the intended benefits of standards-based reform (i.e., improved teaching and learning). Through the provision of appropriate accommodation supports and specially designed instruction, students with disabilities are expected to achieve the same educational outcomes as their peers without disabilities. To facilitate access to the content standards for students with particularly significant cognitive disabilities, some states developed extended standards linked to the original content standards. The following is an example of an Ohio Grade 8 content standard in reading, along with the associated extended standard for students with significant cognitive disabilities: "Cite the textual evidence that most strongly supports an analysis of what the text says explicitly as well as inferences drawn from the text" and "Identify details that support answers to literal questions." Goals that are written as a part of Individualized Education

Programs that are developed for students receiving special education services are expected to be linked to the content standards.

Ongoing Tensions and Concerns

In the United States, content standards are typically developed and validated using an iterative process that involves input from a variety of individuals, including scholars, teachers, and the general public. Some scholars have expressed concern about the development of a particularly broad set of standards that fails to foster depth of student knowledge within each academic discipline. Finally, it is important to note that the impact of content standards on student learning may depend not only on the quality of the standards but on the extent to which teacher professional development, instructional materials, and assessment are aligned to those standards.

Sara E. Witmer and Heather Schmitt

See also Alignment; Common Core State Standards; Curriculum; No Child Left Behind Act; Standards-Based Assessment; State Standards

Further Readings

Browder, D. M., Wakeman, S. Y., Flowers, C., Rickelman, R. J., Pugalee, D., & Karvonen, M. (2007). Creating access to the general curriculum with links to grade-level content for students with significant cognitive disabilities: An explanation of the concept. *The Journal of Special Education, 41*, 2–16. doi:10.1177/0022466907041001010

Porter, A., McMaken, J., Hwang, J., & Yang, R. (2011). Common core standards: The new US intended curriculum. *Educational Researcher, 40*(3), 103–116.

Porter, A. C., Polikoff, M. S., & Smithson, J. (2009). Is there a de facto national intended curriculum? Evidence from state content standards. *Educational Evaluation and Policy Analysis, 31*, 238–268. doi:10.3102/0162373709335465

Schmidt, W. H., Wang, H. C., & McKnight, C. C. (2005). Curriculum coherence: An examination of U.S. mathematical and science content standards from an international perspective. *Journal of Curriculum Studies, 37*, 525–559. doi:10.1080/0022027042000294682

CONTENT VALIDITY RATIO

Validity is the degree to which an instrument measures what it is supposed to measure. Content validity (CV) determines the degree to which the items on the measurement instrument represent the entire content domain. Experts familiar with the content domain of the instrument evaluate and determine if the items are valid. A CV ratio (CVR) is a numeric value indicating the instrument's degree of validity determined from expert's ratings of CV. One rule of thumb suggests that a CVR of at least 0.78 is necessary to deem an item or scale as valid.

In order for a research study to provide accurate and meaningful results, the instrument used to test the hypothesis must be valid. Use of a measurement instrument that is not valid may produce meaningless results.

Methods to Calculate CVR

A CVR can be calculated for each item and overall for an instrument. There are two ways to calculate item and scale (overall) CVR. The first method was developed by Mary R. Lynn in 1986. Experts rate each item using a four-point ordinal scale (1 = *not relevant*, 2 = *somewhat relevant*, 3 = *quite relevant*, and 4 = *highly relevant*). The item CVR is calculated as the number of experts giving a rating of 3 or 4 divided by the total number of experts who evaluated the item. The scale CVR is a proportion of items that met validity (i.e., at least 0.78) out of the total number of items. Figure 1 provides an example of how to calculate item CVR using this method. Figure 2 depicts how to calculate a scale CVR using this method.

A second method to calculate a CVR was developed by C. H. Lawshe in 1975. Experts rate each item using a four-point ordinal scale: 3 = *essential*; 2 = *useful, but not essential*; and 1 = *not necessary*. To calculate an item CVR, the following formula is used: $CVR = (n_e - N/2)/(N/2)$. In this ratio, n_e is the number of content experts who indicated that the item was essential (i.e., a rating of "3"). N is the total number of content experts. The mean CVR of all items computes an overall scale CVR. Figure 3 provides an example of how to calculate item CVR using this method, while Figure 4 demonstrates how to calculate a scale CVR.

Additional CVR Procedures

According to Lynn, measurement instrument should be evaluated by at least six experts. These experts should be individuals who have published,

---

Content relevance scale
1. Irrelevant item
2. Somewhat relevant
3. Mostly relevant
4. Extremely relevant

For Item 1: Three experts rated the item "2" and 7 experts rated it "3"
CVR = Proportion of experts who rate item as content valid (a rating of 3 or 4)/total number of experts who rated it
CVR = 7/10
CVR = **0.70**

For Item 2: One expert rated the item "2" and 9 experts rated it "3"
CVR = Proportion of experts who rate item as content valid (a rating of 3 or 4)/total number of experts who rated it
CVR = 9/10
CVR = **0.9**

For Item 3: 10 ratings of "3"
CVR = Proportion of experts who rate item as content valid (a rating of 3 or 4)/total number of experts who rated it
CVR = 10/10
CVR = **1.0**

Figure 1   Example of calculating item content validity ratio (CVR)

Source: Lynn, M. R. (1986). Determination and quantification of content validity. *Nursing Research, 35*(6), 382–385.

Using the item CVRs in Figure 1, the scale CVR can be calculated as follows:
CVR = the proportion of total items judged content valid
CVR = 2/3
CVR = **0.67**

Figure 2 Example of calculating scale content validity ratio (CVR)

Source: Lynn, M. R. (1986). Determination and quantification of content validity. *Nursing Research, 35*(6), 382–385.

Content relevance
1. Not necessary
2. Useful, but not necessary
3. Essential

For Item 4: Two ratings of "1" and 8 ratings of "3"
CVR = (ne − N/2)/(N/2)
CVR = (8 − 10/2)/10/2
CVR = (7 − 5)/5
CVR = **0.6**

For Item 5: One rating of "2" and 9 ratings of "3"
CVR = (ne − N/2)/(N/2)
CVR = (9 − 10/2)/10/2
CVR = (9 − 5)/5
CVR = **0.8**

For Item 6: 10 ratings of "3"
CVR = (ne − N/2)/(N/2)
CVR = (10 − 10/2)/10/2
CVR = (10 − 5)/5
CVR = **1.0**

Figure 3 Example of calculating item content validity ratio (CVR)

Source: Lawshe, C.H. (1975). A quantitative approach to content validity. *Personnel Psychology, 28,* 563–575. doi:10.1111/j.1744-6570.1975.tb01393.x

Using the item CVRs in Figure 3, the scale CVR can be calculated as follows:
Scale CVR = mean of item CVRs
Scale CVR = 0.6 + 0.8 + 1.0
Scale CVR = 2.4/3
Scale CVR = **0.8**

Figure 4 Example of calculating scale content validity ratio (CVR)

Source: Lawshe, C.H. (1975). A quantitative approach to content validity. *Personnel Psychology, 28,* 563–575. doi:10.1111/j.1744-6570.1975.tb01393.x

presented, and/or are known nationally and internationally for their expertise in the content area. This ensures that the assessment of the validity tool is based on global practices and not standard local practices.

CV should be obtained from experts anonymously to avoid bias. Individuals who are familiar with the person requesting a review of the measurement tool are less likely to provide honest and valuable feedback.

If the CVR is less than 0.78 on an individual item, that item should be revised or deleted. Any feedback provided by experts should be considered in the revisions. If the overall CVR does not meet validity, revisions should be made and the instrument sent to at least six different experts for second review. This process is repeated until the scale CVR meets validity standards. Sending the instrument to different experts increases the rigor of the validating process; it also decreases bias from reviewers who have previously seen the instrument.

Tonya Rutherford-Hemming

See also Validity

Further Readings

Boulet, J. R., Jeffries, P. R., Hatala, R. A., Korndorffer, J. R., Feinstein, D. M., & Roche, J. P. (2011). Research regarding methods of assessing learning outcomes. *Simulation in Healthcare, 6,* S48–S51.

Davis, L. L. (1992). Instrument review: Getting the most from your panel of experts. *Applied Nursing Research, 5,* 194–197.

Lawshe, C.H. (1975). A quantitative approach to content validity. *Personnel Psychology, 28,* 563–575. doi:10.1111/j.1744-6570.1975.tb01393.x

Lynn, M. R. (1986). Determination and quantification of content validity. *Nursing Research, 35*(6), 382–385.

Polit, D. F., & Beck, C. T. (2006). The content validity index: Are you sure you know what's being reported? Critique and recommendations. *Research in Nursing & Health, 29,* 489–497.

Polit, D. F., & Beck, C.T. (2014). *Essentials of nursing research: Appraising evidence for nursing practice* (8th ed.). Philadelphia, PA: Wolters Kluwer.

CONTENT-RELATED VALIDITY EVIDENCE

Validation of test scores involves collecting evidence and developing an argument that supports a particular use (i.e., an inference or decision) of the test scores. For a validity argument to be correct, it must be supported by evidence and be logical and coherent. There are various types of evidence that can be used to support a validity argument, including content-related validity evidence, criterion-related validity evidence, and evidence related to reliability and dimensional structure. The type of evidence needed to support the use of the test scores depends on the type of inference or decision being made. As such, test scores can only be said to be valid for a particular use. If multiple inferences or decisions are to be made based on a set of test scores, multiple types of evidence may be required. Even if a single inference or decision is made, multiple types of evidence may still be required to support the test score use. After briefly reviewing the three types of validity evidence, this entry focuses on the basics of content-related validity evidence, including providing an example of its use.

Types of Validity Evidence

Validity evidence can be classified into three basic categories: content-related evidence, criterion-related evidence, and evidence related to reliability and dimensional structure. Most test score uses require some evidence from all three categories. Content-related validity evidence is evidence about the extent to which the test accurately represents the target domain. For achievement tests, the target domain is most often a particular subject matter domain (e.g., seventh-grade mathematics), and for ability tests, the target domain is most often a particular mental ability (e.g., quantitative reasoning). Criterion-related validity evidence is evidence that relates the test scores to one or more external criterion (often observable behaviors). Evidence related to reliability and dimensional structure are types of evidence about the internal structure of a test (i.e., the composition of the items and subtests). In addition, reliability evidence is evidence about the consistency or reproducibility of the test scores across various test conditions (e.g., raters and time).

Content-Related Validity Evidence

Content-related validity evidence is most important when making an inference about a target domain based on a sample of observations taken from that target domain. Evidence related to both the definition of the target domain and the representativeness or relevance of the sample of observations (items and tasks) taken from the target domain are important aspects of content-related validity evidence. Both types of evidence rely on the judgment of experts and are therefore subjective. Content-related validity evidence is often confused with, or is thought to be the same as, face validity evidence. This confusion is understandable because on the surface the two types of validity evidence have many commonalities.

However, the two types of validity evidence differ in who is making the judgment about validity. When seeking evidence about face validity, the test takers and test users are asked if the test appears to measure what the test developers say the test measures. In contrast, when seeking evidence about content validity, individuals with expert knowledge in the target domain are asked if the test content (items and tasks) represents or is relevant to the target domain.

In the context of ability testing, content-related evidence is evidence about the relevance of the tasks or items to the latent trait or mental ability of interest. In the context of achievement testing, content-related evidence is evidence about the representativeness of the tasks or items to the subject matter domain being measured. Because content-related validity evidence relies on expert judgment and is therefore subjective, it is more appropriate for tests of specific knowledge and skills (i.e., achievement tests) than for tests of mental abilities or latent traits. Defining the target domain and sampling from that domain are easier when specific knowledge and skills are being measured. Defining the target domain and sampling from it are also easier when the knowledge and skills that comprise the domain are stable over time. Content-related validity evidence alone cannot support a particular use of test scores but is one part of the evidence that can be used to support a validity argument around a particular use of test scores.

Content-Related Validity Evidence Study

The goal of content validation work is to establish that the sample of observations (items and tasks) that comprise the test is representative of (or relevant to, if developing an ability test) the target domain. Collecting evidence related to content validity involves four basic steps: (1) identifying and selecting subject matter experts, (2) defining the target domain, (3) developing a procedure to sample observations (items and tasks) from the target domain, and (4) evaluating the effectiveness of the validation work.

When identifying and selecting subject matter experts, test developers should consider a variety of perspectives on the target domain to ensure it is

thoroughly defined and described. In a content-related validity evidence study, the subject matter experts play a critical role and the success of the validation work depends, in part, on their ability to fully and accurately define and describe the target domain. However, subject matter experts should not be the sole source of information used to define and describe a target domain but should be viewed as one of many sources of information that can be used to define and describe a target domain.

Defining the target domain involves fully describing all of the knowledge and skills that comprise the target domain. When describing the knowledge and skills that comprise the target domain, it is important for test developers to be as specific as possible to enable item writers to design and create test items and/or tasks with some ease. Test developers should rely on the subject matter experts, in addition to other sources of information, to describe the knowledge and skills comprising the target domain. Additional sources of information might include previously developed tests and the research literature.

Sampling from the content domain should have a rationale, which itself should be documented. Random sampling is probably not feasible to ensure content coverage. Instead, systematic sampling that ensures the target domain is accurately represented should be considered.

Evaluating the effectiveness of the validation work involves assessing the extent to which the sampling procedure produced items and tasks that are representative of the target domain, such that test scores and the inferences and/or decisions made from those test scores are valid. This work should rely, in part, on the judgments of the subject matter experts. Procedures for quantifying the amount or representative of the content coverage have been developed and should be considered.

An Example: Measuring Seventh-Grade Mathematics Achievement

Test developers have been tasked with creating a measure of students' seventh-grade mathematics achievement. The test will be used to assess students' end-of-year knowledge and skills in seventh-grade mathematics and will measure teacher and/or school effectiveness.

The most obvious subject matter experts when assessing students' end-of-year knowledge and skills in seventh-grade mathematics are teachers of seventh-grade mathematics. Because all students (not requiring accommodations) will be taking this test, it is important to include teachers who teach students at all ability levels, including special education teachers and honors and gifted/talented teachers. Other subject matter experts might include school curriculum directors and mathematics education researchers.

Again, defining the target domain involves fully describing (and documenting) the target domain. In this example, the target domain is seventh-grade mathematics achievement, specifically, the knowledge and skills that comprise the seventh-grade mathematics standards and curriculum. It is often easier to start by identifying the key topics that comprise the target domain. For seventh-grade mathematics, this includes the concepts of ratio, proportion, and slope. Further, subtopics could also be identified, such as the different types of ratios—part–part ratios versus part–whole ratios. In addition to identifying the key topics or concepts (knowledge) that comprise the seventh-grade mathematics standards and curriculum, it may be important to also identify the key uses of those concepts (skills) such as the ability to identify or provide a definition of the concept or to solve problems using the concept.

Once the key concepts (topics) and the key uses of those concepts have been identified, a test blueprint can be developed, and items and tasks can be created that are representative of those key concepts and uses. Item and task development includes creating items and tasks that represent the intersection between each of the three key topics (i.e., ratio, proportion, and slope) and the two key uses (i.e., provide a definition and solve a problem) in the test blueprint, such sample items might include having students provide a definition of a proportion and solve a missing-value proportion problem.

After items and tasks have been developed and assembled into a measure of seventh-grade mathematics knowledge and skills, the extent to which the items and tasks are representative of seventh-grade mathematics knowledge and skills (i.e., the target domain) can be assessed. The subject matter experts should be asked to judge the adequacy of the content coverage. In addition, the adequacy of content coverage can be quantified using percentages. If a particular key topic or concept is found to not have adequate coverage, test developers can request items writers create additional items or tasks until all key topics of concepts have adequate coverage such that the target domain is represented.

Danielle N. Dupuis

See also Construct-Related Validity Evidence; Criterion-Based Validity Evidence; Reliability; Tests; Validity

Further Readings

American Educational Research Association, American Psychological Association, & National Council for Measurement in Education. (2014). *Standards for educational and psychological testing.* Washington, DC: Author.

Downing, S. M., & Haladyna, T. M. (2006). *Handbook of test development.* Mahwah, NJ: Erlbaum.

Hardesty, D. M., & Bearden, W. O. (2004). The use of expert judges in scale development: Implications for improving face validity of measures of unobservable constructs. *Journal of Business Research, 57,* 98–107.

Haynes, S. N., Richard, D. C., & Kubany, E. S. (1995). Content validity in psychological assessment: A functional approach to concepts and methods. *Psychological Assessment, 7,* 238–247.

Lawshe, C. H. (1975). A quantitative approach to content validity. *Personnel Psychology, 28,* 563–575.

CONTINGENCY TABLE ANALYSIS

See Two-Way Chi-Square

CONTROL VARIABLES

In correlational research, a control variable might be labeled a confounding variable or nuisance variable that is "held constant" by statistical means. Suppose we want to know the relations between length of study time and scores on a test of American history, but we are worried that interest in history might be an alternate explanation of the association. If we allowed students to choose and report their own study times for the test, and we also measured the participants' interest in history, we could adjust the relations between study time and test score by statistically holding constant scores on interest in history. In such a study, interest in history would be described as a control variable.

Statistical Control

The mathematics of statistical control is based on correlation and regression, which can be illustrated graphically. In Figure 1, the variance of the distribution of American history test scores is partitioned into 4 areas labeled A, B, C, and D. Partition A is that part of the variance in test scores that is accounted for by neither study time nor interest in history—this is what cannot be predicted by either variable. Partition B is accounted for by study time alone. Partition C is shared by both study time and by interest in history—those more interested in history might spend more time studying, and thus either or both can account for this part of achievement. Finally, Partition D is the variance in achievement accounted for by interest in history alone.

The magnitude of association is indicated by the degree of overlap, that is, by the size of the shared portions. If study time and interest in history do an excellent job of predicting achievement, we would see Areas B, C, and D expand and Area A would shrink. However, if study time and interest in history were highly correlated, they would largely overlap one another, and the area marked C would increase, leading to smaller areas for B and D.

What statistical control does is remove the shared variance. In statistical terms, the *partial correlation* removes the control variable from both other variables of interest. In our example, we could compute a partial correlation between study time and achievement controlling for interest in history. The partial correlation would represent the ratio of B to (A + B), that is, the association of what is left of achievement with what is left of study time once interest in history is removed from both. The *semipartial correlation* removes the control variable from only one of the variables of interest. For example, we could compute the semipartial correlation between study time and achievement, holding constant interest in history for study time only. In this semipartial correlation, the association between study time and achievement would represent the ratio B to (A + B + C + D) because we would remove interest in history from study time, but not from achievement. The semipartial correlation is closely related to the regression coefficient. In essence, the multiple regression equation holds constant or controls each independent variable for all other independent variables.

Pros and Cons

The strength of control variables is that they allow the user to conclude that a focal variable accounts for variance in the dependent variable *above and beyond* the control variables in a regression equation. In our running example, if we computed a multiple regression and the association between time spent and achievement was significant, we could conclude that study time was related to achievement, even after holding interest constant. In other words, interest in history could be ruled out as an alternate explanation of our results. This would help to make a strong case for the value of study time.

On the other hand, suppose that time spent studying is highly correlated with interest in

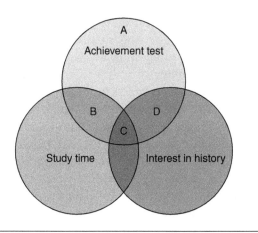

Figure 1   Statistical control through removal of shared variance

history because those most interested in history spent the most time studying. In such a case, the Area C in Figure 1 would become large, Area B would become small, and when we applied the regression model to the data, we would most likely find that time spent studying was not associated with achievement once interest in history was controlled. Should we infer that time spent studying is wasted? Clearly not; it could be that interest leads to studying, which leads to good test scores.

Applications

Control variables may not be advisable when theoretical understanding is the purpose of the research, and several articles have been written about the appropriate use of control variables. In organizational research, authors since 2000 suggest that researchers avoid including control variables in a regression equation simply because the controls are available for the analysis. Control variables should have a clear theoretical role in the analysis that is explained in the article's introduction.

Beyond theoretical justification, there are measurement considerations for the inclusion of control variables. Control variables chosen for the analysis should be measured well and subject to the same standards of reliability and validity as the focal variables. One should avoid using variables that are proxies for the actual variables of interest (e.g., participant sex should be avoided as a proxy for interest in typically masculine or feminine interests).

When control variables are included in the analysis, they should be included in the summary table of descriptive statistics along with the focal variables. Results should be reported both including and excluding the control variables. When control variables are used, care is needed in making inferences because statistical control holds constant things that may be connected in ways not considered by the analysis, such as our example of interest leading to study time leading to achievement.

Michael T. Brannick

See also Causal Inference; Correlation; Descriptive Statistics; Experimental Designs; Multiple Linear Regression; Part Correlations; Partial Correlations

Further Readings

Becker, T. E., Atinc, G., Breaugh, J. A., Carlson, K. D., Edwards, J. R., & Spector, P. E. (2015). Statistical control in correlational studies: 10 essential recommendations for organizational researchers. *Journal of Organizational Behavior.* doi:10.1002/job.2053

Howell, D. C. (2013). *Statistical methods for psychology* (8th ed.). Belmont, CA: Wadsworth.

Meehl, P. E. (1970). Nuisance variables and the ex post facto design. In M. Radner & S. Winokur (Eds.), *Minnesota studies in the philosophy of science* (Vol. 4, pp. 372–402). Minneapolis: University of Minnesota Press.

Pedhazur, E. (1997). *Multiple regression in behavioral research* (3rd ed.). Fort Worth, TX: Harcourt Brace.

Spector, P. E., & Brannick, M. T. (2011). Methodological urban legends: The misuse of statistical control variables. *Organizational Research Methods, 14,* 287–305. doi:10.1177/1094428110369842

Convenience Sampling

Convenience sampling (also known as availability sampling) is a method where the selection of participants (or other units of analysis) is based on their ready availability. This availability is usually in terms of geographical proximity (e.g., students in the researcher's own college or in neighboring colleges) but may involve other types of accessibility, such as known contacts.

As sample selection is based on the researcher's choice, convenience sampling is a form of nonprobability sampling distinct from forms of probability sampling such as (stratified) random sampling or cluster sampling. Convenience sampling differs from quota sampling—another form of nonprobability sampling, in which selection is based on certain identified characteristics—in not specifically seeking representativeness.

Like other nonprobability sampling methods, convenience sampling has certain practical advantages. It does not require an exhaustive list of the study population, which is needed for random sampling, and has clear logistical and resource benefits in terms of travel, cost, and time expenditure. However, these advantages are at the price of certain biases, such as sampling error and undercoverage. Sampling error means that the sampling method provides a sample whose characteristics (e.g., participants' age, educational level, or socioeconomic status) differ systematically from those of the population of interest. Undercoverage means that certain individuals in the population of interest are excluded by the sampling method (e.g., the researcher's interest is in staff in community colleges, liberal arts colleges, and universities, but a convenience sample only accesses staff in community or liberal arts colleges).

If quantitative data are collected, a convenience sample's lack of assured representativeness causes difficulties at the data analysis stage. As the sample is not representative in the way that a probability sample is, using a sample statistic (e.g., a sample proportion) to estimate a population parameter (e.g., a population proportion) is inadvisable, as such an estimate is likely to be biased. Furthermore, using statistical hypothesis tests is questionable, as these assume random sampling. Inferential statistics applied to convenience samples therefore make an assumption that the sample is comparable to a random sample from the same population (an assumption that is normally untestable). In qualitative research, however, this strict empirical representativeness is not normally at issue. What matters here is that members of the sample are relevant to the aims of the study—this is more a notion of theoretical than of statistical generalization and does not require the same concern for empirical representativeness.

> Although convenience sampling has methodological shortcomings, these can be mitigated by:
>
> describing the demographic and other characteristics of the sample in detail, and if possible, comparing these with those of the relevant population, so that readers of the study can evaluate its representativeness;
>
> making efforts to gain the participation of all intended participants, so that response bias or self-selection does not compound a lack of representativeness; and
>
> ensuring that the participants recruited are theoretically relevant to the study, so that selection is not based *solely* on convenience.

Jackie Waterfield

See also External Validity; Quota Sampling; Selection Bias; Simple Random Sampling

Further Readings

Fink, A. (2013). *How to conduct surveys: A step-by-step guide* (5th ed.). Thousand Oaks, CA: Sage.

Lohr, S. L. (2008). Coverage and sampling. In E. D. de Leeuw, J. J. Hox, & D. A. Dillman (Eds.), *International handbook of survey methodology* (pp. 97–112). New York, NY: Erlbaum.

CONVERGENCE

Convergence is a process in statistical analysis describing a series of calculations or guesses for the purpose of ultimately producing a very precise estimate. A simple example of several related equations illustrates the process. Imagine being tasked with solving the following set of equations for X and Y:

$$X + Y = 5, \tag{1}$$

$$X - Y = 3, \tag{2}$$

$$2X + 3Y = 12. \tag{3}$$

Given only Equations 1 and 2, the task easily yields $X = 4$ and $Y = 1$. However, these values do not satisfy Equation 3, for which substituting $X = 4$ and $Y = 1$ would yield 11 rather than 12. In fact, there is no exact solution for X and Y that satisfies all three equations. Still, one may wish to know what estimates of X and Y, $\tilde{X}$ and $\tilde{Y}$, respectively, make all three equations as close to true as possible.

What "close" means in one equation is clear; for Equation 1, for example, $\tilde{X} + \tilde{Y}$ should yield a value close to 5. For more general purposes, however, close must be operationalized across the set of equations by specifying a function that yields a single numerical value operationalizing the discrepancy between the equations' outcome values (5, 3, 12) and the outcome values expected based on the estimates $\tilde{X}$ and $\tilde{Y}$. Such a *discrepancy function*, or *fit function*, may then be used to guide the derivation of optimal values for those estimates.

A simple discrepancy function example, representing an unweighted least squares criterion, would be:

$$F = [5 - (\tilde{X} + \tilde{Y})]^2 + [3 - (\tilde{X} - \tilde{Y})]^2 + [12 - (2\tilde{X} + 3\tilde{Y})]^2.$$

Using this function, we seek $\tilde{X}$ and $\tilde{Y}$ values minimizing F. Readers familiar with multivariable calculus recognize that this could be accomplished analytically, setting to zero the partial derivatives of F with respect to $\tilde{X}$ and $\tilde{Y}$ and solving. Computers, however, are less adept at analytical solutions; fortunately, they are good at using algorithms that employ iterative strategies to derive estimates for unknown quantities.

After choosing initial *start values* for $\tilde{X}$ and $\tilde{Y}$, a computer changes those estimates incrementally, moving in those directions that make F smaller. The process continues adaptively through several *iterations*, altering the estimates in typically smaller increments until F reaches *convergence*. That is, the algorithm stops when F can no longer meaningfully decrease given its incremental changes in $\tilde{X}$ and $\tilde{Y}$, ideally reaching a value close to the analytical minimum; the resulting empirical values of $\tilde{X}$ and $\tilde{Y}$ constitute the estimates according to the criterion used to define F.

Although this is just a simple example, it represents a process that occurs throughout much of statistics. *Maximum likelihood estimation*, for example, employed across many applications (e.g., logistic regression, item response theory, structural equation modeling), seeks estimates for model parameters that optimize a discrepancy function characterizing the likelihood of all observations within a sample of data.

Statistical methods employ many different types of discrepancy functions as well as different search algorithms to optimize them. An algorithm might also fail to converge upon a solution, a result more common with complex models and models with very poor fit to the data. Alternatively, an algorithm might converge but reach a *local minimum* in the discrepancy function rather than the global minimum. This underscores the importance of choosing multiple sets of start values to ensure convergence occurs and that it is to a globally optimum solution for the parameter estimates of interest to the researcher.

Gregory R. Hancock

See also Item Response Theory; Logistic Regression; Maximum Likelihood Estimation; Model–Data Fit; Structural Equation Modeling

Further Readings

Argyros, I. K. (2008). *Convergence and applications of Newton-type iterations*. New York, NY: Springer.

Eliason, S. R. (1993). *Maximum likelihood estimation: Logic and practice*. Newbury Park, CA: Sage.

COOPERATIVE LEARNING

Cooperative learning, sometimes called small group learning, is a teaching strategy that utilizes and emphasizes small learner groups as a core unit that must work together and complete tasks collectively in order to achieve the desired academic goals while providing the learner members with both academic and social learning experiences. Groups typically consist of two to four members. Each learner in a group is responsible for his or her own learning as well as the learning of his or her group mates, creating an atmosphere of cooperative achievement.

Cooperative learning has been described as structuring positive interdependence. Cooperative learning can be conceptualized as placing learners on a team in which the goal is for all members to achieve academic success. This entry explains the differences between cooperative learning and individual learning, then discusses the elements of successfully incorporating cooperative learning in the classroom, the types and techniques of cooperative learning, and its benefits and disadvantages.

Cooperative Learning Versus Individual Learning

Cooperative learning can be understood as contrasting with individual learning teaching approaches. The key difference between cooperative learning and individual approaches to learning focuses on how the learners' learning goals are structured. Learner learning goals specify that how learners are expected to interact with each other and with the instructor. Learners in a cooperative learning environment are able to capitalize on each other's resources and skills by sharing information, evaluating ideas, monitoring work, and checking answers for group members. In cooperative learning, the instructor's role changes from giving information to learners to help them learn to that of a learning facilitator.

In cooperative learning, learners are encouraged and expected to focus on outcomes that are not only beneficial to themselves but also to the other members of the group. In individual learning learners work against each other and toward attainment of an academic goal such as receiving an "A" in the course. Additionally, in individual learning, learners work individually by themselves to accomplish the set learning goals, whereas in cooperative learning, learners work together to improve their chances of success and the success of their teammates.

Elements of Successful Incorporation of Cooperative Learning

Five essential elements have been identified for the successful incorporation of cooperative learning in the classroom: positive interdependence; individual and group accountability; promotive interaction; interpersonal and small group skills; and group processing.

Positive interdependence occurs when members of a group identify a link to each other that connects the success of one with the success of all others. Group members recognize, then, that the efforts of each member are beneficial to everyone and this creates a commitment to all members of the group. In order for positive interdependence to be accomplished:

> Each learner must completely participate within the group.

> Each group member must have a task, role, or responsibility.

> Each group member must understand that each person is responsible for his or her own learning as well as that of the group.

Individual and group accountability requires that the group be certain about goals and able to determine not only the progress toward achievement but also the distinct efforts of each individual member. This includes accountability for each member to contribute his or her share of the work required. In order to have this type of accountability:

> Each learner must achieve and demonstrate content mastery.

> Each learner must be accountable for his or her own work and learning.

> Each learner must actively contribute and not expect the group to "carry" them.

Promotive interaction exists when all members of the group share resources and focus on providing assistance and encouragement for each member's endeavors to learn. Examples of promotive interaction may include oral explanation of how to solve a problem, explanations of how to solve a problem, or peer teaching to classmates. To achieve promotive interactions:

> Face to face interaction is necessary.

> Members must foster the success of other group members.

> Learners must be able to explain to one another what they have learned or are learning.

> Learners must be able to assist one another with understanding and completing assignments.

Interpersonal and small group skills are the skills necessary to perform successfully as part of a group. In cooperative learning groups, students are expected to understand these skills (teamwork) along with acquiring academic content (taskwork). These skills should be seen as a goal and result of cooperative learning and include effective communication skills, interpersonal skills, and group skills. Examples of skills gained through cooperative learning include:

- leadership,
- decision making,
- trust building,
- friendship development, and
- communication
- Conflict management.

Group processing occurs when group members discuss how well they are achieving their goals. Groups need to determine what member actions are beneficial and what actions are counterproductive and decide what behaviors to continue or change. The focus of group processing is to elucidate and advance the group's efficacy and the effectiveness of individual members.

Ultimately, in order for cooperative learning to be successful, two main characteristics must be present:

1. Tasks and reward structures, responsibility of each individual, and accountability of each participant must be clearly distinguished at the beginning and presented to all group members. Individual group members must know exactly what their responsibilities are. There must be individual accountability within the group for each group member's responsibilities.

2. Each group member's responsibility must be such that it can only be completed by that individual member, and as such, each member must actively participate to ensure success for the whole group.

Cooperative Learning Types

Formal Cooperative Learning

Formal cooperative learning is designed, facilitated, and overseen by the instructor over time. Formal cooperative learning is composed of learners working cooperatively to accomplish shared learning goals and to complete defined assignments and tasks. This may occur for as little as one class period or continue for as long as the entire term of the class. In this type of cooperative learning, groups are set for a specific duration and learners contribute to each other's knowledge on

a continuous basis. This type of cooperative learning is usually more appropriate for larger groups of learners.

The instructor's role in formal cooperative learning includes various elements such as preinstructional decisions regarding tasks, objectives, roles, materials, groups, and room assignments; explanations of the tasks and the cooperative learning structure for the students; monitoring the learning and intervening as needed to ensure the task remains on track; and assessing the learning of the individuals and group as it functions.

Informal Cooperative Learning

Informal cooperative learning consists of having learners work together to achieve a joint learning goal in groups formed to last for a brief period, from a few minutes to a class session. In informal cooperative learning, the learners participate in focused discussions before and after the lesson while also participating in pair discussions throughout the lesson. Informal cooperative learning focuses on active involvement of learners in understanding what is being presented as each learner has an individual responsibility to be an active participant in the paired discussions. Informal cooperative learning sets a mood supportive of learning, assists in creating expectations, and provides a closing to an instructional gathering.

During informal cooperative learning, instructors are afforded more time as well as more flexibility to move around the classroom and focus on the learning that is occurring. This can offer instructors additional awareness of how well learners are grasping the concepts presented. When using informal cooperative learning groups and techniques, it is important to ensure that the assignment and the directions are clear and precise and to require groups to produce a specific tangible outcome, such as a written answer. Informal cooperative learning is made up of three types of discussions:

1. Introductory-focused discussion: Instructors assign learners to pairs or triads and explain the task.

2. Intermittent-focused discussions: Instructors divide the lecture into segments. After each segment, learners are directed to partner up with a peer near them and work cooperatively to answer

a question. Each learner is expected to first formulate an individual answer. Then, the two learners share and synthesize ideas into what most likely is a more accurate answer.

3. Closure-focused discussion: Learners participate in a final discussion task in which they summarize what they have learned with a focus on integrating the information into the existing conceptual frameworks.

Cooperative Base Groups

Cooperative base groups are continuous, diverse cooperative learning groups with consistent involvement by members. Characteristically, these groups meet regularly and last for the duration of the class. A good example is a course-long study group. Base groups can participate in and undertake many tasks, including academic tasks, such as reviewing each other's work; personal tasks, which could be assisting each other with resolution of nonacademic issues; routine tasks, such as preparing the classroom for a lesson; and assessment tasks, such as checking each other's perception of the material presented. Members' primary responsibilities include ensuring that all members are progressing academically, maintaining accountability, and providing support, assistance, and encouragement for assigned work.

Cooperative Learning Techniques

There are many varied cooperative learning techniques available. Some cooperative learning techniques utilize learner pairs and other techniques operate with small groups consisting of four or five learners. Cooperative learning techniques have been designed and adapted for any content area making this a versatile teaching approach in both formal and informal cooperative learning settings. Some examples are as follows:

Think–Pair–Share

Think–pair–share requires learners to reflect individually on a presented question or problem. The learner may write down thoughts or simply brainstorm; however, the learner is expected to have developed thoughts or ideas on the posed subject. When prompted, each learner pairs up with a peer to discuss his or her idea(s) and listen to the ideas of his or her partner. In this way, learners are challenged to evaluate their own ideas and that of their peer. Following the pair discussion, the teacher may solicit replies from everybody.

When a teacher uses this method, it alleviates the worry about learners not volunteering because each learner will have already been required to contemplate and discuss at least two ideas (the learner's and learner's partner's) allowing for dialogue and discussion expansion. This technique is particularly well suited for informal cooperative learning as it does not benefit from having set groups.

Jigsaw

The jigsaw technique requires each learner to become not only a learner but also a teacher. Learners are participants of two groups, a primary "home" group and a secondary "expert" group. One way to set this up is to assign each member of the home group a number that corresponds to each member of the other home groups such that each home group has the same numbers (e.g., 1–5). In this way, all of the number 1s will break away and become an expert group (all 1s). Learners then study the assigned material together with the other members of the "expert" group so that all members of the group have learned the assigned topic. The learners then return to their home groups and each learner is responsible for teaching the topic on which the learner became an "expert" while learning about the topic with learner's homogenous group. This cooperative learning technique is most useful in formal cooperative learning groups.

Inside–Outside Circle

This particular cooperative learning strategy is more likely to be used in informal cooperative learning. The physical setup requires learners to form two concentric circles one inside of the other. As the activity takes place, learners in one circle will rotate and face new partners with each rotation which may coincide with each new question or topic. This method is useful when generating new ideas and solving problems.

Reciprocal Teaching

This technique allows for learner pairs to create and hold a dialogue about a text. In this technique, partners take turns reading the text and asking each other questions about the text. This technique allows learners to receive immediate feedback from their partner. Reciprocal teaching allows for learners to use and practice important collaborative learning skills such as clarifying, questioning, predicting, and summarizing. This technique is well suited for informal collaborative learning groups.

Benefits of Cooperative Learning

The benefits of cooperative learning are extensive. This form of learning allows students to develop higher order thinking skills, increase self-esteem, raise satisfaction with the learning environment, foster a positive attitude toward the content, develop more advanced communication skills, and increase social interaction. It also increases student retention and enhances self-management skills.

Cooperative learning strategies contribute to an environment of exploratory and active learning where students are able to clarify concepts and ideas through discussion and debate. Students learn to critique ideas rather than people, learn interpersonal relationship skills, and meet high expectations. As well, this technique allows for task-oriented instruction that is less disruptive and that allows for differentiated instruction to reach students with various learning styles, reduces classroom and test anxiety, and mirrors real-life social and business situations for students to better prepare them for life beyond the classroom.

Disadvantages of Cooperative Learning

Cooperative learning does have its disadvantages. In cooperative learning environments, it is common for low-achieving students to become passive and not focus on the task at hand. There is an increased chance of conflict and an increased need for conflict resolution. Groups may get off task and begin discussing irrelevant information. Higher ability students may not be challenged, whereas lower ability students may always find themselves in need of help and may never experience leadership or "expert" status. There is the risk that one student will take over the group; conversely, there is the possibility of someone not actively contributing and expecting the group to "carry" them.

Lori Kupczynski

See also College Success; Curriculum; Learning Styles; Learning Theories

Further Readings

Aldrich, H., & Shimazoe, J. (2010). Group work can be gratifying: Understanding and overcoming resistance to cooperative learning. *College Teaching, 58*(2), 52–57.

Baker, T., & Clark, J. (2010). Cooperative learning—a double edged sword: A cooperative learning model for use with diverse student groups. *Intercultural Education, 21*(3), 257–268.

Johnson, D. W., & Johnson, R. (1989). *Cooperation and competition: Theory and research*. Edina, MN: Interaction Book.

Johnson, D. W., & Johnson R. T. (2008). Social interdependence theory and cooperative learning: The teacher's role. In R. B. Gillies, A. F. Ashman, & J. Terwel (Eds.), *The teacher's role in implementing cooperative learning in the classroom* (pp. 9–37). New York, NY: Springer.

Johnson, D. W., Johnson, R. T., & Holubec, E. (2008). *Cooperation in the classroom* (8th ed.). Edina, MN: Interaction Book.

Tsay, M., & Brady, M. (2010, June). A case study of cooperative learning and communication pedagogy: Does working in teams make a difference? *Journal of the Scholarship of Teaching and Learning, 10*(2), 78–89.

CORPORAL PUNISHMENT

Corporal punishment is the use of physical force, no matter how light, with the intention of causing a child to experience bodily pain so as to correct or punish the child's behavior. Corporal punishment remains a commonly used practice by parents around the world, but it is also used by teachers throughout the world as a means of punishing children for their misbehaviors. This entry first describes corporal punishment in schools and looks at its legality and prevalence. It then discusses disparities in the use of corporal punishment, the outcomes for children who are subjected to corporal punishment, and efforts to reduce corporal punishment.

School corporal punishment often includes hitting children with an object, such as a wooden paddle, stick, or whip, but also takes the form of slapping, pinching, hair pulling, and ear pulling. Corporal punishment does not refer only to hitting children as a form of discipline; it also includes other practices that involve purposefully causing the child to experience pain in order to punish the child, including washing a child's mouth out with soap, forcing a child to stand in a painful position for long periods of time, making a child kneel on sharp or painful objects (e.g., rice, a floor grate), placing hot sauce on a child's tongue, and forcing a child to engage in excessive exercise or physical exertion. The term *corporal punishment* is synonymous with the term *physical punishment*.

Legality

As of 2016, corporal punishment in schools was prohibited in 128 countries. School corporal punishment is banned from all of Europe and most of South America and East Asia; it is permitted in most countries in Africa and Southeast Asia and in the United States. In the United States, corporal punishment in public schools is legal in 19 states, while corporal punishment in private schools is legal in 48 states (the exceptions are Iowa and New Jersey). Australia, South Korea, and the United States are the only industrialized countries that allow school corporal punishment. In many of the countries that allow school corporal punishment, corporal punishment has been banned from prisons and from the armed services, leaving schools as the last public institutions where corporal punishment is legal, and children the last group of people it is legal to hit.

There is a growing international consensus that corporal punishment of children, whether by teachers or parents, is a violation of children's human rights under the United Nations Convention on the Rights of the Child. The United Nations Committee on the Rights of the Child has concluded that all corporal punishment of children violates children's right to protection from physical and mental violence (per Article 19 of the Convention on the Rights of the Child) and should be banned. As a result, a total of 49 countries have banned all corporal punishment of children, including that by parents.

Prevalence

The United Nations Children's Fund and other organizations have documented that, in some countries, nearly all children (upward of 80% of students) are subject to school corporal punishment on a regular basis; this is true, for example, in Egypt, India, Jamaica, Myanmar, Uganda, and Yemen, among many other countries. Interviews with children and teachers have revealed that school corporal punishment continues even in countries where it is banned, such as in Cameroon, Kazakhstan, Kenya, and South Africa. In the United States, the U.S. Department of Education reported that more than 110,000 children were subject to school corporal punishment in the 2013–2014 school year.

Disparities in Use of Corporal Punishment

Around the world, school corporal punishment is not used equally across all groups of children. Boys, children from racial and ethnic minorities, and children with disabilities are more likely to experience corporal punishment than their peers. In United Nations Children's Fund's Young Lives study, boys were more likely than girls to experience school corporal punishment in each of the four countries studied: Ethiopia: 44% of boys versus 31% of girls, India: 83% versus 73%, Peru: 35% versus 26%, and Vietnam: 28% versus 11%. Indeed, in both Singapore and Zimbabwe, gender discrimination is written into law: Only boys can be subject to school corporal punishment in those countries.

Disparities in school corporal punishment by gender, race, and disability status have been documented in the United States. An analysis of data from all 95,088 public schools in the United States revealed that Black children were much more likely than White children and that children with disabilities were more likely than children without disabilities to be corporally punished in school. The most systematic disparities were for gender, as nearly every school district reported corporally punishing boys at a rate of 3 times that for girls and often times at a rate of 5 times that for girls. These disparities are in contravention of several U.S. federal laws that protect schoolchildren from discrimination on the basis of race, gender, and disability status.

Disparities in the use of school corporal punishment are concerning both because they are unfair and potentially illegal, but also because students who perceive they are being treated in a discriminatory fashion are more likely to engage in negative school behaviors, to have low academic achievement, and to have mental health problems.

Outcomes for Children

Although there is an extensive research literature on the child outcomes linked with parents' use of corporal punishment, whether and how school corporal punishment affects children has not been extensively studied. The studies that do exist have occurred outside the United States.

Some educators may use corporal punishment in an effort to improve children's academic performance and achievement, sometimes indirectly by reducing problem behavior. Yet there is no evidence that school corporal punishment promotes learning and in fact some evidence that it is a hindrance. Research studies conducted in Jamaica and Nigeria each found that children who receive corporal punishment score lower on literacy skills, math skills, executive functioning, and intrinsic motivation.

The strongest evidence of links between school corporal punishment and children's achievement comes from United Nations Children's Fund's Young Lives study of children in four developing countries noted earlier. The study surveyed children in 2011 and again in 2013 and was able to link corporal punishment at age 8 to school performance at age 12, thus eliminating the possibility that the association is a result of children, with low scores eliciting corporal punishment as children's later school performance cannot predict their corporal punishment earlier in time.

Children from each country reported high rates of school corporal punishment (from 20% to 80% of children) when they were 8 years of age, and the more corporal punishment they received at age 8, the lower their math scores were in two samples (Peru and Vietnam) and the lower their vocabulary scores in Peru. Importantly, in none of the countries did school corporal punishment at age 8 predict better school performance at age 12.

One reason that corporal punishment may interfere with children's learning is that children avoid or dislike school because it is a place where they are in constant fear of being physically harmed by their teachers. In the Young Lives study, 5% of students in Peru, 7% in Vietnam, 9% in Ethiopia, and 25% in India who reported a reason for not liking school listed being beaten by teachers as their most important reason. Studies in a variety of countries have revealed that students are afraid of corporal punishment in school and skip days of school or drop out of school altogether to avoid being beaten by teachers.

Students who are corporally punished in school are also more likely to suffer from mental health and behavioral problems. Children who are corporally punished are more likely to have depressive symptoms, to be hostile, and to be aggressive. In the Young Lives study, school corporal punishment at age 8 predicted less self-efficacy 4 years later in Ethiopia and Peru and lower self-esteem 4 years later in Ethiopia and Vietnam.

An important concern with the use of corporal punishment is that it may cause serious injury to children, in large part because objects are so often used to hit children in schools. Some injuries are relatively minor, such as bruises, bumps, and cuts, but others are more major, including broken bones, hematomas, nerve damage, and in rare cases, death. Injuries from school corporal punishment are not restricted to developing countries; in the United States, court cases have documented these same physical injuries from school corporal punishment, including cases of death by excessive exercise as punishment.

Efforts to Reduce Corporal Punishment

Advocates around the world have called for school corporal punishment to be banned because of the research indicating it is ineffective and potentially harmful to children and the fact that it is considered a violation of children's human rights. In the United States, prominent professional organizations such as the American Academy of Pediatrics, the American Bar Association, the American Civil Liberties Union, the American Medical Association, the American Psychological Association, the National Association of Elementary School Principals, and Prevent Child Abuse America have publicly called for school corporal punishment to be abolished in the United States.

If concern for children's welfare is not enough of an incentive, yet another aspect that may motivate countries to consider bans is the costs associated with corporal punishment. In a report prepared for the nongovernmental organization Plan International, researchers calculated that countries lose millions and sometimes billions of dollars each year as a result of various forms of school violence, including corporal punishment. These costs include the long-term costs associated with lower achievement and higher dropout rates, such as lower earnings, higher physical and mental health needs, and higher reliance on social services.

National bans on school corporal punishment are an important step toward reducing the practice, but as noted earlier, corporal punishment continues even in countries where it is illegal, in large part because teachers, parents, and children are often convinced that corporal punishment is necessary for disciplining children. Eliminating corporal punishment will require interventions that teach both adults and children about the harms associated with corporal punishment and about more effective and nonviolent methods of discipline.

There are examples from around the world of successful educational campaigns to reduce school corporal punishment. The Council of Europe has an ongoing campaign called "raise your hand against smacking" (smacking is a term used for spanking in Europe) that is focused on changing public attitudes about corporal punishment. Similarly, a campaign by Plan International known as Learn Without Fear has trained teachers throughout the world in nonviolent discipline and has advocated for bans on corporal punishment in a number of countries. In Uganda, an intervention called the Good Schools Toolkit has been used successfully to train teachers in positive disciplinary methods and thereby reduce the incidence of corporal punishment by 42%.

Changing attitudes about corporal punishment and providing teachers with methods with which they can replace corporal punishment are necessary steps in eliminating school corporal punishment. Schoolwide interventions such as social–emotional learning and positive behavioral interventions and supports are considered effective at reducing students' problem behaviors and creating a positive learning environment for students. Such interventions work to improve student behavior at the school level, thereby obviating the need for school corporal punishment in the first place.

Elizabeth T. Gershoff

See also Adultism; Childhood; Compliance; Cross-Cultural Research; Educational Psychology; Parenting Styles; Punishment; Social Justice; U.S. Department of Education

Further Readings

Committee on the Rights of the Child. (2006). *General Comment No. 8 (2006): The right of the child to protection from corporal punishment and or cruel or degrading forms of punishment (articles 1, 28(2), and 37, inter alia) (CRC/C/GC/8)*. Geneva, Switzerland: United Nations.

DeVries, K. M., Knight, L., Child, J. C., Mirembe, A., Nakuti, J., Jones, R., . . . Naker, D. (2015). The Good School Toolkit for reducing physical violence from school staff to primary school students: A cluster-randomised controlled trial in Uganda. *Lancet Global Health, 385,* e378–e386.

Gershoff, E. T. (2013). Spanking and child development: We know enough now to stop hitting our children. *Child Development Perspectives, 7,* 133–137. doi:10.1111/cdep.12038

Gershoff, E. T., Purtell, K. M., & Holas, I. (2015). Corporal punishment in U.S. public schools: *Legal precedents, current practices, and future policy. Springer Briefs in Psychology Series, Advances in Child and Family Policy and Practice Subseries, 1,* 1–105. doi:10.1007/978-3-319-14818-2

Global Initiative to End All Corporal Punishment of Children. (2015). *Towards non-violent schools: Prohibiting all corporal punishment. Global report*

2015. Retrieved from http://www .endcorporalpunishment.org/resources/thematic -reports/schools-report-2015.html

King, J. B. (2016, November 22). Letter to states calling for an end to corporal punishment in schools. Washington, DC: U.S. Department of Education. Retrieved from https://www.ed.gov/category/keyword/ corporal-punishment

Ogando Portela, M. J., & Pells, K. (2015). *Corporal punishment in schools: Longitudinal evidence from Ethiopia, India, Peru, and Viet Nam* (Innocenti Discussion Paper No. 2015-02). Florence, Italy: UNICEF Office of Research. Retrieved from https:// www.unicef-irc.org/publications/series/22/

Pereznieto, P., Harper, C., Clench, B., & Coarasa, J. (2010). *The economic impact of school violence*. London, UK: Plan International & Overseas Development Institute. Retrieved from plan -international.org/learnwithoutfear

CORRELATION

If one wants to know the degree of a relationship, the correlation between two variables can be examined. Correlations can be quantified by computing a *correlation coefficient*. This entry first describes a concept central to correlation, *covariance*, and then discusses calculation and interpretation of correlation coefficients.

Covariance indicates the tendency in the linear relationship for two random variables to covary (or vary together) that is represented in deviations measured in the unstandardized units in which X and Y are measured. Specifically, it is defined as the expected product of the deviations of each of two random variables from its expected values or means.

The population covariance between two variables, X and Y, can be written by:

$$\begin{aligned} cov(X,Y) &= E[(X - E(X))(Y - E(Y))] \\ &= E[XY - XE(Y) - E(X)Y - E(X)E(Y)] \\ &= E(XY) - E(X)E(Y) - E(X)E(Y) - E(X)E(Y) \\ &= E(XY) - E(X)E(Y) \end{aligned}$$

where E is the expected value or population mean.

Similarly, the sample covariance between x and y is given by:

$$\begin{aligned} s(x,y) &= \frac{1}{N-1}\sum_{i=1}^{n}(x)_i - \bar{x})(y_i - \bar{y}) \\ &= \frac{1}{N-1}\left[\sum_{i=1}^{n}x_iy_i - \frac{(\sum_{i=1}^{N}x_i)(\sum_{i=1}^{N}y_i)}{N}\right] \end{aligned}$$

where N is the number of observations; $\bar{x}, \bar{y}$ are the sample means of x and y.

When one interprets covariances, zero covariances indicate that variables are not linearly related. If they are nonlinearly associated or statistically independent, the covariance is zero. On the other hand, a nonzero covariance indicates the tendency of covarying. If the sign of covariance is positive, the two variables tend to vary in the same direction. If a covariance value is negative, the two variables tend to move in the opposite direction. The covariance is not independent of the unit used to measure x and y, and so magnitude of the covariance depends on the measurement units of two variables. Note that the nonzero covariance does not indicate causation and how strong the association is between two variables.

When considering a variance–covariance matrix, covariances or correlations among observed variables depend on the relationship between latent variables and linear composite variables (i.e., tests consisting of more than one item). The covariance between two composite variables is the sum of the elements of the covariance matrix. It can be written by:

$$\sigma(X,Y) = \sigma(X,Y) = \sum_{i=1}^{p}\sum_{j=1}^{q}\sigma(X_i, Y_j)$$

where p, q are the numbers of variable in X and Y, respectively.

This most commonly computed correlation coefficient is a standardized index of linear association. From the covariance, the correlation coefficient for X and Y is calculated using the following equation:

$$r = \frac{\sum_{i=1}^{N}\frac{x_i y_i}{N-1}}{s(x,y)} = \frac{\sum_{i=1}^{N}x_i y_i}{(s_X s_Y)}$$

The *product moment correlation coefficient* was originally invented by Karl Pearson in 1895 based on the studies conducted by Francis Galton and J. D. Hamilton Dickson in the 1880s. The correlation coefficient ranges from −1 to 1. If its value is 0, the variables have no linear relationship; and if its value is −1 or 1, each variable is perfectly predicted by the other. Its sign indicates the direction of the relationship.

Hyun Joo Jung and Jennifer Randall

See also Autocorrelation; Pearson Correlation Coefficient; Phi Correlation Coefficient

Further Readings

Cohen, J., Cohen, P., West, S. G., & Aiken, L. S. (2003). *Applied multiple regression/correlation analysis for the behavioral sciences*. Mahwah, NJ: Erlbaum.

Galton, F. (1888). Co-relations and their measurement, chiefly from anthropometric data. *Proceedings of the Royal Society of London, 45*, 135–145.

Galton, F. (1889). *Natural inheritance*. London, UK: Macmillan.

Galton, F., & Dickson, J. H. (1886). Family likeness in stature. *Proceedings of the Royal Society of London, 40*, 42–73.

Mulaik, S. A. (2010). *Foundations of factor analysis*. New York, NY: CRC Press.

Pearson, K. (1895). Contributions to the mathematical theory of evolution, II. *Philosophical Transactions of the Royal Society of London, A, 186*, 343–414.

Cost–Benefit Analysis

Cost–benefit analysis (CBA) is a systematic approach used to evaluate the strengths and weaknesses of available options through a critical comparison of benefits and costs. Within the educational environment, this is a strategy used to evaluate the worth of educational programs and determine the added value in relationship to the monetary cost of the program. CBA has two overarching purposes: (1) to determine whether a program, investment, or decision is sound through verifying if its benefits overshadow the costs and by how much and (2) to provide a basis for comparing programs or projects by matching the total expected costs of each option against the total cost of benefits. Although one might assume that money is the driving force behind CBA, it is primarily used as protection for the well-being of individuals affected by the project or program. True economists want to measure the welfare, which is often a challenge because welfare cannot be directly measured. Instead, they use money as an expression of welfare and to assign "worth" to the program, allowing people to make decisions about programs based on this worth. Education is a form of investment in human capital, yielding economic benefits and contributing to the productive capacity of society. In this entry, how CBA is used in educational settings is analyzed. A comparison of CBA and cost-effectiveness analysis (CEA) is also conducted. The steps of conducting a CBA are also provided. Finally, the entry examines how CBA research has supported the importance of quality preschool education programs and concludes with a debate about the overall benefits of CBA in education.

CBA and Education

Educational leaders and policy makers are often faced with determining the best educational programs to serve their students. Investment at any level involves a sacrifice of some type to secure future benefits. CBA is a particularly useful tool for examining these educational programs and interventions. The framework for CBA allows one to compare the costs and benefits to the various policies and/or program alternatives. This technique can be used as an attempt to compare the monetary value of benefits with the monetary value of costs. By calculating the costs and benefits of alternatives in terms of monetary values, it becomes easy to compare components such as rates of return on investment, net differences between costs and benefits, and benefit to cost ratios. The goal, however, would be for educational leaders to select programs that maximized the total benefits relative to costs.

To perform a CBA of alternatives, it is critical to assume that the benefits or outcomes can be valued by their market costs or comparable alternatives. Yet oftentimes programs in the social sciences do not have a market counterpart. For example, if a program is designed to improve student learning, how can one get a market price for student achievement? Benefits of a program, however, can be reflected by increased graduation rates and the added value of students being prepared for future college and career opportunities; it's often difficult to quantify and place a monetary value on all of the benefits of a program.

CBA Versus CEA

The effectiveness of a strategy may be expressed in terms of its actual outcome instead of its monetary value. Monetary measures of resource costs, in this instance, are related to the effectiveness of a program to produce a particular impact or outcome. In cases in which the effectiveness of a program to achieve a particular goal is linked to costs, the method is considered to be a CEA, rather than a CBA. CEA is gaining traction in educational program evaluation, as one might examine various alternatives for raising the literacy level of a population, increasing attendance rates for secondary students, reducing dropout rates, and so on. CEA allows us to rank potential programs according to the significances of their effects relative to their costs but prevents us from equating the costs directly to the benefits. CEA has been utilized to compare educational alternatives related to class sizes, the length of the school day, computer-assisted instruction, and peer tutoring. Oftentimes, however, these analyses only compare the effectiveness of the alternative programs, neglecting to consider the costs associated with the alternative programs.

CBA and CEA are both valuable tools for program evaluation. Although CEA is a method that relates the costs of a program to its key outcomes or benefits, CBA takes that process further by attempting to compare costs with the dollar value of an analysis and can be applied at any time before, during, or after a program implementation. Both CBA and CEA can greatly assist decision makers in assessing the efficiency of a program.

Steps of CBA

The actual process of conducting a CBA is rather sophisticated, with inherent challenges in estimating and calculating program costs and benefits. There are, however, practical steps that can be utilized in this type of analysis. Henry Levin, a leading advocate for the use of CBA in program evaluation, advocates a step-by-step approach to CBA: (a) determine the resources (ingredients) used by the program, (b) determine the costs of the resources on a common metric, (c) measure the monetary costs of all products or outputs from the program, and (d) develop different cost–benefit ratios for all groups involved. Determining costs for individual programs with an educational system, however, has unique challenges. Educational programs are typically not funded by external agencies; therefore, they usually operate within the total district or school budget. It is difficult to determine the actual cost of a program from the overall budget. Personnel, a primary cost within a school district's budget, involves a variety of individuals who frequently work on many projects each day. It is difficult to accurately account for personnel time when individuals are working on multiple projects within environments such as this.

The first step in the CBA process is to identify all the costs and benefits associated with the project or decision. This list should be comprehensive, including all direct costs as well as indirect costs, and other costs such as intangible, opportunity, and the cost of potential risks. Benefits, as well, should be comprehensive, including all direct and indirect revenues and intangible benefits. All items on the list should then be assigned a common unit of monetary measurement. Typically, it's best to take a conservative approach with a conscious effort to avoid bias. Finally, the aggregate costs and benefits should be compared to determine whether the benefits outweigh the costs. If the benefits are favorable, stakeholders might choose to continue with the project or program. If not, they might review aspects of the project to determine whether adjustments such as increasing the benefits and/or decreasing the costs can be made to make the project worthwhile. If adjustments cannot be made, the project or program may be discontinued in the future.

CBA of Preschool Education

One significant area of study has been surrounding preschools. It has been believed that quality early childhood education, particularly for children from low-income households, improves a child's foundation for learning, as well as has the potential to reduce children needing to repeat a grade, being placed in special education, and committing juvenile crimes. As such, this strong foundation may also improve high school graduation rates and students participating in postsecondary educational opportunities, lead to fewer teen pregnancies, and lower the need for public assistance. These outcomes, which may in part be due to receiving a quality preschool education, contribute to the overall benefit of a society. The benefits, however, can be compared with the costs of preschool, to the degree that one can put monetary values on these benefits. Over two decades of research has been conducted through experimental and quasi-experimental research to weigh these results within a cost–benefit framework.

The evaluation of Perry Preschool represents one of the most extensive studies of preschool programs using a cost–benefit approach. In 1963 and 1964, innercity children were randomly assigned to either the preschool intervention treatment group or a control group that did not receive the preschool intervention. During their academic careers and into adulthood, students were periodically surveyed and follow-up evaluations were completed regarding the educational and life outcomes of both the treatment (Perry Preschool) and control (no preschool) groups. Findings revealed that students in the Perry Preschool program were less likely to repeat grade levels or need special education services. Additionally, it was more common for these students to graduate from high school and continue on to postsecondary education. Later, they earned more money and paid more taxes. For every dollar invested in the preschool intervention program, the investment paid almost US$13. This created a cost–benefit ratio of 13:1. Higher tax revenues and lower government support costs associated with the treatment group were attributed to the benefits received.

This method has also been applied to increasing graduation rates for high school students in the United States. Five interventions were identified that reduced dropout rates, thereby increasing the number of students graduating from high school, which included two preschool/early childhood interventions, reducing class sizes in the early grades, increased teacher salaries, and a high school educational reform program. Each intervention included an associated cost for each additional high school graduate, allowing for the cost-effectiveness comparison to be applied. The analysis was extended to a CBA by comparing the fiscal costs to the fiscal benefits, associating the high school completions as a taxpayer benefit from this public sector investment in education. Overall, results indicated that all five interventions benefited the taxpayer and exceeded the costs of the investments made into the programs. By using a method such as CBA, one can obtain research-based evidence that educational interventions are effective but also can be a sound investment for society.

Debating the Benefits of CBA in Education

There remains some controversy regarding the use of CBA in education. CBA requires that all alternative uses of the resources must be known to place value on the resources and identify the cost of the program. In education, however, one may not know all the possible alternative uses of resources. This goes back to the difficulty in obtaining utilization data for personnel to assign costs to the percentage of time they spent on the project.

CBA within educational research serves two primary purposes. First, it is important for school districts to have a greater understanding of how and where money is spent, including activities that receive the most time, money, and/or attention. Second, CBA allows for alternative education reforms or interventions to be compared based on economic costs. Oftentimes, cost analyses seek to expose the hidden costs of school initiatives to help districts implement them with fidelity. The importance of this purpose is relevant, because without the required monetary and personnel support, any school reform initiative is likely to fail. As the per pupil expenditures continue to rise over the past 30 years, education research stands to gain a great deal from the tools of economic analysis such as CBA.

Jana Craig-Hare

See also Policy Evaluation; Policy Research; Program Evaluation; Utilization-Focused Evaluation

Further Readings

Belfield, C., Nores, M., Barnett, S., & Schweinhart, L. (2006). The high/scope Perry preschool program: Cost-benefit analysis using data from the age-40 follow-up. *The Journal of Human Resources, 41*(1), 162–190.

Hummel-Rossi, B., & Ashdown, J. (2002). The state of cost-benefit and cost-effective analyses in education. *Review of Educational Research, 72*(1), 1–30.

Levin, H. (2001). Waiting for Godot: Cost-effectiveness analysis in education. *New Directions for Evaluation, 2001*(90), 55. doi:10.1002/ev.12

Levin, H. M., & Belfield, C. (2015). Guiding the development and use of cost-effectiveness analysis in education. *Journal of Research on Educational Effectiveness, 8*(3), 400–418.

Levin, H. M., & McEwan, P. J. (Eds.). (2002). *Cost-effectiveness and educational policy. Annual Yearbook of the American Education Finance Association.* Routledge.

National Research Council and Institute of Medicine. (2009). Strengthening benefit-cost analysis for early childhood interventions: Workshop summary. In A. Beatty, (Rapporteur), *Committee on strengthening benefit-cost methodology for the evaluation of early childhood interventions, board on children, youth, and families. Division of behavioral and social sciences and education.* Washington, DC: The National Academies Press.

COVARIANCE

See Analysis of Covariance; Correlation

CRAMÉR'S V COEFFICIENT

The Cramér's V (also known as Cramér's ϕ) is one of a number of correlation statistics developed to measure the strength of association between two nominal variables. Cramér's V is a nonparametric statistic used in cross-tabulated table data. These data are usually measured at the nominal level, although some researchers will use Cramér's V with ordinal data or collapsed (grouped) interval or ration data. Although an italicized capital V is most often used as the symbol for the statistic (V), the lowercase Greek letter ϕ with a subscripted c may also be used as follows: ϕ_c. This entry further describes the Cramér's V and discusses its assumptions, calculation, and interpretation. It concludes with an example of the use of the Cramér's V.

The V is a nonparametric inferential statistic used to measure correlation (also known as effect or effect size) for cross-tabulated tables when the variables have more than two levels. It is the effect size statistic of choice for tables greater than 2×2 (read two-by-two). Typical significance statistics for those tables include the chi-square and the maximum likelihood chi-square. The data in columns and rows should be nominal, although the V is frequently used with ordinal variables and collapsed interval/ratio data. Unlike the contingency coefficient, the V can be used when there are an unequal number of rows and columns. For example, the researcher should choose the V when the table has two columns and three rows.

The Cramér's V was developed by Carl Harald Cramér, a Swedish mathematician known for his work on analytic number theory and probability theory. Based on Karl Pearson's chi-square statistic, the V was developed to measure the size of the effect for significant chi-square tables.

The V is a correlation statistic, and as such, it measures the strength of an association between two variables. The V statistic provides two items of information:

> First, it answers the question, "Do these two variables covary?" That is, does one variable change when the other changes? (i.e., are the two variables independent?)

> Second, the size of the V describes the strength of the association. As the V approaches one level, the association is stronger. In a perfect correlation, for every one level of rise in one variable, the other variable would change exactly one level. The value of a V statistic can range only from 0 to +1.0; it cannot be a negative number. (Given that the calculation requires the square root of a number, the result cannot be negative with the standard formula.)

Many statistical computer programs (e.g., STATA, SPSS, and SAS) compute the V statistic as an option to accompany the output of the chi-square statistic, and the significance of V is the same as the significance of the chi-square.

Assumptions

Cramér's V, like virtually all inferential statistics not specifically designed to test matched pairs or related measures, assumes that the sample was randomly selected from a defined population. It assumes subjects were independently sampled from the population. That is, selection of one subject is unrelated to selection of any other subject. Like the chi-square, there must be an adequate sample size for the computed ϕ statistic to be useful. The chi-square demands that 80% or more of the cell-expected values must be at least 5, and if this assumption is violated, neither the chi-square nor a ϕ calculated on the basis of that chi-square can be relied upon. It should be noted that samples smaller than 30 are considered to be very small samples, and small samples are less likely to be representative of the population of interest than larger samples. A sample size of 30 will, in most studies, provide a minimum of 5 for the expected values in all four cells.

Calculation

A great advantage of the V is that it is so easily calculated from the chi-square result. The calculation is as follows:

$$V = \sqrt{\frac{\chi^2 / n}{\min(r-1)\,\text{or}\,(c-1)}}.$$

Where $r - 1$ means the number of rows –1,

$c - 1$ means the number of columns –1,

and min means select the minimum of the two values.

For example, if there are three rows and four columns, $r - 1 = 2$, and $c - 1 = 3$. Thus, the chi-square ÷ n will be divided by the value, 2.

It is important to remember that an effect size statistic is useful only if the original chi-square was statistically significant. It is a mistake to conduct further analysis, such as effect size testing, if the original test of independence on the table fails to produce a significant result. When the chi-square (or Fisher's exact) on a 2 × 2 table is nonsignificant, the range of the confidence interval about the obtained V will contain the value of zero. Thus, calculation of the V is unnecessary because it is, by definition, not significantly different from zero.

Interpretation

Values for the V can range from 0 to +1.0. A value of 1.0 means there is a perfect 1 to 1 correlation between the two variables. Like the Pearson r, the V can be squared to obtain a measure of the amount of variance in the dependent variable that is explained by the independent variable. A V of 0.68 squared results in a value of 0.46, which means that the independent variable accounts for 46% of the variance in the dependent variable.

Although different authors may use different values for weak, moderate, and strong correlation measures, Table 1 can be used as a general guide to interpretation of the strength of effect size represented by various values of the V.

These interpretations are based on the amount of variance in the dependent variable explained by the independent variable. A correlation of +0.29 means that even if statistically significant, only about 8% of the variance in the dependent variable is explained by the independent variable.

Example of Use of the Cramér's V

In this hypothetical example, three large school districts' populations are examined for the number of students achieving high enough scores for college admission on the SAT or ACT. In Districts A and C, students may take their choice of courses so long as they meet the state's minimum graduation requirements. However, in District B (a more affluent district), college preparatory courses are mandatory for graduation. The results are presented in Table 2.

The chi-square test of this table produces the following results: chi-square = 1139.62, $df = 2$, $p < .0001$[2]. There are three rows and two columns.

Table I   Strength of effect size

Between 0 and 0.19	*No Correlation or a Negligible Correlation*
0.20–0.29	Weak correlation
0.39–0.50	Moderate correlation
0.50–0.69	Strong correlation
0.70–1.0	Very strong correlation

Table 2 Chi-square results

	College Score Achieved	College Score not Achieved
District A	1300	1200
District B	2000	120
District C	1098	995

Using the formula for Cramér's V, the following values are required:

Chi-square = 1191.63

Sample size (n) = 6713

Number of rows = 3, Rows – 1 = 2

Number of columns = 2, Columns –1 = 1

$$V = \sqrt{\frac{\chi^2/n = 1191.63/6713 = .177417}{\min(3-1)\,\text{or}\,(2-1) = 1}}$$
$$V = \sqrt{.177414} = .42.$$

The result is interpreted as follows: There was a significant difference among the three districts in the number of students achieving SAT or ACT scores high enough for college admission (chi-square = 1192, df = 2, p < .0001). The effect size of the relationship was 0.43, which is a moderately strong effect size.

Mary L. McHugh

See also Chi-Square Test; Pearson Correlation Coefficient; Phi Correlation Coefficient; Spearman Correlation Coefficient; Two-Way Chi-Square

Further Readings

Norton, B. T. (1978, February). Karl Pearson and statistics: The social origins of scientific innovation. *Social Studies of Science, 8*(1), 3–34.

Vassar-Stats. (2016). *Chi-Square, Cramer's V, and Lambda online calculator*. Retrieved from June 22, 2016, Vassar-Stats website: http://vassarstats.net/newcs.html

CREATIVITY

Over the past 50 years, theory and research on creativity have advanced significantly. These advances can be seen across a number of domains and fields, including business, technology, health care, and design, and the implications for education have been significant. Indeed, scholars now have rich, detailed definitions and conceptions of creativity, considerable knowledge about enhancement of creativity, and comprehensive assessments for use in educational settings. The increased emphasis on creativity in education and the corresponding surge in creativity research have important implications for the definition of creativity and enhancements to creativity.

Scholars agree that a universal definition of creativity needs to encompass more than just the traditional notions of uniqueness and utility, expanding to include ideas such as tangibility, context, and surprise. Furthermore, there are a plethora of established strategies for enhancing creativity in the classroom, from pedagogical techniques such as divergent thinking training and modeling to external resources such as technology use and exposure to and interaction with outside communities. Finally, assessing creativity in the classroom is possible through a variety of instruments and techniques designed to measure creative products, process, people, and environments. This entry reviews definitions of creativity, research on enhancement efforts, and creativity assessments.

Definitions

Creativity is a term embedded in the lexicon, to the extent that it becomes difficult to detach the construct from the widely held myths and stereotypes surrounding it. These misconceptions include the notion that creativity is something we either are or are not born with. Additionally, creativity is often associated with socially isolated and dark or carefree and irrational behavior (such as the "loner" or "hippie" archetypes). Scholars believe many of these misconceptions result from imprecise definitions of creativity. Consequently, in order for research on creativity to be dissociated from these myths, it is important for researchers to clearly define creativity as they intend it to be used. Yet, in one study that examined published creativity research, only a third of articles included explicit definitions of creativity. As a result, scholars in the fields of education and psychology have published several articles attempting to resolve the absence of a definition for creativity.

The traits most commonly and overtly associated with the study of creativity are uniqueness and usefulness. Jonathan Plucker, Ronald Beghetto, and Gayle Dow, in their widely cited definition of creativity published in 2004, added the criteria of tangibility (e.g., an observable product) and the situation or context (acknowledging that whether something can be considered unique or useful is dependent on the existing environment and social framework). Their definition combines these criteria into one comprehensive definition:

> Creativity is the interaction among *aptitude, process, and environment* by which an individual or group produces a *perceptible product* that is both *novel and useful* as defined within a *social context* (p. 90).

Other scholars have provided similar definitions. Using U.S. Patent Office criteria, Dean Simonton asserts that something is creative if it includes some proportion of novelty, usefulness, *and* surprise. Although Plucker and colleagues and Simonton used different approaches to define creativity, their definitions are not mutually exclusive. The most obvious overlap in the two definitions is the emphasis on novelty and usefulness with the shared idea that those two traits alone are insufficient to define creativity.

Given these definitions, there are several models for how to conceptualize creativity, including the "4P model" and "5A model." In the 4P model, creativity includes *people* (the creators themselves and their corresponding personalities and attitudes), *process* (the actual procedures through which original, useful ideas are produced), the creative *product* itself, and *press* (the creators' context and how they interact with it). The 4P conceptualization has been used for several decades, and Vlad Glăveanu expanded and modified that model from a sociocultural perspective to create his 5A framework: *actors* interacting with their social context, creative *action or activity*, *artifacts* (products in cultural context), *audiences* as a component of press, and *affordances*, those activities facilitating interactions between actors and audiences. Regardless of the conceptualization, the key theme across these and other popular models is that creativity is a complex, multifaceted construct, providing multiple pathways for teachers to foster and assess student creativity.

Enhancement

Researchers have identified a number of strategies for enhancing creativity—in addition to barriers within schools that may serve as barriers to the development of student creativity. This section reviews the use of specific teaching strategies, game- and play-based interventions, collaboration, technology, and interaction with outside-of-school communities.

Pedagogical Techniques

First and foremost, teachers can equip students with the correct attitudes about creativity. As previously mentioned, there are several myths surrounding creativity. If teachers debunk these myths for students and teach them that creativity is something that can be learned and achieved deliberately, students will understand that their creative potential is not predetermined.

Teachers can also enhance creativity by encouraging creative ideation, also known as divergent thinking, which is the idea that any given problem has multiple solutions. For example, teachers can train divergent thinking by demonstrating a few different methods for arriving at a solution to a math problem, having students come up with their own hypotheses for science experiments, and instructing students to interpret texts from multiple angles and perspectives. These divergent thinking training approaches enhance creativity by improving the fluency, flexibility, originality, and elaboration of students' ideas.

Another area in which educators can foster student creativity is the area of creative articulation, a concept designed to help explain how creators select potential audiences for their creative work and use communication and persuasion to maximize the value of their creative work in the eyes of those audiences. In the real world, creativity does not stop at the idea or product stages rather continues in a cycle of feedback and revision as the creator or creative team shares their work with various audiences and receives constructive criticism. Yet few opportunities are provided within schools for students to share their creative work and receive feedback. Perhaps more to the point, opportunities for students to learn how to provide constructive feedback are limited. Whenever possible, teachers should provide opportunities for students to share their work with their peers, other educators, and community members, and students should receive guidance and practice as they learn how to provide constructive criticism when evaluating others' creative products.

Teachers can also exhibit and teach creative ideation with a willingness to deviate from the lesson plan to indulge in an unplanned opportunity for learning. For example, when a teacher is explaining themes in a novel, a student might ask a question about how one of the themes directly relates to a current event affecting the school's community. Then, the teacher can choose to disregard the lesson plan, at the risk of not covering all of the novel's themes, to instead facilitate a discussion inspired by the student's question. By taking advantage of this unplanned opportunity, the teacher is providing a more creative and enduring learning experience for the students. When students learn from a teacher who engages with their questions and relevant context in this way, they are also learning from the teacher's willingness to be spontaneous. In this sense, the teacher is modeling creativity.

Creative modeling is one of the most powerful strategies teachers can use to cultivate students' creativity. Recent studies suggest that students who experience creative modeling are more likely to exhibit creative behavior themselves. For example, Xinfa Yi, Plucker, and Jiajun Guo found that when they exposed students to creative models (such as collages and drawings with the same subject matter the students would have to replicate), the students demonstrated significantly more creativity, technical quality, imagination, artistic level, and elaboration, and gave a better general impression on a series of creativity assessments than students who were not exposed to creative models. Modeling creativity is especially effective for disadvantaged students who are less likely to have exposure to creative models outside the classroom. When teachers demonstrate creative behavior themselves, or even when teachers expose students to the creative work of others, students are more likely to be open to new ideas and risk-taking.

Research also shows that game-based and play-based interventions are successful strategies for developing creativity. These types of activities merge real world situations with imagination. This forces students to engage with material creatively yet comfortably, given that games and play are already so integral to students' everyday lives. For example, pretend play, where students are forced to take on roles and perspectives that may not match their own, can advance students' creativity by helping them process their emotions and practice the real-world scenarios. Lessons executed through games and play also provide opportunities for peer collaboration which allows students to enhance creativity in one another.

Collaboration among peers is a mixed blessing for creativity. On the negative side, social pressures can make some students reluctant to contribute to the group's creative work, and group members' ideas may serve as constraints on subsequent idea generation within the group. On the positive side, under the right framework, peers can be an asset to one another's creative processes. When teachers provide a structured environment for collaboration, such as assigning roles within a group or laying out expectations for peer feedback, students are more likely to exchange ideas and problem solve in creative ways that they may not have been able to achieve individually.

External Resources

In addition to teachers and peers enhancing creativity in the classroom, external resources can provide students with distinctive opportunities that facilitate creativity. Teachers often shy away from some of the pedagogical techniques mentioned earlier because of outside pressure to focus on more standardized and concrete achievement; practices that enhance creativity are not necessarily synonymous with those that improve test scores or maximize factual knowledge. So, external resources such as technology and creative communities of practice can help supplement the creativity enhancements the teachers may be unable to directly provide.

Technology can be a helpful tool for fostering student creativity. For example, with video editing software, students are able to explore and express their story-telling abilities through animation or filmmaking, which introduce elements of complexity that can elevate the creative process. Additionally, technological tools like geographic information systems give students a chance to apply and improve their visual–spatial skills. This type of technology has the ability to unlock and develop creativity in areas that students would not normally be exposed to. Therefore, by integrating technology with the curriculum, students can make connections and tap into ideas that traditional teaching methods may not allow for. This can also occur when teachers take students outside the physical setting of the classroom or invite creative practitioners into the classroom.

Students' creativity benefits from exposure to creative and professional communities beyond their schools. For example, if students visit an art gallery to see original artwork and witness the process of the creation of a piece of art, they will develop a new understanding and perspective about how art can be created. Similarly, if a bank manager visits a math class to teach students about how knowledge of interest rates affects loans in the course of solving a real-word problem, students may develop a deeper understanding of the practical uses of math that may lead them to approaching a calculus problem in a different way. Thus, external environments and practitioners offer new and diverse circumstances and scenarios for students to engage with educational material, helping students fulfill their creative potential.

Assessments

Although the conventional wisdom is that high-quality assessments of creativity are not available for use in educational settings, researchers have developed extensive measures of creativity that are appropriate for a variety of uses in classrooms and schools.

Creativity is traditionally assessed from four different perspectives: the assessment of creative products, creative processes (cognition), creative people, and creative environments. Each perspective is marked by a rich history of instrument development and applied assessment within educational settings.

Creative product assessments allow teachers to focus on the general level of creativity of student products or specific characteristics that are associated with creative products. From the specific characteristic perspective, there are instruments such as the Student Product Assessment Form, which allows teachers and students to evaluate products along several dimensions, including originality, attention to audience concerns, and problem focusing. At the other end of the spectrum, the consensual assessment technique involves a general evaluation of a product's creativity by outside raters. These types of assessments lie on different ends of a broad continuum, but these and related product assessments allow educators and students to provide formative and summative feedback to students regarding the creativity of their work.

Creative process measures have traditionally focused on divergent and convergent thinking. Divergent thinking measures, such as the Torrance Tests of Creative Thinking, are traditionally the most popular creativity assessment in schools. Convergent thinking measures include the Remote Associates Test, in which students are provided with three, seemingly unrelated terms and asked to identify how they are related. For example, if the three unrelated terms are *cube*, *skate*, and *cream*, the student should identify *ice* as the word that relates them.

In educational settings, both divergent and convergent thinking measures have been used primarily to identify creative talent. Although convergent thinking measures have fallen out of favor since the 1970s, divergent thinking assessments are experiencing a resurgence, in part due to advances in scoring and score interpretation. However, despite the rich research base on divergent thinking measures, researchers' understanding of creative cognition has expanded beyond the divergent–convergent distinction, and assessments based on these measures have not received as much attention as they deserve, both in experimental and educational settings.

A number of creativity instruments concerning individual characteristics of creators have been developed, and these may be useful for educators in a few different ways. For example, creative personality scales, such as the Gough Creative Personality Scale, may help identify students who have already developed the necessary attitudes for long-term creative productivity. Such measures have also been used as pre-post measures for creativity interventions. For the purposes of identification, instruments such as the Hocevar Creative Behavior Inventory, in which students identify their key accomplishments from a list of possible creative activities, can be useful as they are based on the belief that the best predictor of future creative behavior is past creative behavior. These "person measures" tend to be short and easy to administer, as most are self-report scales.

Given the importance of environmental factors in creative development, the lack of widely used environmental measures (e.g., a creative classroom environment scale) is surprising. Such instruments have been developed for workplace environments, but they have not been studied or widely used in K–12 education settings.

One important limitation of all of these instruments is that many have not been normed with diverse populations of students. The Torrance Tests are an exception, but most other measures have limited evidence of psychometric integrity with economically disadvantaged, non-White students. Given that such students now constitute over half of the K–12 student population in the United States, there is a need for research to address this limitation.

Jonathan A. Plucker and Lorraine Blatt

See also Alternate Assessments; Motivation; Personality Assessment; Surveys; Torrance Tests of Creative Thinking; Triarchic Theory of Intelligence

Further Readings

Plucker, J. A., Beghetto, R. A., & Dow, G. T. (2004). Why isn't creativity more important to educational psychologists? Potentials, pitfalls, and future directions in creativity research. *Educational Psychologist, 39*(2), 83–96. doi:10.1207/s15326985ep3902_1

Plucker, J. A., Guo, J., & Dilley, A. (2017). Research-guided programs and strategies for nurturing

creativity. In S. Pfeiffer (Ed.), *APA handbook of giftedness and talent.* Washington, DC: American Psychological Association.

Simonton, D. K. (2012). Taking the U.S. Patent Office criteria seriously: A quantitative three-criterion creativity definition and its implications. *Creativity Research Journal, 24*(2–3), 97–106. doi:10.1080/10400419.2012.676974

Simonton, D. K. (2016). Defining creativity: Don't we also need to define what is not creative? *The Journal of Creative Behavior, 0*(0), 1–15. doi:10.1002/jocb.137

Yi, X., Plucker, J. A., & Guo, J. (2015). Modeling influences on divergent thinking and artistic creativity. *Thinking Skills and Creativity, 16*, 62–68. doi:10.1016/j.tsc.2015.02.002

CREDENTIAL

See Certification

CRITERION-BASED VALIDITY EVIDENCE

Criterion-based validity evidence is frequently referred to as criterion-based validity, criterion-related validity, or simply criterion validity. In social science research, understanding the psychometric properties of an instrument is essential. These important psychometric properties include reliability and several types of validity. Thus, a researcher must often assess the evidence for the face validity, construct validity, content validity, and/or criterion-based validity of the instruments used in research. Although all forms of validity evidence indicate how well a measure measures what it is supposed to measure, criterion-based validity evidence is related to how accurately one measure predicts the outcome of another criterion measure. If a measure is a valid indicator of a construct of interest, then that measure could be used to predict the values of other measures related to that construct. Therefore, a measure that has high criterion validity would be one in which knowing the value of the predictor variable would allow the researcher to predict the value of the other criterion measure with high accuracy. Furthermore, the criterion-based validity applies to the validity of the predictor variable, not the criterion variable.

Criterion-based validity evidence is often of primary concern in educational research and assessment because educators are frequently looking for ways to determine whether assessment measures will be able to predict success or failure in later educational endeavors. Although other measures of validity are assessed using the opinions of experts and the similarity of a measure to other useful measures of the same construct, criterion-based validity is generally calculated and reported in quantitative measures from correlation and regression analyses. The general term *criterion validity* can include measures of predictive validity, concurrent validity, and postdictive validity. It is important to note that there are several threats to the criterion-based validity of conclusions drawn from the use of instruments that researchers must account for when using measures to predict criterion variable values. The remainder of this entry further describes the three types of criterion-based validity, highlights limitations of criterion-based validity evidence, and demonstrates how to calculate a measure of criterion-based validity.

Types of Criterion-Based Validity

The differences among the three types of criterion-based validity differ primarily in terms of whether the predictor variable precedes, occurs concurrently, or follows the criterion variable. Experiments can be designed to assess any of these three types of criterion-based validity, although the three types are not generally assessed with equal frequency in educational research.

Predictive Validity

Predictive validity is specifically related to how well a predictor variable predicts the values of a future criterion measure. Educational researchers are most often concerned with this type of criterion-related validity because they often want to know how well one can predict whether a student will succeed in later educational endeavors or in their careers. For example, college admissions were, at one time, focused on how well a high school

student's standardized test scores and grade point average (GPA) could predict the likelihood of that student graduating from their college. Thus, the predictive validity of those standardized test scores and GPAs has long been of interest to college admissions departments.

Concurrent Validity

Concurrent validity considers whether two separate measures taken at essentially the same time can predict the value of each other. For example, one might be concerned with whether the interest levels for a social media application of students from one geographic region could be used to predict the interest levels of students from a different region in that same application. Although concurrent validity might often be considered in marketing, it is also important in education. It is often useful to understand issues like how well students' feelings of connectedness to their school might predict the graduation rates and how well graduation rates might predict the sense of connectedness at a school. If they predict each other well, then the two measures have high concurrent validity.

Postdictive Validity

Postdictive validity is an indication of how well a predictor variable can be used to predict the value of a criterion measure taken previously in time. This type of validity is primarily used in studies in which the impact of educational policy might be considered. For example, a researcher might consider how well college GPA could predict whether students attended preschool. Although this postdictive validity of measuring college GPA may not be useful in the ways that predictive validity can be used for selection criteria or to implement programs to change predicted outcomes, postdictive validity can still be useful in determining whether a measure is a good indicator of a construct of interest. So in the aforementioned example, if the construct of interest is writing skills and a researcher knows there is a relationship between writing skills as an adult and college GPA and that there is a relationship between writing skills as a child and preschool attendance, then the criterion-based validity of a measure like college GPA could be considered in terms of the postdictive validity of predicting preschool attendance because it is an indicator of early writing skills. Postdictive validity might also be important when trying to determine which criterion variables might be related to later predictive variables. If a researcher wanted to consider variables related to failure at the college level, the researcher may look at the postdictive validity of college GPA before dropping out for predicting several childhood variables. Once postdictive validity was established for GPA on some of those variables, the relationship between those variables could be further explored.

Limitations of Criterion-Based Validity Evidence

As with all measures of validity, there are threats to criterion-based validity evidence. Several issues surrounding criterion-related validity evidence are important for researchers to keep in mind when making assumptions based on this type of validity. The first is that although criterion-related validity looks beyond simple correlations, it still does not allow one to assume causation between the measures. Although a measure may accurately predict the value of another measure, it cannot be assumed that changes in one measure will therefore cause the values in the other measure to change. In the aforementioned example, one can clearly not conclude that earning a high GPA in college causes one to attend preschool, even if there may be high postdictive criterion-based validity evidence for college GPA predicting preschool attendance. More importantly, the less obviously incorrect conclusion that attending preschool causes one to have a higher college GPA cannot be made. Although it may be true, the criterion-based validity evidence is not enough to indicate this causal relationship. Therefore, in order to draw causal conclusions, the researcher would have to conduct a study with an experimental design. In other words, researchers solely using criterion-based validity evidence can only know that the predictive or postdictive relationship exists. Moreover, the relationship could be caused by the impact of numerous other factors, such as parental education levels or interest in writing, on both measures.

A second threat to criterion-based validity evidence is the use of a restricted range of values for the predictor variables in many of the educational measures used for prediction. A common example of this phenomenon is when colleges use their selection criteria to predict college success in terms of GPA or years to graduate. Generally, those students who apply to the most competitive colleges self-select for the first stage of college admissions. That is, for the most part, only those students who have a relatively high GPA and relatively high standardized test scores apply to the competitive colleges. Thus, when looking at how well the GPA or test scores can be used to predict the outcomes of interest, the values of the predictor variables are generally in the top quarter of the true range for those variables. This restricted range can then suggest stronger correlations than truly exist when considering data from the full range.

A third threat to criterion-based validity evidence is measurement error. Although this validity refers to how well the predictor variable predicts the criterion variable, the researcher is generally interested in a construct represented by the criterion variable measure. If the criterion measure does not have good construct validity (i.e., it does not represent the construct of interest well), then the criterion-based validity is not accurate because the predictor variable is actually predicting the values of something other than a measure of the construct of interest.

Similar to measurement error and a restricted range, selection bias can also lead to false measures of criterion-based validity. If a researcher uses data from a biased sample to determine criterion-based validity, the conclusions may not be transferable to other populations. For example, if a researcher collects data from the five largest school districts in a state to determine the criterion-based validity of state-mandated testing in elementary schools for predicting high school graduation rates, the researcher may find high criterion-based validity. However, the state tests may not actually predict high school graduation rates in small rural districts that were not included in the original study because of their small size.

A final important point to consider is that although criterion-related validity evidence may suggest that one measure can predict the value of another measure, it does not explain why the relationship exists. This concern goes beyond the inability of a researcher to draw causal conclusions about the relationship between the predictor and criterion variables. Regardless of causation, when a measure has high criterion-based validity, it is likely that there are some important relationships between the variables and other related variables. Researchers must look beyond an indication of criterion-based validity to truly understand those relationships.

Calculating a Measure of Criterion-Based Validity

The index of criterion validity is the correlation between the predictor variable and the criterion variable. Although different correlation measures can be calculated depending on whether the variables are continuous, the statistic of primary interest with criterion-based validity evidence is the effect size for the correlation. The effect size of the correlation should be considered in order to understand how well the predictor variable predicts the criterion variable. A statistically significant correlation would only indicate a relationship between the predictor and criterion variables; however, a researcher interested in criterion-based validity evidence is not simply interested in whether the relationship exists. The strength of the relationship, and thus, the effect size, is the statistic of interest with criterion-related validity evidence. If multiple variables are used to predict the value of a criterion variable, the predictor variable with the largest effect size is said to have the most criterion-based validity.

Often researchers are not simply interested in whether a variable has high criterion-based validity but instead are interested in using the variable(s) with high criterion-based validity to calculate predicted values for the criterion variable. In these cases, a regression equation can be used to allow the researcher to calculate the predicted values. When multiple predictor variables can be used, a multiple regression equation can be used to calculate the predicted values of the criterion variable.

Jill Hendrickson Lohmeier

See also Concurrent Validity; Content-Related Validity Evidence; Predictive Validity; Psychometrics; Restriction of Range; Validity

Further Readings

Huang, C. (2012). Discriminant and criterion-related validity of achievement goals in predicting academic achievement: A meta-analysis. *Journal of Educational Psychology, 104*(1), 48–73.

Murphy, K. R., & Davidshofer, C. O. (1988). *Psychological testing: Principles and applications.* Englewood Cliffs, NJ: Prentice Hall.

Nunnally, J. C. (1978). *Psychometric theory* (2nd ed.). New York, NY: McGraw-Hill Education.

Wainer, H., & Braun, H. I. (2013). *Test validity.* Hillsdale, NJ: Routledge.

CRITERION-REFERENCED INTERPRETATION

Criterion-referenced interpretation is the interpretation of a test score as a measure of the knowledge, skills, and abilities an individual or group can demonstrate from a clearly defined content or behavior domain. It is often defined as a contrast to norm-referenced interpretation, where an individual's score only has meaning when it is compared to other individuals' scores. Criterion-referenced interpretations are independent of information based on how the average person performs. This entry further describes criterion-referenced interpretation and its uses, then discusses the design and validation of tests that foster criterion-referenced interpretation. The entry concludes with a look at common misconceptions about criterion-referenced interpretation.

Criterion-reference interpreted scores have been used for a variety of decisions, such as monitoring student achievement, evaluating efficacy of instructional programs, granting licensure and certification, planning individual and group instruction, and identifying possible learning disabilities. Tests that are designed to foster criterion-referenced interpretation of scores include Advanced Placement assessments, driver's license exams, and the Programme for International Student Assessment.

A criterion-referenced interpretation assumes an underlying continuum of content knowledge and behaviors that ranges from none to all encompassing. When the breadth and depth of knowledge and behaviors that comprise the content domain—the criterion—is clearly and completely specified, and a test is constructed with a representative sample of items from the content domain, it is understood that there is a correspondence between an individual's performance on the test and their ability level on the underlying continuum. Thus, if a test is constructed to foster a criterion-referenced interpretation, the inference can be made that an individual who scores 75% on the test knows and is able to demonstrate individual knowledge of 75% of the content domain.

First outlined by Robert Glaser in his 1963 symposium address to the American Educational Research Association, criterion-referenced interpretation gained popularity in the United States in the 1970s, as the development of theories of measurement and test design refined the distinctions between criterion-referenced and norm-referenced interpretations and their uses. Although it is possible under certain conditions to interpret scores from a single test in reference to both a criterion domain and a norming group, doing so rarely leads to satisfactory interpretations because different score interpretations require different test designs. It is important to note that the nature of test score interpretation (criterion- or norm referenced) is a characteristic of the interpretation as enabled by test design, not the test itself. There is a tendency in the measurement and assessment literature to refer to anything not explicitly norm referenced as criterion referenced. Here, the description of criterion-referenced interpretation is consistent with the original intent.

Design and Validation

As with all well-developed tests, in tests designed to foster criterion-referenced interpretation, the purpose, content domain, test specifications, and item specifications are defined. A key component of the content domain that supports criterion-referenced interpretation is that it covers a relatively narrow set of cognitive skills (although this is not a technical requirement), so that the resulting test sufficiently measures performance within the domain. This requires the test developer to define the boundaries of skills relevant to the content domain as well as the types and formats of problems and scoring rules that delineate

membership of appropriate items and tasks. This recognizes natural variability in item difficulty as a function of conceptual difficulty of items and tasks, the complexity of relevant contexts, and recognition of the natural progress of skill levels in the well-defined domain. The result is a pool of carefully constructed items deeply measuring performance to support criterion-referenced interpretations.

Ideally, once the criterion is well defined, items and tasks are generated that cover the entire expanse of the content domain. From this pool of items, a representative sample is drawn to construct the test. The representative sample of items allows for the correspondence between performance on the test and ability on the underlying knowledge continuum to be established. In practice, however, areas of the domain that are more easily measured tend to be overrepresented, even when they are more peripheral content.

Assuming that items are of high quality, ensuring that the items chosen are a representative sample of the content domain is, theoretically, the only concern regarding item selection for fostering criterion-referenced interpretation. Unlike norm-referenced interpretations, criterion-referenced interpretation does not depend on the variability of scores between test takers. Thus, items that are extremely difficult or extremely easy can be included if they address a fundamental skill or knowledge expected of test takers.

Lack of score variability also means that tests designed to support criterion-referenced interpretation are likely to produce low item-total correlations as measures of item discrimination and result in low internal consistency reliability in a classical test theory sense (thus such estimates are inappropriate for scores intended for criterion-referenced interpretation). Other estimates of score consistency are more appropriate, including decision or classification consistency.

The length of the test is dictated by the scope of the content domain and whether score interpretation is for individuals or groups. The broader the content domain, the longer the test will likely need to be in order for the sample of items to adequately cover the domain. Additionally, individual-level score interpretation requires longer tests because each test taker must respond to items that are representative of the entire content domain. However, group- or program-level score interpretations can be supported with fewer items because the content domain only needs to be appropriately represented when scores are aggregated. This means it is possible for each test taker to only respond to items that cover a portion of the domain as long as the entire domain is covered when aggregated to the group- or program level.

A variety of objective and subjective scoring methods can be used to support criterion-referenced interpretation. Selecting the appropriate scoring method largely depends on the nature of the content domain and the target audience. Although a typical scoring method is to calculate the number or percentage of items answered or tasks performed correctly, this method is not the most meaningful for all criterion domains. For instance, the speed of completing the task, such as running a mile or calculating single-digit multiplication, might be of greater importance, especially when the task itself is relatively easy to complete for the intended population. In other contexts, the precision of performance is of greater interest, as when transcribing an interview or using a rubric to score the quality of a test taker's essay. Many standardized tests employ more sophisticated scoring methods using item response theory or Bayesian estimation along with additional scaling considerations to generate final scores. Regardless of the scoring method employed, the theoretical rational and the procedures used to produce the scores need to be well documented in order to support criterion-referenced interpretation.

Although cut scores or performance standards are not required for criterion-referenced interpretation, they are often set in order to aid decisions based on the criterion-referenced interpretation of scores. Performance standards or cut scores categorize test takers into two or more performance or mastery levels. For instance, when score interpretations are used for granting certification, a cut score might be set at 85% correct, whereby test takers who answered 85% or more of the items correctly are granted certification. Although rationale and evidence must be provided to justify the use of cut scores, testing standards dictate circumstances under which cut scores can be established and defended, where to set the cut score is a policy decision based on judgment, often supported with empirical information.

Tests designed to support criterion-referenced interpretation are considered quota free, meaning that the number of test takers expected to score above or below the cut score should have absolutely no bearing on where the cut score is set. Instead, just as scores are interpreted in reference to what students are expected to know and do in a clearly defined criterion domain, cut scores should be set with explicit references to the criterion domain, not the relative performance of a reference group.

The primary validity evidence for interpreting scores from a test in reference to a criterion is a carefully and completely defined criterion domain. The criterion is the content knowledge and performance tasks an individual or group from a specified population is expected to know and be able to do under specified circumstances. This involves specifying whether certain skills or knowledge are of greater importance to the domain, whereas others might be more peripheral. Common procedures for defining the criterion domain include gathering judgments from experts in the domain, mutual consensus from a variety of people associated with the domain, and analysis of research and published works in the domain.

Although tests designed for criterion-referenced interpretation often are used to assess what individuals know and can do at the end of an instructional period, the criterion domain can be defined for any point in the instructional process where it might be useful to measure test takers' current achievement. Each component of the test, including purposes, score interpretations, and uses, is subject to validation, where relevant and appropriate evidence is gathered in its defense.

Common Misconceptions

Tests that are specifically constructed to support criterion-referenced interpretation are commonly referred to as criterion-referenced tests; however, this attribution is misleading. Scores from a single test can be interpreted for multiple purposes. For instance, a score could be interpreted both as a measure of what an individual knows and can do (criterion-referenced interpretation) and as a measure of how individual abilities compare relative to other test takers (norm-referenced interpretation). Although some interpretations might be more appropriate than others based on the design of the test, criterion-reference is an attribute of the interpretation of scores and not the test itself.

Another common misconception regards the multiple definitions of the term *criterion*. With the prevalence of tests that utilize cut scores to categorize test takers into performance or mastery levels, many individuals mistakenly refer to the cut score, performance standard, or mastery level as the criterion (e.g., the criterion passing score). However, the criterion refers to the domain of knowledge and behaviors expected from a defined population under specified circumstances. In an attempt to alleviate possible confusion, the term *domain-referenced interpretation* is sometimes used in place of criterion-referenced interpretation (actually, this has been suggested by measurement specialists numerous times but has not been widely adopted).

A third misconception is treating objectives-referenced interpretations or standards-based assessment interpretations as necessarily criterion referenced. Objectives-based and standards-based score interpretations share many of the measurement and score reporting characteristics as criterion-referenced interpretations in that results offer insight into the behaviors and abilities individuals and groups can currently demonstrate. Many take this similarity to mean that tests designed for objectives-referenced and standards-based score interpretation reveal test takers' knowledge and abilities for specific content domains when, in reality, the scope of the typical standards-based test is far too broad, where many content standards are lightly sampled.

Unlike criterion-referenced interpretation, objectives-referenced and standards-based interpretations do not require as carefully a defined content domain nor items to be a random or representative sample of the domain. Instead, objectives and standards are defined, which themselves are only a subset of the content domain that is expected to be taught. Thus, the inference drawn from the score is no longer what individuals or groups know and can do from the content domain, but what they know and can do from what they were expected to have been taught, in very general terms, because no specific objective or standard is well defined or measured. For school-level accountability, this might suffice as a general indicator; but

for individual-level inferences about knowledge, skills, and abilities, this is insufficient.

Kyle Nickodem and Michael C. Rodriguez

See also Achievement Tests; Cut Scores; Instructional Sensitivity; Norm-Referenced Interpretation; Programme for International Student Assessment; *Standards for Educational and Psychological Testing*; Standards-Based Assessment; Trends in International Mathematics and Science Study

Further Readings

Glaser, R. (1963). Instructional technology and the measurement of learning outcomes. *American Psychologist, 18,* 519–521.

Hambleton, R. K., & Novick, M. R. (1973). Toward an integration of theory and method for criterion-referenced tests. *Journal of Educational Measurement, 10*(3), 159–170.

Hambleton, R. K., Swaminathan, H., Algina, J., & Coulson, D. B. (1978). Criterion-referenced testing and measurement: A review of technical issues and developments. *Review of Educational Research, 48*(1), 1–47.

Popham, W. J. (Ed.). (1971). *Criterion-referenced measurement: An introduction.* Englewood Cliffs, NJ: Educational Technology.

Popham, W. J., & Husek, T. R. (1969). Implications of criterion-referenced measurement. *Journal of Educational Measurement, 6*(1), 1–9.

CRITICAL THINKING

The construct of critical thinking has been widely embraced as a core cognitive skill that should be nurtured and emphasized throughout educational curricula at every grade level. A multitude of definitions have been suggested to describe critical thinking. The general consensus is that critical thinking involves metacognition, or thinking about thinking, to maintain awareness and to reflect and manage one's own thoughts. Moreover, scholars emphasize the importance of recognizing one's own biases and being willing to evaluate the validity of arguments that oppose one's beliefs. Having this willingness implies that a person would have to accept that there is uncertainty about a belief or a solution to a problem and that the person is motivated to examine multiple perspectives or solutions. This entry begins by reviewing the various skills and dispositions incorporated in critical thinking. Next, the entry highlights educational programs designed to teach and improve critical thinking skills. The value and difficulty of assessing critical thinking, as well assessment tools, are then presented. The entry concludes by looking at current and future directions of critical thinking in academia.

Critical Thinking: Skills and Dispositions

With the numerous and variable descriptions of critical thinking, scholars have urged that we must clearly and specifically define critically thinking if we are to systematically assess and promote this construct in educational contexts. In 1990, a leading researcher on critical thinking, Peter Facione, led a panel of expert philosophers in defining critical thinking using the Delphi method. The experts submitted individual definitions of critical thinking, which they analyzed and fine-tuned until they reached a consensus definition. They concluded critical thinking consists of two aptitudes: skills and dispositions on the theory that it is insufficient to expect that a person who has critical thinking skills will simply use them; the critical thinker must also be inclined to practice the skills.

The Delphi consensus definition included six critical thinking skills and seven critical thinking dispositions. The skills are interpretation, analysis, evaluation, inference, explanation, and self-regulation. A critical thinker will interpret, analyze, evaluate, and draw inferences from information to form an evidence-based judgment. Moreover, the critical thinker can explain evidence, theories, concepts, methods, criteria, or contexts that support the judgment. By gathering and evaluating the judgment, the critical thinker can decide what to believe or how to proceed in a given situation. Some scholars call this process analytic reasoning. This type of reasoning involves breaking a concept down into different parts and studying how each part relates to the others. Therefore, analytic reasoning is a cognitive process of coming to an understanding of something believed, through a reasoned process of examining the parts of that belief. If a person is using analytic reasoning, the person is using critical thinking skills.

Critical thinking disposition is categorized as a personality characteristic; disposition indicates how one would approach a problem and use reasoning to solve it. A person with strong critical thinking disposition has high internal motivation to make decisions, solve problems, or evaluate ideas by thinking critically. The Delphi experts identified seven dispositions of critical thinking: inquisitiveness, systemactiy, truth-seeking, open-mindedness, self-confidence, analyticity, and maturity.

These dispositions are derived from a person's learning style, approach to conflicting opinions, and mindfulness in making decisions. Inquisitiveness describes the individual's general desire to learn. Systemacity is the tendency to ask questions in an organized and focused manner. Truth-seeking describes an individual's pursuit of the most accurate knowledge—despite findings that don't support a person's own opinions or self-interest—and continual reevaluation of information, remaining honest and objective throughout the pursuit. Open-mindedness, a common factor in most definitions of critical thinking, indicates individuals' tolerance of views different from their own and sensitivity to their own bias. Self-confidence describes how much trust individuals place in their own reasoning process when arriving at a judgment and their trust in themselves to lead others to a solution. Analyticity is characterized by how individuals apply reasoning and evidence to a proposed solution, while anticipating potential difficulties and remaining alert to the need to intervene. Maturity is the disposition of approaching problems while being mindful of their complexity or poor structure, and that multiple solutions may be plausible yet uncertain, depending on the context and supporting evidence.

Critical thinking disposition involves having willingness to suspend judgment and having the patience to ensure judgments are based on contextual considerations or on reasons that are relevant and consistent with an argument. The critical thinker evaluates conflicting claims and personal biases before arriving at a conclusion and continues to evaluate the conclusion when new information is presented. According to Robert Williams, a critical thinking scholar, a person is deemed proficient in critical thinking if the person's arguments are supported with evidence and if the person can accurately judge whether others' arguments are sufficiently supported. Diane Halpern, a leading researcher on critical thinking, believes critical thinking skills increase a person's chance to succeed in creating and adapting to change.

Teaching and Improving Critical Thinking Skills

Many studies suggest that critical thinking skills can be fostered in children, and one of the most prominent goals of education is to teach students how to think critically about complex topics. Educational programs have begun to invest more time and resources in strengthening 21st-century skills, which include critical thinking and analysis. Critical analytic skills are part of the brain's executive functioning. Executive functioning consists of working memory, inhibition, and cognitive flexibility. Strong critical thinkers use these cognitive processes to transfer reasoning capabilities. For example, the critical thinkers will use their working memory to store and update information. The critical thinkers will use inhibition to maintain an awareness of their own beliefs and biases, which will allow the individuals to identify errors in their thinking and resolve conflicting information instead of making premature judgments. Increased cognitive flexibility means the critical thinker is more able to apply different rules to a situation based on a certain context. Although these brain functions develop naturally in most human beings, research also suggests that games or exercises that target executive functioning can improve critical thinking skills.

Scholars have encouraged tailoring instruction toward verbal reasoning, argument analysis, hypothesis testing, probability assessment, problem solving, and decision making. Additionally, critical thinking can be nurtured outside of formal education. Critical thinking skills and dispositions can be practiced through parent–child or peer–to–peer interactions. For example, parents can challenge their children to take different perspectives or draw inferences by telling stories and asking questions. During play, children can promote critical thinking skills in each other by creating shared goals and achieving goals through communication

and cooperation. Scholars have recommended that teachers and caregivers engage children in conversations with the intent of promoting critical thinking and structure play so that children have the authority to pursue goals through peer interactions.

Encouraging children to reflect on their actions and activities also promotes critical thinking. By prompting a child to consider why an activity occurred, and what was gained from it, the child's metacognitive skills are engaged. Also, children are more likely to have heightened interest in the purpose of the activity if the activity is not imposed on them, and they will be more inclined to think independently in forming arguments about the activity.

Overall, the goal of teaching critical thinking in the classroom is that students use critical thinking skills beyond an in-class exam. The most authentic practice and assessment of critical thinking would take place outside of the classroom, where a student could spontaneously apply critical thinking skills to real-world problems or arguments, without the teacher and other stimuli that might prompt the skills. Students should be observed in a naturalistic setting or simulated scenario, after a semester of instruction, to determine whether the student obtained lasting improvements in skills and dispositions.

Critical Thinking Assessment

A number of articles on the subject suggest that critical thinking is best measured using authentic assessment, where tasks within the assessment are similar to real-world activities. Halpern opined that the most important outcome of critical thinking measures is a person's ability to transfer thinking skills. Projects that have relevance beyond the classroom provide an opportunity for students to show evidence of their higher-order thinking skills. This evidence often takes the form of completed performance assessments. Performance assessments comprise tasks that elicit observations of student performance. However, creating standardized, large-scale assessments of this nature is challenging due to the complexity of items, difficulty in operationally defining abstract constructs, and maintaining objectivity in scoring. To meet these challenges, performance assessments require large amounts of time and resources. Student performances are evaluated using rubrics, where observable behaviors are separated into a series of criteria and scored according the description that best matches the student's performance. Rubric development is challenging because the descriptive adjectives are inherently subjective, and their definitions require extended discussion before a consensus on their meaning can be reached. Moreover, rater training must occur before the raters' rubric scores can be considered valid.

Performance assessments are widely emphasized as summative measures due to their scope, but they also have strong formative value; by reviewing and reflecting on rubric scores, students can understand their strengths and areas for improvement in thinking skills. Moreover, strong thinking skills could be interpreted as both a cause and an effect of completing of a performance assessment. A commonly utilized method of assessing real-word thinking skills is the use of performance items that are set in authentic contexts. For example, constructed-response items based on a given scenario would elicit analytic thinking that is relevant to real-world contexts. Several assessments were designed to measure critical thinking using this method.

The first test designed to measure critical thinking is the Watson Glaser Critical Thinking Appraisal. It was developed in 1964 to select and promote employees into management positions within their occupations. The test is administered using semi-structured interviews that require the employees to use logic to support their views. Scores have been shown to predict reflective judgment. Since the mid-1990s, the Watson Glaser Critical Thinking Appraisal has been more commonly used in educational contexts. In 1985, another logic appraisal test is the Ennis Weir Critical Thinking Essay Test, developed for students. Students are instructed to read an argumentative letter and evaluate errors in reasoning within each paragraph and within the letter as a whole. The scorer uses a guide to assign points to the student's logic. Due to the highly structured nature of the test and scoring system, the test has high inter-rater reliability.

During the 1990 Delphi meeting, the task force developed two tests that measured the aforementioned skills and dispositions. Test development

began with the shared assumption that critical thinking involves the same elements at each stage of human development, from childhood to adulthood. They believed that although the standards for performance differ depending on age, the underlying structure of critical thinking is constant, and these elements can be operationally defined at every level. The two tests that were derived from the Delphi expert consensus are the California Critical Thinking Skills Test, which measures the six critical thinking skills, and the California Critical Thinking Disposition Inventory, which measures the seven dispositions of critical thinking. The basic California Critical Thinking Skills Test has two forms, which make the test suitable for evaluating growth in critical thinking skills. The forms comprise multiple-choice items and span six subscales: interpretation, analysis, evaluation, inference, explanation, and self-regulation. The California Critical Thinking Disposition Inventory has one form, comprising 6-point Likert-type scales that address tendencies toward the seven dispositions. Extensive research has been conducted on the two tests, and they are widely used as a research tool. Advantages of utilizing these tests include increased reliability due to the standardized and objective nature of the tests, and their theoretical basis is founded on the Delphi expert consensus of critical thinking.

Another test measuring critical thinking skills and dispositions is the Halpern Critical Thinking Assessment (2010), which requires students to respond to scenarios through constructed-response items. The test has two forms that consist of 25 everyday scenarios and follow-up items based on five areas of critical thinking: verbal reasoning, argument analysis, hypothesis testing, probability, and problem solving. In the first form, the scenarios are presented with open-ended questions in the first half, followed by a series of multiple-choice questions that pertain to the scenarios. The second form of the test is shorter, comprising only the multiple-choice items. Research on this assessment indicates that the test has high reliability and validity.

Critical Thinking in the 21st Century

With a greater emphasis on teaching 21st-century skills in the classroom and lifelong learning in higher education programs, critical thinking will remain an important focus in the world of academia and in real-world contexts. The research on critical thinking shows that humans are naturally equipped with certain critical thinking skills and dispositions through their executive functioning, and these cognitive processes can be fostered within and outside of the classroom. One of the greatest indicators of strong critical thinking skills and dispositions is whether a person will intentionally apply the same reasoning skills to different contexts, maintaining an awareness of preconceptions and openness to new information. Moreover, subsequent opinions and decisions will be supported with solid evidence, and this evidence will be sought intentionally and continually reevaluated as more information is presented.

Rachel Elizabeth Kostura Polk

See also Constructed-Response Items; Delphi Technique; Metacognition; Multiple-Choice Items

Further Readings

Brown, N., Afflerbach, J., & Croninger, S. (2014). Assessment of critical-analytic thinking. *Educational Psychology Review, 26*(4), 543–560.

Dexter, P., Applegate, M., Backer, J., Claytor, K., Keffer, J., Norton, B., & Ross B. (1997). A proposed framework for teaching and evaluating critical thinking in nursing. *Journal of Professional Nursing, 13*(3), 160–167.

Kuhn, D., & Dean Jr., D. (2004). Metacognition: A bridge between cognitive psychology and educational practice. *Theory Into Practice, 43*(4), 268–273.

Murphy, P., Rowe, K., Ramani, M., & Silverman, L. (2014). Promoting critical-analytic thinking in children and adolescents at home and in school. *Educational Psychology Review, 26*(4), 561–578.

Williams, R. (1999). Operational definitions and assessment of higher-order cognitive constructs. *Educational Psychology Review, 11*(4), 411–427.

CROSS-CLASSIFIED MODELS

Educational outcomes often result from two (or more) clearly hierarchical sampling dimensions, such as when students not only represent themselves but also represent some larger group. In multilevel modeling analyses, the students might be considered "Level 1" but be nested within schools at "Level 2" and would be modeled appropriately using the traditional multilevel model. However, when sampling dimensions are not clearly hierarchical, such as if students at Level 1 are simultaneously nested within more than one Level 2 variable (e.g., both schools and neighborhoods), the traditional multilevel model must be abandoned in favor of a cross-classified model. An understanding of the cross-classified model is critical given the potential curricular and fiscal policy ramifications that could result from incorrectly analyzing nonhierarchical, multilevel educational data. Therefore, this entry provides a brief overview of the cross-classified model and begins by detailing the transition from the traditional multilevel model to the cross-classified model. Then, the unconditional cross-classified model is presented to exhibit how this model partitions systematic variation at all levels, followed by a brief discussion of the random interaction effect. This is followed by a discussion of the complexity involved when estimating and interpreting the effects of predictor variables. The entry concludes with a brief overview of available software to estimate this model.

Before proceeding, it is important to consider that this entry is specific to cross-sectional data with a two-level structure. Specifically, all examples will consider students at Level 1 who are measured at one occasion and belong to one, and only one, Level 2 classification for schools as well as to one, and only one, Level 2 classification for neighborhoods. If, however, a sampling design considers students who attend multiple schools *or* live in multiple neighborhoods, then a multiple membership model would be required. By contrast, if a sampling design considers students to both live in a given neighborhood *and* attend multiple schools, then a multiple membership, multiple classification model would be required.

Transitioning to the Cross-Classified Model

The cross-classified model is similar to the traditional multilevel model in that the primary purpose of both models is to correctly partition all sources of systematic variation to ensure more accurate variance component estimates and, therefore, less biased statistical inference for predictor variables. For example, outcomes from students at Level 1 nested within the same school at Level 2 would be correlated as a result of the systematic variation due to schools. In this nested example, the traditional multilevel model would partition student-level variability from school-level variability prior to including student- and/or school-level predictors. However, when students at Level 1 are sampled from different schools and different neighborhoods at Level 2, it is unlikely that all students who attend the same school live in the same neighborhood or that all students who live in the same neighborhood attend the same school. Thus, the systematic variation due to schools and neighborhoods are not nested but instead are considered *crossed* at Level 2. To estimate the traditional multilevel model on crossed sampling, dimensions would require this model to be severely misspecified (e.g., ignoring either schools or neighborhoods, deleting observations to create a clear hierarchical structure). By contrast, the primary purpose of the cross-classified model is to account for both sources of systematic variation at Level 2 in a single model.

Because estimating the cross-classified model is computationally demanding, especially with increasing model complexity (e.g., student within schools and neighborhoods within cities), it is common to estimate separate traditional multilevel models for each Level 2 classification prior to estimating the cross-classified model (e.g., one model for students within schools, one model for students within neighborhoods). Although the variance components estimated by the traditional multilevel models are biased, they provide useful evidence of whether a cross-classified model could be estimated. Subsequently, the unconditional cross-classified model is estimated to explicitly partition the sources of variability at all levels of analysis, which is where the discussion turns next.

The Unconditional Cross-Classified Model

Consider a continuous outcome such as mathematics achievement, obtained for each student using a nonhierarchical, multilevel sampling design in which students at Level 1 belong to one unique combination of a given school and neighborhood at Level 2. For these data, the unconditional (i.e., no predictors) cross-classified model is:

$$\text{Math}_{i,s,n} = \gamma_{0,0,0} + u_{0,s} + u_{0,n} + u_{0,sn} + e_{i,s,n},$$

$$u_{0,s} \sim N_0, \sigma_{u0,s2},$$

$$u_{0,n} \sim N_0, \sigma_{u0,n2},$$

$$u_{0,sn} \sim N_0, \sigma_{u0,sn2}, \text{and}$$

$$e_{i,s,n} \sim N_0, \sigma_{es,n2}.$$

Here, $\text{Math}_{i,s,n}$ is the observed math achievement for student i who attends school s and lives in neighborhood n; commas are used to separate subscripts to ensure double-digit numbers are indicated clearly (e.g., the math score for student 10 in school and neighborhood 1: $\text{Math}_{10,1,1}$). $\gamma_{0,0,0}$ is the fixed intercept representing the average (or grand mean) math achievement across all students, whereas $u_{0,s}$, $u_{0,n}$, and $u_{0,sn}$ are the random effects for school s, neighborhood n, and the school-by-neighborhood interaction sn, respectively. Given that the random interaction effect is included in this model, random effects $u_{0,s}$ and $u_{0,n}$ represent the school- and neighborhood-specific deviations from the average math achievement of all students, respectively, and these random effects are considered main (or marginal) effects that are averaged across the other Level 2 classification (i.e., $u_{0,s}$ is averaged across neighborhoods and $u_{0,n}$ is averaged across schools). The random interaction effect $u_{0,sn}$ indicates the deviation of average math achievement for a unique combination of school s and neighborhood n from the math achievement that would be predicted by the fixed intercept $\gamma_{0,0,0}$ and random main effects $u_{0,s}$ and $u_{0,n}$. All random effects are assumed independent (i.e., uncorrelated) and normally distributed with a mean of 0 with variances $\sigma u_0, s_2$, $\sigma u_0, n_2$, and $\sigma u_0, sn_2$ for the school, neighborhood, and interaction random effects, respectively; a parenthetical subscript indicates the specific Level 2 classification is held constant (e.g., $\sigma u_0, s_2$ is the random effect variance based on all s schools). Finally, $e_{i,s,n}$ is the residual value representing the deviation of math achievement for student i from the average math achievement of the student's unique combination of school s and neighborhood n. The residual values are assumed independent of the random effects and normally distributed with a mean of 0 and variance $\sigma_{es,n2}$.

As previously stated, the primary purpose of estimating the unconditional cross-classified model is to explicitly partition the sources of variability at all levels of analysis. Once partitioned, intraclass correlations can be calculated to obtain the proportion of variance attributable to each source of variation. In general, these intraclass correlations are calculated as the variance component(s) for the Level 2 classification(s) of interest relative to the total variability in the outcome. For example, the intraclass correlation of math achievement between two students who attend different schools but live in the same neighborhood is:

$$\rho_{s,n,sn} = \text{between school variability total variablity}$$
$$= \sigma u0, s2 \sigma u0, s2 + \sigma u0, n2 + \sigma u0, sn2 + \sigma es, n2.$$

A Note on the Random Interaction Effect

The ability to include the random interaction effect $u_{0,sn}$ is a direct result of having a cross-classification of schools and neighborhoods at Level 2; this effect cannot exist when sampling dimensions are clearly hierarchical and cannot be estimated using the traditional multilevel model. If the random interaction effect is detectable and significant, it allows students who attend the same school to be influenced by their neighborhood and students who live in the same neighborhood to be influenced by their school.

With that said, the ability to actually estimate the random interaction effect in the cross-classified model is dictated primarily by the number of students who have a specific combination of a school and a neighborhood, known more generally as the number of *within-cell replicates* or *within-cell sample size*. Sampling designs with numerous within-cell sample sizes ≤1 (e.g., only one student in a specific school lives in a specific neighborhood) will fail to estimate the random interaction effect (and its variance component $\sigma u_{0,sn2}$). For example, a public school district may give students the option to attend any high school of their

choosing, but even in a large city, it is highly probable that no school will have multiple students from every neighborhood under study. Indeed, small within-cell sample sizes are common in applied educational research and are one of the primary reasons (in addition to unfamiliarity) for why the random interaction effect is estimated infrequently in the literature. However, erroneously omitting a random interaction effect that could have been estimated successfully will result in significantly biased variance component estimates (particularly for the variances of Level 2 classifications), which will in turn result in incorrect statistical inference for predictor effects.

The Conditional Cross-Classified Model

Following the estimation of the unconditional cross-classified model, predictor variables are typically included to explain each source of variability. Including predictor variables in the cross-classified model is similar to the traditional multilevel model with some added complexity, given there are multiple sources of variation at a given level of analysis.

Continuing with the aforementioned example, predicting a student's math achievement using school- and/or neighborhood-level predictors at Level 2 is fairly straightforward. For example, a school's sector (i.e., public *vs.* private) could be included to explicitly explain random school variance $\sigma_{u0,s2}$, whereas a neighborhood's poverty rate could be included to explain random neighborhood variance $\sigma_{u0,n2}$. If the random interaction effect $u_{0,sn}$ was estimated and significant, then an interaction effect between a school's sector and a neighborhood's poverty rate could be included to explain random interaction variance $\sigma_{u0,sn2}$. However, if the random interaction effect was not estimable or nonsignificant, it is unlikely that the sector-by-poverty rate interaction would be detected statistically.

The inclusion of student-level predictors at Level 1 is much more complex because student-level predictors also contain school- and neighborhood-level variability at Level 2. Therefore, including a student-level predictor in a cross-classified model without considering its multiple sources of variability will produce an incorrect estimate for the effect of the student-level predictor, termed a *convergence effect*, that assumes the predictor has an equal effect on all sources of variability. The convergence assumption is explicitly testable. For example, consider using students' psychometric IQ to predict math achievement. To test convergence, the student IQ predictor at Level 1 would be included alongside two newly calculated Level 2 predictors—one representing the average IQ of the students attending each school and the other representing the average IQ of the students living in each neighborhood. When all three IQ effects are included in the conditional model, the school-average IQ effect and neighborhood-average IQ effect are both *contextual effects* that provide an explicit test of convergence. A significant contextual effect indicates the effect of IQ differs between the student, school, and neighborhood, and convergence should therefore not be assumed. When retained in the model, the contextual effects also indicate that after controlling for a student's IQ, there is an additional effect on a student's math achievement score from attending a more intelligent school and living in a more intelligent neighborhood.

Finally, additional random effects for any student-level predictor could also be included in the cross-classified model. For example, the effect of student IQ could vary randomly across different schools and different neighborhoods. In this case, a separate random student IQ variance is calculated across schools and across neighborhoods, with the random student IQ variance across schools predicted by the student IQ-by-school sector interaction and the random student IQ variance across neighborhoods predicted by the student IQ-by-neighborhood poverty rate interaction. Although estimating additional random effects may make sense theoretically, they are typically difficult to estimate in practice given the increased computational demands.

Available Software to Estimate the Cross-Classified Model

The cross-classified model can be estimated using frequentist methods (e.g., restricted maximum likelihood) in SAS, R, SPSS, Stata, HLM, and MLwiN. In addition, Mplus will estimate the cross-classified model as a latent variable model, although this option may be esoteric to those

trained primarily in multilevel modeling. Increasing the complexity of the cross-classified model (e.g., introducing additional sampling dimensions and random effects) will quickly expose the computational ceiling of frequentist-based estimation. Thus, Bayesian methods (e.g., Markov chain Monte Carlo) are often employed because they are more computationally efficient for more complex models. Of the software mentioned, only SAS, R, and MLwiN can be used to estimate the cross-classified model in a Bayesian framework. In addition, individuals with a considerable computational computing background could use SAS/IML or R to create a custom Markov chain Monte Carlo estimator that is specific to their needs.

Ryan W. Walters

See also Bayesian Statistics; Generalizability Theory; Hierarchical Linear Modeling; Markov Chain Monte Carlo Methods; Mixed Model Analysis of Variance

Further Readings

Goldstein, H. (2011). *Multilevel statistical models* (4th ed.). London, UK: Wiley.

Hox, J. J. (2010). *Multilevel analysis: Techniques and applications* (2nd ed.). New York, NY: Routledge.

Raudenbush, S. W. (1993). A crossed random effects model for unbalanced data with applications in cross-sectional and longitudinal research. *Journal of Educational and Behavioral Statistics, 18*, 321–349.

Raudenbush, S. W., & Bryk, A. S. (2002). *Hierarchical linear models: Applications and data analysis methods* (2nd ed.). Thousand Oaks, CA: Sage.

Shi, Y., Leite, W., & Algina, J. (2010). The impact of omitting the interaction between crossed factors in cross-classified random effects modelling. *British Journal of Mathematical and Statistical Psychology, 63*(1), 1–15.

Snijders, T. A. B., & Bosker, R. J. (2012). *Multilevel analysis: An introduction to basic and advanced multilevel modeling* (2nd ed.). London, UK: Sage.

Cross-Cultural Research

Cross-cultural research can be defined as an attempt to compare the use of an intervention or a practice in one culture with a similar intervention or practice in another culture. It also provides a context for the comparative understanding of concepts such as intelligence and motivation across cultures. Cross-cultural research can allow researchers to explore individual differences and diversity issues at a deeper level. This entry discusses the types of research questions that can be answered through cross-cultural research and describes how this research is typically approached.

Cross-cultural research can identify practices that are unique as well as those that are similar across different countries and contexts. Such research can show how learning practices vary in schools and indicate what cultural aspects shape these differences. Cross-cultural research permits the study and comparison of outcomes and conditions for success in different contexts. In education, for instance, numerous research studies have been conducted highlighting the role of parental involvement, teacher training, and school funding in student achievement. However, many of these studies have been conducted in the United States and have not been replicated in other countries. Cross-cultural research would allow researchers to answer questions about how these factors influence student achievement in various contexts around the world.

In attempting to determine to what extent parental involvement influences student achievement worldwide, researchers would look at multiple factors, such as whether there are contextual variables that contribute to the nature of parental involvement in some cultures that are not present in others, what the parent–teacher relationship looks like in different cultures, and how dealing with parental involvement and student achievement manifests itself as an issue in different contexts. Cross-cultural research can enhance understanding of the way certain issues are rooted in schools and yet mediated by the social norms within a culture.

Cross-cultural studies have compared the experience of teaching in different countries, for instance, comparing the learning goals for secondary school students in Canada and Japan and the relative emphasis placed by teachers in the two countries on aspects of critical thinking, problem solving, developing relationships, and taking on responsibility. Teacher narratives have addressed issues such as differences in gender roles in different cultures, and biases students may have about teachers from different countries. Well-designed cross-cultural research can be instrumental in school settings with a large percentage of immigrant students, and findings can be of help to teachers and counselors in building cross-cultural bridges between school and home cultures.

Cross-cultural research typically uses an ethnographic approach. In ethnography, researchers usually take an emic perspective; that is, they study a culture from the perspective of the research participants themselves. This may involve researchers participating in activities of a culture or taking on more of a bystander role. Researchers may also interview or survey participants and collect artifacts or documents as a way of validating the data gathered through observations and controlling for their own biases and assumptions.

Wilfridah Mucherah

See also Cultural Competence; Culturally Responsive Evaluation; Ethnography; Multicultural Validity

Further Readings

Banks, J. A. (2006). *Cultural diversity and education: Foundations, curriculum, and teaching* (5th ed.). Boston, MA: Allyn & Bacon.

Canfield-Davis, K., Tenuto, P., Jain, S., & McMurtry, J. (2011). Professional ethical obligations for multicultural education and implications for educators. *Academy of Educational Leadership Journal, 15*(1), 95.

Li, D., Bai, X., & Li, H. (2014). On cultivating senior middle school students' cross-cultural awareness in English classes. *Studies in Literature and Language, 9*(1), 134–139. doi:10.3968/5437

McAllister, G., & Irvine, J. J. (2000). Cross cultural competency and multicultural teacher education. *Review of Educational Research, 70*(1), 3–24. doi:10.2307/1170592

McDonald, J. K., Goh, M., Brissett, A. A., Yoon, E., & Wahl, K. H. (2007). Working with immigrant students in schools: The role of school counselors in building cross-cultural bridges. *Journal of Multicultural Counseling and Development, 35*(2), 66–79.

Siu, F. W., Brodwin, M. G., Huang, I., Brodwin, E. R., & Kier, C. (2014). International collaborative cross-cultural teaching project: United States and Taiwan. *Journal of Applied Rehabilitation Counseling, 45*(2), 39–45.

VanTassel-Baska, J. (2013). The world of cross-cultural research: Insights for gifted education. *Journal for the Education of the Gifted, 36*(1), 6–18. doi:10.1177/0162353212471451

CROSSOVER DESIGN

The crossover design (also referred to as a replicated Latin square design) refers to a longitudinal study in which participants receive a sequence of treatments that varies based on the group to which the individual is assigned. The groups may be randomly assigned in the case of an experiment or allocated based on some other criteria (e.g., geographic location, classroom) in the case of a nonexperimental study. In its simplest form, the crossover design involves two periods by two treatments. Figure 1 depicts a basic 2 × 2 crossover design with two treatment sequences: AB and BA. As depicted in the diagram, all participants undergo a pretest at the commencement of the study. Then, in the first period of the study, one group of participants receives Treatment A while the other receives Treatment B. At the completion of the first treatment period, participants are administered a posttest. Groups then "crossover," in the second period, so that individuals who started with Treatment A commence Treatment B and those who began with Treatment B undergo Treatment A. Another posttest is conducted after the second period.

More complex variations of the crossover design can include more than two treatments or groups or could involve the use of a treatment in more than one period. The number of waves (or treatment periods) can vary considerably based on the nature of the research question and the length of each treatment. Depending on the design selected, researchers can apply a variety of statistical analyses to determine the impact of period, sequence, carryover, and treatment effects. Designs vary to the extent that they are balanced (i.e., whether or not each treatment is preceded by every other treatment the same number of times) and uniform (i.e., whether each period allocates each treatment to the same number of subjects or whether each subject receives every treatment the same number of times). An example of a balanced uniform crossover design (4 periods × 4 groups) would produce four treatment sequences: ABBA, BAAB, AABB, and BBAA.

Crossover designs have been employed in a wide variety of settings ranging from educational to epidemiological research. The crossover design is primarily used to allow researchers to compare the efficacy or impact of multiple treatments or a combination of treatments and control or placebo conditions. Crossover designs are most appropriate for interventions that are considered temporary, so that multiple treatment options can be tested. Depending on the nature of the treatments, there may be a washout interval between periods to allow the effects of one treatment to wear off before undergoing the next treatment. Clinical trials in medical or pharmaceutical research frequently employ crossover designs to assess the efficacy of different types of medications on a disease or condition. In the social sciences, crossover designs can be used to examine a wide variety of research questions such as the impact of different clinical rotation sequences on examination performance or the effectiveness of different

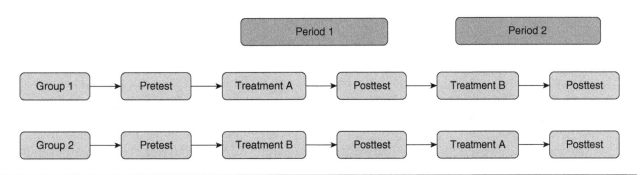

Figure 1   Basic crossover design

psychotherapy approaches on depression. The remainder of this entry discusses the strengths and limitations of the crossover design.

Strengths

A major strength of the crossover design is that it is within subjects, that is, each participant acts as his or her own control, which helps to account for the impact of individual differences and permits a smaller sample size than comparable research designs (e.g., parallel groups). Crossover and parallel groups designs can address similar research questions; however, the latter does so between subjects using a single treatment period, which requires a larger sample size. Another strength of the crossover design is that it provides control over the temporal order of treatments or interventions. The inclusion of multiple combinations of treatments allows for a comprehensive examination of the impact of different sequences.

Limitations

One of the major concerns associated with the crossover design is that the effect of an earlier treatment can produce carryover effects into subsequent periods. These effects can be the result of learning, demand characteristics, or psychological or physical reactions to treatments that persist into subsequent periods. For example, an inadequate washout period between treatments could result in the residual effects of a pharmaceutical treatment from one period impacting the next treatment. Similarly, the psychological state of the participants may systematically differ at the commencement of later periods, if, for example, an aspect of one period induces more psychological stress than another period. An example of learning could occur if a group is taught a particular skill during a treatment period, which they could continue to use in subsequent periods. Regardless of their source, carryover or residual effects from earlier treatments may not be equivalent for the different groups, which could result in researchers being unable to determine the independent impact of each treatment period.

Several options have been put forward to account for these concerns. First, researchers are encouraged to design their studies in a way that allows for interactions between treatments and periods to be detected as well as establishes whether or not the interaction was caused by carryover. This typically requires the use of more complex designs, for example, using the balanced uniform crossover design depicted earlier would provide the researcher with the ability to statistically identify and account for the impact of carryover and sequence effects. However, researchers typically need to balance the risk of carryover and sequence effects against the negative impact of increased study duration (e.g., added cost, higher risk of attrition). In circumstances where it is not feasible to conduct a complex design and carryover effects are suspected, researchers may need to restrict their conclusions to the first treatment period.

*Cindy Suurd Ralph and
Leandre R. Fabrigar*

See also Pretest–Posttest Designs

Further Readings

Jones, B., & Kenward, M. G. (2014). *Design and analysis of cross-over trials*. Boca Raton, FL: CRC Press.

Raghavarao, D., & Padgett, L. (2014). *Repeated measurements and cross-over designs*. Hoboken, NJ: Wiley.

Shadish, W. R., Cook, T. D., & Campbell, D. T. (2002). *Experimental and quasi-experimental designs for generalized causal inference*. Boston, MA: Houghton, Mifflin and Company.

CULTURAL COMPETENCE

Cultural competence in educational inquiry refers to a particular stance or sensibility regarding the cultural and sociodemographic diversity of most American (and many international) educational contexts. This stance is one of proactive awareness of and assumed respect for cultural and sociodemographic diversity. This entry first discusses why cultural competence is important in educational research and how it is reflected in each of the steps of doing research. It then discusses an international study on resilience in children and youth and the ways in which the study exemplified a stance of cultural competence.

A stance of cultural competence assumes that the cultural and sociodemographic characteristics of the students, teachers, and other educators being studied—and of the contexts they inhabit—matter to the quality and the equity of the teaching and learning that takes place in those contexts. Cultural competence in educational inquiry is marked by engagement with difference throughout a study or assessment, from conceptualization to reporting. The stance deliberately includes data gathering activities and analyses of the data that directly engage and inform the particular character of the diversity present in the contexts being studied. This understanding of cultural competence makes it more of a sensibility than an acquired body of knowledge and skills about the specific cultures and other markers of demographic diversity that may be present in an educational inquiry context.

Importance of Cultural Competence in Educational Inquiry

The initial decades of the 21st century have borne witness to the deep challenges of cultural, economic, religious, and geographic diversity around the globe. Many developed countries have become havens for migrants from less developed countries seeking sanctuary from political unrest and violence. Educational institutions, historically and today, remain at the forefront of meaningfully and sustainably integrating diverse peoples into existing societies.

Educational institutions provide safe spaces for engaging with diversity. They further enable the next generations to learn about and from their differences and to develop their own sense of respect for and acceptance of other people and cultures. Therefore, educational research, evaluation, and assessment—in the United States and other countries with diverse populations—are themselves compelled to proactively and meaningfully engage with diversity and difference through the lenses of cultural competence.

Cultural Competence in the Process of Educational Inquiry

A proactive stance of cultural awareness, respect, and engagement will permeate all aspects of an educational inquiry. Most significantly, cultural engagement will be reflected in the inquiry questions asked, the definitions and assessments of key constructs, the processes used to gather and analyze data, and the format and distribution of study reports. Each requires respectful attention to the strands of diversity present in the contexts being studied. For each, the inquirer can ask, "How well does this component of my study, or my assessment process, manifest respect for diversity and meaningful engagement with difference?"

For example, researchers might want to study a web-based mathematics program for middle school students that features visual demonstrations of core mathematical concepts so they can determine how the program's graphics contribute to student learning. Attending to culture, specific study questions could include, "How well do students—who have differing mathematical backgrounds (both quantitatively and qualitatively) and varying levels and kinds of computer experience—develop proficiency in using the program and demonstrate mastery in learning, and how do the program's graphics contribute to these varied learning pathways?" This question requires differentiated assessments of student engagement and learning, differentiated analyses of data, and reporting that is inclusive of all student participants. A culturally competent study design and instrumentation would respectfully track the multiple pathways of engagement and learning in the mathematics program that are demonstrated by students with varying backgrounds and experiences.

Educational assessment activities can be particularly sensitive to cultural and sociodemographic differences, beginning with the definitions of the constructs being measured. These definitions require cultural respect, possibly invoking thoughtful modification of existing assessment instruments and/or the development of study- and context-specific assessments.

Further, in educational evaluation studies, of central importance to a culturally competent and respectful stance is the specification of the criteria developed to make judgments of program quality and effectiveness. Such criteria, which constitute the definitions of a "good" or "effective" program, require development or selection with a culturally respectful and engaged lens.

Cultural Competence in Studying Resilience Across Cultures and Contexts

The construct of *resilience* is often located in theories of child and youth development, with particular relevance to children and youth who experience adversities, such as family disruptions, persistent poverty, or insufficient love or care. The resilience of children and youth is thus a topic of direct relevance to educational theory, inquiry, and practice.

In the first decade of the 21st century, Michael Ungar and Linda Liebenberg led an international team in an iterative, multiphased study designed to develop a culturally respectful measure of child and youth resilience. The researchers in this assessment study conceptualized resilience not only just as a characteristic of the individual but also as the individual's responses to environmental affordances of psychosocial resources. Resilience was specifically defined as "doing well despite adversity," thus encompassing cultural variation in these environmental resources, with specific relevance to the less developed world.

In addition to this explicitly culturally engaged conceptualization of the study's key construct, this research also evidenced cultural competence in its design and implementation processes. The iterative design was implemented as a conversation between the research team and members of local settings in multiple countries. Research team instrument drafts included data from youth and youth worker interviews in local sites.

Further youth interviews accompanied pilot testing of the instrument, invoking a dialogue between resilience as defined on the instrument and resilience as experienced by youth in diverse contexts. The final data analyses were initially performed using Urie Bronfenbrenner's ecological model of development. When this model did not fit the data, the quantitative analyses were reframed using seven key dimensions of resilience derived from extensive interview analyses. The final analysis developed portraits of youth resilience by gender, country, and the degree of social cohesion present in the contexts the youth inhabited.

Jennifer C. Greene

See also Culturally Responsive Evaluation; Joint Committee on Standards for Educational Evaluation; Minority Issues in Testing; Multicultural Validity

Further Readings

American Evaluation Association Statement on Cultural Competence in Evaluation. Retrieved from http://www.eval.org/p/cm/ld/fid=92

Hood, S., Hopson, R., & Frierson, H. (Eds.). (2015). *Continuing the journey to reposition culture and cultural context in evaluation theory and practice.* Charlotte, NC: Information Age Publishing.

Kirkhart, K. (2010). Eyes on the prize: Multicultural validity and evaluation theory. *American Journal of Evaluation, 31*(3), 400–413.

Ungar, M., & Liebenberg, L. (2011). Assessing resilience across cultures using mixed methods: Construction of the child and youth resilience measure. *Journal of Mixed Methods Research, 5*(2), 126–149.

CULTURALLY RESPONSIVE EVALUATION

Culturally responsive evaluation (CRE) is an evaluation approach that places culture and the community of focus at the center of the evaluation, helps to support community empowerment, and has a goal of social justice. This entry explains the reasons for the development of CRE, describes its components, details the process used to conduct CRE and how it contributes to social change, and gives an example of CRE in practice.

Historically, culture has been viewed as "noise" in evaluation—a confounding variable and a subjective factor to be controlled for or discounted. Similarly, the context of an evaluand was considered but treated as separate or distinct. Often, evaluators and program developers indicated that a program was supposed to have the same results regardless of culture and context.

The development of policies and programs has been dominated by people who are not part of the culture and context where those programs have their impact and this disregard and/or ignorance has contributed to perpetuating injustices. Programs have been eliminated because evaluators did not perceive the need for them or were looking at outcomes that were not relevant for the group benefiting from the program. In other cases, context was not considered in decision making around allocation of resources. Some continue to receive programs that may respond to surface needs but fail to solve underlying problems.

CRE has contributed to the field's recognition of the profound influence of culture and context on the evaluand and its intended beneficiaries. It not only considers context but also uses it as data to understand the evaluand and the participants and a compass to direct the program in ways that lead to justice for that community. Cultural context also provides a way to understand the evaluand that reveals how participants experience it and why. It then builds the understanding necessary to identify what justice would mean to and for that community.

CRE Components

There are four main components to CRE: (1) culture, (2) context, (3) responsiveness, and (4) a commitment to social justice.

Culture

Culture is the shared norms and underlying belief system of a group as manifested and guided by its values, rituals, practices, language, institutions, and artifacts. Culture creates and identifies meaning, delineates values and guides how they are turned into action, and shapes the practices and behaviors of a group. For example, one group may value individualism and another collectivism. These values may be applied through individualistic learning rituals or group-oriented education practices.

Culture influences our perception and, thus, how we perform. It also affects what we view as the perceived totality of options for our behavior. A person who values collectivism may benefit and do quite well in a group-oriented and community-focused program and a person who believes intelligence is inherent may see the first sign of difficulty in answering a challenging question in school as a lack of intelligence and, consequently, quit. Therefore, the program strategy may need to change depending on the cultural belief system. The evaluator must consider these dynamics to assist in achieving programmatic goals.

To help ensure cultural sensitivity, the community or beneficiaries of the evaluand are engaged from the start. The people are at the center of CRE. They are the experts in their own experience and belief system. They know what they value, what they need, what practices they engage in, and how best to address and respond to each factor.

Context

There are many cultural realities that constitute the cultural context of an evaluand. These various layers of context include historical, sociopolitical, community, and organizational levels. Historical context includes what has taken place around the evaluand and intended participants over time. History tells the evaluator about the origins and subsequent changes in the evaluand; it can provide deeper understanding of participant needs, past experiences of the community, and roots of the problem.

The sociopolitical context can influence the evaluand in many ways—from decisions around funding allocations to what types of programs are provided to who implements those programs and how. The community context includes the local community's resources and current, collective experiences that are often directed by cultural perspectives. It may include socioeconomic status, collective assets, possible trauma, and available resources. Finally, organizational context includes more localized facets such as who is facilitating the program and how and where the program is implemented. The intersection of all of these constitutes the current cultural context and is, thus, interdependent.

For example, a city may have had a history of financial misconduct. Education was not a priority in the sociopolitical environment and, therefore, has not received sufficient funding to provide the programming necessary for students to meet the statewide goals for reading and math test scores. The community of focus has experienced high rates of school dropout, unemployment, and violent crime. The violence adds additional stress for the students and interferes in their academic performance. As a result of the funding crisis, the city school board decides to lay off more experienced teachers and hire new and young teachers, many of whom do not know or respond to the culture and context of the students. This combination affects if and how certain programs are implemented and how the students perform.

Responsiveness

Responsiveness encompasses a sense of critical consciousness, intentional action, and flexibility. Ostensibly, these three aspects are guided by values including community, relationships, neutralizing power dynamics, social justice, and critical consciousness. CRE evaluators are, therefore, critically self-reflective and strive to hone their social and emotional intelligence in ensuring sound partnerships and data collection efforts. CRE allows for the necessarily organic- and human-centered structure of the program and evaluation to emerge.

Responsive evaluation places stakeholder engagement, relationships, and dialogue at its center. It includes stakeholders throughout the evaluation process and attends to their issues and needs. It is a democratic, empowerment-focused model where the stakeholders dictate the standards and describe the program practices and meaning from their perspective.

The main goal of responsive evaluation is program improvement, which happens through dialogue and relationship building between the different stakeholders. With a reflective mind-set, the evaluator facilitates these dialogues and working alliances. Ideally, those who have a stake in the evaluand will eventually take ownership and make changes through listening and responding to other vantage points and experiences.

The culturally responsive evaluator also learns and integrates the culture of the community for accurate evaluation. The evaluation questions, data collection tools, interpretations and analysis, and influence of dissemination can all be compromised if culture is ignored. Cultural knowledge and integration increases the validity of the tools, data, and analysis as well as the effect of the evaluation as a whole.

In CRE, the evaluation is a conduit not only for relationship building but also for cultural understanding and social justice. Here, the evaluator is both responsive to the stakeholders, particularly the beneficiary community, culture, and context, and responsible for ensuring the results that benefit the community. Furthermore, the relationship building, cultural responsiveness, and resultant data collection and analysis feed into and support empowerment.

Social Justice

The development of CRE has been guided by a desire to support oppressed and marginalized communities. Thus, the evaluation is a tool for social justice, partnering with the communities the evaluand serves to advocate for and with them. The process of the evaluation, from community partnership to advocacy, is itself an intervention, as the evaluand's beneficiaries and community members hold power positions within the evaluation. They craft evaluation questions, inform tool development, and have a say as to whether the evaluation is sound. Ideally, they also partner with the evaluator in advocating for changes, be it regarding the evaluand or sociopolitical context, for their community.

CRE Process

CRE has a prescriptive process in order to achieve its goals. Stafford Hood, Pamela Anderson-Frazier, and Rodney Hopson describe a detailed sequence of steps in conducting CRE. The following is a condensed version of the action steps:

Learn the culture and environment: This step includes both formal and informal assessments, such as spending time in and with the community and conducting semistructured interviews and focus groups, as well as gathering secondary data on the historical, sociopolitical, and cultural contexts.

Engage the people in the process: As with all evaluations, there are a variety of stakeholders who should be considered. However, CRE prioritizes the program beneficiaries and their community.

Develop culturally relevant evaluation design and tools: Here, culture and context are a core part of the evaluation, so the questions and tools consider, integrate, and reflect them.

Conduct the evaluation with the community: Community members are equal partners in the evaluation process, informing evaluation questions, tools, and analysis. Ideally, the evaluator also provides technical support, so members can participate as leaders throughout the evaluation.

Disseminate and advocate: Market lessons learned to foster social justice and a thriving community. The results of the evaluation not only contribute to program improvement but they also help to further the community as a whole.

CRE and Social Change

CRE is not only an approach to evaluation, it is also a tool for achieving social change, particularly with and for disenfranchised communities. Both within the process and as a product, the community is supported and encouraged to manifest its empowerment. This focus and partnership helps to enhance validity and provide data for program improvement tailored to that community and sustainable change through advocacy. Thus, it also involves strategy development both on the levels of program improvement and on the broader social change. Although this type of evaluation often requires additional resources, it is designed to yield more significant results for those who are frequently placed in the margins of society.

CRE in Practice

One example took place in Chicago, IL, with a predominantly low-income Latino community on the west side of the city. The evaluator was contracted to conduct a needs assessment of youth resources, such as after-school youth development programs focusing on STEM, sports, cooking, or the arts. The evaluator and team conducted an analysis of the context, including demographics, resources, sociopolitical issues, and community hardships. With the partner organization, they engaged 20 local parents in shaping the needs assessment process and crafting the assessment tools. They also trained the parents in data collection, and the parents applied their new skills and collected data from 1,500 people in the community. The evaluator, partner organization, and parents then came together and analyzed the data. They found, for example, that over half (60%) of youth whose families were surveyed were not involved in after-school programming and 80% of parents expressed a need for more youth programming in the community. The parents developed recommendations. The evaluator

synthesized these in the report, and the parents used it as a tool for advocating for what they needed in the community.

From the beginning of the evaluation, the evaluator had to consider language, the vulnerability some community members felt around assessment, and the fear that some members had around their immigration status. Also, a significant cultural asset was the strong sense of community and service of the parents. The survey questions, focus group protocol, and overarching process were created with the consideration of language, sensitivity around possible fears, and knowledge of cultural assets.

In bringing the parents together for this assessment, there was more power and potential for broader community engagement, which was needed to galvanize additional members and advocate for filling the gaps in services discovered through the process. This partnership and responsiveness not only helped to ensure valid data were collected more easily and from more people but also the results could be used to meet needs and support community empowerment.

Dominica McBride

See also Advocacy in Evaluation; Cross-Cultural Research; Cultural Competence; Democratic Evaluation; Multicultural Validity; Social Justice; Transformative Paradigm; Values

Further Readings

Amba, T. A. (2006). The practices and politics of responsive evaluation. *American Journal of Evaluation, 27,* 31–43.

Frazier-Anderson, P., Hood, S., & Hopson, R. (2011). Preliminary considerations of an African American culturally responsive evaluation system. In S. D. Lapan, M. T. Quartaroli, & F. J. Riemer (Eds.), *Qualitative research: An introduction to methods and designs* (pp. 347–372). San Francisco, CA: Jossey-Bass.

Greene, J. C. (2005). Evaluators as stewards of the public good. In S. Hood, R. Hopson, & H. Freirson (Eds.), *The role of culture and context: A mandate for inclusion, the discovery of truth, and understanding in evaluative theory and practice* (pp. 7–20). Greenwich, CT: Information Age Publishing.

House, E. (1990). Methodology and justice. *New Directions for Evaluation, 45,* 23–36.

Kirkhart, K. (1995). Seeking multicultural validity: A postcard from the road. *Evaluation Practice, 16,* 1–12.

McBride, D. F. (2015). Cultural reactivity vs cultural responsiveness: Addressing macro issues starting with micro changes in evaluation. In S. Hood, R. Hopson, H. Frierson, & K. Obeidat (Eds.), *Continuing the journey to reposition culture and cultural context in evaluation theory and practice* (pp. 179–202). Charlotte, NC: Information Age Publishing.

Stake, R. (2004). Stake and responsive evaluation. In M. C. Alkin (Ed.), *Evaluation roots: Tracing theorists' views and influences* (pp. 203–217). Thousand Oaks, CA: Sage.

CURRICULUM

The term *curriculum* is widely used among educators at all levels of education. Because of the many ways in which it has been defined, individuals may not be referring to the same concept when discussing curriculum. This entry discusses the common conceptions of curriculum and how these conceptions have changed in recent years.

Often curriculum is described as something that is planned and expected to be taught and learned. However, what is taught (actual vs. anticipated), how something is taught (the type of instructional strategies and medium used to implement what is to be taught), and the degree to which what is taught is actually learned, executed, accomplished, demonstrated, or observed and how it is evaluated are often questions left to evaluator inquiry or form the basis of researchers' studies.

In the mid-20th century, common conceptions of curriculum were plan, system, field of study, experience, and content. Curriculum as a plan refers to what content or skills an educator anticipates teaching. Curriculum as a system refers to the people, processes, and organizational structures that guide planning, teaching, and measuring the taught content.

Curriculum as a field of study refers to the disciplinary emphasis of curriculum as a body of content in its own right to be mastered, which is guided by theory, principles, and practice. Curriculum as experience refers to what learners undergo in an educational system or organization either directly or indirectly as a result of what they are taught by the personnel who provide instructional and measurement activities. Curriculum as content refers to the subject or disciplinary matter and/or psychomotor or affective skills that are taught.

Owing to the influence of postmodernism, conceptions of curriculum that emerged in the later 20th and early 21 centuries were the null, hidden, and transformative curriculums. The null curriculum refers to what is not taught within the subject matter or content, such as particular viewpoints, historical events, or nuanced perspectives. The null curriculum in effect restricts the range of perspectives that are offered to students and results from the educational background of the instructor, the reigning political stance of the locale in which curriculum is taught, or that which is influenced by the preferences of the region, the community, or district where the individual school resides.

The hidden curriculum refers to the values and cultural norms that characterize the learning community, the types of interactions that are permitted or excluded within a particular course which in turn are inherently contextualized by location or time, content or material, and student and instructional members of a learning community that remain openly unacknowledged. Nonetheless, the hidden curriculum is believed to exhibit an influence on both curriculum and student outcomes. From another perspective, the hidden curriculum could be described as the nonverbal experiences that are felt by students because they are transmitted through action, though left unspoken. The hidden curriculum can be inferred by the lack of equal treatment and equality of educational opportunities for all students as well as the practice of tracking and unequal implementation of discipline policies that are in direct conflict with the belief that schools provide equality of opportunities for all of their students.

The transformative curriculum refers to instruction that invites students to question the truth capacity of what they are learning or encourages them to use newly learned information or skills to metamorphose their own thinking and actions.

What is actually taught and how it is taught is also influenced by prevalent societal norms and practices of a particular era in history. Curriculum can be conceived as residing on a continuum. It may be thought of as static and unchanging content such as the didactic, teacher-centered practice of teaching the classics. In contrast, a curriculum that is influenced by societal norms is perceived to be dynamic, fluid, and everchanging.

With the implementation of new forms of technology, including computers and other educational media, researchers such as Robert Kozma and Chris Dede have asserted the potential of technology to promote better achievement and to improve student attitudes toward schooling and learning in general. To be sure, there are wide variations in schools' educational technology, and the way it is used can depend upon the subject matter, learning objectives, teacher proficiency, and infrastructure support at school and district levels. Still, there is little doubt that technology has influenced perceptions of what and how curriculum is implemented.

New opportunities to access information through technology have expanded students' ability to learn outside the classroom, in turn changing the nature of what is seen as curriculum. Educational content is now widely and often freely available on the Internet. As a result, curriculum is no longer limited solely to the subject matter concepts or those activities that an instructor brings to the classroom, laboratory, or clinical-learning environment and plans to teach. Nonetheless, the selection of content that is perceived to be worth knowing is typically influenced by the dominant voices of society, including those who are subject matter experts, textbook publishers, and testing companies.

Linda S. Behar-Horenstein

See also Classroom Assessment; Common Core State Standards; Curriculum Mapping; Curriculum-Based Assessment; Curriculum-Based Measurement; High-Stakes Tests; Instructional Objectives; Instructional Theory; Literacy; State Standards

Further Readings

Dede, C. (1996). Emerging technologies and distributed learning. *American Journal of Distance Education, 10*(2), 4–36. doi:10.1.1.136.1029

Eisner, E. W. (1985). *The educational imagination* (p. 176). New York, NY: Macmillan.

Henderson, J. G., & Gornik, R. (2007). *Transformative curriculum leadership*. Englewood Cliffs, NJ: Prentice Hall.

Joughin, G. (2010). The hidden curriculum revisited: a critical review of research into the influence of summative assessment on learning. *Assessment & Evaluation in Higher Education, 35*(3), 335–345.

Kozma, R. B. (1991). Learning with media. *Review of Educational Research, 61*, 179–221. doi:10.3102/00346543061002179

Kozma, R. B. (1994). Will media influence learning? Reframing the debate. *Educational Technology Research and Development, 42*(2), 7–19.

Ornstein, A. C., & Hunkins, F. P. (2012). *Curriculum: Foundations, principles, and issues* (6th ed.). Boston, MA: Pearson.

CURRICULUM MAPPING

Curriculum mapping involves aligning specific course- and/or grade-level activities toward attainment of specific learning outcomes, which are basically what it is the instructor expects the student to *do*. Curriculum mapping is a process to initiate, review, and validate curriculum alignment. The process results in curriculum maps that provide the visual linkages between course- or grade-level activities and learning outcomes. Curriculum maps also serve as a method of communication among instructors across courses and/or grade levels within educational programs. This entry discusses the development of curriculum mapping, its purpose and benefits, and how mapping takes place.

The learning outcomes can be based on grade-level objectives, program competencies, or standards. Learning outcomes can also refer to learning objectives, ranging from assignment outcomes to course outcomes and course outcomes to program or level outcomes. Curriculum mapping stems from the 1980s work of Fenwick English which began as mere detailing of what instructors were teaching and how it was taught. In the 1990s, the work of Heidi Hayes Jacobs added more depth and breadth to the focus of curriculum mapping.

Curriculum mapping can occur at the course and/or program level. Various studies have examined the value of curriculum mapping, offering tools for effective curriculum mapping and describing/instructor preferences and perceptions of curriculum mapping, but there has been little published research on specific curriculum mapping processes.

Curriculum mapping provides a road map for curriculum planning to achieve previously identified skills, competencies, and/or learning outcomes. Curriculum mapping is a process used in both K–12 and higher education and can be used both within and across grade levels or specific courses. Mapping can involve lesson plans for individual classes or grade-by-grade programmatic planning for an entire school.

Benefits of curriculum mapping include providing short- and long-term goals to meet educational outcomes and identifying gaps and areas for improvement. Curriculum maps are tools to keep faculty focused and can prevent curriculum drift in addition to identifying and preventing curriculum repetition. The curriculum map can identify when concepts should be introduced, reinforced, and mastered within specific courses and/or levels. Curriculum mapping can identify placement of specific assignments, exams, and projects within specific courses, grades, and/or program levels. Attainment of specific learning outcomes can prepare the student for the subsequent course and/or grade level.

Sustained curriculum mapping efforts can improve faculty buy-in/participation and promote curriculum revision when faculty are provided with the resources for curriculum mapping. Curriculum mapping processes need to be outlined with a concrete plan for review and possible revision. Faculty development regarding curriculum mapping procedures and mapping tools, in addition to leadership support and faculty accountability, must be communicated and reinforced. Scheduled mapping discussions within courses, levels, and institutions or programs will ensure maintaining focus and curriculum alignment toward meeting learning outcomes. Mapping also can serve as a process to monitor what faculty do and as an avenue for data collection that can provide valuable assessment and evaluation data for course and/or program improvements.

Examples

The following examples show how curriculum mapping connects the courses at each level and the levels within a program or school.

A K–12 school district could use curriculum mapping to establish leveled competencies for each grade level. Administrators, curriculum personnel, and/or teachers would map the curriculum for each grade level. For each course, they would identify specific concepts to be introduced, reinforced, and mastered to meet specific course learning outcomes. Each course will denote specific assignments, exams, and activities. Attainment of specific course learning outcomes at each level would prepare the student for the next grade level. Faculty and school leaders on each level would review the course maps, ensuring course concepts are taught as the map outlines and any gaps in the course curriculum are identified.

In another example, a school of nursing in an institution of higher education would establish program learning outcomes to meet national competencies for becoming a licensed registered nurse. The nursing program consists of three levels; each level is mapped to meet specific program learning outcomes. Each level contains courses with identified concepts to be introduced, reinforced, and mastered to meet specific course learning outcomes. Attainment of these specific course learning outcomes at each level would prepare the student for the next level. Completing all three levels meets the overall nursing program learning outcomes and prepares the student for the national competencies to successfully pass the licensed registered nurse exam. The school of nursing curriculum committee meets annually to examine and review the course maps as well as the overall program maps to ensure leveled concepts are taught as the map outlines and identifies any gaps in the program curriculum.

Tonya Breymier

See also Concept Mapping; Curriculum; Curriculum-Based Assessment; Curriculum-Based Measurement; Instructional Objectives; Learning Maps

Further Readings

Arafeh, S. (2015). Curriculum mapping in higher education: A case study and proposed content scope and sequence mapping tool. *Journal of Further and Higher Education, 40*(5), 585–611. Retrieved from http://dx.doi.org/10.1080/03098 77X2014.1000278

Ervin, L., Carter, B., & Robinson, P. (2013). Curriculum mapping: Not as straightforward as it sounds. *Journal of Vocational Education & Training, 65*(3), 309–318. Retrieved from http://dx.doi.org/10.1080/18636820.2013.819559

Lam, B., & Tsui, K. (2013). Examining the alignment of subject learning outcomes and course curricula through curriculum mapping. *Australian Journal of Teacher Education, 38*(12). Retrieved from http://dx.doi.org/10.14221/ajte.2013v38n12.8

Shilling, T. (2013). Opportunities and challenges of curriculum mapping implementation in one school setting: Considerations for school leaders. *Journal of Curriculum and Instruction, 7*(2), 20–37. Retrieved from http://www.joci.ecu.edu

Spencer, D., Riddle, M., & Knewstubb, B. (2012). Curriculum mapping to embed graduate capabilities. *Higher Education Research & Development, 31*(2), 217–231. Retrieved from http://dx.doi.org/10.1080/07294360.2011.554387

CURRICULUM-BASED ASSESSMENT

Curriculum-based assessment (CBA) emerged in the 1970s and early 1980s as a novel approach to formative assessment and evaluation. This entry discusses the development of CBA, the two paradigms for CBA, and the four different methods of CBA that fall within those paradigms. CBA was developed for use by teachers to guide educational decisions related to the selection and use of curriculum materials and instructional procedures. Because of its foundation in relevant educational practice, CBA can be a highly useful tool in student evaluation and instructional decisions within a problem-solving framework.

CBA is a collection of assessment and evaluation techniques to test student performance using materials sampled from or based on the local curriculum. CBA was designed to be more instructionally relevant to educators than published assessments because of its high reliance on local curriculum and correspondence with students' daily classroom experiences.

CBA was developed to provide more relevant information to educators because many of the developers perceived that widely used published assessments were too generic to guide local decisions for students. Because these materials were sampled from the local curriculum, CBA was thought to provide the most relevant information to guide decisions about instruction and curriculum. At the time, it was assumed that the most authentic materials for use in assessment were those sampled from the local curriculum and learning environment.

CBA encompasses several assessment and evaluation procedures that use direct observation and other methods to measure student performance with alternate curricula and instructional procedures. There are two related, but distinct, methods to sample and construct CBA materials. First, sub-skill mastery measurement (SMM) is used to divide curriculum goals into short-term, discrete objectives that are assessed sequentially, often in a hierarchical manner. SMM employs mastery measurement, in which performance on one assessment is used to indicate proficiency within one or a few closely related academic domains. Because it assesses mastery of discrete objectives, SMM is useful to evaluate strengths and weaknesses across specific skills. It is also useful to monitor progress over brief periods of time to evaluate educational programs.

The second method is general outcome measurement (GOM). GOM is distinct from SMM in that it samples from the annual curriculum to assess global proficiency relative to achievement across the entire academic year. Although performance is expected to be very low early in the academic year, student performance on successive measurements should increase. In general, GOM assessment scores tend to be more predictive of performance on published norm-referenced assessments than SMM. GOM assessments also lend themselves to triannual screening and longer durations of progress monitoring, which span months rather than weeks.

There are several different types of CBA, representing the two assessment paradigms just discussed. Researchers identified at least four different methods of CBA: CBA for instructional design (CBA-ID), criterion-referenced CBA (CR-CBA), curriculum-based evaluation (CBE), and curriculum-based measurement (CBM). CBA-ID, CR-CBA, and CBE follow an SMM paradigm, while CBM follows a GOM paradigm. Each of these four models are described briefly in the next section.

CBM

CBM is a type of GOM that quantifies student performance in basic academic skill areas through standardized measurement procedures. It was designed to be a reliable, valid, simple, efficient, and inexpensive method for recording the level and rate of student achievement in reading, math, spelling, and written expression. CBM makes use of a GOM assessment paradigm to track progress through the annual curriculum using a series of equivalent assessments. Because it uses GOM, CBM uses measures that are standardized, valid, and reliable.

CBM assessments are designed to be *dynamic indicators* of academic skills, meaning that they assess change over time, are highly sensitive to short-term effects of instruction or intervention, and are correlated with key behaviors that suggest success in an academic domain. This suggests that CBM assessments have high utility in screening and progress monitoring.

CBM was originally designed as a method of curriculum sampling to create equivalent measures for use in screening and progress monitoring. Now, however, most educators use materials that are readily available through assessment companies. These assessments often have established difficulty levels, technical adequacy, and normative information. Reliability and validity of such assessments can be demonstrated more readily with the availability of commercial CBM materials, which give further evidence for the use of such assessments as dynamic indicators of student performance within an academic domain.

Of the four types of CBA, CBM has the most robust research base. First, CBM can be used as an indicator of basic skills development because there is significant reliability and validity evidence. This suggests, as described earlier, that CBM can be used to track progress in skill development. CBM has also been shown to be a reliable and valid method for differentiation between higher and lower performing students in terms of reading achievement, which, again, suggests that CBM reading assessments are useful for screening. To that end, there is significant research to support the use of CBM for academic screening. However, there is also evidence to support the use of CBM for progress monitoring, in terms of both growth in response to instruction and growth in response to intervention activities.

CBA-ID

CBA-ID uses student performance and responsiveness to instruction as a guide for instructional planning, with the goal of delivering instruction that is as efficient and effective as possible. It is used to determine whether instruction is compatible with student skills. Broadly, CBA-ID involves assessing student proficiency in a given content domain and using that information to assess instructional match or tailor instruction to individual student needs. CBA-ID is based on the rationale that student skill deficits are maintained and potentially caused by a mismatch between incoming student skill level and classroom instructional level. The purpose of CBA-ID is to address this mismatch.

CBA-ID makes use of an SMM assessment paradigm to sample student performance within discrete academic objectives. This assessment paradigm is used to measure curriculum mastery for each student, such that instruction is tailored to individuals. CBA-ID operates under the assumption that students learn best when instructional material is neither too difficult nor too easy. Instruction that is at the *instructional level* of a student is challenging enough that students have potential to learn and show clear progress. This is the target level of instruction for CBA-ID.

There is a fairly limited research basis for CBA-ID. Research that has been done, however, supports the idea that instruction that optimizes the ratio of unknown and known information in a given lesson improves engagement, learning rates, and retention.

CBA-ID operates under four basic principles. First, the purpose of CBA-ID is to match assessment with instruction. The rationale behind this principle is that assessment material that is most informative for teachers is material that most closely aligns with material used in the classroom. The classroom is a natural context for assessment in terms of both student learning and teacher instructional practices. If assessment and instruction are matched, valuable information about the effectiveness of both can be inferred.

Second, CBA-ID uses the student's level of knowledge to determine the student's specific areas of weakness. This principle emphasizes the idea that CBA-ID is thoroughly student centered; instruction is focused on filling in each student's knowledge gaps individually. Third, as discussed earlier, CBA-ID places a high focus on correcting the mismatch between instruction and student skill level. This is accomplished through a determination of appropriate instructional match through both level of challenge and rate of instruction.

Finally, CBA-ID operates under the assumption that students benefit from instruction that is appropriately matched to individual skill level, which is assessed through mastery learning. This model of instruction and assessment is in direct opposition to most models of instruction in which the same curricular material is presented to all students at the same rate.

There are four steps to implement CBA-ID. First, the examiner must identify the materials used in the classroom that will be the focus of the assessment. Second, the examiner must determine the student's specific skill deficit using the identified assessment materials. Third, the examiner must determine the necessary modifications to instruction or additional strategies, thereby creating a match between current student skills and instruction. Finally, these changes are implemented and appropriate instructional material is chosen. Student skill development is monitored for progress in mastery of objectives.

CR-CBA

CR-CBA is used to discover the curriculum materials and instructional procedures to optimize the educational program for each individual student. In contrast to CBA-ID, CR-CBA makes use of a mastery criterion. CR-CBA uses sequentially ordered SMM assessments developed from curriculum objectives to determine student skill level and instructional needs by comparing student performance to local normative information. Measures used vary widely, as they are generally created by classroom teachers, but the distinguishing feature of CR-CBA is the comparison of student performance to a normative reference group for interpreting student performance on the skills measured. This criterion is often considered the level of performance necessary for mastery of a given skill.

Implementation of CR-CBA is based on a hierarchical arrangement of skills drawn from a given curriculum and the sequential assessment of these skills. First, examiners must list the desired skills in order, ensuring that all the relevant skills are included and that the order makes intuitive sense. Next, the examiner should create discrete objectives within each skill, writing test items for each objective. The resulting assessment can be used as a pretest, posttest, or assessment of retention before or after instruction takes place.

After taking the assessment, results should be examined to determine the skills or objectives students have mastered and the skills or objectives that represent specific areas of difficulty. In this way, examiners are able to determine whether instruction is appropriately matched to student skill level and whether students have the necessary prerequisite skills for future instruction.

CBE

CBE employs a problem-solving framework in conjunction with repeated SMM assessments to evaluate student skill level and mastery of curricular objectives. It is a hypothesis-testing framework in which information about a student is repeatedly gathered and analyzed to determine where the student's instructional level is relative to the entire curriculum.

CBE can be described as a task analysis model in which a series of interconnected tasks represented curricular objectives. According to this model, a student's instructional placement is determined by the student's position in the maze of tasks; it is the examiner's goal to determine the placement. That is, the examiner must determine the tasks the students mastered and tasks they are ready to learn based on their current performance level.

There are four key steps in CBE. The first step is problem identification, whose purpose is to determine whether the students exhibit a skill deficit according to their current performance level and the expectation according to the curriculum. Problem identification is accomplished through both assessment activities and examination of existing data, such as school-wide screening scores. Both formal and informal assessments can be included in assessment activities.

Second, information gathered through problem identification is analyzed to develop hypotheses about the problem and explain the cause of the observed skill deficit. These hypotheses provide direction for assessment of specific skills. Third, hypotheses are tested with SMM assessments to determine whether they can explain observed skill deficits. If the hypotheses are incorrect, new hypotheses are created and tested in the same way. Finally, hypotheses that are found to be correct are used to inform instructional changes, with the goal of improving the student's observed skill deficit. Student progress is monitored to determine whether instructional changes improve student skill deficits.

Theodore J. Christ and
Danielle M. Becker

See also Curriculum; Curriculum-Based Measurement; Formative Assessment; Progress Monitoring; Screening Tests

Further Readings

Christ, T., Keller-Margulis, M., & Marcotte, A., (2014). The basics of curriculum-based assessment. In S. G. Little & A. Akin-Little (Eds.), *Academic assessment and intervention*. New York, NY: Routledge.

Deno, S. (1985). Curriculum-based measurement: The emerging alternative. *Exceptional Children, 52,* 219–232.

Fuchs, L., & Deno, S. (1991). Paradigmatic distinctions between instructionally relevant measurement models. *Exceptional Children, 57,* 488–500.

Gickling, E., & Thompson, V. (1985). A personal view of curriculum-based assessment. *Exceptional Children, 52,* 205–218.

Hintze, J., Christ, T., & Methe, S. (2006). Curriculum-based assessment. *Psychology in the Schools, 43,* 45–56.

CURRICULUM-BASED MEASUREMENT

Curriculum-based measurement (CBM) has emerged as the most prominent, researched, and influential among a number of curriculum-based assessment methodologies. CBM was developed to index the level and rate of student achievement in the basic skills of reading, mathematics, spelling, and written expression. CBM comprises a standardized set of procedures to administer and score student performance. This entry further describes CBM and then discusses its application in schools, its perceived benefits, and concerns raised about the timed conditions of CBM.

As the name indicates, the measurement content was originally sampled from the local curriculum used for instruction. Students would read, write, or perform mathematical calculations for short durations (1–3 minutes). Performance-based responses contrasted with multichoice-type response formats and curriculum-based content contrasted with the generic content of many published tests. These aspects of CBM were designed to establish more authentic and relevant measures of student performance in the specific learning environment. That information was thought to be useful for teachers to monitor student performance in the annual curriculum and, especially, the performance of students who received special education services.

CBM procedures were designed by Stanley Deno and colleagues to be reliable and valid, simple and efficient, easily understood, and inexpensive. They were also intended to be repeatable. Together, these features provided a measurement procedure for use by teachers to routinely evaluate the effects of an instructional program.

Routine and ongoing evaluations are useful to guide when and whether to change a student's instructional program. That interpretation and use of a data is a type of formative evaluation, and CBM is often described as a formative assessment because it is intended for use to inform instruction. The use of CBM to monitor student progress and evaluate program effects gained substantial popularity and facilitated the emergence of response to intervention, which is a contemporary approach to diagnose learning disabilities. This often entails the use of CBM to develop local norms or compare student performance against benchmark standards to identify those who are at risk or who need supplemental or intensive academic supports.

CBM scores indicate the rate of accuracy performance per unit of time, which is typically in 1-minute intervals. For example, CBM oral reading is a 1-minute oral reading from a grade-level passage. The administrator listens and marks errors and calculates the words read correctly per minute. CBM maze is a 2- to 10-minute silent reading with every fifth or seventh word replaced with a multiple-choice list of three to four alternatives, with the correct word circled by the student. The items completed within the interval are scored to calculate correct selections per minute, which is sometimes replaced by more sophisticated scoring procedures to account for guessing. CBM computation is a 2- to 6-minute interval in which the examinee completes grade-level computation problems. The written work is scored to calculate the digits correct per minute. CBM written expression and CBM spelling are similar with outcomes of correct word sequences and correct letter sequences per minute, respectively.

The CBM rate-based scoring emphasizes the fluency and automaticity of basic skills. This has been widely influential and somewhat controversial. CBM drew attention and focus to promoting accurate and rapid performance of basic skills, such as word identification, computation, writing, and spelling. Fluent performance of the targeted basic skills functions as robust indicators of academic progress and well-being. Benchmark levels of performance and progress were adopted by many educators as key indicators of high-quality instructional programs and student achievement within the early grades.

CBM has been especially popular within the special education community, which serves students with disabilities. Certain disabilities and academic deficits are attributed, in part, by some, to fluency deficits. Many also have attributed the increased sensitivity of CBM procedures to the fluency feature. That is, many have advocated for and used CBM because it was believed to be more sensitive to smaller increments of student achievement and instructional effects than other untimed measurement procedures.

Some educators and researchers reject the concept of fluency for a variety of reasons. One prominent objection is that it is stressful for children to be encouraged to perform quickly and assessed within timed conditions. Although such objections persist, CBM scores predict performance on many untimed and less efficient measures, which include state and national measures of academic accountability along with other national normed tests.

Theodore J. Christ and Kirsten Newell

See also Curriculum; Curriculum Mapping; Curriculum-Based Assessment; Formative Assessment; Progress Monitoring; Response to Intervention

Further Readings

Christ, T. J., Scullin, S., Tolbize, A., & Jiban, C. L. (2008). Implications of recent research curriculum-based measurement of math computation. *Assessment for Effective Intervention, 33*(4), 198–205.

Deno, S. L. (1985). Curriculum-based measurement: The emerging alternative. *Exceptional Children, 52,* 219–232.

Deno, S. L. (2003). Developments in curriculum-based measurement. *The Journal of Special Education, 37*(3), 184–192.

Fuchs, L. S. (2004). The past, present, and future of curriculum-based measurement research. *School Psychology Review, 33*(2), 188–192.

Fuchs, L. S., & Deno, S. L. (1991). Paradigmatic distinctions between instructionally relevant measurement models. *Exceptional Children, 57,* 488–500.

Gersten, R., Clarke, B., Jordan, N. C., Newman-Gonchar, R., Haymond, K., & Wilkins, C. (2012). Universal screening in mathematics for the primary grades: Beginnings of a research base. *Exceptional Children, 78*(4), 423–445.

Hintze, J., Christ, T., & Methe, S. (2006). Curriculum-based assessment. *Psychology in the Schools, 43,* 45–56.

McMaster, K., & Espin, C. (2007). Technical features of curriculum-based measurement in writing: A literature review. *Journal of Special Education, 41*(2), 68–84.

Cut Scores

The setting of cut scores is a specific and precise way of establishing a standard of performance for a test. Standard setting is defined as a process of determining the point on a test's score scale used to establish whether a particular test score is sufficient for some purpose, but it's also the primary test development activity where psychometrics, content, and policy intertwine. Determining the point at which student performance is "good enough" involves a policy directive, understanding of the content, and an evaluation of the reliability and psychometric difficulty of the individual items or of the test as a whole.

Although some have referred to standard setting as "alchemy" given that it relies on human judgment, it is a process that allows policy to interact with content and psychometric considerations. Decisions about performance-level descriptions, panels, and methods should be made by people who understand each of these three areas and inform the workshop facilitation, aligning it with the intended use of the outcomes. Complete standardization is an impossible goal but should be attempted to the degree possible when working with human judgments. This entry first looks at the increased importance placed on standard setting and determination of cut scores in recent years, then discusses the influence of the facilitator, panelists, and method in setting cut scores.

In the movement to standards-based testing in the 1990s and 2000s, standard setting started relying more heavily on written descriptions of the performance levels to determine the cut scores that defined them. As K–12 school systems began using standardized tests for purposes of accountability, multiple cut scores were needed, contrasting with certification and licensure tests that typically only set a pass/fail line. In K–12, policy makers and content experts determined the rigor of each performance level through a written description of the expected knowledge and skill at each level. Later, these descriptions were also used to drive item writing, ensuring that sufficient items were developed that distinguished clearly among the levels.

Using performance-level descriptions in the standard-setting process also standardized the process further, as panelists could focus on those descriptions of knowledge and skills rather than relying solely on their own opinion of sufficient knowledge and skills to meet a performance level. This addition to the process resulted in greater interrater reliability in the cut score recommendations.

Yet, cut scores can still be influenced by three main factors: the facilitator, the panelists, and the method used for standard setting. There are multiple chapters, books, and articles about how to conduct a standard setting workshop, and on the many methods for determining cut scores. Here, the focus is on the parts of standard setting that can have the most effect on cut scores and how they can be standardized to the extent possible.

Facilitator

The facilitator can have an immense effect on the standard setting process. There are obvious ways a facilitator can have a negative impact—for instance, by not being prepared or not explaining the process clearly. However, facilitators can have much more nuanced influence as well. For instance, a facilitator's focus and tone of voice can convey that a particular factor is more or less important.

An example of the effect of the way a facilitator presents information would be in the introduction of impact, or consequence, data. Typically, these data regarding the actual or projected number of students to reach each cut score are provided at the end of Round 2. Panelists will have already made two judgments on where the cut score(s) should be placed. Now they see the results of those placements. A facilitator can place a lot of emphasis on the impact data, discussing the use and any consequences for test takers or others, and caution the panelists to consider the data carefully. Conversely, a facilitator can remind the panelists that they have spent two rounds making reasoned, criterion-based judgments, and these data are shown simply to provide supplemental information. Depending on how the data are presented, the amount of change made to the recommended cut scores in Round 3 can vary considerably.

Before any standard setting workshop, those running the workshop should work closely with policy makers to determine where the emphasis should be placed, how impact data should be presented, and how questions about the standards, test questions, and use of the assessment should be answered. Once an agreement is made on all issues that could influence the cut scores, a script should be prepared that introduces each topic, provides a list of frequently asked questions and answers, and specifies important policy context. The script should be approved by affected policy makers. Then, the script should be used by everyone facilitating that standard setting workshop. For instance, if a workshop is intended to set cut scores on science assessments in three different grade levels, there may be three facilitators. They should all present the information in a common manner.

In addition to a script, having the facilitators practice facilitating with that script is essential.

The standard setting manager should listen to how each facilitator explains the task and introduces each task to ensure they are as similar as possible and match the policy makers' requirements for emphasizing certain areas or responding to policy questions.

The script and rehearsal will greatly reduce the variance caused by a single facilitator, as will have a manager observing all rooms where standard setting is occurring. Final evaluation forms should ask panelists the degree to which they felt free to provide their own opinions versus feeling coerced as well as the primary factors influencing their cut score recommendation.

Panelists

The people brought in to give their judgments on the cut scores can also be hugely influential. Two groups of panelists, given the same instructions, may generate different cut scores. Because of their influence, panelists should be selected carefully. Prior to recruiting, the standard setting manager should determine the target panel. Depending on the assessment, the target panel may be composed primarily of content experts, teachers, or employees in the field of the assessment. Stakeholders may also be desirable, but the primary composition of the panel should be people who understand the construct being assessed and the requirements for the population of test takers.

After qualifications have been determined, the next consideration is demographics. For many assessments, it is important that the standard setting panelists are representative of the general population or at least the pool of qualified candidates. For instance, if the target panel is composed solely of seventh-grade mathematics teachers within a state, the demographic makeup of the panel should be comparable to the demographics of the pool of seventh-grade mathematics teachers in the state.

Within this determination is also the question of how many panelists are needed. Large panels are desirable for ensuring sufficient stakeholders are included, but they can make thoughtful discussion difficult, particularly for individuals who are less outspoken. Thus, large panels are typically divided into smaller tables for discussion purposes.

Recruiting more people and separating them into tables also provides some measure of within-facilitator, cross-panelist variance. Ideal table sizes are no smaller than five people and no larger than eight to encourage participation of all panelists and sufficient numbers for a reliability analysis. Depending on the number of judgments needed, more or fewer panelists may be needed. For example, in a modified Angoff approach, the number of judgments equals the number of items times the number of cut scores. Therefore, a 50-item test with two cut scores will require 100 judgments.

A larger number of panelists are needed to achieve an appropriate level of reliability in the final cut score recommendations. A typical panel would include 30–35 panelists divided into five tables. In a bookmark approach, the number of judgments equals the number of cut scores. Standard setting workshops have been held with as few as eight panelists for a bookmark method but are better with multiple tables. In this case, three tables with six to eight panelists per table is preferred. For a holistic approach, such as with the body of work method, fewer judgments are required, but greater agreement is often desired. In those cases, fewer panelists may be preferred. This method is often conducted with six to eight panelists, although, again, having at least two tables allows for measurement of cross-panel variance.

A final consideration in creating a standard setting panel is the stakes associated with their recommendations and the finality of them. Typically, panels only make a recommendation and then a policy body adopts the final cut scores. Understanding what factors are important to that policy body is important in selecting an appropriate panel. If the workshop is discussed in the news, what reassurances about the people involved in the decision should be given? And, more panelists sounds more rigorous. In a high-stakes arena, the importance of the constitution of the panel cannot be understated.

Method

Finally, even with well-trained facilitators and qualified, representative panels, the cut scores could still differ by method. The most important rule in selecting a method is to ensure that the cognitive task required of the panelists matches the assessment design. For instance, if the assessment was designed as a portfolio of student work or consists primarily of a research paper or essay, a more holistic approach is needed to set cut scores. Conversely, if the assessment requires the students to respond to a large number of multiple-choice items, an item-based approach is more appropriate. For the purpose of this argument, we will focus on an item-based approach.

Even within one class of methods, there are multiple methods to choose from and many modifications or enhancements to that method. Consideration of the test design, relevant features, and both student and panelist cognitive tasks are important in selecting and modifying an assessment.

For example, consider a fourth-grade reading comprehension test comprising 60 dichotomous items. Bookmark is the most common standard setting method used in K–12 testing today. Given the importance of the passage in determining the difficulty of the test question, a traditional bookmark method can obfuscate that connection by separating the passages from the items, requiring the panelist to go back and forth from questions to passages and not see the full set of questions associated with a passage. For instance, a test question that asks the student about the author's purpose could vary in difficulty for a passage where the author clearly states his purpose compared to a passage where the student must infer it from the information the author presents.

In order to keep the focus on the passage, a modification of the bookmark method groups the ordering of test questions within a passage and orders the passages themselves based on overall difficulty of the question set. This format allows panelists to first focus on the difficulty of the passage, discussing various components that contribute to its complexity. Next, they can analyze the interaction of the test question associated with that passage. Only as a later step, panelists would be asked to examine questions across passages in a fully ordered booklet.

In another scenario, consider another test comprising 60 dichotomous items, but now it's a career pathway test given to high school students in a career and technical education program. Given that students take the test at different times of the year and in different years depending on their program and personal goals, it might take an entire year of testing to gain a representative sample of test takers for use in standard setting. Yet, cut scores are needed after the first administration to provide results to that first set of students.

Policy makers often worry about the validity of the impact data with a skewed sample, but it also affects the method chosen. Because the bookmark method requires test questions to be ordered by their psychometric difficulty, using a skewed or nonrepresentative sample to do so can greatly affect the results. In some cases, a modified Angoff method may be a preferred approach as it is not dependent on item difficulty. Some feedback on how the early sample did may be given, but it should be given in the context of the characteristics of those in that sample.

Another possibility is an ordered-item yes/no Angoff method that does provide panelists some information on how the items are ordered based on psychometric difficulty but, unlike the bookmark method, allows for some judgments to be out of line with that ordering. Panelists review each item as compared to the target definition for that cut score and say "yes, two thirds of students meeting this definition would answer this question correctly" or "no, they wouldn't." They record a yes or a no for each item. Typically, they have a pattern of yeses followed by a block of no's, but they can also choose to go out of order for certain items that they feel are misrepresented in difficulty based on the characteristics of the population that initially took the assessment.

Marianne Perie

See also Achievement Tests; Angoff Method; Classification; Common Core Standards; Ebel Method; High-Stakes Tests; Psychometrics; Standard Setting; State Standards; Tests

Further Readings

Cizek, G. (Ed.). (2011). *Setting performance standards: Foundations, methods, and innovations* (2nd ed.). New York, NY: Routledge.

Mee, J., Clauser, B. E., & Margolis, M. J. (2013). The impact of process instructions on judges' use of examinee performance data in Angoff standard setting exercises. *Educational Measurement: Issues and Practice, 32*(3), 27–35.

Perie, M. (2008). A guide to understanding and developing performance level descriptors. *Educational Measurement: Issues and Practice, 27*(4), 15–29.

Perie, M., & Thurlow, M. (2011). Setting achievement standards on assessments for students with disabilities. In G. Cizek (Ed.), *Setting performance standards: Foundations, methods, and innovations* (2nd ed.). New York, NY: Routledge.

Skaggs, G., Hein, S., & Awuor, R. (2007). Setting passing scores on passage-based tests: A comparison of traditional and single-passage bookmark methods. *Applied Measurement in Education, 20*(4), 405–426.

Smith, R. W., Davis-Becker, S. L., & O'Leary, L. S. (2014). Combining the best of two standard setting methods: The ordered item booklet Angoff. *Journal of Applied Testing Technology, 15*(1), 18–26.

Zieky, M., Perie, M., & Livingston, S. (2008). *Cutscores: A manual for setting performance standards on educational and occupational tests.* Princeton, NJ: Educational Testing Service.